CHANGING THE IMMUTABLE

THE LITTMAN LIBRARY OF
JEWISH CIVILIZATION

Dedicated to the memory of
LOUIS THOMAS SIDNEY LITTMAN
who founded the Littman Library for the love of God
and as an act of charity in memory of his father
JOSEPH AARON LITTMAN
and to the memory of
ROBERT JOSEPH LITTMAN
who continued what his father Louis had begun
יהא זכרם ברוך

'Get wisdom, get understanding:
Forsake her not and she shall preserve thee'
PROV. 4:5

The Littman Library of Jewish Civilization is a registered UK charity
Registered charity no. 1000784

CHANGING THE IMMUTABLE

◆

How Orthodox Judaism Rewrites Its History

MARC B. SHAPIRO

Oxford · Portland, Oregon
The Littman Library of Jewish Civilization
2015

The Littman Library of Jewish Civilization
Chief Executive Officer: Ludo Craddock
Managing Editor: Connie Webber
PO Box 645, Oxford OX2 OUJ, UK
www.littman.co.uk

Published in the United States and Canada by
The Littman Library of Jewish Civilization
c/o ISBS, 920 NE 58th Avenue, Suite 300
Portland, Oregon 97213-3786

A catalogue record for this book is available from the British Library

Library of Congress cataloging-in-publication data
Shapiro, Marc B.
Changing the immutable : how Orthodox Judaism rewrites its history / Marc B. Shapiro.
p. cm.
Includes bibliographical references and index.
1. Orthodox Judaism—History. 2. Orthodox Judaism—Philosophy.
I. Title.
BM197.6.S525 2014 296.8'32—dc23 2014022624
ISBN 978–1–904113–60–7

Publishing co-ordinator: Janet Moth
Copy-editing: Lindsey Taylor-Guthartz
Proof-reading: Philippa Claiden
Index: Sarah Ereira
Design, typesetting, and production by Pete Russell, Faringdon, Oxon.
Printed in Great Britain on acid-free paper by
TJ International Ltd., Padstow, Cornwall

Dedicated to my children

Aliza, Yael, Danielle, Joshua, and Jacob

PREFACE

ON 2 MAY 2011 Osama bin Laden was killed by US Navy SEALs. This significant event was memorialized in an iconic photograph in which Barack Obama, Joseph Biden, and Hillary Clinton are receiving an update on the assault (Fig. 1(*a*)). Later in the week, a Brooklyn Yiddish newspaper, *Di Tsaytung*, republished the picture (Fig. 1(*b*)). As can be seen, Clinton (as well as another woman) were removed from the image. While this exaggerated concern for 'modesty' is standard fare in hasidic newspapers and books, it usually goes unnoticed outside their communities. This time was different, however, as the action of *Di Tsaytung* was picked up by numerous news outlets.[1]

Figure 1. The White House, May 2011; Hillary Clinton has been removed from the image below, which appeared in *Di Tsaytung* (Brooklyn), 6 May 2011

(*a*)

(*b*)

[1] The first to call attention to the deletion of the female images appears to have been the blog Failed Messiah, 5 May 2011.

For many, learning about this particular act of censorship was the first exposure to what is part and parcel of a larger phenomenon in the haredi world, namely, the altering and conscious rewriting of Jewish history and thought. I was well into this book when the action of *Di Tsaytung* became public knowledge. However, its discussion, which included commentary and criticism, highlighted for me the need for a detailed investigation of how some in the Jewish world have chosen to rewrite the past to serve the needs of the present.

Milovan Djilas, the famous Yugoslav writer, memorably commented that the hardest thing about being a communist was trying to predict the past. How could people live normal lives when what they knew to be true could be changed the next day, and all evidence of it made to disappear? As a historian, few things are more important to me than preserving the historical record. Yet this book focuses on the actions of those who see nothing sacrosanct about historical memory. Rather, their viewpoint is that history in all its forms, including halakhic history, is to be altered to accord with, and be subsumed into, the current *Weltanschauung* of their segment of Orthodoxy. As in the communist empire, those who want to avoid controversy are best advised to forget that which they once knew and adopt the new version of events, until it is time to trade that in for an even newer version.

This work, while it focuses primarily on books that have been censored, is not intended to be a study in bibliography, but rather a work of intellectual history.[2] I do not cover all the significant examples of censorship. To do so would require a book much larger than the present one, especially as new examples are being produced all the time. My goal is to understand the phenomenon, the mentality that stands behind the ever-increasing censorship, by using representative examples. Together with this, I hope to illuminate many other issues in the pages that follow, not least of which is the conception(s) of truth in traditional Jewish thought.

Those I must thank include Dan Rabinowitz, who runs the Seforim Blog,[3] a venue where much material of interest to this book has appeared. Dan's own writings have also been of great assistance. Menachem Butler and Eliezer Brodt, both of whom are also involved with the Seforim Blog, have each happily shared their vast storehouses of knowledge. Chaim Rapoport, Avinoam Rosenack, Yehudah Mirsky, William Gewirtz, and especially Shimon Steinmetz and Zalman Alpert were helpful to me at various times in

[2] Because I have cited numerous rabbinic figures, I thought it helpful, where possible, to provide the dates for those who are no longer alive. In referring to well-known rabbinic figures, I have added 'R.' before their names the first time they are cited.

[3] <www.seforim.blogspot.com>.

my research. I must also express my appreciation, as I did in the preface to *The Limits of Orthodox Theology*, to an outstanding scholar who wishes to remain anonymous and who was always generous with his time and knowledge. I further thank the Library of the Jewish Theological Seminary of America for graciously permitting me to include images of material found in its collection.

My greatest debt of gratitude actually goes to dozens, if not hundreds, of people whom I have never met and indeed have no idea who they are. I refer to the numerous anonymous writers and commenters on internet sites such as the Seforim Blog, On the Main Line,[4] Behadrei Haredim,[5] and the Otzar HaHochma forum,[6] who over the years have posted much important material relevant to this book, from which I benefited greatly. You know who you are and I just want to say that I am grateful.[7] I also thank the Lucius N. Littauer Foundation and the University of Scranton's Weinberg Judaic Studies Institute for providing me with financial assistance during the writing of this book.

As always, my parents were full of encouragement, with my father constantly enquiring about the book's progress. My in-laws have likewise been a strong source of support. This book could not have been written without my wife Lauren's understanding and patience, and I cannot express my gratitude in words. She has given me a perfect home in which to raise our children. Each of them is special in his or her own way, and it is to them that I dedicate this book.

[4] <www.onthemainline.blogspot.com>.

[5] <http://www.bhol.co.il/forums/topic.asp?whichpage=1&topic_id=585306&forum_id=1364> as well as elsewhere on this site.

[6] <www.otzar.org/forums/index.php>.

[7] In a few cases the internet sites, and the comment sections of blogs, where I first saw a reference were no longer in existence when I checked them in the course of writing this book.

CONTENTS

LIST OF ILLUSTRATIONS

NOTE ON TRANSLITERATION AND TRANSLATION

THE TRANSLITERATION of Hebrew in this book reflects consideration of the type of book it is, in terms of its content, purpose, and readership. The system adopted therefore reflects a broad approach to transcription, rather than the narrower approaches found in the *Encyclopaedia Judaica* or other systems developed for text-based or linguistic studies. The aim has been to reflect the pronunciation prescribed for modern Hebrew, rather than the spelling or Hebrew word structure, and to do so using conventions that are generally familiar to the English-speaking reader.

In accordance with this approach, no attempt is made to indicate the distinctions between *alef* and *ayin*, *tet* and *taf*, *kaf* and *kuf*, *sin* and *samekh*, since these are not relevant to pronunciation; likewise, the *dagesh* is not indicated except where it affects pronunciation. Following the principle of using conventions familiar to the majority of readers, however, transcriptions that are well established have been retained even when they are not fully consistent with the transliteration system adopted. On similar grounds, the *tsadi* is rendered by 'tz' in such familiar words as barmitzvah. Likewise, the distinction between *ḥet* and *khaf* has been retained, using *ḥ* for the former and *kh* for the latter; the associated forms are generally familiar to readers, even if the distinction is not actually borne out in pronunciation, and for the same reason the final *heh* is indicated too. As in Hebrew, no capital letters are used, except that an initial capital has been retained in transliterating titles of published works (for example, *Shulḥan arukh*).

Since no distinction is made between *alef* and *ayin*, they are indicated by an apostrophe only in intervocalic positions where a failure to do so could lead an English-speaking reader to pronounce the vowel-cluster as a diphthong—as, for example, in *ha'ir*—or otherwise mispronounce the word.

The *sheva na* is indicated by an *e*—*perikat ol*, *reshut*—except, again, when established convention dictates otherwise.

The *yod* is represented by *i* when it occurs as a vowel (*bereshit*), by *y* when it occurs as a consonant (*yesodot*), and by *yi* when it occurs as both (*yisra'el*).

Names have generally been left in their familiar forms, even when this is inconsistent with the overall system.

Hebrew sources of general interest have been translated, while those of a more technical nature have not.

ABBREVIATIONS

EJ	*Encyclopaedia Judaica*
HUCA	*Hebrew Union College Annual*
JJS	*Journal of Jewish Studies*
JQR	*Jewish Quarterly Review*
JSIJ	*Jewish Studies Internet Journal*
JSQ	*Jewish Studies Quarterly*
PAAJR	*Proceedings of the American Academy of Jewish Research*
TUMJ	*Torah u-Madda Journal*

Mishnaic and Talmudic Tractates

AZ	*Avodah zarah*
BB	*Bava batra*
Beits.	*Beitsah*
Bekh.	*Bekhorot*
Ber.	*Berakhot*
Bik.	*Bikurim*
BK	*Bava kama*
BM	*Bava metsia*
Eruv.	*Eruvin*
Git.	*Gitin*
Ḥag.	*Ḥagigah*
Ḥal.	*Ḥalah*
Hor.	*Horayot*
Ḥul.	*Ḥulin*
Kel.	*Kelim*
Ker.	*Keritot*
Ket.	*Ketubot*
Kid.	*Kidushin*
Mak.	*Makot*
Meg.	*Megilah*
Men.	*Menaḥot*
MK	*Mo'ed katan*
Naz.	*Nazir*
Ned.	*Nedarim*
Pes.	*Pesaḥim*
RH	*Rosh hashanah*
San.	*Sanhedrin*
Shab.	*Shabat*
Shev.	*Shevuot*
Sot.	*Sotah*
Ter.	*Terumot*
Yev.	*Yevamot*

CHAPTER ONE

INTRODUCTION

THERE IS OFTEN A TENSION between the quest for historical truth and the desire of communities of faith to pass on their religious message. This is because lifestyles and outlooks often change drastically over the generations, while the traditional religious mindset views itself as carrying on the values of the past, the latest link in a lengthy chain. Before the rise of modern historical scholarship, this was an issue that rarely if ever came to the fore. Yet now, when we are so much more attuned to the past, and the study of history is an important part of our lives, there is no escaping the fact that 'tradition' and history are often at odds with each other.

Jacob Katz put the matter bluntly when as a young student in Germany he declared that 'there is no Orthodox history'.[1] One who studies the Jewish past and wishes to be taken seriously as a historian cannot for dogmatic reasons declare ahead of time what his research will reveal. Yet in the eyes of many Orthodox religious leaders, this is precisely the type of history that is needed, and it is what the masses must be indoctrinated in. Call it 'Orthodox history', 'haredi history', or any other name, recent decades have seen a virtual explosion of works of this nature. They all diverge, some drastically, from how history is approached in the academy, and can be seen as a counter-history.[2]

Haym Soloveitchik has described the genre as follows:

Didactic and ideological, this 'history' filters untoward facts and glosses over the darker aspects of the past. Indeed, it often portrays events as they did not happen. So does memory; memory, however, transmutes unconsciously, whereas the writing of history is a conscious act. But this intentional disregard of fact in ideological history is no different from what takes place generally in moral education, as most such instruction seems to entail misrepresentation of a harsh reality. We teach a child,

[1] Katz, *With My Own Eyes*, 82.

[2] I prefer 'Orthodox history' to 'haredi history', since much of what we deal with in this book has nothing to do with the haredi community. Lest the reader misunderstand me, let me clarify that I do not mean that Orthodox Jews cannot also be academic or 'objective' historians. The issue I am concerned with is so-called 'Orthodox *history*', not Orthodox historians, and not all Orthodox Jews write 'Orthodox history' (though all 'Orthodox history' *is* written by Orthodox Jews).

for example, that crime does not pay. . . . Yet we do not feel that we are lying, for when values are being inculcated, the facts of experience—empirical truth—appear, somehow, to cease to be 'true'.[3]

This so-called 'Orthodox history', which insists in viewing the past through the religious needs of the present, is, as we shall see, only the latest manifestation of a lengthy tradition. It is a tradition that long pre-dates our current assumptions about the need for objectivity in telling the story of our past and the importance of absolute truth in our writing.

Jacob J. Schacter was the first to examine this matter in detail, in a lengthy article written in response to the controversy that broke out over my publication of letters from R. Jehiel Jacob Weinberg (1884–1966) to Samuel Atlas (1899–1978).[4] In his article, Schacter called attention to a fascinating essay by David Lowenthal, which is very helpful in understanding the phenomenon of 'Orthodox history'. Lowenthal distinguishes between 'history' and 'heritage' (and if we adopted his terminology we would speak of 'Orthodox heritage').

Heritage should not be confused with history. History seeks to convince by truth, and succumbs to falsehood. Heritage exaggerates and omits, candidly invents and frankly forgets. . . . Heritage uses historical traces and tells historical tales. But these tales and traces are stitched into fables closed to critical scrutiny. Heritage is immune to criticism because it is not erudition but catechism—not checkable fact but credulous allegiance. Heritage is not a testable or even plausible version of our past; it is a *declaration of faith* in the past. . . . Heritage diverges from history not in being biased but in its view of bias. Historians aim to reduce bias; heritage sanctions and strengthens it.[5]

Elsewhere he writes: '[H]eritage is not history at all; while it borrows from and enlivens historical study, heritage is not an inquiry into the past but a celebration of it, not an effort to know what actually happened but a profession of faith in a past tailored to present-day purposes.'[6]

Lowenthal is speaking about the creation of myths in all sorts of communities, and what he says resonates just as powerfully when looking at parts of Jewish society. Yoel Finkelman has also recently discussed how the American haredi community has created a history of eastern Europe that is both nostalgic and inspirational. However, as he also remarks, for this community and for others like it, 'what happened may be less important than what stories we

[3] Soloveitchik, 'Rupture and Reconstruction', 85.

[4] M. B. Shapiro, 'Scholars and Friends'; Schacter, 'Facing the Truths of History'.

[5] Lowenthal, 'Fabricating Heritage', 7–8. Schacter quotes this passage in 'Facing the Truths', 234. See also Shatz, 'Nothing but the Truth?', 163. Lowenthal's book-length treatment is *The Heritage Crusade and the Spoils of History*.

[6] *The Heritage Crusade and the Spoils of History*, p. x.

tell one another about what happened'.[7] As Finkelman notes, occurrences are invented, or covered up, all in the effort to create a tangible group identity, that is, 'for teaching members about what it means to be part of the group'.[8]

Defending the haredi perspective, R. Shimon Schwab (1908–95) famously explained matters as follows:

What ethical purpose is served by preserving a realistic historic picture? Nothing but the satisfaction of curiosity. We should tell ourselves and our children the good memories of the good people, their unshakeable faith, their staunch defense of tradition, their life of truth, their impeccable honesty, their boundless charity and their great reverence for Torah and Torah sages. . . . Rather than write the history of our forebears, every generation has to put a veil over the human failings of its elders and glorify all the rest which is great and beautiful. That means we have to do without a real history book. We can do without. We do not need realism, we need inspiration from our forefathers in order to pass it on to posterity.[9]

[7] Finkelman, *Strictly Kosher Reading*, 99. In the recent anonymous biography of R. Yosef Shalom Elyashiv (1910–2012), *Hashakdan*, i. 12, the author acknowledges that some of the stories he repeats may not be true, but adds that 'they don't tell such stories about me and you'. For him, this is reason enough to include the stories, as their purpose is to inspire the reader so that one day 'it will be possible to tell such stories about us'. See also R. Baruch Shmuel Deutsch's preface to Asher Bergman, *Toledot maran harav shakh*, where he mentions the great spiritual value of knowing the history of the *gedolim* (great Torah leaders), especially when the stories told can be verified. In other words, even stories of questionable veracity can have spiritual value.

[8] Finkelman, *Strictly Kosher Reading*, 99. For a recent study of how great rabbis are portrayed in haredi literature, see Hakak, 'Holy Amnesia'. Hakak notes that some figures in the haredi world have begun to criticize the dominant haredi approach to historical writing. For criticism from the *ḥardal* world, see E. Melamed, *Revivim: nisuin*, 94. *Ḥardal* is a neologism formed from *ḥaredi–le'umi* (lit.: 'fervently Orthodox–nationalistic'), and refers to an ideology that combines Zionism with trends usually identified with the haredi world, such as a conservative approach to halakhah and the attribution of great authority to rabbinic leaders in communal life.

R. Isaac Hutner's (1906–80) criticism of hagiography is often quoted; see his *Paḥad yitsḥak*, 217. See also R. Leopold Greenwald, *Matsevet kodesh*, 138, which criticizes R. Moses Sofer's (1762–1839) grandsons for omitting all mention of the difficulties Sofer encountered when he first became rabbi in Pressburg. See also Greenwald, *Otsar neḥmad*, 69 ff. R. Abraham Isaiah Karelitz, the Hazon Ish (1878–1953), stated that it is important to know the truth about great Torah sages. He further noted in this regard that one need not worry about *leshon hara* (gossip and slander). Just as there is no issue of *leshon hara* when one asks about the quality of a workman, since it is necessary knowledge, so too it is necessary to know about the nature of great Torah sages. See Karelitz, *Kovets igerot ḥazon ish*, vol. ii, no. 133. Yet despite this, we will see that when it came to R. Samson Raphael Hirsch, the Hazon Ish did not want the haredi public to know all of Hirsch's true views; see below, pp. 122–3. See also R. Jacob Saphir, *Even sapir*, introd., pp. 1–2 (unpaginated), who uses the Bible and rabbinic literature to defend his approach of telling the truth about people and communities, even if it is not so flattering.

[9] Schwab, *Selected Writings*, 234. In an interview with Elliot Resnick, R. Nosson Scherman, the general editor of ArtScroll, was asked about his company's whitewashing of history. He replied:

If we accept the judgement of Yosef Hayim Yerushalmi, Schwab's position is actually quite biblical. As Yerushalmi put it, 'The biblical appeal to remember thus has little to do with curiosity about the past. Israel is told only that it must be a kingdom of priests and a holy people; nowhere is it suggested that it become a nation of historians.'[10] Even a biblical book supposedly dedicated to history, the book of Chronicles, is actually far from a detached recording of what happened in the past. This was sensed even in the medieval period, and the commentary attributed to Rashi (1040–1105) points out a number of times that the book of Chronicles has as one of its goals the portrayal of King David in a positive fashion.[11] Rabbinic literature is little different when it comes to recognizing the value of factual history. In the words of M. D. Herr: 'It appears that the Sages understood clearly the superiority and benefits of a fictitious description. In this, they are no different from other great moralistic writers in various times and places.'[12]

Traditionalist scholars, including R. Tsevi Hirsch Chajes (1805–55) and R. Yehudah Herzl Henkin, have also recognized the Sages' efforts at whitewashing misdeeds by biblical figures.[13] It is with clear ideological motives

'Our goal is to increase Torah learning and *yiras shamayim* [fear of Heaven]. If somebody can be inspired by a *gadol b'yisrael* [outstanding Torah leader], then let him be inspired. Is it necessary to say that he had shortcomings? Does that help you become a better person?'; see *Jewish Press*, 6 June 2007. See also my Seforim Blog post, 17 May 2012, where I demonstrated how a translation of a letter by R. Ovadyah Bertinoro (*c.*1445–*c.*1515), published by a haredi press, had deleted Bertinoro's comment that most of the young Jewish women in Palermo were already pregnant at their weddings. The motivation of this censorship was obviously to shield the masses from the knowledge that even in pre-Reform Europe violation of halakhah was a common phenomenon in some places.

[10] Yerushalmi, *Zakhor: Jewish History and Jewish Memory*, 10. On p. 6 he writes: 'For those reared and educated in the modern West it is often hard to grasp the fact that a concern with history, let alone the writing of history, is not an innate endowment of human civilization.'

[11] See Y. H. Sofer, *Berit ya'akov*, 13; Kalimi, *Retelling of Chronicles*, 203–4; Viezel, *Commentary on Chronicles* (Heb.), 245 ff. (called to my attention by Yitzhak Berger). R. Isaac Abarbanel (1438–1508) also noted that Chronicles has an agenda. See Lawee, *Isaac Abarbanel's Stance toward Tradition*, 176–7. A prime example of this is that Chronicles does not mention anything about the David–Bathsheba episode. See also Najman, 'Rewriting as Whitewashing'.

[12] Herr, 'The Sages' Concept of History' (Heb.), 139. See also Rubenstein, *Rabbinic Stories*, 12, which describes the nature of rabbinic 'history' as follows: 'The [rabbinic] storytellers were not attempting to document "what actually happened" out of a dispassionate interest in the objective historical record, or to transmit biographical facts in order to provide pure data for posterity. This type of detached, impartial writing of a biography is a distinctly modern approach. Nowadays we distinguish biography from fiction. . . . In pre-modern cultures, however, the distinction between biography and fiction was blurred. Ancient authors saw themselves as teachers, and they were more concerned with the didactic point than with historical accuracy.'

[13] See Chajes, *Kol sifrei maharats ḥayes*, i. 322–5, and his note on BT *Sot.* 36*b*; Y. H. Henkin, *Benei vanim*, vol. iv, essay no. 9. See also Hirschensohn, *Nimukei rashi*, ii. 55*a*; E. Margaliyot, *Haḥayavim*

that ambiguous figures in the Bible are drawn more sharply in the aggadah. This is not merely in the direction of piety, but also to stress the wickedness of those figures, such as Esau, who do not appear so evil in the biblical text itself.[14] The modern hagiographies follow in this path, at least with regard to the focus on piety.

One should not assume that the contrast between realistic history and hagiography is something only discovered in modern times. We have plenty of examples of medieval scholars who were aware of the rabbinic concern with saving the reputation of biblical figures, but still expressed their preference for the simple reading of Scripture. For example, in commenting on Genesis 35: 22, which mentions that Reuben slept with Bilhah, his father's concubine, R. Abraham Ibn Ezra (1089–1164) states: 'Our Sages explained this beautifully, for "a prudent man concealeth shame" [Prov. 12: 16].'

In this comment, Ibn Ezra is alluding to the interpretation of R. Jonathan (cited by R. Samuel ben Nahmani), who rejects the literal meaning of the verse and instead declares that Reuben's only crime was in moving Jacob's bed from Bilhah's tent to that of Leah.[15] By citing the verse from Proverbs, Ibn Ezra lets the reader know that he understands and sympathizes with this defence of Reuben's honour, even though it is not historically accurate and the 'shame' is quite real.[16] R. Jonathan elsewhere absolves David of the sin of adultery with Bathsheba (2 Sam. 11), claiming that Uriah had issued her a divorce.[17] Despite R. Jonathan's claim, a number of traditional authorities do not accept his approach (which R. Jonathan also uses with reference to a few other biblical figures[18]), and regard David as having sinned in this matter. This, of course, is the plain sense of the biblical story as well as that of Nathan's rebuke (2 Sam. 11–12).[19]

bamikra. Regarding the reverse phenomenon, that of the Sages pointing to negative aspects of biblical heroes even where there is no apparent support for these judgements in the biblical text, see A. Y. Chwat, 'Those Who Are Innocent' (Heb.).

[14] Regarding Esau, see Kugel, *How to Read the Bible*, 138 ff.

[15] BT *Shab*. 55*b*.

[16] Ibn Ezra is more explicit in *Yesod mora*, 7: 9, where he speaks of the 'defilement' of Bilhah, which was the reason Jacob would no longer sleep with her. From the Talmud itself, BT *Shab*. 55*b*, we see that not all the Sages agreed with R. Jonathan's defence of Reuben. His approach is also rejected by R. David Kimhi, *Commentary on the Torah*, Gen. 35: 22, and R. Joseph Bekhor Shor, *Commentary on the Torah*, Gen. 35: 22.

[17] BT *Shab*. 56*a*.

[18] See BT *Shab*. 55*b*–56*a*. R. Moses Kunitz (1774–1837), *Hametsaref*, vol. i, no. 2, assumes that R. Jonathan's viewpoint was not shared by the other Sages.

[19] See Abarbanel, *Commentary* on 2 Sam. 12: 13; R. Judah bar Nathan in *Teshuvot ḥakhmei provans*, no. 71: שגדול חטאו בענין בת שבע כפלי כפלים ואע״פ שרבותי׳ ז״ל הפכו לזכות משפטו שכרם הרבה אבל אין מקרא יוצא מידי פשוטו; R. Isaiah of Trani, *Commentary* on Ps. 51: 1 (but see his opposing view in 2 Sam. 12: 4. Both of R. Isaiah's commentaries appear in the 'Psalms' and 'Samuel' volumes of the *Mikraot gedolot haketer*, published by Bar-Ilan University); Ibn Kaspi, *Adnei kesef*, i, on 2 Sam. 11: 6;

The issues I have discussed in the preceding paragraphs also resonate in general discussions of historiography. To mention only a few sources from antiquity, Cicero declared that there are two rules obligating a historian. The first is that he 'shall not dare to advance a falsity', and the second that 'there is no truth that he shall suppress'.[20] Yet these goals were often not met. Thus, Plutarch presented his *Parallel Lives* 'in a rather idealized fashion, with the intention of conveying moral examples to imitate or avoid'.[21] The other ancient historians acted similarly, for they shared the view 'that the point of history is to celebrate the past . . . and to provide examples of behaviour for the present'.[22] Even Cicero himself, despite his insistence on telling truthful history, 'believed that the past could be—and should be—manipulated and embroidered in order to bring out important moral or exemplary points'.[23]

History as written in the medieval period became even more fanciful and was indeed very similar to 'Orthodox history'. As Ruth Morse has documented, medieval writers did not think that there was a contradiction between telling the truth of what had happened in the past, and altering and recreating aspects of this past, all at the same time. In this conception, the writer is not a passive recorder of the past but one who helps create our image of it. As Morse puts it, 'to ask why medieval writers claimed that what appears to us obviously "invented" material was "true" is another reminder of the incommensurability of our cultures'.[24] She continues:

Malka, *Mikveh hamayim*, vol. vi, 'Even ha'ezer', no. 11; Peniri, *Kol sason*, 260–1. I learnt of R. Isaiah of Trani and Ibn Kaspi from Angel, 'Abarbanel: Commentator and Teacher', 20. See also BT *Ket.* 9*a* (and Rashi, s.v. *ukhema'aseh*), which assumes that Bathsheba was still a married woman when she was with David, and according to one opinion, that she was 'compelled' to have sex with him. BT *AZ* 4*b*–5*a* also assumes that David sinned (though his action was predestined); cf. Tosafot, BT *Yoma* 66*b*, s.v. *mahu*. A good discussion of the issue can be found in Medan, *David and Bathsheba* (Heb.).

[20] *De Oratore*, book 2, ch. 15.

[21] Kelley, *Faces of History*, 46. See ibid. 65, where with reference to Roman historians as a whole, Kelley writes: '[F]or all their professions of truth, none of these historians were "objective" in a modern sense; all were eager to celebrate the moral virtues which had made Rome great and to decry the decline which was threatening its eternal claims.'

[22] Morse, *Truth and Convention*, 94. See also Struever, *Language of History*, 24 (referred to by Morse).

[23] Morse, *Truth and Convention*, 97. It has long been recognized that ancient historians invented the speeches they put into the mouths of various figures. See Metzger, 'Literary Forgeries', 9. See also Veyne, *Did the Greeks Believe in Their Myths?*, p. xi: 'There was a time when poets and historians invented royal dynasties all of a piece, complete with the name of each potentate and his genealogy. They were not forgers, nor were they acting in bad faith. They were simply following what was, at the time, the normal way of arriving at the truth.'

[24] Morse, *Truth and Convention*, 2.

> 'Historical' . . . might be thought of as an exemplary narrative based upon events which had occurred at some point in the past, told in order to move and persuade its audience to imitate the good and eschew the evil, a 'true tale about the past' which included a vast range of what modern readers would regard as invented material and inappropriate, if implicit, moralizing. . . . In the different conceptual space of the Middle Ages, 'true' might mean 'in the main' or 'for the most part' true, or even, 'it could have happened like this'.[25]

Although the writing of history in Western culture has, of course, moved beyond this, 'Orthodox history' still carries on this medieval tradition, a tradition that found expression in numerous pre-modern Jewish historical works.[26] Yet 'Orthodox history' also has other characteristics which are paralleled in modern times by 'Soviet history', where 'truth' was entirely instrumental and what was accepted as fact one day could be entirely rewritten the next.[27]

Historical Truth and Communal Memory

What I am attempting to do in this book is to show how common 'instrumental truth' has been, in particular in the last century. My focus is not primarily on works of history, which is where people usually look for this type of information, but rather on all sorts of texts that are the lifeblood of traditional Jewish communities. We must not forget that for these communities, in particular the haredi community which to a significant extent is a community of scholars, the written word is central. Even the masses in the haredi world are avid consumers of the written word, which is not usually the case in communities where television, sports, or any of countless other pursuits are available for non-intellectuals. In fact, it is precisely because the written word is not reserved for the elites that Orthodox writers and publishers worry about how certain texts will affect those who perhaps cannot 'handle them'. When it is only intellectuals who are doing the reading, ideological censorship is not a pressing concern. However, since the masses are now at risk of being exposed to 'dangerous' material, this has created a phenomenon that as far as I know

[25] Ibid. 6.

[26] This was so not just in historical works, but even in their translations. See Stanislawski, 'The Yiddish *Shevet Yehudah*'.

[27] Soviet history was, of course, at the service of the state, which is a completely different phenomenon from that which I am discussing. With the return of Jews to self-rule in their own land, this type of historical approach was also seen. I think in particular of the creation of the myth, widely accepted in the early decades of the State of Israel and promoted by the government for reasons of realpolitik, that there were no expulsions of local Arabs. Rather, they all left Israel of their own free will, encouraged in this by Arab leaders, with plans to return after the land was conquered by the Arab forces. See Morris, *Birth of the Palestinian Refugee Problem Revisited*.

is not to be found in other religions. I am referring to pious guardians of the faith, usually self-appointed, who take it upon themselves to alter sacred texts, the texts written by great rabbis of the past and cherished by all traditional Jews.[28]

How should a community that prides itself on following the great figures of the past and a treasured historical tradition deal with texts and ideas that reflect a *Weltanschauung* at odds with the current religious climate? As we will see, it is vital for such a community that the events, actions, texts, and ideals of the past be made to conform to the present ideological moment. This book attempts to document how this phenomenon has played out in Orthodox Judaism, in particular in the branch known as haredi Orthodoxy. One can, on occasion, find similar manifestations in the other Jewish denominations and I will refer to a few of them. Yet, as we will see, the motivating factor is entirely different.[29]

The tension between historical truth and maintenance of a communal myth, what Lowenthal has called 'heritage', is seen in a fascinating letter of R. Jacob Israel Kanievsky ('the Steipler', 1899–1985), one of the most outstanding haredi sages of the second half of the twentieth century. He was approached by someone who wanted to write about the Haskalah movement and its devastating effect on traditional Judaism. However, he was not sure how he should deal with the notorious Saul Berlin (1740–94), who forged a volume of responsa and attributed it to the medieval R. Asher ben Yehiel (*c.*1250–1327). Known as the *Besamim rosh*, this volume contains a number of reformist responsa and was clearly designed to undermine rabbinic Judaism.

Kanievsky told him that he should not include anything about Berlin, giving four reasons. The first was the honour due to Berlin's forefathers: he came from an important rabbinic family and it would detract from its honour if Berlin's story became known. Kanievsky's second reason was that perhaps Berlin's soul had already received its punishment and was now cleansed. Therefore, bringing up this episode now could have brought harm to his soul in the world to come.

The last two reasons Kanievsky offered are, I think, the most important and certainly the most relevant for our purposes. Kanievsky wrote that discussion of the episode would be humiliating to those sages who had stood by Berlin, having been taken in by the forgery. In other words, since revealing

[28] Schacter, 'Facing the Truths of History', was the first detailed treatment of ideological censorship. Recently, Shmuel Glick has done some initial work on internal censorship of responsa; see Glick, 'On Alterations' (Heb.).

[29] I have already noted how a recent biography of Saul Lieberman (1898–1983) censors strong criticism of Conservative rabbis. See my *Saul Lieberman and the Orthodox*, 25 n. 25.

the mistake made by these sages would reflect poorly on their judgement in this matter, the historical record needed to be covered up. Kanievsky's final reason was that some people's faith would be weakened by the knowledge that someone who was regarded as a great Torah scholar had become a heretic. He concluded by saying that an article could be written about the destructive influence of the Haskalah without mentioning the names of the Torah scholars who had been led astray.[30]

Kanievsky's last reason is particularly revealing. From his perspective there is no reason for the masses to know about the whole Saul Berlin episode. They are supposed to believe that the more Torah knowledge one has, the greater one becomes. It would damage their faith to read of a great *talmid ḥakham* who abandoned traditional Judaism. Most Torah scholars know about Saul Berlin, and all are well aware of similar people such as the talmudic figure Elisha ben Avuyah, that is, learned men who abandoned the tradition. However, among the masses there are some who cannot handle this information, and it should be kept from them.

Doesn't Everyone Have a Bias?

It hardly needs to be said that all historians have biases. Gershom Scholem famously spoke of the *Wissenschaft des Judentums* scholars' portrayal of Jewish history, which had no room for kabbalah, hasidism, messianism, and antinomianism, not to mention the study of Jewish criminals and the like, as nothing less than 'a form of censorship of the Jewish past'.[31] While nineteenth-century Jewish historians had, to their minds, justifiable reasons not to dwell on such matters, today all responsible historians recognize that this is not the way to approach history, and they are careful not to allow their preconceptions to slant the evidence consciously. Obviously, unconscious bias and distortions abound. However, 'Orthodox history' is in an entirely different category, and as already noted, resembles the 'official' histories found in the Soviet Union, or those commissioned by other communist governments or dictatorships.[32] What all these histories have in common is that certain conclusions are disqualified from the start.[33]

[30] J. I. Kanievsky, *Karyana de'igarta*, vol. i, no. 81. See also Horovitz, *Orḥot rabenu*, i. 285, that Kanievsky assumed that many of the responsa in *Besamim rosh* were authentic, and that Berlin had inserted his forged responsa among them. I believe it is more likely that all the responsa are forged, and that the non-controversial ones were created by Berlin to give 'cover' to the radical responsa.

[31] See Scholem, *Messianic Idea*, 305, 309.

[32] A former editor of the English-language newspaper *Yated ne'eman* told me, in all seriousness, that his job was like that of *Pravda*, in that he determined what the (haredi) masses would read. For more on censorship in haredi newspapers, see Levy, *Haḥaredim*, ch. 19.

[33] For previous studies on Orthodox historiography, see Bartal, 'R. Ya'akov Lifshitz's *Zikhron*

'Orthodox history' also differs from its academic counterpart in that there is conscious recognition that the history being written is part of an ideological agenda, designed to instil the proper education and 'outlook' in the reader. Thus, not only censorship but even outright distortion is permissible, all in the name of a higher truth. One of the most common examples of rewriting, or distortions, we will see is when 'kosher' books, in order for them to remain kosher, need to be 'improved' a bit. I am not talking about books viewed as heretical, which even if not officially banned are regarded as forbidden reading. Rather, I am referring to standard books, part of the traditional Jewish library, which need to be altered in order to remain acceptable in the current religious climate. The point is to fool people into thinking that what they are reading or seeing is authentic, and to prevent them seeing things that would be problematic in the eyes of the censors. In most cases, the alteration is done in such a way that readers do not realize that anything has been changed in the text, for if they were to know it would defeat the whole purpose of the censorship. The acts of censorship, of which we will see many, and telling a story which one knows to be false are simply different stops along the same continuum, all of which have the goal of preserving the faith and self-image of a community.[34]

The altering of the past does not occur simply because people are fearful of what will happen if the masses are exposed to certain things; there is also a more activist outlook. We did not need the totalitarian states to teach us that if you control the past, you have a much easier time controlling the present and the future.[35] This alteration of the past is openly acknowledged by some haredi writers. Thus, on the Dei'ah veDibur website, which carries articles from the haredi newspaper *Yated ne'eman* and advocates the Lithuanian yeshiva worldview, the following appears: 'A related complaint that is sometimes made is that we leave out information. This is true, but the reason is that in our Torah-based scale of values, the harm or embarrassment that can be caused to someone—perhaps a family member or bystander—rates much higher than the needs of the historical record or journalistic objectivity.'[36]

ya'akov' (Heb.); id., 'Shimon the Heretic' (Heb.); id., 'True Knowledge and Wisdom' (Heb.); Rapoport-Albert, 'Hagiography with Footnotes'; Etkes, *Gaon of Vilna* (Heb.), ch. 4; Karlinsky, 'Dawn'; Assaf, *Caught in the Thicket* (Heb.); on p. 22 n. 11, Assaf cites some other relevant studies.

[34] See the earlier comments of Assaf, *Caught in the Thicket* (Heb.), 12, 100, and 35 ff., where he provides a few examples of censorship of the sort to which this book is devoted.

[35] Cf. George Orwell, *Nineteen Eighty-Four*, 35: '"Who controls the past", ran the Party slogan, "controls the future: who controls the present controls the past."'

[36] 'On Writing Biographies of Gedolim', <www.chareidi.org>, on the home page. The article originally appeared in Dei'ah veDibur, 25 May 2005, <http://www.chareidi.org/archives5765/bechukosai/obiogrphbck65.htm>.

The problem with this formulation is that the family member might be embarrassed that his relative attended Yeshiva University or thought highly of R. Abraham Isaac Kook (1865–1935).[37] Thus, the door has been opened to censor and alter history for any subjective reason.[38] The quotation above also refers to potential harm caused to a bystander as a valid reason for censorship. For example, from the haredi perspective the bystander might be harmed spiritually by seeing that a certain sage thought highly of Zionism. So again, we have a justification for not revealing the truth.

The concern with the honour of rabbinic figures can also explain many examples of censorship, and it is basic to the contemporary haredi mindset that matters that do not reflect well on rabbinic leaders should be covered up.[39] What this book hopes to show, however, is how fluid these types of judgements are, and how in one generation a story, halakhic decision, or philosophical viewpoint can be regarded as 'acceptable', while in a later generation that is no longer the case.

The great value that haredi society places on the reputations of rabbinic leaders can be seen in how haredi leaders reacted to R. Nathan Kamenetsky's *Making of a Godol*. In this book, Kamenetsky attempted to portray great rabbinic figures (*gedolim*) in a realistic fashion. He obviously knew that he was moving into dangerous territory with this book, and in his introduction justifies his adoption of the realistic approach, rather than writing hagiography. R. Samson Raphael Hirsch (1808–88) had earlier defended such an approach when it came to examination of biblical figures:

> The Torah never hides from us the faults, errors and weaknesses of our great men. Just by that, it gives the stamp of veracity to what it relates. Were they without passion and without internal struggles, their virtues would seem to us the outcome of some higher nature, hardly a merit and certainly no model that we could hope to emulate. . . . From our great teachers of the Torah . . . we would accordingly learn that it may never be our task to whitewash the spiritual and moral heroes of our past, to appear as apologists for them. They do not require our apologies, nor do such attempts become them. Truth is the seal of our Torah, and truthfulness is the principle of all its true and great commentators and teachers.[40]

[37] Regarding Kook, see Ch. 5 below. What has happened in regard to Kook can be seen in smaller measure with many other rabbis associated with religious Zionism. One example is R. Isaac Herzog (1888–1959). See e.g. Breisch, *Ḥelkat ya'akov*, which has an approbation by Herzog; this was removed in the Tel Aviv, 1992 edition published by Breisch's sons.

[38] See my Seforim Blog post, 25 Oct. 2009, on covering up the facts that R. Shlomo Wolbe (1913–2005) came from an irreligious family and that R. Aaron Kotler's (1891–1962) sister abandoned traditional Judaism.

[39] We also find non-haredi figures who share the haredi concern with rabbinic reputations. See e.g. S. J. Rapoport, *Igerot shir*, ii. 120, on the publication of R. Leon Modena's autobiography.

[40] Hirsch, *Pentateuch*, comment on Gen. 12: 10–13. On Hirsch's approach, see Frisch,

R. Yonah Merzbach (1900–80), a haredi rabbi of German origin, adopted a similar approach when it came to a great twentieth-century Torah scholar, R. Abraham Elijah Kaplan (1889–1924). Kaplan wrote an essay expressing a very positive attitude towards Herzl and Zionism, concluding: 'As my faith in God increased, so grew my connection to Zionism.'[41] Needless to say, such an essay is bound to be uncomfortable reading for today's haredi world.

This essay was later included in a collection of Kaplan's writings published by his son. When asked about the essay, Merzbach replied that he had opposed its sentiments when it originally appeared. Nevertheless, he insisted that it be republished and that Kaplan's 'son and students have no permission to conceal this article'. In words that stand as a challenge to much that we will see in this book, Merzbach further declared: 'We are not to be censors of *gedolei yisra'el* and their holy words.'[42]

Yet despite any such sources that could be cited in support of Kamenetsky's 'realistic approach' to biography, and in opposition to censorship of the life and opinions of great Torah scholars, the response from the haredi world was fast and furious, and resulted in the ban of Kamenetsky's *Making of a Godol*.[43] Yoel Finkelman has summarized the matter quite well:

> Haredi writers of history claim to know better than the great rabbis of the past how the latter should have behaved. Those great rabbis do not serve as models for the present. Instead, the present and its ideology serve as models for the great rabbis. Haredi historiography becomes a tale of what observant Jews, and especially great rabbis, did, but only provided that these actions accord with, or can be made to accord with, current Haredi doctrine. The historians do not try to understand the *gedolim*; they stand over the *gedolim*. Haredi ideology of fealty to the great rabbis works at cross purposes with the sanitized history of those rabbis.[44]

The same concerns that haredi leaders had when it came to Kamenetsky's book were also present in an earlier dispute. This one focused on a comment of R. Israel Lipschutz (1782–1860) in his famous commentary on the Mishnah.[45] Lipschutz records a legend whose upshot is that although people

'R. Samson Raphael Hirsch's Interpretation' (Heb.); id., 'Sins of the Patriarchs', 269 ff. In his commentary on Gen. 9: 24, Hirsch speaks of the need for the younger generation to place a cloak over the lapses of the older generation. However, here he is speaking about how the younger generation should not gloat 'over the "nakedness" of the father', and should take from the elders what is good and noble. He is not talking about creating a mythical righteous past for previous generations.

[41] A. E. Kaplan, *Be'ikvot hayirah*, 91.

[42] See Merzbach's letter in Hamburger, *Harav yonah merzbakh*, 23 n. 21.

[43] See my 'Of Books and Bans'.

[44] Finkelman, *Strictly Kosher Reading*, 122.

[45] Lipschutz, *Tiferet yisra'el*, 'Kidushin' 4: 4.

are accustomed to think of Moses as naturally righteous, in truth, he was born with a terrible nature and only through great effort was able to attain a state of holiness. Although no notice seems to have been taken of this passage during Lipschutz's lifetime, or even in the first decades after his death, some later rabbis were outraged by his inclusion of the legend. In some editions of the commentary, this passage was even deleted.[46]

We find a similar concern with rabbinic honour in many other cases as well. How else is one to explain the fact that the complete autobiography of R. Jacob Emden (1697–1776) has, as of 2015, not yet appeared, though there have been three censored editions? When the complete autobiography does appear, it will be an academic publication, not one designed for the masses. This is because Emden's brutal honesty about both his own life and feelings (including sexual matters), as well as his judgements of other rabbinic leaders, makes this a very problematic book for many in the Orthodox world.

Another example of concern over the honour of rabbinic figures leading to censorship is seen in the *Katuv sham* of R. Abraham ben David of Posquières (Rabad; *c.*1125–98). This book was directed against R. Zerahyah Halevi (twelfth century), who himself had written criticisms of the talmudic codification of R. Isaac Alfasi (1013–1103). Rabad's scholarly battle against R. Zerahyah was long-standing, and the language used most vituperative. In an earlier work directed against R. Zerahyah, Rabad even felt the need to justify his language, stating that he chose to adopt the Spanish approach which, he claims, allows disputants to appear as enemies on the field of Torah battle, while in truth they love each other.[47] Whether Rabad actually can be said to have loved R. Zerahyah, I will leave for others to decide. However, in the first publication of *Katuv sham*, edited by M. Z. Hasidah,[48] one finds a very strange passage, seen in Figure 1.1(*a*).

Isadore Twersky had this passage in mind when he noted that 'Hasidah's manuscript concealed much of this vituperation in code.'[49] Yet Twersky apparently did not realize two important points: first, it is not Hasidah's manuscript that concealed the vituperation, but Hasidah himself. No doubt the reason for this was the concern that in the modern climate Rabad will

[46] See Leiman, 'R. Israel Lipschutz and the Portrait of Moses Controversy'.

[47] See Twersky, *Rabad of Posquières*, 42.

[48] Published in instalments in the weekly *Hasegulah*, beginning in 1933. The various instalments were collected in a one-volume photo-offset of the work, published in Jerusalem in 1969. The passages reproduced in the text are from p. 41 in the 1969 edition (edited by M. Z. Hasidah), and p. 73 in the 1990 edition of Abraham ben David, *Katuv sham*.

[49] Twersky, *Rabad of Posquières*, 121 n. 24.

מא.	ספר	כתוב-שם	להראב"ד	.41
	פרק	ראש--השנה	שלישי	

כתוב-שם:ובפרק ערבי-פסחים ברירנא דר" יוסי ס"ל מצות צריכות כונה ופליגי רבנן עליה,הלכך ליתא להא דר" יוסי ולא לדר" זירא.

אמר אברהם:לעולם מעשה רב בכל-מקום,ודר" זירא אדרבה פליגא,אדשלחו ליה לאבוה-דשמואל לא פליגא,דכיון דאכל מצה הרי נהנה-סס גרונו ומעיו והלא מתעסק שהוא פטור לענין-(ל)שבת,לענין-(ל)חלב-ועריות חייב;ולעולם כל לענין אכילה לא בעינן כונה למצוה,אבל לשאר מצוות בעינן כונה,כפשטה דמתניתן,וכן עיקר.ואע"ג דהא דר" אליעזר ורבי-ם יהושע פלוגת' עליה דר" זירא. :

פרק	<u>פרק יום-טוב של ר"ה</u>	רביעי

כתוב-שם:והאידנא דלית-לן יובלות לא היה צריך הרב לכתוב מכל זה כלום כו

אמר אברהם:ובימי רבי הלא לא היו יובלות ואעפ"כ הוצרך לומר/חוקעין//[אין] אלא כל-זמן שב"ד יושבין,ולא אמר:<u>לא-היו</u> חוקעין,דמשמע-ם שלשעתו היה מורה הלכה;וכן בעיא דר" זירא איך היה שואל על מה שלא היה בימיו ולא בימי אבותיו,אלא כיון שאנו מוצאין שביעית בזמן-הזה מדרבנן,גם יובל בזמן-הזה במקום שיש קדוש-ב"ד מדרבנן,<u>ואם יזמין-ם הבורא שיהיה ב"ד בא"י</u> לקדוש וליובלות <u>ג"כ נתקע כדי לפרסם איסור-יובל בזריעה וקצירה ובהשמטת-קרקעות,</u>ואין להחמיה עליו בזה. :

כתוב-שם:ואין הדברים נראין כן שיהיה ר"ח ז"ל חולק על כל התנאין והאמורא׳

אמר אברהם:ומי הגיד לו דר"ח בא למעט חשבון המקראות,והלא לא בא סס אלא למעט המקראות עצמן,אבל יאמר:ככתוב בתורתיך,ועוד כתי׳ וכן לדברי קדשך ג"פ,וכן לדברי עבדיך-הנביאים ג"פ,ואע"פ שלא הזכיר המקראות עצמן יצא;ומאי דאמר ואמיקנא וכו" ע"ז הדרך אמר,וזה עיקר, ולא כדברי <u>הצרפתי</u>. :

כתוב-שם:והם האריכו להביא ראיות לדבריהם,והם כתובים בספריהם ותשובותיהם.

אמר אברהם:ואם הרבו עוד ראיות מה יועילו להם,וסתם מתני׳ דהכא סםם וסוגיין דמסכת סוכה בענין מקבלת אשה מבעלה ומיד בנה וכו" דקיימא כר" יהודה דוחה כל הראיות שלהם ואין האשה רשאה לברך על סם לולב לפי שאינה באותה מצוה לא מן התורה ולא מדרבנן. :

כתוב-שם:ונ"ל ר" אבהו לרווחא דמילתא אתקין דילמא איכא מאן דסבר כר"י.

אמר אברהם:ואפילו לרבנן,נהי דיצא דיעבד אבל לכתחלה לא מיבעי ליה-לאפסוקי,מדכתיב והעברת שופר תרועה,א"נ ותקעתם תרועה,סםם תרועה יתקעו,דאפקעינהו בחד לישנא,ומ"ה תקון תש"ת תר"ת,א"נ לא דמי הפסקה דאקראי ורשותא,דאי בעי מפסיק ואי בעי לא מפסיק,דכי מפסיק-ם נמי חשיב ליה לחובה על נפשיה,דקביעותא דקביעא עילויה,כעין-מצוה;ם ותו לא מידי. :

כתוב-שם:אבל באמת אין לנו ברכת-התקיעה מדברי-רבותינו,אלא ברכה של תפלה.

אמר אברהם:יש כאן הפוך שטם-יזמי להוא,אי זה דרך עבר רוח-האמת-סם מאת <u>כל הגאונים ז"ל עמודי-עולם</u>,ומאת כמה גדולים וחכמים-וישישים אשר נהגו כמנהג הזה,לדבר אתו,והנה שם השם גפס-בדג בפיו-וזאת עדות על כל בדגמף פוסעפאמף אשר אסף רוח בחפניו להנבא בדגמי, ולהתעות-הפתיים והסכלים,בעדיי-אחרים אשר נתעטר בהם ספר-צימגפח-סם אשר חבר,וברוך יי׳ אשר החיינו,והעיר את רוחי,ועזרני לגלות בדגמף, ולהחזיר עטרה ליושנה,ולהושיבה במקומה,ולא עזב תורת-אמת אשר נתן-ם לנו,ביד לחמכמי;להתעות בהם,כהתעות בלפג שדמתף.ועתה אשוב לדבר על-צבדג אשר כתב בכאן,ואע"פ שהוא דבר מפורסם לכל איש אשר בו רוח-חיים כי איך יצאה מצוה זו מכלל שאר מצות שאין לה ברכה מטבע קצר,ובאי-ם זו ברכה תפטר,וכי מלכיות וזכרונות ושופרות ברכה הן למצות-שופר.סם ועוד: איך הם עובר לתקיעות,והלא יש מהן לפנים ולאחור,שהתקיעות סם באמצע הם,כמו ששנינו:מלכיות ותוקע,זכרונות ותוקע,שופרות ותוקע./:

1ב-מאור לרי"ף תתקמז(זא)מגמ׳כחא.1ה-קידב.3ד-שבת כאא.6א-כסנהדרין סבב.8ב-נ"ל פליגא.9ב-מאור תתקמט(חא)מגמ׳לא.10ד-ר"י בן שאול משמו.11ח-לא-היו משמע בדור הקודם.17ב-מאור תתקנב(חב)מגמ׳לבא.19ד-ר׳ במלחמת.21ה-הרי"ף.22ג-להא,אלא כרבותיו 23ב-מאור לתתקנה(טב)ממשנה לבב.25ג-מבא.28ב-מאור לתתקנז(יא)מגמ׳לדא.30ב-ויקראם יש

השאר בדף-מב.

(*a*)

Figure 1.1 R. Abraham ben David, *Katuv sham*: (*a*) the encoded version in M. Z. Hasidah's edition (Jerusalem: no publisher given, 1969); (*b*) the uncensored version in the 1990 edition (Jerusalem: Hatam Sofer Institute for Manuscript Research)

במאור דף י: ד"ה ומה שנהגו. לרי"ף סי' תתקנו (ראש השנה דף לד:)

כתוב שם: אבל באמת אין לנו ברכת התקיעה מדברי [רבותינו אלא ברכות של תפלה בלבד][59].

אמר אברהם· יש כאן הפוך בני מעין לההוא, אי זה דרך עבר רוח האמת מאת כל הגאונים ז"ל עמודי עולם ומאת כמה גדולים וחכמים וישישים אשר נהגו כמנהג הזה לדבר אתו, והנה שם השם רוח שקר בפיו, וזאת עדות על כל שקריו ופחזותיו אשר אסף רוח בחפניו להנבא שקרים ולהתעות הפתיים והסכלים בעדיי אחרים אשר נתעטר בהם ספר המירוס אשר חבר, וברוך יי' אשר החיינו והעיר את רוחי ועזרני לגלות שקריו ולהחזיר עטרה ליושנה ולהושיבה במקומה, ולא עזב תורת אמת אשר נתן לנו ביד כסילים להתעות בהם כהתעות שיכור בקיאו. ועתה אשוב לדבר על השקר אשר כתב בכאן ואע"פ שהוא דבר מפורסם לכל איש אשר בו רוח חיים, כי איך יצאה מצוה זו מכלל שאר מצות שאין לה ברכה מטבע קצר, ובאי זו ברכה תפטר, וכי מלכיות וזכרונות ושופרות ברכה הן למצות שופר. ועוד איך הם עובר לתקיעות והלא יש מהן לפנים ולאחור שהתקיעות באמצע הם, כמו ששנינו [דף לב.] מלכיות ותוקע זכרונות ותוקע שופרות ותוקע. ושינוי המנהגות מאין לו, ושמא כך התקין רבי אבהו לתקיעות הללו מיושב אבל מעומד שלא להטריח את הצבור מספק לא שהרי יצאו הכל ידי חובתן. והראיה שמביא מילדותו ברכות לצבור וכו' ובזקנותו נשתנה המנהג, השנוי ההוא מאביו יצא ששנה המנהג בעירו על דרך הרב אבן גיאת ז"ל[60] אע"פ שלא היה הוא מודה באותו דבר, אבל רצה אביו להתגדר בדברים זרים ומצא נערים ושאינן בני תורה והנהיגם כרצון רוחו, ואחר כך באו שם אנשי תורה משאר מקומות ולא שמעו למנהגיו הזרים והחזירו המעשה לאמיתו ולמנהגו, וגם הוא קם תחת אביו לשנות דתות ולהחליף מנהגות, ויאבד הוא ואלף כיוצא בו ואות מן ההלכות לא תבטל ומנהג אחד לא ישתנה.

במאור דף יב. ד"ה ואני אומר. לרי"ף סי' תתקסב (ראש השנה דף לד.)

כתוב שם: יש שמדקדקין בשמועה זו על הסדר שאנו נוהגין [היום מה הן][61] כו'.

אמר אברהם: הדקדוק הזה דק לעפר הוא, ואין צורך להשיג עליו. ובאמת וברור אותן שכמיושב הן לערבב, ומכל מקום כבר נפטרו בהם אלא שצריכים לסדר אותן על סדר ברכות ולפיכך מברך עליהם. והם כל דבר שלו שכתב על שמועתו של רבי יצחק [דף טז:] הלא היא כשאר דבריו וחדושיו שלא הצליחו ולא השכילו מעולם ואני קורא אליהם אֲבָל על הניירים שהופסדו בהם ואין צורך להשיב עליהם. ופירוש הערבוב בדרך אמת הוא כדי שאם בא להשטן ישטין על התקיעות הראשונות וכשיעמדו הצבור בתפלה ויתקעו לא ישטין עוד שאין לו רשות להשטין שתי פעמים ותהא תפלת הצבור מקובלת עם זכרון תרועתם. וזהו פירוש הערבוב באמת. ומתוך פירושנו כל דבריו בטלים ונשברים כחרס[62].

במאור דף יב: ד"ה וזו שכתב הרי"ף. לרי"ף סי' תתקס (ר"ה דף לה.)

כתוב שם: וכן נמצא בשאלתות דרב אחאי גאון ז"ל [פרשת בא].

אמר אברהם: שקר העיד על רב אחאי ז"ל, והרב רבי יצחק[63] מסעד לדבריו מרב אחאי ז"ל, ורב האיי גאון ז"ל כך פירש כמו שכתב הרב זלה"ה, והוא העיקר, שאין טעם לברכה באמצע כלל, וכי מברכין על שתי סמיכות זו סמוכה לזו לא בפסחים [פסחים דף קכא.] ולא בחגיגות, וכן בלולב ואתרוג אע"פ שהן נפרדין. ואם שתי מצות הן שח ביניהם למה עבירה בידו והלא מופסקים הן. ובדבריו של זה אין ממש שאמר ממשמש בשל יד ומחזק הקשר שלו וחוזר ומברך ברכת היד ושל הראש, מעתה אין כאן שתים בשל ראש, שקבלת דבי רב אסי[64] כל אימת דממשמשי בהו מברכי [סוכה דף מו.] הלכך אין כאן לא שתים בשל יד (יד) ולא שתים בשל ראש, ומה נעשה לחכמי צרפת[65] שהן תוקעין את עצמן לדבר הלכה.

(b)

not come across very well among readers who see his harsh language.[50] Secondly, while there is a code here, it is not that hard to break, as it is written in *at–bash*.[51] In Figure 1.1(*b*), from a 1990 edition of the work, one can see how the passage looks when decoded.

Let me offer a few other examples of this tendency to cover up matters that might reflect poorly on rabbinic leaders. In 1937 Abraham Isaac Rabinowitz published a small book of hasidic tales. Despite Rabinowitz's good intentions, some felt that he was not careful enough in what he decided to include. One of his stories describes how some of the sons of R. Shneur Zalman Fradkin of Lublin (1830–1902) 'did not behave properly'. After the wife of his eldest son died, the widower remarried. Under the wedding canopy 'R. Shneur Zalman placed his hands on his son's head, and in a weeping voice cried out: "My son, God will help you to become a penitent." And his blessing was fulfilled, because he later travelled to the land of Israel and there he became a great *ba'al teshuvah* and almost a *tsadik*.'[52] When this book was reprinted in 1966, this story, which many would find moving, was omitted.[53] It was not thought proper for the masses to know that a great man like R. Shneur Zalman had children who did not follow in his footsteps, even if at least one of them later mended his ways.[54]

While the instance just mentioned deals with possibly embarrassing family history, we find cases where the embarrassment shielded by censorship relates to the rabbinic sages themselves. Disputes between great rabbis have not been uncommon in Jewish history, yet in the midst of these disputes, accusations have often been made that many in the Orthodox world would

[50] On pp. 2–3 of Hasidah's edition of *Katuv sham*, he notes that he was very troubled by some of Rabad's harsh language and consulted with two sages in Jerusalem about whether he should delete these comments. They instructed him not to alter or omit any of Rabad's words. It is unknown why Hasidah later rejected what these two sages told him.

[51] In the *at–bash* system, the last letter of the alphabet, *tav*, is substituted for the first letter, *alef*, the penultimate letter, *shin*, replaces the second letter, *bet*, and so on. See Trachtenberg, *Jewish Magic and Superstition*, 263.

[52] A. I. Rabinowitz, *Malakhei elyon* (1937 edn.), 40 (no. 4).

[53] See A. I. Rabinowitz, *Malakhei elyon* (1966 edn.), 39. This edition also omits the passage, p. 40 in the original edition, which describes how certain quarrelsome people made R. Shneur Zalman's life miserable, which led R. Shneur himself to move to the land of Israel.

[54] A. I. Rabinowitz, *Malakhei elyon* (1937 edn.), 24, also reports that R. Tsadok Hakohen of Lublin (1823–1900) crossed out the first comment of Tosafot in BT *AZ*, and that this volume is still to be found in R. Tsadok's *beit midrash*. Rabinowitz states that he does not know why R. Tsadok crossed it out. The editor of the 1966 edition did not regard this story as something the masses should see, and it was therefore deleted. For another example, see A. Morgenstern, *Mysticism and Messianism* (Heb.), 259–60, who notes that in the published version of the Vilna Gaon's grandson's introduction to his grandfather's commentary on the Zohar, remarks that depict the Gaon as having little concern with his family were deleted.

now prefer to be forgotten. A good deal of censorship and rewriting of history thus focuses on this area.[55]

Another example when some feel censorship is called for is if a sage egregiously erred in what he wrote; the desire is therefore to cover up this error. I am not referring to a case where the sage is thought to have erred in a theological matter, although there are examples of that as well.[56] I am rather referring to a basic historical error. One instance of this relates to R. Eliezer David Gruenwald (1867–1928), who served as rabbi of the Orthodox community in Satmar in the early part of the twentieth century. His responsa were given to R. David Katzburg (1856–1937) to prepare for publication. Katzburg was a fine scholar in his own right and edited the Hungarian Torah journal *Tel talpiyot*. In going through Gruenwald's writings, Katzburg came upon a responsum in which Gruenwald took another author to task for pointing out an error in the Torah's chapter divisions. Gruenwald saw this as a unacceptable position since these chapter divisions go back to Moses at Sinai and, as with everything else given to Moses, contain all sorts of Torah wisdom.

Katzburg was not sure what to do with this responsum, since to print it would show that the author was ignorant of a pretty basic matter, namely, that the chapter divisions found in the Pentateuch are of Christian origin. He therefore turned to two leading Hungarian scholars, R. Samuel Engel (1853–1935) and R. Mordechai Winkler (1844–1932), asking them how to proceed. Surprisingly, Engel too was unaware of the history of the chapter divisions, and expressed agreement with Gruenwald's view that the chapters were of Jewish origin (although unlike Gruenwald he was unsure if they went back to Moses). Winkler was more careful and suggested that the responsum should not be published before the matter was investigated. However,

[55] This is the motivation of Aharon Sorasky, who in 1991 published a volume, *Yesod hama'alah*, containing hasidic letters from the land of Israel, but omitted documents that focused on an early hasidic dispute. He justified this omission by citing Prov. 25: 2: 'It is the glory of God to conceal a thing.' See Assaf, 'It is the Glory' (Heb.). See also the preface to the Jerusalem, 1987 edition of R. Menahem Mendel of Vitebsk's *Peri ha'arets*. R. Hayim Hezekiah Medini (1833–1904) wrote to Samuel Abba Horodetzky protesting the latter's inclusion, in one of his works, of R. Solomon Luria's (1510–74) strong words of criticism against certain figures (among them R. Joseph Karo (1488–1575)). Medini also cited Prov. 25: 2. See Medini, *Igerot sedei ḥemed*, vol. i, no. 11. In the 17th cent., the rabbis of Venice ordered that a page of R. Meir of Lublin's (1558–1616) posthumously published responsa, *Manhir einei ḥakhamim*, be replaced with a new page because it contained an attack on a deceased rabbi from Mantua and the latter's children had lodged a protest. See Modena, *Ziknei yehudah*, no. 28; Rivkind, 'Dikdukei sefarim', 427–8; Adelman, 'Success and Failure', 497–8. Hebrewbooks.org has two copies of this work; one has the original page (14*a*) and the other is the censored version.

[56] For example, a section from a sermon of R. Ezekiel Landau (1713–93) in which he questioned the authenticity of the Zohar was deleted from a posthumously published volume. This section has recently been published in Kahana and Silber, 'Deists, Sabbatians, and Kabbalists' (Heb.).

Katzburg did not need to investigate anything, as he knew the history of this matter quite well. His only question was whether it was proper to publish a responsum that makes an obvious error. Since Winkler agreed that if Gruenwald was mistaken the responsum should not be published, this is the path Katzburg followed.[57]

A similar example appears in a volume of commentary on the Torah by R. Judah Leib Diskin (1818–98) that first appeared in 2008. Not long after the volume was published, someone noticed that Diskin, who identified with Jerusalem's extremist Orthodox community, quotes from the work *Hakorem*. This was written by the notorious *maskil* Herz Homberg (1749–1841), who by the end of his life had 'incurred the nearly universal hatred of his Jewish contemporaries'.[58] Needless to say, once it became known whom Diskin was quoting, the volume was embargoed and the objectionable passage removed. The people responsible for this censorship acted on the assumption, which I believe is probably correct, that Diskin did not know who Homberg was, and thus mistakenly quoted from his work. By removing the reference to him, the censors felt that they were saving Diskin embarrassment.[59]

Those who practise this sort of censorship would in no way agree with Shaul Stampfer's judgement that their actions show that they presume that they are wiser than the author of the text being censored.[60] From their perspective, it is not at all incongruous to be both a loyal student and a loyal

[57] See G. Oberlander, 'On the Division of the Torah into Chapters' (Heb.), 150–1. Oberlander quotes other leading rabbis who also assumed that the chapter divisions have a Jewish origin. See also Y. H. Sofer, *Menuḥat shalom*, vol. xi, ch. 67.

[58] *EJ*, viii, s.v. 'Homberg, Naphtali Herz'. In contrast to this negative judgement, Rachel Manekin has used archival research to argue that Homberg has been unfairly caricatured. See Manekin, 'Naphtali Herz Homberg' (Heb.). According to Manekin, the negative view of Homberg dates from the 1860s, so it is possible that Diskin's commentary dates from before this time.

[59] For more details of this incident, see my Seforim Blog post, 25 Oct. 2009. For a similar example, see the introduction to Eybeschuetz, *Sar ha'elef*, where R. Aryeh Leib Zuenz (1768–1833) writes that in publishing the work he omitted certain things that he was sure could not have been said by R. Jonathan Eybeschuetz (1690–1764). In one of his famous letters against the Reformers, R. Moses Sofer was mistaken in some of his historical points. When this letter was later reprinted in Sofer's responsa, the section with the errors was removed. Presumably, Sofer's sons were informed about the errors and this led to the omission. See Goldhaber, '"Come, Let Us Go"' (Heb.), 130 n. 36. In an unpublished critique of Dov Eliach's *Sefer hagaon*, p. 27, R. David Tsevi Hillman (1926–2010) requests that publishers delete R. Solomon Kohen's (1828–1905) final comment on tractate *Sukah* in his glosses on the Talmud, *Ḥeshek shelomoh* (printed in the Vilna Talmud), s. v. *hashmatah* to 2*a*, since its obvious error reflects poorly on Kohen.

[60] Stampfer, *Lithuanian Yeshivas*, 11 n. 20. Cf. D. Berger, *Cultures in Collision and Conversation*, 15: 'The observer who affirms untrammeled respect for the rabbinic figure, substitutes his own judgment for that of the rabbi, and then appeals to that rabbi's sanitized image as a model for the posture of which he approves.'

censor. This is because a completely innocuous passage in 1900 could be regarded as embarrassing or religiously problematic a hundred years later. Many of the censors act on the assumption that the authors themselves, were they alive today, would agree with the censorship. Indeed, this is not always a false assumption, and R. Abraham Mordechai Alter (1866–1948), the Rebbe of Gur, even wrote in his will that his successor 'should burn that which will not be good for me'.[61]

Yehoshua Mondshine has described hasidic censorship as follows:

> The phenomenon that hasidim omit things from the writings of their rabbis is not at all rare. They do not see in this any contradiction to the holiness of the words of the *rebbe*, as long as they are certain that their intentions and actions are proper and correspond to the true outlook of their *rebbe*, or when the omission is done out of a concern of damaging the rabbi's honour.[62]

Yet I think that most readers, while understanding what motivates the censors, will nevertheless conclude that the instances of censorship that we discuss in this book are examples of what the Talmud describes as 'a generation that judges its judges'.[63]

Keeping Information from the Masses

The notion that information even from canonical texts should be kept from the masses was, as is well known, an important issue in the medieval and pre-Reformation Church, and was responsible for opposition to translation of the Bible into the vernacular.[64] Jews often think that this was an exclusively Christian phenomenon, and that Jewish thinkers were always in favour of Torah knowledge for all. Yet this was not the case. Just as the Church's concern with vernacular Bibles had to do with the heresy that could come from individuals approaching the sacred texts unmediated, so too there were concerns of a similar nature among Jewish scholars.

I am not speaking here about the study of philosophy or kabbalah that was always viewed as reserved for the elites,[65] but of the Bible itself. With the rise

[61] See Tavyomi, *Evel kaved*, 21.

[62] Y. Mondshine, 'Authenticity of Hasidic Letters' (Heb.), 89. The second reason offered would apparently explain why the discussion of Robinson Crusoe was deleted from the English translation of R. Zalman Sorotzkin's (1881–1966) commentary on the Torah. See On the Main Line, 6 Oct. 2010.

[63] BT *BB* 15*b*.

[64] Deanesly, *The Lollard Bible*. See also Baron, *Social and Religious History*, ix (1965), 55–6. The notion that all Catholic religious figures were opposed to translations is, however, an exaggeration. See Walsham, 'Unclasping the Book?', 147 ff.

[65] The Talmud itself restricts the study of certain mystical matters. See BT *Ḥag.* 11*b*.

of the Haskalah, the Jewish Enlightenment movement, in the late eighteenth century, and the prominent place it gave to Bible study, one sees a counter-reaction from the Orthodox.[66] R. Solomon Kluger (1789–1865) was even asked whether it was permitted to study the Bible intensively. He answers in the affirmative, but his permission is limited to adults. Children are not to be exposed to such study for fear that it will lead them into 'the web of the heretics'.[67]

R. Moses Sofer is reported to have expressed the same attitude with regard to the study of Hebrew grammar: whereas in earlier generations its study was completely proper, once the heretics had begun focusing on it the pious were to keep away.[68] Even the basic study of Jewish law by laymen was frowned upon by some. Thus, it is reported that R. Hayim of Volozhin (1749–1821) refused to give an approbation to the *Ḥayei adam*, a halakhic handbook by R. Abraham Danzig (1748–1820). He did not believe that the masses should have easy access to texts of Jewish law, and thus no longer be dependent on a rabbi.[69] Likewise, R. Hayim Sofer (1821–86) opposed vernacular translations of the halakhic code *Kitsur shulḥan arukh* by R. Solomon Ganzfried (1804–66).[70] A few generations before, in the late eighteenth century, Elhanan Kirchhahn's *Simḥat hanefesh* was burnt by the rabbis of Vilna. The book's 'crime' was that it discussed Jewish laws and customs in the vernacular.[71] In an earlier era, R. Jacob Moelin (*c*.1365–1427) also expressed his opposition to halakhic works in the vernacular.[72] These viewpoints, while no longer popular, have not completely disappeared. Thus, one opponent of the ArtScroll translation of the Talmud offered as his reason the notion that Talmud study is supposed to

[66] In medieval times some rabbis were concerned about teaching the Bible to children. R. Tsemah Gaon (9th cent.) even thought that it could lead to heresy. See M. Breuer, *Asif*, 237 ff. For more discussion on the place of Bible study, see M. Breuer, *Ohalei torah*, 123 ff.

[67] S. Kluger, *Ha'elef lekha shelomoh*, no. 259. Kluger's attitude was adopted by many, and was the focus of Haskalah criticism. See Parush, *Reading Jewish Women*, 65–6. See also R. Simon Glazer's Hebrew introduction to his translation of Maimonides' *Mishneh torah*, 35; J. T. Sofer, *Toledot soferim*, 103 n.

[68] See A. J. Schlesinger, *Lev ha'ivri*, 16 (section 'Yad ha'ivri'). Cf. the almost identical formulations of S. Kluger, *Ha'elef lekha shelomoh*, no. 257 and R. Tsevi Elimelekh Shapira of Dynów, *Ma'yan ganim*, 98. See also Schneebalg, *Shraga hame'ir*, vol. vii, no. 122.

[69] See Shmukler (Shapiro), *Life of R. Hayim of Volozhin* (Heb.), ch. 10 (p. 44). In his note on this passage, at the beginning of the volume, Abraham Elijah Harkavy calls attention to R. Judah Minz's (*c*.1408–1506) comment that there were rabbis who did not use R. Jacob ben Asher's (1270–*c*.1340) halakhic code, *Arba'ah turim* (*Tur*), explaining that this was because it was used by the masses. See Mintz, *Responsa* (Heb.), no. 15.

[70] See H. Sofer, *Kan sofer*, 132. As he put it: הלואי שלא היו נמסרים הדינים לעמי הארץ.

[71] See Carmilly-Weinberger, *Censorship and Freedom of Expression*, 181. See also Zinberg, *History of Jewish Literature* (Heb.), iv. 107, 256.

[72] Moelin, *Responsa* (Heb.), no. 93: 1.

be restricted to the elites, and that ArtScroll frustrates this goal by allowing the masses to participate in this study.[73]

This division between the elites and the masses, so much at odds with modern understandings of how knowledge is to be disseminated, is related to a talmudic concept known as *halakhah ve'ein morin ken*, meaning, 'This is the halakhah, but we do not teach it.' This concept appears a number of times in the Talmud (not to mention in numerous post-talmudic sources),[74] and in one talmudic passage it is given biblical justification from Proverbs 25: 2: 'It is the glory of God to conceal a thing.'[75] According to Nahmanides (1194–1270), the concept can even be seen in the Torah itself.[76] What it means is that although something is technically permitted, the rabbis do not inform the masses of this because of a fear that using this *heter* (permission) could have negative ramifications.[77] As in the case of covering up historical events of the past, here too the elite has the information, yet they make a choice not to allow the masses to have this knowledge.[78] At times, this means that no one avails themselves of the *heter*, but on other occasions it is only the masses who are not given the *heter*, but the elites are free to make use of it.[79]

[73] Gorelik, 'On Printing the Talmud' (Heb.), 39–40. Regarding opposition to the translation of aggadic literature into the vernacular, see Eleazar Mermelstein's articles in *Pinat yikrat*, 5 (Av 5761), 72–90, ibid. 27 (Tamuz 5763), 84–7.

[74] See *Entsiklopedyah talmudit*, vol. ix, s.v. *halakhah ve'ein morin ken*; Fogelman, 'Practical Halakhah' (Heb.); R. Tsevi Hirsch Chajes' note on BT *Shab.* 153*b*; R. Meir Mazuz's introduction to vol. iii of the Ish Matsliah edition of the *Mishnah berurah* (Benei Berak, 2007), 17. The very first *mishnah*, *Ber.* 1: 1, contains an example where the Sages did not reveal the true halakhah 'in order to keep a man far from transgression'.

[75] See BT *Shab.* 153*b*.

[76] See his commentary on Num. 30: 2.

[77] According to R. Joseph Messas (1892–1974), the Sages forbade women being called to the Torah to prevent male sexual arousal. Fearing that the masses would be insulted that the Sages thought so little of their capacity for self-control, the Sages provided them with a false reason for the prohibition. See Messas, *Mayim ḥayim*, vol. ii, 'Oraḥ ḥayim', no. 140, and my Seforim Blog post, 11 June 2012.

[78] See R. Vidal of Tolosa, *Magid mishneh* on Maimonides, *Mishneh torah*, 'Hilkhot isurei biah' 21: 10, who states that Maimonides did not record a certain halakhah in the *Mishneh torah*: כדי להרחיק מהרגל תשמיש. See also Brand, 'Principles of Omission' (Heb.), 53.

[79] See Schachter, *Mipeninei harav*, 153–4, recording that R. Joseph B. Soloveitchik (1903–93) told his students that it was permissible to eat non-Jewish cheese if the rennet had a vegetable base, but that this information was not to be revealed to the masses. See also Yosef, *Ma'yan omer*, ii. 260, that one is permitted to turn on an electric light if for some reason it went off on a festival, but that this should not be made public knowledge. R. Isaac Herzog writes that those who believe that electricity is only rabbinically forbidden on the Sabbath must keep this information from the masses. See Herzog, *Pesakim ukhetavim*, vol. ii, 'Oraḥ ḥayim', no. 67. For an example of *halakhah ve'ein morin ken* when dealing with another scholar, see M. Sofer, *She'elot uteshuvot ḥatam sofer*, vol. ii, 'Yoreh de'ah', no. 338 (end). Here R. Moses Sofer tells us that he was not entirely frank with R. Tsevi Hirsch Chajes, for fear of what the latter would do with Sofer's suggested leniency. In order not to embarrass Chajes, the publisher actually removed his name as the recipient of Sofer's

We find one talmudic example, in *Menaḥot* 36*b*, which shows that even telling an untruth was permitted as part of *halakhah ve'ein morin ken*: 'Ravina related, I was once sitting before R. Ashi when darkness had already fallen and he put on his tefillin, so I said to him, "Is it my Master's purpose to guard them?" "Yes", he replied. I saw, however, that his purpose was not to guard them. He was of the opinion that that was the law,[80] but one should not rule so [in actual practice].'[81] Here we see that in order to prevent others from knowing what the law was, R. Ashi resorted to lying, and this is regarded as acceptable.[82]

Halakhah ve'ein morin ken is a matter that requires its own detailed treatment, and I mention it here because of its relevance to the issue under discussion. If rabbinic leaders are entitled, indeed sometimes called upon, to hide the true halakhah because of fear of the consequences were this information to get into the hands of the masses, it makes perfect sense that this outlook would also be found in non-halakhic matters. In fact, we see from the Talmud that it is not merely with regard to matters of halakhah that there is a distinction between the scholars and the masses. The Mishnah states: 'The story of Reuben [and his father's concubine] is read but not translated.'[83] The intellectuals do not need a translation to understand what the text is saying, but the masses are deliberately kept in the dark in order that Reuben's reputation be preserved.[84]

Another example is mentioned by Rashi, who states that the Torah alters the order of events of Abraham leaving his home and the death of Terah, Abraham's father, in order that 'the matter should not be publicized'. This was done so that people would not conclude that Abraham did not honour his father properly, as he left home before the latter's death.[85] Those with some learning, that is, those who can read Rashi, are let in on the truth, while everyone else is left with a mistaken impression.

letter. That he was indeed the recipient can be seen by examining Chajes, *Darkhei hahora'ah*, part 2, no. 6, in his *Kol sifrei maharats ḥayes*, i.

80 That tefillin are to be worn at night.

81 Lest one fall asleep while wearing the tefillin.

82 See similarly BT *Beits.* 28*b*.

83 *Meg.* 4: 10.

84 It is also possible that the text is not translated so that the masses do not take it literally. Yet there is no evidence that the non-literal interpretation of this episode, advocated by R. Jonathan (see BT *Shab.* 55*b*), was shared by the Mishnah.

85 Rashi on Gen. 11: 32 (based on *Bereshit rabah* 39: 7, but not identical). See also BT *Shab.* 96*b* where R. Akiva reveals that the man who gathered sticks on the Sabbath (Num. 15: 32) was Zelophehad. R. Judah b. Bathyra remarked: 'Akiva! In either case you will have to give an account [for your statement]. If you are right, the Torah shielded him, while you reveal him, and if not, you cast a stigma upon a righteous man.'

Is Truth a Value?

As people go through this book and see the many examples of censorship and distortion, they are bound to wonder: what happened to the value of truth, in particular historical truth? The importance of being truthful is certainly something that Jews regard as significant and teach their children. Here, for example, is a magnet handed out by my children's school some years ago (Figure 1.2).

People might be surprised, therefore, by the evidence brought in this book that when it comes to truth, matters are much more complicated than usually thought. As we will see, for many, the value of truth is seen in a somewhat utilitarian light, and absolute truth may be set aside in many cases. I will postpone a detailed analysis of the role of truth in Jewish tradition, and when falsehood is permitted, to the last chapter. For now, I want to deal with the educational aspect, which is the focus of an essay by Mordechai Breuer entitled 'Concerning Truth in Education'.[86] In this essay he deals with the value of truth in pedagogy, and asks if at times 'educational lies' are acceptable. One of the sources he discusses is by R. Elijah Dessler (1892–1953), who offers a new understanding of 'truth'. According to Dessler, truth should not be understood as identical with certain facts. Rather, 'truth is that which advances the good and brings people to do God's will'.[87] Dessler cites Jacob's lying to his father in order to get the blessing intended for Esau. Since Jacob was doing this entirely for selfless motives, in order to advance God's will, his action must also be regarded as 'truthful'.[88]

Figure 1.2 Joseph Kushner Hebrew Academy magnet, displaying the motto 'The Truth and Nothing but the Truth'

[86] M. Breuer, *Asif*, 260–76. [87] Ibid. 270. [88] Dessler, *Mikhtav me'eliyahu*, i. 94.

Many will claim that Dessler's perspective is not helpful, for all he has done is engage in a semantic game. One could just as easily argue that truth must sometimes be set aside in the name of some more important consideration. Indeed, that is exactly what Dessler is justifying, so why does he insist on holding on to the word 'truth'? Presumably, he does so because of the generally great significance and value of truth in the Jewish tradition. Rather than countenance the rejection of truth, even as an emergency measure (as we will see many do), he is more comfortable redefining what 'truth' means.

It is also possible that Dessler was influenced in his approach by William James' pragmatic theory of truth. Dessler is known to have read non-Jewish writings, and I have noted elsewhere that one of his sermons is lifted from Dale Carnegie's *How to Win Friends and Influence People*.[89] It is not unlikely that he was aware of William James' famous formulation: 'On pragmatic principles, if the hypothesis of God works satisfactorily in the widest sense of the word, it is true.'[90] With this statement, James defines truth in a utilitarian fashion. For Dessler, truth is also to be understood in this manner, yet the focus for him is not on whether something benefits humans, but whether it is in the service of God.

Returning to Breuer, he does not reject the notion of 'pedagogical truth'. Thus, in another essay[91] he cites an article by R. Shlomo Wolbe that speaks of 'hundreds of thousands' of yeshiva students in pre-Second World War Europe, who were entirely devoted to Torah study without any secular learning.[92] The point of this text was to encourage students in Israel to also devote themselves exclusively to Torah study, since they had to replace that which was lost in the Holocaust.

From the standpoint of historical accuracy, the statement is entirely without basis, and indeed, for many years now there have been more young men studying full time in Israel than ever studied in European yeshivas. Yet Breuer sees this as an example of 'pedagogical truth', and he finds this entirely acceptable, as its purpose is not to establish a historical fact, but rather to influence students in a positive direction. In other words, there are different types of truths and 'historical truth' need not be preferred over other sorts of truth (e.g. pedagogical truth, moral truth, etc.). As Breuer puts it: 'It is possible to tell yeshiva students things whose truth is only pedagogical, and as mentioned there is nothing wrong with this. But for the readers of *Hama'yan*, and this includes the yeshiva students among them, one must speak the factual and historical truth.'[93]

[89] M. B. Shapiro, *Saul Lieberman and the Orthodox*, 40–1.
[90] James, *Pragmatism*, 299.
[91] See M. Breuer, *Asif*, 359 n.2.
[92] See Wolbe, 'Contemporary Yeshiva' (Heb.), 38.
[93] M. Breuer, *Asif*, 361.

In other words, when Wolbe tried to pass off 'pedagogical truth' as historical truth on the pages of a journal with which Breuer was involved, that was crossing the line. Typical yeshiva students can be treated in a paternalistic manner and fed all sorts of fraudulent notions, but Breuer regards those who are sophisticated enough to read the semi-academic *Hama'yan* as an elite, and 'pedagogical truth' is no longer acceptable when speaking to them. Although Breuer intended his approach to be supportive of the special 'truths' of the yeshiva world, it would not be surprising if members of this society would regard his approach as incredibly insulting, as people often do when they learn that they have been treated in a paternalistic fashion by those who thought they knew what was best for them.

For his part, Breuer cites biblical passages that seem to support his approach. For example, when Abraham is taking Isaac to Mount Moriah and Isaac asks where the lamb is, Abraham replies that God will show it to them.[94] Breuer sees this as an example of 'pedagogical truth', a truth that gives an answer in accord with the mindset and sophistication of the questioner. Although Breuer does not cite him, R. Azariah de Rossi (*c.*1511–*c.*1578) develops a similar idea in discussing the fantastic story told in the Talmud of how a gnat lived in the emperor Titus' head for seven years, eventually growing into some sort of bird with a brass beak and iron claws.[95] According to de Rossi, the talmudic sages knew that this story was not factual, but was created to impart spiritual lessons. As I will discuss at length below,[96] one is allowed to alter the truth for 'the sake of peace', and based on this de Rossi asserts that certainly one can do so in order to establish peace 'between us and our Father in Heaven'.[97] In other words, falsification of the historical record, or what Breuer calls 'pedagogical truth', is permitted in the name of a higher purpose. As with similar examples in rabbinic literature, de Rossi understands the story about Titus to be a case where the masses will take the tale literally, while the intellectuals will understand that it is merely a pious myth.

What Breuer calls a 'pedagogical truth' was termed a 'necessary belief' by Maimonides (1138–1205). In *Guide of the Perplexed*, iii. 28 Maimonides discusses the difference between what he calls 'true beliefs' and 'necessary beliefs'. 'True beliefs' are those which teach, in a literal fashion, some truth about God, such as His existence, unity, eternity, and omnipotence. Their purpose is to enable one to attain intellectual perfection. 'Necessary beliefs', the basis of which is tradition and not philosophy, are expressed in a figurative manner and fulfil a political function in that, by instilling obedience to the Torah, they regulate the social relations of human beings. In addition, they

[94] Gen. 22: 7–8. [95] BT *Git.* 56*b*. [96] See Ch. 8.
[97] de Rossi, *Me'or einayim*, 103*a* (ch. 16). See Eisen, 'Maharal's *Be'er ha-Golah*', 184.

enable people to acquire noble qualities. For example, the Torah teaches that God is angry with those who disobey Him. Although in truth God does not have the characteristic of anger, the Torah found it advantageous to use this concept for the effect that it would have. It is 'necessary' for the masses to believe that God is angry if they disobey Him, in order for them to keep their behaviour in line. In addition, it is 'necessary' for the masses to believe that God responds instantly to the prayer of someone who is wronged or deceived. For them to believe otherwise would be damaging to their faith.

This notion of 'necessary beliefs' is a basic facet of Maimonides' religious outlook, and a complete discussion of its particulars would go beyond the confines of this study. Suffice it to say that not only does Maimonides identify 'necessary beliefs' in the Torah, but there are also 'necessary beliefs' in his own writings.[98] Maimonides actually tells us right at the beginning of the *Guide* that he will say certain things that do not reflect his true opinion. For the masses, who are not able to see beneath the surface of this work, the 'truths' that they believe in are sufficient to ensure their attachment to the Torah and Jewish life without causing difficulties to their religious faith. The conventional teaching is the 'necessary belief' of Maimonides, while the hidden teaching is the true message.

What is important for us is that Maimonides sees this as an acceptable approach, that is, outwardly advocating a position that will be religiously helpful for many, even though it is not his true opinion. This approach of religious esotericism was popular with numerous medieval thinkers, and even continued in later centuries. To give one modern example, R. Kook writes that one should not publicly express ideas that one believes to be true if they can have negative consequences on those with a different outlook.[99]

Types of Censorship

In speaking of censorship, we must also note that there is a difference between deleting passages when reprinting a text, and not allowing passages to appear when the text is first published. In Orthodox publishing there has long been an assumption that negative personal comments directed against renowned sages should be omitted when publishing a deceased author's work from manuscript.[100] The assumption is that the author would not have

[98] See my *Limits of Orthodox Theology*, 119 ff., and *Studies in Maimonides and His Interpreters*, 85. I plan to elaborate on this point in a future article.

[99] A. I. Kook, *Shemonah kevatsim*, vol. vi, no. 57. Cf. also a letter by Samuel David Luzzatto (1800–65), published in *Otsar neḥmad*, 4 (1863), 129.

[100] Occasionally one finds exceptions to this, e.g. in at least two of the works of R. Elijah David Rabinowitz-Teomim (1843–1905). See my Seforim Blog post, 25 Jan. 2007, and Dan Rabinowitz's post, ibid., 27 May 2010.

wanted this to see the light of day. This explains the common use of ellipses when individuals are criticized.

In speaking of how to present the past, there are also clearly distinctions to be made between leaving out information and fabricating falsehoods. Yet, as we shall see, both paths can find solid support in traditional sources. David Assaf calls attention to the two approaches in his discussion of the apostasy of the son of R. Shneur Zalman of Lyady (1745–1812), the founder of Habad *ḥasidut*.[101] This was, of course, a shocking event, and not something that Habad historians would want to record. Thus we find Hayim Meir Heilman covering up the story in his classic history of Habad, *Beit rabi*. It is the sixth Lubavitcher Rebbe, R. Joseph Isaac Schneersohn (1880–1950), who engages in a full rewrite of the apostasy, which Assaf assumes must be a conscious fabrication. This may be correct; if the Rebbe thought that knowledge of this information would have a negative impact on his hasidim, he certainly could have found justification for creating a 'counter-history'.

Yet perhaps Schneersohn was really convinced of the truth of what he was writing. After all, he strenuously defended the authenticity of the notorious forgeries of hasidic letters found in Kherson, Russia (and his son-in-law and successor, R. Menachem Mendel Schneerson (1902–94), did likewise).[102] Here is an example where the forgeries are so obvious that under normal circumstances one would have to assume that his erroneous defence was motivated by some higher goal. Yet what could that goal possibly be, as no important Habad cause is served by the defence of these letters, and other hasidic leaders had no problem declaring them to be forgeries?

Since there is no apparent reason why Schneersohn had to create a 'necessary truth' in this matter, it is possible that he really believed what he was writing (and Habad hasidim, who generally cannot assume that their *rebbes* erred, are now locked into defending the Kherson archive).[103] All this goes to show that just because an academic historian sees something as obvious, it does not mean that the Lubavitcher Rebbes would come to the same conclusion. In other words, one must be very careful before assuming that such a figure is purposely distorting the truth for some higher cause.

[101] Assaf, *Caught in the Thicket* (Heb.), 30. See also ibid. 67, 69, 108.

[102] Regarding this forgery, see Hillman (ed.), *Letters of R. Shneur Zalman of Lyady* (Heb.), 240–72; Rapoport-Albert, 'Hagiography with Footnotes'; Assaf, *Regal Way* (Heb.), 202–3; Havlin, 'New Light' (Heb.); Hillman, 'On the Kherson Letters' (Heb.); Katzman, 'R. Haim Liberman and the Kherson Letters' (Heb.).

[103] One exception was Haim Liberman, who even assumed that Schneersohn knew that the letters were forged, despite his public defence of them. See Rosenbaum (ed.), *Memorial Book* (Heb.), 140. A leading haredi scholar told me that in his opinion Schneersohn himself was responsible for the forgery, either as the actual forger or in finding someone to perform this function.

I can relate a similar instance that I experienced personally. The last Lubavitcher Rebbe, R. Menachem Mendel Schneerson, had a brother, Yisroel Aryeh Leib, who was not religiously observant, even keeping his store open on the Sabbath. One would think that this would not be a matter for controversy. After all, we are not dealing with ancient history and there are many alive who knew him, including several in the Habad community.[104] In addition, his daughter is alive and well and can testify to this. Yet there is a Habad 'Research Institute' named after 'Rabbi' Yisroel Leib, and on its website he is described as a great *tsadik* and Jewish thinker.[105]

I was certain that this was another example of hasidim consciously covering up uncomfortable facts about their leader's family because they felt that knowledge about the brother would reflect poorly on the Rebbe. After corresponding with the man in charge of the website, in the course of which I presented him with the facts, I came away convinced that he really believed everything he put on his site, and that no facts were going to change his mind. A search of the internet will find other adherents of Habad who have the same perspective, which again should demonstrate that what an outsider might view as a conscious distortion of the facts for ideological purposes can very often be an authentically held belief. There are, to be sure, all sorts of psychological reasons that prevent these people from recognizing the truth, but this does not change the fact that from their perspective the reality they are affirming is a genuine belief.

Examples of distortion and censorship are also seen with another well-known rabbinic figure, R. Joseph B. Soloveitchik (1903–93). As part of the effort to render him 'kosher' for the haredi world, one publication of his novellae describes him on the title page by the honorific title of *gaon av beit din* of Boston, with no hint that he had anything to do with the non-haredi Yeshiva University (see Fig. 1.3).[106]

For those who have no interest in seeing Soloveitchik become accepted in the haredi world, but who still want to make use of his writings, one

[104] See S. S. Deutsch, *Larger than Life*, vol. ii, ch. 7, and my Seforim Blog post, 25 Oct. 2009; <www. mentalblog.com>, 21 Mar. 2006.

[105] 'Rabbi Yisroel Aryeh Leib Research Institute on Moshiach and the Sciences', <www. ryal.org>. According to the biographical section of the website, 'many times he [Yisroel Aryeh] would be the first chosid in Israel to receive the newest publications of Chassidus from New York and other chassidim would get them from him' <www.ryal.org/b.html>. See also Silman, *Scientific Thought in Messianic Times*, 138 ff., for Yisroel Aryeh Leib's (fictional) biography, which goes so far as to say that he 'became known for a special style of studying Chassidus' (p. 142). Silman is the director of the Rabbi Yisroel Aryeh Leib Research Institute on Moshiach and the Sciences.

[106] Shurkin, *Harerei kedem*. Regarding the larger issue of Soloveitchik's image, see L. Kaplan, 'Revisionism and the Rav'.

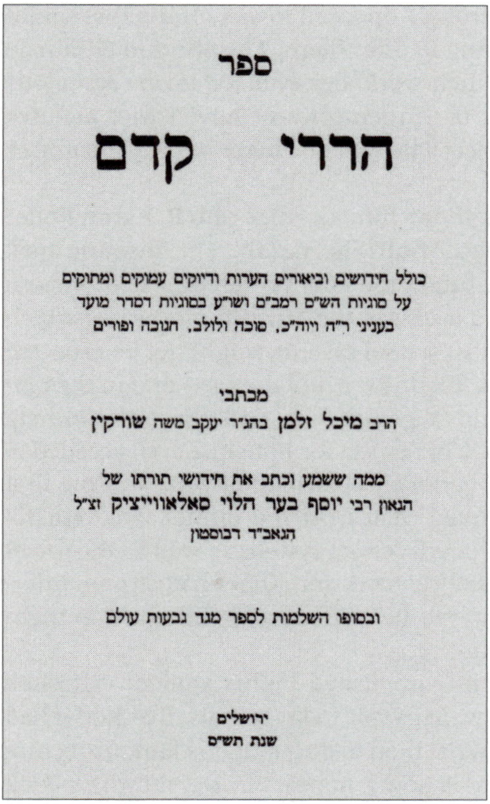
ספר

הררי קדם

כולל חידושים וביאורים הערות ודיוקים עמוקים ומתוקים
על סוגיות הש"ס רמב"ם ושו"ע בסוגיות דסדר מועד
בעניני ר"ה ויוה"כ, סוכה ולולב, חנוכה ופורים

מכתבי
הרב מיכל זלמן בהג"ר יעקב משה שורקין

ממה ששמע וכתב את חידושי תורתו של
הגאון רבי יוסף בער הלוי סאלאווייציק זצ"ל
הגאב"ד דבוסטון

ובסופו השלמות לספר מגד גבעות עולם

ירושלים
שנת תש"ם

Figure 1.3 Title page of R. Michel Zalman Shurkin, *Harerei kedem* (Jerusalem, 2000), omitting any reference to R. Joseph B. Soloveitchik's association with Yeshiva University

approach is to attribute anecdotes he recorded from his father and grandfather (R. Moses and R. Hayim) to 'writings of the students'.[107] A similar phenomenon is the series of anonymously published volumes of talmudic novellae,[108] focused on '*ḥidushei hamasbir*', in which it is never explained that the *masbir* (elucidator) is none other than Soloveitchik.[109] For some, even this

[107] *Hagadah shel pesaḥ mibeit levi (brisk)*, 67–8, 129–30. See also the discussion of this phenomenon on the Behadrei Haredim discussion forum at <www.bhol.co.il/forums/topic.asp?topic_id=929324&forum_id=771>, and <www.bhol.co.il/forums/topic.asp?topic_id=2572392&forum_id=19616> (this last source was called to my attention by Yehudah Mirsky). In the anonymous biography of R. Yehiel Michel Feinstein, *Sar hatorah*, there is no mention that he taught in Soloveitchik's Boston yeshiva, Heichal Rabbenu Hayyim Halevi. Regarding his teaching there, see Farber, *American Orthodox Dreamer*, 43.

[108] These volumes are entitled *Ḥidushei batra*, and it is known that their author is the late R. Hayim Dov Altusky.

[109] One hint to Soloveitchik's identity is that the last four letters of המסביר appear to stand for the initial letters of 'Rabbi Joseph Baer Soloveitchik', with the *mem* and the *heh* perhaps standing for *morenu harav*, 'our teacher, the rabbi'.

is not good enough, and they are strongly opposed to any efforts that might imply that Soloveitchik has something to offer them. The effort to eliminate Soloveitchik from any contact with their world has even led to one egregious example of censorship that brings back memories of how Soviet pictures would be constantly 'updated' to reflect who was no longer in the good graces of the Communist party.[110]

A famous picture of Soloveitchik shows him together with R. Aaron Kotler (1891–1962) and Irving Bunim (1901–80) (Fig. 1.4(*a*)). The meeting took place in 1956 at a dinner to raise funds for Israel's haredi school system (Chinuch Atzmai). Soloveitchik, as a leader of the Mizrahi movement which was involved with the religious Zionist school system, might not be expected to be involved in such an endeavour. Yet this was not the case, and in the previous years he had attended meetings together with Kotler in order to help support Chinuch Atzmai.[111] As a mark of respect for Kotler he even acceded to the latter's request that he serve as honorary chairman of what was the first Chinuch Atzmai dinner in the United States. At the dinner, Soloveitchik spoke about the importance of the haredi school system as well as the greatness of Kotler.[112] It is no secret that Soloveitchik and Kotler had strong differences of opinion in various matters, yet their differences did not stop them from having a respectful relationship.

A biography of Kotler was recently published by his student, Yitzchok Dershowitz.[113] Dershowitz does not want people today to know that Kotler had any relationship with Soloveitchik. What then to do about this famous picture with them appearing together? Here is how it appears in Dershowitz's book (Fig. 1.4(*b*)). By cutting Soloveitchik out, the author does not need to worry that some readers will conclude (correctly) that Kotler could have a respectful relationship with Soloveitchik, even with their strong ideological disagreements.[114]

110 See King, *The Commissar Vanishes*.

111 See Rosensweig, 'Unique Phenomenon', 48.

112 See the text of his speech in A. Bunim, *A Fire in His Soul*, 365–73.

113 Dershowitz, *The Legacy of Maran Rav Aharon Kotler*. Dershowitz's animus towards Soloveitchik is long-standing. On 17 Kislev 5736 (21 Nov. 1975), *Light*, a haredi publication, reproduced Soloveitchik's strong criticism of R. Emanuel Rackman's proposal to revise Jewish marriage law. In the issue of 29 Tevet 5736 (2 Jan. 1976), 16, Dershowitz wrote to protest at Soloveitchik's comments being published 'with the name of the author'. He continued: 'How do you introduce into yeshiva and *heimishe* circles a man who has been intentionally kept (and has kept himself) outside of these very circles for years because of definite past and present damage to the Torah cause through his being the mentor of, and pillar upon whom rest "orthodox nationalists" (Mizrachi) and "orthodox haskalists" (represented by Y.U. and its ideology of "synthesis")[?]'

114 Lawrence Kaplan called my attention to this act of censorship. A picture of Soloveitchik does appear in the book, on p. 355, but here he is together with a group of other rabbis, none of whom are identified, so there was apparently no reason to cut him out. This type of censorship of pictures

(*a*)

(*b*)

Figure 1.4 R. Joseph B. Soloveitchik, R. Aaron Kotler, and Irving Bunim at a Chinuch Atzmai dinner in 1956. The original version appears in (*a*), while (*b*) shows the cropped version that appears in Yitzchok Dershowitz, *The Legacy of Maran Rav Aharon Kotler* (Nanuet, NY, 2005)

Even when it comes to substantive issues, one finds criticism in Orthodox circles for publishing certain material from manuscript. For example, my publication of some of the correspondence of R. Jehiel Jacob Weinberg was assailed by some. This was not because of any personal comments about others that were included, but because Weinberg was shown to have had a very close relationship with Samuel Atlas, a professor at Hebrew Union College. In addition, in these letters Weinberg expressed moral difficulty with certain aspects of halakhah concerning relations between Jews and non-Jews. Weinberg did not reject these *halakhot*, but was honest enough to acknowledge that they troubled him. For some, Weinberg's sentiment was problematic and reason enough to censor the letters, while for others, it was important to publish the letters precisely so people could see that even a great sage is not

is hardly unique, and has already been mentioned in the Preface. Regarding the deletion of the Israeli haredi politician Menahem Porush's image, appearing alongside the Gerrer Rebbe in the original picture, see *Yom hashishi*, 10 Adar 5762 (22 Feb. 2002).

above questioning. As David Berger wrote, 'R. Weinberg has taught us that we are permitted to agonize over these questions, that we are not defying God's will in doing so.'[115]

All the issues that have been described in the previous paragraphs are dealt with in this book. I do not focus on examples of authors censoring or 'correcting' their own writings, however, as this is a different phenomenon. Sometimes this is done precisely because of the sort of pressures that are the motivation for the various types of censorship that will be discussed, but since it is the author himself who makes the change, it is not my concern here.[116] In fact, in many of these cases the author no doubt regretted what he originally wrote, and used the opportunity of a second edition to set matters straight. For example, in the first 'edition' of his *Commentary on the Mishnah*[117] Maimonides cited the mystical work *Shiur komah*. Later, when he concluded that the work was a heretical text, he crossed out the reference.[118]

Another example appears in *Derekh ḥayim* by R. Menahem de Lonzano (sixteenth–seventeenth centuries). In the first edition,[119] he speaks very sharply against certain earlier figures, especially R. Bahya Ibn Pakuda (eleventh century). When he republished this work,[120] he removed these words, which he perhaps regarded as the rash comments of a young man.[121]

I am also not generally concerned with instances when editors tell the readers that they have altered the text. This is interesting from a sociological perspective, but in these cases there is no deception of the reader involved, that is, no attempt to create a fraudulent text. To give one example of this phenomenon, when in 1984 Soncino Press published a revised edition of its *Five Megilloth*, in which all references to non-traditional and non-Jewish

[115] M. B. Shapiro, 'Scholars and Friends'; D. Berger, 'Jews, Gentiles and the Modern Egalitarian Ethos', 89.

[116] A famous instance of this is R. Yehoshua Yeshayah Neuwirth's *Shemirat shabat kehilkhatah*. Certain leniencies found in the first edition are missing from subsequent editions. In ch. 1 of the first edition, for example, Neuwirth permits one to use water heated by solar power on the Sabbath. In the second edition he recommends not doing so (*tov lehimana*, 'it is good to refrain'). See also Eliezer Brodt's Seforim Blog post, 1 Nov. 2011, recording that R. Jacob Meklenburg (1785–1865) referred to Samuel David Luzzatto and Julius Fuerst (1805–73) in the introduction to the first edition of his *Haketav vehakabalah*, but not in the second edition.

[117] Maimonides, *Commentary on the Mishnah*, vol. ii, *San*. ch. 10 (p. 142, seventh principle).

[118] See ibid., n. 42. For sources on Maimonides and *Shiur komah*, see Gurfinkel, 'Maimonides and the Kabbalah' (Heb.), 458–61.

[119] Constantinople (*c*.1575), 20*b*–24*a*.

[120] Venice, 1618.

[121] See D. Kamenetsky, 'The Gaon R. Menasheh of Ilya' (Heb.), 737 n. 12. I say 'perhaps', since it is possible that he removed this section because he was pressured to do so. This would explain why, despite taking it out, in the second edition he still refers the reader to his earlier comments. See also Hacker, 'Controversy over Philosophy' (Heb.), and id., 'Sixteenth-Century Jewish Internal Censorship', 118–19. Lonzano's work was recently republished with additional passages censored. See Brodt, 'Laws of *Birkat hare'iyah*' (Heb.), 926 n. 102.

authors were deleted, the preface informed the reader that the new edition 'reflects the traditional approach as represented by the Rabbis and the Jewish exegetes from the Middle Ages to Modern Times'.[122]

The publishers of other new editions are often not so honest in describing what has been done with the original. One such example is Irving Bunim's book, *Ethics from Sinai*, first published in the 1960s. When it was reprinted in 2000, all references to secular works of literature were removed. In the preface, the publisher explains that 'with the massive changes in the English-speaking Jewish community over the years, the need arose for an updated edition'. We are never told exactly what kind of updating was done. What this sentence really means is that because of the turn to the right in American Orthodoxy, references to secular works of literature are now regarded by many as unacceptable in Torah volumes.

What About Pictures?

The issue of pictures is also an important part of our story, in particular with regard to the issue of women's dress, known as *tseniut* (literally: 'modesty'). As anyone middle-aged or older can attest, and as numerous photographs prove, the standards of *tseniut* in the haredi world have increased in stringency in recent years, and are continuing in this direction.[123]

There is a large book by Rabbi Pesach Eliyahu Falk of Gateshead that presents what are probably the most extreme views of *tseniut* in dress and behaviour ever to appear in English.[124] It is accompanied by a booklet of diagrams showing in minute detail how high a woman's shirt buttons must be, how long the sleeves, how she must carry her handbag, etc. R. Yehudah Herzl Henkin has observed that the ideology of this book is such that it 'prohibits a woman from standing out—and from being outstanding'.[125]

The difficulty, from a purely traditional standpoint, with books like Falk's is that anyone can look at the numerous pictures of rabbis' families in years past and see that their wives and daughters were not dressed in accordance with Falk's prescriptions. For example, you will find women in these pictures

[122] Regarding the updated Soncino books of the Bible, see my *Saul Lieberman and the Orthodox*, 4.

[123] To give just one example of this phenomenon, in 2007 R. Avraham Arbel published his book *Aḥoti kalah*. According to him, when women leave their homes they are forbidden to wear jewellery and should be dressed in worn-out clothes so as not to appear attractive to men. See ibid. 110 ff. This book has approbations from a number of leading rabbis, including R. Ovadyah Yosef, none of whose wives follow(ed) the practices advocated by Arbel. Regarding a recent haredi book that forbids mothers to attend parents' night at school, see my Seforim Blog post, 25 June 2010.

[124] Falk, *Oz vehadar levushah*.

[125] Y. H. Henkin, 'Contemporary Tseni'ut', 37.

whose top button is open. This is so even with R. Eleazar Shakh's (1899–2001) wife,[126] and Shakh was the leader of the non-hasidic haredim in the last two decades of the twentieth century.

The problem is obvious. People will see pictures of how the great *rebetsins* of the past dressed and will assume that they can imitate them. After all, the ultimate validation in traditional society is that great rabbis of the past permitted something. According to this approach, Falk's book, with its new standards, would be severely compromised.

Falk recognizes the problem and discusses it under the heading '"non-kosher" photographs of *chosheve* ['important'] women'.[127] As he explains: 'These books are likewise very detrimental as they appear to contain "live evidence" that in pre-war years the general *frum* public and even *chosheve* people were not careful with aspects of dress that are considered nowadays to be essential.'[128] Seemingly unsure of what to make of these pictures, Falk says that in most cases the picture was taken when the woman was in a private garden, out of the eye of the public. Yet he certainly knows that most of these pictures were taken as family portraits, often at weddings and the like. It is also not uncommon for there to be non-family members in the pictures as well.

That perhaps these '*chosheve*' people had different views of *tseniut* matters is not even considered, and instead the author advocates a different approach, that of removing the pictures from the public eye. 'Hopefully, as a result of this and similar protests, publishing houses who[!] reproduce photographs will in the future either omit inappropriate pictures altogether, or "doctor" the pictures beforehand, thereby ensuring that harmful parts of the pictures are not reproduced.'[129] All I would say is that if you are going to start touching up pictures, you have a lot of work ahead of you. For starters, the typical non-hasidic rabbi's wife in the United States did not even wear a *sheitl* (wig) until the 1970s or later.

Another Type of Censorship

I must also briefly mention the other type of censorship in Jewish history for, as we will soon see, it too connects to the focus of this book. This form of cen-

[126] See her picture in M. Horowitz, *Shehamafte'aḥ beyado*, after p. 64. Her hair is also not covered in the picture. If, during this period of her life, she did not cover her hair it would not be surprising, as this was the case with the wives of many Lithuanian rabbis. However, Dr Efraim Shakh insisted to me that his mother *did* cover her hair, but had to appear uncovered for this official Palestine identity card.

[127] Falk, *Oz vehadar levushah*, 177.

[128] Ibid.

[129] Ibid. 178.

sorship is the one most people are aware of, namely, non-Jewish censorship of Jewish books.[130] This is a complicated subject because there are times when we are not sure whether it was Jews or non-Jews who were responsible for the censorship. One such example is found in R. Ezekiel Landau's talmudic commentary, *Tsiyun lenefesh ḥayah*. In the first edition, published in the author's lifetime,[131] Landau tells his readers that young students should be kept from involving themselves too deeply in Bible study, 'because the heretics also study it for the sake of the language, just as they study other languages'. Landau further explains that it is possible that a boy might have one of these heretics as a Bible teacher and be led astray by him.

This passage was omitted in subsequent editions, of which there were quite a few. Who was responsible for the censorship? R. Joel Teitelbaum (1887–1979), the Satmar Rebbe, placed the blame on the *maskilim*, and thought that subsequent editions were unknowingly based on the censored version.[132] This is not an impossible scenario, yet there is no evidence for it. It is just as likely, if not more so, that the text was altered because of governmental censorship.[133]

Although I will not concern myself in this book with non-Jewish censorship, I would be remiss in not noting that we still suffer from this phenomenon. For example, there are a number of passages in the Talmud that were removed by Christian censors in various editions because they were thought to be insulting to Jesus and Christianity.[134] Many of these censored passages have been printed in an anonymous book called *Ḥesronot hashas*,[135] and are often found in the Soncino translation and the Steinsaltz edition. It is some-

[130] A great deal has been written on this. See the bibliography in Raz-Krakotzkin, 'From Safed to Venice', 93 n. 5. See also id., *The Censor, the Editor, and the Text*. For standard works on the subject, see Popper, *The Censorship of Hebrew Books* and Berliner, *Selected Writings* (Heb.), ii. 9–79.

[131] Prague, 1791, on BT *Ber.* 28*b*.

[132] Teitelbaum, *Vayo'el mosheh*, 416–17 ('Ma'amar leshon hakodesh', ch. 13).

[133] See D. Kamenetsky, 'Approbations' (Heb.), 739 n. 46. Another example where I am not sure who is responsible for the censorship appears in R. David Kimhi's commentary on Ps. 104: 30. Here he mentions both the belief in reincarnation and the philosophers' view that after death the soul does not return to the body. He then records the traditional view of resurrection. In the standard edition of *Mikraot gedolot* the first section of Kimhi's comment has been deleted, and I have not been able to determine when this censorship first occurred. (This example was called to my attention by R. Yisroel Gottlieb.) In Kimhi's commentary on Ps. 91: 6 he denies the existence of demons. Yet this has been deleted from the standard edition of *Mikraot gedolot*. (This example was called to my attention by R. Mordechai Friedman.) The uncensored commentary of Kimhi can be seen in *Mikraot gedolot haketer*, published by Bar-Ilan University.

[134] Regarding these passages, see most recently Schäfer, *Jesus in the Talmud*. For self-censorship of passages that would be insulting to Muslims, see my 'Islam and the Halakhah', 341 n. 33, and my *Studies in Maimonides and His Interpreters*, p. x; see also Weingarten, 'Temple Mount' (Heb.), 158 n. *14.

[135] See also Anon., *Omer hashikheḥah*.

what surprising that the ArtScroll edition of the Talmud, in both Hebrew and English, has not put these passages back. This means that even the ArtScroll Talmud, which has been praised as the pinnacle of Talmud translation, is still a defective edition.[136]

By not reinserting the censored passages, ArtScroll is engaging in self-censorship, not for ideological reasons, which are the focus of this book, but for the sake of good relations between Jews and non-Jews. This sort of self-censorship has a long history, in some places even from an era when books were still in manuscript.[137] There are important rabbinic figures who call attention to such self-censorship. For instance, R. Simeon ben Tsemah Duran (1361–1444), who lived in the pre-printing era, states that R. Jonah Gerondi (*c.*1200–63) altered a passage in one of his books for fear of governmental reaction.[138] R. Joseph Karo assumes the same thing about a passage in the *Arba'ah turim*, the law code by R. Jacob ben Asher (*c.*1269–*c.*1343).[139]

Referring to an earlier era, R. Reuven Margaliyot (1889–1971) suggests that the reason why the Mishnah did not discuss either Hanukah or the future messianic redemption was fear that the Romans would regard such matters as politically subversive.[140] Richard Kalmin even makes the unlikely sugges-

[136] R. Leopold Greenwald claimed that Jews should be grateful to the censors for having removed these passages, which generated so much hatred against the Jewish people. See his letter in H. Bloch, *Anthology* (Heb.), 8. (See Hoffmann, *Der Schulchan-Aruch und die Rabbinen*, 175, for a related point.) Bloch refers to the unpublished writings of a number of prominent 19th-cent. rabbinic scholars who expressed themselves similarly to Greenwald. Yet Bloch's prodigious forgeries are already well established, and these supposed rabbinic writings are without question also fabrications. See my Seforim Blog post, 22 Apr. 2010.

[137] See e.g. M. Kahana, 'Midrashic Manuscripts' (Heb.), 60–1; Rafler, *Netivei me'ir*, 379–80. For an analysis of a 19th-cent. example of internal censorship, see Petuchowski, *Studies in Modern Theology and Prayer*, 193–219.

[138] See Duran, *Magen avot*, 102 (on Mishnah *Avot* 2: 3). Some have argued that R. Menahem Meiri's (1249–1316) writings expressing religious tolerance can also be explained in this way. See Zini's note, ibid. 102; M. Sofer, *Kovets teshuvot ḥatam sofer*, no. 90; Hillman, 'Statements of Meiri' (Heb.); Bleich, 'Divine Unity', 245–6; Kasirer, *Shemitah kemitsvatah*, 93–4. See also Mazuz, 'Article on Shemitah' (Heb.), 305–6, who suggests that Nahmanides wrote something in his Torah commentary because of fear of the government. M. B. Lerner has argued that a couple of talmudic usages of the term *kidush hashem* (sanctification of God's name) are actually examples of internal censorship, designed to avoid the term *ḥilul hashem* (desecration of God's name). See Lerner, 'Formulation' (Heb.), 109–10.

[139] See Karo, *Beit yosef*, 'Ḥoshen mishpat' 266: 1. In this case Karo was mistaken, as only the printed version of the *Arba'ah turim* that he used had been censored. See the textual note in the Makhon Yerushalayim edition. Cf. Rabbinovicz, *Ma'amar al hadpasat hatalmud*, 7 n. 1, 28 n. 25, that copyists in medieval Spain censored texts of the Talmud in accordance with a government decree. See also Langer, *Cursing the Christians*, 113.

[140] R. Margaliyot, *Basis of the Mishnah* (Heb.), 22. As far as I know, no one has made this sort of argument regarding Masada not being mentioned in the Talmud. Most assume that the omission

tion that the reason the Jerusalem Talmud, unlike the Babylonian, records so few disputes between rabbis and heretics was to 'avoid insulting the Bible-reading non-Jews and heretics who were prominent in the Roman world'.[141]

It appears that we even have examples of internal censorship designed to prevent publication of things that could be used to assist Christian arguments. For example, R. Bahya ben Asher (d. 1340) states, following a kabbalistic perspective, that in the 'Time to Come' the prohibition on mixing milk and meat is to be abolished.[142] Yet in three early editions,[143] this passage has been altered, so that the word בטל ('abolished') has been removed from the phrase שכן יהיה איסור בשר בחלב בטל ('thus the prohibition on meat in milk will be abolished'). It is unlikely that the word was removed accidentally, with the two subsequent editions copying the error. Rather, it is more plausible that these are examples of internal censorship so as not to give the Christians 'ammunition', as R. Bahya is speaking about a time when an important biblical commandment will no longer be binding. This could obviously be of use in Christian arguments against the binding nature of the laws of *kashrut*. In fact, this internal censorship is really no different from what we often find in Jewish apologetic and polemical literature where, in order to 'win' the argument, the authors take liberties with the truth.

Another possible example of this type of internal censorship is the following: there are *piyutim* (liturgical poems) that record negative comments about important biblical figures, including the Patriarchs, and these are censored in some manuscripts. The assumption always was that these were suppressed because it was deemed improper to point out the faults of great biblical figures. But Ophir Mintz-Manor has recently argued that the censorship arose out of the Jewish–Christian debate. In an era when Christian writers were criticizing figures in the Old Testament, Jews did not want to give them any more 'ammunition'.[144]

Another example of censorship, and also of self-censorship due to fear of the non-Jews, is found in the Amidah for weekdays. The twelfth blessing is called *birkat haminim*, and focuses on heretics, asking God to uproot them. According to the Talmud, *Berakhot* 28*b*, this prayer was composed by Samuel Hakatan at the request of Rabban Gamaliel II, who flourished at the end of the first century CE. Although Rashi assumed that the blessing was directed

is because the rabbis were not sympathetic to the defenders and/or their suicide. See Ben-Yehuda, *The Masada Myth*, 228–9. See also L. Feldman, 'Masada, A Critique of Recent Scholarship', 226 ff.

[141] Kalmin, *The Sage in Jewish Society*, 74. Kalmin himself acknowledges that this suggestion is improbable.

[142] *Commentary* on Exod. 23: 19.

[143] Venice, 1546; Riva di Trento, 1559; Kraków, 1592. See Chavel's note in his edition of R. Bahya's commentary.

[144] Mintz-Manor, 'Why Give the Heretics a Chance?' (Heb.).

against the early Jewish-Christians,[145] contemporary scholars dispute whether it has any connection to the rise of Christianity.[146]

Early prayer books (*sidurim*) have this blessing directed against the *meshumadim* (apostates) and *minim* (heretics). Maimonides' prayer book reads: **למשומדים אל תהי תקוה כל המינים כרגע יאבדו** ('there will be no hope for the apostates, and the heretics will perish'),[147] and virtually all other geonic and early medieval texts also begin similarly, with many also adding 'Christians' to those who are cursed.[148] Yet very few Ashkenazim ever stop and wonder why the prayer supposed to be directed against the *minim* actually says nothing about them (or about *meshumadim*, for that matter). Instead, it only refers to the *malshinim*, the 'slanderers' or 'informers'.[149] The answer is obvious, and is another example of a change in the *sidur* that originated either in non-Jewish censorship or in self-censorship (depending on the time and place). It might surprise some to learn that there are no Ashkenazi *sidurim*, even among those

[145] See Rabbinovicz, *Dikdukei soferim* (2002 edn.), 'Megilah 17*b*' (p. 98), n. 8.

[146] See van der Horst, *Hellenism–Judaism–Christianity*, ch. 8; Basser, *Studies in Exegesis: Christian Critiques*, 61 ff.; Teppler, *Birkat haminim*; Langer, *Cursing the Christians*, ch. 1. Langer's book is the most complete study of the blessing, dealing with its history from ancient times until the present. Daniel Boyarin has recently presented a new approach. See his *Border Lines*, 67 ff. He assumes that the talmudic account involving R. Gamaliel and Samuel Hakatan is without historical basis, and that the prayer should be dated two centuries after R. Gamaliel.

[147] It appears at the end of *Mishneh torah*, 'Sefer ahavah'.

[148] See Hillman, 'Wording of *Birkat haminim*' (Heb.); Y. Y. Weiss, 'Wording of *Birkat haminim*' (Heb.). Weiss reports that a search of hundreds of manuscript prayer books, from all over the Jewish world, turned up only a few Italian manuscripts that begin with *velamalshinim* in place of *lameshumadim*. These are obviously internally censored texts. Langer found some other manuscripts that begin the prayer similarly. See her *Cursing the Christians*, 202, 208, 275 n. 24. Hillman, 'Wording of *Birkat haminim*' (Heb.), 59, refers to an internally censored manuscript of R. Amram Gaon's prayer book. See also Langer, *Cursing the Christians*, ch. 2 and p. 114, appendix 3; Sh. Sofer, *Sidur*, ii. 138 ff.; Elbogen, *Jewish Liturgy*, 45; Emden, *Luaḥ eresh*, 62; E. Chwat, 'Responsum' (Heb.); Zelcer, 'Shemoneh Esreh in Eretz Yisrael', 118–19.

[149] The word *malshinim*, while not original to the blessing, is found in a few early versions, not in place of *meshumadim*, but in addition to it. See Y. Y. Weiss, 'Wording of *Birkat haminim*' (Heb.), 108; Langer, *Cursing the Christians*, 62. Many current Sephardi versions read: **למינים ולמשומדים אל תהי תקוה**. Regarding developments in the Sephardi version, see Langer, *Cursing the Christians*, 140 ff., 237 ff. R. Jacob Emden's prayer book begins the first line with *velamalshinim*, but instead of *harish'ah* in the next part of the sentence, he substitutes *haminim*. See his *Amudei shamayim*, i. 133*b*. This is also found in some versions of the Ashkenazi *nusaḥ sefarad*. Habad's *Tehilat hashem* prayer book has, in the second part of the sentence, **וכל המינים וכל הזדים**. When Samuel Holdheim was rabbi of the Grand Duchy of Mecklenburg-Schwerin, he changed the version so that instead of *velamalshinim* ('slanderers'), the prayer read *velamalshinut* ('slander'). See A. D. B. Hakohen, *Teshuvat ad"k*, no. 24. For the same approach in David Friedländer's 1786 German translation of the prayer book, see Langer, *Cursing the Christians*, 157. See also Eliezer Landshut's note in Edelman, *Hegyon lev*, 31*a*.

published in the State of Israel, that have returned a more authentic wording to this blessing.[150]

Another famous example of censorship and also self-censorship is found in the Aleinu prayer.[151] The original version reads שהם משתחוים להבל וריק ומתפללים אל אל לא יושיע ('For they bow to vanity and emptiness and pray to a god that does not help'). Leaving aside the issue of whether Jews should still be saying this line, since it is clearly not applicable to many people, such as Muslims and perhaps also Christians,[152] we must note that it was originally removed from the prayer book because of the understanding that it referred to Christians. In fact, this line became an important feature of Christian anti-Jewish polemics,[153] and was commonly discussed by the Jewish apostates who wrote 'exposés' about Judaism.[154]

It did not help matters that some Jews were accustomed to spit after saying the word *varik* ('emptiness'), as it indeed happens to be very similar to the Hebrew word for 'spit'.[155] In 1703 a Prussian royal edict forbade the recital of

150 See M. T. Jacobs, *Bimeḥitsat rabenu*, 50–1, who records that R. Ya'akov Kamenetsky, when praying privately, said the version of the prayer recorded by Maimonides. In explaining the word *velamalshinim* (slanderers), and not realizing that the word is not part of the original prayer, the *Complete ArtScroll Siddur* (ed. Scherman and Zlotowitz), 107, explains that the Sadducees, Boethusians, Essenes, and early Christians 'used their political power to oppress observant Jews and to slander them to the anti-Semitic Roman government'. Quite apart from the improper adjective 'observant' used to distinguish different types of Jews in Second Temple days (as if the Essenes were not observant), or the false claim that Essenes and early Christians had political power, the prayer was certainly not directed against Sadducees, Boethusians, or Essenes, and no one has ever claimed otherwise. The expression *birkat hatsedukin* ('Blessing of the Sadducees') that appears in the standard edition of the Talmud, *Ber.* 28*b*–29*a*, is a censor's corruption of the original *birkat haminim*. See Rabbinovicz, *Dikdukei soferim*, ad loc. A. Davis, *Complete Metsudah Siddur*, 129, also does not realize that the word *velamalshinim* is not original, and states that the blessing 'is directed against the early Christians who informed against Jews to the Roman authorities after the destruction of the Second Temple'.

151 See Berliner, *Selected Writings* (Heb.), i. 46 ff.; Langer, 'Censorship of Aleinu'.

152 As regards Christians, this gets us into the sticky issue of whether Christians worship the same God as Jews, a point that was central to the dispute over the document *Dabru Emet*. See D. Berger, *Persecution, Polemic, and Dialogue*, 392–8.

153 See Scheinhaus, 'Alenu Leschabeach'.

154 See Kalir, 'Jewish Service', 78–9. On these apostates, see Carlebach, *Divided Souls*.

155 The earliest source to mention spitting is Moelin, *Maharil: minhagim*, 'Hilkhot tefilah', no. 3 (p. 438). See also Eisenstein (ed.), *Otsar yisra'el*, viii. 81, 113; Mahler, *Hasidism and the Jewish Enlightenment*, 150. The practice is defended in D. Halevi, *Turei zahav*, 'Yoreh de'ah' 179: 5, but criticized by Bacharach, *Mekor ḥayim*, 97: 2, 132: 2 and A. Horowitz, *Emek haberakhah*, section dealing with laws of prayer, no. 40 (there is no pagination). The Reformer Aaron Chorin abolished the spitting in his congregation. See Greenwald, *Jewish Groups in Hungary* (Heb.), 14. For some, the spitting continued even after the phrase *shehem mishtaḥavim* was no longer recited. See e.g. Hirschowitz, *Minhagei yeshurun*, no. 69. R. Jacob Israel Kanievsky (the Steipler) would spit and add 'may their name be blotted out'. See A. Y. Kanievsky, *Toledot ya'akov*, 177. Barry Freundel recalls from his youth the Yiddish expression *Er kumt tsum oysshpayen*, which means 'He comes

this line. In order to ensure that it be omitted, the edict required that the text of Aleinu be recited out loud so that the recital could be monitored by agents of the government.[156] The edict also specifically forbade Jewish spitting during the prayer.[157] In fact, even before any such restrictions, we know that some Jews would recite this line quietly, and this was obviously done so as to prevent conflict with Christians.[158] As late as 1846 Moravian synagogues were forbidden to recite any prayers that inspired hatred against non-Jews, and Aleinu—the entire prayer, and not just the problematic line—was specifically forbidden.[159]

When, in 1777, an official in Königsberg charged that the Jewish community was not reciting Aleinu aloud, implying that they were quietly adding the offensive line, the community requested that Moses Mendelssohn (1729–86) get involved. He testified as to the antiquity and significance of Aleinu, and that 'only the heathens and their idolatrous worship are referred to in it, and not, as some enemies and slanderers of the Jewish nation falsely contend, the Christians, who like ourselves worship the King of Kings, the Holy One, blessed be He'.[160] While Mendelssohn told the truth in this statement, it was not the complete truth. Obviously, a prayer that pre-dated Christianity could not be said to refer to it in any historical sense, and in this Mendelssohn was correct. But he certainly knew that many of his coreligionists nevertheless saw an allusion to Jesus in the prayer, and for obvious reasons he omitted mention of this.

When the problematic line was first removed from the prayer book, people still recited it by heart. Yet over time the objectionable passage was simply dropped from the standard Ashkenazi liturgy.[161] Only in the twentieth century, with the creation of the State of Israel and the printing of *sidurim* there, did large numbers of Ashkenazim once again start saying the line.[162] In the ArtScroll *Siddur* this sentence is included with parentheses around it. These

at the spitting'. This refers to someone who arrives at synagogue at the very end of the morning prayers. See Freundel, *Why We Pray What We Pray*, 234.

156 Perhaps this is the origin of the widespread practice of singing the opening paragraph of Aleinu aloud.

157 See Altmann, *Moses Mendelssohn*, 307; Elbogen, *Jewish Liturgy*, 72.

158 See *Hagahot haminhagim*, in Tyrnau, *Sefer haminhagim*, 12 n. 14 (regarding the authorship of these notes, see ibid. 17, introd.); Buxtorf, *Synagoga Judaica*, ch. 5.

159 See the report printed in On the Main Line, 8 Nov. 2009.

160 Altmann, *Moses Mendelssohn*, 308.

161 It remained in the Habad liturgy, even if not in print, but for some reason only the first half of the line is recited (with the alternative version ולריק).

162 When R. Moses Feinstein (1895–1986) was asked about saying the line, he replied that he did not 'and one should not alter the practice of our forefathers'. See Shurkin, *Meged giv'ot olam*, 92.

parentheses are a recognition of the fact that the line is not generally said, and I have not seen any widespread efforts in the Orthodox world to ensure that people recite the prayer as it was originally intended to be said. There probably is a feeling among many that whatever the reason it was removed, it is preferable in our times that it should not be reinserted.

Concerning *shehem mishtaḥavim lahevel varik*, it is not just that this is a negative way of referring to one's non-Jewish neighbours. There is something even more significant in this text, which led to its condemnation by Christians and indeed to its becoming an important element in the anti-Jewish propaganda that asserted that Jews mocked Christianity: the numerical value (*gematriyah*) of the word *varik* equals *yeshu* (Jesus).[163]

In its comment on the first appearance of Aleinu, the ArtScroll *Siddur* says the following (based on R. Elie Munk's *The World of Prayer*[164]):

> The inclusion of this verse follows the original version of *Aleinu*. In the year 1400, a baptized Jew, no doubt seeking to prove his loyalty to the Church, spread the slander that this passage was meant to slur Christianity. He 'proved' his contention by the coincidence that the numerical value of וריק, *emptiness*, is 316, the same as ישו, the Hebrew name of their Messiah. This charge was refuted time and again.[165]

In thinking about how to understand this passage, there are only two possibilities. One is that the editors of the ArtScroll *Siddur* are entirely ignorant about the history of this prayer, and how it was a standard view in medieval and early modern times that the word *varik* referred to Jesus. That is possible, but doubtful.

I think it is more likely that they know full well what previous generations of Jews thought, and they know that what was alleged was not 'slander'. However, in an effort to create good relations with non-Jews, and perhaps knowing that many *ba'alei teshuvah* (newly religious Jews) and even some non-Jews use the ArtScroll *Siddur*, they have engaged in a bit of falsehood, quoting something they know is incorrect for the greater good.

In doing this, ArtScroll takes its place in a long line of Jewish apologetic works that misrepresent the truth, all in order to protect the honour (and in earlier times, the property and sometimes even the lives) of Jews.[166] Rabbinic

[163] See Wieder, *Formation of Jewish Liturgy* (Heb.), ii. 453–68, which remains the most comprehensive study of the anti-gentile themes in Aleinu. See also Y. Elbaum, 'Concerning Two Textual Emendations' (Heb.); Yuval, *Two Nations in Your Womb*, 192 ff., 198 ff.

[164] Vol. i, p. 190.

[165] Scherman and Zlotowitz (eds.), *Complete ArtScroll Siddur*, 159. Munk's information about the apostate in 1400 was taken, without acknowledgement, from Ismar Elbogen's classic book on the liturgy, first published in 1913. See Elbogen, *Jewish Liturgy*, 71–2.

[166] See e.g. Zunz, *Die Ritus des synagogalen Gottesdienstes*, 224–5. Sometimes it is not clear if, in apologetic texts, we are confronting deliberate distortion or authentically held beliefs. The most

leaders were in agreement that to accomplish this goal, outsiders were not to be allowed knowledge of certain details found in Jewish texts, and they even permitted falsifying these texts if necessary. As R. Moses Feinstein pointed out, the obvious proof for this is found right at the beginning of countless books published in Europe, where there is a 'clarification' that states that all mention of non-Jews in these books does not refer to Christians but rather to depraved pagans in some far-away place. All Jews knew that this comment was not to be taken seriously. Presumably, this is the reason why, with almost no exception,[167] rabbinic figures never protested this distortion, since it was only the non-Jews who were being deceived.[168]

This last point is one of the major themes of this book, that is, the issue of falsehood in the name of a greater cause. While the cause here is the need to preserve good relations between Jews and their neighbours, there are many other important causes that, as we will see, can be brought to bear in justification of censorship and outright falsehood.

Where is truth in all of this, and does truth have any inherent value? These are important questions, especially since the Talmud states that the seal of God is truth.[169] The issues raised by these questions are among the themes of this book, which focuses on the continuing tension between a commitment to truth and the needs of one's faith community, as the two are sometimes diametrically opposed to one another.

famous example of this is Nahmanides' rejection of the binding authority of aggadic statements in his debate with Pablo Christiani. Quite apart from any academic scholars who hold that Nahmanides was not being frank here, but only expressed himself in this way in order to 'win points' in the debate, this position is also held by a number of traditional scholars. See Eliasburg, *Shevil hazahav*, 27; Medini, *Sedei ḥemed*, vol. vii, 'Pe'at hasadeh', *alef*, no. 70; Y. Kamenetsky, *Emet leya'akov*, 219 n. 1. R. Solomon Elyashiv (1841–1926) claims that one can find this approach with one of the talmudic sages; see S. Elyashiv, *Leshem shevo ve'aḥlamah*, 'Sefer hade'ah', vol. ii, 85*b*–86*a*. For an example of Kalman Schulman, the Hebrew translator of Heinrich Graetz's *Geschichte der Juden*, omitting something that non-Jews might have found objectionable, see E. S. Horowitz, *Reckless Rites*, 215–16, 233 n. 76, 261–2. Schulman also censored his translation of Graetz, with the latter's permission, so that the Orthodox would not be offended. See Shavit and Eran, *The Hebrew Bible Reborn*, 137; On the Main Line, 30 June 2010.

167 One exception I have found is R. Meir Auerbach (1815–78) of Jerusalem. See Hirschensohn, *Malki bakodesh*, iv. 98.

168 See R. Dovid Cohen, *He'akov lemishor*, 33–4. R. Isaac Herzog agreed that distortion of Jewish law was permissible for the sake of good relations between Jews and non-Jews. However, since R. Solomon Luria had a different opinion (and presumably would also oppose the 'clarification' at the beginning of so many books), Herzog thought that the best step would be to omit 'problematic' *halakhot* from any modern summary of Jewish law, rather than actually distorting them. See the discussion of his view in Warhaftig, 'Rabbi Herzog's Approach', 288 ff. Luria's opinion is found in his *Yam shel shelomoh*, *BK* 4: 9.

169 BT *Shab.* 55*a* and parallels.

Jewish Self-Censorship

When did Jewish internal censorship begin? It is impossible to answer this question definitively, but from early on the Bible itself was censored. By this I mean the phenomenon of *kere ukhetiv* (a word is read differently from the way in which it appears in the text).[170] R. David Kimhi (*c.*1160–*c.*1235), among others,[171] is likely correct in claiming that most examples of *kere ukhetiv* are due to confusion about which word should appear,[172] and thus both were recorded. Yet there are some places where it is obvious that other considerations were responsible, and the change of reading is quite ancient.

Although the Bible often uses euphemisms to describe sexual intercourse and other 'touchy' matters,[173] this is not always the case. Thus, Deuteronomy 28: 30, 'A woman shall be betrothed, but another man shall enjoy her', reads in Hebrew אשה תארש ואיש אחר ישגלנה; the last word was not vocalized in the Masoretic tradition, since it was later seen as too explicit, and instead of ישגלנה[174] the word ישכבנה ('will lie with her') was read. The Talmud[175] mentions this *kere ukhetiv*, noting that ישגלנה was thought to be too sexually explicit and thus a more 'tame' word, the root of which means 'lie down' (שכב), was substituted. Verbs with the problematic root שגל also appear elsewhere in the Bible and in each case a verb with the root שכב is read instead.[176]

This instance is only an example of censorship in reading, but we also have examples where at least according to some authorities the biblical text was actually changed. I refer to the phenomenon of *tikun soferim*, which literally means 'correction of the scribes'. The unifying characteristic of almost all of these passages is that before the 'correction', the biblical verse could be regarded as offensive to God or grossly anthropomorphic.

170 The most recent study of this phenomenon, including references to all earlier discussions, is Ofer, 'Ketiv and Kere' (Heb.).

171 See my *Limits of Orthodox Theology*, 101.

172 Introduction to his commentary on the Prophets, and commentary on 2 Sam. 15: 21 and 1 Kgs 17: 14. Kimhi does not mention anything about the *kere ukhetiv* sometimes being used for reasons of 'propriety', as explained in the next paragraph, yet since this reason is offered in the Talmud, I assume that he too accepts it.

173 In some of these cases it is likely that the original biblical text was more explicit than what has been preserved in the Masoretic Hebrew text. See Tov, *Textual Criticism of the Hebrew Bible*, 63, 272.

174 The exact meaning of this word is unclear, but can be understood from the context.

175 BT *Meg.* 25*b*.

176 Nahmanides assumed that the root שגל refers to the sexual act, and therefore rejected Maimonides' view, *Guide* iii. 8, that the reason Hebrew is called the holy tongue is because it has no word for sexual intercourse. See Nahmanides, commentary on Exod. 30: 13. Maimonides' understanding is obviously related to his view, in agreement with Aristotle, that the sense of touch is a 'disgrace to us'. See *Guide* ii. 36, ii. 40, iii. 8, iii. 49, and my *Limits of Orthodox Theology*, 15–16.

I have dealt with this elsewhere, so there is no need to repeat matters here.[177] The only point I will note is that in mentioning one of these *tikun soferim*, Rashi adds that the Sages 'reversed' the passage.[178] There is little doubt that Rashi understood *tikun soferim* literally, and these words of Rashi are authentic, even though not all manuscripts contain them.[179] The words appear in all the standard editions of Rashi, though sometimes in parentheses.

I do not think anyone will be surprised to learn that in the ArtScroll edition of the Pentateuch,[180] as well as in its edition of Rashi,[181] these words are not to be found, not even included in parentheses.[182] Since the passage was regarded as too radical, as it indicates that the text of the Torah has been altered since Moses' day, ArtScroll engaged in a bit of *tikun soferim* of its own![183] Pious Jews study the Torah portion with Rashi every week, and thus have always been exposed to this comment of Rashi. With ArtScroll now the Bible of choice for so many, it is likely that Rashi's comment is now unknown to thousands of otherwise learned Jews, and as with all acts of censorship, that is exactly the point.

Another style of censorship common in the haredi world today is the refusal to mention someone by name who is not regarded as religious enough. One can find plenty of rabbinic precedent for this. Tosafot records an opinion that while R. Meir would cite the insights of his teacher, Elisha ben Avuyah, he would not refer to him by name, for Elisha had left the fold.[184] Thus, no matter how negatively one views a certain individual, this source can be understood to provide justification of those who benefit from his writings without acknowledgement. Similarly, the medieval *Sefer ḥasidim* writes that a

[177] See *Limits of Orthodox Theology*, 98–9, for authorities who assume that *tikun soferim* means actual changes to the original Torah text. For other traditional authors who hold this position, see Pinfer, *Masoret hatorah vehanevi'im*, 6 (see, however, p. 18); I. Epstein, *Judaism*, 195–6.

[178] Commentary on Gen. 18: 22.

[179] See my *Limits of Orthodox Theology*, 98 n. 52. See also Maori, '*Tikun soferim* and *kinah hakatuv*' (Heb.); Avrohom Lieberman, 'Tikkunei Soferim', 231 ff.; A. Mondshine, 'Rashi, Rashbam, and Ibn Ezra' (Heb.).

[180] Scherman (ed.), *Chumash: Stone Edition*.

[181] Herczeg et al. (eds.), *The Torah with Rashi's Commentary*.

[182] They have also been removed from *Mikraot gedolot hamaor*, *Metsudah Chumash/Rashi*, and the Ariel edition of *Rashi hashalem* (Jerusalem, 1986), though in the notes to the latter source it is explained why the passage was omitted.

[183] In ArtScroll's new translation of *Bereshit rabah* in the *Midrash Rabbah, Kleinman Edition*, ii. 23, the following appears: 'The words תיקון סופרים, *a scribal correction*, cannot, Heaven forbid, be taken at face value. There can be no doubt that the Torah as we have it was given to Moses at Mount Sinai and faithfully transmitted ever since.' Yet see above, n. 177, for traditional authorities who do indeed understand *tikun soferim* to mean changes in the Torah text.

[184] BT *Sot.* 12*a* s. v. *aḥerim*.

good Torah insight which is repeated should not be cited in the name of one who causes others to sin.[185]

In a completely different context, but one which also speaks to the issue of using someone's work without mentioning him by name, the Talmud records: '[R. Simeon said:] Who are those whose waters we drink but whose names we do not mention? Rabbi answered him: These are men who wished to uproot your dignity and the dignity of your father's house.'[186] On the previous page, the Talmud refers to an incident where, as a punishment for rebelling against R. Simeon ben Gamaliel, both R. Meir's name and that of R. Nathan were removed from their teachings, with R. Meir being termed 'others' and R. Nathan referred to as 'some say'.[187] Despite this talmudic passage, R. Meir is cited numerous times in tannaitic literature, especially in the Mishnah. This shows that any attempted censorship with regard to R. Meir (or perhaps just his name[188]) was not successful. With reference to this, Tal Ilan has remarked, 'We may expect that if Rabbi Meir was not censored out, other people or other topics probably were, and unfortunately such censorship must have been effective, since it left no trace.'[189]

Regarding the Talmud, although it is true that internal censorship was usually successful, this was not always the case. R. Tsevi Hirsch Chajes cites examples of texts he believes were removed from the Talmud. His proof is that these texts are cited in early rabbinic works, such as *Ein ya'akov*, R. Ahai Gaon's (eighth century) *She'iltot*, and R. Simeon Kayara's (ninth century) *Halakhot gedolot*, yet they do not appear in our edition of the Talmud.[190] Among the texts he mentions is the famous story of Beruriah's end, recorded by Rashi.[191] Commenting on a talmudic passage that speaks of a cryptic 'incident about Beruriah', Rashi records a tale that after Beruriah criticized the rabbinic notion that women are light-headed, her husband, R. Meir, decided to teach her a lesson. He therefore instructed one of his disciples to

185 *Sefer ḥasidim*, no. 977.

186 BT *Hor.* 14*a*.

187 BT *Hor.* 13*b*. See the discussion in Brüll, *Mevo hamishnah*, 216–18; I. H. Weiss, *Dor dor vedoreshav*, ii. 137 (These sources are referred to in a note by Samuel Abba Horodetzky in *Hagoren* (Berdichev) 1 (1897), 62.)

188 In other words, it is possible that there was no attempt to conceal R. Meir's identity, but rather that he was to be mentioned in an indirect manner in order to punish or humiliate him. See also Tosafot, BT *Sot.* 12*a*, s.v. *aḥerim*.

189 Ilan, *Mine and Yours Are Hers*, 52–3.

190 Chajes, *Kol sifrei maharats ḥayes*, i. 342. One text he does not mention is BT *San.* 104*b*, which records R. Judah's statement that the Sages wished 'to add another' to the three kings mentioned in the Mishnah, *San.* 10: 2, who have no share in the world to come. In *Bamidbar rabah* 14: 1 and *Tanḥuma*, 'Metsora' 1, R. Judah is quoted as follows: 'They wanted to include Solomon among them.' It would seem that the text in the Babylonian Talmud has been censored and that the original version is preserved in these midrashic sources. See S. Lieberman, 'Notes on Chapter 1' (Heb.), 163ff.

191 BT *AZ* 18*b* s.v. *ve'ika de'amri*.

seduce her. The student was successful, and when Beruriah learnt the entire story,[192] namely that the seduction was R. Meir's idea, she committed suicide and R. Meir fled the land of Israel in disgrace.

There are a number of strange stories in the Talmud, some of which do not reflect well on the Sages. Yet this is a truly shocking tale, particularly since it is hard to imagine R. Meir attempting to lure his wife into sin.[193] Chajes assumes that in order to spare the honour of R. Meir this story was removed from the Talmud, although it survived in an oral form until it was written down by Rashi.[194] There are also a number of other stories only hinted at in the Talmud which are elaborated upon by Rashi, and it is reasonable to assume that most, if not all, of these elaborations are long-standing traditions.[195]

While Chajes is no doubt correct in most of the examples he gives, not everyone agrees when it comes to the Beruriah story. While Rachel Adler[196] and Daniel Boyarin[197] concur with Chajes that the story dates back to rabbinic times yet was intentionally kept out of the talmudic text, Ilan, David Goodblatt, Dalia Hoshen, Yehudah Herzl Henkin, and Eitam Henkin disagree, assuming that the story is nothing more than a medieval legend.[198]

192 According to one manuscript reading: 'when the matter became known'. See E. Henkin, 'Mystery' (Heb.), 149.

193 See ibid. 140–59; Eleff, *Shirat miryam*, ch. 20.

194 See Chajes, *Kol sifrei maharats ḥayes*, i. 342. There is also another midrashic tale about how a certain R. Meir, while drunk, was intimate with a married woman. R. Yehiel Heilprin assumed that this man was none other than R. Meir the *tana*, husband of Beruriah, and he recorded the story in *Seder hadorot*, s.v. *rabi me'ir*, no. 8. In one recent reprint of *Seder hadorot*, the story has been removed. (R. Solomon Aaron Wertheimer assumes that the R. Meir in this story is not to be identified with the famous *tana*; see id., *Batei midrashot*, i. 184 n. 1.)

195 See R. Heilprin, *Rashi* (Heb.), i. 248–53, ii. 489.

196 R. Adler, 'Virgin in the Brothel'.

197 Boyarin, *Carnal Israel*, 184 ff. Luis Landau might also agree, as he speaks of the story as a tradition that pre-dates Rashi, although he does not specify how old he thinks it is. See id., 'Stories' (Heb.), 117.

198 Ilan, *Mine and Yours Are Hers*, 70 ff.; Goodblatt, 'Beruriah Traditions', 81–2; Hoshen, *Beruria the Tannait*, ch. 4; Y. Henkin, *Benei vanim*, iv. 104 n. 3; E. Henkin, 'Mystery' (Heb.). E. Henkin also assumes that the story post-dates Rashi and was mistakenly interpolated into his commentary. In additional comments on his article on his website, <www.eitamhenkin.wordpress.com>, E. Henkin notes that Hodes, *Al harishonim*, 17, claimed that the story was a forgery inserted into Rashi. In Ilan's more recent book, *Integrating Women*, 189 ff., she adopts a new approach to the story recorded by Rashi. She now claims that it is 'Rashi's personal contribution to the Beruriah tradition'. Ilan assumes that Rashi's 'obvious misogyny' did not allow him to accept a learned woman and '[i]t is to Rashi that we owe the blemished traits of Beruriah's character'. Leaving aside Ilan's assumption about Rashi's alleged misogyny (certainly at odds with how tradition has portrayed him), Rashi was not in the business of making up stories for ideological purposes in the way Ilan imagines. Regarding Rashi and women, see A. Grossman, *And He Shall Rule Over You?* (Heb.), ch. 2. See also Ibn Habib, *She'elot uteshuvot haralbaḥ*, no. 36 (p. 23*a*), who makes the following interesting comment regarding an unusual halakhic approach advocated by Rashi: כנראה שהר' ז"ל כאב הבנות הפך בזכותן בכל.

If it is a medieval legend, then what is the original meaning of the 'incident about Beruriah' mentioned in the Talmud? Unfortunately, we do not know, and according to Ilan it appears that the original story was itself censored by the Talmud.[199]

Ilan has also identified other examples of censorship in classical rabbinic texts, focusing on the representation of women. She points to early layers of texts that contain references to women that were subsequently removed or altered so that a later reader would have no inkling that women were once mentioned. We simply cannot know how many texts were dealt with in this way, since the result of a successful censorship is precisely that all relevant evidence is removed. Ilan makes the following important point:

> Censorship of women from the text is not an institutional action, undertaken by an official body, and it was not necessarily even a conscious one. Many scholars who obliterated women mentioned in texts they handled believed they were emending the text and restoring it to its original, more authentic form.[200]

As an example of the censorship she has in mind, Ilan cites a Tosefta[201] where a halakhic opinion of Beruriah is recorded. Yet when the issue is dealt with in the Mishnah,[202] the attribution of the opinion to Beruriah is omitted. Instead, it is attributed to R. Joshua, who in the Tosefta was the recipient of Beruriah's teaching. According to Ilan, 'it is next to impossible to imagine' that a later editor would attribute something to Beruriah that was originally stated by R. Joshua. 'Thus we clearly see the editor of the Mishnah censoring a tradition in which a woman plays too significant a role.'[203]

Ilan cites other examples of this phenomenon where mention of women has been deleted, and this includes halakhic topics as well. Examples of the latter are when the Tosefta deals with women and both the study of Torah and the wearing of tefillin, two passages that have been altered in the Babylonian Talmud.[204] In other words, the editors of the Talmud changed those passages because they either did not fit with their view of what the halakhah permits or with their conception of the place of women in Judaism. It is also possible that they were altered because they did not fit social reality. In fact, one need not be an academic scholar to come to such a conclusion. As Daniel Boyarin points out, R. Eliezer Waldenberg (1915–2006) also states that since the Babylonian Talmud assumed that women are forbidden to study Torah, it emended the Tosefta to bring it into line with this viewpoint.[205]

199 Ilan, *Mine and Yours Are Hers*, 72–3.
200 Ibid. 54.
201 Tosefta *Kelim (BM)*, 1: 3.
202 Mishnah *Kel.* 11: 4.
203 Ilan, *Mine and Yours Are Hers*, 58.
204 Ibid. 59 ff.
205 *Carnal Israel*, 180–1; Waldenberg, *Tsits eli'ezer*, vol. ix, no. 3. I would hesitate, however, to attribute too much significance to this example, since we can view it not as censorship, but as routine talmudic editing, that is, bringing sources into line with accepted halakhic rulings.

R. Meir Mazuz calls attention to what he thinks is another example of internal censorship in the Talmud. BT *Sanhedrin* 96*b* and *Gitin* 57*b* state that descendants of Haman studied Torah in Benei Berak. Yet the version of *Sanhedrin* recorded in *Ein ya'akov* continues by identifying a descendant of Haman, R. Samuel ben Shilat. According to Mazuz, this is the original text, which was later removed from the Babylonian Talmud. This was done so that R. Samuel and his descendants not be put in danger by someone seeking to fulfil the commandment to destroy Amalek, and who did not know that a Jewish descendant of an Amalekite is to be left alone.[206]

Returning to the Talmud's comment that some people's teachings are cited without mentioning them by name, Maimonides follows this path as well. In his Introduction to *Shemonah perakim*, in explaining why he will adopt insights from non-Jewish philosophers, Maimonides famously states, 'Accept the truth from whoever says it.' Yet immediately following this Maimonides also says that he will not mention these philosophers by name, since doing so 'might make the passage offensive to someone without experience and make him think that it has an evil inner meaning of which he is not aware. Consequently, I saw fit to omit the author's name, since my goal is to be useful to the reader.'[207]

This passage in Maimonides offers carte blanche for Orthodox writers to omit any specific acknowledgement of the sources they are using, as long as there is a possibility that certain readers will find a source objectionable. In my book *Saul Lieberman and the Orthodox* I gave numerous examples of this with regard to Lieberman and other figures associated with non-Orthodox streams of Judaism, and there is no need to repeat myself here.[208] In this book, we will also see examples of this phenomenon with regard to Orthodox figures, in particular R. Abraham Isaac Kook.

206 Mazuz, *Sansan leya'ir*, 18. I think it is more likely that R. Samuel b. Shilat's name was taken out to protect his reputation. Mazuz also notes a textual problem with the talmudic passage, and regarding this see my Seforim Blog post, 22 Apr. 2010. Concerning the dispute as to whether converts from Amalek can be accepted, see O. Yosef, 'On the Issue' (Heb.).

207 Translation in R. L. Weiss and Butterworth, *Ethical Writings of Maimonides*, 60–1. One of Maimonides' sources was Alfarabi's *Fusul al-madani*. See Davidson, 'Maimonides' "Shemonah Peraqim"'.

208 Among the examples I found after *Saul Lieberman and the Orthodox* was published is the mention of Zechariah Frankel, with elaborate titles attached to his name (הרב הגאון החכם הכולל מו"ה), in Rabbinovicz, *Dikdukei soferim*, 'Zera'im', 62 (unnumbered page at the end of the volume). This has been deleted from the Jerusalem, 2002 photo-offset edition of *Dikdukei soferim*. Regarding an approbation by Frankel that was later deleted, see On the Main Line, 18 Mar. 2010. Similarly, Immanuel Loew's name was deleted from the English translation of Pinhas Kehati's commentary on the Mishnah, *Ḥal.* 1: 1; see <www.menachemmendel.net>, 17 May 2006. There are a few similar instances of this sort of censorship in non-haredi works as well. For example, the prayer

To give another example from medieval times to illustrate the point, R. Jacob Anatoli (*c*.1194–1256) had a close relationship with the philosopher Michael Scot (1175–*c*.1232). He quotes him in his *Malmad hatalmidim* and refers to him as 'the sage I befriended'.[209] No doubt sensing how some might react to this, he defends his citing the words of wisdom of a non-Jew, 'for one ought to examine any statement on its own merit, without regard to its author'.[210]

Yet not all were willing to take Anatoli's message to heart. It has been recently noted that when R. Yeruham (*c*.1290–1350), a prominent Provençal halakhist who wrote *Sefer meisharim*, cites a passage from Anatoli referring to Scot, 'the sage I befriended' becomes, in R. Yeruham's retelling, 'the philosophical sages' (*ḥakhmei hameḥkar*). In fact, R. Yeruham's 'first statement in his legal work about his governing method is borrowed indirectly via Anatoli from a Christian scholastic!'.[211] This is the sort of thing that would be censored in modern haredi editions, and we see that already in medieval times R. Yeruham did not feel comfortable letting his readers in on what his source actually said. Despite the fact that the insight originated with Michael Scot, R. Yeruham still felt that it was important and worth citing. Yet, as we will see so often in this book, he took it upon himself to shield his readers from the complete truth.

As we have seen, Maimonides tells us that he is not going to mention the source of his statements because of some people's anticipated reactions. In this book we will see examples where the author does cite the source, seeing no reason for concern about how some readers might respond, even though later editors and printers were indeed very concerned. One example of this is R. Abraham Danzig's *Ḥayei adam*, one of the most popular halakhic handbooks ever published. In the first (1810) and second (1819) editions of his

book edited by Simeon Singer, which for over a century was the standard prayer book in synagogues in Great Britain, had, in its earlier editions, an acknowledgement of thanks to Claude Montefiore (1858–1938), one of the founders of Liberal Judaism in the United Kingdom. This was removed from later editions, where instead an anonymous 'accomplished scholar' was thanked. See Reif, *Judaism and Hebrew Prayer*, 307. Similarly, early printings of Philip Birnbaum's *sidur, Ha-Siddur ha-Shalem*, which was the standard prayer book in Orthodox synagogues in the United States, included words of thanks for non-Orthodox figures such as Louis Ginzberg, Abraham Joshua Heschel, and Simon Greenberg. These too were removed from later editions. One other form of censorship that I do not deal with in this book is the removal of material because of personal animosity. For an example of this, see Leiman, 'Censored Approbations' (Heb.), for R. Judah Leib Maimon's demand that R. Isaac Herzog's approbation be removed from a book.

209 Scot is mentioned by name in the unpaginated introduction, p. 12.

210 Anatoli, *Malmad hatalmidim*, 12 in the unpaginated introduction. The translation comes from Galinsky and Robinson, 'Rabbi Jeruham b. Meshullam', 499 n. 43.

211 Ibid. 499.

work, right at the beginning of the book, there is a reference to Kant and one of his ideas.[212] This citation was excised from the book, beginning with the third edition (1825), which appeared after Danzig's death. Until recent years, when new editions of the *Ḥayei adam* appeared based on the first edition, no posthumous edition of the work contained this passage.

In this case, it is not merely that a reference to Kant in a halakhic work was thought to be improper. Unlike contemporary times, I doubt that in the nineteenth century this alone would have been reason to censor a text. However, the context of the censorship is that the Haskalah had just begun to raise its head in Russia,[213] and I think it is this fact that was responsible for the censorship. In other words, it was unacceptable for Danzig's *Ḥayei adam* to be published in a way that could be used by the *maskilim*.[214] This text, which referred to Kant, could have been used by them to portray Danzig as a *maskil*, or 'modern' Jew, and to show that the study of philosophy was to be welcomed. It was thus dangerous and needed to be removed.[215]

The rise of Haskalah helped end the feud over hasidism. Recognizing that a greater threat was now upon them, the non-hasidim were happy to have the hasidim as allies in upholding the authority of Jewish law. Since then, although there have been some ups and downs, for the most part these two segments of what is today known as the haredi world have got along quite well. So well, in fact, that some do not even want people today to know about the great conflict that hasidism engendered, and how at the end of the eight-

[212] Danzig, *Ḥayei adam* 1: 5. Kant is not mentioned by name but is referred to as 'a great and famous non-Jewish philosopher'. Malbim (R. Meir Leibush ben Yehiel Mikhel Weiser, 1809–79), in his commentary on Lev. 19: 18, refers to הפילוסופים המעיינים, which in context is clearly a reference to Kant. Although Malbim never mentions Kant by name, he deals with Kantian ideas and refers to the titles of Kant's books. See Rosenbloom, *Hamalbim*, 175 ff. As L. Jacobs, *Tree of Life*, 58 n. 17, has noted, Schmelkes, *Beit yitsḥak*, 'Oraḥ ḥayim', 'Petaḥ habayit', p. 1 (unnumbered), also refers to Kant and his Categorical Imperative, yet here too he is not mentioned by name. P. E. Horowitz, *Sefer haberit*, 117*a* (*ma'amar* 20, ch. 25), does refer to Kant by name. So does Haver, *Magen vetsinah*, 12*b*. This source is cited by Brill, 'Writings of the Vilna Gaon', 33. For more recent Lithuanian sages who deal with Kant, however briefly, see Karelitz, *Kovets igerot ḥazon ish*, vol. ii, no. 171; J. I. Kanievsky, *Ḥayei olam*, ch. 24 (the last two sources were called to my attention by Benjamin Brown); Nadel, *Betorato shel r. gedalyah*, 53 n. 3.

[213] See Raisin, *Haskalah Movement in Russia*, 110 ff.

[214] For the battle between traditionalists and *maskilim* concerning the image of the Vilna Gaon, see Etkes, *Gaon of Vilna* (Heb.), ch. 2.

[215] In Danzig's original introduction to his *Ḥokhmat adam*, he mentioned that many were upset because in his *Ḥayei adam* he had criticized various positions of the Vilna Gaon. This introduction was not included in the published version of *Ḥokhmat adam*, and an altered version of it was placed at the beginning of his *Binat adam* (the second part of *Ḥokhmat adam*). See Liberman, *Ohel raḥel*, i. 471–2. This occurred during Danzig's lifetime, and contrary to Liberman, I would assume that Danzig himself was responsible for the altered introduction.

eenth century the Vilna Gaon (1720–97) and other great rabbinic leaders ordered the persecution of adherents of this new movement.

This explains how Betzalel Landau could publish an entire book about the life and teachings of the Vilna Gaon with no mention of his opposition to hasidism, which was such an important part of his later years.[216] This would be unimaginable for someone writing a work of 'pure' history. However, matters are different when an author intends his book to inspire people by means of the Vilna Gaon's life and piety. With such a goal, an author will look differently upon omitting important facts. Thus, if he concludes that reading about the Gaon's persecution of the hasidim could lessen one's opinion of either of the two parties, he will feel justified in omitting this aspect of the Gaon's life.

In contrast to Landau's censorship, and probably motivated by the mitnagdic–hasidic tensions that have arisen anew in Israel, Dov Eliach published a book on the Gaon which discusses his opposition to hasidism in detail.[217] Yet this very author, in an earlier book devoted to R. Hayim of Volozhin, has a chapter purporting to list all of R. Hayim's approbations (*haskamot*). One of these *haskamot* was given to Solomon Dubno (1738–1813) for his edition of the Pentateuch. Dubno is best known for having earlier worked together with Moses Mendelssohn on the *Biur*, the latter's German translation of and Hebrew commentary on the Torah. However, such an association would be troubling to those in the haredi world, where people have been indoctrinated into opposing anything having to do with Mendelssohn. The fact that numerous great Torah sages used Mendelssohn's writings is simply unknown to them.[218] Eliach, who feels it is very important to be honest

[216] B. Landau, *Hagaon heḥasid mivilna*. N. Kamenetsky, *Making of a Godol*, vol. i, pp. xxvii–xxviii, states that his father, R. Ya'akov Kamenetsky, agreed with Landau that he should not discuss the Gaon's battle against hasidism. This testimony is contradicted by Zev Low, who claims that Kamenetsky was very upset with this 'cover-up', as well as with the fact that Landau had not given a correct presentation of the Vilna Gaon's positive attitude towards secular studies. See Low, 'Answer to Criticism' (Heb.), 48–9. The Gaon's support of secular studies is seen in his oft-quoted comment, cited by his student R. Barukh of Shklov: 'To the extent that one lacks knowledge of the other types of wisdom, he lacks a hundredfold in Torah wisdom, since [secular] wisdom and Torah are intertwined.' See R. Barukh's introduction to his translation of Euclid's *Elements*, where he also tells us that the Gaon requested him to translate works of *ḥokhmah* ('wisdom') into Hebrew. Landau, *Hagaon heḥasid mivilna*, 217, 225–6, for obvious ideological reasons, attempts to show that R. Barukh's testimony is unreliable, even though it was published seventeen years before the Vilna Gaon's death. Not only was there no protest from the Gaon or any of his followers, but it is impossible to imagine that R. Barukh would have published something like this in the Gaon's lifetime if it were not true. See Y. Mondshine, *Kerem ḥabad*, iv. 155 n. 8. The sort of ideological distortion in which Landau engages only works when the person whose views are being distorted is no longer among the living and is thus unable to set matters right.

[217] Eliach, *Sefer hagaon*.

[218] See Hildesheimer, 'Moses Mendelssohn'.

when discussing the Vilna's Gaon's opposition to hasidism, is not so forthright when it comes to Dubno. Instead, he takes it upon himself to 'protect' his community from this information, and therefore simply omits R. Hayim's *haskamah* for Dubno from his list.[219]

What I have just described is hardly unique, and we will see many examples of it from different segments of the Orthodox world. The motivation always seems to be the same, namely, that the current generation is not able 'to handle' the truth. As mentioned previously, the censors also often assume that had the author been alive today, he too would have agreed with the censorship of his writings. In a later chapter I examine in detail how followers of R. Abraham Isaac Kook have tried to stop his unexpurgated writings from seeing the light of day. The same phenomenon is also found with regard to Kook's haredi counterpart, R. Abraham Isaiah Karelitz, the Hazon Ish (1878–1953). After his death, a small book he had written entitled *Emunah uvitaḥon* was published. Yet three chapters of the book that contain sharp criticism of certain manifestations of the *musar* movement were not included.[220] Only in 1997 did the censored passages appear.[221] As is usually the case with such matters, one can assume that there was someone who had access to the Hazon Ish's manuscript and did not believe that the master's writings should be kept hidden from the public. It is likely that such a person was responsible for 'breaking the embargo'.[222]

The censorship of the Hazon Ish was due to the fact that the *musar* movement is very much accepted in the Orthodox world and public criticism of it is thought to be improper. There are many similar examples where a person who is originally assailed later becomes very well known and respected. Therefore, when the book with the criticism is reprinted, it is thought best to remove the negative comments. An example of this is that in the first edition of *Vikuaḥ mayim ḥayim* by R. Hayim ben Betzalel (*c.*1520–88), there is strong criticism of R. Joseph Karo and R. Moses Isserles (1520–72) for

219 See Y. Mondshine, '"Silent Approbations"'(Heb.). For another recent book which is also not honest with its readers, see Goldwasser, *Comrade*. This is supposed to be a translation of a Yiddish book. However, the author censored references to Habad and the Lubavitcher Rebbe, both of which are very important in the original. See <www.goldwasserstory.blogspot.com>.

220 The *musar* movement was a religious and ethical movement founded in the 19th cent. by R. Israel Salanter (1810–83). Regarding the Hazon Ish's criticism of the movement, see L. Kaplan, 'Hazon Ish', 157 ff. Kaplan's essay was written before the appearance of the new material in *Emunah uvitaḥon*. See also Brown, *The Hazon Ish* (Heb.), 38–9.

221 See Avni (pseudonym) (ed.), *Ḥazon ha'ish*, 70 ff. Only two of the three censored chapters appear in Karelitz, *Faith and Trust*, trans. Yaakov Goldstein, 250 ff.

222 According to R. Hayim Dov Ber Gulevsky, the Hazon Ish's criticisms of R. Hayim Soloveitchik (1853–1918) were also released in this fashion. See his *Lahat ḥerev hamithapekhet*, 5–6.

their codification of Jewish law. This criticism was removed from subsequent editions.[223]

Another form of censorship relates to translations, where the translators take liberties with the text for various reasons.[224] It is, of course, a truism that every translation is an interpretation. However, even in our post-modern age it should be clear that not every interpretation is correct. Sometimes, the translation is so blatantly inaccurate that we have no choice but to regard it as a conscious alteration.[225]

We will see some examples of this in later chapters. For now, let me offer one case which provides a good illustration of censorship in translation, although I do not believe it is of the ideological type that we will examine later. Rather, it follows in the tradition already mentioned, that of altering the truth because of concerns regarding how it will be viewed by the non-Jewish world—'for the sake of peace', to use a talmudic expression. In this case, it is actually the author himself, Elie Wiesel, who made the changes to his memoir.

Wiesel's *Night* is the most popular of all Holocaust memoirs. It played an enormous role in his rise to fame, which reached its pinnacle in Wiesel being awarded the Nobel Peace Prize. Since then, Wiesel has used his worldwide fame as an ambassador of conscience, speaking out against religious persecution and human rights abuses. In addition to being chosen as part of Oprah Winfrey's Book Club, *Night* is also read each year by thousands of high school and college students.

Until 1996, when Naomi Seidman published 'Elie Wiesel and the Scandal of Jewish Rage',[226] no one had pointed out that there were some significant differences between the Yiddish original, *Un di velt hot geshvign*, published in Buenos Aires in 1956, and the 1958 French translation (and abridgement), *La*

[223] See Elon, *Jewish Law*, iii. 1376 n. 26 (called to my attention by R. Ysoscher Katz). R. Joseph Saul Nathanson (1808–75) was responsible for the deletion; see his approbation in the Żółkiew, 1859 edition. R. Hayim ben Betzalel's uncensored introduction appears in Tchernowitz, *Toledot haposkim*, iii. 93–100.

[224] Regarding the issue of translations in general, and the different audiences addressed in the original as compared to in a translation, see Seidman, *Faithful Renderings*.

[225] For an example of this from the Reconstructionist prayer book, see *Kol haneshamah*, 54. This is its 'translation' of Ps. 147: 19–20: 'God tells the words of tale to Jacob, law and judgments to the people Israel. Has God not done so for all nations? Are there any who do not know such laws?' This is a dishonest translation as the last two sentences are, in the original, not questions but rather non-universalist statements focusing on God's special connection with Israel. This was noted by A. J. Wolf, 'The New Liturgies', 241, who calls attention to other examples.

[226] The essay was reprinted in Seidman, *Faithful Renderings*, 216 ff., and I have cited it from there.

Nuit, done by Wiesel himself. This was soon followed by the 1960 translation into English.

One of Wiesel's great achievements was to show the dignity of the survivor, who is able to go on with his life and join the high echelons of literary and cultural circles. Wiesel is not obsessed with feelings of revenge, and he attempts to show that it is not just he who is able to overcome vengeful thoughts. We see this at the end of *Night* where he describes the first survivors who ventured out of Buchenwald after liberation: 'On the following morning, some of the young men went to Weimar to get some potatoes and clothes—and to sleep with girls. But of revenge, not a sign.'[227]

What would it have done to readers' images of the liberated Jews had they seen what appeared in the Yiddish original, which was only designed to be read by other Jews: 'Early the next day Jewish boys ran off to Weimar to steal clothing and potatoes. And to rape German girls [*un tsu fargvaldikn daytshe shikses*]. The historical commandment of revenge was not fulfilled [i.e. the robbery and rapes were not sufficient revenge].'[228] Seidman writes:

> To describe the differences between these versions as a stylistic reworking is to miss the extent of what is suppressed in the French. *Un di velt* depicts a post-Holocaust landscape in which Jewish boys 'run off' to steal provisions and rape German girls; *Night* extracts from this scene of lawless retribution a far more innocent picture of the aftermath of the war, with young men going off to the nearest city to look for clothes and sex. In the Yiddish, the survivors are explicitly described as Jews and their victims (or intended victims) as German; in the French, they are just young men and women.[229]

There appears to be no escaping the fact that Wiesel altered the historical record—which he presumably portrayed accurately in the Yiddish version—for what he would have no doubt argued is a 'greater cause'. In this, his actions are very much in line with the larger story I tell in this book. Were he writing *Night* today, I doubt that Wiesel would take any creative liberties with the original text. Rather, he probably would simply omit the passage I have referred to. I say this because it is precisely the sort of discrepancy just seen that gives ammunition to Holocaust deniers, who were an insignificant phenomenon when *Night* was first published. Not unexpectedly, Seidman's essay became grist for their mill, as can easily be seen by an internet search.[230]

[227] *Night*, trans. Stella Rodway, 109.

[228] Seidman, *Faithful Renderings*, 221. The words in the second set of square brackets are mine.

[229] Ibid.

[230] For more regarding Wiesel and *Night*, and what genre the book should be categorized as (e.g. 'memoir', 'semi-fictional memoir', 'autobiographical novel', etc.), see Franklin, *A Thousand Darknesses*, ch. 3.

With regard to the Holocaust and the 'creation' of history, it is important to note that the Orthodox have also played their part. The best-known example is the story of how ninety-three Beit Ya'akov girls committed suicide rather than become prostitutes for German soldiers.[231] This story, which we know to be false, first made its appearance during the Second World War. We cannot be sure about the motives of the person who invented it,[232] but I assume that it was designed to raise Jewish awareness of what was happening in Europe. Since then, many gullible people in the haredi world have continued to repeat it.[233] While the story is a complete fabrication, and is known as such by haredi leaders and educators,[234] as far as I can tell no effort has been made in that community to disabuse people of this myth, undoubtedly because of its inspirational message.[235]

231 See Garber, 'The 93 Beit Yaakov Martyrs'.

232 Hillel Seidman claimed that he knew who made the story up. See Schacter and Joseph, 'The 93 Beth Jacob Girls', 104 n. 49. In conversation with me, Seidman would not reveal who this person was.

233 R. Jehiel Jacob Weinberg was even taken in by it, and dedicated his *Das Volk der Religion* to the memory of Sara Schenirer and the ninety-three martyrs.

234 The haredi Holocaust historian, Esther Farbstein, does not even mention it in her book, *Beseter ra'am*. P. Benisch, *To Vanquish the Dragon*, which tells the story of the Beit Ya'akov girls of Kraków, also does not mention the episode. This was noted by Schacter and Joseph, 'The 93 Beth Jacob Girls', 127 n. 110.

235 After describing the story in detail, and showing why it is a fiction, Schacter and Joseph, ibid., conclude (p. 127): 'Maybe it did happen. But, maybe again, it didn't. Could it have happened? Of course.' This makes no sense to me. If, by the word 'could', they mean is such a story a physical possibility, then obviously the answer is yes. But according to this logic, Franklin Roosevelt 'could' have given Hitler the idea to open the extermination camps, and Joseph Stalin 'could' have gone to church every day. Yet this is not how historians operate. The only relevant question is whether there is any evidence that ninety-three Beit Ya'akov girls in Kraków committed suicide. On this point, the evidence collected by Schacter and Joseph demonstrates that the event never took place.

CHAPTER TWO

JEWISH THOUGHT

IN AN EARLIER BOOK, *The Limits of Orthodox Theology*, I probed the outer reaches of traditional Jewish thought and discussed a number of ideas that have made some people very uncomfortable. The phenomenon that this present book documents is also relevant to matters of Jewish thought. It is sometimes hard for people to imagine great figures of a previous era holding vastly different opinions from those that have become commonplace in the Orthodox world. Rather than challenging or explaining unusual views, for some, simply removing these views from the public eye remains a real option. There are also cases where the censor is convinced that the earlier author could not possibly have said what appears in his book. Instead, the objectionable passages are attributed to an 'erring student' or even to a heretic attempting to undermine traditional Judaism. With such a conception, censorship becomes a religious obligation.

A good example of this was seen in the 1975 publication of the commentary on the Torah by R. Judah Hehasid (*c*.1150–1217).[1] R. Judah, a famed pietist, was one of the major figures of medieval Ashkenazi Jewry. While his commentary contains a great deal of noteworthy items, there are also a few passages that would not be expected from a medieval scholar. Recognizing the radical nature of these passages, Y. Lange, the editor, mentions in his introduction that he never had any thought of censoring the text, even though the passages could create confusion for some.[2] He wrote this precisely because he knew that there were those who did indeed want him to delete sections of the commentary.

What was so problematic with this work is that R. Judah Hehasid shows himself as a proto-biblical critic, as he asserts that some verses in the Torah are post-Mosaic.[3] For example, he claims that Genesis 36: 31–9, which contains a list of the kings of Edom 'before there reigned any king over the chil-

[1] Judah Hehasid, *Torah Commentaries* (Heb.).

[2] Ibid. 12–13.

[3] Ibid. 64, 138, 198 (uncensored version). R. Judah Hehasid's view is discussed by Brin, 'Themes' (Heb.); L. Jacobs, *Beyond Reasonable Doubt*, 63–5; Soloveitchik, 'Two Notes', 241 ff.; B. Z. Katz, *A Journey through Torah*, ch. 7.

dren of Israel', post-dates Moses and was added by *anshei keneset hagedolah* (the men of the Great Assembly).[4] R. Judah Hehasid makes another fascinating remark in his commentary on Numbers 21: 17 ('Then sang Israel this song'). He claims that the 'song' referred to is the 'Great Hallel' (Psalm 136). It was only in a later generation that King David removed it from the Pentateuch, together with all the other anonymous psalms written by Moses, and placed them in the book of Psalms.[5]

Having been told about the various 'problematic' passages before publication, R. Moses Feinstein declared that the book contained heresy and could not have been authored by R. Judah Hehasid. It was therefore forbidden to publish the work.[6] Although Lange did publish it, the pressure on him was such that, in opposition to what he originally wrote in his introduction, he now felt forced to publish a second, censored, edition of the commentary.[7] In this new edition, the passages dealing with the Torah's authorship were deleted. This censorship is actually different from most other examples that appear in this book. In the other cases, the censors were aware of the author's views, and for their own reasons chose to censor them. In this case, however, Feinstein really believed that the passages he pointed to were not written by R. Judah Hehasid.[8]

Another medieval scholar who held controversial views regarding the authorship of the Torah was R. Abraham Ibn Ezra, who also believed that the Torah contains post-Mosaic additions.[9] Unlike what happened with R. Judah Hehasid, Ibn Ezra's opinion, which is only hinted at, was never censored. However, R. Joseph Bonfils[10] and R. Samuel Motot,[11] two fourteenth-century commentators who explained Ibn Ezra's cryptic words, *were* censored when

[4] Judah Hehasid, *Torah Commentaries* (Heb.), 198.

[5] Ibid. 184–5.

[6] Feinstein, *Igerot mosheh*, vol. vi, 'Yoreh de'ah' 3, nos. 114–15.

[7] This action, incidentally, could not have satisfied Feinstein, who insisted that the entire commentary was off-limits, since other heretical passages were bound to exist. Feinstein himself pointed to what he regarded as a heretical forgery in that R. Judah Hehasid, *Torah Commentaries* (Heb.), 147–8, asks why homosexuality is forbidden, and then explains that the prohibition is to ensure that men procreate. According to Feinstein, even asking such a question, and offering such a weak explanation, is a sign that the passage could not have been written by R. Judah Hehasid but must have been inserted by a gay-friendly subversive. Yet as R. Chaim Rapoport points out, R. Judah Hehasid is quoted as saying the same thing in another medieval source, and the explanation Feinstein found so weak is also found in Nahmanides, *Sefer haḥinukh* and R. David Ibn Zimra (Radbaz, *c.*1479–1573). See C. Rapoport, *Judaism and Homosexuality*, 155–6.

[8] R. Judah Hehasid is hardly the only medieval authority to have a non-traditional view of the authorship and text of the Torah. See my *Limits of Orthodox Theology*, ch. 7.

[9] See my *Limits of Orthodox Theology*, 107 ff.

[10] Bonfils, *Tsafnat pane'aḥ*, Gen. 12: 6, 22: 14, 36: 31, Deut. 1: 2.

[11] Motot, *Supercommentary* (Heb.), Deut. 1: 2.

their works appeared in a collection of supercommentaries on Ibn Ezra published in Amsterdam in 1722.[12]

Bonfils' commentary had not previously appeared in print, but Motot's had been published in Venice in 1554. It is worth noting that, unlike Bonfils, Motot disagreed with Ibn Ezra and asserted that one must believe that Moses wrote all the apparently anachronistic verses prophetically. In the version of Motot published in 1722, we find not merely censorship but even forgery. While Motot's view was originally offered in opposition to that of Ibn Ezra, in the 1722 edition his view is turned into an *explanation* of Ibn Ezra that removes the radicalism of Ibn Ezra's position.[13]

In this case, the publisher might have even had some justification for his forgery. In his commentary on Deuteronomy 1: 2, Motot reports that there are those who explain Ibn Ezra against his authentic intent in order to bring him into line with traditional views. He concludes that God will reward these (false) interpreters. Thus, by altering Motot's comment regarding Ibn Ezra, the publisher was actually following through on what appears to be Motot's suggestion![14]

Another theologically based censorship can be seen with the important medieval sage R. Samuel ben Meir (Rashbam; *c*.1085–*c*.1158). His Torah commentary is very strongly oriented to the *peshat*, the literal meaning of the text. In line with this, he does not hesitate to offer explanations at variance with the talmudic understanding of certain verses, even in matters of practical halakhah. This does not mean that he rejects the halakhah, only that he regards the halakhah that was passed down from Sinai or that the Sages derived from the verse as not identical to the *peshat*. In other words, there are two truths: halakhic truth and *peshat* truth.[15]

An example of this appears in his commentary on Genesis 1: 5,[16] where he famously explains how, according to the *peshat*, the beginning of day is the morning. This is at odds with the traditional approach that sees the start of

[12] Lazi (ed.), *Margaliyot tovah*.

[13] See my *Limits of Orthodox Theology*, 108 n. 115; Simon, *The Ear Discerns Words* (Heb.), 440.

[14] This point was called to my attentioni by Leor Jacobi.

[15] For a detailed discussion of this topic, with examples from many medieval authorities, see Kasher, *Torah shelemah*, xvii, 286–312.

[16] See also his commentary on Gen. 1: 4, 6, 8, 31. Until recent years, *Mikraot gedolot* Pentateuchs only included Rashbam's commentary from Genesis ch. 18 on; the commentary on Genesis ch. 1 was only printed in the 19th cent. (The commentary on Genesis chs. 2–17 has been lost.) Professor Martin Lockshin has pointed out to me that the omission of Rashbam's commentary on the first chapter of Genesis has nothing to do with censorship, as people often assume. Rather, the single almost complete manuscript of Rashbam's commentary, upon which printed editions were based, only begins at Genesis 18. The commentary on Genesis 1 comes from another manuscript that was not available to the first publishers of *Mikraot gedolot*.

each day in the previous night. This interpretation of Rashbam was strongly attacked by Ibn Ezra in his *Igeret hashabat*.[17] In the preface to this work, referring to Rashbam's view, Ibn Ezra wrote, 'The arm of the scribe who writes this commentary to Scripture should wither and his right eye weaken.'[18]

This curse, enough to frighten away most scribes, has been thought by some to explain why there is only one manuscript in existence that contains Rashbam's commentary on Genesis, chapter 1.[19] Although Ibn Ezra himself often disagrees with the rabbinic understanding of verses, including halakhic matters,[20] in this case he saw Rashbam's explanation as very dangerous to tradition, stating, 'This interpretation will mislead all of Israel, those in the east and those in the west, those near and those far, both the living and the dead.'[21]

It should therefore not surprise us that a recent edition of the *Mikraot gedolot* (Rabbinic Bible) Pentateuch simply removes one of Rashbam's comments explaining his novel view.[22] This came about after pressure was brought to bear upon the publisher. However, not all of Rashbam's 'problematic' comments were removed from this edition. This in turn led to another protest, asserting that the objectionable comments in Rashbam are a heretical interpolation.[23] I assume it is just a matter of time before an edition is published where all traces of Rashbam's position are made to disappear.

One might have thought that the great Maimonides would emerge unscathed from the censor's knife. After all, his books are so well known, as are his views, that it is much more difficult to fool the readership. It is perhaps

[17] See Goodman, *Sabbath Epistle*, which also includes a new edition of the Hebrew text. English translations of the work are taken from here.

[18] Ibid. 4. Regarding what Ibn Ezra saw as so dangerous in Rashbam's interpretation, see Fleischer, 'R. Abraham Ibn Ezra' (Heb.), 164 ff.; Kasher, *Halakhic International Dateline* (Heb.), ch. 22*; Yosef Cohen and Uriel Simon in the appendix to their edition of Ibn Ezra, *Yesod mora vesod torah*, 222 ff. I am following the generally accepted assumption that Ibn Ezra's ire is directed against Rashbam and not at other interpreters, as some have argued. See A. Mondshine, 'On the Relationship between Ibn Ezra's and Rashbam's Commentaries on the Torah' (Heb.); Ta-Shma, *Keneset meḥkarim*, iv. 195; Goodman, *Sabbath Epistle*, preface. For an alternative perspective, see Rottzoll, 'Kannte Avraham ibn Ezra Sh'mu'el ben Me'ir', 98 ff.

[19] See e.g. D. Kahana (ed.), *Rabbi Abraham Ibn Ezra* (Heb.), ii. 45 n. 4 (second numbering). The problem with this view is that we also know of only one manuscript (lost in the Holocaust) of the rest of the commentary on the Torah. For some reason scribes were not interested in copying any of Rashbam's commentary.

[20] See e.g. Lockshin, 'Tradition or Context'; Strickman, 'Abraham Ibn Ezra's Non-Literal Interpretations'.

[21] Goodman, *Sabbath Epistle*, 4. Despite Ibn Ezra's words, R. Ya'akov Kamenetsky cites Rashbam's opinion and concludes that it was only with the giving of the Torah that the day can be said to begin with darkness. See id., *Emet leya'akov* on Gen. 1: 4.

[22] See Levanon, 'The *Sabbath Epistle*' (Heb.), 5.

[23] A copy of this letter of protest is in my possession.

for this reason that a recent edition of the ethical will attributed to Maimonides tells the reader up front that it has omitted a passage 'that will not bring [people] to fear [of God], nor to love [of Him], and it is possible that it will be injurious'.[24] This passage is so famous that it is not the sort of thing that could have been cut out unnoticed.

In the passage, Maimonides writes:

They [the French scholars] do not appear to recognize the Creator, blessed be He, except when they are ingesting boiled ox meat, seasoned in vinegar and garlic, a condiment that they call 'salsa'. . . . Also [they feel near to God] by making of Him a mat for their tongues [to step on], mentioning and speaking about God at all times in anthropomorphic terms. . . . Generally, they have two wives, so that their minds are invariably fixed on sex, eating, and drinking, and on other sensual pleasures. And they believe that in this fashion God is in their presence and that He is listening to them![25]

This is hardly respectful to the (northern) French scholars, to put it mildly. It is also in marked contrast to Maimonides' letter to the sages of Lunel in southern France. In this letter, he not only extols their learning, but also tells them that the future of Torah study is in their hands, as 'the study of the Torah in our communities has ceased. Most of the bigger congregations are dead to spiritual aims, the remaining communities are facing the end.'[26]

Those who are upset that Maimonides has been censored here can, however, rest at ease. Although the letter has been quoted by numerous rabbinic figures, beginning in the sixteenth century,[27] there is no question that, as with a number of other works attributed to Maimonides,[28] it is not authentic. Rather, the first part, which contains words of ethical advice, is by an unknown Italian author and was only joined to the second part some centuries after Maimonides' death.[29] The second part, which is directly addressed to R. Abraham Maimonides (1186–1237), is an obvious forgery,[30] as was noted already by R. Jacob Emden (1697–1776).[31]

[24] Anon., *The* Igeret hamusar *Attributed to Maimonides* (Heb.), 37. Abrahams, *Hebrew Ethical Wills*, vol. i, ch. 5, also omits the second section of the letter, though he acknowledges that it was not written by Maimonides.

[25] Maimonides, *Kovets teshuvot harambam*, iii. 40. I have used José Faur's translation (with slight changes), from his *The Horizontal Society*, i. 367 n. 155.

[26] Maimonides, *Igerot harambam*, ii. 559 (translation in Kobler, *Letters of Jews*, i. 216).

[27] See Anon., *The* Igeret hamusar *Attributed to Maimonides* (Heb.), introd.

[28] See Maimonides, *Igerot harambam*, vol. ii, appendices 1 and 2; Kasher, *Maimonides and the Mekhilta*, 223–32. For the attempts of R. Joseph Kafih and others to add even more works to this list, see my *Studies in Maimonides and His Interpreters*, 76–7.

[29] See Maimonides, *Igerot harambam*, ii. 699.

[30] See ibid. 697–9.

[31] See Emden, *Mitpaḥat sefarim*, 101–2.

There are other instances where authentic writings by Maimonides, and texts written about Maimonides, have been censored for a variety of reasons. Let us begin by looking at Maimonides' great law code, the *Mishneh torah*. Moses Hyamson (1862–1949), a well-known Orthodox rabbi as well as a teacher at the Jewish Theological Seminary of America, published the first two volumes of the *Mishneh torah*. This edition is based on the Oxford manuscript, which contains Maimonides' hand-written attestation and which Hyamson supposedly copied carefully. He also provided an English translation. The first volume was published in Hyamson's lifetime, while the second volume appeared posthumously.

Although this is a twentieth-century work, Hyamson still felt the need to refrain from translating Maimonides' negative references to Jesus.[32] He also engages in censorship for puritanical reasons, of the sort we will see again in Chapter 6. The section 'Hilkhot tefilin' ('Laws of Tefillin') 4: 20–1 contains *halakhot* concerning someone who enters the lavatory or has sexual relations while wearing tefillin. Hyamson was apparently embarrassed by these *halakhot* and refused to render them into English (Fig. 2.1).

While not an example of censorship, it should be noted that Hyamson also took liberties with the *Mishneh torah* in another place. According to Hyamson, his edition 'follows closely the [Oxford] manuscript, line by line and page by page'.[33] This is generally, but not always, true, and in the case to be discussed at present Hyamson was most unfaithful to the text: he actually altered the Hebrew original, and thus misled countless numbers of people who have used his volume. His action, which can best be described as forgery, was part of a much larger tale, although Hyamson did not know this at the time.

For centuries the Ben Asher Codex of the Bible had been preserved in Aleppo. Before arriving there, it had been in Egypt where it was used by Maimonides, who regarded it as authoritative.[34] However, not everyone was convinced that the Aleppo Codex was indeed the one used by Maimonides. The great biblical scholar Umberto Cassuto (1883–1951) went to Aleppo in 1943 and examined the Codex. His conclusion was that it was *not* the text used by Maimonides. One of his main reasons was simple, and apparently incontrovertible: whereas the Aleppo Codex has the so-called Song of Moses (Deut. 32) in 67 lines, Maimonides in the *Mishneh torah*[35] states that it should be written in 70 lines.[36] At least, this is how it appears in the standard printed editions of the *Mishneh torah*. However, all the good manuscripts read

32 See Maimonides, *Mishneh torah*, 'Hilkhot avodah zarah' 10: 1; 'Hilkhot teshuvah' 3: 19, 4: 2.

33 Maimonides, *Mishneh Torah*, ed. Hyamson, preface to vol. ii.

34 See Maimonides, *Mishneh torah*, 'Hilkhot sefer torah' 8: 4.

35 Ibid.

36 See Ofer, 'M. D. Cassuto's Notes' (Heb.), 325–8.

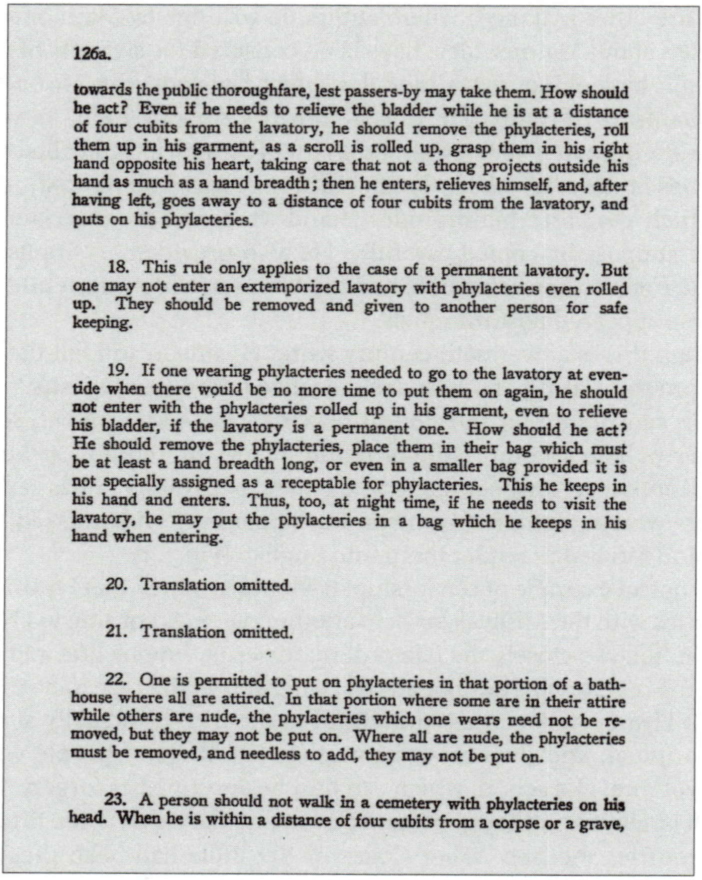

126a.

towards the public thoroughfare, lest passers-by may take them. How should he act? Even if he needs to relieve the bladder while he is at a distance of four cubits from the lavatory, he should remove the phylacteries, roll them up in his garment, as a scroll is rolled up, grasp them in his right hand opposite his heart, taking care that not a thong projects outside his hand as much as a hand breadth; then he enters, relieves himself, and, after having left, goes away to a distance of four cubits from the lavatory, and puts on his phylacteries.

18. This rule only applies to the case of a permanent lavatory. But one may not enter an extemporized lavatory with phylacteries even rolled up. They should be removed and given to another person for safe keeping.

19. If one wearing phylacteries needed to go to the lavatory at eventide when there would be no more time to put them on again, he should not enter with the phylacteries rolled up in his garment, even to relieve his bladder, if the lavatory is a permanent one. How should he act? He should remove the phylacteries, place them in their bag which must be at least a hand breadth long, or even in a smaller bag provided it is not specially assigned as a receptable for phylacteries. This he keeps in his hand and enters. Thus, too, at night time, if he needs to visit the lavatory, he may put the phylacteries in a bag which he keeps in his hand when entering.

20. Translation omitted.

21. Translation omitted.

22. One is permitted to put on phylacteries in that portion of a bath-house where all are attired. In that portion where some are in their attire while others are nude, the phylacteries which one wears need not be removed, but they may not be put on. Where all are nude, the phylacteries must be removed, and needless to add, they may not be put on.

23. A person should not walk in a cemetery with phylacteries on his head. When he is within a distance of four cubits from a corpse or a grave,

Figure 2.1 Moses Hyamson's translation of Maimonides, *Mishneh torah,* vol. ii (Jerusalem: Boys Town Jerusalem Publishers, 1962), p. 126a, showing sections left untranslated

'67 lines'.[37] It is obvious that the printed versions of the *Mishneh torah* (and some manuscripts too) were corrected to agree with the Ashkenazi and Sephardi traditions, according to which the Song of Moses is indeed written in 70 lines.[38]

When we examine the *Mishneh torah* passage in Hyamson's edition, we also find '70 lines'. This is nothing less than forgery as the Oxford manuscript

[37] See the textual note in the Frankel edition of the *Mishneh torah,* 'Hilkhot sefer torah' 8: 4.

[38] See Goshen-Gottstein, 'Authenticity', 33 ff., 46 ff. The Yemenite tradition follows Maimonides' instructions and its Torah scrolls have 67 lines.

has '67 lines'. After mentioning that there are 67 lines, Maimonides lists the first word of each line, and Hyamson copied this part exactly, even though he had just 'corrected' the opening line to read '70'. This created a problem for Chaim Brecher, who assisted Hyamson, because it was his job to add the biblical and talmudic references. He notes that although Maimonides says that there are 70 lines, only 67 'first words' are listed. Apparently not realizing that '70' had been inserted by Hyamson, Brecher assumed that there was a mistake in the manuscript in listing the first words, and he therefore took it upon himself to 'correct' this section.

Why did Hyamson alter the text? Although I assume it was because he thought that the Oxford manuscript contained a scribal error, Samuel Loewinger believed that dogmatic reasons were involved. He also thought that Brecher was part of this 'conspiracy'. Yet as I have noted, it is more likely that Brecher too was taken in by Hyamson. (Therefore, in the following passage, where Loewinger speaks in the plural, I have changed this to the singular). In Loewinger's words, '[he] deliberately changed the reading of the manuscript of the *Mishne Torah* because of [his] exaggerated fear of the possibility of the existence of any differences in the traditions concerning the Torah. It is to be regretted that [he] did not realize that such an approach undermines the faith in "research" of this kind.'[39]

Another example of the censorship of Maimonides relates to his *Treatise on Logic*. In the original Arabic, Maimonides uses the figure of Jesus in giving an example of temporal priority, stating that Moses existed before Jesus. Yet in the three early Hebrew translations that we possess, Jesus has been removed and another name substituted.[40]

The censorship of the *Treatise on Logic* took place centuries ago, before the invention of printing. However, as we have seen with the example from Hyamson, censorship of the 'Great Eagle' has continued into recent times. We will now examine an example from the second half of the twentieth

[39] Loewinger, 'Prolegomenon', p. ix.

[40] See Davidson, *Moses Maimonides*, 319. Davidson's argument, based on the reference to Jesus, is that Maimonides could not have authored this work. On the topic of Jesus, Hillel Zeitlin (1871–1942) wrote some passages that were sympathetic to him, as well as to Christianity as a whole. When Zeitlin's son reprinted his writings, these were removed (as well as some other passages). See Zeitlin, *Rabbi Nahman of Bratslav* (Heb.), 42, and the editorial notes throughout the book. For what could be taken as criticism of R. Nahman of Bratslav and his followers, and was deleted, see pp. 55 n. 84, 56 n. 87, 62 n. 143. For censorship of R. Elijah Benamozegh's (1822–1900) comments in his book *Jewish and Christian Ethics*, compare the photo-offset edition published in Jerusalem in 2000 by the Kest-Lebovits Jewish Heritage and Roots Library with the San Francisco 1873 edition (translated from the French), 53, 59, 61, 96–7, 105. With this book, rather than white passages out, the new edition simply inserted rewritten and reset passages.

century. Since this instance relates to the place of women in society, it is necessary to say something about Maimonides' attitude in this matter, especially since many assume that his view of women was quite negative.

Among medieval writers one can, to be sure, find all sorts of terrible statements about women. Misogyny was common in non-Jewish literature and there are plenty of Jewish counterparts to this. Yet Maimonides is not to be placed in this category. It is true that he often places women together with children and the ignorant, and in some of these passages it is clear that he did not think women had much religious sophistication.[41] When it comes to the study of Torah, he writes: 'Our Sages commanded that one should not teach his daughter Torah, because most women cannot concentrate their attention on study, and they transform the words of Torah into nonsensical matters due to their lack of understanding.'[42] Nevertheless, Maimonides should not be placed with other medieval figures who speak negatively about women. In fact, he is actually one of the most progressive medieval Jewish writers when it comes to views on women.

As is well known, Maimonides was greatly influenced by Aristotle and followed his outlook in numerous ways. In Aristotle's opinion, a woman is defective by nature. It is the man who provides the 'form', while the woman is left to provide the 'matter'.[43] This viewpoint was, it need hardly be said, quite influential in medieval thought. For most medieval thinkers, women were naturally defective, both intellectually and spiritually, and R. Isaac Abarbanel (1437–1508) goes so far as to claim that women are not created in the image of God! After all, the Bible states that God created *man* in His image (Gen. 1: 27). Abarbanel reads this literally, to mean man and not woman, 'for only man can comprehend the secrets of divine wisdom and therefore man alone was the aim of creation'.[44]

Maimonides, however, broke with Aristotle when it came to the latter's view of women. For Maimonides, any judgement to be made about the intelligence of women is due to their social circumstances, living in what was a Taliban-like society. However, they are not *inherently* inferior to men. Maimonides, in fact, asserts that women too are required to obtain knowledge of

[41] See the list of passages in A. Melamed, 'Maimonides on Women', 119–22. Melamed overlooked *Mishneh torah*, 'Hilkhot avodah zarah' 11: 16, where Maimonides states that women and children have 'undeveloped intellects'.

[42] *Mishneh torah*, 'Hilkhot talmud torah' 1: 13.

[43] See the Aristotelian sources and secondary literature cited in Kellner, *Torah in the Observatory*, 284. See also M. C. Horowitz, 'Aristotle and Woman'; Allen, *Concept of Woman*, ch. 2; Maloney, 'The Argument for Women's Difference', 44 ff.; Tuana, *The Less Noble Sex*, 55–6.

[44] Netanyahu, *Don Isaac Abravanel*, 136. See Abarbanel's commentary on Gen. 1: 27. R. Jacob Anatoli had earlier claimed that women are not created in God's image. See Anatoli, *Malmad hatalmidim*, 25*b*, 73*a*.

God and that this is necessary to fulfil various commandments.[45] They are inferior because they have received no education, but this is not something 'hardwired' into them. In the words of Menachem Kellner, according to Maimonides the position of women 'was a function of sociology, not of ontology'.[46] Seen in the context of medieval times, when negative views of women's nature were standard, Maimonides' alternative perspective can be seen as a 'radical egalitarian stance'.[47]

However, the way Maimonides expresses himself could sometimes still be problematic for those who wish to see him as thinking in line with modern ideas. That is the only way I can explain the following example. In his *Letter on Martyrdom*, Maimonides states that the foolishness of the arguments of his opponent is apparent even to 'light-headed women'.[48] Yet when Leon D. Stitskin published a translation of this letter in 1977, at a time when feminism was on everyone's mind in the United States, he removed the reference to women. In its place, he substituted 'the unenlightened'.[49]

While this seems to be a clear example of a politically correct 'translation', Aryeh Newman has defended Stitskin's approach, which he sees as 'judicious'.[50] Although he acknowledges that scholars must have exact translations, he does not believe that this is a requirement for everyone else, for whom a footnote can explain what was removed. He explains the problem

[45] See Maimonides, *Sefer hamitsvot*, positive commandments nos. 1–6, and his words at the end of the positive commandments, *Mishneh torah*, 'Hilkhot yesodei hatorah', chs. 1–4; Harvey, 'Obligation of Talmud'.

[46] Kellner, *Torah in the Observatory*, 293. R. Joseph Kafih held the same view. See S. P. Cohen, 'Maimonides' Relation' (Heb.). See also Rudavsky, 'To Know What Is', 192 ff.

[47] A. Melamed, 'Maimonides on Women', 100. I find the argument of Kellner, Kafih, and Melamed convincing, yet it has been challenged, most recently, by Tirosh-Samuelson, 'Gender and the Pursuit of Happiness'. According to Tirosh-Samuelson, 'Maimonides did not exclude women from the pursuit of happiness, but he maintained that women as a class are incapable of attaining the ultimate end of human life, which is the contemplation of necessary truths' (p. 57). She cites Maimonides' exclusion of women as witnesses (*Mishneh torah*, 'Hilkhot edut' 9: 1) as an example of how he regarded women's cognitive inferiority (p. 69). Yet this is a complete non sequitur since Maimonides is bound to talmudic law, which had already established that only men can serve as witnesses; see BT *Shev.* 30*a*.

[48] Maimonides, *Igerot harambam*, i. 30.

[49] Stitskin, *Letters of Maimonides*, 41. I first saw this example years ago, and it was later also noted by Newman, 'Women, Saints, and Heretics', 78 n. 15. All versions of the Hebrew translation available to Stitskin refer to women, although their wordings are slightly different. (Newman, 'Women, Saints, and Heretics', 78 n. 15, is incorrect in stating that Ibn Tibbon translated this letter.) However, it is interesting to note that in 1984 Yitshak Sheilat published the surviving portion of a hitherto unknown medieval translation of Maimonides' *Letter on Martyrdom* (the original Arabic is lost). See Sheilat, 'Unknown Translation' (Heb.). In this version, the translator does indeed have *amei ha'arets* ('the ignorant') instead of 'light-headed women'. However, as mentioned, Stitskin did not have access to this text.

[50] Newman, 'Women, Saints, and Heretics', 78 n. 15.

with exact translations as follows: '[I]s Maimonides' message transmitted authentically to persons living in the twentieth century, where women have achieved greater equality than before, receive schooling similar to that of males, and regard attributing any disabilities to their alleged lack of responsibility, intellectual inferiority, or absence of education as unacceptable?'[51] In other words, for the reader who is engaged with the text in other than a detached, academic fashion, sometimes a literal translation ends up distorting Maimonides' overall message.

Stitskin's embarrassment at Maimonides' words regarding the intelligence of women, and thus his motivation to censor, was shared by Hyamson, who also translated R. Bahya Ibn Pakuda's *Ḥovot halevavot* into English.[52] In the introduction to this work (p. 29 in Hyamson's translation), R. Bahya states:

> I once questioned a man counted among the learned in the law concerning some of the topics that I have mentioned to you as appertaining to the Science of Inward Duties; and he replied that, on this and like subjects, tradition takes the place of independent thought. 'This', I rejoined, 'can only apply to those who, on account of their small powers of perception and intelligence, lack the capacity for reflection; as, for example, children and feeble-minded persons.'

Anyone who looks at the Hebrew text Hyamson was translating (and of course also the original Arabic) will find that the last sentence should actually read 'women, children and feeble-minded persons'.[53] Since, as we have seen, Hyamson apparently thought that he could do whatever he wished with a text, we probably should be grateful that he refrained from censoring the Hebrew version as well.

One final example of censorship in translations of Maimonides regarding the position of women appears in Eliyahu Touger's new translation of the *Mishneh torah*. In 'Hilkhot talmud torah' (Laws of Torah Study) 1: 13, Maimonides quotes the Sages that if one teaches his daughter Torah, it is as if he taught her *tiflut*. *Tiflut* means 'folly' or 'obscenity'. Yet Touger translates the word as 'tales and parables', which is certainly incorrect. Furthermore, it is hard to believe that the translator actually thinks that this is the proper translation, especially as later in the same halakhah he translates *tiflut* as 'idle things'.[54]

[51] Newman, 'Women, Saints, and Heretics', 79.

[52] Unlike Menahem Mansoor's translation from the original Arabic, Hyamson translated from the medieval Hebrew version.

[53] Yaakov Feldman's translation is also apologetic, as instead of 'women' he has 'unlearned women'. See Bahya Ibn Pakuda, *Duties of the Heart*, p. xxxvii.

[54] This point was made by M. S. Berger, 'Maimonides on Sex and Marriage', 184.

Let us now turn to an act of censorship, not of Maimonides, but of one of the standard commentaries of his *Guide of the Perplexed*. This particular instance is relevant to Orthodox biblical studies as it relates to the historicity of events described in the Bible. Maimonides famously declared that some of these occurrences actually only happened in a dream or prophetic vision. One of these is the visit of the 'men' (angels) to Abraham in Genesis 18.[55] Nahmanides was outraged by Maimonides' opinion, declaring, 'Such words contradict Scripture. It is forbidden to listen to them, all the more to believe in them.'[56]

In this case, Maimonides had to take this view because he did not accept the notion that humans could have any sort of personal dealings with angels, which he identified with the 'separate intellects' rather than as beings whom God sends on various missions.[57] In Maimonides' words: 'Know again that in the case of everyone about whom exists a scriptural text that an angel talked to him or that speech came to him from God, this did not occur in any other way than in a dream or in a vision of prophecy.'[58]

Nahmanides was concerned about what such a view does to the historicity of the Torah. If the angels never really visited Abraham, then they never came to Lot either,[59] meaning that he did not host them in his house, and they did not blind the Sodomites or send Lot out of the city. The entire story of the destruction of Sodom and Gomorrah would also be part of the vision, meaning that the city was never really destroyed. If so, Nahmanides notes, 'Lot could have remained in Sodom.' While this approach would have the virtue of consistency, Nahmanides states that Maimonides incongruously *does* believe that the events described took place, apart from the conversations with angels, which occurred in visions. It is with reference to this understanding of Maimonides that Nahmanides declares that his words contradict the Torah.

In his commentary on *Guide* ii. 46, R. Profiat Duran (*c.*1350–*c.*1415), also known as Efodi, explains that according to Maimonides, the biblical episodes that only 'occurred' in visions or dreams include the story of the Akedah,

[55] See *Guide* ii. 42. In this chapter, Maimonides also states that the stories of Jacob's wrestling with an angel (Gen. 32) and Balaam and the ass (Num. 22) were not historical events. In *Guide* ii. 46 he includes in this category God telling Abraham to count the stars (Gen. 15: 5) and Hosea being told to marry a harlot (Hos. 1: 2). The anonymous medieval *Avat nefesh* (a supercommentary on Ibn Ezra's commentary on the Pentateuch) claims that Ibn Ezra also understood the story of the angels coming to Abraham as a vision. See *Avat nefesh*, Num. 22: 28, available as a typescript on the Otzar HaHochma website (<www.otzar.org>).

[56] Commentary on Gen. 18: 1. R. Abraham Hayim Viterbo (17th cent.) uses almost identical language when referring to this view of Maimonides. See his *Emunat ḥakhamim*, 33*a*–*b*.

[57] See Kellner, *Maimonides' Confrontation with Mysticism*, 272 ff. For Maimonides' other interpretations of 'angels', see Finkelscherer, *Mose Maimunis Stellung*, 29 ff.; A. Altmann, 'Angels and Angelology', *EJ* i, col. 975.

[58] *Guide* ii. 41.

[59] Cf. *Guide* ii. 6.

Abraham's attempted sacrifice of Isaac, as well as the incident of Jonah being swallowed by a great fish. Viewing the Jonah story as non-historical is not particularly radical. The story itself seems artificially constructed in at least one obvious way: many have pointed out that the name Nineveh is related to 'fish'.[60] The irony, which would have been immediately appreciated by the ancients, is that while Jonah refused to go to the 'fish place', the fish came to him.[61] Since the story is structured to a large extent around this play on words, it is unlikely that it was intended to be taken literally.[62] Indeed, it has been claimed that no less a figure than R. Elijah ben Solomon, the Vilna Gaon, independently concluded that the entire tale (not merely the part with the fish) is an allegory.[63] Efodi states his opinion about the Jonah story in one other place, and this appears in all editions of the commentary.[64]

Whether Efodi is correct in claiming that Maimonides regarded the Jonah story as non-historical is not at all clear. Had Maimonides thought this way, I see no reason why he would not have stated as much. After all, this is hardly more radical than asserting the non-literalness of other biblical events, a claim that he makes quite openly. Furthermore, in *Guide* ii. 48, Maimonides writes as if he *does* take the story literally:

When speaking of things the cause of which lies with the volition of animals and their being set in motion by their animal impulses, it says: 'And the Lord spoke unto the fish' [Jonah 2: 11]. This means that it was God who aroused in it that particular volition, not that He turned the fish into a prophet and sent it a prophetic revelation.[65]

[60] See e.g. *Interpreter's Dictionary of the Bible*, iii. 552 (s.v. *Nineveh*).

[61] See Elyakim Ben-Menahem's introduction to Jonah in the *Da'at mikra* edition, 6.

[62] For other arguments in favour of a non-literal understanding, see Uriel Simon's introduction in id., *JPS Bible Commentary: Jonah*, pp. xv–xxi.

[63] See Shashar, 'Should the Book of Jonah be Interpreted Allegorically?' (Heb.). R. Aharon Lichtenstein and R. Avraham Rivlin understand the Vilna Gaon in this way. See the excerpt from Lichtenstein's lecture at <www.aishdas.org>, Avodah Digest, vol. iii, no. 155 (6 Aug. 1999), and A. Rivlin, *Jonah* (Heb.), 43 ff. What makes this interpretation appealing is that, unlike other biblical books explained by the Vilna Gaon, in his commentary on Jonah he only offers an allegorical interpretation, without even implying that there is a literal *peshat*. Others have assumed that the Vilna Gaon's allegory is intended to be an *additional* interpretation, rather than taking the place of the literal meaning. See Y. Rivlin, 'Vilna Gaon's Commentary' (Heb.), 920–1, and Mazuz, *Kise hamelekh*, 66.

[64] Commentary on *Guide* ii. 32. R. Zerahyah ben Yitshak ben She'alti'el Hen also states that the story of Jonah and the fish is not to be understood literally. See *Otsar neḥmad*, 2 (1857), 137. This was also the opinion of R. Tanhum Yerushalmi. See Schussman, 'Allegory' (Heb.), 90 ff. In his commentary on Jonah 1: 1, R. Joseph Ibn Kaspi writes (without mentioning Maimonides): 'Some say that it [the story of Jonah and the fish] took place in a dream and prophetic vision.' See id., *Adnei kesef*, ii. 102. See also A. Rivlin, *Jonah* (Heb.), 34 ff.

[65] See also *Guide* ii. 29 where Maimonides cites a passage from *Bereshit rabah* that assumes the historicity of Jonah being swallowed by the fish.

As far as Efodi is concerned, however, the fact that Maimonides cites a verse from the book of Jonah that seems to be describing a historical event does not mean that he thinks the event actually occurred in 'real time'. In *Guide* ii. 32, Maimonides writes:

> However, we shall find many texts, some of them scriptural and some of them dicta of the Sages, all of which maintain this fundamental principle that God turns who He wills, whenever He wills it, into a prophet—but only someone perfect and superior to the utmost degree. But with regard to one of the ignorant among the common people, this is not possible according to us—I mean, that He should turn one of them into a prophet—except as it is possible that He should turn an ass or a frog into a prophet.

In his commentary on this passage, Efodi understands the last words to be an allusion to Balaam's ass and the fish that swallowed Jonah, to whom God spoke.[66] Just as Maimonides tells us that the story with Balaam's ass only took place in a dream, so too, according to Efodi, this is how one is to understand the story of Jonah and the fish.

Had Maimonides written 'fish', then Efodi's point would be well taken, but what does the mention of a frog have to do with the Jonah story? R. Meir Mazuz points out that the key to understanding Maimonides are his words earlier in the chapter: 'It is not possible that an ignoramus should turn into a prophet, nor can a man not be a prophet on a certain evening and be a prophet on the following morning, as though he had made some find.' According to Mazuz, and I believe he is correct, this is an allusion to Muhammad, who, according to traditional Islamic belief, was an illiterate to whom Gabriel appeared and commanded 'Read' (or 'Recite'). This is what turned him into a prophet. Mazuz concludes: 'It is this sort of "prophet" that Maimonides refers to as an ass or frog.'[67]

The Akedah is in an entirely different category than the Jonah story. Long before Kierkegaard, this was regarded as a central tale of the Bible, focusing as it does on faith in God in the face of an unthinkable demand. The Sages of the talmudic period recognized the centrality of the story, and during the medieval persecutions of European Jewry, Jews turned again and again to the Akedah, drawing all sorts of messages from it.[68] Maimonides himself describes the story as 'the most extraordinary thing that could happen in the world, such a thing that one would not imagine that human nature was

[66] See also Shem Tov ben Joseph Ibn Shem Tov, commentary on *Guide* ii. 32, who offers Efodi's approach as one possible interpretation. (See, however, his commentary on *Guide* i. 2, where this option is not offered.) Efodi's view is rejected by Abarbanel, ad loc.

[67] Mazuz, *Kovets ma'amarim*, 270. This example is not noted in Shamir, 'Allusions to Muhammad'.

[68] See Spiegel, *The Last Trial*.

capable of it'.[69] Thus, Efodi's assertion that, according to Maimonides, the story of the Akedah never really happened would be regarded by traditionalists as radical and unacceptable.

Efodi was not the first to understand Maimonides as teaching that the Akedah was not a historical event.[70] He was preceded in this by R. Isaac Ibn Latif (1210–80),[71] R. Zerahyah ben Yitshak ben She'alti'el Hen (thirteenth century),[72] R. Abraham Abulafia (thirteenth century),[73] and R. Joseph Ibn Kaspi (1279–1340).[74] Efodi's contemporary, R. Eleazar Ashkenazi ben Nathan Habavli (fourteenth century), also understood Maimonides in this fashion and agreed with this interpretation.[75] According to him, if the Akedah had actually happened, one would have expected Abraham to question the command, much as he questioned God when informed of Sodom's coming fate.

R. Jacob Anatoli,[76] R. Moses ben Joshua of Narbonne (commonly called Narboni; d. 1362),[77] and R. Nissim of Marseilles (fourteenth century) also appear to have held that the Akedah was not historical. R. Nissim thought that Ibn Ezra accepted this position as well.[78] The thirteenth-century R. Samuel Saporto feels compelled to reject this view, which presumably means that it was held by more than a few intellectuals.[79] Abarbanel also notes that many scholars held that the Akedah was not historical, a position he rejects.[80]

Although there are a number of interpreters who understand Maimonides to be rejecting the historicity of the Akedah, for at least one person it was too much to have Efodi's commentary, expressing such a view, publicly available. While most of the examples of censorship we examine in this book

[69] *Guide* iii. 24. See also Maimonides, *Mishneh torah*, 'Hilkhot beit habeḥirah' 2: 2, where Maimonides refers to the Akedah as a historical event.

[70] Among modern scholars, Maimonides was understood in this way by Nuriel, *Concealed and Revealed* (Heb.), 154–7, and Y. Leibowitz, *Discussions* (Heb.), 80, 86, 662.

[71] See Ibn Latif, 'R. Isaac Ibn Latif's *Epistle of Repentance*' (Heb.), 62.

[72] See *Otsar neḥmad*, 2 (1857), 125, 127, 138, 141.

[73] See Idel, 'Writings and Teachings' (Heb.), 186–9. It appears that Abulafia agreed with this interpretation. See Idel, *Language, Torah and Hermeneutics*, 62–3.

[74] See his commentary on *Guide* i. 8 (p. 25).

[75] Eleazar Ashkenazi b. Nathan Habavli, *Tsafnat pane'aḥ*, 71–2.

[76] See Anatoli, *Malmad hatalmidim*, 18*a*; M. L. Gordon, 'Rationalism of Jacob Anatoli', 170–1; Ravitzky, 'Thought' (Heb.), 276–7 n. 1.

[77] Commentary on *Guide* iii. 24. See Senior Stern's note in *Hateḥiyah*, 2 (1857), 62.

[78] Nissim ben Moses, *Ma'aseh nisim*, 284 ff.; Kreisel, 'Philosophical-Allegorical Torah Commentary' (Heb.), 307–8. Ibn Ezra, in his commentary on Jonah 1: 1, does appear to be saying that the Akedah story is not historical. For others who understood the Akedah in a non-literal fashion, see D. Schwartz, *Amulets, Charms, and Rationalism* (Heb.), 71–2, 73 n. 14.

[79] *Ginzei nistarot*, 4 (1878), 61.

[80] Commentary on *Guide* i. 8: שמעתי דבת רבים יסכימו עליו. He disputes this opinion in his commentary on *Guide* i. 8 and ii. 42. In his commentary on Gen. 22: 11, he describes this view as 'heresy'. For R. Mordechai Jaffe's attack on this view, see his *Levush pinat yikrat* on *Guide* ii. 46.

are fairly recent, this instance dates from the nineteenth century.[81] Efodi's commentary was printed in its entirety a number of times, beginning with the Venice 1551 edition of the *Guide*. It was only in the Warsaw 1872 edition, published by Isaac Goldman, who was himself a learned man, that Efodi's explanation of Maimonides and the Akedah was regarded as too dangerous to appear in print. It was therefore deleted (together with his remark on Jonah which, as mentioned, also appears elsewhere, even in the 1872 edition).

This censored edition of the *Guide*, which also contains the commentaries of Shem Tov ben Joseph Ibn Shem Tov (fifteenth century), Asher Crescas (fifteenth century), and Abarbanel, has been reprinted numerous times and is a standard work for anyone engaged in serious study of Maimonides' philosophy. Yet its readers are unaware of how nineteenth-century censorship continues to deprive them of what Efodi wrote. In other words, the censorship accomplished that which it set out to do, namely, completely hide Efodi's words from the public and do so in such a manner that no one has any idea that this has happened.[82]

If Efodi had such a radical view, why did Goldman not simply omit the commentary in its entirety? That would have been impossible, since Efodi is a standard, and valuable, commentary on the *Guide*, occupying a place similar to that of Rashi's commentary on the Bible. As such, the commentary had to stay, but that which was too radical was to be removed. This is the pattern we see again and again. Works that are viewed as heretical will be banned. But what is to be done with an 'accepted' work that contains some comments regarded as improper? The answer is to cut these comments out, thus allowing the work as a whole to be saved.[83]

Here is the uncensored page (Fig. 2.2(*a*)) from the Venice 1551 edition together with the censored Warsaw 1872 edition (Fig. 2.2(*b*)).

[81] Lawrence Kaplan was the first to call attention to this censorship. See his 'Rabbi Mordekhai Jaffe', 282 n. 19. Kaplan incorrectly states that Efodi's comment was deleted from all editions after that of Sabbioneta 1553. As mentioned in the text, the comment appears in every edition until Warsaw 1872. I checked the editions published in Jassnitz, 1742, Pressburg, 1856, Żółkiew, 1860, and Lemberg, 1866, all of which were typeset anew. (I was not able to check the Lemberg 1855–6 edition, but since the Lemberg 1866 edition is not censored this was no doubt the case for the earlier Lemberg edition.)

[82] Had people known of Efodi's comment, he would have been cited during the controversy over Nosson Slifkin's books (see below, Ch. 4 n. 35).

[83] Here is another example: R. Yehiel Mikhel Epstein (d. 1706), in the introduction to his *Kitsur shelah*, included an allusion to Shabetai Tsevi as the messiah. This was first noted by R. Jacob Emden. See Naor, *Post-Sabbatian Sabbatianism*, ch. 5. While admirers of Epstein might not have believed this, the issue was so problematic that in later editions the allusion was altered. In one printing the introduction was entirely removed. This censorship allowed the book to remain part of the traditional Jewish library; see Dan Rabinowitz's Seforim Blog post, 1 Nov. 2006. See also

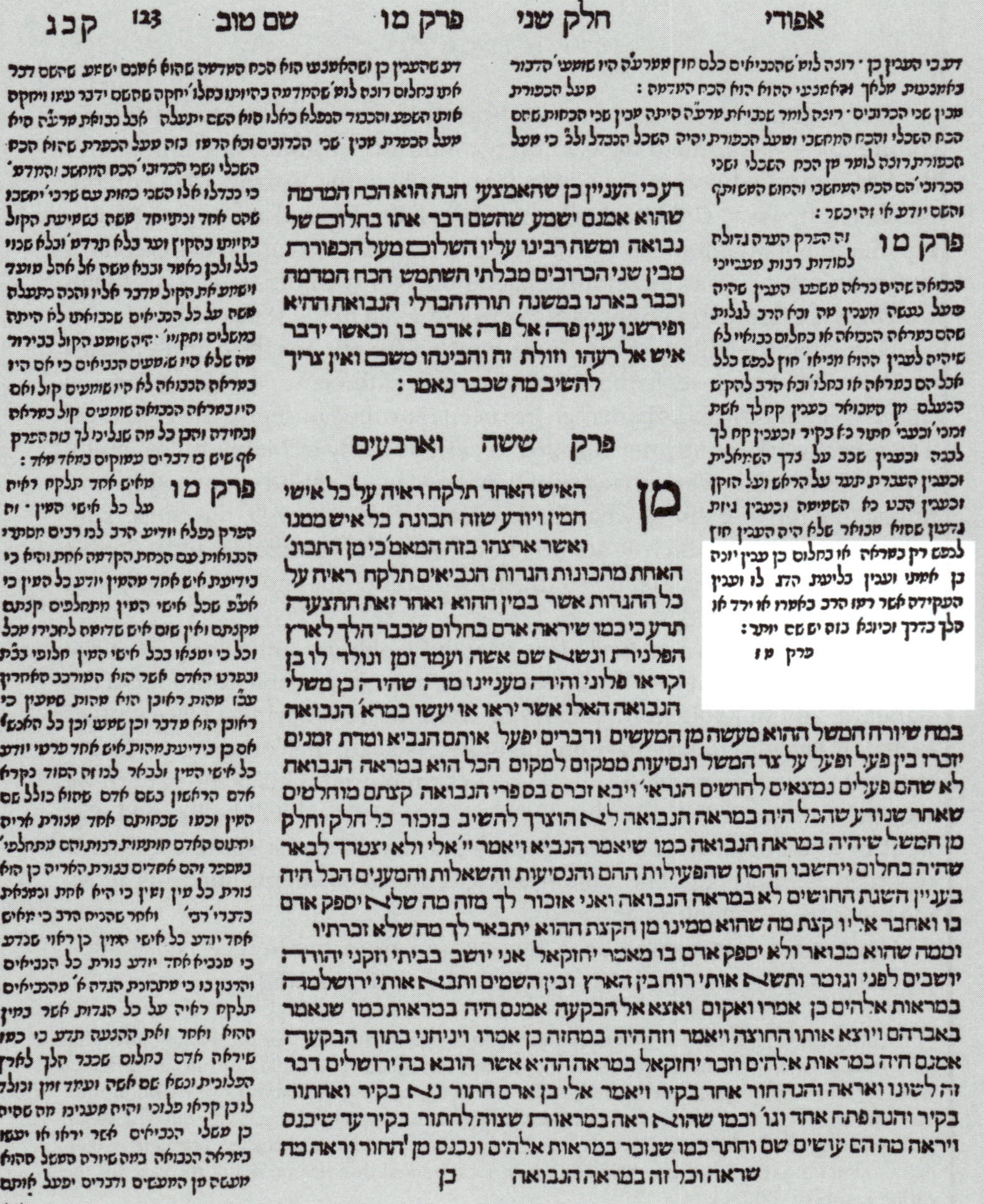
אפודי חלק שני פרק מו שם טוב 123 קכג

רעכי העניין כן שהאמצעי הנה הוא הכח המדמה שהוא אמנם ישמע שהשם דבר אתו בחלום של נבואה ומשה רבינו עליו השלום מעל הכפורת מבין שני הכרובים מבלתי השתמש הכח המדמה וכבר בארנו במשנה תורה הבדלי הנבואות ההיא ופירשנו ענין פה אל פה אדבר בו וכאשר ידבר איש אל רעהו וזולת זה והבינהו משם ואין צריך להשיב מה שכבר נאמר:

פרק ששה וארבעים

מן האיש האחד תלקח ראיה על כל אישי המין ויודע שזה תבונת כל איש ממנו ואשר ארצהו בזה המאמ׳ כי מן התבונ׳ האחת מתכונות הגרות הנביאים תלקח ראיה על כל ההגדות אשר במין ההוא ואחר זאת תתצער תדע כי כמו שיראה אדם בחלום שכבר הלך לארץ הפלנירת ונשא שם אשה ועמד זמן ונולד לו בן וקראו פלוני והירה מענינו מה שהירה כן משלי הנבואה האלו אשר יראו או יעשו במרא׳ הנבואה במה שיורה המשל ההוא מעשה מן המעשים ודברים יפעל אותם הנביא ומדת זמנים יזכרו בין פעל ופעל על צד המשל ונסיעות ממקום למקום הכל הוא במראה הנבואת לא שהם פעלים נמצאים לחושים הנראי׳ ויבא זכרם בספרי הנבואה קצתם מוחלטים שאחר שנודע שהכל היה במראה הנבואה לא הוצרך להשיב בזכור כל חלק וחלק מן המשל שיהיה במראה הנבואה כמו שיאמר הנביא ויאמר יי׳ אלי ולא יצטרך לבאר שהיה בחלום ויחשבו ההמון שהפעולות ההם והנסיעות והשאלות והמענים הכל היה בעניין השגת החושים לא במראה הנבואה ואני אזכור לך מזה מה שלא יספק אדם בו ואחבר אליו קצת מה שהוא ממינו מן הקצת ההוא יתבאר לך מה שלא זכרתיו וממה שהוא מבואר ולא יספק אדם בו מאמר יחזקאל אני יושב בביתי וזקני יהודה יושבים לפני וגומר ותשא אותי רוח בין הארץ ובין השמים ותבא אותי ירושלמה במראות אלהים כן אמרו ואקום ואצא אל הבקעה אמנם היה בבראות כמו שנאמר באברהם ויוצא אותו החוצה ויאמר וזה היה במחזה כן אמרו ויניחני בתוך הבקעה אמנם היה במראות אלהים וזכר יחזקאל במראה ההיא אשר הובא בה ירושלים דבר זה לשונו ואראה והנה חור אחד בקיר ויאמר אלי בן אדם חתור נא בקיר ואחתור בקיר והנה פתח אחד וגו׳ וכמו שהוא ראה במראות שצוה לחתור בקיר עד שיכנס ויראה מה הם עושים שם וחתר כמו שנזכר במראות אלהים ונכנס מן החור וראה מה שראה וכל זה במראה הנבואה כן

לגמרי רק במראה או בחלום כן ענין יונה בן אמתי וענין בליעת הדג לו וענין העקידה אשר רמז הרב באמרו או ירד אל סלם כהנך וכיוצא בזה יש שם יותר:

(*a*)

Figure 2.2 Maimonides, *Guide of the Perplexed*: (*a*) Venice, 1551 edition, showing Efodi's uncensored comment about Maimonides' understanding of the stories of Jonah and the Akedah as non-historical (courtesy of the Library of the Jewish Theological Seminary); (*b*) the Warsaw, 1872 edition, in which Efodi's comment has been deleted

כן שהאמצעי הנה הוא הכח המדמה שהוא אמנם ישמע שהשם דבר אתו בחלום של נבואה, ומרע"ה כ מעל הכפורת (י) מבין שני הכרובים מבלתי השתמש בכח המדמה, וכבר בארנו במשנה תורה הבדלי הנבואה ההיא, ופירשנו ענין פה אל פה אדבר בו, וכאשר ידבר איש אל רעהו, חולת זה, והבינהו משם ואין צריך להשיב מה שכבר נאמר:

פרק מו מן האיש האחד תלקח ראיה על כל אישי המין, ויודע שזה תכונת כל איש ממנו, ואשר ארצהו בזה המאמר, כי מן התכונה האחת מתכונות הגדות הנביאים תלקח ראיה על כל ההגדות אשר במין ההוא, ואחר זאת ההצעה תדע, כי כמו שיראה אדם בחלום, שכבר הלך לארץ הפלונית, ונשא שם אשה, ועמד זמן, ונולד לו בן, וקראו פלוני, והיה מענינו מה שהיה, כן משלי הנבואה האלו אשר יראו או יעשה במראה הנבואה במה שיורה המשל ההוא, מעשה מן המעשים והדברים

שם טוב

כן ושהאמצעי הוא הכח המדמה שהוא אמנם ישמע שהשם דבר אתו בחלום ר"ל שהמדמה בהיותו בחלום יחקה שהשם ידבר עמו ויחקה אותו השפע והכבוד הנפלא כאלו הוא השם יתעלה, אבל נבואת מרע"ה היה מעל הכפרת מבין שני הכרובים וכא הרמז בזה מעל הכפרת שהיא הכח השכלי ושני הכרובים הכח המחשבי והמדמה כי נבדלו אלו השני כחות עם שרבים יחשבו שהם אחד, ונתייחד משה בשמיעת הקול בהיותו בהקיץ וער בלא תרדמה ובלא שנוי כלל ולכן נאמר ובבא משה אל אהל מועד וישמע את הקול מדבר אליו, והנה נתעלה משה על כל הנביאים שנבואתו לא היה במשלים וחקוים והיה שומע הקול בבירור מה שלא היו שומעים הנביאים כי אם היו במראה הנבואה לא היו שומעים קול ואם היו במראה הנבואה שומעים קול במראה ובחידה, והבן כל מה שגליתי לך בזה הפרק אף שיש בו דברים עמוקים במאד מאד:

פרק מו מאיש אחד תלקח ראיה על כל אישי המין. זה הפרק נפלא יודיע הרב לנו רבים מסתרי הנבואות עם הנחת הקדמה אחת, והיא כי בידיעת איש אחד מהמין יודע כל המין, כי אע"פ שכל אישי המין מתחלפים קצתם מקצתם ואין שום איש שדומה לחבירו מכל וכל כי ימצאו בכל אישי המין חלופי בב"ת ובפרט האדם אשר הוא המורכב האחרון, עכ"ז מהות ראובן הוא מהות שמעון כי ראובן הוא מדבר וכן שמעון וכן כל האנשים, אם כן בודעת מהות איש אחד פרטי יודע כל אישי המין ולבאר לנו זה הסוד נקרא אדם הראשון בשם אדם שהוא כולל שם המין, וכמו שהחותם א' מצורת

אפודי

חוץ ממרע"ה היו שומעים הדבור באמצעות מלאך והאמצעי ההוא הוא הכח המדמה: כ מעל הכפורת מבין שני הכרובים. ר"ל שנבואת מרע"ה היתה מבין שני הכחות שהם הכח השכלי והכח המחשבי ומעל הכפורת יהיה השכל הנבדל, ולי נראה כי מעל הכפורת ר"ל מן הכח השכלי ושני הכרובים הם הכח המחשבי והחוש המשותף, והשם יודע איזה יכשר:

פרק מו א זה הפרק הערה גדולה לסודות רבות מעניני הנבואה שהיה נראה מפשט הענין שהיה פועל נעשה מענין מה, ובא הרב לגלות שהם במראה הנבואה או בחלום נבואיי לא שיהיה לענין ההוא מציאות חוץ לנפש כלל אבל הם במראה או בחלום, ובא הרב להקים הנעלם מן המבואר, כענין קח לך אשת זנונים, וכענין חתור נא בקיר, וכענין קח לך לבנה, וכענין שכב על צדך השמאלית, וכענין העברת תער על הראש ועל הזקן, וכענין הבא נא השמימה, וכענין גיזת גדעון, שהוא מבואר שלא היה הענין חוץ לנפש רק במראה או בחלום, וכיוצא בזה יש שם יותר:

אברבנאל

אמודע. הוקשה לרב איך נקרא המודעות למשלים ולא לדברים המפורשים. לכן אמר שהמשלים הם המודעות לפי שיגיעו בעבורם לעניני החכמות. ואמר הרב שכפי זה הפירוש האחרון יהיו מדרגות הנבואה כלם שמנה, ר"ל שבעה מבחלום והם א', ב', ג', ד', ה', ו', ז', כמו שזכרנו, והשמינית היא מדרגת המראה בכלל שיבא יותר עליה להיותה מראה יהיה באי זה אופן שיהיה, ואפי' דבר עמו איש שהיא מדרגה יותר עליונה מהאמרות מהמלאך ומהאלוה. ויש לומר בכאן למה לא זכר הרב ג"כ מדרגת שמיעת הקול במראה מבלי ראות המדבר שהיא עליונה מראיית האיש. והתשובה שכפי זה הפי' האחרון שמיעת הקול שהם הוא עצמו חלום כמ"ש בחלום אדבר בו ולכך לא אמר שהיא עליונה מהחלום כי היא עצמה חלום. וכתב הנרבוני שכפי זה תהיה המעלה המיוחדת למשה על כל הנביאים שהיה מנבא תמיד במראה שישמע דברים מבלתי חידות כמ"ש במראה ולא בחידות ונאמר ויקרא אל משה, ואמר וישמע את הקול מדבר אליו. ואולי הקושיא שזכר הוא שאיך סמנו במדרגות הנבואה שבחלום במדרגה השביעית שיראה בחלום של נבואה כאלו השם מדבר עמו כיון שכל הנביאים זולת מרע"ה היו מתנבאים ע"י מלאך, וא"כ כל הנבואות היו מהמדרגה השנית שהמלאך לא מהשביעית שהיא מהש"י כיון שלא היה השם פעל קרוב בנבואתם. והשיב הרב שכן הוא הענין והאמצעי הוא הכח המדמה שהוא ידמה כאלו השם מדבר עמו ומשה רבינו מעל הכפרת מבין שני הכרובים. ויש לשאול בזה מה רצה הרב לומר כאן. האם היה דעתו שהמלאך הוא הכח המדמה, ומשה היה מנבא בלתו מבלי משל. ולמה א"כ לא אמר דע שהענין כן אבל המלאך הוא הכח המדמה, ואמר שהאמצעי הוא הכח המדמה והם לא יכחישו המקשה. ועוד כי מה כוונת בזה הרב כיון שאף משה היה מנבא בכח המדמה, אם מעט ואם הרבה כמו שפירשתי (על) נגדר הנבואה, אף כפי מה שפירשתי למעלה במדרגות, הנה הש"י הוא שהם רחוקה בנבואה, והמלאך ר"ל השכל הפועל הוא האמצעי בה, לא הכח המדמה, ומה יהיה א"כ כוונת הרב במאמר הזה: ואמרתי בתשובת זה שהמקשה הקשה כאן אם היו ראיית המלאך ושמיעתו בכלל במראה כי היא בכללה מדרגה אחת בלבד כמו שזכר, ובמה נפלאה א"כ נבואת משה רבינו בחלום מנבואת שאר הנביאים שהיו מנבאים כלם במדרגת המראה והיא מדרגה אחת שוה וכוללת בכלם, ואיזה היתרון אשר למרע"ה על שאר הנביאים. ותשובת הרב בה היא כי כן הוא, ר"ל שנבדלה נבואת מרע"ה על כל הנביאים ביותר שאת ויתר עז, ושהאמצעי אשר בו יתרון הנביאים זה על זה הוא הכח המדמה שיש נביא שישתמש ממנו הרבה ויש שישתמש ממנו מעט, ואותו הכח הוא מחקה החקויים והצורות, ומשה רבינו ע"ה היה מנבא מעל הכפורת מבין שני הכרובים, ופי' זה שהפרשים מעל הכח השכלי, ומבין שני הכרובים שהם הכח המחשבי והמדמה. ונראה לי שלא כיון הרב אל דבר מזה, אלא לומר שמשה היה מנבא בהשתמשות חושיו, ובהיותו ער ומקיץ כי היה שומע הקול היוצא מהמקום המקודש ההוא, ולא היו שאר הנביאים כן כי היו בעת הנבואה נרדמים ונופלים ארצה, והוא המורה שלא היתה נבואתו באמצעות הכח המדמה, ולכן המשיך הרב דבריו באומר שכבר כתב בפי' ההלכות שיש בינינו שם:

קרשקש

לדרוש בדברו לכן המטה אשר עלית שם לא תרד ממנה כי מות תמות: (י) מבין שני הכרובים. שהרצון בו השכל הדברי לבד עם התדבקות בשכל הפועל, וכל אותם הנבואות אשר התנבא הגיעו מהש"י כפי רצונו באמצעות השכל הפועל, או היה קול נברא בראו השם אשר ממנו הוכן לו הדבור המגיע לו:

סליק פירוש אברבנאל בעזהי"ת:

Let us now turn to some examples of censorship, not of Maimonides' words or of those of one of his commentators, but of criticism of Maimonides. Maimonides declared that all who believe that God has a physical form are heretics with no share in the world to come.[84] R. Abraham ben David (Rabad) harshly criticized this judgement of Maimonides: 'Why has he called such a person a heretic? There are many people greater and superior to him who adhere to such a belief on the basis of what they have seen in verses of Scripture and even more in the words of those *agadot* which corrupt right opinion about religious matters.'[85]

R. Joseph Albo (*c*.1380–1444) preserves an alternative, and much softened version of Rabad's comment: 'Even though the essential belief is such [i.e. that God is not corporeal], one who believes that God has a form based on his literal understanding of biblical and rabbinic texts is not to be called a heretic.' Missing from this version is Rabad's biting remark that some of the corporealists were even greater than Maimonides. Yet there is no question that Albo's version is not the original text,[86] and I assume that the censoring was done by a follower of Maimonides who was understandably upset by Rabad's comment.[87]

After the early years of controversy over his writings, Maimonides came to occupy a central position in Jewish tradition. It is therefore understandable that harsh criticism of him would be viewed as improper. Even when the criticism was tempered, there were times when it was not allowed in print. For example, some kabbalists taught that as a punishment for what Maimonides wrote in his philosophical writings he was condemned to be reincarnated as a worm. R. Joseph Karo—or rather the *magid* who appeared to him—claimed that although this was indeed Heaven's decree, Maimonides' Torah learning and good deeds protected him so that he was not forced to become a worm, although he did have to go through one reincarnation before reaching heaven. This passage from Karo's *Magid meisharim* was not included when the volume was published.[88]

Naor, *Limit of Intellectual Freedom*, 167–8, regarding the possible alteration of a passage in the *Zohar ḥadash* in order to remove an antinomian-sounding comment.

84 See my *Limits of Orthodox Theology*, ch. 3.

85 Abraham ben David, *hasagah* on Maimonides, *Mishneh torah*, 'Hilkhot teshuvah' 3: 7; translation in Twersky, *Rabad of Posquières*, 282.

86 See D. Kaufmann, *Geschichte*, 487–8.

87 José Faur assumes just the opposite, that the censorship was carried out by the opponents of Maimonides: 'Shocked by his tone, and the harm in terms of public relations that it may cause to the anti-Maimonidean crusade, pious hands rewrote these words' (id., *Horizontal Society*, 418 n. 340). I find this suggestion very unlikely.

88 See Werblowsky, *Joseph Karo*, 31, 170 n. 2. There is reason to believe that what remains of the *Magid meisharim* is only a small portion of the original, and Moshe Idel assumes that the missing sections were suppressed by kabbalists themselves. See his *Kabbalah: New Perspectives*, 19–20.

One of the few figures in recent centuries who had the standing to criticize Maimonides was the Vilna Gaon. While he is often described as a strong opponent of Maimonides' philosophy, Eliyahu Stern has recently argued that his viewpoint on this matter is much more nuanced.[89] One remark of his that led to the assumption that he was unremittingly opposed to Maimonides' philosophy appears in his commentary on Karo's *Shulḥan arukh*.[90] In this work, Karo noted that an incantation recited over one who was bitten by a snake does not have any real effect, but is permitted since it can calm the person. The Vilna Gaon comments:

> This is the view of Maimonides. . . . But all subsequent teachers disagree with him since numerous incantations are referred to in the Talmud. He [Maimonides] followed the accursed philosophy and he therefore wrote that magic, the use of divine names for magical purposes, incantations, demons, and amulets are all false, but they smote him on the head since we find many accounts in the Talmud of the efficacy of divine names and magic. . . . Philosophy, with its many words, misled him to explain all these passages figuratively and to remove them completely from their plain meaning. God forbid, I believe neither in them [i.e. the philosophers] nor their followers. All these matters are to be understood literally, but they also have an inner meaning. This is not, however, the inner meaning given by the philosophers, which we throw to the trash,[91] but of the masters of truth [the kabbalists].[92]

What I have just quoted are the words of the Vilna Gaon as they appear in the first edition of his commentary, published in Grodno, 1806 (Fig. 2.3). This edition was published by two of the Vilna Gaon's sons, thus testifying to its authenticity.[93] One would have thought that the towering significance of the Vilna Gaon would prevent his words from being tampered with,[94] yet this was

[89] See E. Stern, *Genius*, 127ff.

[90] 'Yoreh de'ah' 179: 13.

[91] Eliyahu Stern offers an alternative, and in my opinion incorrect, translation, and I have italicized where we differ. 'Rather, [what I mean] is that everything written follows according to its *sensus literalis* but all of these things have within them a hidden essence [that must be interpreted]. Not the meaning of the *philosophers who toss* [*the* sensus literalis *of the text*] *into the refuse*, but the [inner essence] of the masters of truth.' See E. Stern, *Genius*, 128. Alan Brill's translation is slightly different from Stern's: 'Not the inner meaning of the philosophers who toss [*the true meaning*] to the refuse' (emphasis added). See Brill, 'Writings of the Vilna Gaon', 9.

[92] Most of this translation is taken from L. Jacobs, *A Jewish Theology*, 111–12. Jacobs, as with so many other writers who have quoted this passage, did not know that the standard Vilna text was censored. Allan Nadler was also unaware of this and assumed that Dov Eliach, who cited the original version in *Sefer hagaon*, ii. 588, had altered the Vilna Gaon's words. See Nadler, 'The "Rambam Revival"', 51 n. 39.

[93] See Schischa, 'Order of Publication' (Heb.), 682ff.

[94] The Vilna Gaon's importance was such that for many years the Habad movement engaged in self-censorship so as to avoid publicly criticizing him. In the first edition of the *Tanya*, published by R. Shneur Zalman of Lyady in 1796, and the many subsequent editions until 1900, a comment

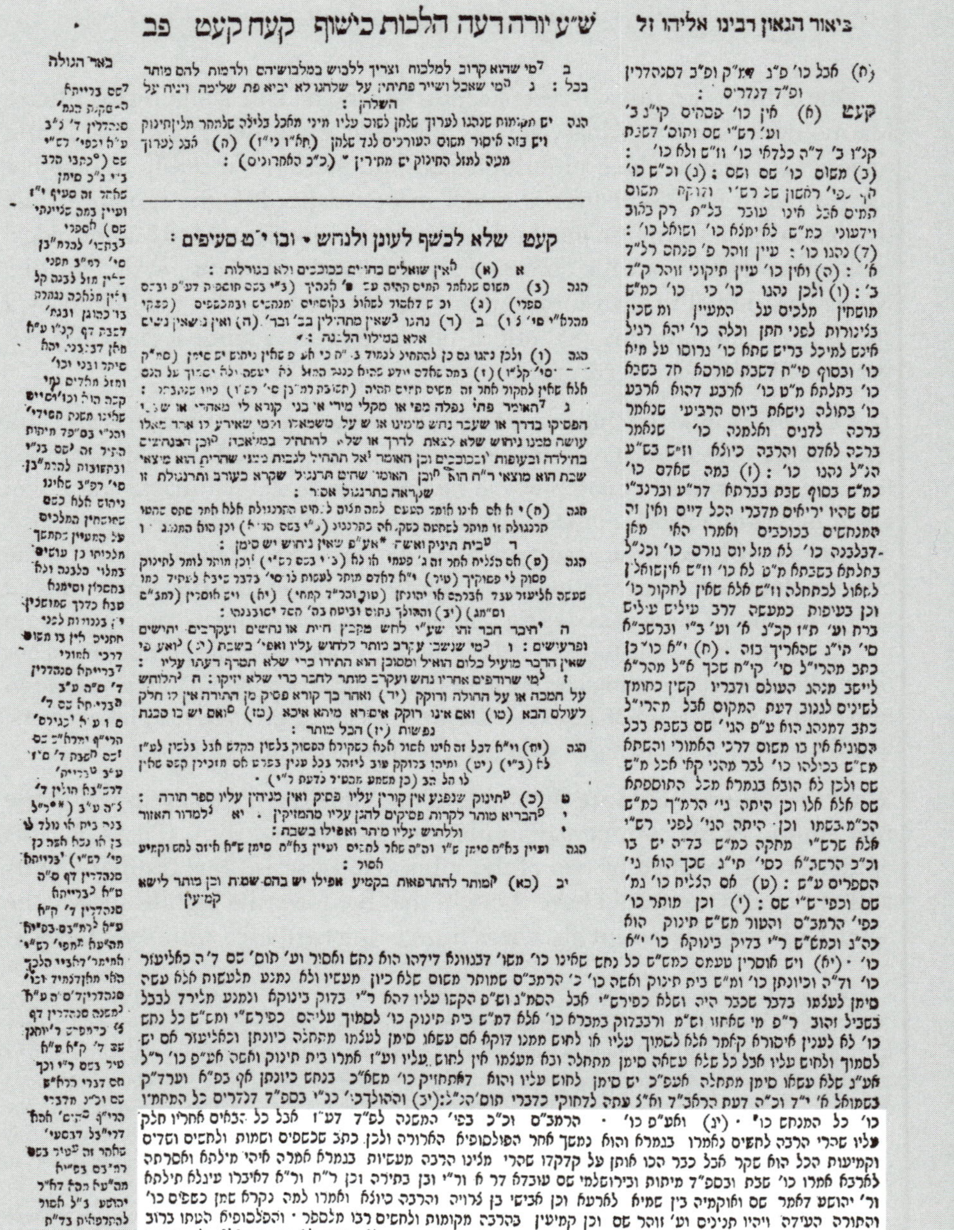

Figure 2.3 R. Joseph Karo, *Shulḥan arukh* (Grodno, 1806), showing the Vilna Gaon's uncensored comment attacking philosophy

Courtesy of the Library of the Jewish Theological Seminary

not to be the case. When the *Shulḥan arukh* was published in Vilna in 1880 by the Romm family,[95] an edition that would soon become standard, the Gaon's description of philosophy as 'accursed' was removed. Furthermore, the reference to throwing the philosophers' meaning 'to the trash' was also changed to something softer: 'Not, however, the inner meaning given by the philosophers, which is in reality only an external meaning [*ḥitsonim*].'

This censorship was perhaps prompted by a claim made by R. Tsevi Hirsch Katzenellenbogen (1796–1868) that the Vilna Gaon's student, R. Menasheh of Ilya (1767–1831), told him that the Gaon's comment was not authentic, but was inserted during publication by someone else. (If this was the reason for the censorship, we can only speculate as to why the entire comment was not deleted.) The *maskilim* jumped on Katzenellenbogen's report, for they too were anxious to claim the Vilna Gaon as one of theirs,[96] a task made more difficult by his harsh attack on Maimonides and defence of 'superstition'. The fact that Katzenellenbogen was himself an adherent of the Haskalah (in its moderate form) is reason enough to cast doubt on his report. Furthermore, his words are contradicted by R. Samuel Luria's eyewitness testimony from the nineteenth century that the autograph manuscript of R. Elijah's commentary corresponded exactly to the text of the first printed edition.[97]

If the Vilna Gaon was censored, we should expect that R. Israel ben Eliezer (*c.*1700–60), the Ba'al Shem Tov, would be given the same treatment. According to a tale recorded in *Shivḥei habesht*,[98] when the Ba'al Shem Tov's wife died his followers wanted him to remarry. He replied: 'Why do I need a wife? For the last fourteen years I refrained from sleeping with my wife, and my son Hersheleh was born by the word [*al pi hadibur*].'[99] It is not clear what 'by the word' signifies. It certainly does not mean divine impregnation, for immediately following this the Ba'al Shem Tov tells his son: 'I know that I gave you a holy soul, for when I joined in union with my wife the heavens shook.'

pointing out the error of 'some scholars who are wise in their own eyes, may God forgive them' was omitted. The reason for the omission is that the viewpoint being criticized, that *tsimtsum* is to be understood literally, was thought by Habad followers to have been held by the Vilna Gaon. See Y. Mondshine, *Likutei amarim*, 15; Moskowitz, 'How is Hasidism "Researched"?' (Heb.), 206 n. 74; Naor, *Limit of Intellectual Freedom*, 202–3.

[95] See Berliner, *Aus dem Leben*, 133–4.

[96] See Etkes, *Gaon of Vilna* (Heb.), ch. 2.

[97] See J. H. Levin, *Aliyot eliyahu*, 43; Dienstag, 'Did the Vilna Gaon Oppose Maimonides' Philosophy?' (Heb.), 255, 257; D. Kamenetsky, 'The Gaon R. Menasheh of Ilya' (Heb.), 735–6 n. 10. The most recent unsuccessful attempt to impugn the authenticity of the Vilna Gaon's comment is Halperin, 'Consultation' (Heb.), 20–1 n. 27.

[98] Kopys, 1815, p. 36*a*.

[99] Ben-Amos and Mintz (trans.), *In Praise of the Baal Shem Tov*, 258.

Presumably, 'by the word' refers to a directive from heaven to cease his asceticism and resume marital relations. It could also refer to some sort of supernatural element that was present when the Ba'al Shem Tov was 'joined in union' with his wife.[100] Yet whatever the story's original intent, when a second edition of the work appeared in Berdichev in 1815, this story of the 'word' was removed.[101] It appears that the publisher felt that the story could be understood in a Christian fashion, and therefore decided to omit it. Also worthy of note is that the Berdichev edition of *Shivḥei habesht* omits the later passage in which the Ba'al Shem Tov speaks of 'joining in union' with his wife, no doubt because the publisher was uncomfortable with the description of their heaven-shaking sexual relations.

In this chapter we have seen examples of censorship of uncomfortable texts that date from medieval times until the eighteenth century.[102] What about earlier material? It is indeed possible that a passage in the Talmud was censored because the idea it expressed was thought to be too radical. *Berakhot* 63*a* states:

> Bar Kappara expounded: What short text is there upon which all the essential principles of the Torah depend? 'In all thy ways acknowledge Him and He will direct thy paths' [Prov. 3: 6]. Rava remarked: Even for a matter of transgression.

A version of this passage is preserved in the sixteenth-century aggadic compilation *Ein ya'akov*,[103] as well as in at least two talmudic manuscripts and one medieval source that adds another sentence to this passage.[104] It records a popular saying that even thieves, when they steal, call upon God (to assist them in their thievery). What happened to this passage? Nahum Rakover suggests that this is an example of internal censorship.[105] In other words, the very mention of a saying that thieves pray for success in their nefarious work was viewed as problematic, and thus was simply deleted from manuscripts.[106]

I know of another example where an ancient text was censored for theological reasons. This time the censorship was carried out by R. Solomon

[100] I assume this is also what is meant when it is reported that the hasidic master R. Yehiel Mikhel Rabinowitz of Zlotshov (d. 1786) was born from 'a spiritual drop, not a physical one'. See Anon., *Beit zlotshov*, ii. 22. I do not think this means a divine impregnation without any sexual intercourse by his father.

[101] See Y. Mondshine, *Shivḥei habesht*, 49.

[102] As for 19th-cent. texts, in recent years many editions of the Mishnah with the commentary of R. Israel Lipschutz (*Tiferet yisra'el*) have removed Lipschutz's *Derush or haḥayim* (found in the Vilna edition, Seder Nezikin) because he accepted modern scientific conclusions about the existence of dinosaurs and a universe much older than Jews traditionally believed it to be.

[103] BT *Ber.* 63*a*.

[104] See Rabbinovicz, *Dikdukei soferim*, ad loc.

[105] Rakover, *Ends that Justify the Means* (Heb.), 55ff.

[106] See pp. 36–7, 45–8 above for other possible examples of internal censorship of the Talmud.

Aaron Wertheimer (1866–1935), famous for his publications of numerous midrashic, geonic, and medieval texts, including material from the Cairo Genizah. He also wrote two volumes of responsa.[107] One of the midrashim he published is named *Midrash alef bet*.[108] Since Wertheimer thought this midrash worthy of publication, one would have assumed that everything in it would be regarded by him as Torah-true. Yet Wertheimer found theological problems in the text, and therefore 'assumed the mantle of official censor'.[109]

For example, in one passage in this midrash, Satan is having a conversation with God. He tells God that he is like Him:

> For You created heaven, I created earth, You created firmaments, I created deeps, You created animals, I created demons . . . You created good things, I created bad things, You created the Garden of Eden, I created Gehenna. . . . The Holy One, blessed be He, said to him, 'Fool who is in the world, you say to Me, "I created Gehenna", so pass into the midst of Gehenna.'

This passage reflects a dualistic conception in which Satan assisted God in creating the world. Wertheimer was obviously not comfortable with this, but not so uncomfortable that it led him to disqualify *Midrash alef bet* as a whole. Instead, he chose to excise the objectionable portion, continuing the pattern that we will see again and again. In this passage, he cut out the dialogue that showed Satan as a co-creator, yet kept the final sentence. However, in order to make this sentence theologically acceptable, he made one small alteration. The 'theologically correct' Wertheimer version reads: 'Fool who is in the world, you say to me, '*You* created Gehenna,' so pass into the midst of Gehenna.'[110]

The fact that the 'new' text does not make any sense was not so important for Wertheimer. What was important is that with this slight alteration, and the excision of the previous section, the text was ready to be published. In truth, even from Wertheimer's perspective there should have been no reason to engage in censorship here, since in the end the midrash itself rejects the notion that Satan has any power. As Deborah F. Sawyer puts it, Wertheimer 'felt so threatened by these ideas, even though they are consequently demolished, that he emended the text to exclude them'.[111]

Another example of Wertheimer's theological censorship is seen when the midrash describes God as placing the children of Israel 'each one upon His neck, each one upon His shoulder, each one upon His throne, each one upon His glory'. The anthropomorphisms were too extreme for Wertheimer, so he

107 Wertheimer, *She'elat shelomoh*.

108 Wertheimer, *Batei midrashot*, ii. 419–59.

109 Sawyer, 'Heterodoxy and Censorship', 121.

110 Wertheimer, *Batei midrashot*, ii. 434.

111 Sawyer, 'Heterodoxy and Censorship', 118.

excised these descriptions. Another example cited by Sawyer is Wertheimer's censorship of a passage that discusses the sexual activity of the righteous in the world to come.[112] These examples are taken from just one of the many texts that Wertheimer edited, meaning that we should suspect that similar censorship exists in the other texts as well.

I do not want to leave the impression that it is only the Orthodox who take liberties with texts in the name of a proper theology, although they, in particular the haredim, are indeed the major 'culprits' in this area. In the Conservative prayer book *Siddur Sim Shalom*,[113] we find the following translation for the blessing in the Amidah that ends *meḥayeh hametim* ('Resurrector of the dead'[114]): 'Praised are You, Lord, Master of life and death.' The Conservative Rabbinical Assembly's earlier *Sabbath and Festival Prayer Book* has 'Who callest the dead to life everlasting'.[115] Conservative Rabbi Ben Zion Bokser (1907–84), in his translation of the prayer book,[116] rendered the passage as 'Who callest the departed to life eternal'.

All of these translations make for very nice blessings. The only problem is that they are not what the blessing in the Amidah is speaking about, and the translators knew this.[117] Yet in order to present congregants with a text that would not violate their theological outlook, an outlook that rejects resurrection, the correct translation was altered, so that God is now 'Master of Life and Death', etc., instead of God the 'Resurrector of the dead'. Similarly, in the prayer for the State of Israel[118] there is a line that reads *reshit tsemiḥat ge'ulatenu*, which means 'the first flowering of our redemption'. Uncomfortable with ascribing any messianic significance to the State of Israel, *Siddur Sim Shalom* 'translates' this line as 'its promise of redemption'.

112 Sawyer, 'Heterodoxy and Censorship', 118–20.

113 p. 107.

114 This is the correct translation of the phrase; see my Seforim Blog post, 27 June 2012.

115 p. 22.

116 p. 52.

117 The Reform *Gates of Prayer* avoids the problem by changing the Hebrew text to read מחיה הכל, which is translated as 'the Source of life', p. 38.

118 p. 417.

CHAPTER THREE

HALAKHAH

HALAKHAH is the central feature of Jewish life, the warp and woof of traditional Judaism. Precisely because of this one should not be surprised—indeed one should expect—that censorship is found here just as in all the other areas I am discussing. In fact, since we are dealing with Jewish law, one would expect there to be more censorship here, in order to prevent what the censor regards as halakhic violations that can be caused by 'problematic' texts.

Let me begin with one of the most famous examples of halakhic censorship. The first edition of R. Moses Isserles' responsa was printed in Kraków in 1640. In this volume, Isserles included a fascinating responsum defending the Jews in Moravia who were accustomed to drink non-Jewish wine.[1] Isserles was not dealing with run-of-the-mill sinners, concerning whom there would be no reason to try to come up with a justification. Rather, the question concerned otherwise halakhically observant people who nevertheless ignored the prohibition against non-Jewish wine. Isserles had previously found it necessary to permit (or at least not protest) when Jews did business with non-Jewish wine, since this was vital for them to make a living.[2]

Since, in pre-modern Europe, water was not generally safe to consume, beer and wine became the basic drinks. We can easily imagine how difficult it was at that time to abstain from non-Jewish wine, a point mentioned by Isserles. The halakhists first confronted this problem in medieval times, and Haym Soloveitchik has described how, despite possible halakhic openings to void the prohibition, the medieval Jews' ritual instinct refused to go that far.[3] Yet a few centuries later things had changed and otherwise pious Jews were indeed violating the prohibition.[4]

[1] The responsum can be found in Isserles, *She'elot uteshuvot harama*, no. 124.

[2] See Meir of Lublin, *She'elot uteshuvot maharam lublin*, no. 50.

[3] See Soloveitchik, *'Yeinam'* (Heb.), 104 ff. However, R. Solomon ben Adret (Rashba, 1235–1310) does speak of Jews who were suspected of drinking non-Jewish wine. See id., *Torat habayit ha'arokh*, 5: 1 (p. 83*b*). See also R. Jacob ben Asher, *Arba'ah turim* (*Tur*), 'Yoreh de'ah' 114: 2. R. Asher ben Yehiel, *She'elot uteshuvot harosh*, no. 19: 16, provides a penance for one who mistakenly drinks non-Jewish wine.

[4] Since the practices of the masses are not influenced by halakhic logic, I am very sceptical of

In order that the communities whose members consumed non-Jewish wine not be regarded as wilful sinners, with all the halakhic consequences this would entail, Isserles was able to find some justification for their behaviour, which he tells us was a continuation of the practice of previous generations. His argument has a few points, the most fundamental of which is that there is no longer a concern that the wine would have been used in an idolatrous ritual. He acknowledges that despite his justification, which is known in rabbinic literature as a *limud zekhut*, what he has proposed is not in accord with the settled halakhah and should not be relied upon.

He is more certain, however, when it comes to one who is ill (but not in any danger (*ḥoleh she'ein bo sakanah*)). In such a case, Isserles has no problem affirming that it is permitted to drink non-Jewish wine. This permission, as well as his justification of those who were healthy and drank such wine, was quite shocking to later halakhists. Many of them feared that Isserles' responsum would weaken the taboo against non-Jewish wine and lead to its consumption.[5] Understandably, there were those who thought that this responsum was too dangerous for publication. It was thus censored from the Amsterdam 1711 edition of Isserles' responsa, published by the renowned scholar R. Aryeh Leib of Amsterdam (*c.*1690–1755).[6]

If a figure as renowned and important as Isserles could have his opinion censored, then it should come as no shock that the same thing happened with

Jacob Katz's argument that it was not the difficulty in observing the prohibition that led to it being ignored. According to Katz, 'Laxity of practice spread in this case because the logic by which permission had been given to trade in wine could be extended to drinking it. . . . [W]hen the legitimacy of trading in gentile wine was broadly accepted, the demands of logical consistency had the expected effect.' Katz, *Tradition and Crisis*, 22.

[5] This is exactly what happened, as R. Israel Silverman, who wrote the Conservative ruling permitting non-Jewish wine, cited Isserles' responsum. R. David Novak responded to Silverman as follows: 'Since he [Isserles] refuses to allow anyone to use his arguments as precedents [*lo lismokh*], I cannot see how anyone after him can legitimately do what Isserles himself said ought not to be done in his name.' See Novak, *Law and Theology in Judaism*, 182. While Novak's point is well taken regarding this case, I must add that the responsa literature is full of examples where halakhists state that their opinions are not to be applied in practice. Yet later authorities routinely ignore this caveat, regarding it as merely an expression of the author's modesty. See Medini, *Sedei ḥemed*, ix. 3687 f. (Arabic numerals (= 'Kelalei haposekim' 16: 47)). In this case, however, it is obvious that Isserles did indeed wish to prevent others from relying on his opinion, and Silverman is guilty of misrepresentation.

[6] See editorial note in *Ets ḥayim*, 9 (2009), 20. R. Jacob Saphir's note in *Halevanon* ('Kevod halevanon' section) (11 Mar. 1869), 85, reports that a manuscript responsum of R. Judah Miller states that R. Tsevi Hirsch Ashkenazi (Hakham Tsevi, 1660–1718), was responsible for the censorship. (Hakham Tsevi was appointed Ashkenazi rabbi of Amsterdam in 1710.) This responsum does not appear in J. Miller, *She'elot uteshuvot rabi yehudah miler*. See Sperber, *Minhagei yisra'el*, ii. 58, who notes the suggestion that R. Moses Hagiz (1672–*c.*1751) was involved with the censorship.

R. Joseph Karo, whose *Shulḥan arukh*, together with Isserles' additions, has played such a central role in Jewish life since its appearance. The issue here was *kaparot*, a ceremony on the day before Yom Kippur in which one's sins are symbolically transferred to a chicken, the propriety of which is a dispute going back to medieval times.[7] No less a figure than R. Solomon ben Adret regarded it as a pagan practice and thus forbidden.[8] Karo was not so extreme in his ruling, as he only wrote that one should refrain from the practice, without bringing in the spectre of paganism. Yet the heading he gave to this section in the *Shulḥan arukh*[9] states that the practice is a foolish custom (*minhag shel shetut*; see Fig. 3.1, taken from the first edition of the *Shulḥan arukh*, Venice, 1564).

The words *minhag shel shetut* appeared in the first eighteen editions of the work, four of them published in Karo's lifetime. Beginning with the Amsterdam 1708 edition these words were omitted. In the new Makhon Yerushalayim edition of the *Shulḥan arukh* the heading is omitted, but is included in a note. Before taking this step, the publishers received the approval of a number of leading Torah scholars.[10] From their perspective, since the current practice is to perform *kaparot*, there is no reason to include Karo's description in the body of his work. R. Yitshak Zilberstein, one of those who urged the censorship, explained that common practice has 'voted' against the *Shulḥan arukh*, 'and Israel, if they are not prophets they are sons of prophets'. Zilberstein also suggested that the censorship that began in Amsterdam was God's will, since in our time there is perhaps no reason to fear a connection between *kaparot* and paganism. After noting that R. Isaac Luria (1534–72) had profound things to say about *kaparot*, Zilberstein refers to a responsum by R. Samuel Aboab (1610–94)[11] who states, without any evidence whatsoever, that the words *minhag shel shetut* were added by the printer. Aboab felt comfortable in saying this, even though the *Shulḥan arukh* appeared four times in Karo's lifetime and he never requested that any changes be made. If Karo is not safe from censorship, and this censorship even received rabbinic approval, I daresay that no text is safe.[12]

In terms of practical halakhah, after the *Shulḥan arukh* the most popular text in Jewish history is R. Solomon Ganzfried's (1804–66) *Kitsur shulḥan*

[7] See G. Oberlander, *Minhag avoteinu beyadeinu*, vol. i, ch. 6.

[8] Solomon ben Adret, *She'elot uteshuvot harashba*, vol. i, no. 395.

[9] 'Oraḥ ḥayim' 605: 1.

[10] See the Holon annual *Zekhor le'avraham* (2000–1), 111–19.

[11] See Morpurgo, *Shemesh tsedakah*, 'Oraḥ ḥayim', no. 23. See also Benayahu, *Yosef beḥiri*, 373.

[12] In private correspondence a colleague, who prefers to remain anonymous, has argued that the example of Makhon Yerushalayim is not as significant as I have made it out to be, as the issue here is not really about an act of censorship, but about reinserting a text that had already been removed.

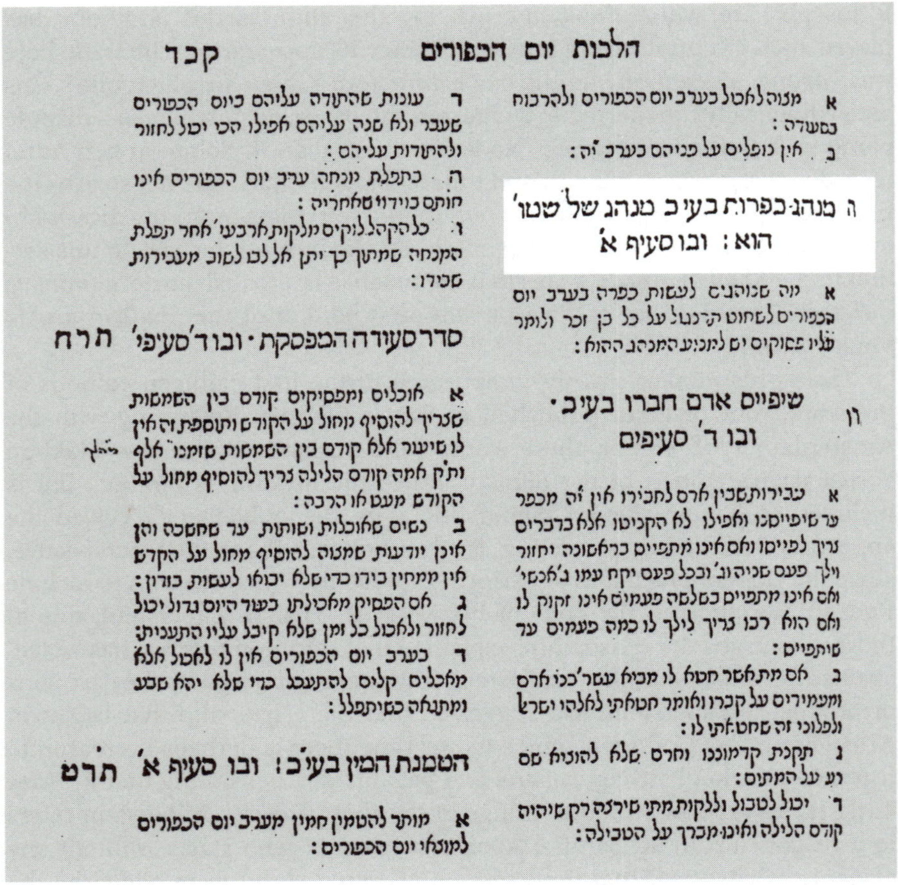

הלכות יום הכפורים קכד

א מצוה לאכול בערב יום הכפורים ולהרבות בסעודה:

ב אין נופלים על פניהם בערב יה:

ה מנהג כפרות בעי״כ מנהג של שטות הוא: ובו סעיף א׳

א מה שנוהגים לעשות כפרה בערב יום הכפורים לשחוט תרנגול על כל בן זכר ולומר עליו פסוקים יש למנוע המנהג ההוא:

ו שיפיים אדם חברו בעי״כ· ובו ד׳ סעיפים

א עבירות שבין אדם לחבירו אין יה״כ מכפר עד שיפייסנו ואפילו לא הקניטו אלא בדברים צריך לפייסו ואם אינו מתפייס בראשונה יחזור וילך פעם שניה וג׳ ובכל פעם יקח עמו ג׳ אנשי׳ ואם אינו מתפייס בשלשה פעמים אינו זקוק לו ואם הוא רבו צריך לילך לו כמה פעמים עד שיתפייס:

ב אם מת אשר חטא לו מביא עשרה בני אדם ומעמידים על קברו ואומר חטאתי לאלהי ישראל ולפלוני זה שחטאתי לו:

ג תקנת קדמונים וחרם שלא להוציא שם רע על המתים:

ד יכול לטבול וללקות מתי שירצה רק שיהיה קודם הלילה ואינו מברך על הטבילה:

ד עונות שהתודה עליהם ביום הכפורים שעבר ולא שנה עליהם אפילו הכי יכול לחזור ולהתודות עליהם:

ה בתפלת מנחה ערב יום הכפורים אינו חותם בוידוי שאחריה:

ו כל הקהל לוקים מלקות ארבעי׳ אחר תפלת המנחה שמתוך כך יתן אל לבו לשוב מעבירות שבידו:

סדר סעודה המפסקת· ובו ד׳ סעיפי׳ תרח

א אוכלים ומפסיקים קודם בין השמשות שצריך להוסיף מחול על הקודש ותוספת זה אין לו שיעור אלא קודם בין השמשות שזמנו״ אלף ות״ק אמה קודם הלילה צריך להוסיף מחול על הקודש מעט או הרבה:

ב נשים שאוכלות ושותות עד שחשכה והן אינן יודעות שמצוה להוסיף מחול על הקדש אין ממחין בידן כדי שלא יבואו לעשות בזדון:

ג אם הפסיק מאכילתו בעוד היום גדול יכול לחזור ולאכול כל זמן שלא קיבל עליו התענית:

ד בערב יום הכפורים אין לו לאכול אלא מאכלים קלים להתעכל כדי שלא יהא שבע ומתגאה כשיתפלל:

הטמנת המין בעי״כ: ובו סעיף א׳ תרט

א מותר להטמין חמין מערב יום הכפורים למוצאי יום הכפורים:

Figure 3.1 R. Joseph Karo, *Shulḥan arukh* (Venice, 1564), with his comment that *kaparot* is a foolish custom

arukh. It has been reprinted so many times that it is hard to imagine that anyone would attempt to censor something in it, yet this has indeed happened. It is one of the ironies of Jewish history that Ganzfried, whose religious views were quite extreme, produced a work that became incredibly popular among all sections of the Orthodox world. One example of what in modern times would be regarded by some as extreme is found in 201:4, where Ganzfried writes:

All those who deviate from the community by casting off the yoke of precepts, severing their bonds with the people of Israel as regards the observance of the Divine Commands, and are in a class by themselves; also apostates, informers, and heretics—for all these the rules of an *onen* and of mourners should not be observed. Their brothers and other next of kin should dress in white, eat, drink, and rejoice that the enemies of the Almighty have perished. Concerning such people, the Scripture states (Psalms 139: 21) 'Do not I hate them, O Lord, that hate Thee?'. Also, (Proverbs 11: 10): 'And when the wicked perish, there is joy.'[13]

In the Lublin 1904 edition of the *Kitsur shulḥan arukh* (and a number of other editions), the halakhah appears, but the words 'apostates, informers, and heretics' have been removed.[14] In the Vilna 1915 edition, the entire halakhah, which simply records that which appears in Maimonides' *Mishneh torah*[15] and the *Shulḥan arukh*,[16] is omitted, so that there are only six sections in the chapter, not seven.[17] In the years following the Second World War, in both the United States and Israel, editions of the *Kitsur shulḥan arukh* have appeared that substitute an entirely new halakhah for what originally appeared in 201: 4.[18] Here are images of (1) the uncensored *Kitsur shulḥan arukh* (Fig. 3.2(*a*)), (2) the Vilna, 1915 edition, where the halakhah has been deleted (Fig. 3.2(*b*)), and (3) the Mosad Harav Kook vocalized edition, where the original halakhah has been deleted but a new halakhah substituted in its place (Fig. 3.2(*c*)).[19]

Why was the original halakhah censored? Jewish literature is full of negative passages against sinners, and unlike similar passages against non-Jews and apostates, there was never governmental censorship of these sorts of texts. I think what we have here is an early example of political correctness in the Orthodox world. The *Kitsur shulḥan arukh* is a work for the masses. In fact, with the expansion of Torah education for girls, they too were taught from this text. The original text in the *Kitsur shulḥan arukh* is not the sort of passage that would be 'helpful' to schoolchildren, and many would regard it as hateful,

[13] I have used the translation (with slight changes) of Goldin, *Code of Jewish Law*, 201: 4.

[14] When the halakhah is recorded in R. Yehiel Mikhel Epstein, *Arukh hashulḥan*, 'Yoreh de'ah' 345: 7, instead of 'apostates' (which for the *Arukh hashulḥan* would mean apostates to Christianity) it has והמהופכים לישמעאלים ('those who become Muslims'). This formulation is obviously intended to prevent Christian enmity, but it cannot be taken seriously.

[15] Maimonides, *Mishneh torah*, 'Hilkhot avelut' 1: 10.

[16] Karo, *Shulḥan arukh*, 'Yoreh de'ah' 345: 8.

[17] There may be earlier editions of the work that also omit the halakhah, but I have not found any.

[18] The substitute halakhah was lifted from Karo, *Shulḥan arukh*, 'Yoreh de'ah' 345: 5, and at least one edition of Ganzfried, *Kitsur shulḥan arukh* substitutes *Shulḥan arukh*, 'Yoreh de'ah' 345: 8. I assume that the substitute *halakhot* were first inserted in various pre-Second World War European editions, but I have not yet found any editions of this type.

[19] The censorship in the Mosad Harav Kook edition was noted in an anonymous comment on the Behadrei Haredim website, at <www.bhol.co.il/forums/topic.asp?topic_id=585306&which page=10&forum_id=1364>. In recent reprintings of the Mosad Harav Kook edition, the censorship has been corrected.

ו מותר ללוות את המת בי"ט א׳ בתוך התחום ובי"ט ב׳ אפי׳ חוץ לתחום ומוהרין ג"כ לחזור לביתם בו ביום · אבל אסור לרכוב ע"ג בהמה כדי ללוות את המת ביו"ט אפי׳ בי"ט שני ואפי׳ האבלים · אבל הקברנים אם אי אפשר להם לילך ברגליהם מותרים לרכוב בי"ט ב׳ ומ"מ לא ירכבו בתוך העיר :

ז מת בליל י"ט ב׳ דמתעסקין בו ישראל אם אין עכו"ם משכימין עשרה בני אדם וקוברים אותו בשעה שהש"ץ אומר פיוטים ואם הוא אדם חשוב שרבים צריכין ללוותו קוברין אותו לאחר יציאה מבהכ"נ קודם האכילה דאיתא במדרש לא תאכלו על הדם שאסור לאכול סעודה קבועה קודם שנקבר המת · ואם א"א להכין כל צורכי הקבורה עד הזמן ההוא קוברין אותו לאחר אכילה :

ח ילד שמת לאחר שלשים יום שידוע שאינו נפל דינו כמו שאר מת אך אם הוא זכר וכחמת איזה סיבה עדיין לא נימול אע"ג ראשתהי אין קוברין אותו בי"ט א׳ משום דצריכין להסיר ערלתו (כדלעיל סי׳ קס"ג) ואין לעשות זאת ע"י עכו"ם אלא משהינן ליה עד י"ט ב׳ דמותר להלינו לכבודו וביום ב׳ מסירין ערלהו וקוברין אותו :

ט תינוק שמת כשהוא ספק נפל (ע"ל סי׳ ר"ג ס"ג) אי לא אשתהי אין קוברין אותו בי"ט א׳ אפי׳ ע"י עכו"ם ומשהינן ליה עד י"ט ב׳ וקוברין אותו ע"י עכו"ם ולא ע"י ישראל ואי אשתהי קוברין אותו בי"ט א׳ ע"י עכו"ם ואם מת בי"ט ב׳ קוברין אותו בו ביום ע"י עכו"ם ולא ע"י ישראל · אם הוא זכר ועדיין לא נימול אפי׳ אשתהי אין קוברין אותו אפי׳ בי"ט ב׳ אפי׳ ע"י עכו"ם אלא משהינן ליה עד לאחר י"ט ומסירין ערלתו וקוברין אותו :

י בשבת וביהכ"פ לא יתעסקו במת כלל אפי׳ ע"י עכו"ם וע"ל סוף סימן קצ"ד :

יא בחוה"מ אין להוציא את המת לבה"ק עד שהקבר מתוקן שלא יצטרכו להעמיד את המטה :

רא דין המאבד עצמו לדעת ושאר רשע שמת · ובו ז׳ סעיפים :

א המאבד עצמו לדעת הוא רשע שאין למעלה ממנו שנא׳ ואך את דמכם לנפשותיכם אדרוש ובשביל יחיד נברא העולם וכל המאבד נפש א׳ מישראל מאבד עולם מלא ולכן אין מתעסקין עמו לכל דבר · לא קורעין ולא מתאבלין עליו ואין מספידין אותו · אבל קוברין אותו ומטהרין אותו ומלבישין אותו תכריכין · כללו של דבר כל שהוא משום כבוד החיים עושין לו · (ולענין אמירת קדיש ע׳ בהת"ם סופר יו"ד סימן שכ"ו ואמרי אש סימן קכ"ב וע׳ תשו׳ רד"ך בית ל׳) :

ב מסתמא לא מחזקינן אינשי ברשיעי · ולכן אם נמצא א׳ חנוק או תלוי וכדומה כל שאפשר לתלות שמא אחר עשה לו זאת לא תלינן ביה :

ג קטן המאבד את עצמו חשוב כשלא לדעת וכן גדול אם נראה שעשה הדבר מחמת רוח רעה או שגעון וכדומה הוי שלא לדעת · וכן אם עשה את הדבר מחמת אונס שהיה מתירא מעינויים קשים כמו שאול שהיה מתירא שמא יעשו בו הפלשתים כרצונם הרי הוא כשאר מת ואין מונעין ממנו שום דבר :

ד כל הפורשים מדרכי הצבור והם האנשים שפרקו עול המצות מעל צוארם ואין נכללים בכלל ישראל בעשייתם אלא הרי הם כבני חורין לעצמן וכן המומרים והמוסרים והאפיקורסים כל אלו אין אוננים ואין מתאבלין עליהם אלא אחיהם ושאר קרוביהם לובשים לבנים ומתעטפין לבנים ואוכלים ושותים ושמחים על שאבדו שונאו של מקום ועליהם הכתוב אומר הלא משנאיך ה׳ אשנא ואומר באבוד רשעים רנה :

ה אם נהרג בין בדינא דמלכותא בין בענין אחר אפי׳ היה מומר מתאבלין עליו דכיון שנהרג בידי אדם ולא מת כדרך כל הארץ הו"ל כפרה :

ו מי שהיה רגיל לעשות עבירה אפי׳ רק לתיאבון ומת אם לא התודה קודם מותו אין מתאבלין עליו אבל אם התודה מתאבלין עליו. אפי׳ היה גנב או גזלן :

ז קטן בן שנה או שנתים שהמיר עם אביו או עם אמו וכת אין מתאבלין עליו *) :

רב הלכות טומאת כהן · ובו ט"ז סעיפים :

א הכהן מוזהר שלא ליטמא למת ואפי׳ נפל שעדיין לא נתקשרו איבריו בגידין חשוב מת (אך אם הפילה תוך מ׳ יום לא חשיב אלא כמיא בעלמא) ולאו דוקא למת שלם אלא אפי׳ לדברים שנפרשים

*) ע׳ דגמ"ר ולפע"ד מעם הש"ע בסי׳ שמ"ה והרמ"א בסי׳ ש"מ הוא משום דבפ׳ היו בודקין סיים דמרדכי סוף דבר־ אומר ר"ת שאין מנהג להתאבל עליו עכ"ל :

15

(*a*)

Figure 3.2 R. Solomon Ganzfried, *Kitsur shulḥan arukh*: (*a*) with 201: 4 uncensored; (*b*) (on page 87) Vilna, 1915 edition, with 201: 4 deleted; (*c*) (on page 88) Mosad Harav Kook edition, with a new halakhah inserted in 201: 4

י בשבת וביוה"כ לא יתעסקו במת כלל אפילו ע"י עכו"ם וע"ל סוף סי' קצ"ד:
יא בחוה"מ אין להוציא את המת לבית הקברות עד שהקבר מתוקן שלא יצטרכו להעמיד את המטה:

רא דין המאבד עצמו לדעת ושאר רשע שמת. ובו ז' סעיפים:

א המאבד עצמו לדעת הוא רשע שאין למעלה ממנו שנאמר ואך את דמכם לנפשותיכם אדרוש ובשביל יחיד נברא העולם וכל המאבד נפש א' מישראל מאבד עולם מלא ולכן אין מתעסקין עמו לכל דבר לא קורעין ולא מתאבלין עליו ואין מספידין אותו אבל קוברין אותו ומטהרין אותו ומלבישין אותו תכריכין. כללו של דבר כל שהוא משום כבוד החיים עושין לו (ולענין אמירת קדיש ע' בח"ס יו"ד סי' שכ"ו ואמרי אש סי' קכ"ב וע' תשובת רד"ך בית ל'):

ב מסתמא לא מחזקינן אינשי ברשיעי. ולכן אם נמצא א' חנוק או תלוי וכדומה כל שאפשר להלות שמא אחר עשה לו זאת לא תלינן ביה:

ג קטן המאבד את עצמו חשוב שלא לדעת. וכן גדול אם נראה שעשה הדבר מחמת רוח רעה או שגעון וכדומה הוי שלא לדעת וכן אם עשה את הדבר מחמת אונס שהיה מתירא מעינויים קשים כמו שאול שהיה מתירא שמא יעשו בו הפלשתים כרצונם הרי הוא כשאר מת ואין מונעין ממנו שום דבר:

ד אם נהרג בין בדינא דמלכותא בין בענין אחר אפי' היה מומר מתאבלין עליו דכיון שנהרג בידי אדם ולא מת כדרך כל הארץ הו"ל כפרה:

ה מי שהיה רגיל לעשות עבירה אפילו רק לתיאבון ומת אם לא התודה קודם מותו אין מתאבלין עליו. אבל אם התודה מתאבלין עליו אפילו היה גנב או גזלן:

ו קטן בן שנה או שנתים שהמיר עם אביו או עם אמו ומת אין מתאבלין עליו*):

רב הלכות טומאת כהן. ובו ט"ז סעיפים:

א הכהן מוזהר שלא ליטמא למת ואפי' נפל שעדיין לא נתקשרו איבריו בגידין חשוב מת (אך אם הפילה תוך מ' יום לא חשיב אלא כמיא בעלמא) ולאו דוקא למת שלם אלא אפילו לדברים שנפרשים ממנו כמו דם וכדומה. וכן אסור ליטמא לאבר שנחתך מן החי אם יש עליו בשר כ"כ שאם היה מחובר היה ראוי להעלות ארוכה ואפי' לאבר של עצמו אסור לו ליטמא. ואסור לכהן *ליכנס לבית שיש שם גוסס ואע"פ שהגוסס הרי הוא כחי לכל דבר ואינו מטמא מ"מ עובר הכהן על לא יחלל שהוא מוזהר שישמור כהונתו שלא יתחלל ושמא ימות זה תיכף:

ב אסור לכהן ליכנס תחת אוהל שיש מת תחתיו אפילו הוא אהל גדול הרבה ואפילו יש שני חדרים אשר בחדר א' יש מת ויש במחיצה המפסקת נקב שיש בו טפח על טפח אסור ליכנס גם לחדר הב' כי נקב טפח על טפח מביא את הטומאה. וכן אם אצל החדר השני יש עוד חדר שלישי וביניהם ג"כ נקב טפח על טפח הולכת הטומאה גם להחדר השלישי וכן לעולם. ונקב העשוי לאורה אפילו אין בו אלא כפונדיון מביא את הטומאה:

ג ולכן במדינתנו שגגות הבתים בולטין לחוץ ברוחב טפח וקי"ל דרוחב טפח מביא את הטומאה. וא"כ זה הקצה מן הגג הוי אוהל להביא את הטומאה. לפי"ז שני בתים סמוכין זה לזה אם יש מת באחד מהן הולכת הטומאה דרך פתח או חלון תחת הקצוות מן הגגין שבולטין לחוץ ונכנסת גם להוך הבית השני דרך חלון או פתח פתוח ואסור לכהן ליכנס גם להוך הבית השני. וכן אפי' כמה בתים הסמוכים זה אצל זה:

ד ואפילו הגגין אינן שוים אלא זה למעלה מזה ואפילו הגג שהטומאה שם בבית הוא גבוה הרבה מן הגג השני או בהיפוך הלכה למשה מסיני הוא דאמרינן חבוט רמי. פי' שאנו רואים כאלו העליון נחבט ונשפל עד למטה ומאחר שאם היה נשפל עד התחתון היה נוגע בו על כן הולכת הטומאה מזה לזה אבל אם יש הפסק ביניהם אפילו כל שהוא שוב אינה הולכת הטומאה:

וכן

פאת . השלחן

*) ע' דגמ"ר ולפענ"ד טעם כב"ע בפי' שמ"ס והרמ"ה בפי' ב"מ הוא משום דכפ' היו נוקין הייס המדבר סוף דבר אומר ר"ת שאין מנהג להתאבל עליו עכ"ל:

אוֹתוֹ תַּכְרִיכִים. כְּלָלוֹ שֶׁל דָּבָר: כָּל שֶׁהוּא מִשּׁוּם כְּבוֹד הַחַיִּים עוֹשִׂים לוֹ (וּלְעִנְיַן קַדִּישׁ--עַיֵּן בְּחָתָם סוֹפֵר יוֹרֶה דֵעָה סִמָּן שכו וְאִמְרֵי אֵשׁ סִמָּן קכב, וְעַיֵּן תְּשׁוּבוֹת רד״ך בַּיִת ל).

ב. מִן הַסְּתָם אֵין מַחֲזִיקִים בְּנֵי אָדָם כִּרְשָׁעִים, וְלָכֵן אִם נִמְצָא אֶחָד חָנוּק אוֹ תָּלוּי וְכַדּוֹמֶה, כָּל שֶׁאֶפְשָׁר לִתְלוֹת שֶׁמָּא אַחֵר עָשָׂה לוֹ זֹאת, אֵין תּוֹלִים בּוֹ.

ג. קָטָן הַמְאַבֵּד עַצְמוֹ חָשׁוּב כְּשֶׁלֹּא לְדַעַת. וְכֵן גָּדוֹל אִם נִרְאֶה שֶׁעָשָׂה הַדָּבָר מֵחֲמַת רוּחַ רָעָה אוֹ שִׁגָּעוֹן הֲרֵיהוּ שֶׁלֹּא לְדַעַת. וְכֵן אִם עָשָׂה הַדָּבָר מֵחֲמַת אֹנֶס שֶׁהָיָה מִתְיָרֵא מֵעִנּוּיִים קָשִׁים, כְּמוֹ שָׁאוּל שֶׁהָיָה מִתְיָרֵא שֶׁמָּא יַעֲשׂוּ בוֹ הַפְּלִשְׁתִּים כִּרְצוֹנָם, הֲרֵי הוּא כִּשְׁאָר מֵת וְאֵין מוֹנְעִים מִמֶּנּוּ שׁוּם דָּבָר.

ד. מִי שֶׁנָּפַל בַּיָּם אוֹ טָבַע בַּנָּהָר אוֹ אֲכָלַתּוּ חַיָּה אֵין מוֹנְעִים מִמֶּנּוּ שׁוּם דְּבַר אֲבֵלוּת. אֲרוֹן שֶׁל מֵת הָעוֹבֵר מִמָּקוֹם לְמָקוֹם, אִם הַשִּׁדְרָה וְצַלְעוֹתֶיהָ שֶׁל הַמֵּת קַיָּמוֹת, עוֹמְדִים עָלָיו בְּשׁוּרָה וְאוֹמְרִים עָלָיו בִּרְכַּת אֲבֵלִים וְתַנְחוּמֵי אֲבֵלִים, אִם יֵשׁ אֲבֵלִים שֶׁמִּתְאַבְּלִים עָלָיו. וְאִם אֵין שִׁלְדּוֹ שֶׁל גּוּף הַמֵּת קַיָּם, אֵין עוֹמְדִים עָלָיו בְּשׁוּרָה וְאֵין אוֹמְרִים עָלָיו לֹא בִרְכַּת אֲבֵלִים וְלֹא תַנְחוּמֵי אֲבֵלִים.

ה. אִם נֶהֱרַג, בֵּין בְּדִין הַמַּלְכוּת בֵּין בְּעִנְיָן אַחֵר, אֲפִלּוּ הָיָה מוֹסֵר מִתְאַבְּלִים עָלָיו, שֶׁכֵּיוָן שֶׁנֶּהֱרַג בִּידֵי אָדָם וְלֹא מֵת כְּדֶרֶךְ כָּל הָאָרֶץ יֵשׁ לוֹ כַּפָּרָה.

ו. מִי שֶׁהָיָה רָגִיל לַעֲשׂוֹת עֲבֵרָה אַחַת רַק לְתֵאָבוֹן וּמֵת, אִם לֹא הִתְוַדָּה קֹדֶם מוֹתוֹ, אֵין מִתְאַבְּלִים עָלָיו. אֲבָל אִם הִתְוַדָּה מִתְאַבְּלִים עָלָיו, אֲפִלּוּ הָיָה גַּנָּב אוֹ גַזְלָן.

ז. קָטָן בֶּן שָׁנָה אוֹ שְׁנָתַיִם שֶׁהֵמִיר עִם אָבִיו אוֹ אִמּוֹ, אֵין מִתְאַבְּלִים עָלָיו.

סִמָּן רב

הִלְכוֹת טֻמְאַת כֹּהֵן

וּבוֹ טו סְעִיפִים

א. הַכֹּהֵן מֻזְהָר שֶׁלֹּא לְהִטַּמֵּא לְמֵת, וַאֲפִלּוּ נֵפֶל שֶׁעֲדַיִן לֹא נִתְקַשְּׁרוּ אֵבָרָיו בְּגִידִים חָשׁוּב מֵת (אַף אִם הִפִּילָה תּוֹךְ אַרְבָּעִים יוֹם, אֵינוֹ חָשׁוּב אֶלָּא כְּמַיִם סְתָם). וְלֹא דַּוְקָא לְמֵת שָׁלֵם אֶלָּא אֲפִלּוּ לִדְבָרִים שֶׁנִּפְרָשִׁים מִמֶּנּוּ, כְּמוֹ דָם וְכַדּוֹמֶה. וְכֵן

especially as by the early twentieth century it would be referring to some of their own relatives who had 'cast off the yoke of precepts'.[20]

When it comes to examining censorship, we are usually confined to looking at different editions of the same work, because unless we are able to see the original manuscript we do not know what has been left out of the published version. R. Shlomo Dayan, the editor of the second volume of *Mayim ḥayim*, the responsa of R. Joseph Messas (1892–1974), admitted to me that he regrets including Messas' controversial responsum[21] in which he ruled that there is no obligation for married women to cover their hair. How many other responsa are there which, because of their unconventional conclusions, never saw the light of day?[22]

Israel M. Ta-Shma calls attention to one such example where, in a manuscript responsum, R. Hayim Eliezer ben Isaac (Or Zarua, 13th cent.) offers an extremely liberal view of the prohibition against eating from new grains (*ḥadash*). Yet this was not included in his published responsa, and indeed was even deleted from one of the manuscripts. Ta-Shma is convinced that this was intended to cover up R. Hayim's liberal opinion, which went against the standard halakhic understanding.[23]

Another such example relates to the binding nature of the *Shulḥan arukh*. R. Hayim of Volozhin records that the Vilna Gaon told him that in matters of halakhah one should not give up one's independent judgement, even if that means opposing a ruling of the *Shulḥan arukh*. This was recorded by R. Hayim in a responsum, but when the responsum was finally published, some sixty years after his death, what the Vilna Gaon had said about disputing with the *Shulḥan arukh* was deleted.[24] In other words, the publisher thought

[20] For another example of removing words from an edition of the *Kitsur shulḥan arukh*, see the notes by Yehiel Domb in *Hama'yan*, 47 (Nisan 5767), 55–6, and Yoel Catane, ibid. 48 (Tishrei 5768), 96. However, in this case the editor apparently erroneously assumed that the deleted words were not authentic.

[21] Messas, *Mayim ḥayim*, vol. ii, 'Oraḥ ḥayim', no. 110.

[22] I am not referring to instances when the author himself decides not to publish something, as was the case with R. Aaron Kotler's responsum supporting the *heter mekhirah* ('sale' of land in Israel during the sabbatical year). See Glick, 'On Alterations' (Heb.), 72 ff. Sometimes the censor comes to regret his action. See Gantz, *Reshumim beshimkha*, 293 (called to my attention by R. Baruch Oberlander). Here it is recounted that R. Moses Gruenwald (1853–1910) wrote a responsum permitting machine matzah. His son, R. Jacob Gruenwald (1882–1941), who was also a great scholar, omitted this responsum when printing his father's *Arugat habosem*. He later confessed, 'All my life I have regretted doing this, and my heart pains me for deleting this responsum from the published work.' It appears that no copies of the censored responsum survive.

[23] See Ta-Shma, *Halakhah, Custom, and Reality* (Heb.), 217 ff. For other examples of such manuscript censorship, see Ta-Shma, 'Review' (Heb.), 350–1; id., *Keneset meḥkarim*, i. 232; id., *Creativity and Tradition*, 44–5 (called to my attention by Ronnie Morris).

[24] Hayim of Volozhin, *Ḥut hameshulash*, no. 9.

that the Vilna Gaon's words were too radical to be made public. Fortunately, this responsum is quoted from the manuscript in *Aliyot eliyahu* by R. Joshua Heschel Levin (1818–83),[25] without which we would not know about this particular instance of censorship.[26]

The examples of censorship just mentioned are motivated by a desire to 'protect' people from ideas that the censors regard as dangerous. For someone committed to halakhah, nothing could be more dangerous than halakhic antinomianism, and this concern would therefore be a virtual invitation to censorship. Certain elements of the hasidic movement have had limited antinomian tendencies,[27] although these have been sublimated. With the exception of the practice in certain hasidic courts to ignore the statutory times of prayer,[28] I do not think that the antinomian stream survives as anything more than a theoretical element of study, even among the followers of Izhbitz–Radzin, one of whose leaders authored some of the most radical sentiments in this regard. R. Mordechai Leiner of Izhbitz (1801–54) went so far as to claim that for the righteous, sins are actually predetermined. When such a person struggles mightily to overcome his evil inclination and is unsuccessful, this failure is itself a proof that his action, while in conflict with halakhah, is nevertheless in line with God's will. The positing of God's will in opposition to halakhah is the essence of antinomianism. To show how subversive this can be, one need only look at how the Izhbitzer understands the biblical narrative of Phineas and Zimri (Num. 25). He turns the story on its head and regards Zimri as a holy man whose 'sin' was actually in accord with God's will. Phineas was not on a level to recognize this and thus killed Zimri.[29]

With this background we can appreciate a comment made by a hasidic thinker, R. Meir Yehudah Shapira (1846–1908).[30] Exodus 18: 13 states: 'And it came to pass on the morrow, that Moses sat to judge the people.' Rashi quotes 'the *Sifrei*'[31] that this was the day after Yom Kippur, and that Moses had

[25] J. H. Levin, *Aliyot eliyahu*, 90–1.

[26] R. Aaron Kotler reported that the Vilna Gaon told R. Hayim of Volozhin that 'until [the generation of] R. Moses Isserles you can dispute with logic, and until [the generation of] R. Asher ben Yehiel you can dispute if you have [talmudic] proofs'. See E. M. Bloch, *Ruaḥ eliyahu*, 90–1. See also E. Rivlin, *Rabbi Joseph Zundel of Salant* (Heb.), 140 n. 8, for a different version of this tradition.

[27] See Y. Mondshine, 'Fluidity of Categories', 301–20.

[28] See L. Jacobs, *Hasidic Prayer*, ch. 4; Wertheim, *Laws and Customs in Hasidism* (Heb.), 88 ff.

[29] M. Leiner, *Mei hashilo'aḥ*, i. 54*a*. For detailed discussion of the antinomian aspect of the Izhbitzer's theology, see Faierstein, *All Is in the Hands of Heaven*, ch. 3; Gellman, *The Fear, the Trembling, and the Fire*, 47 ff.; Magid, *Hasidism on the Margin*, ch. 7.

[30] M. Y. Shapira, *Or lame'ir*, 'Yitro', s.v. *vayehi mimaḥarat* (19*b*–20*a* (second numbering)).

[31] It actually appears in *Mekhilta derabi yishma'el*, 'Amalek (Yitro)', *parashah* 2; the term *Sifrei* was also used for *Mekhilta* in medieval sources. See J. N. Epstein, '*Mekhilta* and *Sifrei*' (Heb.), 112.

descended from Sinai on the previous day. Yet as the Tosafists point out, this would seem to mean that Exodus 18: 12, where Jethro greets Moses, takes place on Yom Kippur.[32] The problem with this is that the verse states that Jethro brought a sacrifice and that he, Aaron, and the elders ate together. Since one would assume that the commandment of fasting on Yom Kippur was already in force,[33] how is this possible?

The Tosafists solve this problem by placing events in a different chronological sequence, so that no one is eating on Yom Kippur. R. Jacob ben Asher recognizes the problem and attempts to solve it by arguing that when the *Mekhilta* (referred to by Rashi as the *Sifrei*) refers to Yom Kippur, it should not be understood literally as the festival on the tenth of Tishrei, but rather as the day that Jethro brought an atonement offering and converted to Judaism.[34] He also claims that the word *kipurim* is a scribal error.[35]

Shapira offers another approach, which he connects to an event said to have occurred with the famed hasidic master, R. Menahem Mendel of Rymanów (1755–1815):

> One time he prayed [*ma'ariv* after Yom Kippur] so early that it appeared to the people around him that it was still daytime. He commanded that they bring him some honey syrup to drink, and this was a wonder to them. The Holy Rabbi said that they should not be astounded by this because he sees in heaven [*begavhei meromim*] that the [heavenly] gates have already closed, and there has already been appeasement through forgiveness of sins. It is now a different time, belonging to the following day.

In other words, R. Menahem Mendel was able to drink on the fast day since he saw that even though there was still daylight, Yom Kippur had really ended.

R. Menahem Mendel's action, and explanation for it, is of course shocking, and deserves further analysis by scholars of hasidism.[36] It certainly is related to the notion expressed by some hasidic leaders that the *tsadik* (hasidic

[32] See *Da'at zekenim miba'alei hatosafot*, Exod. 18: 13.

[33] Both R. Elijah Mizrahi (*c.*1450–1526) and R. Judah Loew (Maharal, *c.*1520–1609), in their commentaries on Rashi, claim that the Yom Kippur prohibitions only came into force the following year. Yet as pointed out in the Ariel edition of Rashi's *Commentary on the Torah*, ad loc., *Midrash tanḥuma*, Exodus, 'Ki tisa' 31, states explicitly that Yom Kippur was commanded immediately upon Moses' descent from Mount Sinai. Nahmanides, commenting on Exod. 18: 13, claims that the words 'the morrow of Yom Kippur' are not to be taken literally to mean the very next day.

[34] For others who adopt this explanation, see Kasher, *Torah shelemah*, xv. 129.

[35] Jacob ben Asher, *Perush hatur ha'arokh al hatorah*, Exod. 18: 13.

[36] R. Solomon Teitelbaum told a story of R. Menahem Mendel of Rymanów ordering that havdalah be recited on the afternoon of Yom Kippur. See his letter published in *Heikhal habesht*, 5 (Kislev 5768), 137–8. While the details of the stories differ, it is likely that they both originate in the same episode.

communal guide) stands above time as reckoned by mere mortals, an idea that was used to justify his praying after the rabbinically ordained times.[37] As for R. Menahem Mendel, suffice it to say that he is reported to have uttered a number of other strange things. To begin with, he is said to have declared that he heard a heavenly pronouncement that he was the *tsadik* of the generation, 'and all that he wishes or requests of God will be fulfilled'.[38] In discussing his previous incarnations, R. Menahem Mendel is recorded to have stated: 'I have already been in the world one hundred times. I am the author of all the true philosophical works, I am Maimonides.'[39] In another incarnation, so he stated, he was the High Priest. Because of this, when R. Menahem Mendel prayed on Yom Kippur he did not say, in describing the Temple service, 'And so he [the High Priest] would say [*vekhakh hayah omer*], "I beg of you, Lord, I have erred, been iniquitous, etc."' Rather, R. Menahem Mendel would recite: 'And so I[!] would say [*vekhakh hayiti omer*] . . .'.[40]

Returning to the incident with R. Menahem Mendel drinking on Yom Kippur, the justification offered, that even though there was still daylight the next day had already begun, enables Shapira to explain how Aaron and the elders also ate on Yom Kippur: 'They saw that the time when they ate was part of the following day.' If R. Menahem Mendel was able to see that a new day had begun even though all outward appearances said otherwise, then one should not be surprised that Aaron and the elders also had this power. In a recent reprint of Shapira's book, published by the author's family in 2002, this entire passage has been omitted. The reprint is a photo-offset, so the omission by whiting out is apparent to all, and shows how uncomfortable his family is with the antinomian potential of his comment.

Another example of a hasidic master altering time appears in R. Abraham Petrokovsky's *Piskei teshuvah*.[41] He reports the following story, which came from his great-uncle:[42] 'One time the holy *admor* [hasidic leader], the *kohen* of Alexander [R. Hanokh Henekh Levin (1798–1870)], sat with him and spoke to him the entire night until it was daylight. He then took the clock and moved the hands back a few hours, and prayed the evening service.' The meaning

37 See R. Israel of Ruzhin, quoted in David Moses of Chortkov, *Divrei david*, 24*a*–24*b*; Menahem Mendel of Kotzk, *Amud ha'emet*, 82–3; Leifer, *Ma'amar mordekhai heḥadash*, 135; R. Noah of Lechovitz, quoted in Jacobs, *Hasidic Prayer*, 53.

38 Menahem Mendel of Rymanów, *Ateret menaḥem*, 34*a*.

39 Ibid. 23*b*.

40 Ibid. It is reported that R. Abraham Joshua Heschel of Apta (1748–1825) would do the same thing. See I. Berger, *Eser orot*, 57*b*.

41 Vol. iii, no. 265. The story also appears in A. M. Rabinowitz, *Sha'arei aryeh*, 74.

42 The Hebrew is ambiguous and can also mean great-great-uncle or someone even further back in time.

Petrokovsky derives from this story is in line with what we have already encountered: 'From here we see that it is not that this holy one prayed after the proper time, but rather through his action he rearranged the heavenly structures [so that his prayer now corresponded to the correct "celestial time"].'

The fact that hasidim in recent years have been uncomfortable with some examples of antinomianism in their tradition is also seen from the following case. R. Menahem Mendel Rabinowitz wrote *Ma'aseh neḥemyah*, which is devoted to the life of R. Nehemiah Yehiel of Bychawa (1808–52), the son of R. Jacob Isaac of Przysucha ('The Holy Jew'; *c.*1766–1814). This work was first published in Warsaw in 1913 and was reprinted in Jerusalem in 1956. In section 54 of the 1956 edition there is a fairly innocuous story about how R. Nehemiah told his assistant to take a particular fish from the water and bring it to his home, and that it was a matter of life and death to remove this fish which had for years been attempting to reach this place.

However, this version is significantly shortened from what appears in the original text from 1913.[43] In the original text, the story with the fish happened on the second day of Rosh Hashanah. R. Nehemiah's assistant is surprised by the request and responds, 'Today is *yom tov*, and it is forbidden to catch [the fish].' It is to this response that R. Nehemiah comments, 'I also know this, but it is a matter of life and death.' The matter of life and death is not explained, but it is clear that a person had been reincarnated in the fish,[44] and by its consumption the soul was able to be perfected. While for R. Nehemiah this made it a matter of 'life and death', for a non-hasid (and also for many hasidim) this was an egregious halakhic violation.[45]

Before hasidism arose, antinomianism was a major feature of Shabateanism, the seventeenth- to eighteenth-century messianic movement. R. Elijah

[43] This example was noted in an anonymous comment on the Otzar HaHochma website, <http://www.bhol.co.il/forums/topic.asp?whichpage=1&topic_id=585306&forum_id=1364>, s.v. *tsenzorah toranit besifrei kodesh*. *Ma'aseh neḥemyah* was reprinted again in Jerusalem in 1987, yet in this edition section 54 appears uncensored.

[44] Hasidim believe that the righteous are often reincarnated as fish. See Nigal, *Magic, Mysticism, and Hasidism*, 58–9.

[45] For another example, see Kattina, *Raḥamei ha'av*, no. 50, s.v. *raḥamim* (p. 15*a*). Here Kattina tells a story of how one Sabbath Elijah the prophet came to the door of Eliezer, the father of R. Israel Ba'al Shem Tov. Even though he showed himself to be a Sabbath violator, nevertheless, Eliezer invited him in for a meal and said nothing about the Sabbath violation so as not to embarrass his visitor. It was because of this kindness that Eliezer merited having the Ba'al Shem Tov as a son. Precisely because this passage is too 'liberal', it was deleted from the Jerusalem, 1950 edition of this book, published by Kattina's grandson. It was also deleted from the Yiddish translation published in Kiryas Yoel in 2009. For this latter point, see Moshe Weiss's letter in *Heikhal habesht*, 32 (Tishrei 5772), 236–7 (called to my attention by Y. Neuwirth).

ben Solomon Abraham Hakohen of Smyrna (d. 1729), the outstanding preacher and author of *Shevet musar* and *Midrash talpiyot*, was himself an adherent of Shabetai Tsevi, long after the latter's apostasy in 1666. This is the subject of a ground-breaking article by Gershom Scholem, who shows that R. Elijah was one of the 'moderate' Shabateans. The 'radicals' believed that the commandments of the Torah were to be entirely revised, since the messianic Torah is different from the Torah of this world. Most famously, this meant that sexual prohibitions were abolished. The 'moderates', on the other hand, argued that while Shabetai Tsevi's apostasy was necessary in order for the messianic drama to play out, this was not to be imitated by others.

> The Jew was expected to remain a Jew. True, a new world-era had undoubtedly been ushered in, the spiritual worlds had undergone *tikkun*, and their structure was now permanently altered; nonetheless, as long as the redemption did not manifest itself outwardly in the realm of objective events in history, as long as the external bondage continued and the phenomenal world remained unchanged, no aspect or commandment of the Torah was to be openly tampered with except for the small number of innovations, such as the cancellation of the fast of *Tish'ah be-Av*. . . . On the whole, it was the view of the 'moderates' that during the transitional period under way, the *kelipot* still retained a good deal of their power, which could only be eliminated by continued performance of the *mitzvot*: the 'façade' of rabbinic Judaism must be allowed to remain temporarily standing, although great changes had already taken place within the edifice.[46]

In *Midrash talpiyot* R. Elijah writes: 'In the Zohar, in a few places, it implies that in the future the messiah will do things that appear repulsive [*devarim nir'im mekho'arim*].'[47] Needless to say, this is a strange passage.[48] As Scholem notes, only in Shabatean literature is the Zohar explained in this way.[49] In his approbation to *Midrash talpiyot*, published in the Lemberg 1875 edition, R. Joseph Saul Nathanson notes this passage and, since he cannot imagine that R. Elijah was himself a Shabatean—he refers to him as a '*tsadik* who

[46] Scholem, *Messianic Idea*, 101–2. Scholem notes that not all of the moderates agreed on the continued cancellation of the Tishah Be'av fast.

[47] s.v. *otiyot mashiaḥ* (p. 33*b*).

[48] Just as strange is that in the great dispute between the hasidim of Sanz and Sadegora, the latter were suspected by at least one author of forging this text in order to justify the rebellious actions of R. Israel of Ruzhin's son, R. Dov Baer of Leovo (*c*.1821–76), who abandoned his hasidim and became a *maskil*. See Zelikovitch, *Shever posh'im*, 62 (printed in id., *Yalkut haro'im*). Only someone who had never looked at the first edition of *Midrash talpiyot*, which pre-dated the rise of hasidism, could make such an accusation. (Even, *Dispute* (Heb.), 27–8, apparently never saw R. Joseph Saul Nathanson's approbation, as he writes that Nathanson accused the Sadegora hasidim of forging the text, when in fact Nathanson blames the Shabateans for this.) Regarding R. Dov Baer, see Assaf, *Beguiled by Knowledge* (Heb.).

[49] Scholem, *Researches in Sabbateanism* (Heb.), 458.

stands in his righteousness'—he assumes that even in the first edition, the Shabateans had already inserted their heresy into the work.[50]

Since Nathanson had declared that R. Elijah could not have written *devarim nir'im mekho'arim*, the publishers of the Lemberg edition of *Midrash talpiyot* altered the text slightly so that it says that the messiah would do 'astounding' or 'frightful things' (*devarim nora'im*). The fact that Nathanson's approbation refers to a text that, after the 'updating', no longer exists, appears not to have bothered the publisher. Indeed, he must have been quite proud of his speculative emendation, and convinced of its accuracy. This can be deduced since by including Nathanson's approbation, which allowed everyone to see what appeared in the original text, the publisher showed that he was different from the other censors who intended to fool the readers.

Nathanson's approbation is significant for another reason, and brings us back to the beginning of this chapter. In addition to the supposed Shabatean forgery in *Midrash talpiyot*, he also calls attention to R. Hayim Lifshitz's *Derekh ḥayim*. This work contains a prayer by Nathan of Gaza (1643–80), the Shabatean prophet,[51] which Nathanson assumes must also be a Shabatean interpolation. His final example of a Shabatean forgery is that 'in the responsa of R. Moses Isserles, printed in Hanau [1710], there is a responsum concerning non-Jewish wine, and in the responsa of Isserles printed in Amsterdam [1711] this [responsum] is not found.' Not having the first edition of Isserles' responsa, printed in Kraków in 1640, or the edition printed in Hamburg around 1710, he was able to assume that the Amsterdam edition was authentic and that Shabateans interested in undermining halakhah had gone to the trouble of inserting a forged responsum into the Hanau edition.[52] It was incomprehensible to Nathanson that Isserles, the defender of halakhah par excellence,[53] was capable of finding any leniency in the matter of non-Jewish wine. It was similarly incomprehensible to R. Abraham Danzig, and he stated that the responsum must have been written by a Moravian troublemaker who slyly inserted it among the authentic manuscript responsa of Isserles.[54]

[50] Nathanson was unaware that this section of *Midrash talpiyot* was actually printed in R. Elijah's lifetime. See Hezekiah Sofer's note in *Datche*, 12 Nisan 5768, 5.

[51] See Tishby, *Paths* (Heb.), 43–4.

[52] Sperber, *Netivot pesikah*, 104 ff., notes some of the confusion Isserles' missing responsum created among halakhists.

[53] In *Shulḥan arukh*, 'Yoreh de'ah' 123: 26, Isserles even quotes an opinion that one who drinks non-Jewish wine by accident should fast for five days. Regarding this passage, see Ehrenreich, 'One Who Drinks Gentile Wine' (Heb.).

[54] Danzig, *Nishmat adam*, 'Hilkhot shabat', *kelal* 69: 3 (in id., *Ḥayei adam venishmat adam hamefo'ar*, ii. 127, 132–3). R. Israel Lipschutz recognizes that the responsum is authentic, but he recommends that its existence be kept hidden from the masses: ואין מגלין אותו אלא לצנועין. See id., *Tiferet yisra'el*, 'Berakhot' 6: 1 (*Yakhin* section).

In addition to Moravia,[55] we know that in Italy many Jews ignored the prohibition against non-Jewish wine, leading R. Joseph Karo and others to condemn the Italian practice.[56] R. Leon Modena (1571–1648) testified that consumption of such wine had been going on for many years before his time, and that great rabbis were among those who drank this wine or did not protest when others did.[57] In his *Historia de' riti hebraici* Modena explained that the prohibition against such wine was only applicable when dealing with idolaters, a category that did not encompass Christians.[58]

Although consumption of non-Jewish wine was opposed by most of the Italian rabbis,[59] a few of them, including R. Samuel Judah Katzenellenbogen of Venice (1521–97), the leading Italian halakhist of his time,[60] were able to provide some justification. Katzenellenbogen even drank this wine himself.[61] Another Italian halakhist, R. Shabetai Be'er (seventeenth century), ruled that

[55] See J. Davis, *Yom-Tov Lipmann Heller*, 83ff. R. Solomon Luria, *She'elot uteshuvot maharshal*, no. 72, mentions Jews who drink non-Jewish wine. He also refers to places where, 'due to our many sins', the practice has become 'completely permitted' (*heter gamur*). See Falk, *Perishah*, 'Yoreh de'ah' 114: 2; D. Halevi, *Turei zahav* on Karo, *Shulḥan arukh*, 'Yoreh de'ah' 114: 3.

[56] See Ya'ari, *Meḥkerei sefer*, 427.

[57] See Modena, *Letters* (Heb.), no. 90. See also Modena, *Ziknei yehudah*, 49; Toaff, *Love, Work, and Death*, 74ff.

[58] See Modena, *Shulḥan arukh*, 47 (the Hebrew trans. of his *Historia de' riti hebraici*). It is possible that this statement was made for apologetic reasons and did not reflect Modena's true opinion, for when directing his words to Jews he strongly opposed drinking non-Jewish wine, and did not drink it himself. See G. Cohen, 'History of the Controversy' (Heb.), 82; Adelman, 'Success and Failure', 9. For evidence of widespread drinking of non-Jewish wine in the Verona ghetto, and a letter of protest from Venice against this (along with an acknowledgement that all was not well in this regard in Venice either), see Modena, *Works* (Heb.), no. 16. For a 16th-cent. Alsatian Jew's report of Jews consuming non-Jewish wine, see D. Kaplan, *Beyond Expulsion*, 61. See also Da Silva, *Peri ḥadash*, 'Oraḥ ḥayim' 496: 16.

[59] R. Samuel Aboab, *Sefer hazikhronot*, section 4, chs. 2–3, responds at length to the justifications offered by those who were lenient regarding non-Jewish wine. See also E. S. Horowitz, 'Early Eighteenth Century', 101–2, who calls attention to a responsum of R. Moses Zacuto (*c.*1620–97) regarding the reliability of a certain Torah scholar who would drink non-Jewish wine when he was travelling. See Zacuto, *She'elot uteshuvot haramaz*, no. 50. See also the non-Italian sources cited in R. Judah Ashkenazi's commentary *Be'er heitev*, 'Oraḥ ḥayim' 272: 2, and R. Hayim Mordechai Margoliyot's commentary *Sha'arei teshuvah*, 'Oraḥ ḥayim' 196: 1 (in the standard editions of the *Shulḥan arukh*).

[60] See Siev, 'R. Samuel Judah Katzenellenbogen' (Heb.).

[61] See K. Schlesinger, 'Controversy' (Heb.); Benayahu, *Relations* (Heb.), 174ff.; Safran, 'Leone da Modena's Historical Thinking', 398 n. 77; Bonfil, *Rabbis and Jewish Communities*, 109; G. Cohen, 'History of the Controversy' (Heb.), 62–90, esp. p. 76. As Soloveitchik, *'Yeinam'* (Heb.), 108, notes, there were Jews in Spain and Germany who also drank non-Jewish wine, but it is not known if any rabbis defended this practice. The same can be said about Rhodes; see Sperber, *Minhagei yisra'el*, iv. 277. R. Hayim Joseph David Azulai (1724–1806) was told that R. Mordechai Tama drank non-Jewish wine. See Azulai, *Ma'gal tov hashalem*, 122. Tama was from Hebron, and while in Amsterdam published the volume of Maimonides' responsa known as *Pe'er hador*.

it is permissible to use non-Jewish wine for kiddush and havdalah (but not for general consumption).[62] The official communal rules of Pisa and Livorno from 1637, while forbidding Jews to eat in non-Jewish inns or taverns, specifically permit Jews to drink non-Jewish wine in small shops.[63] This Italian practice continued, and in a book published in 1872 R. Nahman Nathan Coronel (1810–90) advised those who travel in Italy and see the local Jews drinking non-Jewish wine not to protest.[64]

Apart from Italy, I have found other permissive opinions as well. R. Netanel Weil (1687–1769) of Karlsruhe writes: 'In our time it is not forbidden to drink non-Jewish wine, since those who do not offer wine to idolatry were not included in the decree.'[65] In the nineteenth century there were North African rabbis who also declared that in contemporary times there is no prohibition against drinking non-Jewish wine.[66]

Laxity with regard to non-Jewish wine also spurred a backlash, which not only reaffirmed the binding nature of the prohibition, but attached new significance to it and expanded its parameters. One example of this is the view, already in existence in late medieval times, that a non-Jew is not permitted to even look at a Jew's wine,[67] as this will somehow contaminate it.[68] R. Yair Hayim Bacharach (1639–1702) assumes that a pious person will not drink wine seen by a non-Jew, just as he would not drink wine seen by a menstruant, since both individuals can contaminate through their gaze.[69]

[62] Be'er, *Be'er esek*, no. 109. Abraham Berliner reports that as a result of his opinion regarding non-Jewish wine, Polish Jews mockingly referred to Be'er's book as *be'er esik* (*esik* is Yiddish for 'vinegar'). See Berliner, *Selected Writings* (Heb.), ii. 157. (For another of Be'er's controversial opinions, see Margoliyot, *Sha'arei teshuvah*, 'Oraḥ ḥayim' 33: 2.) R. Nathan Spira (d. 1662) laments how people who ignored the prohibition on non-Jewish wine recited kiddush and havdalah over it. See Spira, *Yayin hameshumar*, 1 (unnumbered). R. Israel Lipschutz, *Tiferet yisra'el*, 'Berakhot' 6: 1 (*Bo'az* section), implies that if one does not have kosher wine or bread upon which to recite kiddush, it is permissible to use non-Jewish wine. See R. Mattathias ben Meir, *Matat yado*, vol. i, no. 45, who responds to Lipschutz.

[63] See Cooperman, '"Trade and Settlement"', 402.

[64] Coronel, *Zekher natan*, 106*a*. Professor Ariel Toaff, who comes from a rabbinic family (his father was chief rabbi of Rome for many years), informed me that until the 1970s, 'my family and almost all other rabbinic families [in Italy] used to drink normally *stam yeinam* [non-Jewish wine] and not kosher wine'.

[65] Weil, *Korban netanel*, 'Beitsah', ch. 1, 5: 9. This liberal position is not found in his responsum on the topic in *Torat netanel*, no. 8.

[66] Messas, *Mayim ḥayim*, vol. ii, 'Yoreh de'ah', no. 66. See also Messas, *Otsar hamikhtavim*, vol. i, no. 454.

[67] It is first recorded by R. Menahem ben Moses Recanati (d. 1571), who refers to it as a *minhag vatikin* (long-established practice). See his *Ta'amei hamitsvot*, no. 360, and Barda, *Revid hazahav*, ii. 28–9.

[68] See Sperber, *Minhagei yisra'el*, iv. 277, and R. Dov Berish Weidenfeld, *Dovev meisharim*, vol. i, no. 124, where Weidenfeld discusses the status of wine seen by a non-Jew through glass.

[69] Bacharach, *Mekor ḥayim*, 'Kitsur halakhot', no. 183 (p. 328). With regard to a menstruant,

R. Judah Loew of Prague (Maharal; 1525–1609) is most famously identified with the increasingly severe approach to non-Jewish wine.[70] He even instituted a special prayer (*mi sheberakh*) for those who abstained from such wine.[71] This action itself shows the problems he had in ensuring observance, since one does not give special recognition to those who observe a law that is taken seriously by all. Indeed, the Maharal specifically mentions that in Moravia not only did the masses drink non-Jewish wine, but so did rabbis.[72] It is probably due to the Maharal's influence in this matter that the prohibition assumed ever more extreme parameters. For example, R. Leib Pisk of Nikolsburg published his *Dimyon aryeh* in Prague in 1616,[73] in which he goes so far as to say that one must accept martyrdom rather than drink non-Jewish wine.[74] A more recent work records the ruling of R. Sheftel Weiss (1866–1944) of Nagysimonyi, Hungary, that given a choice of eating pork or drinking non-Jewish wine, one should consume the pork.[75]

The significance of this issue is demonstrated by its appearance in the late eighteenth century in Saul Berlin's notorious forgery, *Besamim rosh*.[76] In this work, 'R. Asher ben Yehiel' (or another supposed medieval sage, as the responsum is unsigned) states that R. Jacob ben Meir Tam (Rabbenu Tam; *c.*1100–71) declared that the scholars should assemble in order to void the prohibition against non-Jewish wine since it no longer has any connection to idolatrous ceremonies (obviously excluding the Eucharist ritual from any idolatrous connection). The responsum reports that Rabbenu Tam was convinced to shelve his idea since 'R. Simeon' pointed out that wine could once again become central to idolatrous ceremonies. By portraying Rabbenu Tam as retracting his suggestion, on the surface the responsum does not appear radical. However, the basic idea that the prohibition could be voided has been raised. Hundreds of years after 'R. Simeon', when it is obvious that the latter's concern has not materialized, the only logical result would be to return to

Bacharach refers among other sources to Nahmanides' comment that 'if a menstruating woman at the beginning of her issue were to concentrate her gaze for some time upon a polished iron mirror there would appear in the mirror red spots resembling drops of blood . . . just as a viper kills with its gaze' (commentary on Lev. 18: 19).

70 See J. Katz, *Exclusiveness and Tolerance*, 23; Sherwin, *Mystical Theology*, 94 ff.

71 See I. Heilprin (ed.), *Takanot medinat mehrin*, 89 n. 8.

72 See his letter at the beginning of Spira, *Yayin hameshumar*.

73 Regarding the controversy that led him to publish his work, see J. Davis, *Yom-Tov Lipmann Heller*, 83 ff.

74 Pisk, *Dimyon aryeh*, ch. 7.

75 See Tausig, *Beit yisra'el hashalem*, viii. 126.

76 No. 36. For censorship of R. Abraham Bornstein of Sochatchov's (1838–1910) negative judgement of *Besamim rosh* ('it should be burnt even on Yom Kippur that falls on the Sabbath'), see Z. Y. Abramowitz, '*Besamim rosh* in a Hasidic Mirror' (Heb.), 56, and Dan Rabinowitz's Seforim Blog post, 27 Nov. 2006.

Rabbenu Tam's first opinion.[77] In other words, through this responsum *Besamim rosh* has subtly undercut the prohibition against non-Jewish wine, which was exactly Saul Berlin's point.[78]

Let me return to the issue of Shabateanism which has already been mentioned, as the concern about it explains an example of censorship in R. Abraham Danzig's popular *Ḥayei adam*. In the laws of Yom Kippur (144: 20),[79] Danzig refers to a prayer that appears in the anonymous multi-volume work, *Ḥemdat yamim*, which was published in Izmir in 1731–2. An enormous amount has been written about this book, and virtually all academic scholars and many traditionalists are convinced that it is a Shabatean work.[80] Some printers of Danzig's *Ḥayei adam* were also convinced of this, which explains why this reference has been deleted in many editions of the *Ḥayei adam*.[81] Figure 3.3(*a*) shows what the text is supposed to look like, while Figures 3.3(*b*) and 3.3(*c*) show two examples of censored versions.

Although many people continue to regard *Ḥemdat yamim* as a 'kosher' work, those who see it as 'unkosher' have a problem when it is mentioned in a book they are reprinting. Since the author of the book in question was oblivious to *Ḥemdat yamim*'s origin, the motivation for censorship in these cases is also to protect the author's reputation, by preventing people from knowing that he had studied *Ḥemdat yamim*. An example of this concerns the eighteenth-century kabbalist R. Alexander Susskind ben Moses (d. 1793), who in his ethical will urges his sons first to study his own writings, and then to begin study of *Ḥemdat yamim*.[82] In the Zhitomir 1848 edition of the ethical will, *Ḥemdat yamim* is no longer mentioned, and it is now the *Reshit ḥokhmah* of R. Elijah de Vidas (1518–92) that is the first work to be studied after R. Alexander's own. In other editions of the ethical will,[83] *Ḥemdat yamim* is abbreviated as ח"ה, and (mistakenly) as חו"ה, and the abbreviations are never explained.[84]

77 Rabbenu Tam actually had a very stringent view on non-Jewish wine. See R. Reuven Margaliyot's note in his edition of Jacob of Marvège, *She'elot uteshuvot min hashamayim*, 59 n. 1.

78 See also Berlin, *Besamim rosh*, no. 280, that a sick person is permitted to drink non-Jewish wine and eat non-Jewish cheese if it will help him get better, even if he is not in any serious danger, since 'they [the Sages] did not decree against these things in the case of sickness'.

79 In the first edition of the work, published in Vilna in 1810, this passage does not appear. It is, however, found in the second edition (Vilna and Grodno, 1819). The latter edition was published in Danzig's lifetime and contains many additions.

80 See Ya'ari, *Ta'alumat sefer*; Tishby, *Paths* (Heb.), chs. 6–7; Scholem, *Researches in Sabbateanism* (Heb.), 250–88; Fogel, 'Sabbatian Character' (Heb.); Ben-David, '*Ḥemdat yamim*' (Heb.); Y. H. Mizrahi, *Ḥemdat yosef*; Goldhaber, 'Ta'alumah ve'ayin kora lah'.

81 See M. Meir, 'On the "Tefilah zakah"' (Heb.).

82 Alexander Susskind ben Moses, *Tsava'ah*, section 3.

83 e.g. Warsaw, 1913 and Vilna, 1929.

84 For a similar example in the writings of the hasidic master R. Tsevi Hirsch Eichenstein of Zidichov (1763–1831), see Y. Mondshine, '*Ḥemdat yamim* and the Hasidic Masters' (Heb.).

יז מאחר שהעולם מקפידים אם כבה נרו אף שלדעתי אין בו שום חשש דפעמים נכבה מחמת רוח או מחמת חום מ"מ כיון שהעולם מקפידים בזה ראוי לכל אדם ליתן נרו לשמש דלא ישגיח עליו כלל וגם המותר יניח בבית הכנסת דבלא"ה למוצאי יו"כ מבטלין תפלת ערבית מתוך זה ולכן נכון לתקן כמו שכתבתי :

יח אפי' מי שלובש שק מחמת תשובה אסור ללבשו ביו"כ שהוא י"ט וכ"ש אותן הנותנים אבנים או קטניות באנפילאות שקורין (זאקן) ועומדין עליהם משום תשובה שאסור ואף בשאר ימות השנה נ"ל דאסור שזה מדרכי נביאי הבעל כדכתיב עד שפך דם עליהם :

יט המנהג לברך את הבנים קודם שנכנסין לבהכ"נ שאז כבר חל קדושת היום ושערי רחמים נפתחים והנוסח שאנו מברכים ישימך כו' ויה"ר מלפני אבינו שבשמים שיתן בלבך אהבתו ויראתו ותהי' יראת ה' על פניך כל ימי חייך שלא תחטא ותהי חשקך בתורה ובמצות עיניך לנכח יביטו פיך ידבר חכמות ולבך יהגה אימות ידיך יהיו עוסקות במצות רגליך ירוצו לעשות רצון אביך שבשמים ויתן לך בנים ובנות צדיקים וצדיקות עוסקים בתורה ובמצות כל ימיהם ויהיו מקורך ברוך ויזמין לך פרנסתך בהיתר ובנחת ובריוח מתחת ידו הרחבה ולא ע"י מתנות בשר ודם פרנסה שתהיה פנוי לעבודת ה' ותכתב ותחתם לחיים טובים וארוכים בתוך כל צדיקי ישראל אמן :

כ אח"ז ילך לבהכ"נ באימה ורעדה והמנהג בקהלתינו בכל בתי מדרשים להוציא ס"ת מהיכל כמש"כ בכתבי האר"י ז"ל וכבר נדפס בחמדת הימים התפלה שסידר . ואמנם לא כל אדם מבין הדברים רק מי שבא בסוד ה' ומי שא"י הוא להם כדברי ספר החתום ולכן העתקתי מספרים קדמונים תפלה בלשון קל כי בלא"ה לדעת הרבה פוסקים מצות וידוי הוא סמוך ללילה דוקא וראוי לכל אדם וזה נוסחתה ואשרי מי שיאמר אותה גם בשחרית :

הנוסח המוסכם מהפוסקים •

בשם אלהים ועל פי התורה אנחנו מתירים נדרים ושבועות שהאדם אוסר בהם איזה אסור על נפשו · ובכלל מתירים אנחנו נדרים ושבועות שהאדם נודר ונשבע מפי עצמו רק על דברים שבינו לבין עצמו . אבל חס וחלילה לכל איש לחשוב שאנחנו מתירים אלות ושבועות שנשבעים להממשלה ולמקומי המשפט , או אלות ושבועות שנודרים ונשבעים בענינים שבין אדם לחבירו וכמה שנוגע לתועלת זולתנו ולכל איש מאיזה דת וגזע שיהיה , והנדרים והאלות והשבועות שנאמר עליהן בתורה כי לא ינקה השם את שוכר עליהן · מחויבות נשיאות שרירין וקיימין בתוקפן ובלי ישונה . וכל העובר עליהן יענשו חרון אף וחימה להרפות ולדראון עולם :

כל נדרי ואסרי ושבועי ונדויי וחרמי וקונמי וכינויי וקנסי די נדרנא ודי אשתבענא ודי חרמנא ודי אסרנא על נפשתנא מיה"כ שעבר עד יה"כ הזה שבא עלינו לשלום ומיה"כ הזה עד יה"כ שיבא עלינו לשלום נדרנא לא נדרי ושבועענא לא שבועי ונדוינא לא נדויי ותרמנא לא חרמי ואסרנא לא אסרי כולהון אתחרטנא בהון יהא רעוא די יהון שביתין ושביקין לא שרירין ולא קימין ונסלח לכל עדת בני ישר' ולגר הגר בתוכם כי לכל העם בשגג' :

רבון העולמים אב הרחמים והסליחות אשר ימינך פשוטה לקבל שבים ואתה בראת את האדם להטיב לו באחריתו ובראת לו ב' יצרים יצר טוב ויצר הרע כדי שתהיה הבחירה בידו לבחור בטוב או ברע כדי לתת לו שכר טוב על טוב בחירתו כי כן גזרה חכמתך כמ"ש ראה נתתי לפניך היום את החיים ואת הטוב ואת המות ואת הרע ובחרת בחיים · ועתה אלהי לא שמעתי לקולך והלכתי בעצת יצה"ר ובדרכי לבי ומאסתי בטוב ובחרתי ברע ולא די לי שלא קדשתי את איברי אלא טמאתי אותם . בראת בי מוח ולב ובהם חוש המחשבה לחשוב מחשבות טובות והרהורים טובים ולב להבין דברי קדשך ולהתפלל ולברך כל הברכות במחשבה טהורה ואני טמאתי אותם בהרהורים ומחשבות זרות ולא די לי בזה אלא שע"י הרהורים רעים באתי לידי הוצאת זרע לבטלה פעם ברצון ופעם באונס בטומאת קרי המטמא את כל הגוף ומהם בראתי משחיתים ומחבלים הנקראים נגעי בני אדם אוי לי כי תחת המחשבות הטובות שיכולתי לברוא ע"ז מלאכים קדושים שיהיו סניגורים ופרקליטים טובים עלי החתיהם בראתי משחיתים לחבל את עצמי כמ"ש והוכחתיו בשבט אנשים ובנגעי בני אדם · בראת בי עינים ובהם חוש הראות לראות בהם מ"ש בתורה גלקדש אותם בראיית כל דברים שבקדושה והזהרת בתורתך ולא תתורו אחרי לבבכם ואחרי עיניכם אוי לי כי הלכתי אחרי עיני ושמאתי אותם להסתכל בנשים ובכל דבר טומאה· בראת בי אזנים לשמוע דברי קדושה ודברי תורה אוי לי כי טמאתי אותם לשמוע דברי נבלה ולה"ר וכל דבריב האסורים אוי לאזנים שכך שומעות . בראת בי פה ולשון ושניים וחיך וגרון ונתת בתם כח לדבר בהם ה' מוצאות האותיות הקדושים של א"ב אשר בהם בראת שמים וארץ ומלואם ובהם ארגת תורתך הקדושה ובבת הדיבור הבדלת את האדם מן הבהמה ואפי' כבהמה לא הייתי כי טמאתי פי בדברי נבלה בלשון הרע בשקרים ליצנות רכילות מחלוקת מלבין פני חבירו מקלל את חבירו מתכבד בקלון חבירו דברי משא ומתן בשבת ויו"ט בשבועות ונדרים בראת לי ידים וחוש המישוש לעסוק בהם במצות ואני טמאתי עצמי במשמושין של איסור להכות באגרוף רשע ולהרים יד, להכות את ישראל ולטלטל דברים המוקצים בשבת ויו"ט · בראת בי רגלים להלוך לכל דבר מצו' ואני טמאתי אותם ברגלים ממהרות לרוץ לרעה . בראת בי ראש הגויה וחתמת אותו באות ברית קודש להיות עבד נאמן לעבודתך ואני טמאתי אותו בהוצאה זרע לבטלה ובקרי ולהקשות עצמי לדעת שלא במקום מצוה (ונעלתי נעילות אסורות) משמשתי את כל איברי ומצאתי אותם בעלי מומין מכף רגלי ועד ראשי אין בי מתום ועתה ה' אלהי גלוי וידוע לפניך שלא נתכוונתי בכל החטאים והעונות להכעיס אותך ולמרוד כנגדך אך הלכתי בעצת יצרי הרע אשר תמיד בכל יום אורש רשת לרגלי ללכדני ואני עני ואביון תולעת ולא איש כשל כחי לעמוד כנגדו ועמל הפרנסה לפרנס את ב"ב וטרדת הזמן ומקרינ הם היו בעוכרי ולפי שכל זה גלוי וידוע לפניך

כי

(*a*)

Figure 3.3 R. Abraham Danzig, *Ḥayei adam*: (*a*) undated edition with no place of publication, showing the original mention of *Ḥemdat yamim* in 144: 20; (*b*) (on page 101) Pressburg, 1848 edition, with a censored version of 144: 20; (*c*) (on page 102) Vilna, 1924 edition, with a censored version of 144: 20

בידם ומ"מ ע"י עכו"ם נ"ל דמותר כיון שמוחזקים זה למצוה גדולה (עיין בח"א שבת כלל ח' סי' ו') ואם כבו הנרות ביוה"כ אסור לומר לעכו"ם לחזור להדליק ולכן אסור לומר לנכרי לקבל שעוה הנוטף ואפילו לומר לו שיוה"כ שידליק ויקבל השעוה אסור:

טז נוהגין להציע השולחנות ביוה"כ כמו בשבת ונוהגין ללבוש הקיטל שהוא בגד מתים וגם אבל מותר ללבשו:

יז מאמר שהעולם מקפידים אם כבה נרו אף כלדעתי אין בו שום חשש דלפעמים נכבה מחמת רוח או מחמת חום מ"מ כיון שהעולם מקפידים בזה ראוי לכל אדם ליתן נרו לשמש ולא ישגיח עליו כלל וגם המותר יהיה בבה"כ דבלא"ה לפעמים ביוה"כ מבטלין תפלת ערבית מתוך זה ולכן נכון לתקן כמו שכתבתי:

יח אפי' מי שלובש שק מחמת תשובה אסור ללבשו ביה"כ שהוא רש וכ"ש אותן שהולכים אבנים או קסמיות במכפילאות שקורין זאקן ועומדים עליהם משום תשובה שאסור ואף בספר ישועת הסכה נ"ל דאסור שזה מדרכי כהני הבעל כדכתיב עד שפך דם עליהם וכן מנהג הכשרים:

יט המנהג לברך את הבנים קודם שנכנסין לבהכ"נ שאז כבר חל קדושת היום ושערי רחמים נפתחים ואומרים שלכו תברכים ישימך כו' יברכך כו' ויה"ר מלפני אבינו שבשמים שיתן בלבך אהבתו ויראתו ותהי' יראת ה' על פניך כל ימיך שלא תחטא ויהי חשקך בתורה ומצות. עיניך לנכח יביטו. פיך ידבר חכמות. ולבך יהגה אימות. ידיך יהיו עוסקים במצות. רגליך ירוצו לעשות רצון אביך שבשמים. יתן לך בנים ובנות צדיקים וצדיקות עוסקים בתורה ובמצות כל ימיהם. ויהי מקורך ברוך. ויזמין לך פרנסתך בהיתר ובנחת וברוח מתחת ידו הרחבה ולא ע"י מתנת בשר ודם פרנסה שתהיה פנוי לעבודת ה' ותכתב ותחתם לחיים טובים וארוכים בתוך כל צדיקי ישראל אמן:

כ אח"ז ילך לבית הכנסת בשמחה ורעדה והמנהג בקהלותינו בכל בתי מדרשים לאומר ק"ת תהילים. כמ"ש בכתבי האר"י ז"ל ואמנם לא כל אדם מבין הדברים רק למי שבא בסוד ה' ועוד שאין הוא כדברי ספר הסידור ולכן העתקתי מספרים קדמונים תפלה בלשון קל כי בלא"ה לדעת הרבה פוסקים אמת וידוי הוא סמוך ללילה דוקא וראוי לכל אדם לאמרה עם נוסחתה. ואשרי מי שיאמר אותה גם בספרים:

הנוסח המוסכם מהפוסקים

כל נדרי ואסרי ושבועי ונדויי וחרמי וקונמי וקינוסי די נדרנא ודי אשתבענא ודי נדינא ודי חרמנא ודי אסרנא על נפשתנא מיוה"כ שעבר עד יוה"כ הזה שבא עלינו לשלום ומיוה"כ הזה עד יוה"כ שיבא עלינו לשלום נדרנא לא נדרי ושבועתנא לא שבועי וחרמנא לא חרמי ונדוינא לא נדויי ואסרנא לא אסרי כולהון אתחרטנא בהון יהא רעוא די יהון שביתין ושביקין לא שרירין ולא קיימין ונסלח לכל עדת בני ישראל ולגר הגר בתוכם כי לכל העם בשגגה:

רבון העולמים אב הרחמים והסליחות אשר ימינך פשוטה לקבל שבים ואתה בראת האדם להטיב לו באחריתו.

ותאות לו שני יצרים יצר טוב ויצר רע כדי שתהיה הבחירה בידו לבחור בטוב או ברע כדי ליתן לו שכר טוב על טוב בחירתו כי כן נגלה חכמתך: כמו שכתוב ראה נתתי לפניך את הטוב ואת הרע את החיים ואת המות ובחרת בחיים. ועתה אלקי לא שמעתי לקולך והלכתי בעצת יצה"ר ונדדתי לבי ומאסתי בטוב ובחרתי ברע ולא די לי שלא קדשתי את איברי אלא טמאתי אותם. בראת בי מוח ולב ובהם חוש המחשבה לחשוב מחשבות טובות והרהורים טובים ולב להבין דברי קדשך ולהתפלל ולברך כל הברכות במחשבה טהורה. ואני טמאתי אותם בהרהורים ומחשבות זרות. ולא די בזה אלא שעל ידי הרהורים רעים באתי לידי הוצאת זרע לבטלה פעם ברצון ופעם באונס בטומאת קרי המטמא את כל הגוף ובהם בראתי המשחיתים והמחבלים הנקראים נגעי בני אדם. אוי לי כי תחת שהמחשבות טובות שיכולתי לברא ע"י זה מלאכי' קדושים שיהיו סנגורים ופרקליטים טובים עלי המסיתים בראתי משחיתים לחבל את עצמי כמו שכתוב והוכחתיו בשבט אנשים ובנגעי בני אדם. בראת בי עינים ובהם כח הראות לראות בהם מ"ש בתורה ולקרא אותם בראיות כל דבר שבקדושה והזהרת בתורתיך ולא תתורו אחרי לבבכם ואחרי עיניכם. אוי לי כי הלכתי אחרי עיני וטמאתי אותי להסתכל בנשים ובכל דבר טומאה. בראת בי אזנים לשמוע דברי קדושה ודברי תורה. אוי לי כי טמאתי אותם בשמוע דברי נבלה ולה"ר וכל דברים האסורים אוי לאזנים ששמעו שומעות. בראת בי פה ולשון ושניים וחיך וגרון ונתת בהם כח לדבר בהם שמונה אותיות האותיות הקדושים של א"ב אשר בהם בראת שמים וארץ ומלואם ובהם נתת תורתיך הקדושה. ובכח הדבור הבדלת את האדם מן הבהמה. ואפי' כבהמה לא הייתי כי טמאתי פי בדברי נבלה. בלשון הרע. בשקרים. ליצנות. רכילות. מחלוקת. מלבין פני חבירו. מקלל את חבירו. מתכבד בקלון חבירו. דברי משא ומתן בשבת וי"ט. בשבועות ונדרים. בראת לי ידים זריזים שמיטום לעסוק בהם במצות. ואני טמאתי עצמי במישמושין של איסור. להכות באגרוף רשע ולהרים יד להכות את ישראל. ולטלטל דברים המוקצים בשבת וי"ט: בראת בי רגלים להלוך לכל דבר מצוה. ואני טמאתי אותם ברגלים ממהרים לרוץ לרעה. בראת בי ראש הברית וחתמת אותו באות ברית קודש להיות עבד נאמן לעבודתיך ואני טמאתי אותו בהוצאת זרע לבטלה. ובנקרי. ולקשות עצמי לדעת שלא במקום מצוה (ובעלתי בעילות אסורות) ופגמתי את כל איברי ותלאתי אותם בעלי מומין מכף רגלי ועד ראשי אין בי מתום. ועתה ה' אלקי גלוי וידוע לפניך שלא כתכוונתי בכל החטאים והעונות להכעיס אותך ולמרוד כנגדך אך שהלכתי בעצת יצרי הרע אשר תמיד בכל יום פורש רשת לרגלי ללכדני ואני עני ואביון תולעת ולא איש בשל כחי לעמוד כנגדו. ועל שהוכרחתי לפרנס את בני ביתי מטרדת הזמן ויקרי הם היו בעוכרי. ולפי שכל זה גלוי וידוע לפניך כי אין אדם צדיק בארץ אשר לא יחטא לכן ברחמיך הרבים נתת לנו יום אחד בשנה יום אדיר וקדוש יום הכפורים הזה הבא עלינו לטובה לשוב לפניך ולכפר את כל עונותינו ולטהר אותנו מכל טומאותינו כמ"ש כי ביום הזה יכפר עליכם לטהר אתכם מכל חטאתיכם לפני ה' תטהרו. ועתה ראה עמך ישראל אשר לקחת

b)

בהש"מ ואם הפסיק אכילתו בעוד היום גדול יכול לחזור ולאכול כל זמן שלא קיבל עליו תענית בעוד שהוא יום אך יש שכתבו שהמנהג שלאחר שאכלו אסור לאכול דבזה שמפסיקין הוי כאילו קיבל עליו בפה ולכן נכון שקודם בהמ"ז יאמר בפירוש שאינו מקבל עליו עוד התענית ונ"ל דמי שהיה בדעתו כן נמי מותר אבל בסתם אם נהג כך אסור ולא ראיתי מי שנהג כך ויש להחמיר דקבלה בלב הוי קבלה (כן כתב המ"א בסימן תקנ"ג וכן כתב הגר"א דלכ"ע הוי קבלה דלא כרמ"א) :

יג המנהג הפשוט במדינות אלו שלא להטמין המין כעיוה"כ למוצאי יוה"כ דהוי כמכין מיוה"כ לחול :

יד בעוד יום ודאי מדליקין נרות וידליק בחדר ששוכב שם כדי שלא יבא לידי תשמיש ואע"פ שי"א שאין מברכין על הנר ביוה"כ מ"מ המנהג הפשוט שמברכין להדליק נר של יוה"כ ואם חל בשבת פשיטא שמברכין להדליק נר של שבת ושל יוה"כ וגם שהחיינו ואמנם אז לא יברך שהחיינו בבהכ"נ :

טו מצוה להרבות נרות בבתי כנסיות דכתיב ולקדוש ה' מכובד זה יוה"כ שאין בו אכילה ושתיה מצוה לכבדו בנרות וכסות נקיה ונוהגין במדינתנו שכל בעה"ב עושה נר של שעוה לביתו וגם נוהגין לעשות נר בשביל נשמות אביו ואמו שמתו ואמנם גם בזה אדוקים מאד עד שמדליקין אפי' בין השמשות ויש למחות בידם וכ"מ ע"י נכרי נ"ל דמותר כיון שחושבין זה למצוה גדולה (עיין בהלכות שבת כלל ה' סי' ו') ואם נכבו הנרות ביוה"כ אסור לומר לנכרי לחזור להדליקן וכן אסור לומר לנכרי לקבל השעוה הנוטף ואפי' לומר לו עיוה"כ שידליק ויקבל השעוה אסור :

טז נוהגין להציע השולחנות ביוה"כ כמו בשבת ונוהגין ללבוש (הקיטל) שהוא בגד מתים וגם אבל מותר ללבשו :

יז מאחר שהעולם מקפידים אם כבה נרו אף שלדעתי אין בו משום חשש דלפעמים נכבה מחמת רוח או מחמת חום מ"מ כיון שהעולם מקפידים בזה ראוי לכל אדם ליתן נרו לשמש ולא ישגיח עליו כלל וגם המותר יניח בבית הכנסת דכמה פעמים למוצאי יו"כ מבטלין תפלת ערבית מתוך זה לכן נכון לתקן כמו שכתבתי :

יח אפי' מי שלובש שק מחמת תשובה אסור ללבשו ביוה"כ שהוא יו"ט וכ"ש אותן הנותנין אבנים או קטניות באנפילאות שקורין (זאקן) ועומדים עליהם משום תשובה שאסור ואף בשאר ימות השנה נ"ל דאסור שזה מדרכי נביאי הבעל כדכתיב עד שפך דם עליהם וכן מנהג הכומרים :

יט המנהג לברך את הבנים קודם שנכנסין לבהכ"נ שאז כבר חל קדושת היום ושערי רחמים נפתחים והנוסח שאנו מברכים ישימך כו' ויה"ר מלפני אבינו שבשמים שיתן בלבך אהבתו ויראתו ותהיה יראת ה' על פניך כל ימי חייך שלא תחטא ותהי חשקך בתורה ומצות עיניך לנוכח יביטו פיך ידבר חכמות ולבך יהגה אימות ידיך יהיו עוסקות במצות רגליך ירוצו לעשות רצון אביך שבשמים ויתן לך בנים ובנות צדיקים וצדיקות עוסקים בתורה ומצות כל ימיהם ויהי מקורך ברוך ויזמין לך פרנסתך בהיתר ובנחת ובריוח מתחת ידו הרחבה ולא ע"י מתנת בשר ודם פרנסה שתהיה פנוי לעבודת ה' ותכתב ותחתם לחיים טובים וארוכים בתוך כל צדיקי ישראל אמן :

כ אח"ז ילך לבהכ"נ באימה ורעדה והמנהג בקהלתנו בכל בתי מדרשים להוציא ס"ת מהיכל כמש"כ בכתבי האר"י ז"ל · והעתקתי מספרים קדמונים לומר אז וידוי בלשון קל כי בלא"ה לדעת הרבה פוסקים מצות וידוי הוא סמוך ללילה רוקא · וזה נוסחתה · ואשרי מי שיאמר אותה גם בשחרית :

ותקן עוד בכוונת האדם הכבע על עצמו כמו אוכל ולא אוכל וכדומה ולא על הבושת אבל הממשנה מסביע סיאודים לו כין אדם להבינו ותקנה התפלה הזאת :

הנוסח המוסכם מהפוסקים

כל נדרי ואסרי ושבועי ותרמי וקונמי וכנויי וקנסי די נדרנא ודי אשתבענא ודי נדינא ודי חרמנא ודי אסרנא על נפשתנא מיוה"כ שעבר עד יוה"כ הזה שבא עלינו לשלום ומיוה"כ הזה עד יוה"כ שיבא עלינו לשלום · נדרנא לא נדרי ושבועתנא לא שבועי וחרמנא לא

חתם סופר

בקירוב זמן קריאת שמע של שחרית הזמן היותר ונקדם ד' שבועית קודם תקופת ניסן 50 מינוטען אויף 8 אוהר ובכל שבוע צריך להקדים רביע שעה עד שבתקופת ניסן יהי' הזמן המוקדם 50 מינוטען אויף 7 אוהר מד' שבועות קודם תקופת תמוז עד התקופה הזמן המוקדם 50 מינוט אויף 6 אוהר והזמן הזה נמשך במעט השתיות עד ממש סמוך איזה שביעות קודם תקופת תשרי ואז פוחת והולך בכל שבוע בתקופת תשרי הזמן המוקדם 20 מינוטען נאך 7 אוהר ואיזה שבועות לאחר התקופה פוחת בכל שבוע לערך 10 מינוט עד ד' שבועית קודם תקופת טבת עד התקופה הזמן המוקדם אז 50 מינוט אויף 9 אוהר זמן הלילה ד' שבועות קודם תקופת ניסן בין ה' ליו"ד מינוט נאך 6 אוהר ומוסיף רביע שעה לשבוע עד התקופה ואז הוה לילה אוס 10 מינוט נאך 7 אוהר. מד' שבועות קודם תקופת תמוז אזן 9 אוהר אויף 5 מינוטין פאר 9 אוהר ודפחות מעט מעט עד תקופת תשרי 10 מינוט נאך 6. מד' שבועות קודם תקופת טבת עד התקופה 40 מינוטין אויף 5 אוהר. וזאת לדעת דקי"ל מן השקיעה עד צאת הכוכבים כ"ד מינוט או ל"ה מינוט עבדי' הכא לחומרא והכא לחומרא. לכן זמן שאיבת מים למצות אם אפשר לכוון ולראות הרגע מתי נעלמת החמה מעינינו אח"כ יו"ד מינוטן וישאוב ואי לא יחשוב משיעור צאת הכוכבים הנ"ל כאיתו זמן כ"ה מינוטען למפרע וישאוב עד צאת הכוכבים. ולענין הדלקת נרות בשבת וחנוכה בע"ש שצריך להיות לעולם קודם שקיעת החמה והיינו קודם ל"ה מינוטען קודם צאת הכוכבים הנהוג אז לפי חשבון הנ"ל:

אמר הכתוב אמת מארץ תצמח ובתיקוני ד' ע"ב דהוא ר"ת אלף מאתן תשעין כמשפט אתוון דארץ (כאן חסר שתי תיבות) י"ג קרבנות אחר שנבוא אל חשבון בזמן הבית לבביאם אל המקובץ הוא אלף מאתים ותשעים והמה קרבנות ליבור הכאן בחובה:

שס"ה	שבת	ר"ח	פסח	שבועות	ר"ה	יוה"כ	סוכות	ש"ע
ימים בשנה יום יום שני תמידין	נ"ב שבתות שנה מוספי שבת	מוספי ר"ח פרים שנים איל אחד כבשים שבעה חטאת א' י"א פעמים י"ב	מוספי פסח יום יום פרים שנים איל א' שבעה כבשים כבש הבא עם העומר שעיר עזים לחטאת	פרים שנים איל אחד וג' לחם אילים שנים פר אחד ז' כבשים חטאת א', י"ב כבשי עצרת	פר אחד איל אחד כבשים שבעה חטאת אחד	חובות היום פר ושעיר של יו"כ ושעיר הנשרף פר א' ואיל א' כבשים ז' ושעיר הנאכל לערב	מוספי סוכות פרים שבעים כבשים צ"ח י"ד אילים שבעה שעירים	פר אחד איל אחד שבעה כבשים, ושעיר חטאת
שבעה מאות ושלשים.	מאה וארבעה.	מאה ושנים ושלשים	שמונה ושבעים	ארבעה ועשרים	עשרה.	שלשה עשר.	מאה ותשעה ושמונים.	עשרה.

המקובץ מפרט אל הכלל אלף מאתן ותשעין.

והמקובץ מן כל עשרונים שלשה לפר ושני עשרונים לאיל ועשרון לכבש חוץ מן הכבש הבא עם העומר היה מנחתו כפולה שני עשרונים.

למאה וארבעה עשרה פרים שלש מאות וארבעים ושתים עשרונים.	לאילים ארבעים שמונים עשרונים.	לאלף ומאה ושני הכבשים הוא אלף ומאה וארבעה עשרונים עם מנחה כפולה.

והרב הגאון בעל עשרה מאמרות מאמר המדות מדה י"ב ענה ואמר סי' על זה ארץ אשר ה' אלקיך דורש וכו' כי א'ר'ץ הוא אלף מאתן ותשעין מנין הקרבנות וא ש ר הוא מנין אלף וחמש מאות וכו' הוא מספר הוי' ב"ה כי הוא הדורש והוא סי' למלכי צדק מלך שלם למספר הגדול של מ'נ'צ'פ'ך הכ' פשוטה ה' מאות ומ' סתומה שש מאות עם י'ד'ו'ד שהוא מקומו של עולם ג"כ אלף ת"ק וכה תאמר יו"ד פעמים ה' הוא חמשים וי"ו פעמים חמישים הוא שלש מאות ה' פעמים שלש מאות ת"ק והנעלם מן שדי הוא ת"ק כמבואר בכתבי האר"י ז"ל בכוונת יתקדש:

ועתה יתבאר נסכי היין לקרבנות.

שלישית ההין לאיל	רביעית ההין לכבש	חצי ההין לפר
אילים ארבעים ד' פעמים ק"ס לוגין	לאלף ק"ג כבשים ג' פעמים ג' אלף ג' מאות ותשעה לוגין.	לפרים קי"ד ששה פעמים ששה מאות פ"ד לוגין.

גדר המקובץ הוא ד' אלף ומאה ושלש וחמשים לחשבון דחיטך הוא אחד כמו ברחשית ויען דהין היה י"ב לוגין וגדר רביעית הוא שלש מאות ששה וארבעים וא' רביעית ס' בהין שמו בלוגין אחד שמו אחד:

ובספר בחיי איתא על פסוק ומעת הוסר התמיד אלף מאתן ותשעין וגו' לקץ הימין וגו' הוא דאם אברהם אבינו ע"ה שאמר במה אדע דהוא דבר קל נשתעבדו בניו ת"ל שנה אנו שחוטאין במעשה ודיבור ומחשבה אנו לצפות הגאולה לאחר שלש פעמים ת"ל דהוא אלף מאתן ותשעין ובסיום הפסוק אשרי המחכה ויגיע לימים אלף ג' מאות שלשים וחמש כ"ל דקאי על פי דברי קדושו האר"י זלה"ה על כוונת הקדיש ס"ת דיתגדל ויתקדש שמיה רבא הוא אלף מן רבא ונשאר ש'ל'ה וזהו יגדל ש'ל'ה והוא ג' זוצין הגדולות עם ג' אלפים דקטנות עולין ש'ל'ו ע"ש עיי' מ"ח מסכת תפלה ערבית בבריאה כל זה כתוב ומפורש בס' עשרה מאמרות מאמר המדות מדה י"ב ושפירש בפי' יד יהודה שם ומלאתי מסודר בסדר הזה בס' נקרא עולת ראי' כתיבת יד:

Figure 3.4 R. Moses Sofer, *Ḥidushim: seder mo'ed* (Jerusalem, 1894), with uncensored comment on the time of sunset

R. Moses Sofer was another great figure whose writings were censored. According to a text included in his commentary on the Talmud (see Fig. 3.4),[85] which is actually a citation from his teacher R. Nathan Adler (1741–1800),[86] sunset in Frankfurt am Main, for purposes of when the Sabbath starts, occurs 35 minutes before darkness (the same would be true in other parts of Central Europe). To put it another way, this means that the Sabbath ends 35 minutes after sunset, a position that is not in line with the more stringent view identified with Rabbenu Tam, according to which the end of the Sabbath (i.e. darkness) occurs a good deal later than this.[87] How do you ensure that this opinion remains unknown when it appears in Sofer's work? The best solution, as we have so often seen, is simply to omit it. This is exactly what happened in 1954 when Sofer's commentary was reprinted in photo-offset by R. Moses Stern (d. 1997), a well-known Hungarian rabbi. Only in 1997, after Stern was no longer alive, did R. Meir Amsel (1907–2007) reveal that Stern had told him that R. Joel Teitelbaum (1887–1979), the Satmar Rebbe, had 'commanded' him to delete this section.[88]

Yet Stern's action did not go unnoticed. When it was discovered, a group of Brooklyn men who called themselves *anshei yere'im veḥaredim deviliamsburg* ('the God-fearing and pious men of Williamsburg') launched a very strong protest, seeing it as the height of chutzpah (insolence) to tamper with Sofer's writings (see Fig. 3.5).[89] They even connected this with the actions of the Reformers who thought it proper to omit material from the prayer book.

[85] See the end of his *Ḥidushim: seder mo'ed.*

[86] See Plaut, *Likutei ḥaver ben ḥayim*, iv. 3*b*.

[87] It is perhaps strange that Adler's opinion does not distinguish between different times of the year. See A. M. Sofer, *Minhagei raboteinu vehalikhoteihem*, 93. A different perspective is offered in Sofer, *She'elot uteshuvot ḥatam sofer*, vol. i, 'Oraḥ ḥayim', no. 80. For interpretations of Sofer's and Adler's views, not all of which agree with what I have written, see Halberstadt, 'The Time of the End of the Sabbath' (Heb.); H. P. Benisch, 'An Explanation of the Calculation' (Heb.); Pozna, 'An Explanation of the Hatam Sofer's Time Calculation' (Heb.); Y. G. Weiss, 'An Explanation of the Times of Day and Night' (Heb.); Levinger, 'Concerning the Time' (Heb.); Gewirtz, '*Zemannim*', 168–70.

[88] See the editorial comment in *Hamaor* (Sept.–Oct. 1997), 26. Cf. Harfenes, *Yisra'el vehazemanim*, 873. When the censorship was first discovered, Stern claimed that he had nothing to do with it. He placed the blame on an unnamed individual whom he said had access to the volumes and carried out the censorship on his own. This information appears in Stern's 'open letter' dealing with the issue, a copy of which Professor Shnayer Leiman was gracious enough to send me. In this letter, Stern also states that regardless of what the practice was in Pressburg (Bratislava), Budapest, and Vienna, in the name of Orthodox unity it is best if all those in the United States adopt Rabbenu Tam's view as to when the Sabbath ends.

[89] Despite what appears in the placard (see Fig. 3.5), we have evidence that in the 20th cent. the Sabbath in Pressburg ended later than the time given by Sofer. See H. P. Benisch, *Hazemanim bahalakhah*, i. 213, ii. 442 ff. (According to R. Leopold Greenwald, who studied in Pressburg, in the United States the Sabbath ended 30 minutes after sunset. See Greenwald, *Maharil uzemano*, 47–8.)

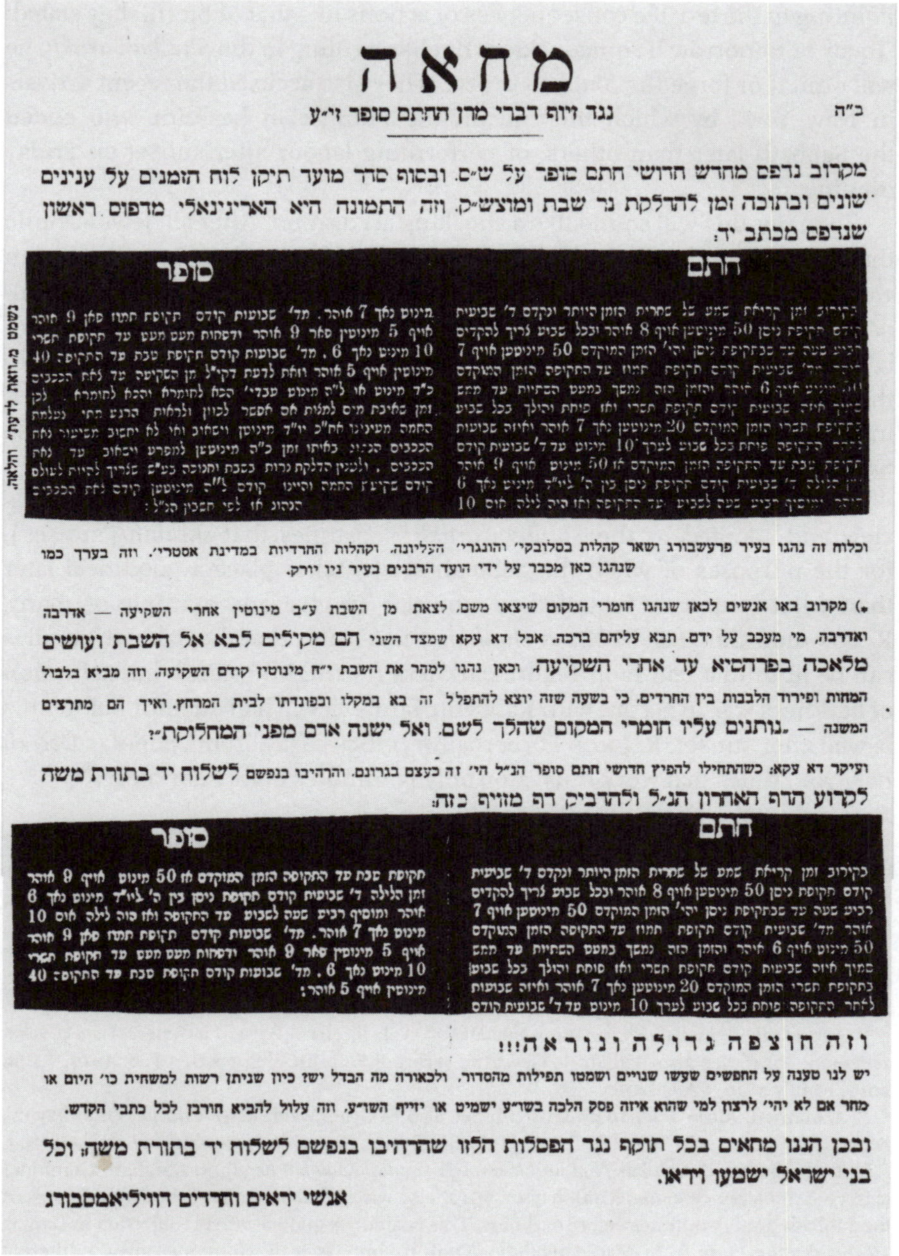

מחאה

ב״ה

נגד זיוף דברי מרן החתם סופר זי״ע

מקרוב נדפס מחדש חדושי חתם סופר על ש״ס. ובסוף סדר מועד תיקן לוח הזמנים על ענינים שונים ובתוכה זמן להדלקת נר שבת ומוצש״ק. וזה התמונה היא האריגינאלי מדפוס ראשון שנדפס מכתב יד:

סופר	חתם

וכלוח זה נהגו בעיר פרעשבורג ושאר קהלות בסלובקי׳ והונגרי׳ העליונה. וקהלות החרדיות במדינת אסטרי׳. וזה בערך כמו שנהגו כאן מכבר על ידי הועד הרבנים בעיר ניו יורק.

*) מקרוב באו אנשים לכאן שנהגו חומרי המקום שיצאו משם. לצאת מן השבת ע״ב מינוטין אחרי השקיעה — אדרבה ואדרבה, מי מעכב על ידם. תבא עליהם ברכה. אבל דא עקא שמצד השני הם מקילים לבא אל השבת ועושים מלאכה בפרהסיא עד אחרי השקיעה. וכאן נהגו למהר את השבת י״ח מינוטין קודם השקיעה. וזה מביא בלבול המחות ופירוד הלבבות בין החרדים. כי בשעה שזה יוצא להתפלל זה בא במקלו וכפונדתו לבית המרחץ. ואיך הם מתרצים המשנה — ״נותנים עליו חומרי המקום שהלך לשם. ואל ישנה אדם מפני המחלוקת״?

ועיקר דא עקא: כשהתחילו להפיץ חדושי חתם סופר הנ״ל הי׳ זה כעצם בגרונם. והרהיבו בנפשם לשלוח יד בתורת משה לקרוע הדף האחרון הנ״ל ולהדביק דף מזויף כזה:

סופר	חתם

וזה חוצפה גדולה ונוראה!!!

יש לנו טענה על החפשים שעשו שנויים ושמטו תפילות מהסדור. ולכאורה מה הבדל ישז כיון שניתן רשות למשחית כו׳ היום או מחר אם לא יהי׳ לרצון למי שהוא איזה פסק הלכה בשו״ע ישמיט או יזייף השו״ע. וזה עלול להביא חורבן לכל כתבי הקדש.

ובכן הננו מחאים בכל תוקף נגד הפסלות הלזו שהרהיבו בנפשם לשלוח יד בתורת משה, וכל בני ישראל ישמעו וידאו.

אנשי יראים וחרדים דוויליאמסבורג

Figure 3.5 Placard protesting against R. Moses Stern's censorship of R. Moses Sofer's commentary

Pointing to the terrible consequences of actions like that of Stern, they stated: 'Today or tomorrow if someone does not like a ruling in the *Shulḥan arukh*, he will omit it or forge the *Shulḥan arukh*.' They also accused the recent arrivals in New York, by which they meant the Hungarian hasidim who ended the Sabbath later than others, of performing labour after sunset on Friday evening.

To many, this will sound like a shocking accusation. After all, Jews assume that the Sabbath begins at sunset, so how could these pious Jews have been working after this time? Yet the truth is that in previous centuries it was standard practice in many places in Europe for people to continue to perform labour well after sunset on Friday. In some areas, this practice continued into the twentieth century,[90] and the placard against Stern is evidence that even in the post-Second World War years there were still some who started the Sabbath after sunset.

The post-sunset start to the Sabbath, in accord with Rabbenu Tam's view and adopted by the *Shulḥan arukh*,[91] assumes that *shekiah* ('sunset'), for the purposes of when the Sabbath starts, takes place a good deal later than what is usually regarded as sunset.[92] To give one example of many, R. Solomon Ganzfried's *Kitsur shulḥan arukh* states that the Sabbath candles can be lit until a half hour before darkness (i.e. night).[93] Since his definition of darkness was in accord with Rabbenu Tam's view,[94] half an hour before this is well after sunset. R. Jacob Lorberbaum (1760–1832), in his popular *Derekh haḥayim*, states that work must stop only 15 minutes before darkness.[95]

[90] See H. P. Benisch, *Hazemanim bahalakhah*, vol. ii, ch. 46. In the Vienna Schiffshul, founded by Sofer's son-in law, R. Solomon Spitzer, candle-lighting was after sunset, even in the years following the First World War. See R. Avraham Ya'akov Bombach's testimony in *Otserot hasofer*, 16 (2006), 74–5. See also R. Shmuel Wosner (b. 1913 in Vienna), *Shevet halevi*, vol. i, no. 47.

[91] *Shulḥan arukh*, 'Oraḥ ḥayim' 261: 2. Elsewhere in the *Shulḥan arukh* Karo seems to reject the opinion of Rabbenu Tam. See Greenwald, *Maharil uzemano*, 49; Ajdler, 'Talmudic Metrology VII', 28 ff.

[92] See H. P. Benisch, *Hazemanim bahalakhah*, vol. ii, chs. 46, 51; Harfenes, *Yisra'el vehazemanim*, 872 ff. See also William L. Gewirtz's series of Seforim Blog posts, 3 Feb. 2010, 7 Apr. 2010, 10 July 2010, 3 Aug. 2010.

[93] Ganzfried, *Kitsur shulḥan arukh*, 75: 1. See also E. Gruenwald, *Keren ledavid*, 'Oraḥ ḥayim', no. 79.

[94] See Braun, *She'arim metsuyanim bahalakhah*, 75: 1.

[95] Lorberbaum, *Derekh haḥayim hashalem*, 19*a* (*zeman hadlakat nerot*). R. Abraham Gombiner (*c.*1637–83), *Magen avraham*, 'Oraḥ ḥayim' 331: 2, also writes that sometimes they would not start the Sabbath until 15 minutes before darkness. This position is quoted without objection in Danzig *Ḥokhmat adam*, 149: 6. In *Magen avraham*, 'Oraḥ ḥayim' 235: 3, R. Gombiner gives a different formulation, stating that people would perform labour until approximately half an hour before darkness. See also Rabinowitz-Teomim, *Seder eliyahu*, 79, for his report of his visit to Galicia, where they did not light the Sabbath candles until כמעט קרוב ללילה.

The practice of beginning the Sabbath after sunset is pretty much extinct today, and had become significantly less common by the beginning of the twentieth century. There is no need here for me to examine how this came about, and why the viewpoint of the *ge'onim* (later adopted by the Vilna Gaon and R. Shneur Zalman of Lyady), which claims that the Sabbath begins at (or very close to) sunset and ends somewhat earlier than the time advocated by Rabbenu Tam, emerged victorious.[96] Suffice it to say that of all the developments in Jewish religious life in the past few hundred years, this is certainly one of the most important, as it involved a significant alteration of how the most significant aspect of Jewish life was practised. As Shlomo Sternberg put it: 'We are in the strange situation that as far as one of the most fundamental issues of *Halachah* is concerned, the onset of the Sabbath, universal Jewish practice today is contrary to the explicit ruling of the *Shulhan Aruch*. We also know that universal practice today is contrary to the common practice in Eastern Europe in the last [nineteenth] century.'[97] Acceptance of the *ge'onim*'s opinion about when the Sabbath begins and ends is also significant from another angle, as it means that today 'most people perform melakha [work] on Motza'ei Shabbat [Saturday evening] at a time when, according to most Rishonim [medieval rabbinic authorities] and the Shulchan Arukh, doing so constitutes a Shabbat violation, punishable with sekila [stoning].'[98]

I am aware of another example of Stern's censoring of Sofer's writings.[99] In Sofer's responsa on 'Oraḥ ḥayim', first published in Pressburg in 1855,[100] he refers to the Vilna Gaon as having emended a text, 'as was his wont' (*kedarko*) (Fig. 3.6(*a*)). In 1958, Sofer's responsa were reprinted by Stern, and as one can see in Figure 3.6(*b*), the word *kedarko* has been removed, no doubt because it was thought to be disrespectful to the Vilna Gaon.

Since R. Moses Sofer was censored when what he wrote was thought to be problematic, we can expect that the same thing would happen with his leading student, R. Moses Schick (1807–59). We have the testimony of R. Issachar

[96] See H. P. Benisch, *Hazemanim bahalakhah*, vol. ii, chs. 44–6. N. Kamenetsky, *Making of a Godol*, i. 657, quotes his father, R. Ya'akov Kamenetsky, as follows: 'Only the popularity of *Mishnah berurah* [first published in 1892 (5652), ninety-six years after the Gaon's demise!] which ruled that one must be very careful [יש ליזהר מאד] to refrain from all work immediately after sunset, led to the universal embrace of the Gaon's *psaq*' (brackets in original). See I. M. Hakohen, *Mishnah berurah*, 261: 23.

[97] Sternberg, 'Bein haShemashot', 18. Contrary to others who have written on the topic, Sternberg argues that Rabbenu Tam's opinion, later advocated by the *Shulḥan arukh*, was never adopted in practice in any medieval community. He believes that it was only in the second half of the 16th cent. that people began to do work and light Sabbath candles after sunset.

[98] Rimon, '"Tosefet Shabbat": Adding Time onto Shabbat'.

[99] This censorship was noted by Mazuz, *Arim nisi: yevamot*, 56.

[100] *She'elot uteshuvot ḥatam sofer*, vol. 1, 'Oraḥ ḥayim', no. 101.

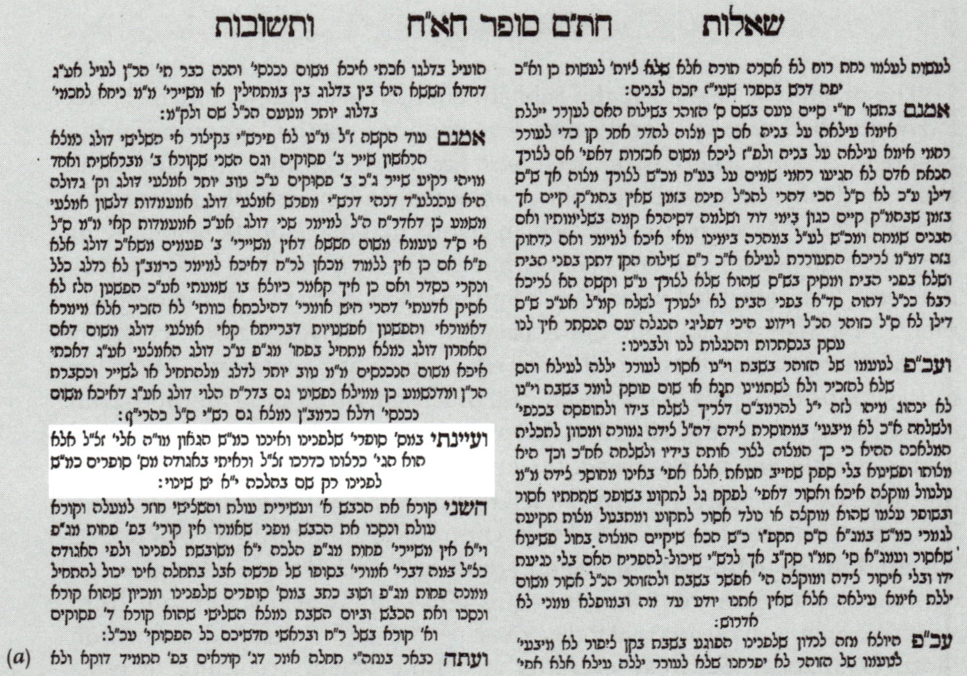

(a)

(b)

Figure 3.6 R. Moses Sofer, *She'elot uteshuvot ḥatam sofer*, vol. i, 'Oraḥ ḥayim', responsum no. 101: (*a*) Pressburg, 1855 edition, showing the uncensored version; (*b*) 1958 edition (New York: R. Moses Stern), with the word *kedarko* deleted

Solomon Teitchtal (1885–1945) that his father-in-law, R. Jacob Joseph Ginz (1854–1925), possessed the manuscripts of Schick's responsa. (Schick had been his teacher.) In one of these responsa, Schick explained that he did not recite the hymn 'Shalom aleikhem' on Friday night, because he followed the example of his teacher R. Moses Sofer, who also did not recite it. Schick offered the same reason to explain why, when his wife gave birth, he did not hang 'holy names' designed to protect her on the walls. When R. Jekutiel Judah Teitelbaum (1808–86), the rabbi of Sighet, saw these responsa in manuscript, he told Ginz that since the general practice was not in accord with what Schick wrote, these responsa should be omitted in order to protect Schick's honour, and that is what was done.[101] R. Meir Stein (d. 1933) further reports that he was shown twenty-two responsa from Schick that were not included with the responsa published after his death. The reason for this was that in these responsa Schick expressed a more tolerant attitude towards the Hungarian Status Quo communities than appears elsewhere in his writings.[102]

Turning to the Sephardi world, we find an example of censorship in the writings of R. Joseph Hayim of Baghdad (1832–1909). R. Joseph Hayim remains one of the most influential Sephardi halakhists, and is unusual in that he also wrote a halakhic work in the vernacular (Arabic), designed to be read by women.[103] In this book (ch. 17), he discussed the matter of women covering their hair, a practice whose obligatory nature has been the subject of some dispute in recent years.[104] The fundamental issue is whether there is an obligation for married women to cover their hair at all times and places, or only in a society in which this is the norm. According to the latter assumption,

[101] See J. H. Schwartz (ed.), *Zikaron lemosheh*, 173. For another example of censorship of Schick's responsa, see N. Ben-Menahem, 'Maḥaloket-Beregsas'.

[102] Status Quo is the 'term applied to those communities in Hungary which after the schism that occurred at the Hungarian General Jewish Congress of 1868–69 . . . did not join the Neologist organization or the Orthodox communities', *EJ* xv, col. 347, s.v. 'Status Quo Ante'. See Weingarten, 'Responsa That Were Concealed' (Heb.), 97. R. Solomon Tsevi Schück (1844–1916) had previously argued that R. Moses Schick's strong negative comments about the Status Quo communities (e.g. Schick, *She'elot uteshuvot maharam shik*, 'Oraḥ ḥayim', no. 307) were dictated by the needs of the hour, but were not permanently applicable. See Schück, *She'elot uteshuvot rashban*, vol. i, 'Oraḥ ḥayim', no. 62. In support of this assumption, Schück could have noted that in 1875 Schick sent a responsum to R. Jonah Tsevi Bernfeld (1834–91), the Status Quo rabbi of Debrecen (Schick, *She'elot uteshuvot maharam shik*, 'Yoreh de'ah', no. 170). It is clear from this letter, and especially from the titles given to Bernfeld, that Schick regarded him as a colleague no different from his other rabbinic colleagues. See also Ferziger, 'The Road Not Taken'.

[103] *Kanun al-nisa*. The title page says that it was printed in Livorno, but this is not correct. See Hayim, *Laws for Women*, 4 (unnumbered), where the matter is explained.

[104] See Broyde, 'Hair Covering and Jewish Law', 97–179.

פסקי הלכות

מרן הרב משה פיינשטיין
ר"מ דמתיבתא תפארת ירושלים

בענין הליכה במקל בשבת ויו"ט לסומא ולאדם שקשה לו לילך זולתו

יום א' כ"ה שבט שדמ"ח
לנכדי היקר חביבא דנפשאי הרה"ג מוהר"ר מרדכי טענדלער שליט"א
בברכת שלום וברכה וכט"ס.

בענין שאלתך אודות איזה אשה סומא בברא־פארק, ה' ישלח לה רפואה שלימה, אם מותרת לילך במקל ברה"ר בשבת.

הנה יש לעיין בענין הכללי של הליכה במקל בשבת ויו"ט לאינשי שקשה להם ללכת בלא מקל, דבש"ע או"ח סימן ש"א סעיף י"ז איפסק בחיגר שאפשר לו לילך זולתו היינו בלא מקל אסור, ופשוט שהוא אף שרק בקושי הולך בלא מקל נמי אסור דאי לא כן פשיטא דהרי הוא ככל אדם, אלא דאף שקשה לו ההליכה בלא מקל כיון דעכ"פ יכול לילך בם בלא מקל אסור לילך במקל, ובסעיף י"ח איפסק בחיגר שאפשר לו לילך זולתו היינו בלא מקל אסור, ופשוט שהוא אף שרק בקושי הולך בלא מקל נמי אסור דאי לא כן פשיטא דהרי הוא ככל אדם, אלא דאף שקשה לו ההליכה בלא מקל כיון דעכ"פ יכול לילך גם בלא מקל אסור לילך במקל, ובסעיף י"ח איפסק גם שסומא אסור לו לצאת במקל, והוא מגמ' ביצה דף כ"ה דת"ר אין הסומא יוצא במקלו ופרש"י דהרי דרך חול וזילותא דיו"ט הוא, וברא"ש שם איתא משום דהסומא אין לו צורך למקל להלוכו אלא לתרוצי סוגיא עביד, ובמג"א שם ס"ק כ"ח כתב בטעם איסור סומא כיון דיכול לילך בלא מקל, ונראה דהוא פירוש על טעם הרא"ש, אבל הא לכאורה תמוה מאחר דהיתר דאינו יכול לילך כלל בלא מקל הוא משום דכמנעלים דידיה חשיבא כמפורש ברא"ש שם, מ"ט לא יתחשבו גם כבמנעלים דידיה בשביל זה שיותר טוב לו לילך במקל מחמת כל איזו סיבה שהיא, נהי שמנעלים ממש אף כשניחא לו יותר לילך בלא מנעלים אלא יחף או בכריכת (*a*)

Figure 3.7 R. Moses Feinstein's responsum on the use of a walking stick on the Sabbath: (*a*) version published in the journal *Am hatorah* (1986) in which the words 'Boro Park' appear; (*b*) version in *Igerot mosheh*, vol. viii, 'Oraḥ ḥayim' 5: 19, in which the words 'Boro Park' have been deleted (Jerusalem: Rabbi D. Feinstein, 1996)

כ״ט, ומיהו אם הבת קטנה צ״ע אם יעשה הגדול חטא בשביל הקטן, דהא אין מצווין להפרישו וכו׳. ללכת חוץ לתחום בשבת לנקום נקמת אביו שרי [נימוקי הרמ״ה דיני בושת סימן כ״א], וצ״ע דהא לא עדיף מצורך מצווה, דאסור לילך חוץ לתחום.

נראה דהא דמקשה המג״א מהא שאין אומרים לאדם חטא כדי שיזכה חברך, הוא רק לענין איש אחר. אבל להאב הוא דין עצמו, שמחוייב מכל-שכן ממה שמפורש בקידושין דף ל׳ ע״ב דמחוייב להשיא לביתו. שלכן ודאי מחוייב לראות שתהיה אשה כשרה לדת ישראל, ופשוט שהוא אף בבת קטנה. ורק לאחרים שייך קושיא זו, וספקתו בס״ק כ״ט בקטנה. וספקת המג״א מחמת שאין מצווין להפרישה תמוה מאד, הא העיקר הוא שלא ישאר מומר בגדלותו, שבשביל זה וודאי מצווין להפרישו, אף לקטן, אם יבוא מזה גם לעבור בגדלותו, וצע״ג.

ומה שכתב ללכת חוץ לתחום לנקום נקמת אביו, פלא. וכי היכן מצינו שיש בכלל מצווה לנקום, אף שהוא לכבוד אביו. ואולי כוונתו בדין גואל הדם על שהרג את אביו, למאן דאמר (סנהדרין מ״ה ע״ב) מצווה בגואל הדם, וצע״ג.

סימן ש״ז

סעיף ח׳

דבר שאינו מלאכה וכו׳ מותר לישראל לומר לעכו״ם לעשותו בשבת, וכו׳, או מפני מצווה. ובהגה, ועי׳ לעיל סי׳ רע״ו ס״ב דיש מקילין אפילו במלאכה דאורייתא. ובט״ז סק״ד, כתב ב״י בשם הגמ״ר וכו׳, אבל אם אפשר לעשותו (ע״י ישראל) כגון בר״ה דיכול להביא ע״י מחיצות בני אדם, שריא אמירה לעכו״ם. והיכא דאיכא למימר דילמא אתי לאיחלופי בר״ה אסור אמירה לעכו״ם אפילו באיסור דרבנן, אפילו לדבר מצווה וכו׳, עכ״ל. והקשה ב״י על זה, שזה סותר מ״ש קודם לכן בסמוך, שאם אפשר לעשותו כגון בר״ה דיכול להביא ע״י מחיצת ב״א שרי, וצ״ע. ומר״ח ז״ל תירץ דזה מיירי מחצר לחצר שלא עירבו, ואתו לאחלופי להוציא מרה״י לר״ה, ושם ליכא תקנתא דמחיצה של בני אדם, דאסור אמירה לעכו״ם, עכ״ל. ולעד״נ דמחיצת בני אדם מועלת גם ברשות הרבים לעניין הוצאה מרשות היחיד, דכל שעומדים ב״א מן הפתח היוצא לרשות הרבים ולהלן, ה״ל כל אותו צד שבין האנשים כרה״י, וא״כ מותר להוציא לשם מרה״י, כדין מרה״י לרה״י.

לכאורה יש לומר כוונת הב״ח, דמחיצה של אנשים מועיל ברשות הרבים. וכן יודה שמועיל גם מרשות היחיד לרשות הרבים, אם היה מחיצה של בני אדם. אבל אין מועיל מחיצה של בני אדם, מרשות היחיד לרשות היחיד שלא עירבו, משום שעכ״פ הוא רשות אחר, אף שעשה עוד מחיצה בתוכה. ולא שיטעה לחלק בין אמצע רשות הרבים, לבין מרשות היחיד לרשות הרבים, ולא קשיא לפי זה קושית הט״ז. ואף שימצא שיהיה חמור מרשות היחיד לרשות היחיד, מאשר מרשות היחיד לרשות הרבים, אינו כלום, דאזלינן בתר טעמא.

סעיף ד׳

אסור לחשוב חשבונות, אפילו אם עברו, כגון כך וכך הוצאתי על דבר פלוני, ודווקא שעדיין שכר הפועלים אצלו, אבל אם פרעם כבר, מותר.

עדיין שכר הפועלים אצלו, לכאורה איירי שלא ישתנה כלום מצד מחשבתו, משום שידוע כמה חייב להפועלים. ומכל מקום אסור, מאחר שעדיין שייך לחשוב בזה, ואינו כדבר העבר לגמרי. דלא כדראיתי באיזה מקום, שהוא דווקא משום דאפשר שישתנה על ידי חשבונותיו.

סימן יט

סומא אם מותר לצאת במקל בשבת

יום א׳ כ״ה שבט שדמ״ת

למע״כ נכדי היקר הרה״ג מוהר״ר מרדכי טענדלער שליט״א.

בעניין מה ששאלת אודות אשה סומית, ה׳ ישלח לה רפואה שלמה במהרה, אם מותרת לילך במקל ברה״ר בשבת.

הנה בעצם העניין דהליכה במקל בשבת וי״ט לאינשי שקשה להם ללכת בלא מקל, בשו״ע או״ח סימן ש״א סעיף י״ז איפסק בחיגר שאפשר לו לילך זולתו, היינו בלא מקל, דאסור. ופשוט שהוא אף שרק בקושי הולך בלא מקל, נמי אסור. דאי לא כן, פשיטא, דהרי הוא ככל אדם. אלא דאף שקשה לו ההליכה בלא מקל, כיון דעכ״פ יכול לילך גם בלא מקל, אסור לילך במקל. ובסעיף י״ח איפסק גם שסומא אסור לו לצאת במקל, והוא מגמ׳ ביצה דף כ״ה ע״ב, דת״ר אין הסומא יוצא במקלו. ופרש״י, דהווי דרך חול, וזילותא די״ט הוא. ובראש״ש שם (סי׳ ה׳) איתא משום דהסומא אין לו צורך למקל להילוכו, אלא לתרוצי סוגיא עביד. ובמג״א שם ס״ק כ״ח, כתב בטעם איסור סומא, כיון דיכול לילך בלא מקל, ונראה דהוא פירוש על טעם הרא״ש.

אבל הא לכאורה תמוה, מאחר דההיתר דאינו יכול לילך כלל בלא מקל, הוא משום דכמנעלים דידיה חשיבא, כמפורש ברא״ש שם, מ״ט לא יתחשבו גם כמנעלים דידיה בשביל זה שיותר טוב לו לילך במקל, מחמת איזו סיבה שהיא. וי״ל דנהי שמנעלים ממש, אף כשניחא לו יותר לילך בלא מנעלים, אלא יחף, או בכריכת סדין וכדומה, נמי מותר לצאת במנעלים - הוא משום דמנעלים הוא לבוש. שלבד עניין הליכה, הוא בגד ככל בגדים. אבל המקל, שאין בו עניין לבישה, וכל עניין חשיבות בגד הוא מצד

when women generally go around with uncovered heads, there is no such obligation.

R. Joseph Hayim states that in Europe married Jewish women generally did not cover their hair.[105] He quotes the justification offered by European Jews that since all women, Jewish and non-Jewish, go about with uncovered hair, this does not arouse sexual thoughts in men. He concludes: 'These are their words which they answer for this practice, and we do not have a reply to push off this answer of theirs.'[106] In other words, R. Joseph Hayim acknowledges that the practice of European Jewish women to go around with uncovered hair can be justified, and is not to be regarded as sinful. When R. Joseph Hayim's book was translated into Hebrew,[107] the sentence just quoted was deleted. By doing so, a significant halakhic opinion was removed from the public eye—exactly the aim of the censor.[108]

R. Sofer, R. Schick, and R. Joseph Hayim were among the leading halakhic authorities in the nineteenth century, with R. Joseph Hayim also continuing into the first years of the twentieth century. R. Moses Feinstein and R. Shlomo Zalman Auerbach (1910–95) held these roles in the second half of the twentieth century. As with their predecessors, both of them were also to suffer from censorship. Feinstein is known for his refusal to countenance the establishment of an *eruv* in any part of Brooklyn, although there is a great deal of dispute over how strong this opposition was. The main argument of those who see Feinstein as an uncompromising opponent is that he regarded Brooklyn as a real *reshut harabim* (public thoroughfare), meaning that an *eruv* cannot be established there.[109]

Yet in a 1984 responsum, concerning the use of a walking stick by a blind woman in Boro Park, Brooklyn, Feinstein explicitly states, in his conclusion, that today there is almost no real *reshut harabim*. From here we see that, at least in this responsum, when it came to carrying on the Sabbath he did not regard Brooklyn as a *reshut harabim*. The beginning of the responsum is shown in Figure 3.7(*a*), as it appeared in the journal *Am hatorah*.[110] When it was reprinted in a posthumously published volume of *Igerot mosheh*, the collection of Feinstein's responsa,[111] the reference to Boro Park was omitted (see Fig. 3.7(*b*)). This was apparently done in order to create the fiction that Feinstein was adamant about Brooklyn being a *reshut harabim*. The appear-

105 What follows is taken from Sasson, 'The Ben Ish Hai and Women's Hair Covering'.

106 Translation ibid. (with slight changes).

107 Hayim, *Ḥukei hanashim*.

108 Sasson also calls attention to ideologically based additions to the text in the English translation of the book, *Laws for Women*.

109 Feinstein himself stated on a number of occasions that Brooklyn is a *reshut harabim*. See the sources in *Igerot mosheh* cited in the Eruv Online blog, at <eruvonline.blogspot.com>, 23 Jan. 2006.

110 *Am hatorah*, 11 (1986).

111 Vol. viii, 'Oraḥ ḥayim' 5: 19.

ance of 'Boro Park' in the responsum would have created problems for this position, but these disappear once 'Boro Park' is deleted.[112]

R. Shlomo Zalman Auerbach is reported to have said that if a person is troubled by something, he can tell his spouse all the details, including mentioning other people by name. According to Auerbach, in such a case one need not be concerned with the issue of *leshon hara* (malicious gossip). The 'problem' with this ruling is that no such leniency was ever mentioned in earlier sources. Furthermore, R. Israel Meir Hakohen (1838–1933), the Hafets Hayim, whose formulation of the relevant *halakhot* has achieved widespread acceptance, explicitly forbids *leshon hara* between spouses.[113] Rather than point out that in this matter Auerbach differed from the Hafets Hayim, it was easier to simply censor Auerbach's viewpoint when the work it originally appeared in was reprinted in a new edition.[114]

Since I have just mentioned the Hafets Hayim, the following point is also worth noting. In his son R. Aryeh Leib Cohen's biography of the Hafets Hayim, he describes his own involvement in the writing of the *Mishnah berurah*, a work that became the most influential halakhic text in modern times.[115] He also notes that this explains some contradictions in the work, since what

[112] This example was noted by Eruv Online, at <eruvonline.blogspot.com>, 10 Oct. 2005. See also ibid., 23 Jan. 2006.

[113] I. M. Hakohen, *Ḥafets ḥayim*, 49, 153–4, 156 ('Hilkhot leshon hara' 1: 8 (in the *Be'er mayim ḥayim* section), 8: 10, 14). Much of what the Hafets Hayim includes in his halakhic codification of *leshon hara* was not regarded by earlier sources as having real halakhic standing. See Brown, 'From Principles to Rules'. Not noted by Brown is R. Jacob Emden's view that you can speak *leshon hara* about someone who has 'sinned' against you. See his note on Mishnah *Avot* 1: 17 in the Vilna Romm edition of the Talmud, and the complete version of this note (from manuscript) published in Emden, *Megilat sefer*, 6 (first pagination). For R. Abraham Isaac Kook's rejection of Emden's point, see Kampinski, *Bein shenei kohanim gedolim*, 137.

[114] See Baris, 'Place and Identity' (Heb.), 299 n. 62; Eliyahu, '*Leshon hara* between Husband and Wife' (Heb.). R. Mordechai Gross accepts Auerbach's view. See Gross, *Om ani ḥomah*, vol. ii, no. 87. Gross reports that the Hazon Ish also held this opinion. See also R. Hayim Rabi's letter in Y. Cohen, *Ukeneh lekha ḥaver*, 632–4. Even the Hafets Hayim held out the possibility that some examples of *leshon hara* between husband and wife (and even others) might be permissible, as he writes: ואפשר דהוא הדין אם כונתו בספורו להפג את דאגתו מלבו, הוי כמכוין לתועלת על להבא, in I. M. Hakohen, *Ḥafets ḥayim*, 180 ('Hilkhot leshon hara' 10: 14 in the note). This means that Auerbach's lenient position is not that distant from the Hafets Hayim's, since Auerbach himself certainly never permitted purely malicious *leshon hara*. See Y. Cohen, *Ukeneh lekha ḥaver*, 640.

For a responsum by Auerbach that was altered by the family because it appeared too 'Zionist', placing the State of Israel in the halakhic category of *malkhut yisra'el* (Jewish sovereignty), see Mashiah, *Rabbi Shlomo Zalman Auerbach's Halakhic Philosophy* (Heb.), 162 ff. Regarding censorship in Auerbach's writings dealing with the laws of the sabbatical year, in particular the *heter mekhirah*, see Guttel, 'Heaven Forbid This Should Be Done' (Heb.); Chaim Rapoport's Seforim Blog post, 23 Oct. 2007; Yitzchak Jacobovitz's Seforim Blog post, 31 July 2008.

[115] Introduction to I. M. Hakohen, *Mikhtevei harav ḥafets ḥayim*, 42–3.

he wrote did not always agree with what his father had written. Not only was this passage removed from at least one printing of the biography,[116] but after it had appeared in the first edition of R. Yehoshua Yeshayah Neuwirth's (1927–2013) classic *Shemirat shabat kehilkhatah*, Neuwirth deleted it from all subsequent editions.[117]

Earlier I mentioned the responsa volume *Besamim rosh*. While the book's responsa are attributed to R. Asher ben Yehiel and other great medieval scholars, the work actually has a Reformist tendency and is aimed at undermining traditional Judaism. However, this was not apparent to all, which explains how the book became accepted by much of the rabbinic world.[118] Even with the book's acceptance, two responsa stood out as particularly shocking, so that when the volume was published for the second time in Kraków in 1881, they were removed.[119] The first responsum is no. 345. Here we learn that it is no sin to commit suicide if one feels that life is too difficult or even because of poverty, as these circumstances could lead one to sin. The Jewish opposition to suicide, we are told, is only directed against 'philosophical' suicides. The other responsum, no. 375, offers guidelines on when travel in a carriage is permitted on the Sabbath. It is actually not as radical as a number of other responsa in *Besamim rosh* that one might have assumed would also have been excised.[120] Yet this topic was very relevant at the time of the censorship, and religious laxity in this area would have had significant consequences.

As we have seen throughout this chapter, there are those who censor halakhic positions they find objectionable. While they sometimes do this by actually deleting material from books, the most common way is simply not to mention these opinions in halakhic discussions. However, R. Shlomo Zalman Auerbach felt that this too was unacceptable, and he stated that articles on halakhic topics should not omit lenient opinions.[121] Similarly, R. Hayim Kanievsky instructed the publisher of a new volume of writings

[116] See Benayahu, *Yosef beḥiri*, 376 n. 24.

[117] See Schacter, 'Facing the Truths of History', 225. There were many halakhically substantive changes between the first and later editions of Neuwirth's book. See the references at <www.menachemmendel.net> in the blog entry for 11 June 2013.

[118] I hope to discuss *Besamim rosh* and the rabbinic reactions to it in a future article. In the meantime, the relevant secondary literature is referred to in Fishman, 'Forging Jewish Memory'.

[119] It is said that the hasidic leader R. Ezekiel Halberstamm of Shinova was responsible for this. See Z. Y. Abramowitz, '*Besamim rosh* in a Hasidic Mirror' (Heb.), 58.

[120] To give just one example, see no. 348, which totally rejects the prohibition of *kitniyot* on Passover and suggests that it arose due to Karaite influence. Regarding Karaites and halakhic censorship, see Glick, *Window* (Heb.), 268, which notes that a responsum of R. David Ibn Zimra was deleted from an edition of R. Betsalel Ashkenazi's (*c*.1520–*c*.1594) responsa because of its moderate position regarding the Karaites.

[121] See Stepansky, *Ve'alehu lo yibol*, ii. 216.

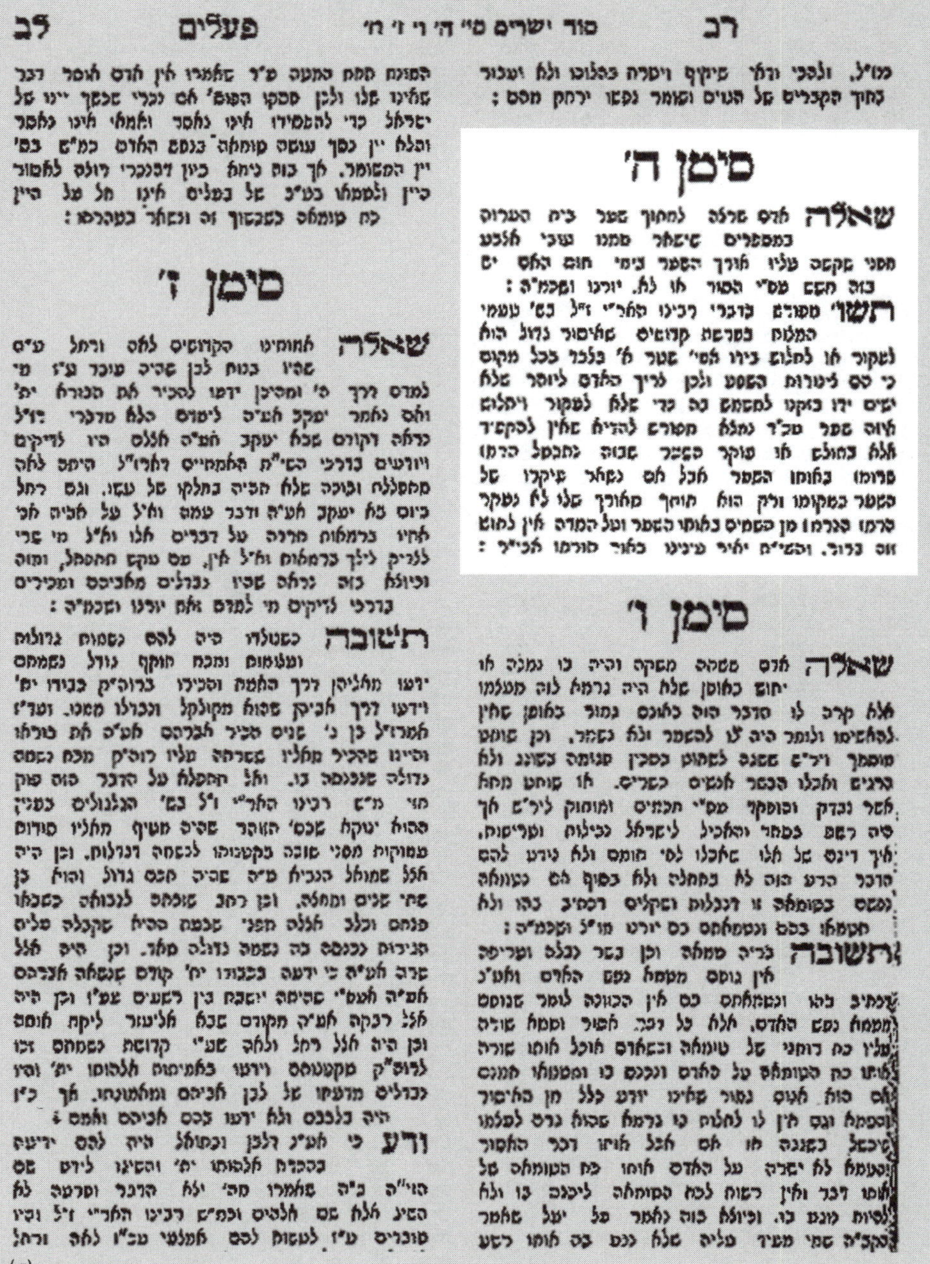

רב סוד ישרים סי׳ ה׳ ו׳ ז׳ ח׳ פעלים לב

מו״ל, ולפי ודאי שיקוף ויסריח בהלוכו ולא יעבור
בתוך הקברים של הגוים ושומר נפשו ירחק מהם ;

סימן ה׳

שאלה אדם שרוצה לחתוך שער בית הערוה
במספרים שישאר ממנו שיעור אצבע
מפני שקשה עליו אורך השער בימי חום האם יש
בזה חשש עפ״י הסוד או לא. יורנו ושכמ״ה :

תשובה מפורש בדברי רבינו האר״י ז״ל בס׳ טעמי
המצות בפרשת קדושים שאיסור גדול הוא
לעקור או לתלוש בידו אפי׳ שער א׳ בלבד בכל מקום
כי יש ליניקות השפע ולכן צריך האדם ליזהר שלא
ישים ידו בזקנו למשמש בה כדי שלא לעקור ויתלוש
ואזה שער שכ״ד נמצא מפורש להדיא שאין להקפיד
אלא בתולש או עוקר השער שבזה נתבטל הכחו
שרשו באותו השער אבל אם נשאר עיקרו של
השער במקומו ורק הוא תוחך מאורך שלו לא נעקר
שרשו ושרשו מן השמים באותו השער ועל המדה אין לחוש
זה כלל. והשי״ת יאיר עינינו באור תורתו אכי״ר :

סימן ו׳

שאלה אדם ששהה משקה והיה בו נמלה או
יתוש באופן שלא היה נראה לנו מתחלתו
אלא קרב לו הדבר הזה כאונס גמור באופן שאין
לאפשרו ולגמור היה לו להשמר ולא נשמר. וכן שוחט
שוחט ויר״ש שהגה לשחוט בסכין פגומה בשוגג ולא
הרגיש ואכלו הבשר אנשים כשרים. או שוחט מתא
אשר נבדק ונפסק עפ״י חכמים ומוחזק ליר״ש אך
היה רשע בסתר והאכיל לישראל נבילות וטריפות,
איך דינם של אלו שאכלו לפי תומם ולא נודע להם
הדבר הרע הזה לא בתחלה ולא בסוף אם נגעו
נפשם בטומאה זו דנבלות ושקצים דכתיב בהו ולא
תטמאו בהם ונטמאתם בם יורנו מו״ל ושכמ״ה ;

תשובה נבילה טמאה וכן בשר נבלה וטריפה
אין גורם טמאת נפש האדם ואע״ג
שכתיב בהו ונטמאתם בם אין הכוונה לומר שגורם
טמאת נפש האדם, אלא על דבר איסור וטמא עולה
עליו כח רוחני של טומאה ובאדם אוכל אותו שורה
אותו כח הטומאה על האדם ונכנס בו ומטמאו אמנם
אם הוא אנוס נגמר שאינו יודע כלל מן האיסור
וטמאה וגם אין לו לחוש כי גרמא שהוא גרם לעצמו
שיכשל בשגגה או אם אכל אותו דבר האסור
וטומאה לא ישרה על האדם אותו כח הטומאה של
אותו דבר ואין רשות לכח הטומאה ליכנס בו ולא
לנסות מגע בו. וכיוצא בזה נאמר אל יעל שאמר
הקב״ה שמי מעיד עליה שלא נכנס בה אותו רשע

הטומאה משם נתעה ע״ד שאמרו אין אדם אוסר דבר
שאינו שלו ולכן פסקו הפוס׳ אם נכרי שנסך יינו של
ישראל כדי להפסידו אינו נאסר ואמאי אינו נאסר
והלא יין נסך עושה טומאה בנפש האדם כמ״ש בס׳
יין המשומר. אך בזה ניחא כיון דהנכרי רוצה לאסור
היין ולטמאו בע״כ של בעלים אינו חל על היין
כח טומאה כשנסך זה וכאשר בארנו :

סימן ז׳

שאלה אמותינו הקדושים לאה ורחל ע״ה
שהיו בנות לבן שהיה עובד ע״ז מי
למדם דרך ה׳ ומהיכן ידעו להכיר את הבורא ית׳
ואם נאמר יעקב אע״ה לימדם הלא מדברי רז״ל
נראה דקודם שבא יעקב אע״ה אצלם היו צדיקים
ויודעים בדרכי השי״ת האמהיים דאמר״ל הימה לאה
מתפללת ובוכה שלא תהיה בחלקו של עשו. וגם רחל
כיום בא יעקב אע״ה ודבר עמה וא״ל על אביה אני
אחיו ברמאות אמרה על דברים אלו וא״ל מי שרי
לצדיק ליהך ברמאות וא״ל אין, עם עקש תתפתל, ומזה
וכיוצא בזה נראה שהיו גדולים מאביהם ומכירים
בדרכי צדיקים מי למדם את יורנו ושכמ״ה :

תשובה כשנולדו היה להם נשמות גדולות
ועצומות ונכח תוקף גודל נשמתם
ידעו מאליהן דרך האמת והכירו ברוה״ק בבורא ית׳
וידעו דרך אביהן שהוא מקולקל ונבדלו ממנו. ועד״ז
אמרז״ל בן ג׳ שנים הכיר אברהם אע״ה את בוראו
והיינו שהכיר מאליו שהרחה עליו רוה״ק מכח נשמה
גדולה שנכנסה בו. וא״ל והתפלא על הדבר הזה שוק
ממ״ש רבינו האר״י ז״ל בס׳ הגלגולים כענין
שהוא יעקב שבס׳ הזוהר שהיה מטיף מאליו סודות
עמוקות מפני שובה בקטנותו לנשמה דגדולות. וכן היה
אצל שמואל הנביא ע״ה שהיה חכם גדול והוא בן
שתי שנים ומחצה, וכן רחב שזכתה לנבואה כשבאו
פנחס וכלב אצלה מפני שבמה הבית שקבלה עליה
הגרים נכנסה בה נשמה גדולה מאד. וכן היה אצל
שרה אע״ה כי ידעה בכבודו ית׳ קודם שנשאה אברהם
אע״ה אעפ״י שהיתה יושבת בין רשעים עש״ו וכן היה
אצל רבקה אע״ה מקודם שבא אליעזר ליקח אותה
וכן היה אצל רחל ולאה שע״י קדושת נשמתם זכו
לרוה״ק מקטנותם וידעו באמיתות אלהותו ית׳ והיו
נבדלים מדעתו של לבן אביהם ומאמונותיו. אך כ״ז
היה בלבבם ולא ידעו בהם אביהם ואמם :

ודע כי אע״ג דלבן ובתואל היה להם ידיעה
בהכרת אלהותו ית׳ והשיגו לידע שם
הוי״ה ב״ה שאמרו מה׳ יצא הדבר ופרעה לא
השיג אלא שם אלהים וכמ״ש רבינו האר״י ז״ל והיו
עובדים ע״ז לעשות להם אמצעי עכ״ו לאה ורחל

(*a*)

Figure 3.8 R. Joseph Hayim, *Rav pe'alim*, vol. iv, 'Sod yesharim', no. 5, in which he permits the trimming of beards: (*a*) Jerusalem, 1912 edition, uncensored; (*b*) (on page 116) undated reprint, censored version; (*c*) (on page 117) Jerusalem, 1980 edition (no publisher given), where responsum no. 5 has been omitted and the responsa renumbered

כנז"ל. ולהכי ודאי שיקיף ויטרח בהלוכו ולא יעבור בתוך הקברים של הגוים ושומר נפשו ירחק מהם:

סימן ה'

סימן ו'

שאלה אדם ששתה משקה והיה בו נמנה או יחוש באופן שלא היה גרמא לזה מעצמו אלא קרה לו הדבר הזה באונס גמור באופן שאין להאשימו ולומר היה לו להשמר ולא נשמר. וכן שוחט מוסמך וירא שמים שגגה לשחוט בסכין פגומה בשוגג ולא הרגיש ואכלו הבשר אנשים כשרים. או שוחט מתא אשר נבדק והופקד עפ"י חכמים ומוחזק לירא שמים אך היה רשע בסתר והאכיל לישראל נבילות וטריפות. איך דינם של אלו שאכלו לפי תומם ולא נודע להם הדבר הרע הזה לא בתחלה ולא בסוף אם נטמאה נפשם בטומאה זו דנבלות ושקצים דכתיב בהו ולא תטמאו בהם ונטמאתם בם יורנו מו"ל ושכמ"ה:

תשובה בריה טמאה וכן בשר נבלה וטריפה אין גופם מטמא נפש האדם ואע"ג דכתיב בהו ונטמאתם בם אין הכוונה לומר שגופם מטמא נפש האדם. אלא כל דבר אסור וטמא שורה עליו כח רוחני של טומאה וכשאדם אוכל אותו שורה אותו כח הטומאה על האדם ונכנס בו ומטמאו אמנם אם הוא אנוס גמור שאינו יודע כלל מן האיסור והטמא וגם אין לו לתלות בו גרמא שהוא גרם לעצמו שיכשל בשגגה אז אם אכל אותו דבר האסור והטמא לא ישרה על האדם אותו. כח הטומאה של אותו דבר ואין רשות לכח הטומאה ליכנס בו ולא להיות נוגע בו. וכיוצא בזה נאמר על יעל שאמר הקב"ה שמי מעיד עליה שלא נגע בה אותו רשע והדבר יפלא והלא ז' בעילות בעל אך הענין כי בעילות שלו מאחר שהיו באונס גמור לא נגע בה כח הקליפה והרע של הזוהמא שלו ולא שרתה הקליפה עליה:

וכה"ג הפליתי בס"ד על מ"ש רז"ל המניח אוכל תחת המטה ששורה עליו רוח רעה. ואמרתי אם הניח אדם אוכל של חבירו תחת המטה שלא בידיעתו וזה המניח הוא איש זר שאינו בנו ולא אשתו ולא עבדו של בעל האוכל כדי שנאמר ידם כידו אין שורה עליו רוח רעה האמור על אוכל המונח תחת המטה ע"ד שאמרו אין אדם אוסר דבר שאינו שלו ולכן פסקו הפוס' אם נכרי שכשך יינו של ישראל כדי להפסידו אינו נאסר ואמאי אינו נאסר והלא יין נסך עושה טומאה בנפש האדם כמ"ש בס' יין המשומר. אך בזה ניחא כיון דהנכרי רוצה לאסור היין ולטמאו בע"כ של בעלים אינו חל על היין כח טומאה בשכשוך זה ונשאר בטהרתו:

סימן ז'

שאלה אמותינו הקדושים לאה ורחל ע"ה שהיו בנות לבן שהיה עובד ע"ז מי למדם דרך ה' ומהיכן ידעו להכיר את הבורא ית' ואם נאמר יעקב אע"ה לימדם הלא מדברי רז"ל נראה דקודם שבא יעקב אע"ה אצלם היו צדיקים ויודעים בדרכי הש"ת האמתיים דארז"ל היתה לאה מתפללת ובוכה שלא תהיה בחלקו של עשו. וגם רחל ביום בא יעקב אע"ה ודבר עמה וא"ל על אביה אני אחיו ברמאות חרדה על דברים אלו וא"ל מי שרי לצדיק לילך ברמאות וא"ל אין, עם עקש תתפתל, ומזה וכיוצא בזה נראה שהיו גדלים מאביהם ומכירים בדרכי צדיקים מי למדם זאת יורנו ושכמ"ה:

תשובה כשנולדו היה להם נשמות גדולות ועצומות ומכח תוקף גודל נשמתם ידעו מאליהן דרך האמת והכירו ברוה"ק כבודו ית' וידעו דרך אביהן שהוא מקולקל ונבדלו ממנו. ועד"ז אמרז"ל בן ג' שנים הכיר אברהם אע"ה את בוראו והיינו שהכיר מאליו ששרתה עליו רוה"ק מכח נשמה גדולה שנכנסה בו. ואל תתפלא על הדבר הזה פוק חזי מ"ש רבינו האר"י ז"ל בש' הגלגולים בענין ההוא ינוקא שבס' הזוהר שהיה מטיף מאליו סודות עמוקות מפני שזכה בקטנותו לנשמה דגדלות. וכן היה אצל שמואל הנביא ע"ה שהיה חכם גדול והוא בן שתי שנים ומחצה. וכן רחב שזכתה לנבואה כשבאו פנחס וכלב אצלה מפני שבעת ההיא שקבלה עליה הגירות נכנסה בה נשמה גדולה מאד. וכן היה אצל שרה אע"ה כי ידעה בכבודו ית' קודם שנשאה אברהם אע"ה אעפ"י שהיתה יושבת בין רשעים עע"ז וכן היה אצל רבקה אע"ה מקודם שבא אליעזר ליקח אותה וכן היה אצל רחל ולאה שע"י קדושת נשמתם זכו לרוה"ק מקטנותם וידעו באמיתות אלהותו ית' והיו נבדלים מדעתו של לבן אביהם ומאמונתו. אך כ"ז היה בלבבם ולא ידע בהם אביהם ואמם:

ודע כי אע"ג דלבן ובתואל היה להם ידיעה בהכרת אלהותו ית' והשיגו לידע שם הוי"ה ב"ה שאמרו מה' יצא הדבר ופרעה לא השיג אלא שם אלהים וכמ"ש רבינו האר"י ז"ל והיו עובדים ע"ז לעשות להם אמצעי עכ"ז לאה ורחל לא למדו מלבן כלום אלא ידיעתם היתה ברוה"ק מקטנותם מתמת גודל קדושת נשמתם:

סימן ח'

שאלה למה דוד הע"ה לא נכתב שמו בתוספת יו"ד אלא רק בדברי הימים ובשיר השירים שהם בכלל כתובים אבל בנביאים לא נכתב בו יו"ד יורנו ושכמ"ה:

תשובה

(b)

גדי"ל. ולהכי ודאי שיקיף ויערה בכללו ולא יעבור בתוך הקברים של הגוים ושומר נפשו ירחק מהם :

סימן ה'.

שאלה. אדם ששתה משקה והיה בו נמלה או יתוש באופן שלא היה גרמא לזה מעצמו אלא קרה לו הדבר הזה באונס גמור באופן שאין להאשימו ולומר היה לו להשמר ולא נשמר. וכן שוחט מוסמך ויר"ש שטעה לשחוט בסכין פגומה בשוגג לא הרגיש ואכלו הבשר אנשים כשרים. או שוחט מתא אשר נבדק והופקד עפ"י חכמים ומוחזק ליר"ש אך היה רשע בסתר והאכיל לישראל נבילות וטריפות. איך דינם של אלו שאכלו לפי תומם ולא נודע להם הדבר ברע הזה לא בתחלה ולא בסוף אם נטמאה נפשם בטומאה זו דנבלות ושקצים דכתיב בהו ולא תטמאו בהם ונטמאתם בם יורנו מו"ל ושכמ"ה :

תשובה. בריה טמאה וכן בשר נבלה וטריפה אין גופם מטמא נפש האדם ואע"ג דכתיב בהו ונטמאתם בם אין הכוונה לומר שגופם מטמא נפש האדם. אלא כל דבר אסור וטמא שורה עליו כח רוחני של טומאה וכשהאדם אוכל אותו שורה אותו כח הטומאה על האדם ונכנס בו ומטמאו אמנם אם הוא אנוס גמור שאינו יודע כלל מן האיסור והטמא וגם אין לו לתלות בו גרמא שהוא גרם לעצמו שיכשל בשגגה או אם אכל אותו דבר האסור והטמא לא ישרה על האדם אותו כח הטומאה של אותו דבר ואין רשות לכח הטומאה ליכנס בו ולא להיות נוגע בו. וכיוצא בזה נאמר על יעל שאמר הקב"ה שמי מעיד עליה שלא נגע בה אותו רשע והדבר יפלא והלא ז' בעילות בעל אך הענין כי בעילות שלו מאחר שהיו באונס גמור לא נגע בה כח הקליפה והרע של זוהמת שלו ולא שרתה הקליפה עליה :

וכ"הג. העליתי בס"ד על מ"ש רז"ל המניח אוכל תחת המטה ששורה עליו רוח רעה. ואמרתי אם הניח אדם אוכל של חבירו תחת המטה שלא בידיעתו וזה המניח הוא איש זר שאינו בנו ולא אשתו ולא עבדו של בעל האוכל כדי שנאמר ידם כידו אין שורה עליו רוח רעה האמור על אוכל המונח תחת המטה ע"ד שאמרו אין אדם אוסר דבר שאינו שלו ולכן פסקו הפוס' אם נכרי שכשך יינו של ישראל כדי להפסידו אינו נאסר ואמאי אינו נאסר והלא יין נסך עושה טומאה בנפש האדם כמ"ש בס' יין המשומר. אך בזה ניחא כיון דהנכרי רוצה לאסור היין ולטמאו בע"כ של בעלים אינו חל על היין כח טומאה בשכשוך זה ונשאר בטהרתו :

סימן ו'.

שאלה. אמותינו הקדושות לאה ורחל ע"ה שהיו בנות לבן שהיה עובד ע"ז מי למדם דרך ה' ומהיכן ידעו להכיר את הבורא ית' ואם נאמר יעקב אע"ה לימדם הלא מדברי רז"ל נראה דקודם שבא יעקב אע"ה אצלם היו צדיקים ויודעים בדרכי השי"ת האמתיים דאחז"ל היתה לאה מתפללת ובוכה שלא תהיה בחלקו של עשו. וגם רחל ביום בא יעקב אע"ה ודבר עמה וא"ל על אביה אני אחיו ברמאות הרבה על דברים אלו וא"ל מי שרי לצדיק לילך ברמאות וא"ל אין, עם עקש תתפתל, ומזה וכיוצא בזה נראה שהיו נבדלים מאביהם ומכירים בדרכי צדיקים מי למדם זאת יורנו ושכמ"ה :

תשובה. כשנולדו היה להם נשמות גדולות ועצומות ומכח תוקף גודל נשמתם ידעו מאליהן דרך האמת והכירו ברוה"ק כבודו ית' וידעו דרך אביהן שהוא מקולקל ונבדלו ממנו. ועד"ז אמרז"ל בן ג' שנים הכיר אברהם אע"ה את בוראו והיינו שהכיר מאליו שרתה עליו רוה"ק מכח נשמה גדולה שנכנסה בו. ואל תתפלא על הדבר הזה פוק חזי מ"ש רבינו האר"י ז"ל בס' הגלגולים בענין ההוא ינוקא שבס' הזוהר שהיה מגיד מאליו סודות עמוקות מפני שזכה בקטנותו לנשמה דגדלות. וכן היה אצל שמואל הנביא ע"ה שהיה חכם גדול והוא בן שתי שנים ומחצה. וכן רחב שזכתה לנבואה כשבאו פנחס וכלב אצלה מפני שבעת הביאה שקבלה עליה הגירות נכנסה בה נשמה גדולה מאד. וכן היה אצל שרה אע"ה כי ידעה בכבודו ית' קודם שנשאה אברהם אע"ה אעפ"י שהיתה יושבת בין רשעים עע"ז וכן היה אצל רבקה אע"ה מקודם שבא אליעזר ליקח אותה וכן היה אצל רחל ולאה שע"י קדושת נשמתם זכו לרוה"ק מקטנותם וידעו באמיתות אלהותו ית' והיו נבדלים מדעתו של לבן אביהם ומאמונתו. אך כ"ז היה בלבבם לא ידעו בהם אביהם ואמם.

ודע כי אע"ג דלבן ובתואל היה להם ידיעה בהכרת אלהותו ית' והשיגו לידע שם הוי"ה ב"ה שאמרו מה' יצא הדבר ופרעה לא השיג אלא שם אלהים וכמ"ש רבינו האר"י ז"ל והיו עובדים ע"ז לעבות להם אמלאי עכ"ז לאה ורחל לא למדו מלבן כלום אלא ידיעתם היתה ברוה"ק מקטנותם מחמת גודל קדושת נשמתם :

סימן ז'.

שאלה למה דוד המע"ה לא נכתב שמו בתוספת יו"ד אלא רק בדברי הימים ובשיר השירים שהם בכלל כתובים אבל בנביאים נכתב בו יו"ד יורנו ושכמ"ה :

תשובה

(c)

by R. Yehiel Mikhel Epstein (1829–1908) to include everything, including his permission to turn on electric lights on festivals.[122]

Let me conclude with a case that has been cited as an example of halakhic censorship, but which does not really fall into this category. Here are images from R. Joseph Hayim's responsa, *Rav pe'alim* (Fig. 3.8(*a–c*)), showing both the first and two later editions.[123] On the face of it, what we are confronted with here seems no different from the many other examples we have seen. In the first edition, R. Joseph Hayim states that there is no prohibition against trimming one's beard, a potentially problematic assertion for a kabbalist. Furthermore, this position is contradicted by what he writes in his pseudonymous *Torah lishmah*.[124] We can thus easily understand why some people would want to censor what R. Joseph Hayim wrote in *Rav pe'alim*.[125]

Yet in this instance, a strong case has been made that the responsum in question, which was included in a volume published after Hayim's death, is not authentic. A number of Baghdadi scholars reported that this information came from Hayim's son,[126] and while it is possible that he was mistaken, or even lying, it appears that those who omitted the responsum were indeed convinced that it was not authentic. In the words of R. Mordechai Eliyahu (1929–2010): 'If there was some chance, even the most far-fetched possibility, that this responsum was written by R. Joseph Hayim, they would have decided to leave it in, as it was already printed.'[127] This example is therefore different from most other cases we have seen, in which the censors *are* aware of the truth, but nevertheless decide that their goals are best served by removing material from the public eye.

122 See Y. M. Epstein, *Kitvei ha'arukh hashulḥan*, preface, 'Oraḥ ḥayim', no. 7.

123 In one of the later editions, shown in Figure 3.8(*c*), the publisher has replaced responsum no. 5 with what used to be no. 6, no. 6 with what used to be no. 7, and no. 7 with what used to be no. 8. On the following page in the responsa volume (not shown here) responsum no. 8 is omitted and the numbers begin with no. 9.

124 No. 215. There is no longer any doubt that R. Joseph Hayim is the author. For the most recent discussions, see Zohar, 'Halakhic Work' (Heb.), 40–2; Ben-David, *Shevet miyehudah*, 213–36; O. Yosef, *Yabia omer*, vol. ix, 'Oraḥ ḥayim', no. 96; M. Koppel, Mughaz, and Akiva, 'New Methods'; R. Avraham Motze's comments in *Vaya'an shemuel*, 9 (2006), no. 50; Zabihi, *Ateret paz*, vi. 43–4; Deblitzky, 'Responsa of R. Joseph Hayim' (Heb.); Hillel, *Ben ish ḥai*, 410 ff.

125 For an example of recent censorship of R. Shabetai Be'er's testimony that there were great kabbalists who cut their beards, see the Bein Din Ledin blog, 1 July 2010.

126 See R. Mordechai Eliyahu's letter in Hayim, *Hod yosef*, 97.

127 Ibid. See also Hillel, *Vayashav hayam*, i. 286–7. On the other hand, Yosef, *Yabia omer*, vol. ix, 'Yoreh de'ah', no. 10: 5; Y. H. Sofer, *Keneset ya'akov*, 152; Abba Shaul, *Or letsiyon*, vol. iii, no. 17: 6; Y. Yosef, *Ein yitsḥak*, iii. 214; and R. Meir Mazuz, note in *Peninei haparashah* (5771), no. 570, believe that the responsum is authentic.

CHAPTER FOUR

RABBI SAMSON RAPHAEL HIRSCH

THERE IS NO DENYING the enormous impact of R. Samson Raphael Hirsch on Orthodox Jewish life and thought. However, notwithstanding the great admiration for Hirsch among all segments of Orthodoxy, for some this admiration was mixed with ambivalence. On the one hand, Hirsch saved German Orthodoxy—or at least this was what many thought. This alone entitled him to a great deal of respect among all segments of Orthodoxy. On the other hand, his *torah im derekh erets* philosophy, which required Jews to take part in Western civilization while remaining faithful to Judaism, was diametrically opposed to the ideology of traditionalist Orthodoxy as it developed in eastern Europe and Hungary.

With few exceptions, the rabbinic leaders in these lands, most notably R. Moses Sofer, wanted their followers to remain far removed from the culture and civilization of the wider 'non-Jewish' world. They saw the opportunities of emancipation as a recipe for religious disaster, and viewed a more secluded Jewish life as the most religiously secure.[1] Hirsch, on the other hand, perceived the ghetto as something that the Jews had been placed in against their will, and he therefore welcomed emancipation. For him, the greatest sanctification of God's name was the pious Jew who also worked as a doctor, lawyer, government employee, and the like.[2]

As mentioned, due to his success in strengthening German Orthodoxy, one finds great respect for Hirsch in all circles, including among east European rabbinic leaders.[3] For instance, R. Abraham Mordechai Alter, the Rebbe of Gur—a staunch antagonist of secular studies—would not allow himself to

The original version of much of this chapter, an essay entitled 'Samson Raphael Hirsch and Orthodoxy: A Contested Legacy', was written for publication in *The Paths of Daniel: Studies in Judaism and Jewish Culture Presented to Rabbi Professor Daniel Sperber*, edited by Adam Ferziger for publication by Bar-Ilan University Press © Bar-Ilan University, Ramat Gan, Israel.

[1] See M. Breuer, *Asif*, 164 ff.

[2] See ibid. 167 ff.

[3] See my 'Samson Raphael Hirsch and Orthodoxy'.

pen a criticism of the *torah im derekh erets* philosophy. As he put it, 'one must be very careful to protect the honour of Rabbi Hirsch'.[4] This is one of many examples of traditionalist admiration for Hirsch which was combined with a repudiation of his educational philosophy. Even the extremist R. Hayim Eleazar Shapira (1872–1937), the Rebbe of Munkács, was able to see something positive in German Orthodoxy's system of education, since, as with the red heifer of old, though it contaminates the pure, perhaps it can also 'purify the impure'.[5]

For some east European rabbinical figures, admiration for Hirsch was not always accompanied by an appreciation of what his philosophy was all about. R. Barukh Ber Leibowitz (1864–1939), the famed *rosh yeshivah* (head of the academy) in Kamenitz, is the best-known example of this. In 1934 or thereabouts, he was asked by a young German rabbi, Shimon Schwab (1908–95), if the Hirschian approach was still valid.[6] Leibowitz's reply assumed without question that Hirsch's philosophy was a *hora'at sha'ah*, an emergency measure designed to save German Orthodoxy. As he saw it, German Orthodoxy was so intertwined with German society and culture that Hirsch could not ignore this. It was, however, incomprehensible to Leibowitz that this engagement with the non-Jewish world could actually be something that Hirsch had desired.[7] Never having read Hirsch's writings on *torah im derekh erets*, it is not surprising that he would say this. Leibowitz's position in this matter was also shared by the Lubavitcher Rebbe, R. Joseph Isaac Schneersohn,[8] and R. Yekutiel Aryeh Kamelhar (1871–1937);[9] presumably they too had never read Hirsch's writings on the topic.

Hirsch and Post-Second World War Haredi Jewry

In thinking about haredi attitudes towards Hirsch, the first thing to observe is that he has entered the pantheon of *gedolim* in the haredi world. The strongest proof of this is that Hirsch is the subject of a biography published in

[4] See Grunfeld, *Three Generations*, 48–9; Sorasky, *History* (Heb.), 147; Levi, 'Rabbi Samson Raphael Hirsch', 11.

[5] M. Goldstein (ed.), *Tikun olam*, 144. See also H. E. Shapira, *Divrei torah*, 4: 93. Regarding Shapira, see Nadler, 'War on Modernity'. Numbers 19 describes a ceremony in which the ashes of a red heifer are mixed with water and sprinkled on an individual who is ritually impure. This person is thereby rendered pure, while the one who performed the sprinkling becomes impure.

[6] Regarding Schwab's question, which he posed to a number of east European sages, see my '*Torah im Derekh Eretz*', 85–6.

[7] See B. B. Leibowitz, *Birkat shemuel*, vol. i, 'Kidushin', no. 27.

[8] Schneersohn, 'Critique' (Heb.). For R. Menachem Mendel Schneerson's negative evaluation of Hirsch's writings, which he regards as 'apologetics', see his *Igerot kodesh*, vol. xx, no. 7558, pp. 130–1.

[9] See Kamelhar, *Dor de'ah*, i. 3. See also Y. Mondshine, *Hatsofeh ledoro*, 136.

the ArtScroll series of 'significant Torah personalities',[10] which in America is the ultimate haredi stamp of approval.[11] In fact, due to this acceptance in the haredi world, it has become standard to refer to him as 'Rav Hirsch'. This is ironic, because in Germany itself the German Orthodox often referred to him as simply 'Hirsch'.

Like the American haredi community, the Israeli haredim have also accepted Hirsch. On the one hand, this is understandable, as Hirsch's family and followers were among the founders of the anti-Zionist Agudat Yisra'el. Many of them also remained supporters of the organization when they came to Palestine/Israel. Yet by the mid-1960s Mordechai Breuer—the great-grandson of Hirsch—called attention to the changing ideological winds in the haredi world, and published what can best be described as an open letter entitled 'Agudat Yisra'el and Western Orthodoxy'. There he spoke about how the German Orthodox *torah im derekh erets* outlook was no longer welcome in Agudat Yisra'el circles.

Even with the development at which Breuer pointed, however, it was not a matter of the Agudah simply rejecting the Hirschian ideology. Matters were more complicated than this, as the Agudah wished to keep Hirsch in its pantheon of sages, even as it rejected a basic facet of his outlook. Yet how could a rabbi who advocated *torah im derekh erets* be considered a *gadol* by the wider Agudah population, which was opposed to this ideology?

Before even looking at this question we must remember that there were two other aspects of Hirsch's thought which were of great importance to the nascent haredi ideology. The first was *Austritt* (i.e. religious separatism and, where possible, formal secession from the general community in order to avoid any connection with non-Orthodox rabbis and institutions). This—together with *torah im derekh erets*—was one of the foundations of Hirsch's ideology. It is true that Agudat Yisra'el in eastern Europe never adopted a policy of strict *Austritt* vis-à-vis the non-Orthodox, and this was also the case in the State of Israel (unlike the approach of the Edah Haredit,[12] which in pre-state days was aligned with Agudat Yisra'el). Yet the fact that Hirsch advocated creating Orthodox communities that were independent of the broader Jewish population was very useful in establishing his legitimacy among the haredim. As might be expected, both Hirsch and his *Austritt* ideology are often cited in haredi polemics against non-Orthodox (and insufficiently Orthodox) forms of Judaism in the State of Israel and the Diaspora.

[10] See <www.artscroll.com/Categories/bia.html>. The book is Klugman, *Rabbi Samson Raphael Hirsch*.

[11] Regarding ArtScroll, see Stolow, *Orthodox by Design*.

[12] The Edah Haredit is a separatist anti-Zionist Orthodox community in Israel.

Another element of Hirsch's thought was his proto-anti-Zionism, seen most prominently in his famous letter to Jacob Lifshitz. Here he writes that what R. Tsevi Hirsch Kalischer (1795–1874) saw as a great mitzvah, that is, encouraging mass settlement in the land of Israel, he regards as not a small sin.[13] This too was, in the pre-Second World War era, very much in line with a segment of Agudah thinking, and helped solidify Hirsch's reputation in haredi circles.

Yet despite the elements of Hirsch's thought that supported haredi ideological positions, for those who wished to place Hirsch in the pantheon of haredi sages, the problem remained: what should be done with the other pillar of his thought, *torah im derekh erets*? It is not as though this could be ignored, especially as there were plans, in the early days of the State of Israel, to translate Hirsch's writings into Hebrew. In addition, there were other comments in his works that would create great problems on the 'haredi street' if they appeared in Hebrew. In Letter Eighteen of his *Nineteen Letters*, for instance, Hirsch sharply criticizes Maimonides, using a style that is not acceptable within haredi society when relating to a venerable rabbinic sage of the past.[14]

The *Nineteen Letters* (also known as *Igerot tsafun*) had already appeared in Hebrew in 1890, but had long been unavailable. In 1948 the Netzah publishing house released this work in a new translation. This was the first step in Netzah's plan to publish the collected writings of Hirsch in Hebrew, and thus introduce the wider Agudah world to his thought. In this edition, Hirsch's criticism of Maimonides appears, but the following sentence was deleted: 'Therefore, many conclusions could be and were drawn, but before drawing them, people should have asked themselves, "Is Moses the son of Maimon, or Moses the son of Mendel [Mendelssohn], really identical with Moses the son of Amram?"'[15]

This was thought to be too strong an attack on Maimonides, especially as he was lumped together with Mendelssohn, and that is why it had to be removed. In fact, Netzah did not take this step on its own but received the encouragement of R. Abraham Isaiah Karelitz, the Hazon Ish, who was the most authoritative haredi rabbinic figure in the decade after the Second World War. We learn the story from R. Joseph Abraham Wolf (d. 1979), a graduate of the Berlin Rabbinical Seminary who was involved with Netzah. Although his

[13] See Hirsch, *Shemesh marpe*, 216. See also ibid. 211 for his letter to Kalischer.

[14] For recent discussions of Hirsch's criticism of Maimonides, see Gottlieb, 'Counter-Enlightenment', 279 ff.; Kohler, *Reading Maimonides' Philosophy*, 311 ff.

[15] Hirsch, *Nineteen Letters*, trans. B. Drachman, 193.

background was that of German Orthodoxy, upon settling in the land of Israel he became a prominent haredi educator who was very close to the Hazon Ish.

According to Wolf, he had been asked to translate the *Nineteen Letters*. He consulted with the Hazon Ish because he was not sure what to do with a very harsh comment by Hirsch against Maimonides. Wolf felt that the harshness of Hirsch's comment was due to the fact that the Reformers in Hirsch's days had taken to viewing themselves as the spiritual heirs of Maimonides.[16] Wolf added, however, that the Jewish world had changed greatly since the time when Hirsch made his comment. He also noted that Hirsch never again returned to such criticism of Maimonides, or for that matter, any early authority. The implication of this, according to Wolf, is that Hirsch must have regretted what he wrote and in his mature years he would not have approved of such strong language.[17]

It thus appeared to Wolf that the passage should not be translated. However, not wishing to make such a decision on his own, he turned to the Hazon Ish. The latter told Wolf that he was 'obligated' to alter passages such as this, or to omit them entirely. The Hazon Ish added that if anyone were to criticize Wolf for doing this, Wolf should state publicly whose instructions he was following.[18]

When Netzah reprinted the *Nineteen Letters* in the late 1960s,[19] it was felt that even more text had to be censored. Thus, all criticism of Maimonides, including three whole paragraphs devoted to this theme, were cut out.[20] Here is an example of what was regarded as 'acceptable' just twenty years earlier, but had now come to be deemed unsuitable in a book written by a *gadol* such as Hirsch:

This great man, to whom and to whom alone, we owe the preservation of practical Judaism to our time, is responsible, because he sought to reconcile Judaism with the difficulties which confronted it from without, instead of developing it creatively

[16] Regarding this phenomenon, Hirsch himself wrote: 'True that Maimonides' 'Guide' was burnt. He would have been the first to consign his book to the flames had he lived to see the manner in which it has been—and still is—abused.' See Hirsch, *Judaism Eternal*, ii. 240.

[17] A. Wolf, 'From His Holy Words' (Heb.), 4. See my Seforim Blog post, 6 May 2010.

[18] Although in the end it was Hayim Weissman, not Wolf, who translated the volume, I assume that it was the Hazon Ish's reply to Wolf that guided Netzah in the censorship. An introductory essay by Wolf appears in Netzah's second edition of the *Nineteen Letters*.

[19] The volume does not record the year of publication. The National Library of Israel catalogue lists it as having appeared in 1967, followed by a question mark. This edition was reprinted in Benei Berak in 1989.

[20] See pp. 92–3 in the original (Fig. 4.1(*a*)) and compare to p. 105 in the reprint (Fig. 4.1(*b*)). For another example of how criticism of Maimonides was deleted, see pp. 96–7 in the original and compare to p. 108 in the reprint.

from within, for all the good and the evil which bless and afflict the heritage of the father. His peculiar mental tendency was Arabic–Greek, and his conception of the purpose of life the same. He entered into Judaism from without, bringing with him opinions of whose truth he had convinced himself from extraneous sources and—he reconciled.[21]

What this deletion means is that the reader of Letter Eighteen in Netzah's updated translation of the *Nineteen Letters* will be completely unaware of Hirsch's strong criticism of Maimonides. This, of course, is the point. Only a careful reader might note that on page 105 the space between the second paragraph and the third is a little larger than it should be, and that the first two words of the third paragraph have been altered (Fig. 4.1(*b*)). Otherwise, there is no way to know that anything has been removed, and that is what makes it a successful censorship.

Netzah also carried out other acts of censorship in the *Nineteen Letters*. These were thought to be unnecessary when Netzah's first translation appeared, but were later regarded as essential in order to prevent the haredi readership from being scandalized. The Hazon Ish's recommendation to censor was stated with regard to Hirsch's criticism of Maimonides, but we have no evidence that he said anything about the other examples of censorship carried out by Netzah. One of these is also found in Letter Eighteen of the *Nineteen Letters*, and focuses on Hirsch's critical view of Jewish mysticism. Hirsch does not seem to be criticizing kabbalah per se, but rather what kabbalistic learning had become for many.[22] Yet by the 1960s even the following was viewed as too radical and had to be deleted:

A form of learning came into existence concerning which, as a layman, I do not venture to express a judgment, but which, if I comprehend aright the little that I know, is an invaluable repository of the spirit of Bible and Talmud, but which has been, unfortunately, misunderstood, and what should have been eternal, progressive development, was considered a stationary mechanism, and the inner significance and concept thereof as extra-mundane dream-worlds. This learning came into existence, and the mind turned either to the external ingenious development of the Talmud, or to this learning, which appealed to the emotions as well. Practical Judaism, which, comprehended in its purity, would perhaps have been impregnated

[21] Hirsch, *Nineteen Letters*, 181–2.

[22] See Munk, 'Rabbiner Hirsch als Rationalist der Kabbala'; I. Grunfeld's introduction to his translation of Hirsch's *Horeb*, pp. cxx–cxxix; M. Breuer, *Modernity within Tradition*, 67–8; Danziger, 'Rediscovering the Hirschian Legacy', on Joseph Elias's translation of the *Nineteen Letters*. Elias's response and Danziger's rejoinder appear in *Jewish Action*, 57 (Fall 1996), 60 ff. Unlike the other authors cited, Danziger understands Hirsch to have had a negative view of kabbalah.

with the spiritual, became in it, through misconception, a magical mechanism, a means of influencing or resisting theosophic worlds and anti-worlds.[23]

Any negative comments of Hirsch with regard to east European Jewry had to be covered up as well. Therefore, although in the first letter of his *Nineteen Letters* he refers negatively to Torah knowledge 'acquired from Polish teachers',[24] in the Netzah translation, including the first edition,[25] this passage becomes a criticism of Talmud study carried out 'with lack of understanding and depth'. The passage was even softened a bit in Jacob Breuer's reworking of Bernard Drachman's 1899 translation, and here the passage refers to study carried out 'in an old-fashioned Cheder'.[26] This is, of course, what Hirsch meant, but it is telling that there is no mention of 'Polish', which, incidentally, has been reinserted in Joseph Elias's edition of Drachman's translation ('Polish-Jewish teachers'), along with a note by the editor explaining that Hirsch did not mean to belittle east European Jewry.

Mordechai Breuer called attention to a further example of Netzah's censorship. Here, in a passage dealing with Jewish education from another of Hirsch's works, Hirsch's mention of *torah im derekh erets* is deleted![27] Let us not forget that *torah im derekh erets* was the central value of Hirsch's life. One can only wonder at the absurdity of trying to keep Hirsch 'kosher' by nullifying his entire educational philosophy. This is so even if the 'nullification' is accomplished by arguing that times have changed and Hirsch's views are no longer applicable, or even that Hirsch himself only intended *torah im derekh erets* as an emergency measure without any permanent validity.

This latter notion is a central feature of the haredi myth of Hirsch, and for many it is what allows him to be accepted.[28] I have already mentioned its appearance in the writings of R. Barukh Ber Leibowitz, and Leibowitz's understanding is actually quoted in one of the translations of Hirsch produced by Netzah.[29] Although in this example the publisher does not actually

[23] Hirsch, *Nineteen Letters*, 187.

[24] Ibid. 2. The original is 'unter polnischer Leitung'.

[25] There is no evidence that the Hazon Ish gave his approval to this particular alteration.

[26] Hirsch, *Nineteen Letters*, trans. Breuer, 23.

[27] M. Breuer, 'Review of Recent Books' (Heb.), 68.

[28] See Swift, '"External Books"' (Heb.), 207; Wolbe, *Alei shur*, i. 296: Jakobovics, *Zekhor yemot olam*, ii. 132. Unlike the authors just mentioned, R. Yoel Schwartz, a leading haredi writer, presents an accurate description of what Hirsch meant by *torah im derekh erets*. See his *Life of Rabbi Samson Raphael Hirsch* (Heb.), 38 ff. Yet he concludes his discussion as follows (p. 42): 'Despite what has been written about the viewpoint of Rabbi Samson Raphael [Hirsch], one must be aware that for many generations this has not been the outlook of the Torah greats.' See also the publisher's preface to the Netzah edition of some of Hirsch's educational essays: Hirsch, *Yesodot haḥinukh*.

[29] See the publisher's note on R. Jehiel Jacob Weinberg's essay on Hirsch, printed at the beginning of Netzah's edition of Hirsch, *Bema'gelei shanah*, iii. 16.

93 הרב .שמשון ב״ר רפאל הירש

על היסוד הרוחני של המצוות, שברובן — לאחר שאינן מאשרות את פרטי חלכות המצוה כתוכן שלה — אינן עומדות בפני הבקורת, אינן מאירות ומבארות את המצוה, ועל כן אינן יכולות להלוות אליה במעשה, בחיים ובבאור ההלכה.

התשקפות האלה היו עד ימינו-אנו לנחלת אותם האנשים הרוצים לדעת ביחוד את רוח וטעם המצוות. אבל ביניהם ובין ההלכות המחיבות למעשה אין כל קשר, ועל כן ירדו בעיניהם ערך המצוות כאילו מחוסרות הן כל רוח ויסוד, והם בזים להן.

ראה-נא, בנימין יקירי. במקום שהם יתיצבו על קרקע היהדות, וישאלו את עצמם: היות והיהדות מעמידה לנו את הדרישות האלה, מהי השקפתה על יעוד האדם? במקום שיבינו ראשית כל את המצוות לפי התנ״ך והש״ס, וישאלו אחר כך את עצמם: מהי המהות ומהו טעם המצוה הזאת? סגלו האנשים האלה לעצמם השקפה מחוץ ליהדות, ורצו למשוך ולהתאים את היהדות אליה. הם יצרו להם דעות קדומות על המצוות, בלי לשים לב למהותן האמיתית לכל חלקיהן ופרטיהן.

ומה היו התוצאות?

כשההשקפות האלה גרמו באופן טבעי שאנשים אשר נדמה להם שכבר הגיעו לתכלית הדעת יראו את עצמם פטורים מלקיים את המצוות, היות ומטרתן לפי השקפתם היא רק להדריך את בני האדם אל הדעת, ויחשבו שעל אחת כמה וכמה אינם חייבים ללמוד את הלכות המצוות המופיעות לעיניהם כמחוסרות רוח ויסוד —, נהפכו אנשים אחרים, שהעמיקו להבין מהם את היהדות, לאויבי הרוח הפילוסופית הזאת.

הבאים אחריהם נהפכו לאויבי כל רוח חוקרת, ולאויבי הפילוסופיא בפרט. כמה מאמרים שלא חדרו לעומקם[97] שמשו בתור כלי זין כדי לדחות כל נסיון להבין את רוח התלמוד. נוסף לזה, לא הבחינו בין שאלת „מה נאמר בזה?״ ל„מדוע נאמר הדבר הזה?״; ואף את המצוות מסוג ה„עדות״ הוציאו מכלל הרוח, למרות שלפי מהותן הן נועדו אך ורק כדי להוליד שאר-רוח. כשם שבתקופה יותר מאוחרת, מאמר שלא ירדו לעומקו (סנהדרין כ״ד א׳ תוספ׳ בד״ה בלולה) גרם להם להתרחק לגמרי

97) למשל ב״ר לך לך מ״ד, ת״כ אמ׳ י״ג ט׳, ועוד. המאמר „לא דרשינן טעמא דקרא״ שלעתים קרובות שמעתיו כטענה בוכוחים שהיו לי, אין משמעותו אלא הכלל הנכון בהחלט שאסור לנו להשתמש בטעם המצוה שאנו מצאנו אותו על פי השערתנו, בבואנו לפסוק הלכה למעשה, דוקא מפני שאין הטעם הזה אלא השערה בלבד.
ר׳ הרמב״ן על התורה קדושים י״ט י״ט, ועוד.

(*a*)

Figure 4.1 R. Samson Raphael Hirsch, *Igerot tsafun*: (*a*) the 1948 edition (Tel Aviv: Netzah); (*b*) the 1967(?) edition (Benei Berak: Netzah), with three paragraphs deleted

בהישגיהם המזהירים בשטח תבנת התורה, אם כי לא כל לומדי התורה זכו גם לתפוס בשלמות את רוחה.

בבתי הספר הלא־יהודיים עצב הנוער היהודי את רוחו בכוון פילוסופי ועצמאי. צעירינו שאבו את ידיעותיהם על הפילוסופיא היוונית ממקורות ערביים. הם ראו את תכלית יעודם בהשגת האמת הצרופה. רוחם הערה ראתה את עצמה מנוגדת ליהדות, היות ולא הכירו את מעלת רוחה; השקפת עולמם — בנגוד להשקפת העולם היהודית, הקוראת והמזרזת למעשים ופעילות, והרואה אף בדעת אמצעי לפעולות.

התקופה ההיא הולידה איש בעל שאר־רוח, שהתחנך בעת ובעונה אחת על ברכי היהדות הצרופה ועל ברכי חכמת ערב. עליו היה קודם כל למצוא פשרה כדי לאחות את הקרע בתוך עצמו; ולאחר שעלה הדבר בידו, הוציא את מסקנות מלחמתו הפנימית לרשות הרבים, ועל ידי זה היה למורה, לכל אלה שנבוכו באותה המלחמה.

הודות לאיש הדגול הזה ורק הודות לו, נשמרה היהדות המעשית עד ימינו. אבל מפני שמסקנתו היתה פ ש ר ה, ולא התפתחות יוצרת של היהדות מתוך עצמה, ומפני צורת פשרתו, צצו מתוכה כל מיני תוצאות חיוביות ושליליות.

כוון רוחו המיוחד לו היה ערבי־יווני, וכך היתה גם השקפתו על החיים הוא חדר לתוך היהדות מחוץ, הביא אתו השקפות מרחוק ובא אתן ליד פשרה. השלמות העצמית על ידי הכרת האמת, מטרה עליונה היא בעיניו והחיים המעשיים משועבדים לה. ידיעת ד׳ — מטרה היא לו, ולא אמצעי. מכאן — חקירות על מהות ד׳, והיהדות קשורה לפי שיטתו באופן יסודי לתוצאות החקירות האלה. המצוות משמשות בשיטתו רק כמדריכים, אמנם נחוצים ומועילים, בדרך הדעת, כדי לשמור עלינו מטעויות — ואחדות מהן נועדו אפילו לדעתו, רק כדי לשמור עלינו מטעויות חלקיות וחולפות בשטח האמונה הפוליתאיסטית. על פי השיטה הזאת נהפכו המשפטים והמצוות לכללי החכמה, החוקים — לכללי הבריאות, שמטרתם לעורר את הרגש ולהגן עלינו מפני תעתועי הזמן; חלק ממצוות העדות — מיועדות לפיה לשמש גורם לחקירה וכו׳. לשיטתו אין יסוד כל המצוות בעצם הויתם הנצחית של הענינים, אין המצוות נובעות מתוך יחס נצחי אל האדם ומיועדו לעולמי עד, ואין הן מיועדות להנציח על ידי מעשה סמלי את הרעיון האצור בתוכן; אבל על ידי זה נשמט היסוד הכללי של המצוות. והוא, המורה הגדול שערך באופן שיטתי את הלכות התלמוד, הביע בחלק האחרון של ספרו הפילוסופי השקפות

בהישגיהם המזהירים בשטח הבנת התורה, אם כי לא כל לומדי התורה זכו גם לתפוס בשלמות את רוחה.

בבתי הספר הלא־יהודיים עצב הנוער היהודי את רוחו בכוון פילוסופי ועצמאי. צעירינו שאבו את ידיעותיהם על הפילוסופיא היוונית ממקורות ערביים. הם ראו את תכלית יעודם בהשגת האמת הצרופה. רוחם הערה ראתה את עצמה מנוגדת ליהדות, היות ולא הכירו את מעלת רוחה; השקפת עולמם — בנגוד להשקפת העולם היהודית, הקוראת והמזרזת למעשים ופעילות, והרואה אף בדעת אמצעי לפעולות.

השקפות מסויימות היו עד ימינו־אנו לנחלת אותם האנשים הרוצים לדעת ביחוד את רוח וטעם המצוות. אבל ביניהם ובין ההלכות המחיבות למעשה אין כל קשר, ועל כן ירדו בעיניהם ערך המצוות כאילו מחוסרות הן כל רוח ויסוד, והם בזים להן.

ראה־נא, בנימין יקירי. במקום שהם יתיצבו על קרקע היהדות, וישאלו את עצמם: היות והיהדות מעמידה לנו את הדרישות האלה, מהי השקפתה על יעוד האדם? במקום שיבינו ראשית כל את המצוות לפי התנ"ך והש"ס, וישאלו אחר כך את עצמם: מהי המהות ומהו טעם המצוה הזאת? סגלו האנשים האלה לעצמם השקפה מחוץ ליהדות, ורצו למשוך ולהתאים את היהדות אליה. הם יצרו להם דעות קדומות על המצוות, בלי לשים לב למהותן האמיתית לכל חלקיהן ופרטיהן.

ומה היו התוצאות?

כשההשקפות האלה גרמו באופן טבעי שאנשים אשר נדמה להם שכבר הגיעו לתכלית הדעת יראו את עצמם פטורים מלקיים את המצוות, היות ומטרתן לפי השקפתם היא רק להדריך את בני האדם אל הדעת, ויחשבו שעל אחת כמה וכמה אינם חייבים ללמוד את הלכות המצוות המופיעות לעיניהם כמחוסרות רוח ויסוד — נהפכו אנשים אחרים, שהעמיקו להבין מהם את היהדות, לאויבי הרוח הפילוסופית הזאת.

הבאים אחריהם נהפכו לאויבי כל רוח חוקרת, ולאויבי הפילוסופיא בפרט. כמה מאמרים שלא חדרו לעומקם[97] שמשו בתור כלי זין כדי

97) למשל ב"ר לך לך מ"ד, ת"כ אמ' י"ג ט', ועוד. המאמר „לא דרשינן טעמא דקרא" שלעתים קרובות שמעתיו כטענה בוכוחים שהיו לי, אין משמעותו אלא הכלל הנכון בהחלט שאסור לנו להשתמש בטעם המצוה שאנו מצאנו אותו על פי השערתנו, כבואנו לפסוק הלכה למעשה, דוקא מפני שאין הטעם הזה אלא השערה בלבד.

ר' הרמב"ן על התורה קדושים י"ט י"ט, ועוד.

advocate Leibowitz's interpretation, the fact that it is quoted signals to readers that this is an acceptable interpretation of Hirsch.[30]

There are other examples that can be brought to illustrate the difficult relationship between the haredi world and Hirsch. For instance, Hirsch advocated the creation of a religious laity, and he insisted that not everyone needed to devote his life to Torah study or become a rabbi. Yet the notion that one could, as a first choice, serve God by having a profession, rather than exclusively through Torah study, is not something that fits in with the haredi *Weltanschauung* of recent decades. The following note appears in the Netzah edition of Hirsch's writings:

> These words of Rabbi Samson Raphael Hirsch need to be understood against the background of his era. They were stated in order to save the youth who had separated, or whose parents had separated them, from the study of Torah, and who were almost in the arms of Haskalah and assimilation. This is not the case today when we have been worthy of a new generation of youth whose soul longs for Torah precisely in a yeshiva setting. There are many parents whose ideal is to see their sons advancing in the study of Torah and intensively pursuing this. There are also numerous young women of valor who place upon themselves the burden of earning a livelihood, precisely in order that even after marriage their husbands will not be disturbed from their studies.[31]

The ambivalent haredi view of Hirsch can be seen with regard to his understanding of the binding authority of aggadic literature and the extent of the Sages' scientific knowledge. From geonic times until the present there has always been a 'school' of traditional thought that argued that aggadah did not have the same binding authority as halakhah, and that individual *agadot* could therefore be rejected. This 'school' also claimed that talmudic passages dealing with scientific matters do not contain any special knowledge received from Sinai. In other words, when the Sages spoke about science, they were simply expressing the most advanced knowledge of their time. Hirsch shared these positions and strongly defended his stand in two Hebrew letters addressed to the mystic and German Orthodox activist R. Hile Wechsler (1843–94).[32]

These letters to Wechsler, however, are absent from the book *Shemesh marpe*, which appeared in 1992. This volume contains a wide range of Hirsch's writings that were either penned originally in Hebrew or translated into Hebrew from German. Referring to the omission of the Hirsch–Wechsler letters from this volume, Lawrence Kaplan writes:

[30] See also R. Yehudah Leib Orlean's essay, printed as an introduction to Hirsch, *Bema'gelei shanah*, vol. iv.

[31] Ibid. i. 180.

[32] The letters appear in M. Breuer, *Asif*, 279–5. Regarding Hirsch and aggadah, see also Danziger, 'Rediscovering' and rejoinder, above, n. 22.

In my memorable phone conversation with Rabbi [Shimon] Schwab . . . our conversation at one point turned to the recent important collection of writings of Rabbi Hirsch, *Shemesh Marpeh*, edited by Rabbi Eliyahu Klugman and published by Rabbi Schwab himself. . . . I took the opportunity to express my surprise that these two letters of Rabbi Hirsch to Rabbi Wechsler were not included in the volume, which purports to include all of Rabbi Hirsch's major Hebrew writings, published and unpublished. Rabbi Schwab replied—and I am citing him practically verbatim—'Yes, you are correct. The editor [Rabbi Klugman] consulted with me, and I advised him not to publish them. I told him that the letters are controversial and likely to be misunderstood, and that his publishing them would just bring him unnecessary grief [*tzoros*].'[33]

In recent years an attempt has been made—completely without merit, it must be stressed—to impugn the authenticity of these letters. With Hirsch now a part of the haredi world's pantheon of sages, it was unacceptable for him to diverge so sharply from current haredi *da'as torah*.[34] This came to the fore very clearly in the so-called Slifkin Affair, in which the books of the young scholar Nosson Slifkin were banned. One of the reasons offered for the ban was his approach to scientific errors in the Talmud, in which he adopted the very same view as that advocated by Hirsch.[35]

Confronted by Hirsch's clear statements, R. Moshe Shapiro, an influential Jerusalem haredi rabbi, declared that there is no evidence that the letters were indeed written by Hirsch.[36] He based this conclusion on the fact that we do not have Hirsch's original letters, only copies made by someone before the letters were sent to Wechsler. We do, however, have Wechsler's original letters, in which he responds to Hirsch. Based on his answers it is absolutely clear that he is responding to the very letters of Hirsch of which copies still exist.[37]

In truth, it is very difficult to imagine that even Shapiro believed the position that he was advocating. Rather, it is more likely that he was engaged in another form of censorship. Since he found it impossible to cover up Hirsch's views as expressed in his letters to Wechsler, the next best choice was to declare the letters inauthentic. Just as the censor knows the truth and still chooses to cover it up, so too we should not be surprised if people go even one

[33] L. Kaplan, '*Torah u-Madda*', 28 n. 25.

[34] *Da'as torah* refers to the authoritative opinion of haredi sages on both halakhic and non-halakhic matters.

[35] Complete details of the so-called 'Slifkin Affair' can be found on Slifkin's website, <www.zootorah.com/controversy>.

[36] See M. Shapiro, *Afikei mayim*, 68 n. 87. This section of the book is written by one of his students, but reflects Shapiro's viewpoint.

[37] See Mordechai Breuer's comments quoted in Slifkin's response to Shapiro, on Slifkin's website, <www.zootorah.com/controversy/ResponseToRavMosheShapiro.pdf>.

step further and disingenuously claim that a text is falsely attributed or even forged in order to destroy its authority and thus remove it from the public eye. This, of course, is exactly the same goal as that of the typical censor.[38]

Another example of censorship concerning Hirsch is seen with regard to the issue of head covering for men. While today this is a basic sign of an observant Jew (the Syrian community being perhaps the one exception to this statement), it was not always the case. No less a figure than the Vilna Gaon believed that it was only a custom to cover one's head,[39] and there are sources for this view in talmudic and medieval literature as well.[40] In modern Germany, Orthodox Jews did not regard head coverings as essential, except during prayer and when reciting blessings and eating. German Orthodox Jews also often wore a hat when outside, which was a common manner of dress in wider German society.[41] Some covered their heads at home, but others saw no need for this,[42] and heads were never covered at the university or places of work.[43]

Today, however, this is exactly the sort of thing that some in the haredi world do not want their followers to know about, as it destroys the illusion of religious uniformity among Orthodox Jews in this matter. The problem is that R. David Tsevi Hoffmann (1843–1921), the leading halakhic authority in Germany in the early twentieth century, describes this phenomenon in his responsa.[44] He was a teacher at Hirsch's school in Frankfurt, and writes that for the non-Torah subjects the students did not cover their heads. In other words, Orthodox students at an Orthodox school sat bareheaded in class.[45] Let us also not forget that this was not simply any Orthodox school, but the school

[38] Slifkin reports that Shapiro later changed his tactics. Instead of denying the authenticity of the letters, he asserted that 'Rav Hirsch is not from our Beis HaMidrash'. In other words, Hirsch's opinion on these matters does not carry any weight. See <www.zootorah.com/controversy/ResponseToRavMosheShapiro.pdf>.

[39] See his commentary, *Be'ur hagra*, on Karo, *Shulḥan arukh*, 'Oraḥ ḥayim' 8: 6.

[40] See Zimmer, 'Men's Headcovering'; Laderman, 'What Do Jewish Artistic Findings Teach Us about Head Covering for Men?' (Heb.).

[41] See Deshen, *R. Shimon Kohen of Frankfurt* (Heb.), the picture after p. 38, which shows a group of Orthodox Jews in Frankfurt posing outside for a wedding picture. The women are wearing wigs and the men are bareheaded. See also M. Y. Schlesinger, 'Young Men Wearing a Tallit' (Heb.), 112.

[42] See M. Breuer, *Modernity within Tradition*, 9: 'He [R. Selig Aviezri Auerbach] did not like it when we covered our head with a skullcap or a hat at home, except for prayers or meals.'

[43] This was also a common practice in the United States. Schachter, 'Pearls' (Heb.), 320, records that R. Joseph B. Soloveitchik recommended to his son-in-law, R. Aharon Lichtenstein, that he not wear a *kipah* at his interview for admission to Harvard. He was concerned that the interviewer might harbour antisemitic sentiments.

[44] Hoffmann, *Melamed leho'il*, vol. ii, no. 56.

[45] This was also the case with R. Victor Schonfeld's Orthodox Day School in London. See Taylor, *Solomon Schonfeld*, 17. On p. 52, Taylor reports, without documentation, that Chief Rabbi Joseph Hertz once attended a non-Jewish event without a head covering.

run by the separatist community of Frankfurt, the same community that was regarded by many of the other German Orthodox as extremist.[46]

The practice Hoffmann describes continued into the Nazi era. Mordechai Breuer wrote to me as follows:

> I left the Hirsch school in Frankfurt in 1934. The rule of uncovered heads while studying 'secular' subjects (a concept which should not have actually been used at a school adhering to the principle of Torah Im Derech Eretz) was enforced without exception (it was not enforced upon teachers who served as rabbis in one of the local synagogues). However, during the last years of the school's functioning, when the impact of the Nazi regime became increasingly palpable, pupils and teachers reacted by covering their heads in 'secular' subjects as well.[47]

Hoffmann further reports that the first time he came to Hirsch's home, Hirsch requested that he take off his hat, leaving him bareheaded.[48] Hirsch explained that in Germany it was regarded as disrespectful to visit an important person without removing one's hat. Thus, if a non-Jewish teacher saw him enter the home wearing his hat, he would assume that Hoffmann had failed to display his respect for the director of the school. This information was provided by Hoffmann as part of a responsum focused on the issue of taking an oath in court while bareheaded.[49] He concludes that while it is better to have your head covered while taking an oath, which after all, is a religious matter, if the judge forbids this one is permitted to take the oath without a head covering. In his responsum, he also discusses the general issue of covering one's head, notes that in Hungary the rabbis were very strict about this, and quotes the Vilna Gaon, whom we have mentioned already, as saying that even when dealing with religious matters, covering the head is not a commandment but merely a commendable practice.

Hoffmann's *Melamed leho'il* was reprinted in 1954 without any changes to the original text. Yet when it was reprinted in Israel in the late 1990s, the responsum regarding head covering was thought to be problematic because of the information it revealed. This was particularly so as the new edition of *Melamed leho'il* was published as part of the Leibowitz–Kest edition of Jewish books. This was an endeavour to reprint hundreds of important works cheaply so that yeshiva students could have access to them. As *Melamed leho'il*

[46] Fred Margulies, who was a student at the Berlin Orthodox Adass Jisroel school from 1934–8, informed me that there too the students only covered their heads for religious subjects. He also recalled going to R. Alexander Altmann's (1906–87) home to ask him a halakhic question, Altmann was one of the leading Orthodox pulpit rabbis in Berlin, yet he answered the door without a head covering.

[47] See my Seforim Blog post, 11 June 2007.

[48] I assume that this refers to the moment when he greeted Hirsch and entered his home, but not that he would remain bareheaded once inside.

[49] Hoffmann, *Melamed leho'il*, vol. ii, no. 56.

is one of the most important works of twentieth-century responsa, it was included in the project.

What then could the publisher do with the 'problematic' responsum, especially as the new edition was simply a photo reprint? The solution was to white out the responsum in question and to 'correct' the heading at the top of the page (see Fig. 4.2). The responsum was also removed from the table of contents, so that it skips from number 55 to 57.[50] The irony of this particular example of censorship is that it is likely that many people who owned the uncensored *Melamed leho'il* skimmed through it without even bothering to read the responsum in question. In the case of the new edition, however, those who see the blank space will certainly be motivated to locate an uncensored edition in order to find out what is missing.

Another example of censorship in the area of head covering can be seen in a picture of Isaac Breuer (1883–1946).[51] Breuer was Hirsch's grandson and a leading figure in Agudat Yisra'el. He was also a lawyer by profession and wrote a very interesting autobiography which, among other things, describes his growing disillusionment with the Agudah and its lack of recognition of the enormous significance of Jewish settlement in the land of Israel.[52] In 1988 this autobiography appeared, entitled *Mein Weg*. It is in German and contains a picture of Breuer which is by now well known, since it had earlier appeared in the *Encyclopaedia Judaica* (Fig. 4.3(*a*)).[53] An academic collection of Hebrew essays devoted to Breuer also appeared in 1988.[54] Here, however, the picture we have just mentioned appears with a *kipah* (skullcap) placed on Breuer's head (Fig. 4.3(*b*)). It is not known who was responsible for this 'touching up', but the motivation was probably that Orthodox Jews in Israel would find it difficult to relate to a bareheaded religious thinker.

Here is another example of a photograph touched up to add a head covering, and in this case it is not from Germany. It shows Israel Brodski (1823–88, Fig. 4.4(*a*)), a member of a wealthy Russian Jewish family known for its philanthropy. Brodski himself donated money so that the Volozhin yeshiva could

[50] The censored reprint has a preface by a descendant of Hoffmann, also named David Tsevi Hoffmann. Another family member claims that R. Yosef Shalom Elyashiv recommended to this David Tsevi Hoffmann that the responsum be deleted. While I cannot say whether this report is true, it must be noted that when this descendant reprinted *Melamed leho'il* in a new edition in 2010, nothing was censored.

[51] This example was called to my attention by Lipman Phillip Minden.

[52] See I. Breuer, *Darki*, ch. 14; M. Morgenstern, *From Frankfurt to Jerusalem*, 231 ff., 299 ff.

[53] *EJ* iii, col. 1364. The picture also appears in I. Breuer, *Weltwende*, back cover, and in Anon., *Die Samson-Raphael-Hirsch-Schule*, 183.

[54] Horwitz (ed.), *Isaac Breuer* (Heb.). I have no doubt that Horwitz was unaware that the picture she published had been altered.

נ"ה.

ש א ל ה:

אי מותר לבנות גדר לבית עלמין מאבנים של ע"ז שלהם שנהרס.

ת ש ו ב ה:

לא פירש בשאלתו אי נהרס ע"י נכרים או ממילא. והנה בנהרס ע"י נכרים פשיטא דנתבטל, ואפילו נהרס ממילא נתבטלו האבנים ע"י מכירה לישראל כמ"ש בי"ד סי' קמ"ו סעיף ח'. ומ"ש מר דכתב רמ"א סי' קמ"ו סעיף ה' וז"ל אומות שלנו וישמעאלים שאינם עע"ז אינם יכולים לבטל עכ"ל ט"ס נזדמן לו בדברי רמ"א דבאמת לא כתב רמ"א רק ישמעאלים שאינם עע"ז אינם יכולים לבטל, רק הש"ך בסי' קכ"ד ס"ק י"ב כ' דהוא הדין כל גוי שאנו מוחזקין בו שאינו עע"ז, מ"מ מן הסתם מורה הש"ך דגוים שלנו יכולין לבטל, ואף שכ' שם ס"ק ט' דגוים בזמן הזה לאו עע"ז הן, היינו דוקא לענין ניסוך דאין יינן אסור בהנאה משום דאין מנסכין יין לע"ז וכמ"ש הח"ס בכמה דוכתי. גם הטעם דמקילין בסחורה בדברים שצריכין לעבודתם שכ' הש"ך סי' קנ"א ס"ק ז' אינו ענין לכאן דאף דנכרים משתפין שם שמים ודבר אחר ונכרים אינן מצווין על השיתוף וכמו שהארכתי בזה בספרי: דער שלחן ערוך וכו' (בלשון אשכנז) מ"מ לישראל הוי שיתוף ע"ז גמורה והמשתף יכול לבטל ופוק חזי כל האחרונים שקלו וטרו בענין ביטול ע"ז ולא משתמיט חד מינייהו למימר דנכרים שלנו אינם יכולים לבטל, ועוד אי אמרינן דאינן יכולין לבטל מפני שאינן עע"ז א"כ בית תפילה שלהם אינו אסור משום משמשי ע"ז. ואין לומר דלחומרא אמרינן דהם עע"ז דזה הוי תרי חומרי דסתרי אהדדי דהוי עע"ז ואעפ"כ אינן יכולין לבטל משום דאינן עע"ז, אתמהה. וכבר ישב על מדוכה זו הגאון מו"ה מענדל קארגוי זצ"ל שנשאלה שאלה לפניו אי עצים ואבנים של בית תפלה שלהם שסתרו אותו מותרין בהנאה ואם הם מותרין לצורך בנין בית הכנסת והעלה דמותרין משום דנתבטלו, ואף דלצורך מצוה מאיס מ"מ ע"י שינוי שקבען בבנין פקע האיסור מהם. ומ"מ כ' שם דלמעשה לקבוע אותן אבנים בכותלי ביהכ"נ אף שמדינא מותר מ"מ בעיני העולם יהא כדבר תימא ולזות שפתים ע"כ הוא נותן שם עצה שלא יקנו הקהל האבנים אלא יעשו קציצה (אַקקאָרד) עם ראש הבנאים והוא קונה העצים והאבנים מבית ע"ז ואין צריכין לעכב על ידו עיי"ש בספר גידולי טהרה בשו"ת סי' ל"ד.—

והנה בנ"ר קיל יותר דבית הקברות אין בו קדושה והכותלים אינן לצורך מצוה רק לשמור מקום הקברות ואין כאן לזות שפתים ע"כ נ"ל להתיר בפשיטות.

נ"ו.

ש א ל ה:

אי רשאי לישבע בערכאות שלהם בגילוי ראש.

ת ש ו ב ה:

אין לי פנאי להאריך כעת. אבל עיין בכנה"ג לי"ד סי' קנ"ז דמיקל בשעת הדחק. ועיין בבית לחם יהודה ושער אפרים שהביאו זה ורומז על שו"ת

ועיין גם בבית הלל לי"ד סי' קנ"ז דהיו נותנים שוחד שלא יצטרכו לישבע בגילוי ראש. והנה בעת הזאת הרבנים היראים במדינות אונגארן מחמירין מאד בענין גלוי ראש, עיין הבירור מש"ס ופוסקים בשו"ת נחלת בנימין סי' ל'. והנה הגר"א בהגהותיו לס"י ח' ס"ק ב' העלה שאין איסור אפילו להוציא אזכרה בג"ר אלא מירת חסידות. ומ"ש שם בתשובת נחלת בנימין שאם בבית חנוך שמו לחוק שצעירי ישראל צריכין לישב דוקא בפריעת ראש ועושין כן ע"ר אביהם וראשי הערה, זה איסור גמור משום ובחוקותיהם לא תלכו. הנה בק"ק יראים דפפד"מ בבית החינוך שנתיסד מהגאון ר' שמשון רפאל הירש זצ"ל (שאני הייתי מורה שם ב' שנים וחצי) יושבים התלמידים בשעת לימוד שאר המדעים בפריעת ראש, ורק בשעת לימוד תורה מכסים ראשם (וכן הוא המנהג בבית הספר בהאמבורג) וזה נעשה שם עפ"י תקנת הרה"ג מו"ה ש"ר הירש זצ"ל. ובפעם ראשון שבאתי לביתו של הרה"ג ש"ר הירש בכובע על ראשי, אמר לי שכאן הוא דרך ארץ להסיר הכובע מעל הראש כשבאין אל אדם חשוב, ואולי יראה מורה אחר (יש בבית החינוך שם גם הרבה מורים א"י) שאני איני מסיר הכובע מעל הראש לפני ראש בית החינוך (דירעקטאָר) היה מחשב זה כאילו אני מבזה אותו. וכזה וכיוצא כזה אין בו משום בחוקותיהם. — ואם כן בנידון דידן אם השופט נותן רשות לכסות הראש בשעת השבועה מה טוב, וכל אחר בוראי לכתחלה צריך לבקש מהשופט לכסות ראשו ויאמר כי הוא מצווה לכסות ראשו בכל דבר שבקדושה והשבועה הוא לו בלתי ספק דבר קדושה. אמנם אם השופט אינו רוצה לתת לו רשות א"צ לקבל עליו אפי' עונש ממון ויכול לישבע אפילו בגילוי ראש, וכן פסק מהרא"י בפסקים וכתבים לסי' ר"ג, ע' שו"ת יריעות שלמה חלק א' ועיין בכור שור לשבת דף קי"ח ע"ב דהיכא שנראה מתוך מעשיו דלאו משום חוקותיהם שרי וע' בשו"ת חיים שאל ח"ב סי' ל"ה (דפוס ליוואָרנא) אי רשאי לברך בגילוי ראש וגם מדבר שם אי יש לו על ראשו פעריקקע, פסקים וכתבים של מהרא"י סי' ר"ג מתיר לישבע בגילוי ראש (אך צריך לי לעיין שם בפנים).

נ"ז.

ש א ל ה:

ראובן חייב לשמעון לשלם סכום מעות לזמן מוגבל, והוא ממאן לשלם ונגשו שניהם אל השופט (בערכאות) והשופט חייב את ראובן לשלם המעות עם חמשה פראָצענט צינזען מיום המוגבל עד זמן פרעון, אם מותר לשמעון לקבל אותן צינזען, או אסור משום רבית.

ת ש ו ב ה:

מה שפתח מכ"ת בכהא דהיתירא ואמר שהפראָצעססצינזען אינם שוים בעיניו, וגם התחבולות ראובן איננו כי אם להפטר מהתובע ועל זה דוה לבו ולא על פרוטי הצינזען, ואין כאן קציצת רבית, כל זה אינו כדאי (אף אם יהיבנא לי' סברתו) אלא שאינה רבית קצוצה. אמנם ודאי לא יצא מידי רבית מאוחרת שהרי השופטים הטילו על החייב רבית מפני מעותיו של זה שהיו בטילות אצלו, ומה לי אם נותן הרבית על פי דבר השופט או נותן לו מרעתו מתנה בשביל שעיכב מעותיו אצלו.

(a)

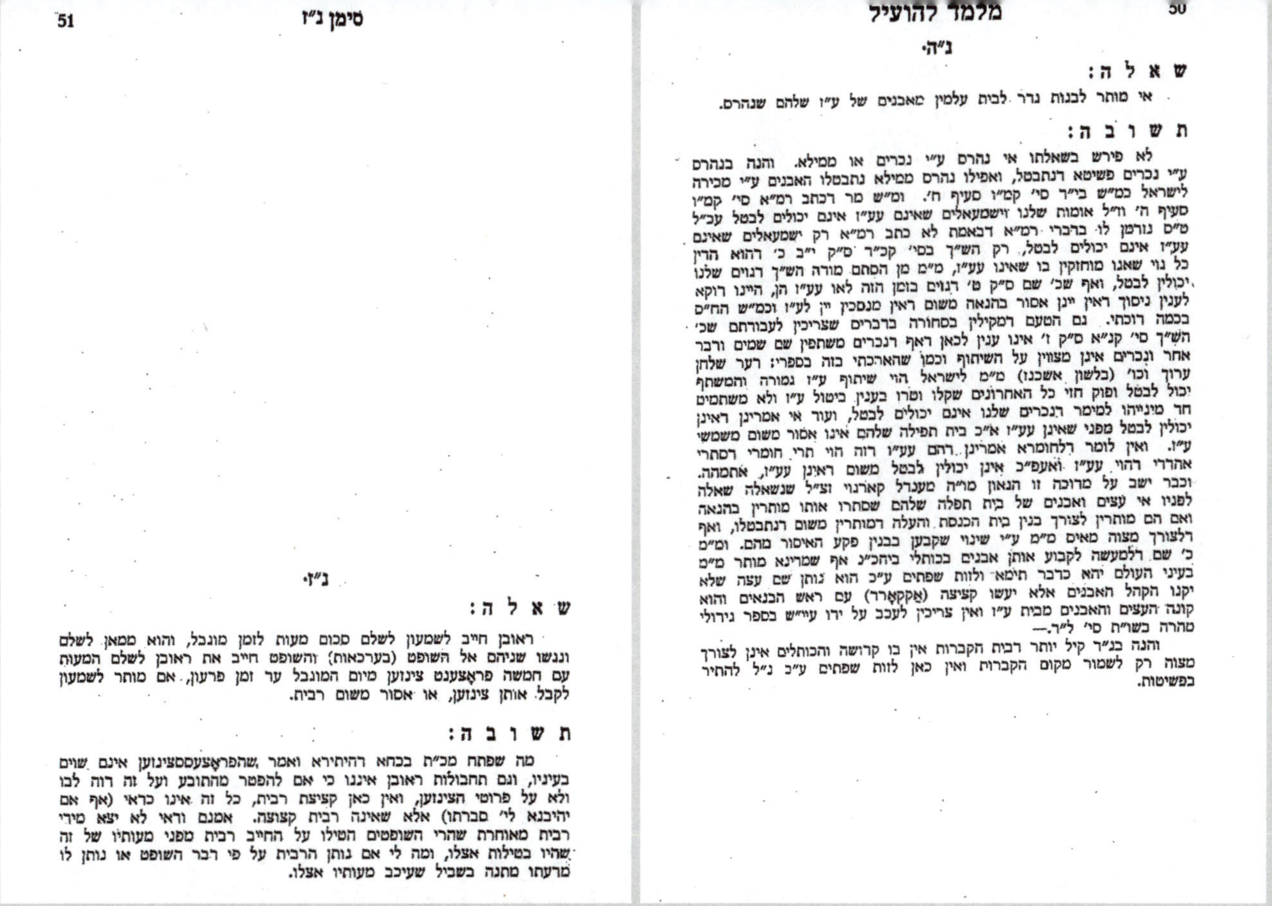

50 מלמד להועיל

נ"ה׳

ש א ל ה :

אי מותר לבנות גדר לבית עלמין מאבנים של ע"ז שלהם שנהרס.

ת ש ו ב ה :

לא פירש בשאלתו אי נהרס ע"י נכרים או ממילא. והנה בנהרס ע"י נכרים פשיטא דנתבטל, ואפילו נהרס ממילא נתבטלו האבנים ע"י מכירה לישראל כמ"ש בי"ד סי׳ קמ"ו סעיף ח׳. ומ"ש מר דכתב רמ"א סי׳ קמ"ו סעיף ה׳ וז"ל אומות שלנו וישמעאלים שאינם עע"ז אינם יכולים לבטל עכ"ל ט"ס גורמן לו בדברי רמ"א דבאמת לא כתב רמ"א רק ישמעאלים שאינם עע"ז אינם יכולים לבטל, רק הש"ך בסי׳ קכ"ר ס"ק י"ב כ׳ דהוא הדין כל גוי שאנו מוחזקין בו שאינו עע"ז, מ"מ מן הסתם מודה הש"ך דגוים שלנו יכולין לבטל, ואף שכ׳ שם ס"ק ט׳ דגוים בזמן הזה לאו עע"ז הן, היינו דוקא לענין ניסוך דאין יינן אסור בהנאה משום דאין מנסכין יין לע"ז וכמ"ש הח"ס בכמה דוכתי. גם הטעם דמקילין בסחורה בדברים שצריכין לעבודתם שכ׳ הש"ך סי׳ קנ"א ס"ק ז׳ אינו ענין לכאן דאף דנכרים משתפין שם שמים ודבר אחר ונכרים אינן מצווין על השיתוף וכמו שהארכתי בזה בספרי: רער שלחן ערוך וכו׳ (בלשון אשכנז) מ"מ לישראל הוי שיתוף ע"ז גמורה והמשתף יכול לבטל ופוק חזי כל האחרונים שקלו וטרו בענין ביטול ע"ז ולא משתמיט חד מינייהו למימר דנכרים שלנו אינם יכולים לבטל, ועוד אי אמרינן דאינן יכולין לבטל מפני שאינן עע"ז א"כ בית תפילה שלהם אינו אסור משום משמשי ע"ז. ואין לומר דלחומרא אמרינן דהם עע"ז דזה הוי תרי חומרי דסתרי אהדדי דהוי עע"ז ואעפ"כ אינן יכולין לבטל משום דאינן עע"ז, אתמהה. וכבר ישב על מדוכה זו הגאון מו"ה מענדל קארגוי זצ"ל שנשאלה שאלה לפניו אי עצים ואבנים של בית תפלה שלהם שסתרו אותו מותרין בהנאה ואם הם מותרין לצורך בנין בית הכנסת והעלה דמותרין משום דנתבטלו, ואף דלצורך מצוה מאים מ"מ ע"י שינוי שקבען בבנין פקע האיסור מהם. ומ"מ כ׳ שם דלמעשה לקבוע אותן אבנים בכותלי ביהכ"נ אף שמדינא מותר מ"מ בעיני העולם יהא כדבר תימא ולזות שפתים ע"כ הוא נותן שם עצה שלא יקנו הקהל האבנים אלא יעשו קציצה (אַקקאָרד) עם ראש הבנאים והוא קונה העצים והאבנים מבית ע"ז ואין צריכין לעכב על ידו עיי"ש בספר גידולי טהרה בשו"ת סי׳ ל"ד.—

והנה בנ"ד קיל יותר דבית הקברות אין בו קדושה והכותלים אינן לצורך מצוה רק לשמור מקום הקברות ואין כאן לזות שפתים ע"כ נ"ל להתיר בפשיטות.

51 סימן נ"ז

נ"ז׳

ש א ל ה :

ראובן חייב לשמעון לשלם סכום מעות לזמן מוגבל, והוא ממאן לשלם ונגשו שניהם אל השופט (בערכאות) והשופט חייב את ראובן לשלם המעות עם חמשה פראָצענט צינזען מיום המוגבל עד זמן פרעון, אם מותר לשמעון לקבל אותן צינזען, או אסור משום רבית.

ת ש ו ב ה :

מה שפתח מכ"ת בכהא דהיתירא ואמר ,שהפראָצעססצינזען אינם שוים בעיניו, וגם תחבולות ראובן איננו כי אם להפטר מהתובע ועל זה דוה לבו ולא על פרוטי הצינזען, ואין כאן קציצת רבית, כל זה אינו כדאי (אף אם יהיבנא לי׳ סברתו) אלא שאינה רבית קצוצה. אמנם ודאי לא יצא מידי רבית מאוחרת שהרי השופטים הטילו על החייב רבית מפני מעותיו של זה שהיו בטילות אצלו, ומה לי אם נותן הרבית על פי דבר השופט או נותן לו מדעתו מתנה בשביל שעיכב מעותיו אצלו.

(*b*)

Figure 4.2 R. David Tsevi Hoffmann, *Melamed leho'il*, vol. ii, no. 56: (*a*) (on page 134) 1954 edition (New York: Hermon), showing the discussion of head covering; (*b*) Israeli edition from the late 1990s (Jerusalem: Foundation for the Advancement of Torah Study), with the controversial responsum removed

(*a*) (*b*)

Figure 4.3 Isaac Breuer: (*a*) photograph published in the *Encyclopaedia Judaica*, with no head covering (Jerusalem: Keter, 1972); (*b*) the same picture as it appears in Horwitz (ed.), *Isaac Breuer* (Heb.) (Ramat Gan: Bar-Ilan University, 1988), with a *kipah* added

(*a*) (*b*)

Figure 4.4 Israel Brodski: (*a*) photograph with no head covering, from Leoni (ed.), *Volozhin: The Book of the City and of the Ets Hayim Yeshiva* (Heb.) (Tel Aviv: Organization of Volozhin Alumni in Israel and Abroad, 1970); (*b*) the same photograph as it appears in Plato, *Bishevilei radin* (Petah Tikvah: Makhon 'Bishevilei Hayeshivot', 2001), with a *kipah* added

establish its *kolel* for young scholars.[55] This *kolel*, known by Brodski's name, remained open even after the yeshiva was closed in 1892.[56] Should it surprise us that when this picture was recently included in a haredi work, a *kipah* was placed on Brodski's head (Fig. 4.4(*b*))?[57]

Another instance of censorship dealing with head coverings relates to Italy, where just as in Germany, it was common for men not to cover their

[55] A *kolel* is an institution that supports a group of men so they can devote themselves to full-time study of Talmud and rabbinic literature.

[56] See Leoni (ed.), *Volozhin* (Heb.), 146. The picture comes from this page as well. For more on the Brodski *kolel*, see N. Kamenetsky, *Making of a Godol*, ii. 1219–20.

[57] The picture comes from Plato, *Bishevilei radin*, 31. I thank Dan Rabinowitz for calling my attention to this example. R. Jehiel Jacob Weinberg recently also had a *kipah* placed on his head; see my Seforim Blog post, 29 Aug. 2012.

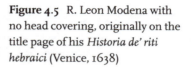

Figure 4.5 R. Leon Modena with no head covering, originally on the title page of his *Historia de' riti hebraici* (Venice, 1638)

heads.[58] This practice is described and defended by R. Leon Modena, who mentions how he would sometimes go about without a head covering himself.[59] There is also a famous picture of Modena which shows him bareheaded (Fig. 4.5).[60] R. Moses Gentili (Hefets; 1663–1711), author of the biblical commentary *Melekhet maḥshevet*, was another rabbi whose pictorial image (Fig. 4.6(*a*)) appears to show him bareheaded (although this is not entirely certain). He is also beardless, which again was a common practice in Italy, even among rabbis.[61] This picture appeared at the beginning of the first edition of his book (Venice, 1710).[62] When the book was reprinted in Königsberg in 1860, the ambiguity about the head covering was unacceptable, and an obvious *kipah* was put on his head. The new picture also aged him, and this was because the printer misunderstood what is written under the original picture. There it states is that he is מא"ו years old, and the double apostrophe signals that the meaning of the Hebrew letters is 'forty-six'. Yet the printer in

58 See Delmedigo, *Matsref leḥokhmah*, ch. 22, p. 26*a*.

59 See Modena, *Ziknei yehudah*, nos. 21–2; Safran, 'Leone da Modena's Historical Thinking', 383.

60 This picture first appeared on the title page of his *Historia de' riti hebraici*. 'He is depicted bareheaded, reflecting Modena's statement in his responsum on head covering that he uncovered his head when speaking to noblemen. Since this book addressed a king, Modena has shown respect by baring his head.' Mann (ed.), *Gardens and Ghettos*, 247.

61 See E. S. Horowitz, 'Early Eighteenth Century', 95–115. From a later period, pictures of Samuel David Luzzatto and the one surviving picture of R. Elijah Benamozegh show them bareheaded.

62 D. Rabinowitz, 'Yarmulke', 230 n. 29, writes: 'S. Y. Agnon, in his autobiography [*A Simple Story*], recorded that he was shocked as a child in Galicia to see this portrait of R. Hefetz, a Rabbi, bareheaded, beardless, with shoulder-length hair.' There are two mistakes here. First, *A Simple Story* is a work of fiction, not autobiography. Second, there is nothing in the story about Gentili being bareheaded. The relevant sentence reads: 'Rabbi Moses Hefetz, his hair unrabbinically long and his chin unrabbinically beardless . . .'. See Agnon, *A Simple Story*, 15. (In the original Hebrew, the word 'unrabbinically' does not appear.)

(*a*) (*b*)

Figure 4.6 R. Moses Gentili: (*a*) apparently with no head covering, from his *Melekhet maḥshevet* (Venice, 1710); (*b*) with *kipah* added, from *Melekhet maḥshevet* (Königsberg, 1860)

Königsberg mistakenly understood מא״ה to mean *me'ah*, 'one hundred', as if there were no apostrophes (Fig. 4.6(*b*)). Therefore, in addition to adding the *kipah*, he aged Gentili by more than fifty years![63]

My final examples regarding head coverings appear in the biography of the Lubavitcher Rebbe, R. Menachem Mendel Schneerson, written by Shaul Shimon Deutsch.[64] Deutsch was able to locate a picture of the Rebbe from his student file at the University of Berlin, which he subsequently published. This photo had never before been seen publicly, and in it the Rebbe is bareheaded (Fig. 4.7(*a*)). This should not be surprising considering what we have already seen about German Orthodoxy. Deutsch also published a

[63] This mistake was first pointed out by Samuel David Luzzatto; see his note in *Halevanon*, 26 Tishrei 5627, 301–2. See also D. Rabinowitz, 'Yarmulke', 230–1; A. Hakohen, 'R. Moses Hefets' *Melekhet maḥshevet*' (Heb.), 271 n. 15; On the Main Line, 18 Mar. 2009; <notrikon.blogspot.com>, 31 Dec. 2012.

[64] S. S. Deutsch, *Larger than Life*, vol. ii, ch. 11. Deutsch also shows other alterations in pictures of the Rebbe, such as turning his light-coloured hat into black and darkening the colour of his suit. The picture of the Rebbe from his student file has recently been published with a *kipah* inserted on his head. See Weingort, *Hagadah*, 53.

(*a*) (*b*)

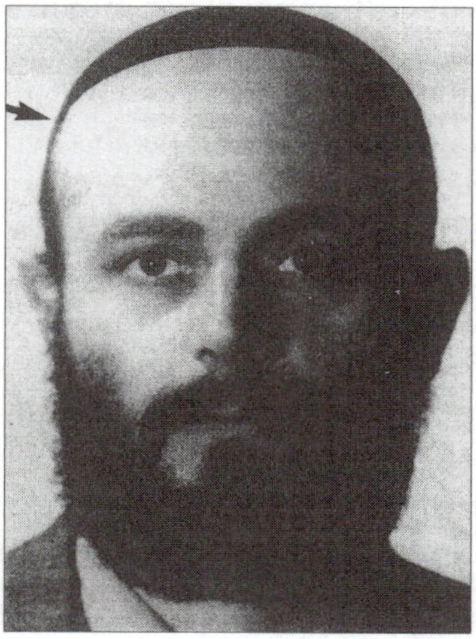

(*c*)

Figure 4.7 R. Menachem Mendel Schneerson, the Lubavitcher Rebbe: (*a*) and (*b*) with no head covering; (*c*) with a *kipah* added (arrow inserted by Deutsch). These pictures appear in Deutsch, *Larger than Life* (New York: Chasidic Historical Productions, 1997)

picture of the Rebbe's United States passport, and here too he is bareheaded (Fig. 4.7(*b*)). A third picture he included is of the Rebbe's previously published naturalization photograph, but this time a *kipah* had been added to his head (Fig. 4.7(*c*)).[65]

If we return to the Netzah publishing house, we can observe that while it was issuing German Orthodox works it also became quite expert in the art of

[65] For another picture of the Rebbe in which a *kipah* was added, see <failedmessiah.com>, 17 Feb. 2012. The original picture appears at <www.tinyurl.com/nhblo3j>. See also the pictures of the Rebbe here <www.therebbebook.com> in the MMS Personal Files. For examples of *kipot* placed on relatives of the Rebbe, see <www.mentalblog.com>, 5 June 2007.

censorship. This means that one cannot rely on any of its editions or translations without examining the original. The unstated rationale behind its acts of censorship is always the same, namely, to ensure that almost nothing from the German Orthodox world is published that reflects a different *Weltanschauung* from the post-Second World War haredi worldview.[66]

A typical example of this may be seen in how Netzah dealt with one of Jacob Rosenheim's (1870–1965) essays. Speaking about Hirsch, Rosenheim wrote that he showed 'tolerant, cautious reserve (if judged by the moral rigour of the divine Law and of rabbinical teaching) towards those very objectionable forms of conduct of the sexes on the parquet floors of the salons, towards **תערובת נשים עם אנשים**[67] [and] towards **קול באשה ערוה**[68] at public examinations in the higher grades'.[69] Rosenheim's point was that because of the mindset of his community, Hirsch was forced to compromise on these issues. Yet the very notion that such compromises are possible would not reflect well on Hirsch in the haredi world. This passage was therefore simply excised in the Netzah translation.[70]

Other examples of Netzah's censorship appear in its publications of the writings of R. Jehiel Jacob Weinberg, Isaac Breuer, and Ahron Marcus (1843–1916). In one of Weinberg's essays on Hirsch, he points out that the notion that Hirsch advocated secular studies for professional reasons alone is 'a distortion of the historical truth'.[71] When this essay was reprinted (without acknowledgement of where it first appeared),[72] Weinberg was made to say—in direct opposition to his authentic comment—that the notion he criticized 'is not the entire historical truth'.[73]

Later in this essay, Weinberg mentions that Hirsch showed a certain sympathy for Moses Mendelssohn.[74] Despite the fact that many great sages wrote

[66] Discomfort with German Orthodoxy is found throughout the haredi world. For example, in the obituary of R. Joseph Dunner in the London *Jewish Tribune*, no mention was made that he was a graduate of the Berlin Rabbinical Seminary. Instead, it stated that he attended 'the beis medrash of Harav Yechiel Yaakov Weinberg'. See Menachem Butler's Seforim blog post, 13 Apr. 2007. To my knowledge, this is the first time in history that the Berlin Rabbinical Seminary has been referred to in this way. Weinberg was himself quite upset when one of his students attempted to downplay his relationship with the Seminary. See Weinberg, *Kitvei hagaon*, ii. 354.

[67] The mixing of the sexes.

[68] 'A woman's voice is considered nakedness [i.e. licentious]' (BT *Ber.* 24*a*).

[69] Rosenheim, *Samson Raphael Hirsch's Cultural Ideal*, 60. (I have corrected the punctuation to agree with the original German, *Das Bildungsideal S. R. Hirschs*, 65.)

[70] Rosenheim, *Rabi shimshon rafa'el hirsh*.

[71] Weinberg, 'Torat haḥayim', 191.

[72] See Breuer, 'Review of Recent Books' (Heb.), 71.

[73] Introductory essay to Hirsch, *Bema'gelei shanah*, ii. 16.

[74] Ibid. 192. Weinberg adds that perhaps this was only a matter of literary politeness. In his larger essay on Hirsch, in Weinberg, *Seridei esh*, iv. 367, Weinberg removed this speculation.

positively of the man and his works,[75] in the haredi world Mendelssohn has been elevated into one of the worst enemies of traditional Judaism.[76] Weinberg's comment about Hirsch and Mendelssohn is therefore simply excised, as is a complete paragraph that discusses the relationship of Hirsch and Mendelssohn (and which criticizes Isaak Heinemann (1876–1957) for blurring the difference between the two). A final example from this essay is that in discussing how to enable traditional Judaism to thrive among those who are living in a modern Western society, Weinberg criticizes the solutions offered by those whom he characterizes as being of 'small mind and limited vision'.[77] This disparaging judgement of certain haredi ideologues was also excised.

Weinberg also wrote an essay on the talmudic historian Isaac Halevy (1847–1914),[78] which was reprinted by Netzah,[79] and here too we find the same pattern. For example, on the very first page Weinberg compares Halevy negatively to R. David Tsevi Hoffmann, pointing out the problems with Halevy's harshly polemical style. In the Netzah reprint this is censored from Weinberg's essay, and that is just from the first page. Much more falls by the wayside in subsequent pages, wherever Weinberg chooses to criticize Halevy. While some of the censored material might perhaps have been acceptable, even for Netzah, in a volume not intended to honour Halevy, most of what was removed could never have been printed in any haredi work, simply because Weinberg's objective and critical style is not what haredi readers have come to expect.

[75] See Hildesheimer, 'Moses Mendelssohn'.

[76] See A. B. Rosenberg, *Tsava'at aba*, 8*a*, no. 40, in the name of R. Shalom Roke'ah of Belz (1781–1855), that Mendelssohn was even worse than 'the known evil one' (Jesus?). While the latter's soul will eventually receive a *tikun* (rectification), this is not the case for Mendelssohn or anyone who studies his works. R. Levi Yitshak of Berdichev (1740–1809) supposedly said that Mendelssohn has to spend over eighteen million years in hell. See On the Main Line, 26 June 2012.

[77] Weinberg, 'Torat haḥayim', 199.

[78] See Weinberg, *Seridei esh*, iv. 249–66.

[79] M. Auerbach (ed.), *Memorial Book* (Heb.), 119–30.

CHAPTER FIVE

RABBI ABRAHAM ISAAC KOOK

WHEN IT COMES to Orthodox rewriting of the past so as to align it with the present, the figure of R. Abraham Isaac Kook stands out. During his lifetime, and especially after his assumption of the Chief Rabbinate of Eretz Yisra'el in 1921, Kook was regarded by most of the Orthodox as one of the world's leading rabbinic figures. In Palestine, there were those who even regarded him as *the* pre-eminent figure, the *gedol hador* ('greatest scholar of the generation') par excellence.

There were, of course, some who did not look so kindly upon Kook, and their opposition was long-standing. Not long after Kook's arrival in Palestine in 1904 he began making waves with his tolerant attitude towards the non-religious *ḥalutsim* (pioneers). Indeed, it soon became apparent that not only was Kook tolerant of them, but he even regarded the *ḥalutsim* as having a significant role, in both a physical and theological sense, in the building up of the land of Israel.

The opposition to Kook was centred in Jerusalem, where some members of the Old Yishuv,[1] anti-Zionist in the extreme, stopped at nothing to defame him.[2] Matters got so bad that the British authorities put two of his leading antagonists in jail.[3] The campaign against him was also pursued by the extreme anti-Zionists in Europe, most of whom were in Hungary.

What was it that created such animosity? The fact that Kook was willing to work with the non-religious Zionists would have been enough to tarnish his reputation in certain circles. Yet, as indicated, Kook did not merely work with the non-religious, but even provided a theological *raison d'être* for their

[1] The Old Yishuv was the community of Ashkenazi Jews in the land of Israel that originated before the first great *aliyah* at the end of the 19th cent.

[2] For details, see Schatz, 'Beginning of the Campaign' (Heb.); M. Friedman, *Society and Religion* (Heb.); Bezalel Naor's introduction to his translation of A. I. Kook, *Orot*.

[3] See M. Friedman, *Society and Religion* (Heb.), 229–30. One of those imprisoned was Meir Heller. Some letters from him focusing on his opposition to Kook appear in T. H. Friedman, *Tsevi ḥemed*, 47 ff.

very existence, explaining how they had an important contribution to make to the rejuvenation of the Jewish people in the pre-messianic era. The controversy really heated up after publication of his book *Orot* ('Lights') in 1920. In a work full of provocative formulations, the most controversial was the famous chapter 34 (in the section 'Orot hateḥiyah', 'Lights of Renascence'), where Kook claims that the exercise of the young *ḥalutsim* raises up the Shekhinah, the divine presence, 'just as it rises through songs and praises uttered by David, king of Israel, in the book of Psalms'.[4]

Kook's 1925 speech at the inauguration of the Hebrew University of Jerusalem also became a cause célèbre.[5] What was reported in the anti-Zionist Orthodox press—and it is impossible to know whether the original reports were purposeful distortions—was that he declared, with reference to the new university, 'For Torah shall go forth from Zion, and the word of the Lord from Jerusalem' (Micah 4: 2). Kook's clarification of what he had actually said did little to change the minds of those who had already decided that he was a heretic, but it was not without any impact. For example, R. Joseph Messas, rabbi of Tlemcen, Algeria, had seen a vitriolic attack on Kook in the Hungarian periodical *Beit va'ad leḥakhamim*, which focused on what Kook was alleged to have said at the inauguration. Finding the report difficult to believe, Messas wrote to Kook. After learning from Kook what the latter had actually said, Messas turned his sharp pen on the editor of the Hungarian journal, who in Messas's eyes was now guilty of the terrible sin of defaming a Torah scholar.[6]

Most of the leading sages in the land of Israel, such as R. Tsevi Pesah Frank (1873–1960),[7] R. Yehiel Michel Tukatchinsky (1872–1955), R. Isser Zalman Meltzer (1870–1953), R. Moses Mordechai Epstein (1866–1934), R. Hayim Yehudah Leib Auerbach (1883–1954, the father of R. Shlomo Zalman Auerbach), and numerous others were on Kook's side during the raging disputes. This does not mean that they shared all, or even most, of Kook's opinions, but they still regarded him as the rav of Jerusalem and many viewed him as the most distinguished scholar in the country. Even the famed R. Solomon Eliezer Alfandari (*c.*1822–1930), while strongly opposed to Kook's ideas,[8]

[4] On the controversy, including discussion of *Orot*, ch. 34, see Naor's introduction to his translation of A. I. Kook, *Orot*. One source he does not mention is R. Hayim Hirschensohn's (1857–1935) defence of Kook in id., *Ḥidushei harav ḥayim hirshenson*, vol. iii, no. 23.

[5] See Leiman, 'Rabbi Abraham Isaac ha-Kohen Kook: Invocation'; Naor, *When God Becomes History*, 98 ff.

[6] See Alharar, *Likhvodah shel torah*, 41–56.

[7] See his letter in Hirschensohn, *Malki bakodesh*, iv. 43–4.

[8] See A. Rosenberg, *Mishkenot haro'im*, iii. 1089 ff. Alfandari was idolized by one of Kook's leading denigrators, R. Hayim Eleazar Shapira. See M. Goldstein, *Mas'ot yerushalayim*.

nevertheless wrote to R. Jacob Moses Harlap (1883–1951) that economic sanctions should be enforced against those who were defaming Kook.[9]

As the years passed, Kook's reputation underwent changes. For the first few decades after his death he was regarded as a somewhat other-worldly figure, and his vision of religious Zionism had hardly any influence. This changed with the 1967 Six Day War, which saw the emergence of the messianic wing of religious Zionism under the leadership of Kook's son, R. Tsevi Yehudah Kook (hereafter, 'R. Tsevi Yehudah', 1891–1982). After 1967 the academic world also began to take a great interest in Kook, and many previously unpublished works of his began to appear in print. By a few decades after the Six Day War there was little question that Kook was the most studied, and influential, Orthodox Jewish thinker of the twentieth century.

Part of the great attraction of academics to Kook is precisely his radical ideas, which are now focal points of research. The growing awareness of the contents of Kook's writings has been one factor making it difficult for many in the haredi world to relate to him in a positive fashion. It is also no accident that as Kook began to assume great importance for the religious Zionist community, especially the settlers—for whom he became the central religious thinker—his reputation began to suffer in the emerging haredi society. With the exception of certain extremist groups in Jerusalem and Hungary, almost all Orthodox Jews regarded Kook as one of the *gedolim* in the first half of the twentieth century, even if they did not share his philosophy. This is why he was invited to attend the 1914 Agudat Yisra'el convention in Germany, which due to the outbreak of the First World War never took place, leaving Kook stranded in Europe until the end of hostilities. However, by the last quarter of the twentieth century it was obvious that Kook did not belong to the canon of *gedolim* of the haredi world.

It is interesting that two of the most important figures in haredi society during the last thirty years, R. Shlomo Zalman Auerbach and R. Yosef Shalom Elyashiv, came from the community that supported Kook, and never wavered in their positive feelings towards him.[10] Yet despite this, the strength of the anti-Kook sentiment was too strong to be beaten back, even by these two leaders of the haredi world. The fact that Kook had become central to the religious Zionist enterprise meant that haredi ideologues, who put a great deal of effort

[9] A copy of the letter appears in Y. Harlap, *Shirat hayam*, 434. See also Naor's translation of A. I. Kook, *Orot*, 230 n. 89.

[10] For Auerbach's relationship with Kook, see Kinarti, *Or shelomoh*. Elyashiv supported the firing of a Makhon Yerushalayim editor who refused to include passages from Kook's writings. See the interview with R. Yosef Buxbaum, the director of Makhon Yerushalayim, in *Besheva*, no. 104 (5 Aug. 2004), available at <www.inn.co.il/Besheva/Article.aspx/3142>. See also Anon., *Hashakdan*, i. 47; Anon., *Yisa shalom* (n.p., 2012).

into the delegitimization of religious Zionism, now needed to distance themselves from Kook as well.

This change in perception of Kook created an enormous problem for the haredi world. Because in the past Kook had been regarded as a prominent sage, he had written numerous approbations[11] for works of leading Torah scholars. Even R. Abraham Isaiah Karelitz, the Hazon Ish, when first arriving in the land of Israel, addressed a halakhic question to Kook, referring to him by the honorific title *hod kevod maran, shlita.*[12] He is also known to have stood up for the entirety of Kook's lengthy speech when the latter came to Benei Berak to speak at the cornerstone-laying ceremony of the Beit Yosef (Novardok) yeshiva.[13] Although the Hazon Ish's view of Kook became more negative after this,[14] widespread recognition of his earlier, more positive view, not to mention the great esteem in which many other sages held Kook, challenged the recent haredi *Weltanschauung*. To counter this, the censors in haredi society have been very busy. In fact, Kook has been the victim of more censorship and simple omission of facts for the sake of haredi ideology than any other figure.

When books are reprinted by haredi and anti-Zionist publishers Kook's approbations are routinely omitted.[15] In the Hebrew introduction to my *Saul Lieberman and the Orthodox*, I told of meeting one such publisher in Harvard's Widener Library. He had come there in order to find rare books to reprint. Upon looking at one of the books he had published, I immediately noticed that there was a blank space where one would have expected an approbation. Quickly finding a copy of the original in the Harvard stacks, I saw that it was Kook's *haskamah* that was removed. I approached the man and told

[11] *Haskamot* in Hebrew. The singular is *haskamah*.

[12] See B. Z. Shapira (ed.), *Igerot lare'iyah*, 448–9, and see p. 591 for pictures of the Hazon Ish's letters. Both of the Hazon Ish's letters to Kook have recently been reprinted, but the phrase *hod kevod maran shlita*, which appeared in one of these letters, has now been deleted. See A. I. Karelitz, *Genazim ushe'elot uteshuvot ḥazon ish*, i. 126.

[13] See Kohen, *Pe'er hador*, ii. 32; Horovitz, *Orḥot rabenu*, v. 172; Neriyah, *Bisedeh hare'iyah*, 247.

[14] See Horovitz, *Orḥot rabenu*, v. 172; Brown, *The Hazon Ish* (Heb.), 220 ff. The Hazon Ish instructed a book dealer not to carry Kook's philosophical writings. See Kohen, *Pe'er hador*, ii. 34; Brown, *The Hazon Ish* (Heb.), 227. Yet even with regard to Kook's philosophical works, the Hazon Ish sometimes expressed a more positive view, depending on whom he was speaking to. See Efrati, 'Two Visits' (Heb.). The way in which the Hazon Ish referred to Kook changed considerably between his arrival in Palestine and a few years later. For example, in a letter from 1937 the Hazon Ish conspicuously avoids using the normal phrases of praise for great rabbis, and writes simply הרב קוק ז"ל. The other rabbis mentioned in this letter have the title *gaon* attached to their names. See A. I. Karelitz, *Genazim ushe'elot uteshuvot ḥazon ish*, ii. 100.

[15] As a sign of increasing extremism in the haredi world, even the name of the revered R. Tsevi Pesah Frank has been removed from an approbation. See Dan Rabinowitz's Seforim Blog post, 22 Jan. 2007.

him that I understood that he regarded Kook as a heretic. However, the author of the book thought that Kook was a great man, which is why he had solicited his *haskamah*. 'What then gives you the right to take it out?', I demanded to know. The publisher's reply left me speechless. He told me that the author is now in heaven where he knows the truth about Kook, that Kook was not a righteous man but in fact a heretic, 'and he is therefore happy with what I have done'.[16]

Sometimes, the censorship of Kook is nothing less than comical. For example, in 1994 the family of the late R. Isaac Kossowsky (1877–1951) published a volume of his writings.[17] Kossowsky, who lived in Johannesburg from the 1930s, was a brother-in-law of R. Hayim Ozer Grodzinski (1863–1940). Like his brother-in-law, Kossowsky had a great deal of respect for Kook, as did the Lithuanian sages in general. Upon Kook's death Kossowsky delivered a very long eulogy, and he referred to Kook as 'the high priest among his brothers' (cf. Lev. 21: 10). Right at the beginning of his talk, he speaks of the great importance of eulogies, and how the speaker must make the listeners aware of the great loss they have suffered, and the special nature of the one being mourned.

Incredibly, in direct contradiction to these very words, the eulogy as it is printed does not mention who its subject is. It is entitled 'From a Eulogy for One of the Rabbis'. Throughout the eulogy, Kook's name, or anything that could identify him, is removed, leaving us with a wonderful eulogy for an unnamed rabbi. It is hard to imagine a greater undermining of the role of a eulogy, as elaborated upon by Kossowsky. Yet such is the environment in the haredi world that the editor, a descendant of Kossowsky, thought that censoring the eulogy was appropriate.[18]

In addition to removing all identifying references to Kook, the editor took other liberties as well. For example, when Kossowsky mentions how the great rabbis who supported the return to Zion—Mordechai Eliasberg (1817–89), Samuel Mohilever (1824–98), Isaac Jacob Reines (1839–1915), as well as the Mizrahi movement as a whole—battled against the secular Zionists, this too was removed, replaced by generic 'great rabbis' who are now the battlers against the secularists. The original eulogy contains a few pages discussing Kook's greatness, following which Kossowsky notes that although Kook was

[16] There are hasidic stories with similar themes. See e.g. Sorasky, *Marbitsei torah*, vi. 270–1 (called to my attention by Gershon Buchinger).

[17] Kossowsky, *She'elat yitsḥak*. The eulogy discussed appears on pp. 235–8. It was deleted entirely from the 2006 edition of *She'elat yitsḥak*. See Glick, *Kuntres*, iii, no. 3690.

[18] The uncensored eulogy, published from manuscript, appears in A. Elbaum and A. Elbaum, *Dabar ledor*, 52–63.

the subject of attacks, 'even his strongest opponents had to admit' his great righteousness. All this is omitted in the censored version, which, however, does include these words: 'And now that he is no longer with us, Orthodox Jewry is orphaned and with a hurt heart we cry out: who will bring us his replacement? . . . When a righteous man dies, he dies only for his generation.' The last sentence comes from the Talmud, *Megilah* 15*a*, and its meaning is that even though the righteous man is dead, his soul and name survive. Yet today, as we see in this censored eulogy, while the soul might survive, the name certainly does not!

The fear of associating with Kook, and of showing how great rabbis of the past who today are regarded as mainstays of the haredi world were on friendly terms with Kook and even admired him, is a reflection of the extremism that has taken root in haredi Judaism. In the case just mentioned, and this is a pattern that is constantly repeated, it is a descendant or other family member of the deceased rabbi who made the choice to censor his writings. In many of these cases of censorship, an outsider would not have the courage to do such a thing. However, family members, who are presumed to have the best interests of the author at heart, have often concluded that in our day and age, in order to spare the author (or his family) embarrassment, they must distance him from Kook. Others are worried that the author will not be 'accepted' in haredi circles if his relationship with Kook is known, or that people might not understand the original context of the author's relationship with Kook and therefore use this information 'improperly'.[19]

I have already noted that during Kook's lifetime there was strong opposition to him on the part of some members of the Old Yishuv. What is often overlooked is that the majority of the Old Yishuv was actually in R. Kook's corner during the great dispute. One need only look at the list of those individuals and yeshivas that welcomed Kook's appointment as rav of Jerusalem to see the support he commanded in the Old Yishuv.[20]

R. Tsevi Pesah Frank was one of the leading rabbinic figures who stood with Kook. In a letter to R. Hayim Hirschensohn, we get a glimpse of his anger at the opposition Kook was confronting:

> The Gaon, our Master RAY [Rabbi Abraham Isaac] Hakohen Kook was accepted here as Rav [rabbi] by the majority of the Holy Community here. It is well known that the members of the Kollel Ungarn [Hungarian *kolel*] are envious of our Russian

[19] See David Glasner's Seforim Blog post, 15 Feb. 2008. For censorship of Glasner's grandfather's name (R. Akiva Glasner (1886–1956)) because of his Zionism, see Glick, *Kuntres*, iii, no. 3632.

[20] See B. Z. Shapira (ed.), *Igerot lare'iyah*, 156–68. The yeshivas were Ets Hayim, Hayei Olam, Me'ah She'arim, Torat Hayim, and Sha'ar Hashamayim.

and Polish brethren. . . . They write and sign tens of thousands of letters to America and the entire world in the name of all the Ashkenazim in Jerusalem . . . that R. Hayyim Sonnenfeld is the Rav here, when all see and know that R. Hayyim Sonnenfeld was never, and will not be, the Rav, for he is an old, frail man for whom it is not possible to get involved in the affairs of the town. . . . The Gaon, our Master RAY Kook is the Rav here. All the largest institutions are under his presidency.[21]

There is a good deal more in this letter, in which he blasts the Jerusalem extremists for their activities, but even from this short excerpt one gets a sense of how a figure revered by the haredim regarded Kook. I do not mean to imply that the entire Lithuanian Torah world related positively to Kook, as this was not the case. Two notable figures who were strongly opposed to Kook, viewing him as nothing less than an enemy of Torah Judaism, were R. Joseph Rozin (1858–1936) and R. Elhanan Wasserman (1874–1941).[22] As can be expected, their statements are often reprinted by the anti-Zionist Orthodox. What the latter are *not* prepared to reprint are the letters sent to Kook by his good friend, R. Zelig Reuven Bengis (1864–1953), who after Kook's death became chief rabbi of the anti-Zionist Edah Haredit, the same group that caused Kook so much pain.[23]

One aspect of the haredi response to Kook has been to write him out of the Torah world completely. Sometimes this is hard. For example, what is one to do with the fact that the renowned R. Elijah David Rabinowitz-Teomim (the Aderet) was Kook's father-in-law, and that Kook wrote a volume dedicated to his memory?[24] The biographical introduction in one of Rabinowitz-Teomim's posthumously published books simply refuses to mention that Kook was his son-in-law.[25] Another haredi biography of Rabinowitz-Teomim quotes from Kook's volume but never mentions the author's name.[26] This

[21] Hirschensohn, *Malki bakodesh*, iv. 43–4 (trans. Naor in A. I. Kook, *Orot*, 224–5).

[22] For Rozin's attack on Kook in which he characterizes him as a heretic, see A. Rosenberg, *Mishkenot haro'im*, iii. 1109. Wasserman called Kook a *rasha* (evil man). See his *Yalkut ma'amarim umikhtavim*, 152. A photograph of the handwritten letter appears in the back of the volume. Wasserman's attack was provoked by false information. He mistakenly believed that Kook encouraged financial support of the Zionist Keren Hayesod. See E. Henkin, 'Rabbi Abraham Isaac Kook's Relationship with the Keren Hayesod' (Heb.), 75–6.

[23] See B. Z. Shapira (ed.), *Igerot lare'iyah*, nos. 143, 192, 358. See also ibid., no. 142, for a letter to Kook from R. Pinhas Epstein (1889–1969). Epstein later became *rosh beit din* of the Edah Haredit. Both Epstein and Bengis address Kook as *av beit din* of Jerusalem.

[24] A. I. Kook, *Eder hayekar*.

[25] Rabinowitz-Teomim, *Over oraḥ*. Speaking of Rabinowitz-Teomim, in 1984 his autobiography, *Seder eliyahu*, was published. In 2010 it was reprinted, but this time it was heavily censored to remove all sorts of comments about his family and aspects of the rabbinic world. See Dan Rabinowitz's Seforim Blog post, 27 May 2010.

[26] Rabinowitz-Teomim, *Ḥidushei hagaon ha'aderet*. The Ponovezh yeshiva had many manuscripts written by Rabinowitz-Teomim, yet they never published them. This may have been due to

approach of not mentioning Kook by name, and only referring to his books, is also followed in various haredi halakhic works.[27]

The same 'problem' mentioned with regard to Rabinowitz-Teomim also occurs with R. Shlomo Zalman Auerbach, who became an enormously influential figure in the haredi world. Yet both he and his father, R. Hayim Yehudah Leib Auerbach (1886–1954), were great admirers of Kook, with the younger Auerbach referring to Kook in 1979 as 'our rabbi, may the memory of the righteous be a blessing' (רבנו זצ"ל).[28] Yet one will not find any mention of this in the haredi biographies of Auerbach, nor do they mention that Kook officiated at Auerbach's wedding in 1930.[29]

Kook's followers have not been silent in the face of all the distortions of the historical record. One important thing they did was to publish the volume *Igerot lare'iyah* ('Letters to Rabbi A. I. Kook'), which contains over five hundred pages of letters from leading rabbinic figures to Kook, showing how they related to him. Amihai Kinarti has also performed a valuable service in publishing four booklets documenting the close and respectful relationships with Kook enjoyed by four outstanding sages of nearly unimpeachable credentials in the haredi world: Rabbis Hayim Ozer Grodzinski, Isser Zalman Meltzer, Tsevi Pesah Frank, and Shlomo Zalman Auerbach.[30]

fear of how certain extremists would react in view of the close relationship between Rabinowitz-Teomim and Kook. See E. Melamed, *Revivim: gedolei yisra'el*, 70.

27 For an example, see Kasirer, *Shemitah kemitsvatah*. When R. Yitshak Ratsaby has to refer to Kook, he writes הרא"ק, standing for 'Rabbi Abraham Kook'. Many examples of this can be seen by doing a search of his books on Otzar HaHochma. See also Ratsaby, *Olat yitsḥak*, ii. 440. Most people would have no idea who this is, which is exactly the point. The anonymous *Shemitah kemitsvatah* (n.p., 2006), written against the *heter mekhirah* (the temporary sale of farmland to a non-Jew during the sabbatical year, thus allowing a Jew to work the land), refers numerous times to Kook's responsa volume, *Mishpat kohen*, but refuses to mention him by name. This refusal leads to the following bizarre wording: 'And so wrote the *Mishpat kohen* in his book *Shabat ha'arets*' (p. 16; called to my attention by David Zilberberg).

28 See his 1979 letter in Neriyah, *Likutei hare'iyah*, iii. 101.

29 See Neriyah, *Likutei hare'iyah*, iii. 99–100; Kinarti, *Or shelomoh*, 18; Y. Eliyahu and R. Eliyahu, *Hatorah hamesamaḥat*, 41. Kook was the *shadkhan* (matchmaker) for Elyashiv's marriage, and officiated at it as well. See Anon., *Hashakdan*, i. 47; Anon., *Yisa shalom*, 20. The latter source has a picture of Elyashiv's *ketubah*, the particulars of which were filled in by Kook himself. See also Melamed, *Revivim: gedolei yisra'el*, 131. For another example of how Kook is ignored, see Rosenblum, *Reb Shraga Feivel*, who neglects to mention that R. Shraga Feivel Mendlowitz (1886–1948) was a great admirer of Kook and even taught a class on Kook's teachings. See Low, 'Answer to Criticism' (Heb.), 49. Rosenblum's ignoring of Kook is also mentioned by Mendlowitz's grandson, Menachem Mendlowitz, in his lecture 'The Complexity of Greatness: My Grandfather, Rav Shraga Feivel Mendlowitz', available at <http://www.torahinmotion.org/store/products/complexity-greatness-my-grandfather-rav-shraga-feivel>.

30 Respectively *Hare'iyah veha'aḥi'ezer*, *Az nidberu yir'ei hashem*, *Ateret tsevi*, and *Or shelomoh*. See also Kampinski, *Bein shenei kohanim gedolim*, which deals with the relationship between Kook and R. Israel Meir Hakohen (the Hafets Hayim).

What about R. Jacob Moses Harlap? He was a saintly figure who was also Kook's leading disciple and, with the possible exception of R. Tsevi Yehudah, there was no one who was more attached, both emotionally and intellectually, to Kook.[31] From the moment that Harlap was introduced to Kook in 1904 while on a visit to Jaffa,[32] his entire personality became subsumed into that of Kook. In fact, Harlap's entire approach to Judaism can be seen as a set of footnotes to the teaching he received from his master, Kook. It was Harlap who came to Kook's defence when the controversy over *Orot* heated up, publishing his *Tovim me'orot*, which attempted to explain some of the controversial passages. This latter publication led to him becoming an object of attack in *Kol hashofar*,[33] an anonymous and infamous pamphlet that blasted Kook. Harlap also sent two long letters in defence of Kook's ideas in *Orot* to R. Hanokh Tsevi Levin (1870–1935), with the intention of influencing Levin's brother-in-law, R. Abraham Mordechai Alter, the Rebbe of Gur.[34]

Yet the popular haredi biographer Aharon Sorasky, in discussing Harlap, describes how he was an outstanding student (*talmid muvhak*) of R. Joshua Tsevi Michel Shapira (1840–1906), without even mentioning one word about Harlap's connection to Kook, whom he regarded as his primary teacher. Sorasky also neglects to record that Harlap succeeded Kook as *rosh yeshivah* of Merkaz Harav, Kook's yeshiva.[35] The problem Sorasky had to confront is obvious: if Harlap was a great Torah leader (*gadol*), how can it be that he revered Kook? This would, understandably, lead people to think that they too should share Harlap's reverence. Sorasky's solution was therefore simply to omit any mention of Harlap's connection to Kook. In this case the problem was made more difficult for Sorasky because his discussion of Harlap appears in his biography of R. Yisrael Alter (1895–1977), the Rebbe of Gur. Sorasky informs us that in the early years of his 'reign', Alter would study kabbalah every Friday with Harlap. It would not help Alter's image in the haredi world if it were known that he was influenced by the outstanding disciple of Kook who, at the time the two studied together, was serving as *rosh yeshivah* of Merkaz Harav. Therefore, Sorasky is careful to inform the reader that Harlap's kabbalistic knowledge came from Shapira, without any indication that Kook's influence, kabbalistic and otherwise, was the primary force in Harlap's life.

Another great follower of Kook was R. Yitshak Arieli (1896–1974), author of the talmudic work *Einayim lamishpat*. He was appointed by Kook to serve as

[31] See e.g. H. Lifshitz, *Shivḥei hare'iyah*, 277.

[32] See Tsoref, *Life of Rav Kook* (Heb.), 119. It was R. Tsevi Pesah Frank who made the introduction.

[33] pp. 7ff.

[34] The letters are printed in *Me'avnei hamakom*, 13 (2001), 66–72.

[35] Sorasky, *Pe'er yisra'el*, i. 270–1, 317. See Melamed, *Revivim: gedolei yisra'el*, 35–6, 236.

mashgiaḥ ruḥani (spiritual guide) of Merkaz Harav. Yet in the 2006 reprint of one of the volumes of *Einayim lamishpat*, published by Arieli's grandchildren, a paragraph in his preface in which he speaks about Kook[36] and Merkaz Harav has been omitted.[37] Furthermore, in the biographical introduction there is no mention of Arieli's connection to Kook or his yeshiva.[38]

Seeing what has been done with Kook's followers, Harlap and Arieli, one can only imagine the lengths that people go to blot out any connection between Kook and those rabbis who, while friendly with him, were not in Kook's 'camp'. One energetic soul, Moshe Maimon Alharar, has published a volume devoted to refuting the newspaper *Yated ne'eman*'s slanderous distortion of what Kook said at the dedication of the Hebrew University.[39] The book also deals with Alharar's attempts to get the paper to issue a simple retraction. These attempts failed, even after those in charge of the paper were shown that what they had printed was false. As in so many other cases, the truth was not as important to this newspaper as making sure that Kook is seen as a figure who is outside the Torah world. If it is necessary to repeat falsehoods and destroy Kook's reputation in order to achieve that goal, then this is a price that *Yated ne'eman* is willing to pay, and which it believes is halakhically warranted.

The delegitimization of Kook can be found throughout the haredi world, in newspapers, works of Torah scholarship, and children's books. Let me offer an illustrative example. Over the last generation a wonderful new edition of Maimonides' *Mishneh torah* has appeared, known as the Frankel edition. An enormous amount of work went into its production, as may be seen in the many commentators referred to in the index, as well as in the significant manuscript work undertaken to produce a high-quality text. Conspicuously absent from the commentators referred to in the index is Kook, who often discusses Maimonides in his many volumes of responsa. The editors even chose

36 He refers to Kook as גאון ישראל וקדושו מרנא ורבנא רבי אברהם יצחק הכהן קוק זצ״ל.

37 Yitshak Avi Roness informs me that this volume (on *Berakhot*) was reprinted earlier by Arieli himself without any omissions. The matter is somewhat complicated by the fact that before reprinting the volume on *Berakhot*, Arieli also reprinted his *Einayim lamishpat* on *Kidushin*, and here he did remove a positive reference to Kook. Details on this will appear in a forthcoming article by Roness.

38 See Melamed, *Revivim: gedolei yisra'el*, 87. Melamed notes that in 1998 another edition of *Einayim lamishpat* was also censored to remove mention of Kook. R. Yosef Shalom Elyashiv expressed his displeasure at the most recent censorship, leading the publisher to recall the books and correct matters by reinserting the deleted material. See Melamed, *Revivim: gedolei yisra'el*, 89. See also Anon., *Hashakdan*, ii. 106; Anon., *Yisa shalom*, 38–9. Melamed also points out that a recent biography of R. Elijah Romm (1872–1919; Rosenthal, *To'afot re'em*) avoids any discussion of Romm's close relationship with Kook. See Melamed, *Revivim: gedolei yisra'el*, 82–3. For censorship of R. Aryeh Levin's (1885–1969) close connection to Kook, see ibid. 99–101.

39 Alharar, *Likhvodah shel torah*.

to ignore Kook's book, *Shabat ha'arets*, which is a commentary on *Mishneh torah*, 'Hilkhot shevi'it' ('Laws of the Sabbatical Year').[40]

Other efforts at delegitimization are more pernicious, and here I refer to the issue of Kook's *haskamot* (approbations), referred to earlier in this chapter. For hundreds of years it has been the practice for traditional authors to request great rabbinic figures to write a *haskamah* for their book, asserting, in essence, that it is a valuable work and that scholars would benefit from studying it. While most of the earliest *haskamot* were designed to protect the financial interest of the publisher, by forbidding anyone to reprint the book, the genre was later transformed so that *haskamot* became almost exclusively testimonies to the religious acceptability of the author and his book.

Understandably, many rabbis wished to adorn their books with *haskamot* from Kook. He is known to have written some 283 of them during his lifetime, which I believe makes him the most prolific writer of approbations until the late twentieth-century explosion of printing allowed other figures to pass this mark with ease.[41] The problem for opponents of Kook is that these *haskamot* show him as a great sage respected by the Torah community at large. The way to counter this is by removing his *haskamot*, thus rewriting history in the process. Although it is probably the case that some printers who remove the approbations are not motivated by anti-Kook extremism, but by business considerations—the reprint will not sell in certain places if it contains Kook's *haskamah*[42]—the damage to Kook's legacy is the same. If the

[40] R. David Tsevi Hillman, who was very involved with the Frankel edition, justified the omission of Kook by noting that the Hazon Ish and R. Hayim Kanievsky also do not refer to him. See his letter, which I published in the Seforim Blog, 11 Jan. 2008. In response to the Frankel edition, the followers of Kook issued their own, much larger, index: see Kahana, Ra'anan, and Blum (eds.), *Index of the Commentaries* (Heb.), and R. Aryeh Stern's preface to vol. i. R. Shlomo Zalman Auerbach criticized an author who wrote about the laws of *shemitah* and did not refer to Kook. See Neriyah, *Likutei hare'iyah*, iii. 98.

[41] See the list of his approbations in Kook, *Haskamot hare'iyah*, 129–39.

[42] Business considerations of this sort are nothing new. For example, in the 19th cent. the comments of the *maskil* Hayim Zelig Slonimsky were removed from an edition of the *Mishneh torah*, but only for those volumes that were to be sent to Poland. See Dienstag, 'Maimonides' *Mishneh torah*' (Heb.), 53. The publisher of the 19th-cent. Vilna edition of the Talmud refused to include at least one of R. Jacob Emden's negative comments against hasidim. This was presumably done so as not to hurt sales. See Yeshayah Asher Zelig Miller's letter in *Or yisra'el*, 42 (Tevet 5766), 249. (See also M. M. S. Goldstein, 'Studies' (Heb.), 205, who claims that the passage was omitted because Emden's comment against the hasidim was not harsh enough!) A responsum critical of Agudat Yisra'el was removed from many copies of R. Judah Gruenwald's *Zikhron yehudah*, i, no. 200. This was done so that the volume could be sold at the 1923 Agudah convention in Vienna. See Schischa, 'Responsa' (Heb.), 48–9. In 2005 Makhon Harav Matsliah in Benei Berak published separate editions of R. Elijah Levita's *Hatishbi*. One of the editions omitted the notes of R. Solomon Tsevi Schück, who is not acceptable in most Hungarian Orthodox circles.

book in question is newly typeset then it is quite easy to omit the *haskamah*, and no one will be the wiser. One example of this is seen in R. Joseph Patsanovsky's classic *Pardes yosef*. This work, the first volume of which appeared in Piotrków in 1930, contains a *haskamah* from Kook.[43] In various subsequent editions, including one titled *Pardes yosef hashalem* ('The Complete *Pardes yosef*'!),[44] the *haskamah* has been removed. This latter book, since it is reset as opposed to being photo-offset, has no difficulty in creating the illusion that nothing is missing.[45]

I mentioned earlier how a reprinted book had a blank space where Kook's *haskamah* appeared in the original edition. This is a problem that arises with cheap photo-offset printing. Here, the only way that the *haskamah* can be removed without affecting the rest of the work, and without calling attention to the omission, is if it occupies an entire page all by itself. A good example of this is seen in R. Reuven Margaliyot's (1889–1970) *Nefesh ḥayah*, a commentary on the *Shulḥan arukh*.[46] He sent the book to Kook for a *haskamah*, and Kook replied not only with an approbation, but appended a series of learned notes. His letter was given its own page, and his name was adorned with abundant rabbinic praise.[47] Yet when this valuable book was reprinted in approximately 1980 (no place or date is given), Kook's *haskamah* was removed, leaving the *haskamot* of R. Meir Arik (1856–1926) and R. Moses Babad undisturbed, as they appear on another page. The reader has no way of knowing that anything has been removed, which is exactly what the censor hopes for.[48]

However, what can be done when Kook's *haskamah* does not occupy its own page but appears together with *haskamot* by other rabbis? When R. David Tsevi Kamin's *Beit david*[49] was reproduced by photo-offset in the late 1960s,

43 Patsanovsky, *Pardes yosef*, i. 333–4.

44 Professor Shnayer Z. Leiman has quipped that it should rather be called *Pardes yosef heḥaser* (*shalem* means 'complete', while *ḥaser* means 'deficient').

45 Another newly typeset edition of the work, *Pardes yosef hashalem vehamefo'ar*, does include Kook's approbation. See Dan Rabinowitz's Seforim Blog post, 23 Nov. 2011.

46 Margaliyot, a legendary scholar and bibliographer, was fortunate to meet Kook shortly before the latter died. It was then that Kook encouraged him to publish his edition of the Zohar, which soon became the standard edition. See his introduction to this work.

47 רבינו הגדול גאון ישראל וקדושו עמוד הימיני מרן אברהם יצחק הכהן הי"ו מרא דארעא דישראל.

48 These are some other books from which Kook's *haskamah* was removed: Shochet, *Beit yedidyah*, in the Brooklyn, 1992 reprint; Amram Gaon, *Seder rav amram hashalem*, in the Jerusalem, 1993 reprint; M. Goldstein, *Yabia omer*, in an undated reprint (no place of publication listed); Walk, *Ein eli'ezer*, in the Brooklyn, 1990 reprint; Wilstein, *Ḥayei hamishnah*, in the undated Jerusalem reprint (R. Jacob Moses Harlap's *haskamah* was also removed); Yeloz, *Yesh me'ayin*, ii, in the Brooklyn, 2002 reprint; Rippman, *Keter kehunah*, in the Jerusalem, 1989 reprint.

49 The date on the title page is 1919, but the *haskamot* are dated a couple of years later.

the simplest approach was taken, namely, leaving out the entire first page of *haskamot*. While this meant also omitting the other rabbis' approbations—including those of R. Joseph Hayim Sonnenfeld (1848–1932) and R. Isaac Yeruham Diskin (1839–1925)—it was obviously thought that this was the price that had to be paid to keep Kook out. In the original edition of this book there was a second page of *haskamot*, but presumably since it would be regarded as disrespectful to include these *haskamot* while omitting those by Sonnenfeld and Diskin, all the approbations were removed.[50]

The same thing happened with one of R. Aaron Kagan's books. Kagan was the son-in-law of R. Israel Meir Hakohen, the Hafets Hayim, and a great admirer of Kook, whom he refers to as *maran* ('our master'). In 1928 he published an open letter in opposition to those heaping abuse on Kook. He begins by noting that until then he had never protested against the attacks because his father-in-law, who also thought highly of Kook,[51] believed it was best not to give the extremists any publicity. Kagan further reports that since the Hafets Hayim's feelings for Kook were well known, the opponents of Kook would not dare to say anything against him in the Hafets Hayim's presence.[52] Yet the disrespect for Kook had become so bad that Kagan now felt that he was required to speak out. He also noted, with regard to those defaming Kook, that one who insults a Torah scholar has no share in the world to come, and must be placed under a ban.[53]

In 1923 Kagan published the second volume of his *Avodat hakorbanot*, and it was reprinted in Tel Aviv in 1928. This work is devoted to the sacrificial laws, a subject near to the Hafets Hayim's heart,[54] since as a *kohen* (priest) he hoped to be personally involved with it in the imminent messianic era.[55] In both the 1923 and 1928 editions Kook's *haskamah* appears on one page together with the approbations of R. Raphael Shapiro (1837–1921), the head of the Volozhin yeshiva, and R. Hayim Ozer Grodzinski. The approbations also

[50] The book was reset and republished in Jerusalem in 1997 and 2001. The publisher took advantage of this and put all of the *haskamot* back in, with the exception of Kook's. This book and the omission of the *haskamot* are discussed by Rafler, *Netivei me'ir*, 435–6.

[51] According to R. Tsevi Yehudah, the lengthy approbation of Kook's father-in-law, R. Elijah David Rabinowitz-Teomim, for the Hafets Hayim's *Likutei halakhot* was actually written by Kook. See *Linetivot yisra'el*, ii. 17; Neriyah, *Siḥot hare'iyah*, 123–4. This information would appear to be contradicted by Rabinowitz-Teomim, *Seder eliyahu*, 100.

[52] See also Neriyah, *Siḥot hare'iyah*, 126–7, for two stories regarding how the Hafets Hayim reacted when meeting those who attacked Kook.

[53] See Kagan's letter in B. Z. Shapira (ed.), *Igerot lare'iyah*, 565–6.

[54] See his introduction to Kagan, *Avodat hakorbanot*.

[55] See what the Hafets Hayim told R. David Cohen (the Nazir; 1887–1972), recorded in Cohen, *Mishnat hanazir*, introd., 10–11.

appear in the 1979 and 1984 photo-offset reprints. Yet in both the undated and the 2001 reprints of Kagan's book, Kook's *haskamah* was removed. In fact, the entire page of approbations was removed, since the publishers did not want to delete Kook's *haskamah* (i.e. white it out) and leave the others in. By cutting out the entire page the other *haskamot* have been lost. But as already mentioned, by adopting this approach people will not suspect what has been done to the book, which is obviously not the case when everyone can see a blank space on the page. The only *haskamah* that remains in these censored editions is that of the Hafets Hayim.

Kagan's book was reprinted in Jerusalem in 2002 with beautiful new type, and this will become the standard edition. Here too the *haskamot* by Kook, Shapiro, and Grodzinski are missing. With this new edition, one would have expected a publisher who chose to omit Kook's *haskamah* to include the approbations of Grodzinski and Shapiro. Undoubtedly, the publisher used one of the censored editions for his new edition, and assumed that other than the Hafets Hayim's letter no other *haskamot* had been received. Such is the effect of censorship that even the 'innocent bystanders', in this case Shapiro and Grodzinski, are condemned to have their *haskamot* lost to posterity along with that of Kook.

Other printers were not prepared to pay the price described above, namely, cutting out the 'acceptable' *haskamot* in order that Kook's should not also appear. I have already mentioned the cruder tactic in which the *haskamah* is taken out, leaving a blank space in its place.[56] An example of this may be seen in the Brooklyn, 1992 reprint of R. Abraham Samuel Tsevi Zilberstein's *Korban shemuel* (see Fig. 5.1).[57] Further examples of this way of removing Kook's *haskamot* appear in a number of other books, of which I will mention a few.

In the second volume of R. Elhanan Jakobovitz's *Even shimon*, a letter from Kook is included at the beginning of the work. The author refers to Kook with elaborate titles of respect.[58] Yet anyone who examines the Brooklyn,

[56] Yonatan Meir called my attention to the following interesting point: the writings of R. Joseph Isaac Schneersohn contain a number of letters to Kook, complete with the flowery titles one would expect. For one of the letters, however, someone had access to the computer file and removed all of the titles, so that now the letter is addressed to קוק, no more and no less. I have no doubt that this was not done by the editors responsible for publication, but by a troublemaker. See Schneersohn, *Igerot kodesh*, vol. xiii. 217 (no. 4715).

[57] The *haskamot* that Zilberstein printed in this volume were actually given for his earlier work, *Karnot hamizbe'aḥ*. The story I tell above, pp. 145–6, regarding the removal of Kook's *haskamah* revolved around Zilberstein's *Korban shemuel*.

[58] מאורן של ישראל זצוק"ל, see Jakobovitz, *Even shimon*, 2.

הסכמות

מהר"ג הגאון המובהק זקן גאון הגאונים חריף העצום ומפורסם ע"ש תבל בעשר ספריו הנוראים כש"ת מו"ה **אברהם אהרן יודעלעוויץ** זצ"ל רב הכולל לאגודת הקהלות **בנויארק** בעהמ"ח עשרה ספרים גדולים ונוראים ספרי שו"ת **בית אב** וספרי **דרש אב** וכו'

בעזהי"ת, כבוד ידיד עליון יתרומם ויתנשא, ה"ה גאון ע"ה ובנגב הרבה חריף ומחודד ומפולפל ומלמיח לילים ופריקים. בסברות זכים ולחים. ממש כחריפי דפומבדיתא בשעשועי דאורייתא. לעילא לעילא מכל ברכתא. ה"ה ר' **אברהם שמואל צבי** זילבערשטיין רב **בטאראנטא קענעדע**. יהיה לו ולכל החוכים על דגלו וברכה. עד עולם.

אחדש"ט ושתה"ר. הדפיס מספרו **קרנות המזבח** הגיעני, ורב נחת ועונג היה לי בקראי בהם, ראיתי גודל חכמתו ואומץ חריפותו, סברותיו שנונים, ומבהיקים כפז ופנינים, אשרי לו ככה, מ"ד ישא ברכה, ואשר ינקש ממני **הסכמה** על ספרו הוא אך למותר. כי הכסיל לא **יבין את דברין** ולא ישכיל ולא יבין על מה ולמה אנכי מהללו, והאיש אשר **יבין** דברי תורה בעיניו יראה **כי ספרו** הוא כולו עוטה אורה בחכמה וסברא. יקרה וטהורה, ואינו צריך לדידי ולשבחי, **ובפה מלא אומר אשריך עיר טראנטא שזכית לרב כזה.** ויהא רעוא משמי שמיא דירים רישיה אכולא ברכא, וילמוד תורה כחפצו ומפיק אוהב כאמן להוגי תורה ולירא' ד' ולחושבי שמו.

נאום הק' **אברהם אהרן יודעלעוויץ**

רב הכולל לאגח"ק דניוארק יצ"ו בעהמ"ס שו"ת בית אב ודרש אב. (עיין אריכות פלפולי תורה הנדפס בקרנות המזבח)

מהר"ג הגאון הגדול חריף ונקי עסקן כללי המפורסם ע"פ תבל כש"ת מו"ה **מאיר שפירא** שהיה אבד"ק **פיטרקוב** ואח"כ ר"מ **בישיבת לובלין** זצ"ל בעהמ"ס שו"ת **אור המאיר**.

ב"ה עש"ק וירא **תרפ"ז** לפ"ק ניויארק.

שוכ"ט לכבוד הרב הגאון החריף ונקי במ"ס פאר יקדושים ובלר מטעי היחם כש"ת כש"ת מו"ה **אברהם שמואל צבי זילבערשטיין** שליט"א ומלפנים אבד"ק ביידעטשין, ואבד"ק **וויעזבניק** בפולין וכעת רב **בטאראנטא**.

זה עתה הביא לו בנו היקר נ"י קונטריסו הנחמד **קרנות המזבח** וראיתי אמריו כי נעמו, בנויים על אדני תריכות ובקיאות בסברות ישרות, ומטעמי הפלפול וראויים הם לאי שאוהבים ויפילו על פני תבל ויתענגו בהו שוחרי תורה ואוהבי תושיה ובהרעיפו על קונטרסו ראיתי ראשית דבריו לזה נדפס כבר שם] והערותי מזה בשו"ת **אור המאיר**, יתפס הפנאי הקצר יהי **השם** את כתה"ר **וידעו נא רבים להוקיר ערכו** ידידו דוש"ת.

הק' **מאיר שפירא**

אב"ד פיעטרקוב (ואח"כ בלובלין)

מהר"ג הגאון המובהק החריף המפורסם עיניו כיונים על אפיקי הש"ס והפוסקים שהיה אבד"ק **האריסבורג ובספרינגפיעלד מאסס**. וכעת אבד"ק **סינסינעטי**. ויו"ר **לאגודת הרבנים** נאה"ב. ונשיא **אגודת ישראל** נאה"ב.

בעזהשי"ת יום ג' לחדש טבת **תרפ"ז ספרינגפילד מאסס**. „בו ירוה נחת" לפ"ק.

אל כבוד ידידי הרב הגאון בנן של קדושים סדרן ומפולפל וכו' וכו' כש"ת מוה"ר **אברהם צבי הירש זילבערשטיין** שליט"א, ברכה ושלום.

אחדש"ט:

לא הייתי בניתי ימים אחדים. ובניתי עמוס הבני בעבודה. ע"כ אחרתי המענה ויסלח נא. הקונטרסים מדף י"ג עד מ"א הגיעוני. ופה ושם עיינתי, ואחזתי **בקרנות מזבחו**. זרקתי מדם הקדשים ופה ושם ראיתי „אמורי בנוה" ממולאים בפלפולי דאורייתא, ונסיכי יין התורה, המשמח לבב אנוש. והראוי להעלות על מזבח הדפוס. „ועל יסודותיו" מלאתי יש „די לשיריים" ולקיים תן לחכם ויחכם עוד, ואומר על כן הילו לאורייתא תדירא. יוסיף להיות עוסק בתורת ד' ולהתברך בכל טוב סלה:

ידידו הכותב ומותם לכבוד התורה,

אליעזר בהרה"ג ר' בוכם בנוח זצ"ל **זילבר**.

הגאון המובהק החריף האריך כאן מאד בפלפולא דאורייתא והוא נדפס **בקרנות המזבח**, וסיים וכל זה כתבתי בחפזי כי מכתבים לעשרות עוד עלי לכתוב להיום. ידידו,

אליעזר זילבר

Figure 5.1 R. Abraham Samuel Tsevi Zilberstein, *Korban shemuel* (Brooklyn: Copy Corner, 1992), with Kook's *haskamah* whited out

1993 reprint of this volume will have no way of knowing to whom these words of reverence refer, since although Kook's letter is included, his name at the beginning (in the letterhead) and at the end (the signature) has been removed, leaving two blank spaces.

The publisher who reprinted R. Eliezer Tsevi Zigelman's *Naḥalei emunah* in Brooklyn in 1983[59] also wished to avoid cutting out an entire page of approbations, of which Kook's was the very first. Fortunately for him, he did not have to leave a blank space, since he was able to lift the approbation from R. Shalom Mordechai Schwadron (1835–1911), which appeared at the end of the volume and took up roughly the same amount of space,[60] and substitute this for Kook's *haskamah*. By means of photographic alteration, the publisher also ensured that there is no evidence of any missing lines in the place where Schwadron's *haskamah* originally appeared.

The same method was used in the London, 1967 reprint of the commentary by R. Yehudah Ashlag (1885–1954) on R. Hayim Vital, *Ets haḥayim*, vol. 2. In the original Jerusalem, 1930 edition, Kook's *haskamah* appears on the first page, with R. Joseph Hayim Sonnenfeld's *haskamah* on the second page. In the 1967 reprint, Kook's *haskamah* is nowhere to be found, and that of Sonnenfeld takes its place.[61] In R. Isaiah Joseph Margolin's *Hama'aseh vehamidrash*, Kook's *haskamah* is the very first, and under it come those of Sonnenfeld and R. Elijah Klatzkin (1852–1932; Fig. 5.2(*a*)). However, in the Brooklyn, 1992 reprint, Kook's *haskamah* is missing and Sonnenfeld's is at the top (Fig. 5.2(*b*)). In reprinting the volume, all the publisher had to do when he removed Kook's *haskamah* was move Sonnenfeld's up, and the empty space at the bottom is filled by a *haskamah* from R. Moses Mordechai Epstein which originally appeared on the following page. In other words, with Kook's *haskamah* gone, everyone 'moves up' and no one is the wiser, since the *haskamot* on the following page end in the middle, leaving the remainder of the page blank.

These examples are obviously of a different sort from those in which the author himself removes Kook's *haskamah*. A famous instance of this is found with R. Isaac Hutner (1906–80). After studying in the Slobodka yeshiva in

[59] The book originally appeared in Lublin, 1935, and was reprinted without any censorship in Jerusalem, 1968.

[60] I say 'roughly' since the publisher also had to insert fairly large gaps between the paragraphs in order to enable the approbation to fill up the space. In addition, the page of *haskamot* that used to appear first has been moved, and the first *haskamot* are now those given by hasidic figures.

[61] In the London, 1967 reprint of vol. i of Ashlag's commentary on Vital's *Ets haḥayim*, Kook's *haskamah* was also removed. Interestingly, there is at least one example where Sonnenfeld's *haskamah* was taken out. See A. Elbaum, 'Alterations' (Heb.), 37.

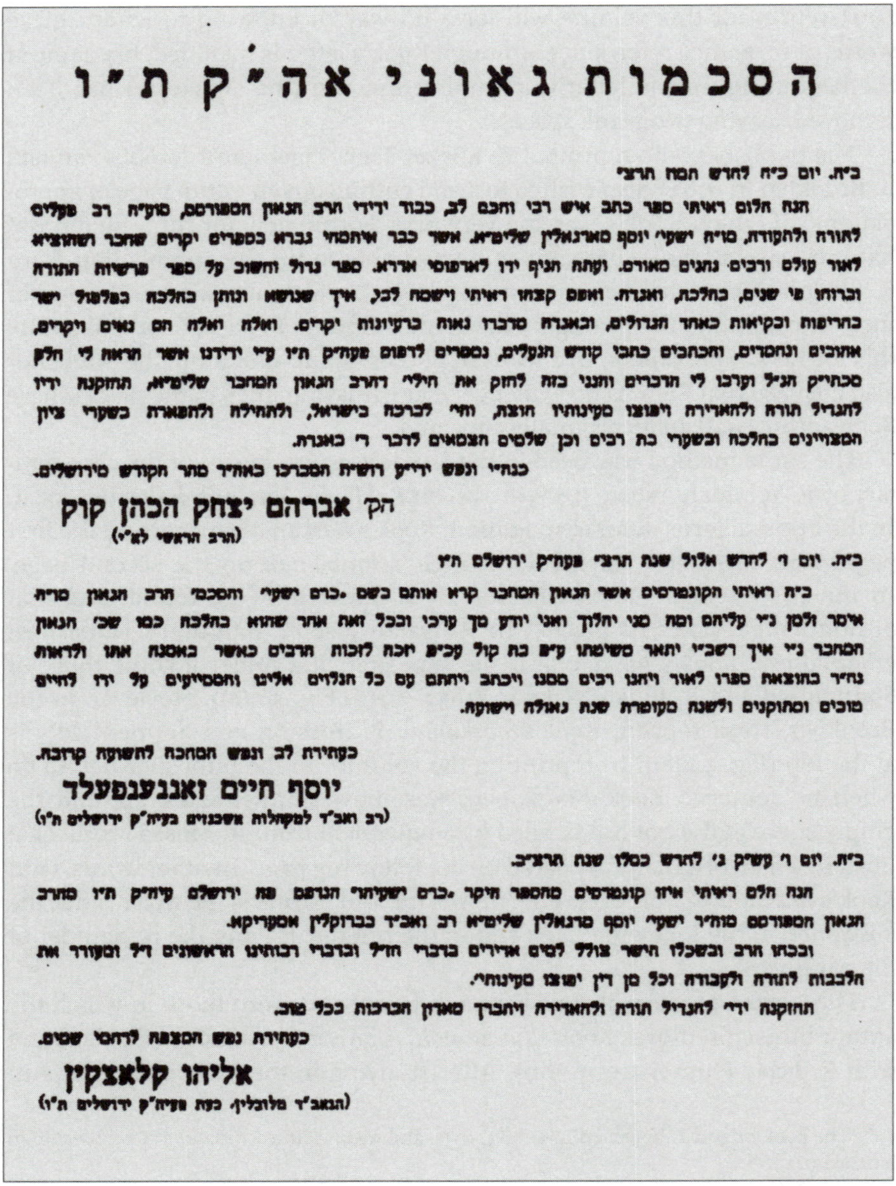

הסכמות גאוני אה״ק ת״ו

ב״ה. יום כ״ח לחדש תמוז תרצ״ז

הנה חלום ראיתי ספר כתב איש רבי וחכם לב, כבוד ידידי הרב הגאון המפורסם, סוע״ה רב פעלים לתורה ולתעודה, כו״ה ישעי׳ יוסף מארגאלין שליט״א. אשר כבר איתמחי גברא בספרים יקרים שחבר ושהוציא לאור עולם ורבים נהנים מאורם. ועתה הניף ידו לארפוסי אדרא. ספר גדול וחשוב על ספר פרשיות התורה וברוחו פי שנים, בהלכה, ואגדה. ואשם קצתו ראיתי וישמח לבי, איך שנושא ונותן בהלכה בפלפול ישר בחריפות ובקיאות כאחד הגדולים, ובאגדה מרבה נאוה ברעיונות יקרים. ואלה ואלה הם נאים ויקרים, אהובים ונחמדים, והכתבים כתבי קודש הנעלים, נמסרים לדפוס פעה״ק ת״ו ע״י ידידנו אשר תראה לי חלק מכתי״ק הנ״ל וקרבו לי הדברים והנני בזה לחזק את חילי׳ דהרב הגאון המחבר שליט״א, תחזקנה ידיו להגדיל תורה ולהאדירה ויפוצו מעינותיו חוצה, והי׳ לברכה בישראל, ולתהלה ולתפארת בשערי ציון המצויינים בהלכה ובשערי בת רבים וכן שלמים הצמאים לדבר ד׳ באגדה.

כנתיי ונפש ידידו הדו״ש הסברכו באו״ד סתר הקודש סירושלים.

הק׳ **אברהם יצחק הכהן קוק**
(הרב הראשי לא״י)

ב״ה. יום ד׳ לחדש אלול שנת תרצ״ז פעה״ק ירושלם ת״ו

ב״ה ראיתי הקונטרסים אשר הגאון המחבר קרא אותם בשם ״כרם ישעי׳״ והסכמי הרב הגאון מרי״ת איסר ולמן נ״י עליהם ומה מני יהלוך ואני יודע מך ערכי ובכל זאת אחר שהוא בהלכה כמו שכי׳ הגאון המחבר נ״י איך רשב״י יתאר משיטתו ע״פ בת קול עכ״פ יזכה לזכות הרבים כאשר באמנה אתו ולראות נח״ר בהוצאת ספרו לאור ויתנו רבים ממנו ויכתב ויחתם עם כל הנלוים אלינו והמסייעים על ידו לחיים טובים ומתוקנים ולשנה מקוטרת שנת גאולה וישועה.

כעתירת לב ונפש המחכה לתשועה קרובה.

יוסף חיים זאנגענפעלד
(רב ואב״ד למקהלות אשכנזים בעיה״ק ירושלים ת״ו)

ב״ה. יום ד׳ עש״ק ג׳ לחדש כסלו שנת תרצ״ב.

הנה הלם ראיתי איזו קונטרסים מהספר היקר ״כרם ישעיהו״ הנדפס פה ירושלם עיה״ק ת״ו מהרב הגאון המפורסם מוה״ר ישעי׳ יוסף מרגאלין שליט״א רב ואב״ד בברוקלין אמעריקא.

ובכחו הרב ובשכלו הישר צולל למים אדירים בדברי חז״ל ובדברי רבותינו הראשונים ז״ל ומעורר את הלבבות לתורה ולעבודה וכל מן דין ישוצו מעינותיו.

תחזקנה ידיו להגדיל תורה ולהאדירה ויתברך מארון הברכות בכל טוב.

כעתירת נפש המצפה לרחמי שמים.

אליהו קלאצקין
(הגאב״ד מלובלין. כעת פעיה״ק ירושלים ת״ו)

(*a*)

Figure 5.2 R. Isaiah Joseph Margolin, *Hama'aseh vehamidrash*: (*a*) Jerusalem, 1937 edition with Kook's original *haskamah*; (*b*) 1992 version (Brooklyn: Copy Corner), with the *haskamah* removed

הסכמות גאוני אה״ק ת״ו

ב״ה. יום ז׳ לחרש אלול שנת תרצ״ פעה״ק ירושלם ת״ו

ב״ת ראיתי הקונטרסים אשר הגאון המחבר קרא אותם בשם ״כרם ישעי״ והסכמ׳ הרב הגאון מו״ה איסר זלמן נ״י עליהם ומה מני יהלוך ואני יורע סך ערכי ובכל זאת אחר שהוא בהלכה כמו שכ׳ הגאון המחבר נ״י איך רשב״י יתאר משיטתו ע״פ בת קול עכ״פ יזכה לזכות הרבים כאשר באמנה אתו ולראות נח״ר בהוצאת ספרו לאור ויחנו רבים ממנו ויכתב ויחתם עם כל הנלוים אלינו והמסייעים על ידו לחיים טובים ומתוקנים ולשנה מעוטרת שנת גאולה וישועה.

כעתירת לב ונפש המחכה לתשועה קרובה.

יוסף חיים זאננענפעלד

(רב ואב״ד למקהלות אשכנזים בעיה״ק ירושלים ת״ו)

ב״ה. יום ו׳ עש״ק ג׳ לחרש כסלו שנת תרצ״ב.

הנה חלם ראיתי איזו קונטרסים מהספר היקר ״כרם ישעיהו״ הנרפס פה ירושלם עיה״ק ת״ו מהרב הגאון המפורסם מוה״ר ישעי׳ יוסף מרגאלין שליט״א רב ואב״ר בברוקלין אמעריקא.

ובכחו הרב ובשכלו הישר צולל למים אדירים בדברי חז״ל ובדברי רבותינו הראשונים ז״ל ומעורר את הלבבות לתורה ולעבורה וכל מן רין יפוצו מעינותי׳.

התוקנה ירי׳ להגדיל תורה ולהאדירה ויתברך מארון הברכות בכל טוב.

כעתירת נפש המצפה לרחמי שמים.

אליהו קלאצקין

(הגאב״ד מלובלין, כעת פעיה״ק ירושלים ת״ו)

ב״ה. ירושלים צום השביעי יהפך לנו לששון ולשמחה תרצ״א לפ״ק.

ראיתי קונטרסים מהחבור כרם ישעי׳. מעשה ידי הרב הגאון המפורסם בשערים. מו״ה ישעי׳ יוסף מרגאלין שליט״א, רב ואב״ר בברוקלין. וראיתי כי הוא כרם חמר, מלא רבר, הרבה הרב המחבר, להביא רברי ראשונים ואחרונים, וצולל בכשרון רב, לעומקא, ומעלה פנינים מרבריהם, ומחרש בשכל נכון ובפנים מסבירות ואורג מהלכה לאגרה ומאגרה להלכה, ובדברי האגרה, הוא מעורר את הלבבות לתורה, ולעבורה, ורבריו באגרה יקרים ונעימים, וכל מן רין יפוצו מעינותיו, ואשרי התלמירי חכמים היוצאים מבית כנסת לבית מררש, ובית מררש לבית כנסת, יתקבלו רבריו לתהלה ולתפארת.

הכ״ר המרבר למען התורה והרעה.

משה מרדכי עפשטיין

(אב״ר ור״מ ישיבת חברון ״כנסת ישראל״
כעת בעיה״ק ירושלים ת״ו)

(*b*)

Lithuania, Hutner went to Palestine to study at the yeshiva's Hebron branch. While there he came under the influence of Kook. Yet after coming to the United States in 1934 and later becoming head of the Chaim Berlin yeshiva, he moved in a different ideological direction. He even stopped hanging a picture of Kook on the wall of his sukkah.[62]

In 1932 Hutner published his *Torat hanazir*, which carried a *haskamah* from Kook together with approbations from R. Hayim Ozer Grodzinski and R. Abraham Dovber Kahana Shapiro (1870–1943), the chief rabbi of Kovno. When he reprinted the book in 1965 Hutner removed all the approbations. It is obvious that the issue was Kook's *haskamah*, but so as not to be seen as insulting his memory, he removed the others as well. *Torat hanazir* was reprinted by photo-offset in 1980, supposedly without Hutner's permission.[63] This time Grodzinski's *haskamah* was put back in, occupying a complete page. It appears underneath the original heading that reads 'Letters of the *Ge'onim*', even though now only one letter appears. The *haskamot* of Shapiro and Kook shared a page in the original edition, so short of whiting out Kook's *haskamah*, it was easiest to omit this page in its entirety. This same procedure was followed in the 2003 reprint that appeared in Israel.

The 1965 printing of Hutner's book is not the sort of censorship I am concerned with, as Hutner, whose views continued to develop, certainly had the right to remove Kook's *haskamah* from his own book. Yet despite Hutner's removal of the *haskamah*, I would be remiss not to note that he still retained his great love for Kook and remained under his influence. This can be seen from his 1962 letter to R. Tsevi Yehudah, where he writes that he regards himself as a student of Kook and that his appreciation of him only grows with age.[64] As far as I am aware, however, despite what he wrote to R. Tsevi Yehudah, Hutner does not mention Kook even once in his writings.

As already mentioned, the controversy over Kook originated not merely in his actions, namely his support of the Zionist movement, but also in what he wrote. It is important to note that the conflict would have been even more bitter had Kook been entirely open about his ideas, ideas that would have led to more loss of rabbinic support. Kook was aware of this and was frank in acknowledging that while on the one hand he felt the need to speak his mind, that is, to proclaim the truth, at the same time he was hesitant to do so.

[62] See Hillel Goldberg, *Between Berlin and Slobodka*, 76.

[63] Another version claims that Hutner sold the rights to reprint the book.

[64] Neriyah, *Bisedeh hare'iyah*, 437 (pp. 419–38 are devoted to Hutner's relationship with Kook); B. Z. Shapira (ed.), *Igerot lare'iyah*, 585. Hutner once visited Yeshivat Hakotel in Jerusalem. While there he told R. Yeshayahu Hadari that if one were to remove Kook's influence upon him, he would lose half of what he was (heard from Hadari).

Whether this was because he did not want to create controversy, or because he was concerned with the negative effect some of his ideas might have on the masses—throughout his career both considerations are present—it is clear that he was conscious of his self-censorship. In fact, after meeting with R. Abraham Mordechai Alter, the Rebbe of Gur, he agreed to put into words his regret that he had not adequately explained his more provocative formulations in *Orot*.[65] This agreement shows that Kook recognized that some of his formulations were not suitable for the masses. Yet you can never please everyone, and R. Hayim Hirschensohn was among those who were disappointed by what they regarded as Kook's caving in to Alter's pressure. Kook, for his part, attempted to reassure Hirschensohn that although he had perhaps compromised too much in order to create peace, nothing was lost in terms of the substance of his ideas.[66]

This recognition that even Kook engaged in self-censorship is important to the story of what became of his writings after his death. It is only in recent years that a number of groundbreaking articles have appeared that give us great insight into the process of editing Kook's writings, and the different forms of censorship that have been applied to them.[67] Much of what we know in this area is only due to the uncensored publication of Kook's *Shemonah kevatsim*. This work created great conflict among Kook's followers, with many opposing any release of Kook's writings that would show him differently from how he appears in the works edited by R. Tsevi Yehudah and R. David Cohen, the famed Nazir. Since many of Kook's published philosophical works originate in *Shemonah kevatsim*, its appearance is an opportunity finally to see what Kook wrote without, as it were, going through his gatekeepers.

[65] Kook's letter about this appears in Tsuriel (ed.), *Otserot hare'iyah*, i. 404. Alter actually misunderstood Kook's intention. He assumed that Kook was 'nullifying' his problematic words, as Alter put it in his famous letter describing his meeting with Kook. See Alter, *Osef mikhtavim*, 70; *Shabat hare'iyah*, 92 (2009), 4, see <http://www.yeshiva.org.il/midrash/shiur.asp?id=12264>. The suggested texts of how Kook's clarification should be worded, in both Alter's and Kook's handwriting, have survived and were recently offered at auction. See the Asufa Auction House catalogue (Torah works), Dec. 2009, no. 518.

[66] See Hirschensohn, *Malki bakodesh*, iv. 130*a*–*b*; A. I. Kook, *Igerot hare'iyah*, iv, no. 1184. Hirschensohn defended Kook's equation of physical exercise carried out for the sake of the nation with the recitation of psalms. See Hirschensohn, *Ḥidushei harav ḥayim hirshenson*, iii. 33*a*.

[67] See Rosenack, 'Who's Afraid of Rav Kook's Hidden Writings?' (Heb.); id., 'Hidden Diaries'; Y. Meir, 'Lights and Vessels' (Heb.); U. Abramowitz, 'The Mission, the Monopoly, and the Censorship' (Heb.); Silber, 'Ha'arafel betaharato'; Munitz, 'Editing' (Heb.). This latter article is derived from Munitz's doctoral dissertation, 'R. Kook's Circle and the Editing of His Works' (Heb.). An analysis of the censorship of Kook's writings within the larger context of 'freedom of information' and the 'public's right to know' appears in T. Friedman, 'Does the Public Have a Right to Know?' (Heb.).

The hesitation to publish Kook's writings in an 'unedited' fashion did not arise after his death. We know that even in Kook's lifetime R. Tsevi Yehudah preferred that certain material not appear in print.[68] Udi Abramowitz has called attention to the fact that Kook published *Rosh milin* without telling R. Tsevi Yehudah about it beforehand, wishing to present him with a fait accompli.[69] The Nazir, who was appointed by Kook to edit *Orot hakodesh*, tells us that certain passages were kept out of print because R. Jacob Moses Harlap, Kook's senior disciple, was afraid of the criticism that would ensue were these provocative theological musings to be published.[70]

As can be seen from articles by Yonatan Meir and Udi Abramowitz, Kook clearly harboured great ambivalence about the activities of his 'censors'. R. Tsevi Yehudah, in line with his fearful attitude, suggested to his father that the material in *Orot*, chapter 34, about the spiritual value of exercise be omitted, obviously sensing its explosive character. However, Kook replied to him that his suggestion was 'not due to fear of heaven, it is due to fear of flesh and blood'.[71] When R. Yitshak Arieli also suggested that the passage be omitted, Kook was adamant in his refusal, regarding this suggestion as akin to a prophet suppressing his prophecy.[72] In fact, if chapter 34 was to be censored then chapter 33 would presumably have to be 'edited' as well, since in this chapter Kook also speaks of the significance of a healthy body, going so far as to say:

> We dealt so much in soulfulness, we forgot the holiness of the body. We neglected physical health and strength, we forgot that we have holy flesh, no less than holy spirit. . . . Our return will succeed only if it will be—with all its splendid spirituality—also a physical return, which produces healthy blood, healthy flesh, mighty, solid bodies, a fiery spirit radiating over powerful muscles. With the strength of holy flesh, the weakened soul will shine, reminiscent of the physical resurrection.[73]

The most R. Tsevi Yehudah could do to soften the impact of chapter 34 was to declare that his father did not have yeshiva students in mind when speaking of the value of strengthening oneself physically.[74]

[68] See U. Abramowitz, 'The Mission, the Monopoly, and the Censorship' (Heb.), 137 ff.

[69] Ibid. 139.

[70] David Cohen, *Mishnat hanazir*, 91.

[71] T. Y. Kook, *Siḥot harav tsevi yehudah al sefer orot*, 34. See also Agnon, *Sefer, sofer vesipur*, 352, citing R. Tsevi Yehudah; Hoch, 'The Politics of Redemption', 118.

[72] See Carmy, 'Dialectic, Doubters, and a Self-Erasing Letter', 227 n. 2.

[73] Translation in A. I. Kook, *Orot*, trans. Naor, 189. Regarding Kook and the human body, see Shasha, '"A Burning Spirit"' (Heb.).

[74] Remer, *Gadol shimushah*, 56. There are two editions of this work. The 1984 edition has a great deal of material from R. Tsevi Yehudah that was not included in the 1994 edition. Among the

Some years after the publication of *Orot*, Kook gave an interview to the newspaper *Do'ar hayom*.[75] Here he states that his positive view of exercise has not changed. He also speaks of the value of sports, which he regards as a holy matter (*davar shebikdushah*), and in particular the Maccabi sports organization. 'We must return to our nation the strength of the warriors of Judah, which is vital for the building of the people and the land. . . . We say that "the King [i.e. God] desires life",[76] therefore we must fight against the obstacles in our path, we must build up our strength, and channel it to building the nation.'[77]

Although, as mentioned, Kook was hesitant to censor his own writings, he was well aware of why R. Tsevi Yehudah was uncomfortable with publishing his works 'unedited'. According to the Nazir, on occasion Kook himself would, in the same breath, state that it is impossible for him not to express his ideas, but then add that he did not want to create disputes.[78] It is reported that on another occasion Kook was asked if certain texts should be excluded from *Orot hakodesh*. He replied that in his opinion everything should be printed, 'but you must ask my "censors"'.[79] In at least one case, the censors' fear of

deleted passages is the following (p. 68): 'The Hazon Ish was not the *gedol hador*. The *gedol hador* and halakhic decisor *par excellence* was my father, of blessed memory. In Vilna there were other laymen who were *ge'onim*, R. Shalom David Rabinowitz, R. Yerucham Fishel Perla, R. Moses Kreines, and others. . . . Even if he [the Hazon Ish] was a *gadol*[!], he was not the halakhic decisor for this generation and generations to come.' A source in the Merkaz Harav yeshiva informed me that R. Avraham Shapira (1914–2007) was responsible for this particular deletion.

[75] 30 Tishrei 5687 (no. 22). The interview is reprinted in B. Kluger, *Min hamakor*, 89 (unnumbered). As far as I can tell, none of the many discussions of *Orot*, ch. 34, have noted this interview. See ibid. 119 (unnumbered), for a placard signed by both Kook and Sonnenfeld in opposition to Saturday soccer matches. See also Kook's letter in Anon., *Afikei torah*, 285, where he responds to a false rumour that he permitted such matches, and Wasserman and Henkin, *Striking Root* (Heb.), 98 ff.

[76] *Melekh ḥafets baḥayim*. The words come from an addition to the Amidah during the Ten Days of Penitence. In a recently published letter to H. Ansbacher of Germany (see Naor's introduction to his translation of A. I. Kook, *Orot*, 41 ff.), Kook writes that his words about exercise were not directed to his own generation, but to a more spiritually refined future era. This strikes me as an apologetic answer that does not reflect Kook's real sentiments and goes against the plain sense of the text of *Orot*. Furthermore, in the dispute over this chapter, Kook and R. Tsevi Yehudah had plenty of opportunity to promote this defence publicly, yet this was never done. Kook also does not adopt this approach in other private letters in which he deals with the controversy over *Orot*.

[77] A placard, signed by Sonnenfeld and R. Elijah Klatzkin, describes Kook's view—actually, a somewhat distorted portrayal of Kook's outlook—as heretical and arising from non-Torah sources. It concludes: 'The King desires life, he does not desire the wicked, who in their lives are called dead.' According to the placard, these rabbis also prohibited attendance at soccer matches. See B. Kluger, *Min hamekor*, iv. 75 (unnumbered). (For R. Ben Zion Uziel's (1880–1953) speech at the World Maccabi sports competition held in Palestine, see Uziel, *Mikhmanei uzi'el*, 481–3.)

[78] David Cohen, *Mishnat hanazir*, 91.

[79] H. Lifshitz, *Shivḥei hare'iyah*, 296.

publishing even continued after the book was printed. I am referring to Kook's *Arpilei tohar*, of which the first eighty pages (five-sixths of the complete work) were printed in Jaffa in 1914; with the outbreak of war, publication was halted. The pages were hidden from view, and Kook was prevailed upon not to complete publication.[80] There were, however, copies that circulated, and many years later R. Tsevi Yehudah gave a complete copy of the manuscript to Professor Rivka Schatz-Uffenheimer. This is what enabled the later 'editing' of *Arpilei tohar* to be exposed.[81]

As noted previously, the issue of how to publish Kook's writings has led to great controversy among his followers. There are those who have pushed for release of everything. Others have argued that some of his works are not appropriate for this generation, and that which is published must go through careful 'editing', which usually involves a good deal of censorship.[82] It is ironic that followers of Kook, who (justifiably) complain so much about how their teacher is censored and distorted in haredi works, have actually done the same thing to him. It is true that there are times when it is possible that Kook himself would not have wanted certain information publicized, such as when he spoke of the 'wickedness' of his adversary, R. Joseph Hayim Sonnenfeld.[83] Yet almost all of the censorship relates to the realm of ideas. It focuses on Kook's philosophy, especially its antinomian elements,[84] or his innermost struggles and self-perception, which sometimes shows him in near (or perhaps even actual) prophetic rapture.[85]

As mentioned, some of Kook's followers thought that his ideas were too radical, not necessarily in themselves, but that in this day and age—one of limited spiritual achievements—if these ideas were to get out they could be spiritually dangerous. As the Nazir put it, explaining why he felt obligated to

[80] See Y. Meir, 'Lights and Vessels' (Heb.), 170 ff. There is little doubt that in this case it was R. Tsevi Yehudah who convinced Kook not to publish the volume. See Meir, ibid.

[81] See Segal, 'Orot be'ofel', 20–1.

[82] According to Munitz, 'R. Kook's Circle and the Editing of His Works' (Heb.), 5, today there is actually a committee of rabbis that determines which parts of Kook's writings are to be censored and altered.

[83] See Rosenack, 'Who's Afraid of Rav Kook's Hidden Writings?' (Heb.), 260.

[84] The most complete study of antinomianism in Kook's writings appears in an unpublished article by Ari Chwat, which he kindly shared with me.

[85] See Rosenack, 'Who's Afraid of Rav Kook's Hidden Writings?' (Heb.), 261 ff., 273; id., *Prophetic Halakhah* (Heb.), 182 ff.; Garb, 'Prophecy, Halakhah, and Antinomianism' (Heb.), 267–7; S. Cherlow, *Tsadik* (Heb.), chs. 6, 8; Bin-Nun, 'Inspiration of the Holy Spirit' (Heb.), 356 ff. Bin-Nun argues that, in speaking of Kook, the proper category is not prophecy but *ruaḥ hakodesh*, a lower level of divine inspiration. R. Tsevi Yehudah and R. Shalom Natan Ra'anan, Kook's son-in-law, believed that Kook had supernatural knowledge. See Remer, *Gadol shimushah* (1984), 132; id., *Gadol shimushah* (1994), 116; note in *Iturei kohanim* (Tamuz 5761), 45; H. Lifshitz, *Shivḥei hare'iyah*, 283; A. Shapira, *Ḥag hasukot*, 106. R. Jacob Moses Harlap thought likewise; see E. Melamed, *Revivim: gedolei yisra'el*, 37.

censor a passage in *Orot hakodesh*, 'The generation is not yet ripe.'[86] While it is also possible that the censors were—and continue to be—afraid of renewed attacks on Kook, which in turn may lower his rabbinic status, the first explanation is the more significant one. As Rosenack puts it:

> At first, R. Kook's disciples sought to protect him from the rage of the Old Settlement rabbis and his other adversaries. Little by little, however, as his image grew more distant and became more established following his death, the editors began to try to protect us—the readership—from R. Kook's revolutionary ideas . . . [and] the revelation of his thought in all its grandeur.[87]

A good example of what I have just described can be seen in Kook's *Arpilei tohar*, mentioned above. This work finally appeared in 1983, under the imprint of the Rabbi Tsevi Yehudah Kook Institute. There are many interesting things in this text, and perhaps the most provocative is when Kook discusses how Jewish law can be updated. He writes:

> At times, when there is need to transgress the way of the Torah, and there is no one in the generation who can show the way, the thing comes about through breaching. Nevertheless, it is better for the world that such a matter come about unintentionally. Only when prophecy rests on Israel is it possible to innovate such a matter as a 'temporary measure'. Then it is done with express permission. With the damming of the light of prophecy, the innovation comes about through a long-lasting breach, which saddens the heart with its externals, but gladdens it with its inner content.[88]

In other words, when continued adherence to a certain halakhah will have negative consequences, and there is no formal mechanism to abolish the law, Providence ensures that people begin to violate this halakhah. Looking at matters from the outside, at the 'externals', people are of course saddened by the violation, since it appears to be a rebellion against halakhah. Yet those who can see what is really happening, who recognize the 'inner content', realize

[86] See Rosenack, 'Hidden Diaries', 118. The passage referred to by the Nazir appears in A. I. Kook, *Shemonah kevatsim*, vol. iv, no. 17, and here Kook refers to himself in prophetic terms. The censored version is in A. I. Kook, *Orot hakodesh*, i. 157. In the preface to *Orot hakodesh*, the Nazir tells us that all changes in the text until p. 320, which includes the passage just mentioned, were done in consultation with Kook. Yet there is reason to believe that even in the first 320 pages Kook was not as involved as the Nazir suggests. See D. Schwartz, *Religious Zionism* (Heb.), 200, for a passage from the Nazir's diary where we see that only on a few occasions did Kook have any input in the editing of *Orot hakodesh*. See also Rosenack, 'Who's Afraid of Rav Kook's Hidden Writings?' (Heb.), 289.

[87] Rosenack, 'Hidden Diaries', 147.

[88] A. I. Kook, *Shemonah kevatsim*, ii, no. 30, and the first printing of id., *Arpilei tohar*. The translation is in id., *Orot*, trans. Naor, 56.

that matters are being directed by the Divine, in what is a necessary adjustment to halakhic practice. In time, what used to be regarded as a violation becomes accepted, even among the halakhists.

This is exactly the sort of passage that makes the conservative followers of Kook very nervous. Thus, when *Arpilei tohar* was published in its entirety in 1983 a couple of slight changes were made which do not simply soften the text, but actually give it a completely opposite meaning. No longer does the long-lasting breach sadden the heart with its 'externals' and gladden it with 'its inner content'. Rather, in the censored version 'the breach' ('long-lasting' has been removed) saddens the heart with its 'essence', but gladdens it with its 'purpose'.[89] While the second change is not so significant, to state that the halakhic breach saddens the heart with its 'essence' is the exact opposite of what Kook actually wrote, which is that it is only the externality of the halakhic violation that brings sadness. What the censors have done is 'distance the essential nature of the outbreak from any substantive connections with its beneficial effects'.[90]

The chief editor of *Arpilei tohar* was none other than Yitshak Sheilat, later to be known as a great Maimonidean scholar. He defended the propriety of his censorship, which was guided by senior rabbis of the Merkaz Harav yeshiva. He saw his actions as simply part of his job as an editor. As he put it, 'If a word is added or an expression is improved for the sake of clarification, or due to respect, what sin is there in this? Isn't there a concept of *tikun soferim* mentioned with regard to our Holy Torah? See *Tanḥuma*, "Beshalaḥ", chapter 16 and the commentators there.'[91]

This is quite an amazing statement, tying his 'editing' to *tikun soferim*. In fact, the *Midrash tanḥuma* cited by Sheilat is one of the sources that understands the concept of *tikun soferim* literally, namely, that the Men of the Great Assembly actually changed the words of the Torah.[92] Sheilat sees himself, and other editors, as following this path in that they have the freedom to alter the original text when this is done for the right reasons. In this case, Sheilat tells us that the reason is so that people should not be led to the false belief that violation of the Torah can be justified. 'If one is looking for religious legitimization for sins, let him go to the false prophets, to Shabetai Tsevi and his sect, but do not touch the anointed ones of God.'[93] In other words, the religious needs of the present provide the justification for altering a text of the past.

The only regret expressed by Sheilat is that he did not note in the introduc-

[89] A. I. Kook, *Arpilei tohar*, 15.

[90] Ross, 'Can the Demand for Change in the Status of Women be Halakhically Legitimated?', 490 n. 20. See also ead., *Expanding the Palace of Torah*, 205.

[91] Sheilat, '"Orot" me'ofel', 47.

[92] See my *Limits of Orthodox Theology*, 98 ff.

[93] Sheilat, '"Orot" me'ofel', 47.

tion that changes were made to the text. As he explains, he was persuaded not to do so by those who were assisting him in the editing.[94] These men understood better than he that telling people up front that you are giving them a censored text completely undermines the censor's goal. I do not know if Sheilat was aware of the irony of his censorship of *Arpilei tohar*, as it was with regard to this very work that Kook wrote to R. Tsevi Yehudah, telling him that he wanted *Arpilei tohar* to appear without any editing or reworking, and that this would be very beneficial to readers.[95] In another letter to R. Tsevi Yehudah, he mentions that he corrected some of the wording in this book, but did not find anything that should be deleted.[96]

Another example of censorship in *Arpilei tohar* is the following: in the original version, Kook spoke of the great value of intensive study joined with *menuḥah* (rest) and *tiyul*.[97] The latter term appears to mean wandering, walking, or even hiking. That is, it refers to a physical pursuit connecting one to nature, which is the dialectical counterpart of the intensive intellectual activity inside the *beit midrash*.[98] This, of course, fits in very well with Kook's advocacy of physical exercise, discussed above. This model is also a standard component of religious Zionist youth groups in Israel, in which hiking trips around the country also have important historical and spiritual components.[99]

These hiking trips are not a new thing, as we see from the Nazir's diary. Here he describes a lengthy, and quite dangerous, multi-day hike that he and two fellow students at Merkaz Harav yeshiva undertook in 1926, with the goal of visiting various historical–spiritual sites.[100] The Nazir even hoped that this would lead to his attaining divine inspiration (*ruaḥ hakodesh*).[101] It would seem, therefore, that Kook's advocacy of *tiyul* should not be a cause of concern in the censor's eyes. Yet in the 1983 edition of *Arpilei tohar*, *tiyul* has been altered to read *tiyul ruḥani*, which means 'spiritual wandering'.[102] I do not deny the possibility that this conservative understanding is what Kook had in mind, even though it is not entirely clear what 'spiritual wandering' is supposed to mean. It is also possible that *tiyul* could mean free-floating meditation, as opposed to study.[103] Yet precisely because the matter is ambiguous,

[94] See Segal, 'Orot be'ofel', 25.

[95] Kook, *Igerot hare'iyah*, vol. ii, no. 687.

[96] Ibid., no. 693. See above, n. 80, regarding R. Tsevi Yehudah convincing Kook not to publish this work. In Kook's eyes, it was better not to publish it than to alter the text to make it more 'acceptable'.

[97] The passage is also found in A. I. Kook, *Shemonah kevatsim*, ii, no. 112.

[98] See Silber, 'Ha'arafel betaharato', 295.

[99] See Friedfertig, *Kum hithalekh ba'arets*, 19 ff., and also A. I. Kook, *Igerot hare'iyah*, iv, no. 1205.

[100] David Cohen, *Mishnat hanazir*, 80 ff.

[101] Ibid. 80.

[102] A. I. Kook, *Arpilei tohar*, 43.

[103] Dr Jonathan Garb offered this suggestion. See also A. I. Kook, *Eder hayekar*, 15, who refers to ספרי טיול, שמעיינים בהם בדרך ארעי. In id., *Igerot hare'iyah*, iii, no. 791, he refers to טיול עיוני הרגשי נפשי שכלי רזי, and in *Shemonah kevatsim*, i, no. 731, he speaks of the soul's טיולה הפנימי.

inserting the word *ruḥani* prevents readers from drawing their own conclusions as to what Kook had in mind.[104]

Let us turn to some other writings by Kook. Since he was a great spiritual figure, it is not surprising that he had some affinity for other such powerful personalities. In one of his early works, Kook even wrote that Jesus had great charismatic power.[105] While he also criticized Jesus, the simple mention of anything positive regarding the latter was too much for his opponents, and his supposed love of Christianity became one of the points on which they attacked him.[106]

Kook also had some interesting things to say about Spinoza. According to Kook, Spinoza had 'admirable power', and 'his soul was infused with the notion of divine unity'. He added that it is possible 'to extract from this thick-rinded fruit a substance of lasting worth, once cleansed and refined'.[107] Yet the most provocative things Kook said about Spinoza have only recently appeared in print. Based on a newly published text we can even say that Kook 'embraced certain elements of Spinozism, which he felt came back to life in a purified form in Beshtian Hasidism, especially Habad'.[108]

The relevant passage begins as follows:

> The Spinozist system, with all its dross, is the complete opposite of the light of Israel. Therefore, it was the hand of God that fell upon the righteous rabbis of Amsterdam to remove him from Israel. It [Spinoza's system] engendered the modern age with all its evils, including antisemitism, so that Spinoza and Bismarck are comparable to Balaam and Haman.

This passage appears in three editions of Kook's recently published writings.[109] It continues with a section that deserves to be quoted in full, since it is omitted from two of the three editions, with no indication of the censorship.[110]

104 See Segal, 'Orot be'ofel', 25. Sheilat, '"Orot" me'ofel', 47, insists that his addition clarifies the meaning of the passage, and the fact that people disagreed with him in this regard shows how important such a clarification is. Yet intellectual honesty requires that such a clarification be placed in brackets or in a note, rather than altering the reading of the text. As early as the Middle Ages, Rabbenu Tam strongly criticized those who altered a text because of a difficulty, rather than offering their 'correction' as a suggestion while keeping the original text intact. See my *Between the Yeshiva World and Modern Orthodoxy*, 193.

105 See A. I. Kook, *Ma'amrei hare'iyah*, 5–6.

106 See Naor's introduction to A. I. Kook, *Orot*, 50–1; id., *When God Becomes History*, 40 ff., 122 ff.

107 A. I. Kook, *Ikvei hatson*, 134–5, trans. in Yaron, *The Philosophy of Rabbi Kook*, 47.

108 Naor, 'Plumbing Rav Kook's Panentheism', 87 n. 22. In his recently published *Kevatsim miketav yad kodsho*, ii. 73–4, Kook points to the positive in Spinoza's pantheism, while acknowledging its limitations.

109 A. I. Kook, *Kevatsim miketav yad kodsho*, i. 146; id., *Pinkas 13*, 85; and id., *Pinkesei hare'iyah*, i. 292. The latter two censored editions were published by the R. Tsevi Yehudah Kook Institute.

110 Only in A. I. Kook, *Kevatsim miketav yad kosho*, i. 146, does the passage appear. In general, *Pinkas 13* has been severely censored. The sections from this book that were removed appear in

In addition to its value in helping us understand Kook's view of Spinoza, it shows us that Kook was well aware of the process whereby theological views are rendered acceptable in the Orthodox world—if a recognized authority figure (*gadol*) advocates a position, then it is 'in'—and the dangers this presented in his eyes.

If he had not been expelled, he would have mingled with the totality of Israel and written major compositions that would have been accepted like the *Guide* [*of the Perplexed* of Maimonides], the *Kuzari* [of Judah Halevi], and the like. And certainly, along with this, he would have composed some Torah novellae [*ḥidushim*] on halakhah or aggadah according to his ability. These would have led to the acceptance of his theological views, and would, heaven forbid, have exploded the foundations of Israel. But these consequences would have been revealed in days to come and in many circumstances. Since, with all this, he was of the seed of Israel, there is in his inwardness some fundamental principle that after much refinement should enter the camp. Mendelssohn began to refine him, but did not complete his *tikun*. But the Ba'al Shem Tov refined him, without knowing whom he was refining, because he did not need his [Spinoza's] source, because he drew the knowledge from its inner source and refined it. The work is not yet done. It is gradually being done, and when it is finished he [Spinoza] will emerge from accursed and become blessed [*barukh*, punning on his first name].[111]

This censorship of Kook's ideas regarding Spinoza followed the earlier action of the Nazir, who excised Kook's mention of 'Spinozist' from *Orot hakodesh*, replacing it with 'pantheistic'.[112] The Nazir recognized that Kook was treading a fine and dangerous line in his attraction to Spinoza. He actually claimed that 'his own approach can "rescue" Kook's thought from the "dangers" of the Spinozian pantheism latent within it'.[113] Because of this provocative assessment of Kook's relationship to Spinoza, the Nazir's comment, which Dov

Kevatsim miketav yad kodsho, i. 93 (no. 35*a*), 95–7 (nos. 38*a–c*), 124–6 (no. 87*a*), 127–8 (no. 88*a*), 129–31 (nos. 89*a–b*), 132–7 (nos. 91*a–b*), 143 (nos. 110*a–d*), 146 (no. 117; this is the section on Spinoza that I have quoted). For some of these passages it is not clear what the censors found problematic. In *Pinkesei hare'iyah*, i, *Pinkas 13* is included. Here, all of the passages censored earlier, with the exception of the one dealing with Spinoza, now appear in full. In 2010, *Pinkesei hare'iyah*, ii, was published by the R. Tsevi Yehudah Kook Institute. This contains a heavily censored version of a work by Kook known as *Linevokhei hador*, which was mysteriously placed on the internet in 2010. See my Seforim Blog post, 29 Oct. 2010; E. Henkin, 'Rav Kook's *Linevokhei hador*' (Heb.), and Henkin's post at <ravtzair.blogspot.com>, 30 June 2010.

111 *Kevatsim miketav yad kodsho*, i. 146. Most of the translation comes from S. Rosenberg and Ish-Shalom (eds.), *The World of Rav Kook's Thought*, 449.

112 Compare A. I. Kook, *Orot hakodesh*, ii. 399, with id., *Shemonah kevatsim*, i, no. 96.

113 D. Schwartz, *Faith at the Crossroads*, 64.

Schwartz published from the manuscript of the Nazir's diary,[114] was omitted when the diary appeared in print in 2005.

Yoel Elhanan points to what he regards as an example of censorship by Kook's followers, related to Herzl.[115] Before discussing this, I must note that among Orthodox thinkers there were different views as to how to relate to Herzl. Some, such as R. Abraham Elijah Kaplan (1899–1924), R. Jehiel Jacob Weinberg, and Dr Isaac Breuer wrote about him in a very positive way, believing that any religious defects were due to his background and not something he could be blamed for.[116] Weinberg actually saw him as something of a penitent. Needless to say, this was also the view of the Mizrahi movement. On the other hand, for the Hungarian extremists Herzl was the epitome of evil. For them it was no longer the issue of Herzl the man, but what he represented. That this negative view of Herzl did not remain solely the possession of Ashkenazi extremists is seen in the fact that R. Avraham Yosef, chief rabbi of Holon and the recipient of a salary from the Zionist state, ruled that parents must not name their children Herzl, as this name was held by an 'evil man'.[117]

Returning to Kook, in his famous eulogy for Herzl, Kook characterized him as the one who helped usher in the era of the messiah son of Joseph, which will precede the coming of the messiah son of David and with it the ultimate redemption.[118] However, despite this very public eulogy, in the fourth volume of Kook's letters, published in 1984,[119] we do encounter something interesting with regard to Herzl that led to Elhanan's assumption of censorship. This volume was edited by R. Ben Zion Shapira, the son of R. Avraham Shapira, who succeeded R. Tsevi Yehudah as *rosh yeshivah* of Merkaz Harav,

[114] D. Schwartz, *Faith at the Crossroads*, 64–5.

[115] See Elhanan, 'How to Build Herzl's Temple' (Heb.). 'Yoel Elhanan' is actually a pseudonym.

[116] See my *Between the Yeshiva World and Modern Orthodoxy*, 147–8.

[117] Sela, 'R. Avraham Yosef: Do Not Name a Son "Nimrod" or "Herzl"'. Yosef is the son of R. Ovadyah Yosef (1920–2013), who used to hold the highest rabbinic position in the State of Israel.

[118] See Naor, *When God Becomes History*, 3 ff. (also containing a translation of the eulogy). The original appears in A. I. Kook, *Ma'amrei hare'iyah*, 94–9. See also Gerber, *Enlightenment Revolution* (Heb.), 64 ff.

[119] R. Tsevi Yehudah did not publish any more volumes of Kook's letters after vol. iii, which appeared in 1965. Vol. iii ends with Kook's return to Palestine after the First World War, which began a period of great conflict with the extremist Orthodox. His private correspondence from this time would be very illuminating, but perhaps because of his harsh judgements against his opponents, R. Tsevi Yehudah did not wish to publish these letters. There is no question that vol. iv, published after R. Tsevi Yehudah's death, omitted many letters. I should also note that while the second edition of B. Z. Shapira (ed.), *Igerot lare'iyah* (letters to Kook), has many more letters than the Jerusalem, 1986 edition, in at least one case the second edition censored material that appears in the first edition. See my *Between the Yeshiva World and Modern Orthodoxy*, 52 n. 7.

and who was known to be less enamoured of the mystical path of Kook and his students.[120]

As is the case with a number of other examples of censorship, Elhanan felt confident in identifying this one because the relevant letter[121] was also published elsewhere in its entirety, in R. Hayim Hirschensohn's *Malki ba-kodesh*.[122] Writing to Hirschensohn, Kook mentioned that a great synagogue should be built right next to the Western Wall. He envisioned it as being under the authority of great sages and without any party affiliation. When Kook's missive appeared in the fourth volume of his letters, the following sentences were omitted:

> This would complete the vision of Herzl in *Altneuland* concerning the temple [*hatempil*] to be erected not exactly on the site of the Holy Temple. He prophesied and knew not what he prophesied! There should be such a house close to the location of the Holy Temple until the Lord appears in His glory and there will be fulfilled all the good promises concerning His people and His world that were conveyed through the prophets of truth and righteousness.[123]

According to Elhanan, this passage was removed from the version of Kook's letter included in his collected letters because Kook's followers were once again trying to protect his image. Yet, in this case, it turns out that Elhanan is incorrect and there was no censorship involved. At my request, R. Ari Chwat, director of Beit Harav Kook in Jerusalem, checked the text of the letter in their possession (which is not in Kook's handwriting), and it too is missing the passage just quoted, as is an alternative copy of the letter he located. In other words, when the volume of Kook's letters was published, the editors did not have this passage before them.[124] Eitam Henkin plausibly suggests that the passage Hirschensohn printed was added by Kook shortly before the letter was sent, and was therefore not included in the transcription that had already been made for the archive.[125]

Despite Kook's eulogy for Herzl, it must be noted that, as with much else, his view of Herzl is not simple. For example, in one letter published in *Igerot hare'iyah* we find Kook agreeing that a religious school should take part in a celebration of Herzl's birthday, but only because 'we must not increase

[120] Shapira's outlook, which some regarded as a complete abandonment of the religious philosophy of both Kook and R. Tsevi Yehudah, was part of the reason a group broke off from Merkaz Harav and formed the yeshiva Har Hamor under the direction of R. Tsevi Tau. See Sheleg, *The New Religious* (Heb.), 48 ff.; Rosen-Tsevi, 'Emergent Metaphysics' (Heb.), 421–45.

[121] A. I. Kook, *Igerot hare'iyah*, iv, no. 994.

[122] Hirschensohn, *Malki bakodesh*, iv. 3*a*.

[123] I have used the translation in Naor, *When God Becomes History*, 135, with slight changes.

[124] Through an examination of the letters, E. Henkin arrived at this conclusion independently. See E. Henkin, 'Was a Comment about Herzl Censored?' (Heb.).

[125] Ibid.

discord'. This is hardly an endorsement of Herzl. Yet in the very next letter Kook speaks of Herzl as one 'whose memory is sanctified, as with his spirit he raised up the flag of the nation'.[126] In another letter, which Kook wrote to his father-in-law, R. Elijah David Rabinowitz-Teomim, and which R. Tsevi Yehudah refused to publish,[127] Kook justifies his appearance at a memorial event for Herzl. In this letter he does not argue for Herzl's great significance. Rather, he claims that because of his position as rabbi of Jaffa he felt obligated to speak at the event, for to refuse to do so would have created a great deal of controversy. He also notes that in his remarks he did not say anything positive about Herzl himself.[128]

Why would R. Tsevi Yehudah not publish Kook's letter to Rabinowitz-Teomim? I think it is because his own view of Herzl did not have any of the nuances or complications found in the writings of his father. When R. Tsevi Yehudah looked at Herzl he saw only the positive. He also placed a great amount of significance on Herzl, going so far as to say that 'our existence and the structure of our life [in the State of Israel] all come from Herzl'.[129] R. Tsevi Yehudah even had a picture of Herzl in his home, which hung next to that of the Hafets Hayim.[130] With this in mind, we can understand why R. Tsevi Yehudah refused a student's request that he elucidate Kook's eulogy for Herzl. As the student explained, and this viewpoint is generally shared by R. Tsevi Yehudah's followers, even the significance granted to Herzl in this eulogy does not represent Kook's final '*erets yisra'el*' outlook. Rather, and in contrast to *Orot*, the eulogy is a reflection of Kook's diaspora thought, which had not yet been revised.[131]

[126] A. I. Kook, *Igerot hare'iyah*, i, nos. 295–6. See also ibid., no. 294, and vol. ii, no. 571, for other positive references to Herzl.

[127] He did, however, give a copy of the letter to Yossi Avneri, who discussed it in his article 'Rabbi A. I. Hakohen Kook' (Heb.), 56–7.

[128] See A. I. Kook, *Ginzei re'iyah*, iii. 16–18; Filber, *Kokhvei or*, 170–4. On one occasion Kook even forbade a synagogue to recite a memorial prayer for Herzl. See Ogen (ed.), *Asher hayah*, 82. This source is referred to in <www.yoel-ab.com/katava.asp?id=111>.

[129] See his lecture 'Herzl' (Heb.), 35. See also T. Y. Kook, *Linetivot yisra'el*, i. 15, ii. 533; H. A. Schwartz, *Mitokh hatorah hago'elet*, ii. 286–7. R. Tsevi Yehudah's words of encouragement to those attending a special ceremony at the grave of Herzl appear in a note in *Iturei kohanim* (Tamuz 5762), 25.

[130] See Remer, *Gadol shimushah* (1994), 54; note in *Iturei kohanim* (Tamuz 5762), 46; Aviner, *Tsevi kodesh*, 152; *Iturei yerushalayim* (Kislev 5769), 89; Wolberstein, *Mashmia yeshuah*, 252–3; Melamed, *Revivim: gedolei yisra'el*, 299. R. Tsevi Yehudah even spoke positively about the intermarried Max Nordau, who in his eyes was a *ba'al teshuvah*. See T. Y. Kook, *Linetivot yisra'el*, ii, no. 115 (pp. 593–4); id., *Siḥot harav tsevi yehudah: bamidbar*, 324–5; note in *Iturei kohanim* (Tamuz 5755), 37–8.

[131] Remer, *Gadol shimushah* (1994), 59. It is reported that R. Tsevi Yehudah believed that only advanced students should study this eulogy. See note in *Iturei kohanim* (Sivan 5757), 29. R. Tsevi

I want to return now to the issue of the alteration of Kook's words in *Orot* and other texts edited by R. Tsevi Yehudah, as well as in *Orot hakodesh*, edited by the Nazir.[132] While some have attached the label of censorship, with all of its negative connotations, to the actions of R. Tsevi Yehudah and the Nazir, I question whether this is proper. This is because Kook himself gave the job of editing his writings to these two who, together with Harlap, were his closest disciples.[133] When the Nazir met with Kook a few days before his death, the latter specifically mentioned that if Harlap says 'to take out three words' this could be done, and that he relied on the two of them.[134]

Even if Kook would not have agreed with every one of the changes—and since he mentioned 'three words' apparently this pointed to his desire that the changes be very minor—the fact remains that R. Tsevi Yehudah and the Nazir *were* given authority by Kook to make changes. It is therefore difficult to speak of the books they published as having been censored, as opposed to 'edited'.[135] In fact, we must even speak of *Orot* as 'edited', although it appeared in Kook's lifetime, because even if Kook agreed with the changes made by his son, it was R. Tsevi Yehudah who was the moving force in this area.[136] Furthermore, there is no evidence that Kook concerned himself much with his son's editorial decisions in *Orot*. Having been granted editorial authority by his father, it makes perfect sense that R. Tsevi Yehudah would refuse to permit another of Kook's disciples, R. Moshe Gurwitz, to publish any of Kook's writings.[137] In reflecting on R. Tsevi Yehudah's editing, Udi Abramowitz has

Yehudah's interest in not disseminating Kook's diaspora thought, which would later be superseded by his more advanced vision, is no doubt the reason why he instructed his students not to include three of Kook's earliest essays in id., *Ma'amrei hare'iyah*. See the editor's introduction to *Ma'amrei hare'iyah*, 14 n. These essays originally appeared in the rabbinic journal *Hapeles*, and while friendly towards Zionism, were not in line with the dialectical position vis-à-vis Zionism later adopted by Kook. See T. Y. Kook, *Or linetivati*, 281; id., 'Explaining' (Heb.); U. Abramowitz, 'Ideology' (Heb.), 69; Ben-Artzi, '"The Old Will Be Renewed"' (Heb.), 11 n. 10; id., 'First Teaching' (Heb.), 75. Kelner, *Milon hare'iyah*, 388 ff., offers an alternative perspective.

[132] One interesting example from A. I. Kook, *Orot hakodesh*, iii. 297, is the deletion of Kook's explicit reference to homosexuality (*mishkav zakhar*). See Naor, *From a Kabbalist's Notebook*, 168 n. 12.

[133] Regarding Kook's relationship with R. Tsevi Yehudah, see U. Abramowitz, 'Ideology' (Heb.); id., 'The Mission, the Monopoly, and the Censorship' (Heb.), 129 ff. For examples of R. Tsevi Yehudah's editing, see Rosenack, 'Who's Afraid of Rav Kook's Hidden Writings?' (Heb.), 268 ff.; U. Abramowitz, 'The Mission, the Monopoly, and the Censorship' (Heb.), 142. Regarding the Nazir's editing, see D. Schwartz, *Religious Zionism* (Heb.), 198–233; Dison, '*Orot hakodesh* Re-edited' (Heb.).

[134] David Cohen, *Mishnat hanazir*, 95.

[135] As Neriah Guttel has shown, even the halakhic work *Shabat ha'arets*, which appeared in 1910, was heavily edited. See Guttel, 'Craftmanship and Art' (Heb.).

[136] See Munitz, 'Editing' (Heb.), 133 n. 32.

[137] R. Tsevi Yehudah wrote that after his father's death he had exclusive authority when it came to editing the latter's writings. See his letter in *Orot ha'emunah*, 148: הנה אזהרתו התקיפה של אאמו"ר הרב

concluded that 'by concealing thousands of philosophical passages written by his father, Rabbi Zvi Judah exerted a more powerful influence on the interpretation of Rav Kook's writings than any form of textual emendation could have given him'.[138]

It is of course interesting to examine what editorial changes R. Tsevi Yehudah and the Nazir made, as this enables us to get a sense of how they felt they needed to protect Kook and perhaps of how their ideas differed from those of their teacher.[139] For example, there is the famous chapter 45 of *Orot* ('Orot hateḥiyah') where Kook begins: 'Just as wine cannot be without dregs, so the world cannot be without wicked people.' Kook continues to elaborate on this point, writing, in the original: 'The exile weakened the life force of the nation and our dregs decreased greatly, to the point where the survival of the nation is endangered because of so few wicked people, and for lack of a broad grasp of life.' When *Orot* was published, R. Tsevi Yehudah cut out the words 'so few wicked people'.[140] In this example, the essential message of the chapter remains even without the words that R. Tsevi Yehudah omitted. Yet it is obvious that R. Tsevi Yehudah did not want this message to be unduly emphasized.[141]

Kook also wrote of the righteousness of the righteous (*tsidkat hatsadikim*) being supported in each generation by the wickedness of the wicked (*rish'at haresha'im*), 'who in truth are not wicked at all, as long as they cling with their heart's desire to the collectivity of the nation'.[142] Yet when this text appeared in *Orot* ('Orot hateḥiyah'), chapter 20, gone was any reference to the *resha'im* as not being really wicked. The 'edited' formulation describes how the righteous are supported by those who, *despite* their wickedness, still have an attachment to the nation. In this case, R. Tsevi Yehudah's 'correction' entirely inverts what

זצ"ל בשעותיו האחרונות, לפני הסתלקותו מעלינו ממצב חייו אשר בעולמנו זה, הלא היתה שסידור הכתבים והטיפול בהם יהיה דוקא על ידי בפיקוח שלי, ואחריות פקודתו זו הנוראה מוטלת עלי בכל עוזה מבלי להקל בה. Yet as we have seen, this is not entirely accurate, as Kook also gave Harlap and the Nazir a role in the editing.

138 U. Abramowitz, 'Ideology' (Heb.), 1 (English section).

139 In addition to sources cited throughout this chapter, see also D. Schwartz, *Challenge and Crisis* (Heb.).

140 The original text appears in A. I. Kook, *Shemonah kevatsim*, iv, no. 25.

141 This is noted by Ari Chwat in his unpublished article, 'Question of Antinomianism' (Heb.).

142 A. I. Kook, *Shemonah kevatsim*, ii, no. 283 (trans. in A. I. Kook, *Orot*, 285 n. 129). In a passage published after R. Tsevi Yehudah's death, Kook writes that 'there is no sin and iniquity in the world that does not also have sparks of holiness'; see A. I. Kook, *Me'orot hare'iyah*, 67 (cited in U. Abramowitz, 'Ideology' (Heb.), 66). In *Shemonah kevatsim*, v, no. 9, Kook writes: 'Every sin and transgression of a *tsadik* goes to strengthen the power of the holy.' This passage was altered when the text was published by R. Tsevi Yehudah in A. I. Kook, *Orot hateshuvah*, 11: 6. For R. Tsevi Yehudah's comment on R. Tsadok Hakohen of Lublin's similar antinomian language, see U. Abramowitz, 'Ideology' (Heb.), 60.

Kook intended when he declared that those who attach themselves to the nation are not really wicked at all.[143]

Speaking of sinners, Abramowitz has noted that R. Tsevi Yehudah, when he published *Orot hateshuvah*, omitted the antinomian-like passage that 'all the sins of Israel strengthen the holy in the world'.[144] Another example worth noting is that Kook wrote of 'sparks of light' that can be found in Christianity, Buddhism, and even paganism.[145] Yet when this text was published in *Orot*, all that appeared were general comments speaking of sparks of light in all the 'various beliefs'.[146] In this case, as in many others, the meaning remains the same even after the 'editing'. However, lacking the explicit references in the original version, it is hardly as powerful.[147]

Let me cite two additional examples, which Avinoam Rosenack has already noted, as further illustrations of how R. Tsevi Yehudah and the Nazir were indeed prepared on occasion to alter Kook's text so that it came to mean something entirely different from what he originally intended.[148] Kook wrote as follows: 'Prophecy and divine inspiration come *from* the inner core of man,[149] and from within him they emanate to all that concerns the entire world. This is the case of aggadah, for it flows from the soul of man, presenting itself also in the external aspect of the world.'[150] In other words, prophecy, divine inspiration, and aggadah 'remain in the domain of absolute subjectivity'.[151] When the Nazir published this text in *Orot hakodesh*,[152] a couple of slight changes enabled him to alter the meaning of the passage entirely. According to the edited version, Kook writes: 'Prophecy and divine inspiration come, *by word of God, to* the inner core of man.'[153] This change was made in Kook's lifetime, and according to the Nazir had the approval of Kook.[154] Even if this was so, we

[143] See U. Abramowitz, 'Ideology' (Heb.), 26. In the same chapter of *Orot*, R. Tsevi Yehudah softened Kook's criticism of religious separatism. In A. I. Kook, *Shemonah kevatsim*, ii, no. 283, Kook refers to those who support separatism as 'doing the work of Amalek'. In *Orot*, ch. 20, this was altered so that the criticism is only of the *ideology* of separatism, which is referred to as a 'deed of Amalek'. See my 'Samson Raphael Hirsch and Orthodoxy'.

[144] A. I. Kook, *Shemonah kevatsim*, v, no. 9. See U. Abramowitz, 'Ideology' (Heb.), 72–3.

[145] A. I. Kook, *Shemonah kevatsim*, i, no. 167.

[146] A. I. Kook, *Orot*, 131.

[147] For many similar examples, see Munitz, 'Editing' (Heb.). Munitz argues that R. Tsevi Yehudah's changes to *Orot* almost never involve a complete alteration of meaning, but tend to stress certain matters and tone down others. He too, however, acknowledges that there are occasions when the meaning is indeed changed by R. Tsevi Yehudah. See ibid. 140.

[148] See Rosenack, 'Who's Afraid of Rav Kook's Hidden Writings?' (Heb.), 267 n. 65.

[149] מפנימיותו של אדם (italics added).

[150] A. I. Kook, *Shemonah kevatsim*, v, no. 127; I have altered the translation that appears in Ish-Shalom, *Rav Avraham Itzhak HaCohen Kook*, 55.

[151] Ibid.

[152] Vol. i, section 16 (p. 23).

[153] נבואה ורוה"ק באים, בדבר ד', לפנימיותו של אדם (the Nazir's changes are noted in the text by italics).

[154] See above, n. 86, where I note that this assertion is problematic.

must also realize that in cases like this it is not that Kook changed his view, but that he acceded to the wishes of others who wanted to shield him from assault.[155]

Kook wrote: 'Literature, painting, and sculpture[156] aim to bring to realization all the spiritual concepts impressed deep in the human soul.' These words were published by Kook in 1903.[157] Yet when R. Tsevi Yehudah republished this text as part of Kook's commentary on the Song of Songs,[158] the beginning of the passage was altered to read: 'Literature, its depiction and sculpting'.[159] The reason for the change is clearly to cover up Kook's positive feelings for the visual arts.[160] This was done even though R. Tsevi Yehudah would later publish Kook's very encouraging letter to the Bezalel Academy of Arts and Design in Jerusalem. In Kook's mind, the pursuit of art in the land of Israel shows that the spirit of the people of Israel has been revived. This in turn will 'nurture the sensitivity for beauty and purity with which the precious children of Zion are so blessed, and it will uplift many depressed souls, giving them a clear and illuminating view of the beauty of life, nature and work, and the honor of labor and diligence'.[161]

It is precisely this sort of 'editing' that has left people wondering whether Kook would have agreed with what his followers have done. It has also fuelled the demands to publish the actual writings of Kook, rather than edited versions, so that people can examine his unvarnished words. Regarding R. Tsevi Yehudah's role in the editing, it is hard to see how this is in line with the message of a dream he reported in which Kook appeared to him. In this dream, R. Tsevi Yehudah asked his father if perhaps the generation was not yet ready for his teachings. He replied, 'There is no need to cover up and restrict the light. It will not cause any harm, and there is absolutely no need to fear or be anxious.'[162]

155 See Rosenack, 'Who's Afraid of Rav Kook's Hidden Writings?' (Heb.), 290.

156 הספרות ציור והחטוב.

157 A. I. Kook, 'Teviat ein ayah', 352. The passage also appears in Lewin (ed.), *Alumah*, 43 and A. I. Kook, *Kevatsim miketav yad kodsho*, i. 40. My translation comes from Mirsky, 'Intellectual and Spiritual Biography', 390.

158 A. I. Kook, *Olat hare'iyah*, ii. 3.

159 הספרות, ציורה וחיטובה.

160 Regarding Kook and art, see Zuckerman, 'On Art' (Heb.); Tseviali, 'Rabbi Abraham Isaac Hakohen Kook' (Heb.).

161 A. I. Kook, *Igerot hare'iyah*, i, no. 158 (p. 204), trans. in Z. Feldman, *Rav A. Y. Kook: Selected Letters*, 193. In this letter, Kook also calls attention to the halakhic problem of sculpting a complete human face, and offers a suggestion on how this difficulty can be overcome. For a series of quotes from Kook on art, including his evaluation of Rembrandt, see <www.orot.com/art.html>. See also the series 'Exploring the Role of Art and Creativity Through the Teachings of Rav Kook', at <http://www.atid.org/resources/art/ravkook.asp>. For R. Tsevi Yehudah's encouragement of art, see Remer, *Gadol shimushah* (1994), 78.

162 T. Y. Kook, *Or linetivati*, 317. See also U. Abramowitz, 'The Mission, the Monopoly, and the Censorship' (Heb.), 137 ff.; Wolberstein, *Mashmia yeshuah*, 61. There were other times when Kook

In thinking about how R. Tsevi Yehudah edited his father's writings, we must also bear in mind that while he regarded himself as the 'absolute continuation' of his father,[163] R. Tsevi Yehudah actually differed from Kook in a few significant ways. I say this even though Kook himself wrote that R. Tsevi Yehudah 'is virtually one with me' and thus understood him better than anyone else.[164] There is no question that Kook's and R. Tsevi Yehudah's relationship was not merely that of a father and son, but also a deep spiritual kinship. Yet despite this, Kook and R. Tsevi Yehudah did not see eye to eye on all matters. For instance, Kook had a much more positive view of secular culture than his son, who envisioned a Torah-only culture.[165] They also differed when it came to hasidism and in particular on the role of the *tsadik*, which found a very sympathetic ear in Kook. R. Tsevi Yehudah, however, had a much more negative view of this and therefore did not publish his father's many comments dealing with the *tsadik*.[166]

Although I am sure that R. Tsevi Yehudah understood his father better than anyone, it must also be acknowledged that he was not always correct in matters relating to Kook. For example, he suspected that Kook's early essay, 'Afikim banegev', which appeared in 1903 in the rabbinic journal *Hapeles*,[167] had been tampered with by the editor.[168] The fact that Kook himself, in the thirty years after he published this essay, never mentioned anything about it having been altered did not dissuade R. Tsevi Yehudah from making his claim, but it is certainly reason enough for the dispassionate observer to disregard the accusation.[169]

The censorship carried out by Kook's followers is designed to preserve his reputation in the Orthodox world. Yet R. Moshe Tsuriel, a great follower of Kook whose *Otserot hare'iyah* is an indispensable collection of Kook's

appeared to R. Tsevi Yehudah in a dream. See Remer, *Gadol shimushah* (1994), 115; Wolberstein, *Mashmia yeshuah*, 54–5, 63, 336, 407. R. Tsevi Yehudah stated that even after his father's death he continued to consult him about how to run his yeshiva. See *Iturei yerushalayim* (Kislev 5770), 11. R. Tsevi Yehudah also kept a notebook in which he mentioned the various souls he met in his dreams. See *Iturei yerushalayim* (Adar 5770), 5.

163 See Neriyah, *Bisedeh hare'iyah*, 295.

164 See A. I. Kook, *Igerot hare'iyah*, i, no. 102. The letter is from 1907 and pre-dates Kook's relationships with Harlap and the Nazir.

165 See Rosen-Tsevi, 'Emergent Metaphysics' (Heb.), 428.

166 See U. Abramowitz, 'Ideology' (Heb.), ch. 1. According to Abramowitz (p. 35), there are 'hundreds' of such texts that were kept 'under wraps' by R. Tsevi Yehudah.

167 The essay is reprinted in Tsuriel (ed.), *Otserot hare'iyah*, ii. 77–130.

168 See T. Y. Kook, 'Explaining' (Heb.); the article also appears in Weinman, 'Mishnah rishonah'.

169 See Ravitzky, *Messianism, Zionism, and Jewish Religious Radicalism* (Heb.), 131 ff.; Weinman, 'Mishnah rishonah', 71. In a letter written in 1909 to his son-in-law, Kook recommends that he read his essays in *Hapeles*. See Kook, *Otserot hare'iyah*, i. 380.

writings, has engaged in another sort of censorship, one designed to enable Kook's ideas to enter the haredi world unannounced. In his *Otserot ha'agadah*, which collects comments on talmudic passages from a wide range of scholars, one finds ideas cited in the name of 'Rabbi A. Hakohen'.[170] This is not a household name, as are the other scholars Tsuriel quotes. Tsuriel explained to me that this R. A. Hakohen is none other than Kook. Similarly, R. Shmuel Brazil quotes Kook's saying that 'the righteous do not complain about wickedness, but increase righteousness. They do not complain about heresy, but increase faith.' Yet rather than mention Kook as the source, the passage is attributed to 'a certain *gadol*'.[171]

In adopting this approach, Tsuriel and Brazil could point to Maimonides as a precedent. In *Shemonah perakim*, Maimonides states that he will not mention non-Jewish philosophers by name, since doing so 'might make the passage offensive to someone without experience and make him think that it has an evil inner meaning of which he is not aware. Consequently, I saw fit to omit the author's name, since my goal is to be useful to the reader.'[172] In other words, it is more important for the ideas to be spread, even if the originator of these ideas has to go unmentioned.[173]

The censorship carried out by Kook's followers also extends to the writings of R. Tsevi Yehudah. In the following example we are fortunate that two groups were working on the same text, otherwise we would never have known that anything was amiss, since the censors were not helpful enough to add an ellipsis to alert the reader that something had been taken out.

In 1989 R. Tsevi Yehudah's *Or linetivati* was published.[174] This is modelled after the elder Kook's *Orot*, and includes selections of R. Tsevi Yehudah's ideas, culled from various sources. The following year the first volume of his collected letters, *Tsemaḥ tsevi*,[175] was published. Only with the latter pub-

[170] See pp. 468, 481, 485, 493. The passages are all taken from A. I. Kook, *Ein ayah* on BT *Ber*. Additional references to 'Rabbi A. Hakohen' appear in Tsuriel (ed.), *Otserot hamusar*, 236, 1344, and id., *Derishat tsiyon*, 28. In id. (ed.), *Otserot hatorah*, 46, he refers to 'Rabbi Tsevi Hakohen', and this is R. Tsevi Yehudah Kook. Tsuriel informed me that the source of the passage is T. Y. Kook, *Siḥotav shel harav tsevi yehudah hakohen kuk al perek kinyan torah*, 59. Another reference to 'Rabbi Tsevi Hakohen' appears in Tsuriel, *Leket mehegyonei hatorah*, 927. Tsuriel informed me that the source of this passage is Anon., *Erets tsevi*, 202.

[171] Brazil, *Besha'arei hamo'adim*, 249. Kook's saying appears in id., *Arpilei tohar*, 39 (= id., *Shemonah kevatsim*, ii, no. 99). This was called to my attention by R. Moshe Weinberg.

[172] Translation in R. L. Weiss and Butterworth, *Ethical Writings of Maimonides*, 60–1. For other relevant sources, see S. A. Fish, *Davar*, 144 ff.

[173] See above, pp. 28–9, regarding R. Joseph B. Soloveitchik.

[174] The text to which I will refer appears on p. 211.

[175] The text to which I will refer appears on p. 24.

lication was it possible to recognize the censorship that had occurred in *Or linetivati*. Both the complete passage, from *Tsemaḥ tsevi*, and the censored text from *Or linetivati*, appear in Figure 5.3. In the original letter, written in 1910, R. Tsevi Yehudah speaks of Leo Tolstoy (1828–1910) in a very exalted way. He describes him as growing ever closer to God, a 'true saint among the nations of the world, full of holiness and righteousness and closeness to God'. He even puts the acronym *shlita* after his name. This acronym, signifying that the bearer of it should live a long and good life, is only attached to important names. Yet here, R. Tsevi Yehudah inserted it after mentioning a non-Jew. I do not know of another example of this in the whole of rabbinic literature.[176] Obviously, the editors of *Or linetivati* were troubled by R. Tsevi Yehudah's effusive praise for Tolstoy, and that is why they took out the entire section.

What the editors did not know, or perhaps knew and chose to ignore, was that in an era when so many of the Russian populace, including the intellectuals, were expressing antisemitic feelings, Tolstoy spoke out against the 1903 Kishinev pogrom. He also penned these words, in his 1891 essay 'What is a Jew?': 'The Jew is that sacred being who has brought down from heaven the eternal fire and has illumined with it the entire world. He is the religious source, spring, and foundation out of which all the rest of the peoples have drawn their beliefs and their religions.'[177]

Salo W. Baron comments that Tolstoy's essay 'achieved wide circulation several years before his death in 1910'.[178] R. Tsevi Yehudah's letter dates from a few months before Tolstoy's death, in other words, from a time when Tolstoy's reputation in the Jewish community was at its height. As can be seen from the extract that appears in Figure 5.3(*a*), R. Tsevi Yehudah's admiration for Tolstoy focused on his general approach to life, rather than his connection to Jewish matters (or the fact that he had studied Hebrew with a rabbi[179]). However, this admiration would not have been so profound if not for Tolstoy's reputation as a philosemite.[180] Many years later R. Tsevi Yehudah continued

[176] R. Tsevi Yehudah also attached *zikhrono livrakhah* ('may his memory be a blessing', the phrase that accompanies the name of someone who has died) to Arthur Balfour's name. See *Lisheloshah be'elul*, 1: 64, included in T. Y. Kook, *Nefesh hare'iyah*, 56.

[177] Hertz, *A Book of Jewish Thoughts*, 135.

[178] Baron, *Russian Jews Under Tsars and Soviets*, 164.

[179] See Noyes, *Tolstoy*, 268.

[180] Tolstoy's attitude was actually more complex. See Schefski, 'Tolstoi and the Jews'. As Schefski puts it, Tolstoy had 'an inconsistent policy on the Jewish religion, vacillating between praise and condemnation' (p. 5). It must be noted, however, that the 'condemnation' is found in personal diary entries and letters. We have many examples of historical figures whose private reservations about aspects of Judaism and/or Jews did not affect their exemplary public statements and actions.

כד צמח צבי

למקור החיים, להכללים היותר אדירים של החיים ולכל הפרטים ופרטי־הפרטים, לבורא לכלל הבריאה ולכל נברא; ובפרט לכל השלם יותר ועומד במעלה יותר עליונה במעלות הבריאה, לכל הנברא בצלם, לכל בן עמו, בן ישראל. – "ואהבת לרעך כמוך" וזהו "כלל גדול בתורה". כי על כן מושג האהבה הוא מהמושגים היותר עליונים, מהיסודות בהשקפת־העולם והכרת־המציאות, ונמצא הוא באפן חשוב מאד ב"הלכות יסודי התורה" ובסוף "הלכות תשובה" של הרמב"ם וב"מורה־נבוכים" וב"כוזרי", והוא יסוד שיטת־המוסר החשובה מאד של אותו האדם הגדול והנפלא, החסיד האמתי שבאוה"ע, הממולא בקדושה וצדקות וקרבת אלהים טָלְסְטָי שליט"א. אמנם, בזה האחרון היתה מצומצמת מתחילה על "אהבת הבריות" וגם זה היה מצד כלליות האהבה המתפשטת מן הבריאה על הברואים ומן היצירה על היצורים, אבל לפי הנראה לי ולפי הידיעות שקבלתי ממנו הוא הולך ומתעלה ומתרומם – כדין זקני ת"ח – וגם "אהבתו" נתעלתה לאהבת־ד' עליונה, לצמאון־לאל־חי אדיר ונשגב. וכן ב"אדר היקר" נמצא מבואר יפה ענין האהבה ג"כ בתור מושג עליון, פנימי, עיקרי, טבעי־אמתי. ועוד. בכל המקומות הנזכרים יש לעַיֵן ולהתעמק ולמצא את מושג האהבה האמתי העליון, גם מצד אהבת ד' וגם מצד אהבה אנושית. את פרטי מראי־המקומות קשה לי לצַיֵן לע"ע.

אוסיף ואֹמר אֹדות מה שכתבתי בזה על מושג הטוב ומושג האהבה מצד עליוניות הכלליות, כי זוהי, כמדומה לי, אמתת הכונה של מאמר חז"ל: "גדול כחם של נביאים, שמדמים צורה ליוצרה" (אך לא אדע עוד אם זה מכוון ומיושב כראוי בגוף הדברים, כי שכחתי את מקומם). תמוהים ומופלאים הם הדברים האלה בעיני רבים, דלכאורה קשה מהו דמיון הצורה ליוצר ואדרבה הלא היוצר לצורה מדמים הם ולא להפך, וגם יסוד הגדלות בזה אינו מיושב כ"כ. אבל באמת לפי דברינו זהו עיקר גדלות כחם של נביאים, שהם אינם באים בדרך למודי לדון מן הבריאה על הבורא – אשר זהו דרך חקירה אנושית בלבדה – אלא מתוך שנפשם מתעלית למרומי שמי ד', מתוך ההכרה העליונה בהדר גאון ד' ועזו, ההכרה בכלליות המציאות והאהבה, בקיצור מתוך קרבתם אל ד', אל היוצר, מתוך כך, ודוקא מתוך־כך, יכולים הם להבין ולהכיר, להסתכל ולדעת את הצורה, את הבריאה, ומתוך כך הם יכולים לחיות בתוך הבריאה, בתוך הצורה, בעולם הזה; ומתוך כך הם מבינים ומכירים, מסתכלים ויודעים, חיים ומסדרים את חייהם. ודוקא מתוך כך ולא סגי בלאו הכי, כי חיים שאינם אלהיים אינם חיים כלל, ודוקא מתוך התרוממותם למרומי ה"עולמות העליונים" ומתוך הכרתם ואהבתם את היוצר, את מקור הצורה, הם באים לאהוב ולהכיר את הצורה. זהו למעלה מבחי' "מבשרי אחזה אלוהַ", להפך: ממחזה אלוה אדע

(*a*)

Figure 5.3 Letter from R. Tsevi Yehudah Kook: (*a*) as published in *Tsemaḥ tsevi*, (Jerusalem, 1990) referring to Tolstoy; (*b*) as published in *Or linetivati* (Jerusalem, 1989), with the passage on Tolstoy removed

קלה | מֻשָּׂג הָאַהֲבָה הַכְּלָלִי

"ואהבת לרעך כמוך זה כלל גדול בתורה", את מושג האהבה בתוך כלל כל התורה, יש לתפוש במובן המחלט היותר כללי, היותר עליון ואדיר, שהוא עיקר יסוד ושורש אהבת השי"ת, "האהבה העליונה". מתוך כך, מתוך התעלות מושג האהבה במובן הכללי הזה מתמלא האדם כולו, בכל מלוא ישותו, חסד ואצילות, ואהבה נמרצה לד' אדון כל היצורים רבון כל העולמים ולכל העולמים ולכל היצורים שלו. אהבה נמרצה וצמאון וגעגועים למקור הטוב, למקור החיים, להכללים היותר אדירים של החיים ולכל הפרטים ופרטי הפרטים, לבורא, לכלל הבריאה ולכל נברא; ובפרט לכל השלם יותר ועומד במעלה יותר עליונה במעלות הבריאה, לכל הנברא בצלם, לכל בן עמו, בן ישראל, – "ואהבת לרעך כמוך" וזהו "כלל גדול בתורה".

כי על כן מושג האהבה הוא מהמושגים היותר עליונים, מהיסודות שבהשקפת הָעולם והכרת המציאות. ונמצא הוא באופן חשוב מאד בהלכות יסודי התורה ובסוף הלכות תשובה של הרמב"ם ובמורה נבוכים וב"כוזרי". וכן ב"אדר היקר" נמצא מבואר יפה ענין האהבה גם כן בתור מושג עליון, פנימי, עיקרי, טבעי אמיתי ועוד. בכל המקומות הנזכרים יש לעיין ולהתעמק ולמצוא את מושג האהבה

to speak very highly about Tolstoy, going so far as to refer to him as a *ba'al teshuvah* (penitent).[181]

I have no doubt that if asked, the censors would reply that it is not that they have any problem with what their teacher said, God forbid. If he said it, then it must be true. However, they obviously believe that the public will not understand how he could have spoken in this way about Tolstoy, and this will tarnish his reputation. So by censoring him, they are actually doing him a favour, by helping to preserve his reputation. While this does not make the censorship any more acceptable, it does show that not all censorship comes from a bad place. While most censorship is designed to keep 'dangerous' views and personalities out of the public eye and is motivated by opposition to these things, there is a different form of censorship. As we have also seen with Kook, this censorship is motivated not by opposition to the figure being censored, but out of reverence for him, and a desire to ensure that this reverence is shared by as many as possible.

This approach is elaborated upon by R. Ya'akov Ariel, a leading student of R. Tsevi Yehudah, with reference to Kook's writings. In justification of the refusal by some of Kook's followers to publish certain of his writings, Ariel claims that it is important to allow Kook's already-published works to achieve wide acceptance, thus establishing his place in the Torah world. Only then, he states, should his writings be the subject of no-holds-barred academic

[181] T. Y. Kook, *Judaism and Christianity* (Heb.), 25. For more words of admiration for Tolstoy, see id., *Siḥot harav tsevi yehudah al sefer orot*, 158. See also id., *Linetivot yisra'el*, i. 19; Anon., *Lezikhro*, 40; T. Y. Kook, *Siḥot harav tsevi yehudah: bamidbar*, 122; H. A. Schwartz, *Mitokh hatorah hago'elet*, ii. 132; Remer, *Gadol shimushah* (1994), 64. R. Tsevi Yehudah often noted his father's comment, stated with regard to Nietzsche, that there are great souls among the non-Jews. See T. Y. Kook, *Siḥot harav tsevi yehudah*, 133–4. See also T. Y. Kook and David Cohen, *Dodi litsevi*, 61, where R. Tsevi Yehudah speaks of the value of reading the works of 'the wise and pious of the nations'. See, similarly, T. Y. Kook, *Bama'arakhah hatsiburit*, 124 (which mentions Tolstoy). (Regarding Tolstoy, see also Greenwald, *Aḥ letsarah*, 6–7, who blasts a 'Modern Orthodox' rabbi for discussing Tolstoy during a funeral eulogy. He notes that in previous years 'everyone knew' that only a secularist or a Reformer would do such a thing.) While Tolstoy was a great admirer of the Jews, the opposite was the case with Dostoevsky. See D. Goldstein, *Dostoevsky and the Jews*. Yet Hillel Zeitlin was so impressed with Dostoevsky that he compared him to R. Nahman of Bratslav and even referred to him as 'the Russian *gaon*', though the term *gaon* is usually reserved for Torah scholars. Zeitlin's son, Aaron, deleted this passage when he republished the text. See Zeitlin, *Rabbi Nahman of Bratslav* (Heb.), 48 n. 25. While the elder Zeitlin saw similarities between Nietzsche and R. Nahman, his son Aaron wished to cover this up, and thus deleted his father's identification of the *Übermensch* (*ha'adam ha'elyon*) with R. Nahman's *tsadik*; see ibid. 59 n. 117. Another mention of *ha'adam ha'elyon* became *ha'adam hayehudi ha'elyon* in A. Zeitlin's edition; see ibid. 61 n. 129. A. Zeitlin also excised his father's mention of the great Polish poet Juliusz Słowacki; see ibid. 72 n. 27. For more regarding A. Zeitlin's 'editing' of his father's work, see Y. Meir, '*The Book of Visions*' (Heb.), 171–2.

research. He compares this to earlier scholars who were criticized in their lifetimes (no doubt referring to Maimonides, R. Moses Hayim Luzzatto (1707–46), and R. Jonathan Eybeschuetz, among others); after their authority had been accepted, no amount of scholarly research could alter their standing. As for the natural desire of scholars to write about all that interests them, Ariel states: 'Researchers are also commanded to be careful, and therefore it is permissible for them to overcome their healthy and natural intellectual curiosity for the sake of public responsibility.' If these reasons are not enough to deter scholars, Ariel adds the following: 'Every *gadol* in Israel only published a *selection* of his writings. There is no value in publishing *all* the writings.'[182] Needless to say, these sentiments are rejected by all academic scholars, who are adamant that in seeking to understand someone's thought, *everything* he wrote is valuable.

Contrary to Ariel, R. Yoel Bin-Nun, another student of R. Tsevi Yehudah, has recently argued that while R. Tsevi Yehudah's reluctance to allow his father's 'unedited' manuscripts to appear in print was justified at the time, there is no longer a reason to adopt this approach today. He adds that Kook's opponents will never recognize him as a religious authority. Therefore, any new publication of theologically daring material has no relevance to them. As for the religious Zionist world, Kook's position there is so strongly established that access to his entire uncensored writings, 'the complete truth', as Bin-Nun puts it, will in no way damage his image.[183]

182 Ariel, 'Conquering Curiosity' (Heb.), 44. To get a sense of where Ariel is coming from, the following is also noteworthy. He sensed that in Hagai Segal's article in *Nekudah*, 'Orot be'ofel', subtle criticism of R. Avraham Shapira was expressed for his role in preventing the publication of Kook's writings. Ariel writes: 'One asks questions of a rabbi. This is the way of Torah. However, one does not criticize. This is the way of cheap journalism.'

183 Bin-Nun, 'Inspiration of the Holy Spirit' (Heb.), 374.

CHAPTER SIX

SEXUAL MATTERS AND MORE

THROUGHOUT HISTORY, one of the prime considerations leading to censorship has been the issue of sex, namely, what is and what is not allowed to be shown and said. Since Judaism has a very conservative sexual ethic, Jewish history has also seen its share of censorship in the sexual realm. While it is probably true that the impact of Christian society has had some influence on the development of puritanical attitudes, this is hardly the entire story. Furthermore, the haredi world has developed in such a way that its standards of modesty are far removed from anything that is found even in the most conservative Christian circles.

For example, Israeli haredim have a difficult time in bringing awareness of breast cancer to their communities, because the word 'breast' will never appear in their publications. This is the sort of extreme fastidiousness when it comes to language that, as far as I know, has no parallels outside this community. Similarly, in all the controversies over gay pride parades that have taken place in Israel, the words 'gay' or 'homosexual' have never appeared in the Israeli haredi press.[1] (The American haredi press has different standards in this regard.) The Israeli haredi media use euphemisms to name the events, but never actually tell the readers who organizes these parades. Rape and other sexual crimes are also not mentioned. In fact, someone whose only source of news was the Israeli haredi papers would never have learnt exactly what precipitated Bill Clinton's impeachment or the resignation and prison sentence of Israel's President Moshe Katzav.[2]

In many ways, contemporary Orthodox society, and not just the haredi world, is much less comfortable with images of the human body than was the case among Jews in the past. For example, Figure 6.1(*a*) is from the beautiful

[1] A friend comments: 'I think the explanation for this is (also) rooted in the fact that the written language (Hebrew, with biblical paraphrasing throughout) is more circumspect and literary than the spoken one, so there is an automatic sense that one does not write as explicitly as one speaks.'

[2] Regarding an English dictionary published for haredi schools, from which 'inappropriate' words had been removed, see Alderman, 'The Charedi Custom of Excise'.

edition of Maimonides' *Mishneh torah* published by Immanuel Athias in Amsterdam in 1702. This was an important edition because there was no censorship in Amsterdam, meaning that the book was 'complete'. One could never imagine this *Mishneh torah* title page being reprinted by any traditional press today, as it would be regarded as lacking in modesty. In fact, when a set of this *Mishneh torah* recently came up for auction, the picture of the title page printed in the catalogue was censored (Fig. 6.1(*b*)).[3] Similarly, a reprinting of Karo's *Shulḥan arukh* with a title page like the one that appeared in the Venice edition of 1577–8 (Fig. 6.2(*a*)) or the Amsterdam edition of 1698 (Fig. 6.2(*b*)) would also be unimaginable today.

In recent years, many excellent editions of important books have appeared. In the introductions the editors include pictures of the title pages of previous editions, as part of a discussion of the history of the work's printing. This is done to give the reader the impression that the new edition is 'scientific', and that the earlier editions have been examined. When R. Mordechai Jaffe's (1530–1612) classic *Levush*[4] was recently reprinted the same model was followed. The problem was that the title page of the first and second editions[5] of one of the sections, both of which appeared in Jaffe's lifetime, had 'problematic' images (Fig. 6.3(*a*)). In the new edition's introduction,[6] the page is represented thus (Fig. 6.3(*b*)).[7] Needless to say, anyone who sees this will only wonder about what is being covered up.

There are many such 'immodest' title pages, printed by a variety of publishing houses by both Jews and non-Jews, as anyone who peruses a Judaica auction catalogue can attest. Although any publisher who put these images on a title page today would never be able to sell his books, that was not the case in earlier years. Publishers, always concerned about sales above all else, would never have added these pages if they had thought it would hurt their sales. In fact, I am unaware of any evidence that rabbinic leaders ever expressed opposition to the appearance of female images on these title pages.[8]

[3] *Judaica Jerusalem*, auction catalogue, 15 Mar. 2001, 69. For another example of 'immodest' images censored from an edition of the *Mishneh torah*, see my Seforim Blog post, 25 Mar. 2012.

[4] While each section of the work has a different title (e.g. 'Levush hatekhelet', 'Levush ateret zahav'), it is commonly referred to as simply the *Levush*.

[5] Lublin, 1590 and 1603. The title page in the text is from the 1603 edition. The images in this woodcut had earlier appeared in the Prague 1526 haggadah, a Pentateuch published in Ichenhausen in 1545, and a *Seder seliḥot* published in Heddernheim in 1546. See Wengrov, *Haggadah and Woodcut*, figs. 19*a*, 19*b*.

[6] Jaffe, *Levush pinat yikrat*, published in 2000.

[7] This example was noted by Dan Rabinowitz in his Seforim Blog post, 23 Nov. 2005.

[8] Many years later, R. Abraham Isaac Kook expressed strong opposition to including pictures of women in a *maḥzor* (festival prayer book). See A. I. Kook, *Oraḥ mishpat*, 'Oraḥ ḥayim', no. 21: 2 (called to my attention by R. Baruch Oberlander).

משנה תורה
הוא
הי״ד החזקה
להרמבם זצל
חלק ראשון
באמשטרדם
ברפוס ובמצות הבחור הנחמד עמנואל
הישיש הנכבד כהר״ר יוסף עטיאש
שנת והמכתב מכתב אלהים הוא

(*a*)

(*b*)

Figure 6.1 Title page of Maimonides' *Mishneh torah* (Amsterdam, 1702): (*a*) original; (*b*) censored version in the *Judaica Jerusalem* auction catalogue (Jerusalem: Agudat Hovevei Yuda'ikah, 2001)

The elaborate title pages disappeared, not because of any rabbinic decrees, but because styles of book publishing changed. The only example of a title page that I know of that was controversial is that of the responsa of R. Joel Sirkes (1561–1640), published in Frankfurt in 1697 by a non-Jewish printer (Fig. 6.4). In this case Menahem Mendel Krengel reports that the leading rabbinic scholars of that generation condemned the title page. He does not say that this was because of the topless women on the lower right corner. After all, as mentioned, there are numerous books that have title pages showing women in various states of undress. Rather, he claims that the rabbis' ire was aroused by the idolatrous (i.e. mythological) symbols said to appear here.[9]

[9] Azulai, *Shem hagedolim hashalem*, ii, s.v. *bayit ḥadash*, in Krengel's note. This would explain why another version of this edition contains a different title page.

(*a*)

(*b*)

Figure 6.2 Title page of R. Joseph Karo's *Shulḥan arukh*: (*a*) Venice, 1577/8 edition with details enlarged to right; (*b*) Amsterdam, 1698 edition

Courtesy of the Library of the Jewish Theological Seminary

(*a*)

(*b*)

Figure 6.3 Title page of R. Mordechai Jaffe's *Levush*: (*a*) Lublin, 1603 edition; (*b*) 2000 reprint (Jerusalem: Zikhron Aharon), showing the censored image

שאלות
ותשובות
שחיבר
הרב הגדול המפורסם מופת הדור רבן של כל בני
הגולה כמוהר"ר יואל סירקשזצ"ל רב המחבר בית חדש
אשר האיר העולם מכבוד הוד והדר תפארתו בעירואם
בישראל ק"ק קראקא יע"א ושם בנה בית חדש · ועוד
מצא כביר ידו בשאלותיו ובתשובותיו והיו גנוזים עד הנה
שהובאו לדפוס ע"י הגבירה החסידה הרבנית מהמנוח
הגאון המפורסם מאור הגדול כמוהר"ר מאיר שטערן
זצ"ל שהיה משכן כבודו בק"ק אמשטרדם בערת קדושה
אשכנזים י"ץ לרב ולמ"ץ והיא בת הגאון המפורסם מאור
הגדול כמוהר"ר מענדלן בס זצ"ל מק"ק קראקא
שהיה חנותו פה ק"ק פרנקפורט לאב"ד
ור"מ ולמ"ץ ונדפס בתכלית היופי
בהשגחה גדולה
פרנקפורט
דמיין
FAMA
IMMORTA
STI
בשנת
חכמת נסים בנחה ביתה לפ"ק
נדפוס המסונה הדוןיהןנוולישט

Figure 6.4 Title page of R. Joel Sirkes' *She'elot uteshuvot habaḥ* (Frankfurt, 1697)
Courtesy of the Library of the Jewish Theological Seminary

This no doubt refers to the figures on the right and left, which are representations of the Greek gods Zeus and Poseidon (the latter even holding his trident!).[10] At the bottom of the picture one can also find two small crosses, something that escaped the notice of the Jews involved in the publication.[11]

Although the way the women are dressed in this title page was not the reason for its removal, this does not mean that some people did not think it improper to display women in this fashion. Yosef Hayim Yerushalmi has called attention to the fact that there is an image of a topless woman in two haggadahs (Prague, 1526 and Mantua, 1560).[12] Yet in a haggadah published in Venice in 1603 the woman has been turned into a man. In case anyone might be confused, the words above the picture actually state that this is a man (see Figs. 6.5 and 6.6).[13] This change was made for reasons of modesty, even though, it must be noted, Venice editions had plenty of 'immodest' pictures. In more recent reprints of the Prague 1526 haggadah, the problematic pictures have simply been deleted.[14]

Here is an example of modern puritanical sentiments. The book *Minḥah belulah*, by R. Menahem Abraham Rapa Porto (d. 1624), was published in Verona in 1594. At the end of the volume he printed his family's coat of arms (Fig. 6.7(*a*)). Here is how the coat of arms looked when the book was reprinted in Benei Berak in 1989 (Fig. 6.7(*b*)). When the coat of arms was again reprinted in 2010 (Fig. 6.7(*c*)),[15] the women (apparently mermaids) had been turned into men.[16]

[10] Another pagan image found on a number of 16th- and 17th-cent. Jewish title pages is that of Venus rising naked from the waters on a seashell. See M. J. Heller, *Printing the Talmud*, 25 n. 1. For Mars and Minerva on title pages, see M. J. Heller, *Studies*, ch. 1.

[11] Dan Rabinowitz explains how this woodcut, produced by Christians, found its way to Sirkes' responsa; see D. Rabinowitz, 'Two Versions' (Heb.). Rabinowitz disputes Krengel's report that that the title page was condemned by the rabbis. He also denies that there is any Christian symbolism on the page.

[12] Yerushalmi, *Haggadah and History*, pl. 41.

[13] I have used the images that appear in Dan Rabinowitz's Seforim Blog post, 1 Dec. 2005.

[14] The Venice Haggadah of 1629 was recently reprinted by a haredi outreach organization, and here too one finds censorship of the puritanical sort, such as lengthening women's sleeves and filling in cleavage. See <www.holyhyrax.blogspot.com>, 10 Apr. 2008. See also E. S. Horowitz, 'Between Cleanliness and Godliness', 39 n. 37; Horowitz's Seforim Blog post, 22 Mar. 2013, and Dan Rabinowitz's Seforim Blog post, 14 Mar. 2013.

[15] Hamburger, *Hayeshivah haramah befiorda*, i. 390.

[16] See my Seforim Blog post, 25 Mar. 2012, where I credit Michael Silber and the blog 'On the Main Line', who first called attention to these examples. One exception to all the censorship of title pages is Pollak, *Vayakem edut beya'akov*, published by the brothers Moses and Solomon Katz in 1595 (Fig. 6.8(*a*)). When this volume was reprinted by photo-offset in Brooklyn sometime in the 1990s, the title page was left intact. Yet it was censored when placed on Otzar HaHochma (Fig. 6.8(*b*)).

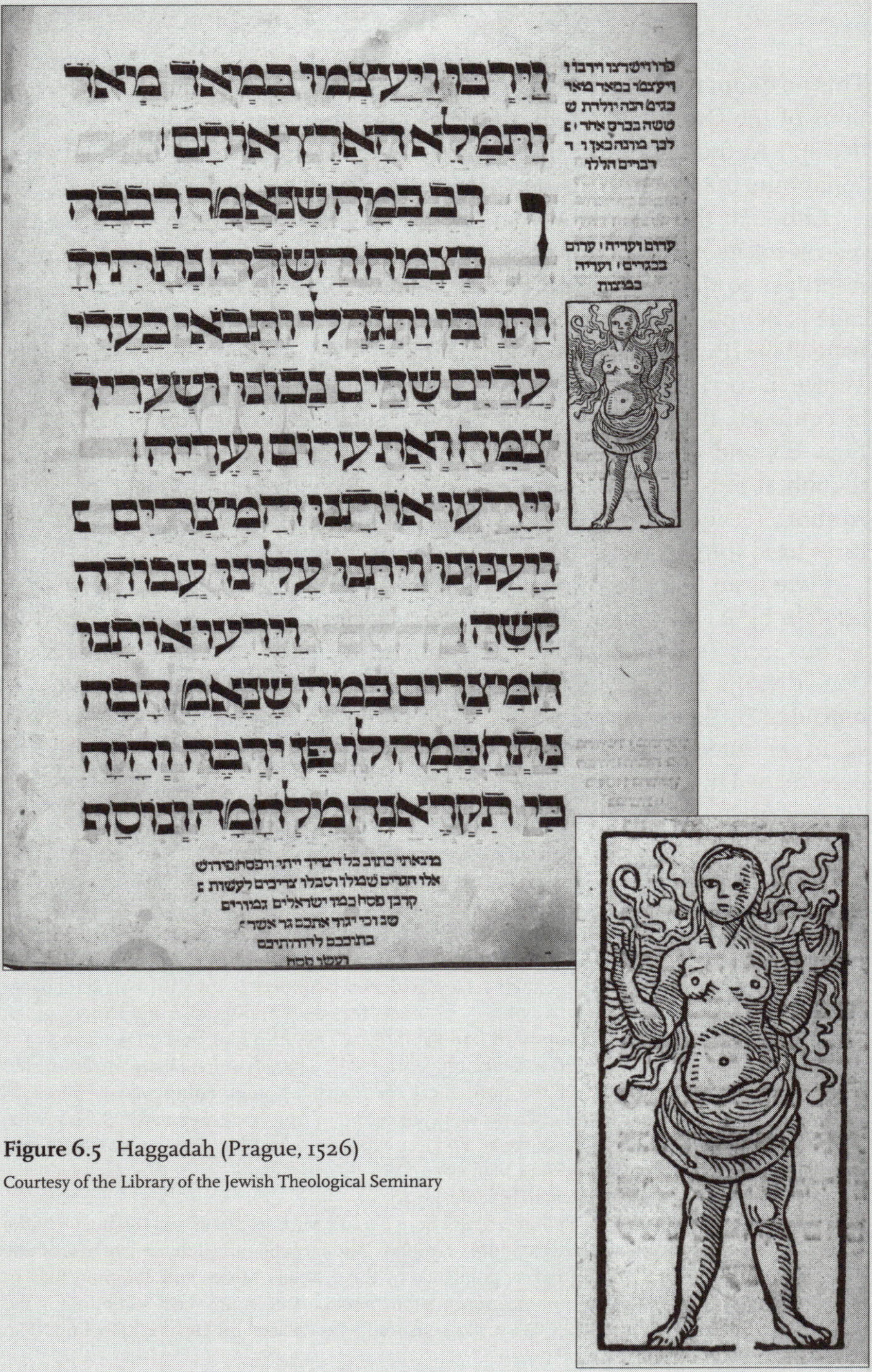

Figure 6.5 Haggadah (Prague, 1526)

Courtesy of the Library of the Jewish Theological Seminary

צורת איש ערו' וערי'

ורב כמה שנאמר רבבה כצמח
השדה נתתיך ותרבי ותגדלי
ותבואי בעדי עדיים שדים נכונו
ושעריך צמח ואת ערום ועריה
וירעו אותנו המצרים ויענונו ויתנו
עלינו עבודה קשה׃ וירעו אותנו
המצרים כמה שנאמר הבה
נתחכמה לו פן ירבה והיה כי
תקראנה מלחמה ונוסף גם הוא על
שונאינו ונלחם בנו ועלה מן הארץ׃
ויענונו כמה שנאמר למען ענותו
בסבלותם ויבן ערי מסכנות לפרעה
את פיתום ואת רעמסס׃ ויתנו עלינו
עבודה קשה כמה שנאמר ויעבידו

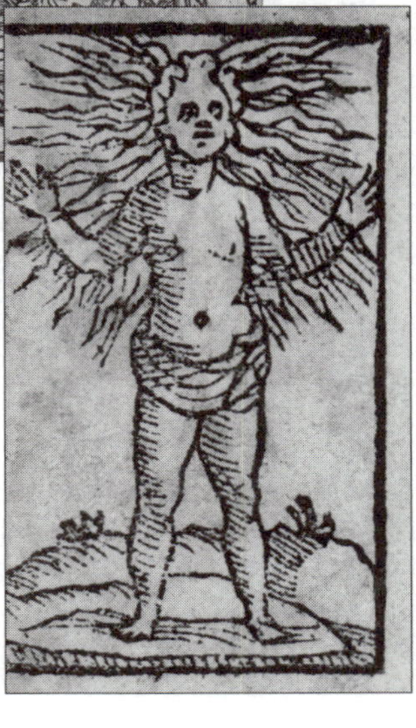

Figure 6.6 Haggadah (Venice, 1603)

Courtesy of the Library of the Jewish Theological Seminary

(*a*) (*b*) (*c*)

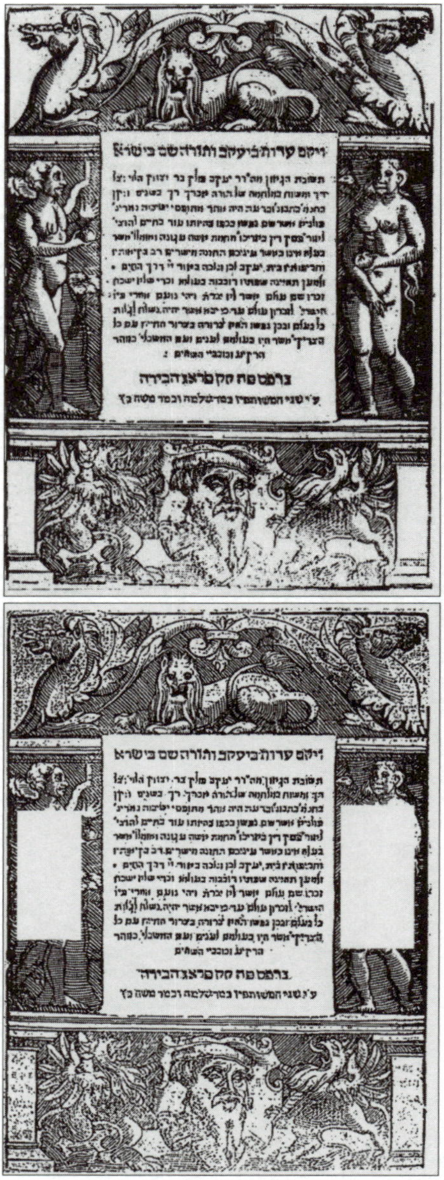
(*a*) (*b*)

Figure 6.7 (*left*) R. Menahem Abraham Rapa Porto, *Minḥah belulah*: (*a*) Verona, 1594 edition showing the original coat of arms; (*b*) 1989 reprint (Benei Berak: SLA), with 'mermaids' covered up; (*c*) version reproduced in Hamburger, *Hayeshivah haramah befiorda* (Benei Berak: Ashkenazi Heritage Institute, 2010), with the 'mermaids' transformed into men

Figure 6.8 (*right*) Title page of R. Jacob Pollak's *Vayakem edut beya'akov* (Prague, 1595): (*a*) original version; (*b*) censored version on Otzar HaHochma

In recent years, it is not simply immodestly dressed women but the very presence of *any* woman, or even young girl, in pictures that has become problematic in certain circles. Thus, as mentioned in the Preface, images of women are deleted from pictures, even in the case of important female political figures.[17] This is in line with recent haredi conceptions of modesty. In fact, in some haredi publications a woman's first name is never mentioned, which explains why R. Hayim Kanievsky told the author of a biography of the Hazon Ish not to mention the names of the Hazon Ish's sisters.[18]

The parallel to these haredi efforts to ensure modesty in visual images is Catholic efforts to cover human genitalia in art. Girolamo Savonarola (1452–98) is remembered as a prime mover in this, and the movement later picked up steam in the Counter-Reformation with the so-called 'fig-leaf campaign'. Michelangelo's sculptures were shielded from view and a later painter covered up 'indecent' parts of both his famous *Last Judgement* and the ceiling frescoes in the Sistine Chapel.[19]

In Chapter 1 I mentioned the phenomenon of *kere ukhetiv*, and how words with the root שגל were thought to be too explicit, leading to the substitution of a 'tamer' word when read aloud. In line with this approach, the Sages were also puritanical in their own discussions about sex and used a variety of euphemisms. What is significant, however, is that despite this general tendency, one finds exceptions and there are some very explicit, almost obscene, sexual references. Thus, while we find the fastidious use of the words 'eat',[20] 'speak', 'talk',[21] and 'do work'[22] to designate sexual activity, we also find the following passage:

> R. Johanan said: The limb [*ever*] of R. Ishmael son of R. Jose was as a bottle of nine *kabs* capacity. R. Papa said: R. Johanan's limb was as a bottle containing five *kabs*, others say, three *kabs*. That of R. Papa himself was as [large as] the wickerwork baskets of Harpania (BT *Bava metsia* 84*a*).

[17] See the Ishim ve-Shitos blog, 26 June 2008, which shows how a famous picture of the Hafets Hayim sitting near two women has been altered in this fashion.

[18] See T. Yavrov, *Ma'aseh ish*, iii. 5–6. Kanievsky also reports that the Hazon Ish and his own father, the Steipler, never called their wives by their first names. For criticism of Kanievsky, see Hen, *Haketav vehamikhtav*, 226–7, who makes the point that both the Bible and Talmud show no hesitation in mentioning women by name.

[19] See Carmilly-Weinberger, *Fear of Art*, 15 ff.; Stollhans, 'Michelangelo's Nude Saint Catherine'; Connor, *The Last Judgment*, ch. 12. When the Sistine Chapel was restored, Pope John Paul II instructed that several of the post-Michelangelo loincloths be removed.

[20] See Boyarin, *Carnal Israel*, 117.

[21] See Mishnah *Ket.* 1: 8 (R. Assi's opinion); Boyarin, *Carnal Israel*, 121; Paul, *Divrei shalom*, 217–18.

[22] See Paul, 'An Akkadian-Rabbinic Sexual Euphemism'. See also E. Z. Melamed, '*Lishna me'alya* and *kinuyei soferim* in Talmudic Literature' (Heb.), 138–9.

While the Soncino Talmud translates *ever* as 'waist', this appears to be a puritanical rendering, as it appears obvious that the meaning of *ever* in this passage is 'penis'.[23]

Another example of the Soncino translation's prudishness appears in *Avodah zarah* 44*a*. Here the Talmud speaks of Queen Maccah, mother of King Asa. She is said to have made an 'abominable image', and the Talmud explains that this was an object that intensified licentiousness: 'It was a kind of phallus that she made and was vaginally penetrated by it [*nivelet lo*] every day.' The Soncino translation has: 'It was a kind of phallus with which she had daily connection.' Elaine Chapnik notes:

> Translating *niv'elet* as having 'daily connection' betrays the translator's prudish discomfort with the Queen's masturbation. The Soncino Talmud's implication, that she was engaging in ritual idol worship with no sexual overtones, is utterly inconsistent with the text.[24]

If twentieth-century writers felt constrained in how they could translate texts, this was certainly the case during the Victorian era, whose name is synonymous with prudishness. Here is what a nineteenth-century English translation of the Mishnah tells us about its policy; in reading it one must remind oneself that we are dealing with a translation designed for intelligent adults, not naive schoolchildren.

> The Treatise Nidda not being suited to the refined notions of the English reader, has not been printed; and for the same reason the Hebrew in some places has been substituted for the English. In Treatise Yebamoth it has been deemed necessary to omit, for similar reasons, Chapters VI. and VIII., as well as several sections in the same Treatise; the omissions being indicated by asterisks.[25]

There are numerous examples that could be cited where a refined sense of propriety affected the translation, and these do not always have to do with sex.

[23] See the ArtScroll translation and note, ad loc.; Boyarin, *Carnal Israel*, 197; id., *Socrates and the Fat Rabbis*, 182. Shimon Steinmetz called the following to my attention: BT *MK* 18*a* states that Pharaoh's *parmashtak* was a cubit and a span. Soncino relies on a speculative etymology to translate this as 'shock of hair'. This translation is offered even though the standard understanding (e.g. in the *Arukh*, Rashi, and Jastrow, *Dictionary*) is that the word means 'penis'.

[24] Chapnik, '"Women Known for These Acts"', 87. See also ibid. 85–6, where Chapnik points to another example. Shimon Steinmetz called my attention to the Soncino translation of BT *Yoma* 19*b*. The Talmud states ואבעול כמה בתלותא בנהרדעא, and Soncino translates this as 'how many virgins were *embraced* in Nehardea!' (emphasis added). ArtScroll more accurately translates: 'a number of virgins were *bedded* in Nehardea' (emphasis added), but a more exact translation is 'were deflowered'. See Sokoloff, *Dictionary*, 202.

[25] De Sola and Raphall, *Eighteen Treatises from the Mishna*, preface, p. iii n. 1.

For example, Philip Birnbaum (1904–88), whose translation of the prayer book was the most popular Orthodox *sidur* in the pre-ArtScroll era, was unable to write the word 'urine' (which appears in 'Pitum haketoret', a talmudic text[26] recited every Sabbath and by some people every day). Instead, he just kept the Hebrew words *mei raglayim*, knowing that most people would not know what this means.[27]

One finds a similar lack of comfort with words that appear in the Tahanun prayer: *veshiketsunu ketum'at hanidah*. R. Joseph H. Hertz (1872–1946) translates this as 'They held us in abomination, as of utter defilement.'[28] Birnbaum translates: 'They utterly detest us.'[29] R. Jonathan Sacks, in his new translation of the *sidur*, renders it as 'They abhor us as if we were impure.'[30] One can find similar renderings in almost all other translations, the intent of which is to blur the correct meaning, which is: 'They abhor us as the ritual impurity of a menstruating woman.'[31]

This concern with propriety is also seen in M. Rosenbaum's and A. M. Silbermann's popular translation of Rashi on the Torah. In his commentary on Genesis 49: 24,[32] Rashi writes:

Our Rabbis interpreted 'His bow remained in strength' [Gen. 49: 24] as referring to his [Joseph's] vanquishing of his evil inclination concerning his master's wife. [The evil inclination] is called 'a bow' because the semen is shot like an arrow. 'His arms were bedecked with gold' [ויפזו זרעי ידיו], [ibid.]: [This means that] they [his hands] sent forth [ויפוצו], that is, the semen [הזרע] went out from between his fingers [מבין אצבעות ידיו].

[26] BT *Ker.* 6*a*.

[27] Birnbaum, *Ha-Siddur ha-Shalem*, 32, 408. See On the Main Line, 16 Oct. 2007. R. David de Sola Pool's search for an 'acceptable' word led him to mistranslate *mei raglayim* as 'refuse water'. See id. (ed. and trans.), *Traditional Prayerbook*, 120, 329. As early as medieval times we find the apologetic notion that *mei raglayim* means water from a spring named *raglayim*! See Anon., *Kol bo*, ed. D. Avraham (Jerusalem, 1990), ii. 228 (*perush pitum haketoret*). The Bible actually preserves a crude word for urine; see 2 Kgs 18: 27 and Isa. 36: 12. In these instances *meimei ragleihem* is substituted for the word that appears in the Bible (i.e. it is the *kere*). Judg. 3: 24 and 1 Sam. 24: 4 contain euphemisms for relieving oneself. See BT *Yev.* 103*a*.

[28] Hertz, *Authorised Daily Prayer Book*, 179.

[29] Birnbaum, *Ha-Siddur ha-Shalem*, 114.

[30] Sacks, *Koren Siddur*, 150. Scherman and Zlotowitz (eds.), *Complete ArtScroll Siddur*, 131, translate: 'They abhor us like menstrual impurity.' This too is an incorrect (apologetic?) translation, as the focus is not on menstruation *per se*, but on the menstruating woman. The phrase *ketum'at hanidah* comes from Ezek. 36: 17. In Scherman (ed.), *Tanach*, ArtScroll's Hebrew–English Bible, the verse in Ezekiel is translated properly: 'like the contamination of a menstruous woman'.

[31] Daniel Sperber has recently argued for removing these words from the prayer book. See id., *On Changes in Jewish Liturgy*, 46–7.

[32] In many editions, Rashi's comment appears at the end of v. 26.

Rashi's interpretation is apparently that of the midrashic work *Bereshit rabah*, which states that the semen went out from his fingernails.[33] This could mean that Joseph masturbated, and that this is what enabled him to resist Potiphar's wife. Although it does not cite the Joseph story, the medieval pietistic work *Sefer ḥasidim* states that one should indeed masturbate if this is the only way of preventing oneself from engaging in forbidden sexual relations.[34] R. Tsadok Hakohen of Lublin cites this view of *Sefer ḥasidim* and adds that this explains Joseph's behaviour.[35]

Alternatively, Rashi is simply summarizing a passage in *Sotah* 36*b*, where the Talmud records R. Meir's comment on the words **ויפזו זרעי ידיו**: 'He stuck his hands in the ground so that his semen came out between his fingernails.'[36] The element of sticking his hands in the ground does not appear in *Bereshit rabah* and may be a different understanding of how Joseph overcame his lust (although many traditional commentators assume that the stories in *Bereshit rabah* and *Sotah* are describing the same occurrence, perhaps wishing to disabuse people of the notion that Joseph might have masturbated). In addition, it is not clear whether in *Sotah* the semen and the fingernails are supposed to be understood literally.[37] Perhaps the entire passage is just a poetic way of describing Joseph conquering his lust. If the passage is to be understood literally, it presumably means that Joseph's spilling of seed is not to be regarded as intentional.[38]

The M. Rosenbaum–A. M. Silbermann translation of Rashi, which began to appear in 1929, apparently understood Rashi to mean that Joseph mas-

[33] *Bereshit rabah* 98: 20: נתפזר זרעו ויצא לו דרך צפרניו. See similarly JT *Hor.* 2: 5. Note, however, that while the midrash uses the word צפרניו, 'his fingernails', Rashi uses **אצבעות ידיו** 'his fingers'.

[34] *Sefer ḥasidim*, no. 176. For authorities who agree with *Sefer ḥasidim*, see C. Rapoport, *Judaism and Homosexuality*, 140 n. 11.

[35] T. Hakohen, *Yisra'el kedoshim*, 148 (10: 27): יש גם כן בהוצאת זרע לבטלה דהותר במקום יצר רע הגובר, כמו שאמרו בספר חסידים סימן קעו עיין שם. והא דיוסף מסתמא היה כן.

[36] This understanding of Rashi is found in *Tosafot hashalem*, v. 74.

[37] See *Teshuvot hage'onim*, no. 26.

[38] That is how the passage has been understood by a number of commentaries. See e.g. R. Samuel Edels (Maharsha; 1555–1631) on BT *Sot.* 36*b*, who feels the need to stress that 'certainly Joseph was careful not to touch his member'. See also Azulai, *Petaḥ einayim*, 'Nidah' 13*a*; Kunitz, *Ben yoḥai*, 71. Some guilt, however, is attached to Joseph by R. Isaac Luria. R. Hayim Vital quotes Luria, in the name of R. Kalonymos, as stating that Joseph sinned in his mind, and the drops of semen went out from his fingers. Because Joseph did not consummate the sexual act with Potiphar's wife, his bones could be buried in the land of Israel, but not his body. See Vital, *Sha'ar hapesukim*, Numbers, ch. 12 (p. 34*a*). From another text by Vital, we see that Luria meant that the semen literally came out through the fingers; see Vital, *Likutei torah nevi'im ukhetuvim*, 'Vayeḥi', p. 52*a*. See also Hayim, *Ben yehoyada*, 'Sotah' 36*b*. R. Moses Valle (d. 1777), a leading member of R. Moses Hayim Luzzatto's circle, states explicitly that Joseph 'spilled his seed needlessly', though he also omits any account of how this came about. See Valle, *Or olam*, 769.

turbated. This explains why this section of Rashi is not translated, even though the Hebrew text is complete. Another example of the Rosenbaum–Silbermann edition's prudery appears in Genesis 25: 1. Commenting on the verse recording that Abraham took Keturah as a wife, Rashi states that Keturah is Hagar but was called Keturah 'because she bound up her opening, for she did not have sexual relations with any man from the time she separated from Abraham'.[39] While Rosenbaum and Silbermann translate the beginning of Rashi's comment, that she was named Keturah because her deeds were as beautiful as incense (*ketoret*), the second option, mentioned above, is simply omitted in the translation.[40]

In his commentary on Genesis 3: 1, Rashi states that the serpent saw Adam and Eve 'naked and engaging in sexual intercourse before the eyes of all, and he desired her'. Rosenbaum and Silbermann 'translate' this as 'he saw them naked and unashamed and he coveted her', once again sparing the reader a sexually explicit comment. In Genesis 25: 26 Rashi states that Jacob was formed from the first drop of Isaac's semen and Esau from the second. In Genesis 49: 3 Rashi comments on the words 'Reuben, you are . . . the first of my vigour': 'This is his first drop, for Jacob had never had a seminal emission.' These last two passages are not translated in Rosenbaum–Silbermann.

Other examples of 'uncomfortable' comments by Rashi that remain untranslated in Rosenbaum–Silbermann are those on Genesis 18: 8, 11, which refer to Sarah's menstrual cycle, Genesis 19: 5, which states that the Sodomites wished to have homosexual sex with the visiting angels, and Genesis 24: 16, which tells us that Rebecca was not merely a virgin, but had also not engaged in unnatural sex, unlike 'the daughters of the gentiles who would preserve their virginity but were promiscuous in unnatural ways [lit. 'elsewhere', i.e. anal sex]'. One final example: in his commentary on Genesis 32: 14 (32: 15 in other editions), Rashi discusses the frequency of the sexual act for various people and animals, and this too is not translated in the Rosenbaum–Silbermann translation.[41]

Another interesting text, which from the standpoint of sexual propriety is absolutely shocking, appears in Rashi's commentary on Genesis 2: 23. The verse states that after Eve was created Adam said: 'This time, it is bone of my bones and flesh of my flesh.' The Talmud quotes R. Eleazar on this verse:

[39] In this example, as in all others mentioned below, Rashi is quoting comments of the talmudic sages.

[40] This was called to my attention by Nathan Lamm.

[41] A few of these examples are noted by Lawee, 'From Sepharad to Ashkenaz', 423 n. 148. I have not checked the entire Rosenbaum–Silbermann translation of Rashi, but based upon what I have noted already, I assume that other sexual references have also been omitted from their translation.

'This teaches that Adam had intercourse [*sheba adam al*] with every beast and animal but found no satisfaction until he had intercourse with [*sheba al*] Eve.'[42] This text was notorious in medieval times, and both Nicholas Donin (thirteenth century) and Jerònim de Santa Fe (fifteenth century) quoted it in their attacks on the Talmud as a particularly obscene rabbinic passage.[43]

Rashi lived well before these attacks and thus had no reason not to cite R. Eleazar's explanation, but it should not be surprising that some translations of Rashi share Donin's and de Santa Fe's abhorrence—or at least fear that their readers will have this reaction—and refuse to provide a literal translation of the passage. Thus, in A. J. Rosenberg's translation[44] the passage is rendered as: 'This teaches us that Adam came to all the animals and the beasts [in search of a mate], but he was not satisfied until he found Eve.' In order to spare sensitive ears, the reader is not informed that there was any sexual activity taking place. The same blurring of meaning is found in Rosenbaum and Silbermann's translation ('Adam endeavored to find a companion among all cattle and beasts'), as well as in two other popular translations of Rashi.[45]

It is true that there is a whole series of supercommentaries on Rashi that reinterpret Rashi's aggadic explanations (and thus the Talmud and Midrash as well) in a non-literal fashion. Yet in this case, only considerations of prudishness can explain such a step in a translation, especially as even among many traditional commentators Rashi's words have been understood literally. One such commentator is pointed to by none other than the ArtScroll translation of Rashi,[46] with the explanation that the prohibition on bestiality 'did not come into effect until after the creation of Eve'.

As Eric Lawee has shown, the literal understanding of Rashi's (and the Talmud's) comment was standard in medieval Ashkenaz, while 'to a one, Spanish supercommentators urged a reading according to which Adam's intercourse with beasts was cognitive, not carnal'.[47] By the seventeenth century it is almost impossible to find any interpreter who takes the passage literally. Lawee also points out that while R. Elijah Mizrahi (*c.*1450–1526), in his

42 BT *Yev.* 63*a*.

43 See Lawee, 'Reception of Rashi's *Commentary*', 46 ff.

44 A. J. Rosenberg (trans.), *Mikraot gedolot: bereshit*.

45 *Metsudah Chumash/Rashi*; Ben Isaiah and Sharfman (trans.), *Pentateuch and Rashi's Commentary*.

46 Herczeg et al. (eds.), *Torah With Rashi's Commentary*. As Eric Lawee has noted, in the ArtScroll English Talmud only the non-literal interpretation is mentioned. See Lawee, 'Embarrassment and Re-embracement', 206–7.

47 Lawee, 'From Sepharad to Ashkenaz', 394–5. One source not mentioned by Lawee is R. David Maroka Martika, who lived no later than the 15th cent. See Martika, *Zekhut adam*, 16.

commentary on Rashi, *does* interpret the text literally, in the 1862 Warsaw edition of the work, which until recent years was the standard edition, this passage was excised.[48] By this time the only acceptable reading of this passage in Rashi was to treat it like the Song of Songs, where the words must be understood allegorically. Mizrahi's literal understanding was simply too scandalous and thus had to go.

When the Church censored this passage, seeing it as blasphemous, no less a figure than Johann Reuchlin (1455–1522) came to Rashi's defence. Reuchlin interpreted Rashi to mean that 'Adam came to each beast and animal but his sensuality was not aroused until he saw his wife'.[49] Presumably unaware of those Jewish interpreters who understood Rashi literally, Reuchlin claimed that 'Rashi's words had been twisted by devils[!] to incite Christians against Jews'.[50] It is of course most ironic that Reuchlin defended Rashi against what he believed to be devilish misinterpretations, when, in fact, these interpretations were offered by outstanding rabbinic scholars who would have been more than a little piqued that a non-Jew was telling them that they were distorting Rashi's words.

The fact that the Church chose to censor this comment of Rashi shows that it was not only anti-Christian texts that were subjects for deletion. One can also cite other passages of a sexual nature that offended the Christian censors and were therefore removed. Examples include *halakhot* in Maimonides' *Mishneh torah* and R. Jacob ben Asher's *Arba'ah turim* recording the permissibility of 'unnatural intercourse'. It is possible that these *halakhot* were also found in the original version of R. Joseph Karo's *Shulḥan arukh*, but since the first edition was also subject to censorship, we can only assume as much. It was left to R. Moses Isserles to add the missing *halakhot*.[51]

Until now I have dealt with post-biblical texts that created problems, but the difficulty is as old as the Bible itself. The Song of Songs presents a great challenge for those who are uncomfortable with references to female anatomy and romantic relationships. But it is also an opportunity for translators to use all sorts of euphemisms and circumlocutions. Those who can read the Bible in its original Hebrew see what the text actually says, but those who rely on translations are subject to the whims of the translators.

The ArtScroll edition of Song of Songs translates it in accordance with the midrashic understanding.[52] For example, 'your two breasts' (4: 5, 7: 4) become either 'Moses and Aaron' or the 'Tablets of the Law'. This is exactly

[48] Lawee, 'From Sepharad to Ashkenaz', 419. It has been reinserted in E. Mizrahi, *Ḥumash hare'em.*
[49] Walton and Walton, 'In Defense of the Church Militant', 397.
[50] Ibid.
[51] See Karo, *Shulḥan arukh*, 'Even ha'ezer' 25: 2; Raz-Krakotzkin, 'From Safed to Venice', 113.
[52] Scherman and Zlotowitz (eds.), *Shir ha-Shirim*.

the approach adopted by the Targum in its 'translation' of the Song of Songs. In ArtScroll's commentary the literal meaning is also given. Yet in the ArtScroll *Siddur, Chumash,* and *Passover Machzor* only the interpretative meaning is offered. The reason given for this is that 'The literal meaning of the words is so far from their meaning that it is false.'[53]

The ArtScroll *Siddur* and *Machzor* are, I think, the first ones in history to adopt such an approach, but the sentiments expressed by ArtScroll are not new. This can be seen from what happened when the Rabbinical Council of America (RCA) published a *sidur* in 1960.[54] This prayer book, translated by R. David de Sola Pool (1885–1970), was placed under a ban by the Agudas HaRabbonim (rabbinical association) of the United States and Canada. One of the reasons given for the ban was that the Song of Songs was translated 'in a secular and vulgar fashion' and even included 'obscenities' (*nibul peh*).[55] Since the so-called obscenities are actually just translations of the Hebrew, I assume that Agudas HaRabbonim wanted the translator to use euphemisms. (As far as I know, no one has ever suggested the publication of an 'updated' Hebrew version of the Song of Songs, so that Hebrew speakers are not exposed to the original words.)

Although the RCA translation was attacked for being too explicit, even this version engaged in subtle censorship for puritanical reasons. For example, Song of Songs 1: 13 states: *bein shadai yalin*. This means 'he lies between my breasts'. ArtScroll, in the literal translation that accompanies its midrashic 'translation', softens the passage a bit, but still writes 'bosom'. Yet in the RCA *sidur*, gone are the 'breasts', and instead the lover rests 'on my heart'.

Another example of puritanical sentiments influencing a biblical translation can be seen in Joseph Magil's *Linear School Bible*.[56] Magil's Pentateuch

[53] Gold (ed.), *The Complete ArtScroll Machzor: Pesach*, 567. See my Seforim Blog posts, 14 Nov. 2011 and 20 Nov. 2011.

[54] De Sola Pool (ed. and trans.), *Traditional Prayerbook*.

[55] See *Hapardes* (Feb. 1961), 1 (unnumbered). Another reason given for the ban was the presence of faulty translations, including translations that contradict both halakhah and the accepted *peshat*, as well as translations that could lead people to heresy. The reference to heresy refers to the translation of the *Berikh shemeih* prayer (p. 241), which translates *bar elahin* not as 'angel' but 'son of God'. The RCA *sidur* translates the opening words of the Kaddish as 'Exalted and hallowed be God's great name in this world of His creation. May His will be fulfilled.' This has some similarity to the Lord's Prayer (Matt. 6: 9–10, King James Version): 'Our Father which art in heaven, Hallowed be thy name . . . Thy will be done in earth . . .'. The RCA *sidur* translation 'May His will be fulfilled' is a clear error, as the Aramaic simply means '[In the world that he created] according to His will'. The similarity between the RCA *sidur*'s translation of the Kaddish and the Lord's Prayer is hardly an accident. De Sola Pool, in his book *The Kaddish*, 21 ff., 111 ff., had earlier discussed the relationship between the Kaddish and the Lord's Prayer, concluding that 'the agreement between them is so close and so exact in main features and in almost all details, that their essential unity of origin is undeniable' (p. 112).

[56] I thank Dr Sam Kahan for bringing this Bible to my attention.

was first published in 1905 and was followed by similar linear translations of other biblical books. In the preface to the work, Magil writes that his intention is to have his edition used as 'a school book and a companion to all those desiring to study the Bible in its original language without regard to age or sex'. What then to do about certain 'problematic' passages? Magil tells us that he has left untranslated those passages 'not suitable for translation from the modern stand-point of nicety. For the same reason, a word was sometimes purposely rendered incorrectly[!], the correct rendering being given in the footnotes.'

The passages which Magil does not translate, giving us only the Hebrew, are Genesis 38: 8–30 (the story of Judah and Tamar), 39: 7–18 (Joseph and Potiphar's wife); Leviticus 15 (physical secretions including menstruation), 18: 6–23, 19: 20–2, 20: 10–21 (sexual crimes); Numbers 5: 11–31 (the *sotah* (adulterous woman); Deuteronomy 22: 13–29 (accusation that a bride is not a virgin), 23: 1–3 (sexual crimes, the law of a *mamzer*,[57] and one whose private parts are maimed), and 23: 10–15, 18–19 (nocturnal emissions, hygiene in the war camp, harlotry).

Magil's concern with propriety is also seen in other verses that speak of sexual relations. For example, Genesis 29: 30 speaks of Jacob 'going into' Rachel, and Magil turns this into Jacob marrying her. While the translation is not exact, one could argue that it expresses the sense of the verse. Yet this puritanical approach also leads to (intentional) error. An example of what Magil has in mind when he speaks of giving 'incorrect' translations appears in Numbers 31: 17, where the Israelites are commanded to kill the Midianites, including 'every woman that hath known man by lying with him'. Magil's translation refers to 'every woman that has ever been married', and, as promised in the preface, gives the correct translation in the footnote.[58]

One final example is worth noting, since it appears not only in Magil but also in many other translations, both earlier and later, up to the present day. This illustrates well the continuing concern with 'propriety' and the feelings of the reader. 1 Samuel 25 describes David's confrontation with Nabal, and in verse 22 David speaks of not leaving anything with Nabal, even a *mashtin bekir*. The typical English translation renders this as 'one male'. Anyone desiring an accurate translation can turn to the King James version, where the words are correctly rendered as 'any that pisseth against the wall'.[59]

[57] The offspring of certain forbidden sexual relationships.

[58] Since the footnote appears on the same page as the text, I wonder why Magil saw any value in his approach.

[59] It is not just Jewish translators who showed their puritanical sense. For example, in Marcus Dods's 1881 translation of Augustine's *City of God*, which was the standard English version for

Before moving on, let me also note that we have at least one famous example of self-censorship regarding the matters of which we have been speaking. This comes from R. Jacob Emden, who must have realized that one of his comments was too much, even for him. In the first edition of his *Migdal oz*, Emden quoted a Jewish man who had had sexual relations with a non-Jewish woman, and the woman told him that she had more sexual pleasure with a circumcised man than with one who was uncircumcised.[60] This passage, which Gershom Scholem described as 'near obscenity, especially in a prayer book',[61] was deleted by Emden himself from most of the copies of the first edition of this work, and the uncensored copies are now a collector's item.[62]

Let us now turn to some examples where texts dealing with personal matters were altered. While the authors were prepared to share these stories, later publishers, and even copyists of manuscripts, were more reticent. For example, a passage in R. Joseph Karo's *Magid meisharim* that mentions his sex life was deleted from manuscripts, obviously for puritanical reasons.[63] In the hasidic work *Malakhei elyon*, edited by Abraham Isaac Rabinowitz,[64] there is a description of what led R. Tsadok Hakohen of Lublin to divorce his wife. According to the tale, his wife 'extended her hand' to a non-Jewish military figure who came to drink wine in her father's establishment. This probably means that she gave him her hand to kiss, as was the custom in those days. This entire story was removed from the second edition of the work,[65] no doubt because it was thought that it provided 'too much information'.

There is also another passage regarding R. Tsadok that was censored. This text is interesting because it illustrates how certain hasidic disciples thought it

many years, a section of book 14, ch. 26, dealing with the sexual relationship of Adam and Eve, is left untranslated. In Clement of Alexandria's *The Instructor*, a large section of book II, ch. 10, dealing with sex in marriage, was not translated in the Edinburgh 1867 edition. An editorial note informs the reader that 'for obvious reasons, we have given the greater part of this chapter in the Latin version' (p. 244). In the Edinburgh 1869 translation of Clement's *Stromata*, the entire book III remains untranslated. (My colleague Dr Eric Plumer brought these examples from Christian literature to my attention.) Another example of Christian puritanical censorship is seen in the Venice, 1574 edition of Maimonides' *Mishneh torah*, where references to unnatural sexual intercourse (*shelo kedarkah*) were deleted. See the Frankel edition's lengthy textual note on 'Hilkhot melakhim' 9: 7, which lists all the examples.

60 Emden, *Migdal oz*, 2*b*. See also p. 3*a*, for another comment about non-Jewish women preferring intercourse with a circumcised man.

61 Scholem, *Researches in Sabbateanism* (Heb.), 657. *Migdal oz* is regarded as part 3 of Emden's prayer book.

62 See Kestenbaum's auction catalogue, Sept. 2006, p. 35, where an uncensored edition of the three-volume prayer book was expected to be sold for between $20,000 and $25,000. It ended up selling for $43,660. See the auction result at <www.kestenbaum.net/prc_0906.php>.

63 See H. L. Gordon, *Maggid of Caro*, 116.

64 p. 19 (no. 12).

65 Jerusalem, 1966.

was important to record everything about their master, even if they could only allude to certain matters. From the standpoint of contemporary mores, some of what they recorded is precisely *not* the sort of thing that should be preserved for posterity. According to the story, R. Tsadok was observing *yahrzeit*, the anniversary of the death of a close relative, and was leading the prayers for the congregation. 'Something happened, which I am not able, and I do not want to tell, and those who were there certainly remember what happened then. He was terribly distressed by it, and in the Amidah he was groaning and sighed greatly.'[66] Apparently, what this means is that R. Tsadok broke wind, and those who were praying with him were aware of this.[67] It is no surprise that this strange text was removed when the work was reprinted.

In the previous two cases moderns might assume that the original text included too much information and that the later censorship is understandable. The next example, however, is just the opposite, and it is the original text that is more in line with contemporary mores. In a published letter from R. Elhanan Wasserman to R. Eliezer Silver (1882–1968) describing the death of R. Hayim Ozer Grodzinski, Wasserman writes: 'A short while before his death . . . he said: "You know that it is not good."'[68] The first thing to notice is that an ellipsis is provided. This is significant, as usually haredi censorship does not provide any indication that words are missing. So what has been deleted? In the original letter it mentions that Grodzinski held his wife's hand.[69] Although the haredi world is opposed to all public displays of affection, one would think that even in that world this particular act of censorship would be regarded as downright cold-hearted. For what could possibly be objectionable in recording that in his last moments, Grodzinski reached for the hand of his wife, with whom he had shared some fifty-seven years?[70]

There is another fascinating text to which I would like to call attention. It too deals with a woman although, again, the context is not sexual. This example is particularly interesting since it shows that even in the early nineteenth century, the publisher was troubled by something that certainly would bother a modern reader. I refer to the phenomenon of a husband striking his wife, which unfortunately is not unknown in Jewish history.[71]

66 A. I. Rabinowitz, *Malakhei elyon* (Warsaw edn.), 24 (no. 29).

67 See Karo, *Shulḥan arukh*, 'Oraḥ ḥayim' 103: 3: 'If one has an eruption [of air] while he prays, if it is from below it is a bad omen for him.'

68 Wasserman, *Kovets ma'amarim ve'igerot*, ii. 97.

69 I thank Chaim Landerer for this information. The letter is preserved at the Agudath Israel Archives in New York.

70 For censorship of a song by the famous hasidic composer Yom Tov Ehrlich, see David Assaf's blog, Oneg Shabbat, 21 Sept. 2012. Among other 'problematic' verses, Ehrlich had written of R. Akiva's love for his wife.

71 See Avraham Grossman, 'Medieval Rabbinic Views'; id., *Pious and Rebellious* (Heb.), ch. 10; Graetz, *Silence is Deadly*; Teherani, *Amudei mishpat*, i. 147 ff.

Today, such behaviour is regarded with abhorrence, as it would have been by most Jews throughout the generations. There are numerous halakhists, from medieval times to the present, who speak of the utter horror of wife-beating. Yet for the sake of historical accuracy we must note there were also some authorities, a minority to be sure, who thought that at times a husband *was* permitted to hit his wife if he thought this was necessary in order to keep her 'in line'.

Even when permission was given to hit one's wife, it did not mean that the woman was ever regarded like property, and that she could be abused at will for any reason at all. Those who permitted wife-beating generally saw this as a way of forcing her to follow religious law.[72] Viewing a wife as subservient, much as one views a child vis-à-vis a parent, opened the door to 'corrective' measures, which for some included physical violence. For example, both R. Israel Isserlein (1390–1460) and R. David Ibn Zimra explain that a husband can beat his wife if she behaves in a sinful way because 'she is under his control'.[73]

[72] See e.g. R. Jonah Gerondi, *Igeret hateshuvah*, ch. 5: 'He who beats his wife transgresses two negative commandments, unless he is striking her to reprove her for her sins'; and R. Eliezer of Metz, *Sefer yere'im*, no. 217: 'A man should be very careful not to raise his hand against his fellow, even his wife, but if he intends to chastise her or to guide her, or to chastise or guide his fellow in the right way, it is permitted, as it is said, "A whip for the horse, a bridle for the ass, and a rod for the fool's back" [Prov. 26: 3].'

[73] Isserlein, *Terumat hadeshen*, no. 218, and Ibn Zimra, *She'elot uteshuvot haradbaz*, no. 888: אם [היא] עושה דברים בלתי הגונים לפי תורתינו יש לו רשות ליסרה ולהכותה להחזירה למוטב כיון שהיא ברשותו. For a similar justification, see R. Elijah Capsali (*c.*1483–1555), *Me'ah she'arim*, ch. 43, who thinks that one is *obligated* to hit one's wife if this is the only way to stop her from cursing one's parents. We see that this is his opinion because he states that in this case, if the husband does not hit her he will be punished (i.e. heavenly punishment). Virtually all those who permit husbands to beat their wives are speaking of cases where the wife is guilty of some specific sin. However, there are exceptions. For example, R. Samuel Hanagid (11th cent.) writes that a husband should beat his wife 'if she dominates you as a man and raises her head'. See A. Grossman, 'Medieval Rabbinic Views', 55; id., *Pious and Rebellious* (Heb.), 381. (R. Samuel Hanagid's words appear in his *Ben mishlei*, 117 (no. 419), which is a poetic wisdom text, modelled on the book of Proverbs, not a halakhic work.) In *Magen elokim*, 64, the author (apparently R. Isaac Aboab (15th cent.)), as part of his marital advice, recommends not speaking too much to one's wife, showing her an angry face, and hitting her. R. Samuel Jaffe (16th cent.), famous for his commentaries on the Jerusalem Talmud and Midrash, states that by virtue of the husband's authority, he has the right to strike his wife (and children) with a stick and strap. See S. Jaffe, *Yefeh mar'eh*, on JT *Bik.* 3: 5 (p. 93*a*). Because this viewpoint is so extreme, R. Nissim Abraham Ashkenazi (d. 1860), *Neḥmad lemar'eh*, 197*b*, assumed that Jaffe must only be referring to a case when a wife curses her husband, and that he could not possibly be giving the husband carte blanche for such behaviour. See also Adelman, '"Law and Love"', 295–6: 'Archival materials from the sixteenth-century Roman Jewish community confirm these findings with descriptions of wife-beating as a sometimes acceptable part of Jewish family life, "hitting her in the manner in which women, modest virgins, and those who observe the rules are chastised". One wife was warned that if she was not obedient to her husband he would be able "to do with her as the Torah permits".'

It should have been apparent to all that even limited permission given to hit wives would lead to terrible abuses, but that is not how everyone saw matters. A responsum from the geonic period even states that if a woman is beaten by her husband she should remain quiet, as this is the way a modest women behaves.[74] (R. Eliezer Papo (1785–1828) also offered this advice many years later, adding that by accepting upon herself the 'judgement of heaven'(!), the wife can look forward to reward in the world to come.[75])

Maimonides writes that if a woman does not fulfil her household duties, for which she is religiously obligated, she can be beaten.[76] Upon this ruling, R. Abraham ben David (Rabad, Maimonides' great critic), exclaims that he never heard of such a thing, that it is permissible to beat a woman.[77] According to many, Maimonides means that the court can beat the woman, not the husband. Yet this is hardly clear and does not appear to be how Rabad[78] or R. Vidal of Tolosa (fourteenth century)[79] understood the ruling. Meiri and R. Solomon Luria state explicitly that Maimonides means the husband. Luria explains that Maimonides sees this case as parallel to the way in which a master can physically discipline his slave.[80] Yet he adds that unlike a slave, according to Maimonides a wife can only be treated this way when her misbehaviour also constitutes a religious infraction, as, for example, refusing to perform her household duties.[81]

R. Nissim Gerondi (1320–76) quotes an unnamed *gaon* who also stated that a husband could beat his wife in the circumstances described by

[74] This responsum also states that a wife must feed her husband, even from her hand to his mouth, and stand up when he enters the room. See Lewin (ed.), *Otsar hage'onim*, 'Ketubot', no. 428, pp. 169–70. The responsum is attributed to R. Yehudai Gaon (8th cent.), but Grossman doubts that this is accurate. He assumes that the text is part of the genre of non-normative Jewish literature that was influenced by Muslim writings. See A. Grossman, *Pious and Rebellious* (Heb.), 377–8.

[75] Papo, *Pele yo'ets*, 6*b* (letter *alef*, s.v. *ahavat ish ve'ishah*). Shockingly, Papo's advice is even repeated by contemporary rabbis in their books on *shelom bayit* (domestic peace). See Zakai, *Shelom bayit*, 118; Y. Hakohen, *Shalom ohalekha*, 27; Ayash, *Beitkha shalom*, 136.

[76] Maimonides, *Mishneh torah*, 'Hilkhot ishut' 21: 10.

[77] R. Menahem Meiri, who like Rabad was from Provence, does refer to beating one's wife, and discusses whether it is permissible to hit her with a stick when she is a *nidah* (menstruant). See Meiri, *Beit habeḥirah*, 'Nidah', 279, 'Ketubot', 24. See also Tosafot, *Ketubot* 63*a*, s.v. *rav*. Rabad's own solution to a 'misbehaving' wife is also not in line with modern sensibilities. He states that one can cease sustaining her, including feeding her, until she submits.

[78] See A. Grossman, *Pious and Rebellious* (Heb.), 384.

[79] See his *Magid mishneh*, 'Ishut' 21: 10.

[80] כמו שכופה הרב את עבדו במקל ורצועה בעניין המלאכה ה"נ בעל לאשתו. S. Luria, *Yam shel shelomoh*, 'Bava kama' 3: 21. For Meiri's statement, see *Beit habeḥirah*, 'Ketubot', 259–60.

[81] Ibid. Luria himself rejects Maimonides' opinion. See also R. Samuel Eliezri, *Melekhet shemuel*, 98–9, who asserts that Maimonides means that the husband beats the wife, not the court.

Maimonides,[82] and Maimonides' ruling could well be reflecting this viewpoint.[83] Centuries after Maimonides, R. Moses Isserles ruled that a man may not beat his wife, adding that this is sinful and not a Jewish trait. However, he also stated that if she needlessly curses her husband or degrades his parents, actions which are both halakhic violations, and does not heed his rebuke, it is permissible to hit her if this will stop her improper behaviour.[84] Isserles' ruling will cause people great discomfort today, and it is almost impossible to find a modern halakhist who adopts this opinion.[85] As early as the nineteenth century, R. Hayim Palache of Izmir (1788–1869) understood the danger of Isserles' position, since any man who wished to beat his wife could use Isserles' reason as a pretext. In other words, as long as beating one's wife is permitted in *any* circumstances, it leaves all women vulnerable. Therefore, Palache concluded that 'in our day' it is never permitted to use physical force against one's wife.[86] While Palache's outlook is certainly admirable, one would assume that even in Isserles' day there were men who were prepared to beat their wives for all sorts of reasons, and if challenged would claim

[82] See his commentary on BT *Ket.* 63*b* (p. 26*b* in the Alfasi pages).

[83] See A. Grossman, *Pious and Rebellious* (Heb.), 385. In *Igeret hakodesh*, in Nahmanides, *Works* (Heb.), vol. ii, p. 336, the author writes ואין ראוי לריב עמה ולא להכותה על ענין תשמיש. This language seems to imply that there is no actual prohibition on hitting one's wife, only a moral imperative to refrain from doing so. Charles Mopsik claims that this work was written by R. Joseph Gikatilla (1248–*c.*1325). See Mopsik, *Lettre sur la sainteté*, 13 ff.

[84] Isserles' gloss on Karo, *Shulḥan arukh*, 'Even ha'ezer' 154: 3. See also Isserles' gloss on *Shulḥan arukh*, 'Ḥoshen mishpat' 421: 13. His ruling is based on Isserlein, *Terumat hadeshen*, no. 218. (See also Solomon ben Adret, *She'elot uteshuvot harashba hameyuḥasot leramban*, no. 102.) R. Moses Provencal agrees with Isserles that a wife can be beaten to stop her improper behaviour. See Provencal, *She'elot uteshuvot rabenu mosheh provintsalu*, vol. i, no. 77. However, an early copyist was uncomfortable with what Provencal wrote and inserted a few words, bracketed in the published edition, that do not reflect Provencal's outlook: ואולם אם יתברר שהיא היתה מרגלת הקטטה ובשביל כך הי' מכה אותה [אע"פ שאינו רשאי] הפסידה מזונותי' משיצאה עד שתשוב אליו. Some authorities rule that if you see a man sinning it is permitted to beat him as well, if this will stop his sinful action; see M. Jaffe, *Levush ir shushan*, 'Ḥoshen mishpat' 421: 13; S. Luria, *Yam shel shelomoh*, 'Bava kama' 3: 9.

[85] There are some exceptions. See e.g. H. J. D. Weiss, *Vaya'an david*, vol. iii, 'Even ha'ezer', no. 102, where R. Hayim Joseph David Weiss concludes that one can beat one's wife to prevent her from sinning, but only if she is going to violate a biblical prohibition. See also R. Shlomo Korah, *Teshuvah kahalakhah*, no. 38, who permits a man to beat his wife if she curses him to his face. R. Aharon Yehudah Grossman claims that since women and children do not have completely developed intellects, 'therefore sometimes both of them need to be hit in order to educate them'. See A. Y. Grossman, *Vedarashta veḥakarta* (2008), vol. v, part 2, p. 529. He also points out, ibid., p. 528, that while Maimonides permits using a *shot* (which means 'whip' or 'rod') on one's wife, he forbids doing this with a student, with whom one can only use a small strap. See Maimonides, *Mishneh torah*, 'Hilkhot talmud torah' 2: 2.

[86] Palache, *Kaf haḥayim*, 1: 11; id., *Tokhaḥat ḥayim*, 'Emor' (p. 30*b*). See also Medini, *Sedei ḥemed*, vol. v, 'Ma'arekhet heh', no. 5 (p. 1962).

that they were provoked by their spouses' misdeeds, the very misdeeds that Isserles rules are sufficient grounds for beating one's wife.

What does all this have to do with internal Jewish censorship? In 1806 the commentary on the Torah by R. Jacob ben Asher (*c.*1269–*c.*1343) was published for the first time, and was reprinted a few times after this. Yet it was only in 2006, when the commentary was published in a critical edition, that readers learnt that the 1806 edition had omitted something that appears not only in the manuscript used for this edition, but also in the two other existing manuscripts of this commentary.

When Leah gave birth to her first son, she called him Reuben, 'Because the Lord hath looked upon my affliction' (Genesis 29: 32). She called her second son Simeon, 'Because the Lord hath heard that I am hated' (Genesis 29: 33). R. Jacob ben Asher explains that before Reuben was born, Jacob used to beat Leah, and this is what she meant by God *looking* upon her affliction. Once Reuben was born he no longer beat her, but would still scold her, which is why with Simeon's birth she spoke of God *hearing* that she is hated.[87] Seeing the patriarch Jacob portrayed as beating his wife was so troubling to the editor in 1806 that the easiest way to handle the problem was simply to omit it.[88]

It is interesting that a similar passage by R. Jacob ben Asher appears in the standard *Ba'al haturim* commentary by him on Genesis 3: 12. The verse states: 'The woman whom Thou gavest to be with me, she gave me of the tree, and I did eat.' According to R. Jacob ben Asher, this means that 'she hit me with [a branch of] the tree until I acquiesced to her [and ate the fruit]'.[89] Unlike the previous example from R. Jacob ben Asher, this explanation is not unique to him, as it also appears in works by the Tosafists[90] and R. Jacob of Vienna

87 Jacob ben Asher, *Perush hatur ha'arokh al hatorah*, Gen. 29: 32.

88 David Assaf called attention to I. Berger, *Eser orot*, 36*b*, no. 22, who quotes R. Israel ben Shabetai Hapstein (1733–1844), the Maggid of Kozienice, concerning a strange practice of hitting a bride until her tooth falls out. See Assaf, *Caught in the Thicket* (Heb.), 37. While it is hard to know what to make of this report, it is noteworthy that in all subsequent editions, and even in some copies of the 1907 edition, this section has been deleted. Regarding beating one's children, in some manuscripts of the Vilna Gaon's famous letter to his family, he states that at times children should be beaten 'with cruel blows'. These words were removed from other manuscripts. See Eliezer Brodt's Seforim Blog post, 3 Mar. 2013. Another possible example of censorship is found in *Sefer ḥasidim*, no. 274. The early editions state that if a man touches his wife he should wash his hands before touching a Jewish book. By the 19th cent. we find editions where 'his wife' is no longer mentioned, and instead it states that if a man touches his own skin he should wash before touching a book. It is possible that this was an intentional alteration of the text of *Sefer ḥasidim*. This point was made in an anonymous comment on the haredi website 'Behadrei Haredim' at <www.bhol.co.il/forums/topic.asp?topic_id=585306&which page=19&forum_id=1364>.

89 The basis for the exegesis is the phrase 'she gave me of the tree', instead of 'she gave me of the fruit of the tree'.

90 *Moshav zekenim al hatorah*, Gen. 3: 12; *Tosafot hashalem*, i, Gen. 3: 12.

(fourteenth century),[91] and is also reflected in a poem by Immanuel of Rome (1261–1328).[92] This is such a strange comment,[93] even more than the previous one, that I find it hard to believe that any medieval authority would have offered it on his own. Presumably, there was some midrashic source, since lost.[94]

Another example of censorship with regard to the position of women is seen in R. Elhanan Wasserman's famous *Ikveta dimeshiḥa* (Footsteps of the Messiah). This work was first published in Yiddish,[95] and as the title suggests, offers Wasserman's musings regarding what he thought was the era before the arrival of the messiah. A major theme is the need to hold on to Torah in the traditional sense, in an era in which the irreligious have achieved great power and their lifestyle poses a great threat to Orthodox Judaism.

In this book, Wasserman also gives advice on how to create a happy marriage. He writes:

> The Sages said, 'Come down a step in choosing your wife.'[96] [This means] that one should marry a woman who is on a lower level than him, for the world is based on 'And he shall rule over you' [Gen. 3: 16], [and] 'that every man should rule in his own house' [Esther 1: 22]. If she will be on a higher level than him, then she will rule at home, and the Sages already said, 'One whose wife rules him, his life is no life.'[97] This is counsel for all times, how to live a happy life.

This text appears in section 27 of *Ikveta dimeshiḥa*, which has been printed a number of times. However, in all but a few of the Hebrew editions this pas-

91 Jacob of Vienna, *Peshatim uferushim*, 11.

92 Immanuel of Rome, *Maḥberot*, 400 (no. 22).

93 In his edition of Jacob ben Asher, *Ba'al haturim al hatorah*, 19 n. 110, Ya'akov Koppel Reinitz refers to Jacob Reifman's comment that R. Jacob ben Asher's explanation should be deleted, as it was inserted by those intending to mock the Torah. See Reifman, 'Some More Flowers' (Heb.); Sulam, 'Supplements' (Heb.), 145–6. This is a variation of the often expressed apologetic notion that various controversial statements in rabbinic writings are products of an 'erring student'. Yet as Reinitz points out, all manuscripts contain the passage in question. In addition, Reifman did not know that this explanation also appears in other early texts. See also Yehudah Hershkowitz, 'Note' (Heb.). R. Joseph Hayim, *Od yosef ḥai*, 'Ki tetse', 110, was obviously troubled by the passage, and therefore suggests, without any supporting evidence, that the text should be emended so that instead of שהכתני, 'she hit me', it should read שנגעתני, 'she touched me'. See also S. Ashkenazi, *Alfa beita tinyeta dishemu'el ze'ira*, i. 210–13.

94 R. Israel Meir Hakohen, *Shem olam*, part 2 (*Nefutsot yisra'el*), ch. 5 (p. 67), mistakenly states that the passage appears in the Midrash. Another strange comment by R. Jacob ben Asher appears in id., *Ba'al haturim al hatorah* on Gen. 29: 31. Here he states that Jacob suspected that Leah had been sexually promiscuous before their marriage. For R. Elijah David Rabinowitz-Teomim's shocked response, see ibid. 42–3 (second pagination).

95 A reprint of the original Yiddish appears in Wasserman, *Yalkut ma'amarim umikhtavim*, 32–76.

96 BT *Yev.* 63*a*.

97 See BT *Beits.* 32*b*.

sage is missing.[98] The reason is obviously because Wasserman's words would appear incredibly sexist to contemporary readers, even among many in the haredi world.[99]

Let me conclude this chapter by returning to the subject of sex, and pointing out that had it not been for an act of censorship, Israel Najara's (*c.*1555–*c.*1625) *Ya-h ribon*, one of the most beloved Sabbath hymns, would probably never have achieved popularity. R. Hayim Vital (1543–1620), in his *Sefer haḥezyonot*, records that while drunk Najara engaged in homosexual acts. He also mentions that Najara had sexual relations with a non-Jewish woman. Because of this, Vital wrote that 'the hymns that he has composed are in themselves good, but whoever speaks to him and whatever leaves his mouth is forbidden, because he always used foul language and was a drunkard his whole life'.[100]

In early editions of the book, Najara's name was deleted, and it is possible that it was even deleted from the manuscript used for the first edition. It was only with the 1954 publication of *Sefer haḥezyonot*, from Vital's own autograph manuscript, that the report about Najara became known. Had this information been public knowledge in earlier years, it is unlikely that Najara's hymn would ever have been adopted, even though, as we have seen, Vital asserted that his hymns are without objection. Yet even after the publication of the uncensored *Sefer haḥezyonot*, we should not be surprised that a 2002 edition of the work published by a Jerusalem yeshiva continues to omit Najara's name.[101] To do so is a lot easier than explaining to people why such a man's hymn should still be sung.

[98] The passage is even censored in Wasserman, *Kovets ma'amarim ve'igerot*, which reinserts other passages that had been censored.

[99] This point was made in an anonymous comment on the haredi website Behadrei Haredim at <www.bhol.co.il/forums/topic.asp?topic_id=585306&whichpage=2&topic_id=1364>.

[100] Vital, *Sefer haḥezyonot*, 34, trans. in Faierstein, *Jewish Mystical Autobiographies*, 71.

[101] See Dan Rabinowitz's Seforim Blog post, 3 May 2006. R. Ya'akov Moshe Hillel knows of the accusations against Najara but refuses to elaborate. See id., *Vayashav hayam*, ii. 145–6: גם גברא רבה דכוותיה לא יצא נקי מן החשד, ולא נמלט מן הביקורת החריפה כנגדו הכתובה וחרותה לדורי דורות. והשתיקה יפה כי אחרי מות קדושים אמור. On the general issue of Lurianic kabbalah and homosexuality, see Magid, 'Constructing Women from Men'. For censorship of Jiri Langer's work dealing with homoeroticism, see Halper, 'Coming Out of the Hasidic Closet', 190 n. 3.

CHAPTER SEVEN

OTHER CENSORED MATTERS

Non-Jews

Texts dealing with non-Jews are an area where internal censorship, and of course non-Jewish censorship, has abounded. Usually the motivation for internal censorship was because the texts in question speak negatively about non-Jews, and Jews rightly feared how non-Jews would react. Often, the original text can be found in manuscripts, but when the book was printed the publisher deleted the anti-gentile comments.[1] At other times, the changes were even made to the manuscript.[2] There were also occasions when changes were made between one edition and another. Here is an interesting example, where in the first edition of the *Entsiklopedyah talmudit* ('Talmudic Encyclopaedia')[3] a passage from Maimonides was included that from a modern perspective is terribly immoral (Fig. 7.1(*a*)).[4] It was not long before the passage was replaced. Here is how it appears in the current edition of the *Entsiklopedyah talmudit* (Fig. 7.1(*b*)).

There have also been times when certain texts have been censored or altered, not because of concern about how non-Jews will react upon seeing how negatively they are portrayed, but for almost the exact opposite reason. The texts were originally quite 'universalist', but confronted with non-Jewish persecution, universalist notions became very problematic to many Jews, and this is what led to the alterations.

The most famous example of this comes from the Mishnah, *Sanhedrin* 4: 5, which states: 'Only one man was created, to teach that one who destroys a

[1] See e.g. Spitzer, 'Was *Sefer maharil* Censored?' (Heb.), 84.

[2] See pp. 36–7 above.

[3] *Entsiklopedyah talmudit*, iii, col. 297.

[4] This censorship was noted in an anonymous comment on the haredi website Behadrei Haredim at <www.bhol.co.il/forums/topic.asp?cat_id=38&topic_id=2752360&forum_id=19616>. Maimonides wrote in *Mishneh torah*, 'Hilkhot isurei biah' 12: 10:

> If an Israelite has intercourse with a gentile woman, whether she is a minor three years and one day old or an adult, whether she is married or unmarried, even if the Israelite is only nine years and a day old, once he wilfully has intercourse with her, she is liable to be put to death, because an offence has been committed by an Israelite through her, just as in the case of an animal.

R. Jehiel Jacob Weinberg had already expressed dismay over this view of Maimonides. See my *Between the Yeshiva World and Modern Orthodoxy*, 182 n. 47.

single Jewish person is regarded by Scripture as if he had destroyed the entire world, and one who saves a single Jewish person is regarded by Scripture as if he had saved the entire world.' Ephraim E. Urbach showed that the original version of this *mishnah* referred to 'a single person', and that 'Jewish' is a later insertion.[5] It is almost certain that the addition of 'Jewish' was ideologically based, designed to limit the universalist message found in the original version.

Along these lines, in the chapter on R. Abraham Isaac Kook we saw how R. Tsevi Yehudah Kook's very positive comments about Tolstoy were censored. The 'problem' in that case was that certain individuals thought that R. Tsevi Yehudah's reputation would suffer if people learnt that he so admired a non-Jewish personality. Even the published works of such an open-minded scholar as Samuel David Luzzatto suffered in this regard. Thus, while in an Italian work he spoke of all humans as brothers, in the Hebrew translation this became 'all Jews'.[6]

The same 'problem' is seen in other texts. For example, in manuscripts of a work by R. Jacob Moelin (*c.*1365–1427), a passage was deleted that records that Moelin greeted the non-Jews he met upon leaving the synagogue.[7] R. Moses Hagiz, who is most famous for his relentless assaults on the Shabateans, was also a friend of the great Christian Hebraist, Johann Christoph Wolf (1683–1739). He even mentions Wolf in the introduction to his *Mishnat ḥakhamim*,[8] where Wolf's name appears in large print followed by the wish 'May the Lord in his mercy lengthen his days' (Fig. 7.2). As Elisheva Carlebach remarks, 'Hagiz made no secret of his pride in his relationship with Wolf.'[9] When *Mishnat ḥakhamim* was reprinted in 1864, an alert publisher removed the mention of Wolf, thus 'leaving the impression that Hagiz was praising some Jewish scholar!'.[10]

We find something similar with *Hatishbi* by R. Elijah Levita (1469–1549), first published in Isny in 1541. In the introduction, Levita speaks glowingly about his Christian printer (and scholar in his own right), Paul Fagius (1504–49), going so far as to say 'From Paul to Paul there has arisen none like Paul.' Levita also expresses the ecumenical hope that each will call 'to his God'. This type of language is not unexpected coming from Levita, who had close relationships with many Christian scholars, even living for ten years in

[5] Urbach, *Me'olamam shel ḥakhamim*, 561–77. For the earliest textual witness to support Urbach's conclusion, see Kellner, 'New and Unexpected Evidence' (Heb.).

[6] See Gopin, 'An Orthodox Embrace of Gentiles?', 176.

[7] See Spitzer, 'Was *Sefer maharil* Censored?' (Heb.), 84.

[8] p. 4*a*.

[9] Carlebach, *The Pursuit of Heresy*, 264.

[10] Ibid. 337 n. 25. See On the Main Line, 11 June 2009.

שאין בו מעשה[164], וכל שכן שהמודווג בעצמו עמהם בכלל הלאו, כשהוא מיחדה לו לאשה[165] ואין הלאו אלא כשבא עליה דרך חתנות ואישות[166]. ולא יעשה אדם שושבין לגוי משום לא תתחתן בם, ליתן עליהם בלא תעשה[167], ואינו אלא אסמכתא בעלמא, שהאיסור של שושבינות הוא מגזרת חכמים והסמיכוהו על הכתוב[168].

הבא על הגויה בפרהסיא, בין דרך חתנות ובין דרך זנות, קנאים פוגעים בו וממיתים אותו[169]. בבת ישראל הנבעלת לגוי נחלקו ראשונים: יש סוברים שאין קנאים פוגעים בה, לפי שהולד כמותה והוא כשר[170], ויש סוברים שאף בה יש דין של קנאים פוגעים[171].

בביאת זנות — בי"ד של חשמונאים גזרו על הבא על הגויה דרך זנות, ועונשו בכרת מדברי קבלה[172].

גויה אינה בכלל הלאו שנאמר על קדשה*, שבפירוש נאמר: לא תהיה קדשה מבנות ישראל[173], ואל תתמה היאך תהיה הישראלית הקדשה ביאתה בזנות בלאו[174] והגויה מדברי סופרים, שאיסור העריות הוא בגזרת הכתוב ודבר שאין לו טעם בכל פרטיו[175].

כתבו ראשונים שישראל שבא על הגויה בין קטנה בת שלש שנים ויום אחד בין גדולה, בין פנויה בין אשת איש, ואפילו היה קטן בן תשע שנים ויום אחד, כיון שבא על הגויה בזדון, הרי זו נהרגת, מפני שבאה לישראל תקלה על ידה, כבהמה, ודבר זה מפורש בתורה, שנאמר: הן הנה היו לבני ישראל בדבר בלעם וגו'[176] וכל אשה יודעת איש למשכב זכר הרגו[177].

בין שמנה-עשר-דבר* שגזרו תלמידי שמאי והלל נמנית אף גזירה על בנותיהן[178], ונחלקו אמוראים אם פירושו שגזרו טומאת נדות על בנותיהן[179] או שגזרו על יחוד* עם הגויה[180]. הלכה שגזרו על היחוד[181].

ישראלית שנבעלה לגוי דרך זנות, יש סוברים שמן התורה ביאת היתר היא, ואינה אסורה אלא מדרבנן מגזירת בי"ד של שם[182], ולא שמענו שיהיה עונש כרת בה, כמו בישראל הבא על הגויה, שכן בנה של ישראלית ימשך אחריה ויהיה ישראל[183], ואין סברא לומר שיש בה איסור-עשה* משום הוציאוה ותשרף[184], האמור בגזרת בי"ד של שם[185]. ויש מן האחרונים שכתב להיפך, שהנבעלת לגוי יש בה איסור מן התורה, ישעל גוי שבא על הישראלית אמרה תורה כי יסיר את בנך מאחרי ה'[186].

גוי שבא על בת כהן פוסלה מן התרומה, וכן פוסל את הכהנת והלויה והישראלית בביאתו מן הכהונה, שנאמר: ובת כהן כי תהיה אלמנה וגרושה וזרע אין לה ושבה אל בית אביה וגו'[187], מי שיש לו אלמנות וגירושין בה, יצא גוי שאין לו בה אלמנות וגירושין[188], ואפילו לדעת הסוברים שבנה מן הגוי כשר[189].

יש מן הראשונים סובר שביאת גוי אין שמה ביאה, והיא כביאת בהמה, כיון שהתורה הפקירה זרעו, שנאמר: אשר בשר חמורים בשרם וזרמת סוסים זרמתם[190], ולכן אשת איש שזנתה ברצון עם הגוי אינה חייבת מיתה על ביאתו, וכן אין האשה מוזהרת ביהרג ואל יעבור בביאתו, וכן אין האשה נאסרת על הבועל הגוי לכשיתגייר כדרך שנאסרת על הבועל ישראל[191], ויש מוסיפים שאף לבעלה

אהע"ז שם; רמ"א בשו"ע שם בשם יש חולקים. 164 ע"ע לאו שאין בו מעשה. 165 החינוך מצוה תכז. 166 ע"ז שם; רמב"ם שם; חינוך שם. וע"ע שבע אומות מחלוקת בז' אומות, אבל בשאר אומות בגיותם לר' שמעון מפורש בגמ' שם דרך חתנות. 167 ירושלמי ע"ז פ"א ה"ט. 168 מרה"פ שם. 169 רמב"ם איסו"ב שם ה"ד, ע"פ משנה סנהדרין פא ב. וע"ע בועל ארמית: בפרהסיא, על פרטי הדינים. 170 רמב"ן במלחמות סנהדרין פ"ח; תשו' ב"י אהע"ז דיני גיטין סי' י, והביאו כברכ"י אהע"ז סי' ד סי"ד; שו"ת חת"ם אהע"ז ח"ב סי' פב. 171 הגהות מרדכי יבמות פ"ד סי' קח בשם ר' אברהם הגדול מרגנשבורג, והביאו בשו"ת תרומת הדשן סי' ריט ורכג ובמהרי"ק שורש קעה. ועי' חזון איש אהע"ז סי' נט אות י. 172 ע"ע בועל ארמית, ושם אם גזרו על עצם האיסור או שגזרו על חיוב מלקות, ועי"ש פרטי הדברים. 173 דברים כג יח. 174 ע"ע קדש; קדשה. 175 מ"מ אישות פ"א ה"ד, ועי"ש בשם ר' משה הכהן שלא כ"כ והוא חלק עליו, וע"ע הנ"ל. 176 במדבר לא טו. 177 שם יז. רמב"ם איסו"ב פי"ב ה"י, ועי"ש במ"מ שלא מצא לו מקור ומהפסוק אין ראיה כי שם אפילו לא נבעלו רק ראויות לביאה נהרגו. 178 שבת יז ב. 179 עי' לחלן: בטומאה וטהרה. 180 ע"ז לו ב. 181 רמב"ם איסו"ב פכ"ב ה"ג; טוש"ע אהע"ז כב ב. וע"ע יחוד. 182 תוס' יבמות טז ב ד"ה קסבר ומה א ד"ה יצאו, ע"פ ע"ז לו ב; חי' הר"ן סנהדרין עד ב. ועי' תוס' רי"ד ע"ז שם שבי"ד של שם נקרא דאורייתא. 183 חי' הר"ן שם. 184 בראשית לח כד. 185 תוס' קדושין עה ב ד"ה ור' ישמעאל. 186 אבני מלואים סי' טו ס"ק א, ועי"ש שיישב בזה קו' התוס' על הסובר עכו"ם הבא על בת ישראל הולד ממזר, וצ"ב שהרי אין האיסור בשאר אומות אלא דרך חיתון. 187 ויקרא כב יג. 188 יבמות מה א ורש"י וש"נ; רמב"ם איסורי ביאה פי"ח ה"ב; טוש"ע אהע"ז סי' ד סי"ט וסי' ו ס"ח. 189 תוס' יבמות שם ד"ה יצאו. וע"ע אכילת תרומה: איסורה לחללה, שיש למרים מפסוק אחר, וע"ע זונה וע' חללה. 190 יחזקאל כג כ. עי' יבמות צח א. 191 ע"ע אשת איש: איסורה לבעלה. ר"ת בתוס' כתובות ג ב ד"ה ולידרוש ושמ"ק שם ובתוס' סנהדרין עד ב ד"ה והא. ועי' תוס' שנץ סוטה כו ב בשם ר"ת לאיסור. (a)

Figure 7.1 *Entsiklopedyah talmudit*, iii, col. 297: (*a*) original text (1953), with the passage from Maimonides; (*b*) 'corrected' text without the passage from a later edition

שאין בו מעשה[164], וכל שכן שהמזדווג בעצמו עמהם בכלל הלאו, כשהוא מיחדה לו לאשה[165] ואין הלאו אלא כשבא עליה דרך חתנות ואישות[166]. ולא יעשה אדם שושבין לגוי משום לא תתחתן בם, ליתן עליהם בלא תעשה[167], ואינו אלא אסמכתא בעלמא, שהאיסור של שושבינות הוא מגזרת חכמים והסמיכוהו על הכתוב[168].

הבא על הגויה בפרהסיא, בין דרך חתנות ובין דרך זנות, קנאים פונעים בו וממיתים אותו[169]. בבת ישראל הנבעלת לגוי נחלקו ראשונים: יש סוברים שאין קנאים פונעים בה, לפי שהולד כמותה והוא בשר[170], ויש סוברים שאף בה יש דין של קנאים פונעים[171].

בביאת זנות — בי"ד של חשמונאים גזרו על הבא על הגויה דרך זנות, ועונשו בכרת מדברי קבלה[172].

אף על פי שכל הבועל אשה לשם זנות בלא קדושין לוקה מן התורה, לפי שבעל קדשה[173], אין הדברים אמורים אלא בבת ישראל, אבל נויה אינה בכלל הלאו שנאמר על קדשה, שבפירוש נאמר לא תהיה קדשה מבנות ישראל[174], ולא אסרה תורה אלא דרך חתנות, אבל הבא על הגויה דרך זנות, איסורו מדברי סופרים, גזרה שמא יבוא להתחתן[175]. ואל תתמה האיך תהיה הישראלית הקדשה ביאתה בזנות בלאו, והנויה מדברי סופרים, שאיסור העריות הוא בגזרת הכתוב ודבר שאין לו טעם בכל פרטיו[176]. ויש מהראשונים סוברים שעיקר האיסור הוא מן התורה, אלא שבית דין של חשמונאים גזרו שיתחייב מלקות[177].

אהע"ז שם; רמ"א בשו"ע שם בשם יש חולקים. 164 ע"ע לאו שאין בו מעשה. 165 החינוך מצוה תכז. 166 ע"ז שם; רמב"ם שם; חינוך שם. וע"ע שבע אומות מחלוקת בז' אומות, אבל בשאר אומות בגיותם לר' שמעון מפורש בגמ' שם דרך חתנות. 167 ירושלמי ע"ז פ"א ה"ט. 168 מרה"פ שם. 169 רמב"ם איסו"ב שם ה"ד, ע"פ משנה סנהדרין פא ב. וע"ע בועל ארמית: לפרהסיא, על פרטי הדינים. 170 רמב"ן במלחמות סנהדרין פ"ח; תשו' ב"י אהע"ז דיני גיטין סי' י, והביאו בברכ"י אהע"ז סי' ד סי"ד; שו"ת חת"ם אהע"ז ח"ב סי' פב. 171 הגהות מרדכי יבמות פ"ד סי' קח בשם ר' אברהם הגדול מרגנשבורג, והביאו בשו"ת תרומת הדשן סי' ריט ורכג ובמהרי"ק שורש קעה. ועי' חזון איש אהע"ז סי' נט אות י. 172 ע"ע בועל ארמית, ושם אם גזרו על עצם האיסור או שגזרו על חיוב מלקות, ועי' שם פרטי הדברים. 173 עי' רמב"ם אישות פ"א ה"ד, וע"ע קדש: קדשה, ושם אם במיוחדת לכך או אף שאינה מיוחדת. 174 דברים כג יח. 175 רמב"ם איסורי ביאה פי"ב ה"ב; טור סי' טז. 176 מ"מ אישות שם. 177 חידושי הר"ן סנהדרין

בין שמנה־עשר־דבר* שגזרו תלמידי שמאי והלל נמנית אף גזירה על בנותיהן[178], ונחלקו אמוראים אם פירושו שגזרו טומאת נדות על בנותיהן[179] או שגזרו על יחוד* עם הגויה[180]. הלכה שגזרו על היחוד[181].

ישראלית שנבעלה לגוי דרך זנות, יש סוברים שמן התורה ביאת היתר היא, ואינה אסורה אלא מדרבנן מגזירת בי"ד של שם[182], ולא שמענו שיהיה עונש כרת בה, כמו בישראל הבא על הגויה, שכן בנה של ישראלית ימשך אחריה ויהיה ישראל[183], ואין סברא לומר שיש בה איסור־עשה* משום הוציאוה ותשרף[184], האמור בגזרת בי"ד של שם[185]. ויש מן האחרונים שכתב להיפך, שהנבעלת לגוי יש בה איסור מן התורה, שעל גוי שבא על הישראלית אמרה תורה כי יסיר את בנך מאחרי[186].

גוי שבא על בת כהן פוסלה מן התרומה, וכן פוסל את הכהנת והלויה והישראלית בביאתו מן הכהונה, שנאמר: ובת כהן כי תהיה אלמנה וגרושה וזרע אין לה ושבה אל בית אביה וגו'[187], מי שיש לו אלמנות וגירושין בה, יצא גוי שאין לו בה אלמנות וגירושין[188], ואפילו לדעת הסוברים שבנה מן הגוי כשר[189].

יש מן הראשונים סובר שביאת גוי אין שמה ביאה, והיא כביאת בהמה, כיון שהתורה הפקירה זרעו, שנאמר: אשר בשר חמורים בשרם וזרמת סוסים זרמתם[190], ולכן אשת איש שזנתה ברצון עם הגוי אינה חייבת מיתה על ביאתו, וכן אין האשה מוזהרת ביהרג ואל יעבור בביאתו, וכן אין האשה נאסרת על הבועל הגוי לכשיתגייר כדרך שנאסרת על הבועל ישראל[191], ויש מוסיפים שאף לבעלה

פב א, ועי' אבני מלואים סי' טז ס"ק ד. וע"ע בועל ארמית ושם ציון 2. 178 שבת יז ב. 179 עי' להלן: בטומאה וטהרה. 180 ע"ז לו ב. 181 רמב"ם איסו"ב פכ"ב ה"ג; טוש"ע אהע"ז כב ב. וע"ע יחוד. 182 תוס' יבמות טז ב ד"ה קסבר ומה א ד"ה יצאו, ע"פ ע"ז לו ב; חי' הר"ן סנהדרין עד ב. ועי' תוס' רי"ד ע"ז שם שבי"ד של שם נקרא דאורייתא. 183 חי' הר"ן שם. 184 בראשית לח כד. 185 תוס' קדושין עה ב ד"ה ור' ישמעאל. 186 אבני מלואים סי' טז ס"ק א, ועי"ש שיישב בזה קו' התוס' על הסובר עכו"ם הבא על בת ישראל הולד ממזר, וצ"ב שהרי אין האיסור בשאר אומות אלא דרך חיתון. 187 ויקרא כב יג. 188 יבמות מה א ורש"י וש"נ; רמב"ם איסורי ביאה פי"ח ה"ב; טוש"ע אהע"ז סי' ד סי"ט וסי' ו ס"ח. 189 תוס' יבמות שם ד"ה יצאו. וע"ע אכילת תרומה: איסורה לחללה, שיש למדים מפסוק אחר, וע"ע זונה וע' חללה. 190 יחזקאל כג כ. עי' יבמות צח א. 191 ע"ע אשת איש: איסורה לבעלה. ר"ת בתוס' כתובות ג ב ד"ה ולידרוש ושמ"ק שם ובתוס' סנהדרין עד ב ד"ה והא. ועי' תוס' שנץ סוטה כו ב בשם ר"ת לאיסור.

(b)

הקדמת המחבר ד

מיעקב אבינו · ולכן ראוי לשלב שם הוי״ה ואד״נות כזה **יאהדונהי** כי היא עיקר הכוונה הנזכרת בכל פעם שאדם מזכיר השם ברוך הוא · ולפיכך בספרים הנדפסים במקו׳ הי״ת מרשימים שתי יוד״ין רמז ליו״ד ראשונה משם הוי״ה ב״ה ויו״ד אחרונה משם אד״נות · והיא אחת מהכוונות דיש בפסוק פא״י · א״ת ידיך אלא יודיך ע״פ השילוב הנזכר · דוק ודעהו · ובאותו זמן שאל שאלני האיש מה רמז יש במכתבים הקדמונים · שנהגו לכתוב שלש יודי״ן · ונדלתי להעלות בכתב קצת ממה שנרמז בהם :

והנה במסיבות העתי׳ נהיה כי באתי אל בית האדון המלומד הגדול המופלא ומופלג בדרישת שלימות החכמות ואדקת חשקו באסיפת כל ספרי החכמה והמדע · וכבר יצא מוניטון שלו בעולם בספרים שהדפיס כעין ספר יוחסין · ה״ה הדרשן המפורסם בעיר הגדולה ומהוללה המבורג יע״א נקרא בשמו הטיב הפרופעסיר דאקטור **יוחנן קרישטוף וואלף** האל ברחמיו יאריך ימיו בטוב ובנעימות כאות נפשו · ובטובו וחסדו · העלה אותי אל עלייתו · מקום המעולה ומקודש בכמה אלפי אלפים ספרים מכל אומה ולשון · לא די מספרים שכבר יצאו לאור הדפוס · רק שכל ספרי בני עמינו הקדמונים שהן בכתיבת יד · משתדל בעבודם · ומוציא עליהם הון רב כדי להיותם בבית גנזיו כאודם פטדה וברקת · בזהב אופיר משוקעת · כי אצלו יקר מחכמה ומכבוד · כל כלי יקר שפתי דעת · מהחכמים הראשונים · היפים מגד עצמם · מבלי תמרוק ומרקחת · ומכלל ספריו ראיתי מקרא גדולה כתובה ע״ג קלף דחזותא מוכיח שהוא כתב ישן נושן יותר מאלף שנה · וסדר כתיבתה היא אחד מקרא ואחד תרגום בזה אחר זה · ובמקום שם הוי״ה ב״ה כתוב שלש יוד״ין ❜ ובמקרא אחרת כיוצא בה אשר יש אתו · כתוב שלש יוד״ין · שתים למטה · ואחת למעלה · כעין זה ❜❜ · ותמהתי על שמראה · וגם הגדיל התימא האדון החכם · למה היו רומזים שלשת היוד״ין · ואני זכרתי את אשר נדלתי להמשכיל המנוח הנז״ל · והשבתי לשואלי דבר מתאיין של דברים כפי מה שמקובל אצל זקני ישראל הקדמונים · דהיו כותבים באופן זה לשם הי״ת · כדי לנהוג בו קדושה יתירה באותיותיו · כי חיות הנה · ויש בהן קדושה מעולה · ולפיכך היו כותבין ג׳ יוד״ין שעולין למ״ד · שכן שם הוי״ה ב״ה עם ארבע אותיותיו עולה שלשים · ומאחר דמאתו י״ת בא כל שפע לעליונים ולתחתונים · ובפרט לזרע יעקב ישראל ישורון לפיכך נכתב בשלש יוד״ין · דישכן בג׳ שמות מפסוק היחוד · ה׳ · אלהינו · ה׳ · והן רמז לשלש יוד״ין דברכת כהנים דאינון סגולתא · יו״ד יברכך · יו״ד יאר · יו״ד ישא · והן כנגד השלש יוד״ן דיש בשם הוי״ה ב״ה כשנכתב באופן זה יו״ד ה״י וא״ו ה״י · והוא הנקרא שם ס״ג דהג׳ יוד״ן שבו · מעידין על עלת כל העלות · דאתמר עליה (בישעיה מ״ד) אני ראשון ואני אחרון · ומבלעדי אין אלהים · דאיהו ראשון ואחרון · ומבלעדיו אין אלהים · והכי איתא בזוהר בראשי׳ דכ״ב שורה ד׳ז״ל ועוד תלת זמנין אתמ׳ בהאי קרא אני אני דאית בהון א · א · א · י · י · י דאתרמיז ביו״ד · ה״א · וא״ו · ה״י · יו״ר · ה״א · ו י ו · ה״א · ואית בהון תלת ווי״ן ו׳ו׳ו׳ דאחיה · ואני · ואין · דאתרמיזו באלין במהן וכו׳ עי״ש עד והאי רזא לא אתמסר לכל חכימיא ונביאה וכו׳ · והן כמה הג׳ יוד״ין דאיתנהו בקרא דקרי ולא כתיב · ה׳ מלך · ה׳ מלך · ה׳ ימלוך · לדעת כי הוא היה הווה ויהיה ומלכותו בכל משלה · ובאשר מה שכתבתי לעיל הוא אחד מהרמזים שרומזי׳ על התקשרות הי״ת ותורתו · עם ישראל לאן מרעיתו · כי אותנו לקח להיות לו לעם נחלה · ומה נחלה אין לה הפסק · כך לעם נחלה כל״ם · ישמע חכם ויוסיף לקח · דאם תחקור תמצא דאחד מע״ב שמות הוא שלש יוד״ין · והוא הכ״ב · במספר הע״ב :

ועוד

Figure 7.2 R. Moses Hagiz, *Mishnat ḥakhamim* (Wandsbeck, 1733), showing his reference to the Christian Hebraist Johann Christoph Wolf

the home of Cardinal Egidio da Viterbo (1469–1532). Levita also publicly defended his teaching of Torah to non-Jews.[11] In a later edition of *Hatishbi*, produced by a publisher uncomfortable with such relationships between Jews and non-Jews, the passage dealing with Fagius was omitted.[12]

As mentioned, the more normal form of censorship when it comes to non-Jews is the removal of things that could create problems in Jewish–gentile relations. We see this also when dealing with translations. It is certainly true that every translation incorporates interpretation, but there are cases where it is obvious to every reader that the translator has moved beyond his assigned role and has actually entered the text by significantly altering the original version. Often this is done for apologetic purposes and is of a piece with the examples of censorship on which this book focuses, in that the translator does not want the readers to know what appears in the original. Unlike other examples of censorship, when it comes to alterations in translation there is an inner crowd and the outsiders. Those who can read the original are allowed full entry to the author's intention. Those who do not know Hebrew, who have not earned their admission, as it were, are regarded by the translator as not worthy of receiving all that the author had to say.

Many of the alterations in translations concern the portrayal of non-Jews. Yet we should not exaggerate in this area. For example, Ran HaCohen goes too far when he refers to Martin Buber (1878–1965), in his *Hasidic Tales*, as engaging in 'a drastic adaptation of the text . . . to "politically correct" conventions'.[13] What Buber did was translate the Hebrew/Yiddish *arel* (literally 'uncircumcised') into German as 'peasant'. For HaCohen, the use of *arel* in the original 'represents the non-Jew by reference to his body—to his genitals—[and] stresses instead his (spiritual) impurity, not to say filth'.

While HaCohen claims that the term 'peasant' 'could be non-Jewish but didn't have to [be]', and that this is an example of Buber's blurring of ethnic and religious identity, it is obvious that when one of Buber's hasidic tales speaks of a 'peasant' without any further identification, that a non-Jew is meant. The 'peasant' is the classic example of a simple non-Jew, and it is nit-picking to suggest that in a work of the type Buber was publishing that the text has suffered any distortion by having 'peasant' instead of 'uncircumcised'. Even in an academic translation it is acceptable to render *arel* as 'a gentile', as that, and nothing more, is its typical meaning in Hebrew and Yiddish, and

11 See Aranoff, 'Elijah Levita', 21.

12 Maramarossziget (1910?); this was later reprinted with additional notes in Benei Berak, 1976. These editions also omit Levita's mention of 'the Cardinal' (Egidio da Viterbo) s.v. *metatron*, yet they do not omit him s.v. *notarikon*.

13 HaCohen, 'The Hay Wagon Moves to the West', 7. All quotations are from this page.

31 BOOK OF ESTHER

9 THE JEWS DEFEND THEMSELVES

Now in the twelfth month, which is the month Adar, on the thirteenth day of the same, when the king's commandment and his decree drew near to be put in execution, in the day that the enemies of the Jews hoped to have rule over them, the Jews gathered themselves together in their cities throughout all the provinces of the king Ahasuerus, to lay hand on such as sought their hurt; and no man could withstand them; for the fear of them was fallen upon all the peoples.

And all the princes of the provinces, and the satraps, and the governors, and they that did the king's business, helped the Jews; because the fear of Mordecai was fallen upon them. For Mordecai was great in the king's house, and his fame went forth throughout all the provinces; for the man Mordecai waxed greater and greater.

Mordecai
From a drawing by E. M. Lilien

מגלת אסתר ט 30

ט

ט

א ובשנים עשר חדש הוא־חדש אדר בשלושה עשר יום
בו אשר הגיע דבר־המלך ודתו להעשות ביום אשר
שברו איבי היהודים לשלוט בהם ונהפוך הוא אשר
2 ישלטו היהודים המה בשנאיהם: נקהלו היהודים
בעריהם בכל־מדינות המלך אחשורוש לשלח יד
במבקשי רעתם ואיש לא־עמד בפניהם כי־נפל פחדם
3 על־כל־העמים: וכל־שרי המדינות והאחשדרפנים
והפחות ועשי המלאכה אשר למלך מנשאים את־
4 היהודים כי־נפל פחד־מרדכי עליהם: כי־גדול מרדכי
בבית המלך ושמעו הולך בכל־המדינות כי־האיש
5 מרדכי הולך וגדול: ויכו היהודים בכל־איביהם מכת־
6 חרב והרג ואבדן ויעשו בשנאיהם כרצונם: ובשושן
הבירה הרגו היהודים ואבד חמש מאות איש:

7
פרשנדתא ואת
דלפון ואת
8 אספתא: ואת
פורתא ואת
אדליא ואת
9 ארידתא: ואת
פרמשתא ואת
אריסי ואת
ארידי ואת
י ויזתא: עשרת
בני המן בן־המדתא צרר היהודים הרגו ובבזה לא
שלחו

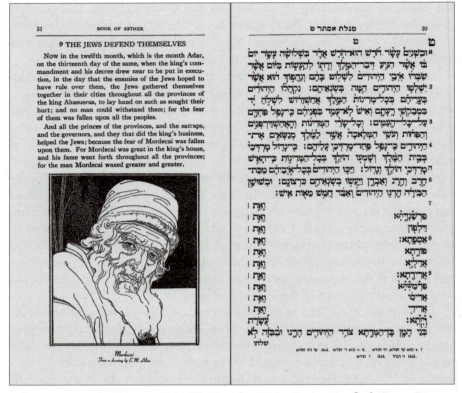

Figure 7.3 Morris Silverman (ed.), *The Complete Purim Service* (Hartford, Conn.: Prayer Book Press, 1947), showing the partial translation of Esther 9

even a circumcised non-Jew is referred to this way. (I would, however, recommend an explanatory footnote the first time the term appears.)

In the following example, from an American Purim Megillah,[14] the censorship in translation is not motivated by concern about how non-Jews will react, but is an early example of political correctness before the term even existed. The year of publication was 1947, right after the Holocaust. The problem was chapter 9 of the book of Esther, which describes the killing of Haman's sons and thousands of other Persian enemies. These mass killings might have suggested some similarities to what had just occurred with the Jews of Europe. Since the book of Esther is read in synagogue, the Hebrew could not be removed, but the English omits material that might trouble the Jewish conscience (Fig. 7.3).[15]

14 Silverman (ed.), *Complete Purim Service.*

15 I thank Sheldon Bootin for bringing this to my attention. (There are a few other missing

Haskalah

Texts regarding the Haskalah and hasidism, two of the major Jewish developments in modern times, were understandably also subject to censorship. Let us begin with Moses Mendelssohn, the man who is often regarded as the founder of the Haskalah. R. Moses Sofer famously referred to Mendelssohn by the abbreviation רמ"ד, which stands for Rabbi Moses Dessau (Dessau being Mendelssohn's birthplace). This appears in his ethical will, in which he tells his children not to use Mendelssohn's writings.[16] He also referred in this way to Mendelssohn in a letter,[17] and in another letter twice refers to him as החכם רמ"ד, 'the wise man Rabbi Moses Dessau'.[18] In other words, despite his negative feelings about Mendelssohn, he was still willing to grant him titles of respect.[19]

Sofer's negative view of Mendelssohn is hardly a secret, yet it is also well known that a number of Sofer's students, in particular R. Moses Schick, did not follow their teacher in his condemnation of Mendelssohn.[20] For those who saw Mendelssohn as the embodiment of evil, the title 'rabbi' which Sofer assigned to him was difficult to stomach. R. Akiva Joseph Schlesinger (1837–1922) even wrote—and it is difficult to imagine that he intended this seriously—that the *resh* stood for *rasha* (evil one)![21]

In a pattern that is all too familiar, some member of the family—as only he would have had access to the actual manuscript of Sofer's ethical will—altered the text so that the *resh* was lengthened into a *ḥet*. This *ḥet* stands for *ḥakham* ('wise man'), which has less significance than the Hatam Sofer calling Mendelssohn 'rabbi'. As Professor Michael Silber has put it: 'It is clear

passages, but it is not clear why they were deleted.) In the preface we are told that this translation comes from the *Abridged Bible* published by the Jewish Publication Society (JPS). (It was actually published by the United States government, using the JPS translation, under the title *Readings from the Holy Scriptures*.) In this abridged Bible, however, the book of Esther appears in its entirety. For two earlier Jewish bowdlerized versions of the book of Esther, see E. S. Horowitz, *Reckless Rites*, 24, 43–4, and also 106, 133.

16 A. J. Schlesinger, *Tsava'at mosheh*, 2*a*.

17 M. Sofer, *She'elot uteshuvot ḥatam sofer haḥadashot*, no. 6.

18 M. Sofer, *She'elot uteshuvot ḥatam sofer*, vol. ii, 'Yoreh de'ah', no. 338.

19 A colleague suggested that the ר in רמ"ד does not stand for 'rabbi' but '*reb*'. I find this most unlikely, but even if this were so, the title *reb* also implies some measure of respect.

20 See Hildesheimer's comprehensive article, 'Attitude of the Hatam Sofer'. R. Mordechai Benet was Sofer's senior and greatly respected by him. In an 1832 biography, Benet's son reported that his father 'knew the books of R. Moses Dessau very well', but this line was omitted when the biography was reprinted in 1929. See M. Miller, *Rabbis and Revolution*, 370 n. 89.

21 A. J. Schlesinger, *Tsava'at mosheh*, 10*b*. In the first edition of this work, as well as in other works, Schlesinger showed that he was aware that the *resh* stood for 'rabbi'. See Hildesheimer, 'Attitude of the Hatam Sofer', 155 n. 50.

that a clumsy line was drawn down a *resh* of RMD to make it look like a *ḥet*. The Hatam Sofer's *ḥets* are in the shape of a tent, this one is rounded off.'[22] The truth of Silber's observation can be seen by examining the autograph manuscript (Fig. 7.4).[23]

Naphtali Herz (Hartwig) Wessely (1725–1805) is another early *maskil* concerning whom there has been great dispute in the Orthodox world. R. Ezekiel Landau (1713–93) is famous for condemning him and his writings,[24] though a number of equally well-respected sages quoted Wessely approvingly. Many of these citations are referred to in the introductions to two recently published volumes of Wessely, one of which was actually banned.[25]

With this difference of opinion regarding Wessely, it should not be surprising that when the writings of the great *musar* personality, R. Simhah Zissel Ziv of Kelm (1824–98), were published,[26] references to Wessely were deleted.[27] Similarly, the first edition of *Ahavat david* by R. Eleazar Fleckeles (1754–1826) contains a letter from Wessely, which has disappeared from the photo reprint of this volume recently published in Brooklyn.[28] It could be that the simple mention of Wessely was enough to bring about this particular censorship. However, it is also possible that something else was problematic. In this letter, Wessely cites R. Jonathan Eybeschuetz as stating that if people do not want to believe in kabbalah this is not objectionable, since it is not part of the foundations of Jewish faith.[29]

Solomon Dubno (1738–1813) was one of Mendelssohn's collaborators

[22] Private communication. See also Hildesheimer, 'Attitude of the Hatam Sofer', 154 n. 45.

[23] The image comes from Strasser and Perl (eds.), *Mosheh alah lamarom*, 62. For further evidence that the proper reading is *resh*, see Hildesheimer, 'Attitude of the Hatam Sofer', 143 ff. See also On the Main Line, 30 Mar. 2011, for a German version of the ethical will that was published a month after Sofer's death: it reads 'R. Mose aus Dessau'. Some also mistakenly claimed that the proper reading was ובספרי חמד, meaning that Sofer was telling his children not to read romantic novels. See Hildesheimer, ibid. 146 ff. See also I. H. Weiss, *Zikhronotai*, 58 n. 27. Yet substituting the word חמד for רמ"ד destroys the rhyming sequence of the passage, since רמ"ד should be pronounced Ramad (like other acronyms such as Rambam, Tanakh, etc.): ובספרי רמ"ד, אל תשלחו יד, עולמי עד, אז רגלך לא ימעד. I thank R. Moshe Maimon for this point. See also Schischa, 'Bibliographical Notes' (Heb.), 78, and R. Joseph Naphtali Stern's letter in *Yeshurun*, 29 (2013), 758–9.

[24] See Flatto, *Kabbalistic Culture*, 7 ff.

[25] Wessely, *Sefer hamidot*, id., *Yein levanon*. For the ban on *Sefer hamidot* see Dei'ah veDibur, 4 Sept. 2002, 'Book Written by Haskalah Figure and Disguised as Mussar Distributed Among Chareidim', <http://www.chareidi.org/archives5763/rosh_yk/index.htm>.

[26] Simhah Zissel Ziv of Kelm, *Ḥokhmah umusar*.

[27] See the introduction to Wessely, *Yein halevanon*, 28 (citing R. David Tsevi Hillman, who has seen the manuscript essays).

[28] A friend who spoke to the publisher of the new photo reprint informed me that the publisher claimed that he was not responsible for the censorship, as in the copy of the book he used the 'problematic' pages had already been removed.

[29] For the two censored pages, see On the Main Line, 24 Feb. 2010.

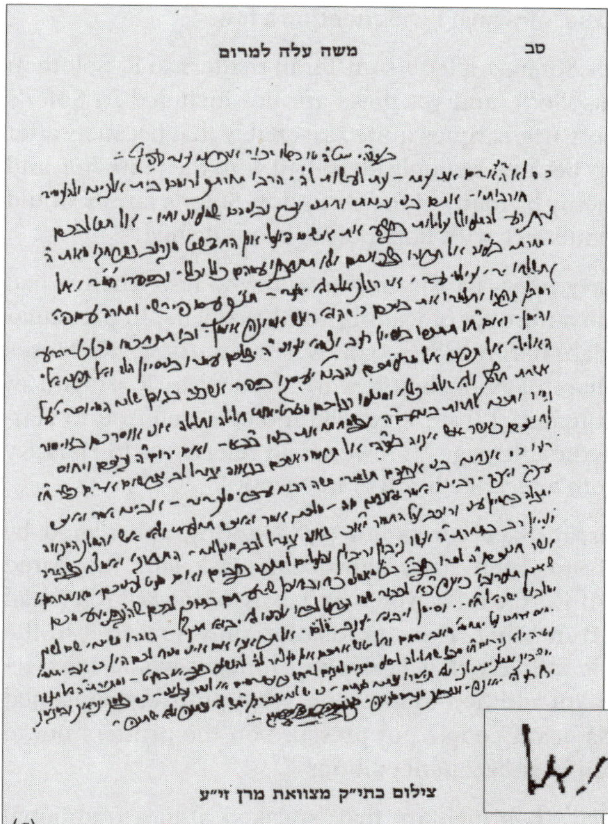

(*a*)

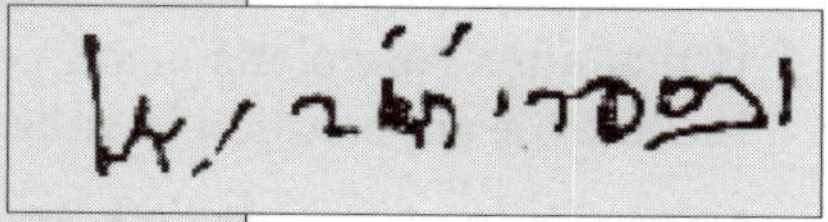

(*b*)

Figure 7.4 (*a*) Autograph manuscript of R. Moses Sofer's ethical will; (*b*) R. Moses Sofer's reference to 'Rabbi Moses Dessau' (Mendelssohn) enlarged with the *resh* having been turned into a *ḥet*

on his Torah translation and commentary, being responsible for most of the commentary on Genesis and part of Exodus. Dubno later broke with Mendelssohn and returned to eastern Europe, where he made plans to publish a commentary on the entire Torah. Among the approbations he received was one from R. Hayim of Volozhin. In 1991 Dov Eliach published a biography on R. Hayim, with a chapter that purports to list all of R. Hayim's approbations.[30] After all we have seen so far, it should come as no shock that one *haskamah* is missing (the one given to Dubno). Yehoshua Mondshine sees this act of censorship as a perfect illustration of a generation that judges its judges.[31] In other words, instead of following the lead of its sages, the current generation attempts to foist its own ideas upon them.[32]

30 Eliach, *Avi hayeshivot*, 627–39.

31 Cf. BT *BB* 15*b*.

32 Y. Mondshine, '"Silent Approbations"' (Heb.), 154. Regarding the Eliach censorship, see also Assaf, *Caught in the Thicket* (Heb.), 43 ff.; and see above, pp. 51–2.

Similar examples abound, of which I will mention a few.

1. We know that R. Moses Sofer sent letters on Torah matters to R. Solomon Judah Rapoport (1790–1867), and yet these are not included in Sofer's responsa. Shmuel Weingarten argues quite reasonably that because, after Sofer's death, Rapoport became strongly identified with the *maskilim*, and was thus seen as an enemy by many of the Orthodox, Sofer's family would not permit his correspondence with Rapoport to be published.[33]

2. Abraham Elijah Harkavy (1835–1919) was a *maskil* who nevertheless had close relationships with a number of leading Torah scholars, in particular R. Naphtali Tsevi Judah Berlin (1816–93). When, in 1909, R. Moses Samuel Shmukler (Shapiro) published a work devoted to R. Hayim of Volozhin, he included material from Harkavy, and even referred to Harkavy's contribution on the title page.[34] However, all references to Harkavy have been removed from a recent edition of this work.[35]

3. *Te'udah beyisra'el* by Isaac Baer Levinsohn (1788–1860), considered by many to be the 'manifesto of the eastern European Haskalah',[36] appeared with the approbation of R. Abele Poswoler (1764–1836), *av beit din* (head of the rabbinical court) in Vilna. This approbation only appeared in the first edition. Since it is unlikely that Levinsohn himself would have removed such an important addition to his book, what probably happened is that after Poswoler's death people put pressure on the printers not to include the approbation in subsequent editions.[37]

4. An example of a *maskil*'s commentary that 'sneaked' into a traditional work, and has only recently been taken out, is the anonymous commentary on *Shulḥan arukh*, 'Yoreh de'ah', known as *Miluim*. This commentary was first published in the nineteenth-century Vilna Romm edition of the *Shulḥan arukh*, and on the page identifying the commentaries it states that the author of this work wishes to remain anonymous. Today, virtually no one knows who the author was, although when the commentary first appeared we are told that the rabbis were very upset.[38] That is because its author was Mordechai Plungian (1814–83),[39] a *maskil* who worked for the

[33] Weingarten, 'Responsa That Were Concealed' (Heb.), 94–5. For the removal of Chajes' name from Sofer's published responsa, presumably on account of his Haskalah sympathies, see below, Ch. 8, n. 10.

[34] Shmukler (Shapiro), *Life of R. Hayim of Volozhin* (Heb.).

[35] See Dan Rabinowitz's Seforim Blog post, 20 Nov. 2006.

[36] Levisohn, 'Early Vilna *Haskalah*', 52.

[37] See ibid. 52 n. 37.

[38] See I. A. Z. Margulies, *Amudei arazim*, 43*a*.

[39] See Maimon, *Midei ḥodesh beḥodsho*, v. 132; A. D. Levin, *Otsar igerot kodesh*, no. 66 (who refers to Plungian by the derogatory terms *menuval* and *min gamur*).

publisher.[40] R. Jacob Israel Kanievsky was one of the few in recent times who did know about Plungian's authorship,[41] and I think that it is due to his strong opposition to its inclusion in any new editions that the *Miluim* has been removed in the newly typeset editions of the *Shulḥan arukh*. In some of the previous photo-offset editions this commentary was whited out.

5. The first edition of *Sedei ḥemed* by R. Hayim Hezekiah Medini (1833–1904) had references to articles that appeared in the 'enlightened' newspapers *Hamelits* and *Hatsevi*. These were taken out in the edition that appeared after the author's death.[42]

6. I cite this next example because the explanation that was later altered sounds as though it could have been offered by a *maskil*. Yet it was actually stated by R. Moses Sofer, as we are told by none other than his grandson, R. Solomon Sofer. In answer to the question of why there is no mention of the Hanukah miracle in the Mishnah, the Hatam Sofer said that it was because R. Judah the Prince, the editor of the Mishnah, was from the Davidic line and was upset with the Hasmoneans for improperly seizing the monarchy.

   This explanation appeared in the first edition of R. Solomon Sofer's *Ḥut hameshulash*.[43] However, when Sofer later issued a second edition of this book,[44] he added something that did not appear in the original, and removed the maskilic flavour from the Hatam Sofer's explanation. According to the 'new' elucidation, R. Judah the Prince's omission of the Hanukah miracle was based on his *ruaḥ hakodesh* (divine inspiration), which was also how the Mishnah as a whole was composed.[45]

[40] Plungian was also responsible for a section of the abridged *Yefeh to'ar* commentary that was included in the Vilna Romm edition of the *Midrash rabah*. Regarding him, see Werses, 'Mordechai Plungian' (Heb.).

[41] See J. I. Kanievsky, *Karyana de'igarta*, vol. i, no. 253. He records the written testimony of his father-in-law, R. Shemariah Karelitz (the father of the Hazon Ish). See also Anon. (ed.), *Zekhor ledavid*, ii. 120.

[42] See Benayahu, 'R. Hayim Hezekiah Medini' (Heb.), 196 (brought to my attention by Chaim Landerer). Here are some more examples: R. Hanokh Zundel Luria's very respectful reference to Moses Mendelssohn was removed from the Pressburg, 1859 edition of Luria's *Kenaf renanim*; see Perl, *Pillar of Volozhin*, 84 n. 122. (See also ibid. 37, for an apparent censorship of Mendelssohn's name in a work by R. Naphtali Tsevi Judah Berlin.) In R. Jacob Tsevi Meklenburg's *Haketav vehakabalah*, published in his lifetime (Leipzig, 1839), there is a preface in which he praises Wessely and Samuel David Luzzatto. When the book was reprinted after his death, the preface was removed, possibly due to these references. See Posen, '"When Torah Scholars are Engaged in a Halakhic Dispute, Who Are You to Interfere?"' (Heb.), 60 n. 18.

[43] Paks, 1887, p. 31*a*.

[44] Munkács, 1894.

[45] See *Ḥut hameshulash*, 2nd edn., p. 36*a*; Avraham Kosman, 'Is There a Tractate "Hanukah"?'

7. In the 1989 reprint of volume 2 of R. Judah Leib Krinsky's *Meḥokekei yehudah*, originally published in 1928, numerous letters at the beginning of the book are omitted, including those from R. Judah Leib Fishman (Maimon; 1875–1962), Nahum Sokolow (1859–1936), Samuel Posnanski (1864–1921), Baer Ratner (1852–1917), and Abraham Elijah Harkavy. A few letters from traditional rabbis and scholars were also omitted, because they had the unfortunate fate of being printed on the same page as the objectionable letters. For this example, and many others, the copy of the book that has been included on the Otzar HaHochma website is the censored version. Since we are in a new technological age and Otzar HaHochma has become *the* library for many, one can only hope that in the future Otzar HaHochma will make the effort to ensure that the books it places online are uncensored. Fortunately, in this instance the copy on HebrewBooks.org has not been altered.[46]

8. While the instances just mentioned have to do with the Orthodox censoring references to *maskilim*, we also find the reverse. For example, the standard edition of R. Hayim Joseph David Azulai's *Shem hagedolim*[47] omits certain kabbalistic passages. This was done by the publisher, Isaac Ben Jacob, in order to make the book appear more 'enlightened'.[48]

Hasidism

With regard to censorship in the history of hasidism, abundant examples can be cited. I quoted Yehoshua Mondshine's comments in this regard in the introduction, and they bear repeating here:

(Heb.), 13; and Eliezer Brodt's Seforim Blog post, 25 Dec. 2011. One source Brodt neglects to mention is M. Adler, *A Hasmonean and His Sons* (Heb.), 111 ff.

[46] In an example where Otzar HaHochma itself was responsible for the censorship, Yosef Avivi's article, 'R. Hayim Vital's *Ets ḥayim*' (Heb.), was deleted from the version of *Tsefunot* that appears on Otzar HaHochma.

[47] Vilna, 1853.

[48] See Vaknin, 'Ben Ya'akov's Deletions' (Heb.); E. H. Koppel, 'Concerning Ben Ya'akov's Deletions' (Heb.); Anon., 'Maskilic Changes' (Heb.). In his talmudic commentary, first published in Prague in 1791, R. Ezekiel Landau spoke of the danger of freethinkers and self-styled kabbalists. See *Tsiyun lenefesh ḥayah* on BT *Ber.* 28*b*. This passage was omitted in the next (posthumous) edition (Żółkiew, 1824), and subsequent editions were based on the censored one. I cannot entirely explain this act of censorship, since if the problematic part of the passage was the criticism of self-styled kabbalists, why would the criticism of freethinkers be omitted too? For a similar censorship of one of Landau's sermons, see Kahana and Silber, 'Deists, Sabbatians, and Kabbalists' (Heb.). Regarding censorship of R. Moses Kunitz's 'enlightened' biography of R. Judah the Prince, see my Seforim Blog post, 14 Nov. 2011. For censorship of R. Naphtali Tsevi Judah Berlin's positive references to R. Yehiel Mikhel Pines, see E. Henkin, 'Ban' (Heb.), 20–1.

The phenomenon that hasidim omit things from the writings of their rabbis is not at all rare. They do not see in this any contradiction to the holiness of the words of the *rebbe*, as long as they are certain that their intentions and actions are proper and correspond to the true outlook of their *rebbe*, or when the omission is done out of a concern of damaging the rabbi's honour.[49]

Some of the censorship was due to a change in the outlook of non-hasidic Jews. While it was acceptable among this group to attack hasidism and its leaders in the first years of the new movement, once hasidism became mainstream and an integral part of traditional Judaism, such attacks made for uncomfortable reading and were prime targets for censorship. One example is R. Jacob Emden's attack on hasidism in the first edition of his *Derush tefilat yesharim*.[50] This was omitted in the Kraków, 1911 edition.[51] Halakhic criticism of hasidic leaders was also censored. For example, R. Naphtali Tsevi Judah Berlin expresses himself strongly in opposition to a viewpoint of R. Shneur Zalman of Lyady, stating flatly that it is not true and can be ignored, as his arguments were only intended to intimidate the scholarly reader (Fig. 7.5(*a*)).[52] Here is how the page looks in certain editions, where the offending comment has been removed, as well as the name of the responsum's recipient (Fig. 7.5(*b*)).

Yet even as hasidism became more mainstream, family members were sometimes still embarrassed by their relative's connection with the movement, and this also led to censorship. For example, R. Tsevi Hirsch Horowitz (d. 1817), who succeeded his father, R. Pinhas Horowitz (1730–1805), as rabbi of Frankfurt, was an opponent of hasidism. Multiple sources report that because of this he took out all references to hasidic leaders in his father's writings, in particular those citing R. Dov Baer of Mezeritch (*c.*1710–72), who had a significant influence on R. Pinhas.[53]

A famous example of hasidic censorship relates to a sermon of the Belzer Rebbe's brother, R. Mordechai Roke'ah (1902–50), delivered in January 1944 on the occasion of the emigration of the Rebbe, R. Aaron Roke'ah (1880–1957), and his family from Hungary. In the sermon, R. Mordechai reassured anyone who might be thinking that the Rebbe was leaving them because he was fearful for the future. According to R. Mordechai, this was not the case at

[49] Y. Mondshine, 'Authenticity of Hasidic Letters' (Heb.), 89. Mondshine's article was a response to Haran, 'Praises of the *Rebbe*' (Heb.). Haran responded to Mondshine; see his 'Atarah leyoshnah'. See also Karlinsky, *Alternative History* (Heb.).

[50] p. 23*b*.

[51] p. 25*b*. See Schacter, 'Rabbi Jacob Emden', 15.

[52] N. T. J. Berlin, *Meshiv davar*, ii, no. 61. This example is noted in Glick, *Kuntres*, iii, no. 4082. For another example of censorship in Berlin's *Meshiv davar*, see Eliezer Brodt's Seforim Blog post, 5 Mar. 2014.

[53] See Y. N. Heschel, 'On the Holy Work *Panim yafot*' (Heb.), 137–8.

Figure 7.5 R. Naphtali Tsevi Judah Berlin, *Meshiv davar*, vol. ii, no. 61: (*a*) original text (Warsaw, 1894), recording his opposition to R. Shneur Zalman of Lyady's opinion (*b*) censored text with the comment (and addressee) removed, from a recent reprint

שו"ת הלכות בכור סימן ס סא סב משיב דבר
סימן סא
סימן סב
רש"י גדר האמצעי שבאוזן דמשמעו דהסחוס הוא בולט בגובה.
ובאמת אינו כן. מש"ה הוסיף הט"ז אותו קושי הוא גדר בעומק
האוזן אבל החתך מוכרח להיות דוקא בשפת האוזן שהוא במקום
נראה. ולא למעלה דהוי מום שבסתר. וכבר הרגיש גם מעכ"ה
נ"י בזה. וכבר הודיעני רב אחד שנמלא נדפס באיזה ספר השגה
על הוראה זו של הגאון מלאדי ז"ל ושכחתי שם הספר.
ומה שדרש מעכ"ה נ"י ממני ע"ד חומרת האחרונים ז"ל לאסור
החלב מבהמה האוכלת חמץ בפסח. אם כך הוא בבילת
תרנגולת האוכלת חמץ. ומלבד שמע"כ נ"י חילק בטעם יפה. עוד
יש חילוק היותר פשוט. דחלב הוא או מדם שבהמה או ככל דבר
היוצא מן החי מגופו ובשרו כדאיתא בבכורות ד"ו. דמש"ה עלה
עס"ד לאסור חלב באכילה. משא"כ בילה היא פירשא בעלמא כמ"ש
התוס' חולין דס"ד בד"ה שאם ריקמה. דלולי דרשת חז"ל פי'
(ח"ב) ב

(*b*)

all, and he reported that the Rebbe foresaw that 'rest and tranquility will descend upon the inhabitants of this land [i.e. Hungary]'.[54] A few months after the publication in February 1944 of this sermon, which was one of the last Jewish works printed in Hungary, the deportations to Auschwitz began. Not surprisingly, when this sermon was reprinted in 1967 as part of a biography of the Belzer Rebbe,[55] the section showing how hopeful the Rebbe was for the future of Hungarian Jewry was deleted. As Esther Farbstein comments, 'It was difficult for the authors of the biography to admit that the Rebbe erred in his assessment of the situation.'[56]

Sometimes descriptions of hasidic life, especially its unconventional or even antinomian aspects, were thought not fitting to be reprinted.[57] This explains why Ahron Marcus's German work on hasidism was not completely translated into Hebrew,[58] why a reprint of a book on the Chernobyl dynasty deleted six chapters on the Maiden of Ludmir, the only female hasidic *rebbe*,[59] and why posthumous editions of R. Yekutiel Aryeh Kamelhar's work on hasidism, *Dor de'ah*, removed a section dealing with the antinomian views of R. Simhah Bunim of Przysucha (1765–1827). According to Yehoshua Mondshine, this latter censorship was 'largely as a result of the remarks by R. Meir Jehiel Halevi of Ostrowiec, to the effect that Przysucha hasidism had long abandoned the practice of "digression" and was now toeing the line advocated by R. Isaac Meir of Gur (author of *Ḥidushei harim*), urging a return to the full rigour of the *Shulḥan arukh*'.[60]

In *Or lashamayim* by R. Meir of Apta (d. 1831),[61] we are mysteriously told that due to a 'hidden reason', the 'righteous ones of the generation' had commanded that an explanation in the commentary be removed. In the approbation of R. Menahem Mendel, R. Meir's son-in-law, he states that he removed the comment himself because of the 'hidden reason'. The fact that we are told that something was removed is itself significant, and goes against the general pattern. But what was the reason for the passage being deleted? Ahron Marcus reports a hasidic tradition that R. Meir of Apta had explained, based on a hint in a biblical verse, that the messiah would arrive in the year 1962.[62] Presumably, the deletion was so as to not depress the people who would learn

[54] Trans. in L. Kaplan, 'Daas Torah', 59. Kaplan's discussion of the episode is based on Piekarz, *Polish Hasidism* (Heb.), 373–434.

[55] B. Landau and Ortner, *The Holy Rebbe of Belz* (Heb.).

[56] Farbstein, *Beseter ra'am*, 97 n. 149. Farbstein's judgement is actually too soft, as it is not merely that the authors refuse to admit that the Rebbe erred in his 'assessment', but that the future developments showed that his *ruaḥ hakodesh* was faulty. For a defence of the Belzer Rebbe, see Ortner, *Devar ḥen*, 304 ff.

[57] See above, p. 90 ff.

[58] See Assaf, *Caught in the Thicket* (Heb.), 35–6. He notes that when the Hebrew translation was reprinted, even more material was deleted. See also Kitsis, 'A. Marcus's *Hasidism*' (Heb.).

[59] See N. Deutsch, *The Maiden of Ludmir*, 58.

[60] Y. Mondshine, 'Fluidity of Categories', 319.

[61] 'Balak', s.v. *mah*.

[62] Marcus, *Hasidism* (Heb.), 59.

from the book, published in 1860, that the redemption was still so far off.

In the early nineteenth century we find another example of internal censorship in a hasidic text. In a letter, R. Shneur Zalman of Lyady wrote that while 'according to the Torah, the [material] needs of a man's wife and children take precedence over others, they do not take precedence over the needs of the *tsadikim* and especially the *tsadikim* in the Holy Land'. This outlook was regarded as too extreme, and in 1814, when this letter was reprinted by R. Shneur Zalman's own hasidim, the passage just quoted was removed.[63]

Internal hasidic battles also led to censorship. The conflict between R. Hayim Eleazar Shapira, the Rebbe of Munkács, and R. Issachar Dov Roke'ah (1851–1926), the Rebbe of Belz, is well known. In one responsum, Shapira even attacks Roke'ah by writing that there was no need for the halakhic authorities to deal with a certain issue, because all they needed to write was 'let him go to Belz, and everything is permitted'. In certain editions, the words 'to Belz' are simply whited out.[64]

Another example of censorship relates to the figure of R. Nahman of Bratslav (1772–1810), who was controversial even among hasidim. In the first edition of *Midrash pinḥas*, which records the teachings of R. Pinhas Shapiro of Koretz (1726–91), there is a negative comment about R. Nahman's character (Fig. 7.6),[65] which has been deleted from later editions.[66]

There is a very interesting example where the censorship, if we can call it that, was carried out by R. Israel Meir Hakohen (the Hafets Hayim), the author of the work involved. His volumes on personal morality and proper speech became classics in their time. Attached to one of these volumes is a work entitled 'Sefat tamim'. In chapter 4 the Hafets Hayim records a story that took place in the days of the Ba'al Shem Tov about a man who was reincarnated as a horse in order to pay off his debt. This is noteworthy, as the Hafets Hayim was one of the leaders of the non-hasidic segment of Jewry, and yet in this case he did not shy away from mentioning the Ba'al Shem Tov. The text appears in Figure 7.7(*a*).[67]

[63] See Loewenthal, 'Women and the Dialectic of Spirituality', 13 n. 20.

[64] See Glick, *Kuntres*, ii, no. 2309. See M. Goldstein, *Mas'ot yerushalayim*, 87*b*–88*b*, for Shapira's criticism of Slobodka students and his negative view of R. Moses Mordechai Epstein. This was removed in subsequent editions of the book. This is another example where followers, in order to protect their teacher's reputation, take it upon themselves to act as censors.

[65] The book is not paginated. The passage appears as no. 10 in the third numbering. As R. Pinhas Shapiro died in 1791, when R. Nahman was still a young man and before he had much of a following, the negative comment attributed to him is apparently apocryphal.

[66] For an example where very strong criticism of secular studies was deleted from a hasidic text, see Anon., 'Concerning *Be'er mayim ḥayim*' (Heb.).

[67] I. M. Hakohen, *Shemirat halashon*, 'Sefat tamim' 41*a*. The Hafets Hayim retells the same story, including the mention of the Ba'al Shem Tov, in id., *Maḥaneh yisra'el*, ii, ch. 6.

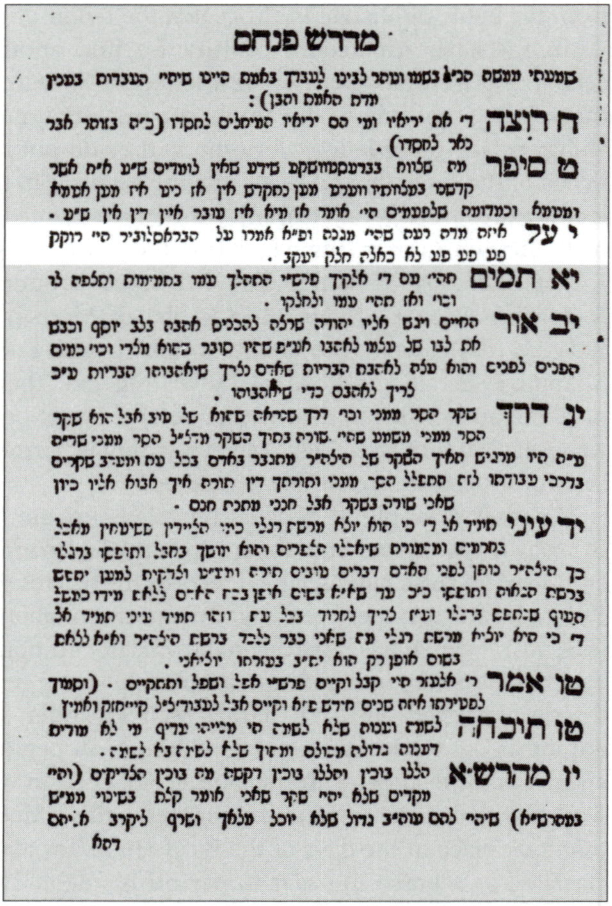
מדרש פנחס

ח רוצה

ט סיפר

י על

יא תמים

יב אור

יג דרך

יד עיני

טו אמר

טז תוכחה

יז מהרש״א

Figure 7.6 R. Pinhas Shapiro, *Midrash pinḥas* (Lemberg, 1872), showing his negative comment about R. Nahman of Bratslav

The story that the Hafets Hayim refers to appears in the anonymous *Shivḥei habesht*,[68] but as Yehoshua Mondshine has noted,[69] the Hafets Hayim's source is R. Eliezer Papo's *Pele yo'ets*, which also records the tale.[70] Neither *Shivḥei habesht* nor *Pele yo'ets* is the sort of text to which the Ashkenazi non-hasidic world would generally refer. In Figure 7.7(*b*) we can see how the text of 'Sefat tamim' looks in the standard reprinted version. Here, instead of mentioning the Ba'al Shem Tov, the story quoted by the Hafets Hayim is said to have occurred 'in earlier times'. In order to make sure that the page ends on the same word as the original, which is crucial in a photo-offset, the printer had to make some alterations, starting as early as the third line of the paragraph. This was done in order to allow him to add an extra line, which is the

[68] p. 103. [69] See Y. Mondshine, 'Sipurim vegilguleihem', no. 62. [70] p. 30*b*, s.v. *gezel*.

only way the additional Hebrew letters would fit. The original edition has twenty-five lines and the altered edition has twenty-six. Inserting the new letters was easy, as they could be taken from anywhere else in the book. Yet even with all this preparation he still did a sloppy job, as the inserted word (*harishonim*) does not remain within the left margin. A careful reader would notice this and realize that something is not right with the text.

Many have assumed that what we have here is an example of anti-hasidic censorship of the Hafets Hayim's work.[71] Yet as Shmuel Ashkenazi has shown,[72] we find this change in two editions that were produced in the Hafets Hayim's lifetime. Since one cannot imagine that the printer would have made this change on his own, we must assume that it was the Hafets Hayim himself who did so. Ashkenazi is presumably correct in suggesting that the Hafets Hayim originally thought that the ריב״ש referenced was, as is usually the case, R. Isaac bar Sheshet (1326–1408). When he later learnt that it referred to the Ba'al Shem Tov, he did not want such a reference to appear in his work and made the change.[73]

Zionism

The issue of Zionism provides another opportunity for the rewriting of history and for the censors to go to work. This is especially the case as attitudes towards Zionism have split the Orthodox world in modern times unlike any other matter.[74] While there were Orthodox Jews and rabbinic leaders who supported political Zionism, and many of these were supporters of the Mizrahi movement, it appears to me (and others) that the majority of the rabbinic elite was opposed to Zionism in its early years.[75] Because so much was at stake in this dispute, unsavoury tactics were often used. If R. Meir Bar-Ilan (1880–1949) is to be believed, this included even tampering with the text of a letter of R. Hayim Soloveitchik so that his condemnation of the Zionists was made even stronger.[76]

[71] In addition to the sources mentioned by Ashkenazi (in his Seforim Blog post, 2 June 2010) and Mondshine ('Sipurim vegilguleihem', no. 62), see also M. Katz, 'An Alteration' (Heb.).

[72] See his Seforim Blog post, 2 June 2010.

[73] Regarding the Hafets Hayim's attitude towards hasidism, which though generally positive was also critical, see R. Aryeh Leib Cohen (the Hafets Hayim's son), 'Ways and Opinions' (Heb.).

[74] See Luz, *Parallels Meet*.

[75] I say this with full cognizance of the fact that R. Tsevi Yehudah Kook famously opened the holy ark and in front of the Torah scrolls declared that most of the great rabbis had not been opposed to Zionism, but rather were silent on the issue. See Remer, *Gadol shimushah* (1994), 29–30; Wolberstein, *Mashmia yeshuah*, 192.

[76] Bar-Ilan, *From Volozhin to Jerusalem* (Heb.), i. 244.

שפת תמים פרק ג ד

מא 81

ותשבר כד על המבוע זו כרס לאחר שלשה ימים
כריסו נבקעת ומוסרת לפה ואומרת לו היליך מה
שגזלת ושחמדת ונתת לי [ועכל לומר שזהו כונת הכתוב
במשלי י' ופי רשעים יכסה חמס] גם אחז"ל שעבור
זה החטא מאכילין אותו שם חול דק ושיניהם נשברות
כמו שנאמר שיני רשעים שיברת ובשהם אינם רוצים
לאכול משיב להם הקב"ה מדוע כשהייתם אוכלים
גזל בעוה"ז היה מתוק בפיכם · ואפי' אחר כל
העונשים לא יהיה לו תקנה גמורה עד שישוב בגלגול
להשיב הגזלה · וראיתי בספרים מעשה נפלא שהיה
בימי הריב"ש שבא אחד בגלגול סוס והיה עובד בכל
כחו כדי לשלם את חובו. וזהו מן הגלגולים הקשים
ולפעמים יצטרך לבוא עוד הפעם לאותו העולם לחזור
ולהסבבות כדי לפרוע את גזלתו כמו שמובא בכמה
מקומות וכן כתב הגר"א במשלי על הפסוק מציל
נפשות עד אמת · וכזה ביארתי המדרש בקהלת על
הפסוק שמח בחור בילדותיך ויטיבך לבך וגו' ודע כי
על כל אלה יביאך האלקים במשפט משל לאחד שברח
מפני

(*a*)

Figure 7.7 R. Israel Meir Hakohen, *Shemirat halashon*, 'Sefat tamim' 41*a*: (*a*) Vilna, 1879 edition, showing the reference to the Ba'al Shem Tov; (*b*) later edition, with the reference deleted and the text rearranged

שפת תמים פרק ג ד מא

שזהו כונת הכתוב במשלי י׳ ופי רשעים יכסה
חמס] גם אחז״ל שעבור זה החטא מאכילין אותו
שם חול סדק ושייסה נשברות כמו שנאמר שיני
רשעים שיברת והשסה אינם רוצים לאכול משיב להם
הקב״ה מדוע כשהייתם אוכלים גזל בעוה״ז היה
מתוק בפיכם . ואפי׳ אחר כל העונשים לא יהיה
לו תקנה גמורה עד שישוב בגלגול להשיב הגזלה .
וראיתי בספרים מעשה נפלא שהיה בימים הראשונים
שבא אחד בגלגול סוס והיה עובד בכל כחו כדי
לשלם את חובו . וזהו מן הגלגולים הקשים ולפחות
ילטרך לבוא עוד הפעם לאותו העולם לחזור ולהבראות
כדי לפרוע את גזילתו כמו שמובא בכמה מקומות
וכן כתב הגר״א במשלי על הפסוק מליל הפסוח
מד אמה . וכזה בילרתי המדרש בקהלת על הפסוק
שמח בחור בילדותך וייטיבך לבך וגו׳ ודע כי על
כל אלה יביאך האלקים במשפט משל לאחד שברח
שאי
יא 11

(*b*)

With the creation of the State of Israel there was a lot of excitement in much of the rabbinic world. Many rabbis expressed themselves in ways that would later bring embarrassment to their families, as the state never developed in as religious a fashion as was hoped. For instance, shortly after the establishment of the state, R. Eliezer Waldenberg published his three-volume *Hilkhot hamedinah* ('Laws of the State'). This work deals with all sorts of halakhic issues relevant to running a modern state, and bears witness to Waldenberg's great optimism and joy in the new State of Israel, which he regarded as the 'beginning of the redemption'.[77] After his death, when it became obvious that Waldenberg's family would never republish this work, an anonymous person took it upon himself to do so. Rather than being thankful that Waldenberg had an admirer willing to shoulder the publishing expenses, the family attempted to stop publication with an appeal to the *beit din* of the Edah Haredit.[78]

Another example concerns R. Isaac Meir Patsiner (1888–1960), the son-in-law of the famous R. Isser Zalman Meltzer. In 1956, the same year that he was appointed to the Israeli Chief Rabbinate's *beit din hagadol*,[79] he published the second volume of his *Parashat hamelekh*. In his introduction to this work he speaks very positively about the State of Israel, stating that it is the 'beginning of the redemption'. When this book was reprinted in 1983, these sentiments were no longer to be found.[80]

The great fear of Zionism also led to censorship of R. Tsadok Hakohen's classic *Tsidkat hatsadik*. This work was originally published in a censored version in 1902, a couple of years after his death, and it was only in 1968 that the complete text was published.[81] In one originally censored passage, R. Tsadok elaborates on the importance in Judaism of identifying with the nation of Israel.[82] He notes that a person can convert to Judaism knowing nothing

[77] Waldenberg, *Hilkhot hamedinah*, i. 8.

[78] See Anon., 'Mystery' (Heb.).

[79] See Yitshak Goldschlag's obituary of Patsiner, *Shanah beshanah* (1961), 370.

[80] This was noted by Shaul Shiff in an article in the online *Hatsofeh*. (This newspaper, which ceased publication some years ago, no longer has an internet presence.) Another example worth noting is that the name of R. Judah Kowalsky (1862–1925), a well-known Mizrahi rabbi, was deleted from the responsa of R. Abraham Bornstein. See Don-Yihye, *Anshei torah umalkhut*, 395; Katzman, 'The Gaon R. Judah Leib Gordon' (Heb.), 664 n. 27.

[81] Those passages censored from the first edition of *Tsidkat hatsadik* (1902) were preserved in a copy of the book, having been handwritten by one of R. Tsadok's students. See Borschel-Dan, 'Visiting Gershom Scholem'.

[82] No. 54. It is not always clear what was regarded as problematic in other censored passages. I think no. 69 was censored because in this text R. Tsadok points to something positive that accrues when 'wicked Jews' assimilate. Also censored were no. 163, which expresses antinomian sentiments, and no. 146, perhaps because it implies that R. Joshua ben Hananiah did not control his sexual urges as much as R. Eliezer.

about the religion, to the extent that he still worships idols, but as long as he regards himself as a member of the people of Israel, the conversion is valid.[83] Similarly, R. Tsadok explains that despite any sins one may commit, one remains in the fold as long as one does not turn one's back on the Jewish people. Following a view earlier advocated by R. Yom Tov Ishbili (Ritva; *c.*1250–1330), R. David Ibn Zimra,[84] and R. Jacob Emden,[85] R. Tsadok disagrees with Maimonides' well-known opinion in his *Igeret hashemad* that one need not give up one's life if forced to convert to Islam. R. Tsadok claims that one must indeed suffer martyrdom in such a circumstance, since adoption of Islam means abandonment of the nation of Israel and the assumption of a different identity. He contrasts conversion to Islam, which is not an idolatrous religion yet entirely removes a Jew from his people, with those Israelites in earlier times who worshipped idolatry but still identified with the nation of Israel. Unlike the convert to Islam, the ancients were not severed from their people. All of these comments were problematic in that they could lend support to the secular Zionist perspective that put the stress on national, rather than religious, identity. They were therefore omitted.

Here is an example where we see an act of censorship in R. Joshua Joseph Hakohen's *Ezrat kohanim*, which appeared in Warsaw in 1873. The original text appears in Figure 7.8(*a*), while the 1971 censored version is shown in Figure 7.8(*b*). The censored passage relates to the permissibility of offering sacrifices even without the existence of the Temple. While this is a halakhic matter that was discussed by great sages before the existence of the Zionist movement, in later years discussions of this sort became identified with religious Zionist figures. I have no doubt that this is the reason why the passage was censored in the reprinted version, which happened to be produced by a man in Monroe, New York, a centre of the Satmar hasidic sect.[86]

The haredi 'problem' with Zionism is also visible in the way in which the ArtScroll publishing house dealt with the writings of R. Shlomo Yosef Zevin (1888–1978). Although an adherent of Habad hasidism, Zevin was also an unabashed religious Zionist.[87] In his classic *Hamo'adim bahalakhah*

83 רק בקריאת שם ישראל די; ibid., no. 54.

84 See Ibn Zimra, *She'elot uteshuvot haradbaz*, nos. 344, 1163. Ibn Zimra quotes Ishbili.

85 Emden, *Migdal oz* (1874), 28*b*.

86 The introduction to vol. i of the work, 'Mevo hamikdash', pp. 3*b*–4*a*, is also censored, removing the author's argument that the Temple will be rebuilt before the coming of the messiah. The Jerusalem, 2002 edition, which was reset, is also missing the passage seen in Figure 7.8(*a*). However, this edition includes the complete introduction, which, as noted, is missing in the censored version.

87 Zevin's Habad background was that of the Bobruisk branch, not Lubavitch. With the end of Bobruisk, Zevin transferred his allegiance to Lubavitch, but he never adopted the Lubavitch anti-

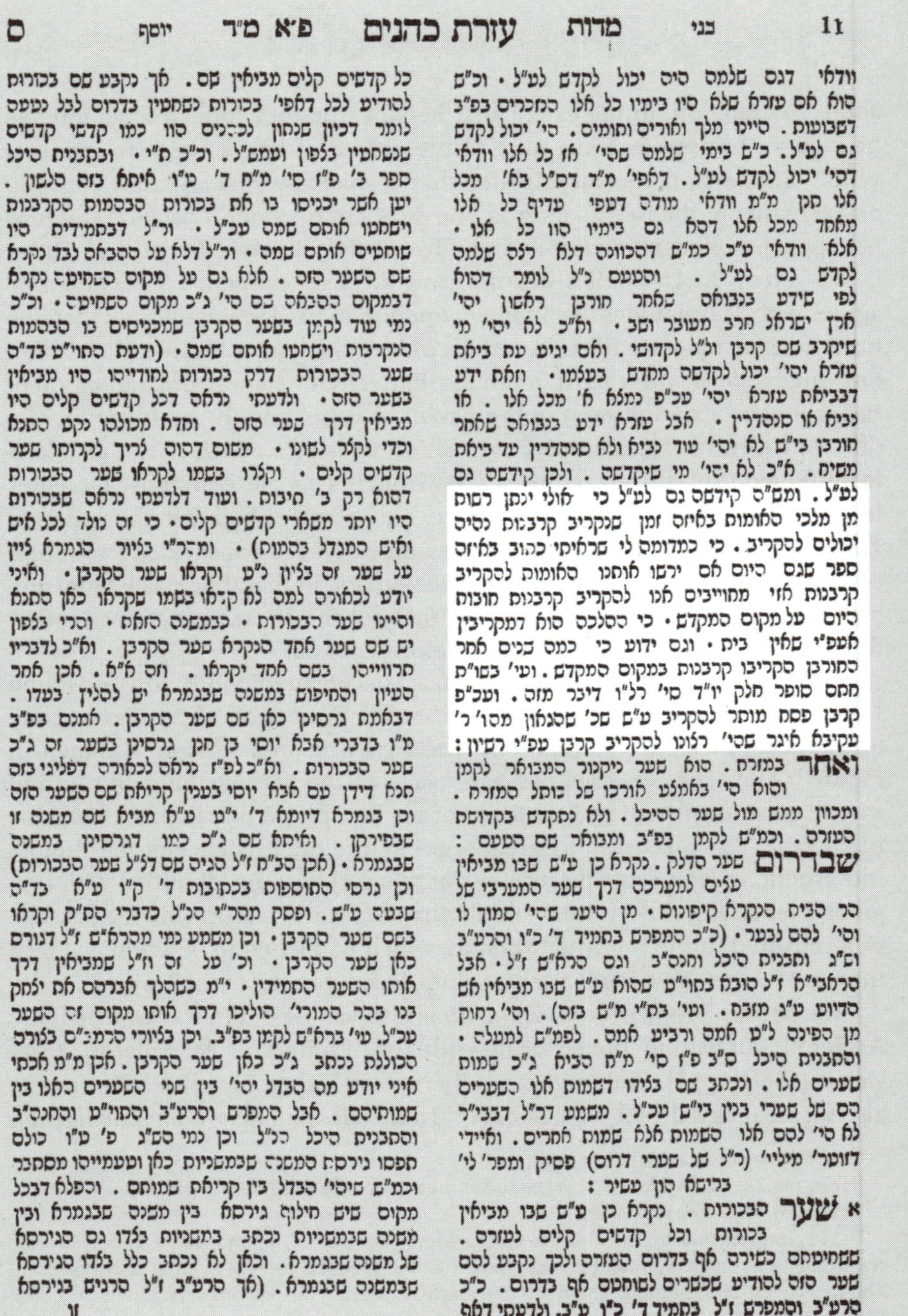
יא בני מדות עזרת כהנים פ"א מ"ד יוסף ס

ולכן קידשה גם לע"ל. ומה"ט קידשה גם לע"ל כי אולי ינתן רשות מן מלכי האומות באיזה זמן שנקריב קרבנות ונהיה יכולים להקריב. כי כמדומה לי שראיתי כתוב באיזה ספר שגם היום אם ירשו אותנו האומות להקריב קרבנות אזי מחוייבים אנו להקריב קרבנות חובות היום על מקום המקדש. כי הלכה היא דמקריבין אעפ"י שאין בית. וגם ידוע כי כמה שנים אחר החורבן הקריבו קרבנות במקום המקדש. ועי' בשו"ת חתם סופר חלק יו"ד סי' רל"ו דיבר מזה. ועכ"פ קרבן פסח מותר להקריב ע"ש שכ' שהגאון מהו' ר' עקיבא איגר הסי' רצונו להקריב קרבן עפ"י רשיון:

(*a*)

Figure 7.8 R. Joshua Joseph Hakohen, *Ezrat kohanim:* (*a*) Warsaw, 1873 edition, showing the discussion of the possibility of offering sacrifices in the absence of the Temple; (*b*) 1971 edition (Monroe, NY: I. Lowy), with the passage removed

ודאי דהא שלמה היה יכול לקדש לע"ל. וכ"ת הא אם עזרא שלא היו בימיו כל אלו המנויים בפ"ב השבועות. היינו מלך ואורים ותומים. הי' יכול לקדש גם לע"ל. כ"ש בימי שלמה שהי' אז כל אלו ודאי הי' יכול לקדש לע"ל. דאפי' מ"ד דס"ל בא' מכל אלו סגי מ"מ ודאי מ"מ דעפי עדיף כל אלו מאחד מכל אלו דהא גם בימיו הוו כל אלו. אלא ודאי ע"כ כמ"ש דהכוונה דלא רצה שלמה לקדש גם לע"ל: והטעם נ"ל לומר דהוא לפי שידע בנבואה שאחר חורבן ראשון יהי' ארץ ישראל חרב מעובר ושב. וא"כ לא יהי' מי שיקרב שם קרבן ול"ל לקדושי. ואם יגיע עת ביאת עזרא יהי' יכול לקדשה מחדש בעצמו. ואת"ל ידע דבביאת עזרא יהי' עכ"פ כמלא א' מכל אלו. או נביא או סנהדרין. אבל עזרא ידע בנבואה שאחר חורבן בי"ש לא יהי' עוד נביא ולא סנהדרין עד ביאת משיח. א"כ לא יהי' מי שיקדשה. ולכן קידשה גם לע"ל.

ואחד במזרח. הוא שער ניקנור המבואר לקמן והוא הי' באמצע אורכו של כותל המזרח. ומכוון ממש מול שער ההיכל. ולא נתקדש בקדושת העזרה. וכמ"ש לקמן בפ"ב ומבואר שם הטעם:

שבדרום שער הדלק. נקרא כן ע"ש שהו מביאין עצים למערכה דרך שער המערבי של הר הבית שנקרא קיפונוס. מן השער ההי' סמוך לו הי' נכנס לעזר'. (כ"כ המפרש בתמיד ד' כ"ו והרע"ב ות"ג ותבנית היכל ותוס"ב וגם הרמב"ם ז"ל. אבל הראב"ד ז"ל סובר בחיבורו שהוא ע"ש שהו מביאין אש הדיוט ע"ג מזבח. ועי' בס"י פ"ש בזה). והי' רחוק מן הפינה ל"ה אמה ורביע אמה. לפמ"ש למעל'. ובתבנית היכל ה"ב פ"ז הי' מ"מ הביאו ג"כ שמות שערים אלו. וכתב שם בצידו דשמות אלו השערים הם של שערי בנין בי"ש עכ"ל. משמע דר"ל דבבי"ר לא הי' להם אלו השמות אלא שמות אחרים. ואיידי דעסקי' מילי' (ר"ל של שערי דרום) פסיק, ומפרש לי' בריישא הון עתיר:

א **שער** הבכורות. נקרא כן ע"ש שהו מביאין בכורות. וכל קדשים קלים לעזרה. שאחיטתם כשירה אף בדרום העזרה ולכן נקבע לשם שער זה להודיע שכשרים לשוחטם אף בדרום. כ"כ הרע"ב והמפרש ז"ל בתמיד ד' ל"ו ע"ב. ולדעתי דאף כל קדשים קלים מביאין שם. אך נקבע שם בכורות להודיע לכל דאפי' בכורות נשחטין בדרום לכל הפחות לומר דכיון שנתון לכהנים הוו כמו קדשי קדשים שנשחטין בצפון וקמ"ל. וכ"כ ת"י. ובתבנית היכל ספר ב' פ"ז הי' מ"מ ד' ע"ו איתא גם שלמון.

יען אשר יכניסו בו את בכורות הבהמות שקרבנות וישחטו אותם שמה עכ"ל. ור"ל דבתמידיה הוו שוחטים אותם שמה. ור"ל דלא על השחיטה לבד נקרא שם השער הזה. אלא גם על מקום השחיטה נקרא דבמקום השחיטה שם הי' ג"כ מקום השחיטה. ור"ל נמי עוד לקמן בשער הקרבן שמכניסים בו הבהמות הנקרבות וישחטו אותם שמה. (ודעת הפרי"ע בד"ה שער הבכורות דרק בכורות לחודייהו הוו מביאין בשער הזה. ולדעתי נראה דכל קדשים קלים הוו מביאין דרך שער הזה. ותדע מדאתו מקום השחיטה וכדי לקצר לשום. משום דהוה צריך לקרותו שער קדשים קלים. וקצרו בשמו לקראו שער הבכורות דהוא רק ב' תיבות. ועוד דלדעתי נראה שבכורות הוו יותר מצוי' מקדשים קלים. כי זה נולד לכל איש ואיש המגדל בהמות). ומהרי"ו בליקוט הגמרא ליין על שער זה בגליון ל"ע וקראו שער הקרבן. ואיני יודע לכאורה למה לא קראו בשמו שקראו כאן המשנה והיינו שער הבכורות. כהמשנה הזאת. והרי בצפון יש שם שער אחד שנקרא שער הקרבן. וא"כ לדבריו תרוייהו בשם אחד יקראו. וזה א"א. אבן אחר העיון והחיפוש במשנה שבגמרא יש לסלק כעדו. דבאמת גרסינן כאן שם שער הקרבן. אמנם בפ"ב מ"ו בדברי אבא יוסי בן חנן גרסינן בשער זה ג"כ שער הבכורות. וא"כ לפ"ז נראה לכאורה דפליגי בזה תנא דידן עם אבא יוסי בענין קריאת שם השערי' הוא וכן בגמרא דיומא ד' י"ט ע"א מביא שם משנה זו שבפירקין. ואיתא שם ג"כ כמו דגרסינן במשנה שבגמרא. (אבן הכ"מ ז"ל הגיה שם וצ"ל שער הבכורות) וכן גרסי התוספות בכתובות ד' ק"ו ע"א בד"ה שבעה ע"ש: ופסק הרמב"ם כלל כדברי הת"ק וקראו בשם שער הקרבן. וכן משמע נמי מהרמב"ם ז"ל דגרס כאן שער הקרבן. וכ' על זה וז"ל שמביאין דרך אותו השער התמידין. י"א כשהלך אברהם את יצחק בנו בכור המורי' הוליכו דרך אותו מקום זה השער עכ"ל. עי' ברמ"ם לקמן בפ"ב. וכן בליקוטי הרמב"ם בגמרא הסוללם נכתב ג"כ כאן שער הקרבן. אבן מ"מ אכתי איני יודע מה הבדל יהי' בין שני השערים כאלו בין שמותיהם. אבל המפרש והרע"ב והתוי"ט והתוס"ב והתבנית היכל כ"ל וכן נמי הש"צ פ' פ"ו כולם ספמו גירסת המשנה שבמשניות כאן ועמייהו משמע וכמ"ש שיהי' הבדל בין קריאת שמותם. והנלא דבכל מקום שיש חילוף גירסא בין משנה שבגמרא ובין משנה שבמשניות נכתב במשניות בצדו גם הגירסא של משנה שבגמרא. וכאן לא נכתב כלל בצדו הגירסא שבמשנה שבגמרא. (אך הרע"ב ז"ל הביאו בגירסא

ע

(*b*)

Zevin discusses the obligation to tear one's garment upon seeing the desolate cities of the land of Israel. He assumes that this is no longer required, as the cities are now under Jewish rule. In his discussion, Zevin refers to 'the rise of the State of Israel (how happy we are to have merited this!)'.[88]

Such an expression of happiness with regard to the state, the creation of which brought much of biblical Israel under Jewish control, was regarded as too Zionist by those involved in the translation commissioned by ArtScroll, and was therefore omitted from the English translation.[89] Here again we see the pattern we have seen so often. Recognizing the great value of Zevin's Torah writings, ArtScroll desired to translate them. However, in order to keep Zevin 'kosher' in today's haredi world, it was thought that the only feasible approach was to delete problematic passages. By censoring Zevin, ArtScroll presumably feels that it is 'saving' him for those benighted individuals who would want nothing to do with Zevin were they to know of his Zionism. Preserved from this peril, they can now benefit from his writings (and ArtScroll can also make money from the books).[90]

Zionism. Significantly, Zevin's descendants have never tried to hide his Zionism. See e.g. the biographical introduction to Zevin, *Le'or hahalakhah*, 37.

88 Zevin, *Hamo'adim bahalakhah*, ii. 442 (end of the chapter on 'The Destruction').

89 *The Festivals in Halachah*, translated by Shlomo Fox-Ashrei. The editor was Uri Kaploun, and the 'contributing editor' was Meir Holder. See ii. 294.

90 For further details on the censorship of Zevin, see my Seforim Blog post, 14 Oct. 2013.

CHAPTER EIGHT

IS THE TRUTH REALLY THAT IMPORTANT?

THE READER who has made it this far and seen all the examples of censorship and distortion is probably wondering, what ever happened to truth? Isn't this an important value in the Jewish tradition, and if so, how do so many people, many of whom are quite pious, justify their actions? It is to these questions that we now turn in this concluding chapter, and we will see that the matter is not a simple one at all.

We must begin by emphasizing that under normal circumstances truth is indeed a very important value in Judaism.[1] Numerous talmudic passages speak of this, and I will cite only four: Mishnah, *Avot* 1: 1: 'The world stands on three things: on justice, on truth, and on peace'; Talmud, *Shabat* 55*a*: 'The seal of the Holy One, blessed be He, is truth'; *Sanhedrin* 92*a*: 'Whoever dissembles in his speech is as though he had engaged in idolatry'; *Sanhedrin* 103*a*: 'Four classes will not appear before the presence of the Shekhinah. . . . The class of liars, as it is written, "He that telleth lies shall not tarry in my sight" [Psalm 101: 7].'

The thirteenth-century anonymous work *Sefer haḥinukh* regards lying as 'abominable',[2] and generally speaking, no traditional Jewish thinker would disagree.[3] After all, there is an explicit biblical verse that states 'Keep thee far from a false matter' (Exodus 23: 7). Another verse states: 'Lying lips are an abomination to the Lord' (Proverbs 12: 12). However, as we shall see, rabbinic

[1] See J. Gerondi, *Sha'arei teshuvah*, section 3: 178–86; Anon., *Orḥot tsadikim*, ch. 22; I. M. Hakohen, *Sefat emet*, ch. 6; M. N. Friedman, *On Truth and Falsehood* (Heb.); Scheinfeld, *Olam hasheker*; Aratan, *Torat hamidot*, part 3; Karelitz, *Emunah uvitaḥon*, ch. 4, no. 13; Tobolski, *Midevar sheker tirḥak*; Y. H. Fish, *Titen emet leya'akov*; N. Yavrov, *Niv sefatayim*; Silver, *Emet keneh*; Littwack, *Midevar sheker tirḥak*; Y. H. Sofer, *Hadar ya'akov*, vol. vi, no. 17.

[2] No. 74.

[3] R. Nahman of Bratslav has a very unusual position. According to him, 'Falsehood is only with the mouth, but not in writing.' See id., *Sefer hamidot*, s.v. *emet*, no. 50. R. Nahman's opinion is also shared by Zilberger, *Atsei zayit*, vol. ii, no. 23 (end): אין איסור כלל בכתיבה. Abulafia, *Yad ramah* on BT *BB* 172*a* (no. 108), and Tosafot, BT *BB* 94*b*, s.v. *hakhi*, state explicitly that writing is also included under 'Keep thee far from a false matter'. See H. S. Abraham, *Devar torah*, ii. 352; Waldenberg, *Tsits eli'ezer*, xv, no. 12.

literature also leaves us with a number of exceptions to the strong affirmations of truth.[4]

Ibn Ezra mentions that on occasion even prophets will tell untruths.[5] One example he gives is that Abraham says to those who accompanied him when he intended to offer Isaac as a burnt offering: 'I and the lad will go yonder and we will worship and come back to you' (Genesis 22: 5).[6] Abraham was not yet ready to tell Isaac and the others the truth, and thus uttered this falsehood. Ibn Ezra further notes that had Abraham told the truth, 'Isaac would quite possibly have fled.'

The issue of truth-telling in a halakhic context came to the fore in a dispute between R. Moses Sofer and R. Tsevi Hirsch Chajes. The issue that precipitated it was the question of delayed burial. In 1772, Duke Friedrich of Mecklenburg-Schwerin, responding to the possibility of burying people prematurely when they were still alive, issued an order requiring the Jews in his realm to wait three days before burying their dead. We know that a Jewish apostate had influenced the duke in this matter, convincing him that the practice of early burial was not of great importance in Judaism. The local Jewish community, believing that this ordinance violated Jewish law, wrote to both R. Jacob Emden and Moses Mendelssohn, requesting their expert opinions. The plan was to use these opinions in their efforts to have the law revoked.[7]

Emden replied that one could not abandon the traditional Jewish practice of immediate burial because of a far-fetched concern that someone who appears dead is really alive. In his German letter to the duke, Mendelssohn agreed with Emden that delaying burial was in opposition to Jewish law. This letter was sent for the sake of Jewish solidarity, but did not reflect Mendelssohn's true view, which appears in a Hebrew letter he sent to the community leaders. Here he said that the duke's requirement was *not* against Jewish law. After calling attention to the various times when it is permitted to postpone a burial, Mendelssohn added that if in these cases the rabbis permitted a body to lie unburied overnight, 'then certainly if there remains the slightest doubt that he may still be alive [he should not be buried]'.[8]

Mendelssohn also argued that the contemporary practice of immediate burial was actually opposed to ancient Jewish tradition. The old Jewish

[4] For an analysis of the differences in this regard between Jewish and American law, see Resnicoff, 'Lying and Lawyering'. The complexity of our topic is seen in R. Judah Leib Margaliyot's formulation, *Tal orot*, 6*b*: ואין דבר מתועב כמו השקר, והותר מכללו לשופטי ארץ כשהם משתדלים ע״כ להוציא דין אמת לאמתתו.

[5] Commentary on Gen. 27: 19.

[6] See also Gen. 22: 8 where, in response to Isaac asking about the lamb to be offered, Abraham replied, 'God will see to the sheep for His burnt offering.'

[7] My description of events is based on Altmann, *Moses Mendelssohn*, 287 ff. See also Samet, *Heḥadash*, ch. 7.

[8] See Samet, *Heḥadash*, 165.

practice was to place the dead in caves and catacombs where the body was watched for three days in order to see if there were any signs of life.[9] In other words, according to Mendelssohn, what the duke wanted was nothing more than that the Jews return to their old way of doing things.

In the decades after Mendelssohn, there were many reform-minded Jews who supported this step and viewed it as in line with modern medical science. It was in response to these reformist sentiments that Sofer took a strong stand in opposition to any altering of the traditional practice. He expressed this opinion in a letter to Chajes, who appeared to think there was nothing wrong with delaying burial if it was thought medically necessary.[10] In this letter, Sofer asserted that one who does not bury a corpse immediately has violated two Torah commandments, one positive and one negative.

In Chajes's reply he claims that Sofer is mistaken in his assumption that one would violate two Torah commandments, as the only violation is of a negative prohibition.[11] To this, Sofer responds that according to Nahmanides one does indeed violate a positive commandment. Therefore, he was within his rights in claiming so. Furthermore, Sofer notes, since there is no practical difference whether or not a prohibited act is in violation of one or two Torah commandments, 'it is good to raise [i.e. intensify] the prohibition'.[12] In other words, in order to discourage halakhic violation, it is advisable to make the sin appear worse than it really is, or at least worse than most authorities regard it to be.

This notion of intensifying the level of a prohibition has already been dealt with by Moshe Samet and Jacob Katz, both of whom stress this point as an important aspect of Sofer's battle against nascent Reform Judaism.[13] I will have a good deal more to say on this, but first we must note Chajes's reply to Sofer.[14] He insists that it is not proper to 'raise the prohibition' in the fashion done by Sofer. He acknowledges that the talmudic sages would sometimes exaggerate the level of a prohibition, for instance, stating that one is subject to the heavenly death penalty for certain violations. Yet this was only by way of

9 See the post-talmudic tractate *Semaḥot*, ch. 8.

10 M. Sofer, *She'elot uteshuvot ḥatam sofer*, vol. ii, 'Yoreh de'ah', no. 338. Chajes' name, as the recipient of the responsum, was removed when Sofer's responsa were posthumously published. This was presumably because of his sympathies for the Haskalah.

11 Chajes, *Kol sifrei maharats ḥayes*, i. 265–6.

12 Ibid. 269–70.

13 Samet, *Heḥadash*, 218 ff., 458 ff.; J. Katz, *Halakhah in Crisis* (Heb.), 79. See also Kosman, 'Central Role' (Heb.), 76 ff., who discusses Sofer's use of this approach in one area of the Sabbath laws. Samet, *Heḥadash*, 218, assumes that Sofer's second responsum to Chajes, where he mentions 'raising the prohibition', was excluded from Sofer's posthumously published responsa due to 'religious correctness'.

14 Chajes, *Kol sifrei maharats ḥayes*, i. 270 n.

threats to put the fear of sin into people, as had already been pointed out by Maimonides.[15]

Chajes understands Sofer to be including in his 'raising the prohibition' the notion that one can also say that something is biblically prohibited when in reality the prohibition is only rabbinic. Chajes sees this as a violation of the prohibition against adding to the Torah, as well as a violation of the biblical commandment to keep far from a false matter. The fact that one might have a good reason for the deception is not sufficient in his eyes to sanction any distortion. He concludes: 'The Sages were always careful to clarify which matters were from the Torah and which were rabbinic, even when there was no practical legal distinction.'[16]

Regarding Chajes's objection that Sofer's approach violates the biblical command against telling a falsehood, this chapter will show that the prohibition is far from absolute. Since Sofer's false statement—assuming it was indeed false—had an important purpose, this would make it permissible in the eyes of many authorities. Furthermore, it is most unlikely that Chajes is correct in assuming that Sofer believed that one can describe something as biblically prohibited when this is not the case. In fact, Sofer is careful to point out that his description of delayed burial as a violation of two commandments is not technically incorrect, since Nahmanides did, after all, hold this opinion.[17] Had Sofer thought that telling a falsehood about a commandment was acceptable when it came to influencing the masses to follow religious law, he would not have had to justify his position by citing Nahmanides.

Yet even if Sofer did not hold the position attributed to him by Chajes, there were others who did. We can thus speak of a fundamental dispute about

[15] Maimonides, *Commentary on the Mishnah*, ii, *San.* 7: 4 (pp. 121–5). See also id., *Mishneh torah*, 'Hilkhot teshuvah' 3: 14, where the version in most manuscripts is: כדי להתרחק מהן ולהזהר מהן. Another relevant example is *Mishneh torah*, 'Hilkhot sotah' 3: 2. Here Maimonides states that the court tells the suspected adulteress the story of Reuben and Bilhah (Gen. 35: 22) according to its literal meaning, namely, that Reuben had sexual relations with his father's concubine. According to one approach in BT *Shab.* 55*b*, however, this never actually happened. In order to encourage the woman's repentance, the court is permitted to speak falsely in this case. (However, see above, Ch. 1 n. 16, for the Talmud's recording of the view that Reuben indeed had sexual relations with Bilhah. Perhaps Maimonides accepted this view.) R. Simeon ben Tsemah Duran notes that the Sages exaggerated when describing sins that cause a person to lose his share in the world to come. See id., *Ohev mishpat*, ch. 10. On the Sages' exaggerations, see Israeli, *Mitsvot zemaniyot*, 507; Isaac bar Sheshet, *She'elot uteshuvot harivash*, no. 171; D. Halevi, *Turei zahav*, 'Yoreh de'ah' 116: 4; Dehan, *Dibrot ya'akov: ketubot*, 2 ff.; Y. H. Sofer, *Hadar ya'akov*, v. 29–30; Wreschner, *Seder ya'akov*, 21 ff. (first numbering); Y. Yosef, *Ein yitsḥak*, iii. 151 ff. See also Kafih, Commentary on *Mishneh torah* (Heb.), 'Hilkhot shabat' 17: 10 (p. 355): אלא דמה שאמרו חייבין עליה משום רה"ר, דרך הפלגה, ולעולם מדרבנן כלומר כרמלית היא.

[16] Chajes, *Kol sifrei maharats ḥayes*, i. 270 n.

[17] This point is stressed by R. Moses Feinstein; see his *Dibrot mosheh: ketubot*, 247.

whether rabbinic figures are obligated to tell the truth in their halakhic decisions, or whether, on the contrary, the most important thing is to keep the people in line. According to the second approach, if a rabbi feels that the only way to secure religious stability in his community is to tell the masses falsely that something is prohibited, even biblically prohibited, then this would be acceptable.

This dispute has great contemporary relevance as well as historical interest. For example, in the controversy about the halakhic validity of women's prayer groups, there were some who thought that the prohibitions issued against these groups, while formulated in halakhic terms, were actually 'public policy' prohibitions. In their classic article on the topic, Dov and Aryeh Frimer cite many sources related to this issue, concluding that 'the consensus of codifiers maintain that public policy considerations, no matter how justified, do not entitle the rabbinic authority to misrepresent halakah'.[18]

Yet the Frimers also cite sources, including R. Solomon ben Adret,[19] and from more recent times, R. Ovadyah Yosef[20] and R. Hayim Kanievsky,[21] who disagree with this, believing that it *is* permissible to 'misrepresent the reason for or source of a prohibition'.[22] Some authorities they cite also hold that one may 'upgrade' a rabbinic prohibition to a biblical one,[23] which, as we saw, was how Chajes (apparently) misunderstood Sofer's intent. The Frimers also refer to many sources that claim that just as one is permitted to deviate from the truth in order to maintain peace (as we will soon see), the same logic applies to 'misrepresenting halakha in order to maintain peace between *kelal Yisrael* [the Jewish people] and the Almighty'.[24] In other words, there is a strong trend in the tradition that would permit misrepresentation and outright falsification of the halakhah if a good purpose were served by doing so. We will soon confront a number of explicit talmudic examples in support of this position. I will also present a number of cases from post-talmudic authorities that do likewise. In contrast to the Frimers' claim, it is apparent to me that the consensus is that one is indeed permitted to misrepresent halakhah for important reasons.[25] Those authorities who have a different perspective appear to be contradicted by the talmudic passages we will see.

[18] Frimer and Frimer, 'Women's Prayer Services', 39. Among the sources they do not cite, mention should be made of R. Moses Schick's responsum, printed in *Tsefunot*, 6 (5750), 93 (regarding why Schick would not sign the 1866 Mihalowitz decrees); Herzog, *Pesakim ukhetavim*, iv, 'Yoreh de'ah', no. 20.

[19] Solomon ben Adret, *She'elot uteshuvot harashba*, vol. i, no. 43.

[20] See his letter at the beginning of Y. Yosef, *Yalkut yosef: hilkhot bikur ḥolim ve'avelut*, 7–8.

[21] See Frimer and Frimer, 'Women's Prayer Services', 67.

[22] Ibid.

[23] See ibid. 65.

[24] Ibid. 67.

[25] In support of their claim, Frimer and Frimer (ibid. 63), cite Maimonides' ruling in *Mishneh torah*, 'Hilkhot mamrim' 2: 9, that a court that states that a rabbinic prohibition is biblical has

It is true that for some of these passages there are alternative interpretations, and it would be a worthwhile project to examine them. However, this is not my intent at present, as I am interested in the strand of Jewish tradition that countenances falsehood. As for the alternative explanations, some of them twist the sources beyond recognition, all in order to avoid the conclusion that the Sages would countenance any form of falsehood, especially in halakhic matters. The fact that some commentators went to such extremes is itself illustrative of the importance of truth in the tradition, and I see this as a good thing. Yet all of their mental gymnastics cannot obscure the fact that there is another tradition as well, one that will undoubtedly make many uncomfortable. Nevertheless, this approach deserves to be understood in a sympathetic manner as well, and to be recovered, as it were, from well-intentioned attempts to explain it away.

Returning to the issue of attributing biblical authority to rabbinic laws, R. Menahem Meiri claims that the Talmud itself sometimes does so.[26] Although Meiri does not explain why this is done, he undoubtedly assumes that the Talmud wished to strengthen rabbinic laws that were not being sufficiently observed. Meiri notes that the Talmud states that honouring a step-parent is a Torah law, when in reality it is only a rabbinic command. Human psychology being what it is, one can assume that step-parenting in ancient times was as difficult, and often thankless, as it is today. Thus, according to Meiri, the Talmud 'raised' the prohibition to encourage people to offer the proper respect to a step-parent.

The same motive would also apply to another example he offers: the prohibition of work on *ḥol hamo'ed*. Meiri assumes that this is only rabbinic, although from the Talmud one could conclude that it is a Torah prohibition.[27] According to Meiri, the reason the prohibition was 'raised' must have been in order to encourage its observance. This was necessary, for as we see from the following passage in the Jerusalem Talmud, *ḥol hamo'ed* was not taken as seriously as the Sages would have liked.

Said R. Ba bar Mamel, 'If there were someone who would be appointed with me for the stated purpose . . . I would permit people to do work on *ḥol hamo'ed*. . . . Have

violated the commandment against adding to the Torah. No one would dispute this. Yet the authorities who assert that it is permitted to lie would either claim that Maimonides is only referring to a court, not an individual decisor, or they would make an exception for extreme cases in which religious standards need to be supported. After all, the examples we will see from the Talmud do not intend to say that one may lie about halakhah as a matter of routine, but only that authorities have this option in extreme cases. There is no reason to assume that Maimonides would disagree.

[26] See his *Beit habeḥirah*, BT *Ket.* 103*a*.

[27] Meiri cites BT *MK* 11*a*. See also BT *Ḥag.* 18*a*.

they not prohibited doing work on *ḥol hamo'ed* only so that people will eat and drink and labour in the Torah? But they eat and drink and squander their leisure.'[28]

To see how this notion that one is permitted to misrepresent the halakhah in the name of a higher cause played out in more recent times, let us look at an interesting responsum by R. Elijah Rusoff, a twentieth-century American halakhist.[29] The case is as follows: a person was sitting *shiva* and the last day of his mourning was on the Sabbath. Not knowing much about Jewish law, he asked Rusoff if he had to sit *shiva* on that day. He explained that he was anxious to get back to his shop, since his wife did not know how to run it properly. After seeing how the man regarded *shiva* more seriously than the Sabbath, and seeking to prevent him from working on this day, Rusoff falsely told the man that he must also sit *shiva* on the Sabbath and observe all mourning practices, with the one exception being that he could wear leather shoes.

Rusoff informs us, however, that after giving this answer he began to question whether he had acted properly. He wondered if he had violated the commandment to keep far from a false matter, even though the false information he had provided was in order to prevent the man from desecrating the Sabbath. Among the sources he cites to defend his action is *Avodah zarah* 59*a*, where R. Yohanan declares something forbidden for people 'who are not students of the Torah', even though in truth there is no prohibition. This brings us back to the issue of *halakhah ve'ein morin ken* that was discussed in Chapter 1.[30] As we saw, there are certain matters that, although permissible, the Sages did not wish the masses to know about. On occasion, the Sages even lied to prevent this knowledge from getting out.[31] In line with this, there is another important talmudic source which Rusoff does not cite, even though it speaks to this issue. In *Gitin* 62*a* we are told that one may lie to an *am ha'arets* (one who was not careful with the laws of purity) about a certain halakhic consequence since that is thought to be a good way to prevent him from spreading his ritual impurity.[32]

Rusoff quotes another important passage in defence of his action, from R. Eliezer of Metz's (twelfth century) *Sefer yere'im*.[33] R. Eliezer explains that the commandment of keeping far from a false matter applies only when the lie will damage one's neighbour, as in court proceedings. Yet 'falsehood that does not have negative repercussions was not forbidden by the Torah'.

[28] JT *MK* 2: 3. This passage is not cited by Meiri.

[29] Rusoff, *Ugat eliyahu*, 14*b*.

[30] See p. 21.

[31] See above, p. 22, where I refer to BT *Men*. 36*b*.

[32] This is the simple meaning of the text, though R. Moses Sofer has a different interpretation, according to which no falsehood is involved. See M. Sofer, *Ḥidushei ḥatam sofer: gitin*, ad loc.

[33] No. 235.

Thus, according to R. Eliezer, white lies are permissible,[34] though obviously not recommended because of the bad character traits they would encourage. However, in the example discussed by Rusoff, there was no reason to be concerned about this since there was a good reason not to be honest. Based on the sources he quotes, Rusoff's conclusion is that one need not tell the truth if one has the opportunity to save another from sin.[35] Rusoff further declares that had he not lied to the questioner, and thus saved him from desecrating the Sabbath, he would have violated the commandment not to put a stumbling block in front of the blind.[36]

Returning to the dispute between Sofer and Chajes, even Chajes, who opposed 'raising the prohibition', admitted that there were times when the Sages would not tell the masses the actual halakhah, but rather give them a more stringent ruling.[37] Chajes cites *Ḥulin* 15*a* as an example of this. Here we see that Rav would teach one halakhah to his students, but when speaking to the ignorant masses he was cautious and told them the more stringent opinion as a precautionary measure. Chajes is certainly correct in this, but it then follows that his criticism of Sofer is only about the latter's words. That is, had Sofer simply advocated a strict ruling without any explanation there would be no reason to object. What Chajes finds problematic is only the misrepresentation of the source of the prohibition.

Any discussion of the permissibility of lying for a good purpose has to take into account Maimonides, who, I believe, provides good support for this position. In the introduction to the *Guide*, Maimonides tells us that at times he will contradict himself, and the contradictions will be such that the masses will not sense them. He did this, no doubt, so that the masses should not be confronted with issues that would create religious difficulties for them. In other words, Maimonides tells us that he will say things that are not true because certain people 'can't handle the truth' (to use the famous phrase from

[34] Those who find this conclusion problematic might be inclined to say that there is still a rabbinic prohibition against white lies, though R. Eliezer does not do this. See below, n. 62.

[35] R. Yitshak Zilberstein discusses the same sort of case as Rusoff and comes to an identical conclusion. See Goldschmidt, *Zikaron basefer*, 106, who disagrees. For another example where a rabbi permits one to lie in order to lessen somebody else's halakhic transgression, see Rudnik, *Sedeh yitsḥak*, 149 ff.

[36] For an earlier example of lying in order to keep people from sin, see my Seforim Blog post, 11 Jan. 2008. There I discuss how R. Isaac Grishaber (d. 1815) falsely claimed that R. Ezekiel Landau had retracted his permission to eat a type of sturgeon. Regarding this, see also Schnitzker, 'Revealer of Secrets' (Heb.); Sinclair, 'Fictitious Retractions'. See also Y. Yosef, *Yalkut yosef: sova semaḥot*, ii. 141–2 n. 8, that if a father will violate the Sabbath on account of his son's circumcision, the *mohel* should tell him that the baby is not healthy enough for a Saturday circumcision, and that it must be postponed until Sunday. See also Hamami, *Minḥat avraham*, no. 11 (p. 96).

[37] Chajes, *Kol sifrei maharats ḥayes*, i. 331 (*Mevo hatalmud*, ch. 26).

the film *A Few Good Men*).[38] Determining exactly what the esoteric teachings of Maimonides are has been central to the study of the *Guide* since medieval times, and the existence of an esoteric level has also been recognized by traditionalist scholars.[39]

Maimonides can thus be seen as in line with the position that absolute truth can be waived in the interest of religious conformity. In fact, if Maimonides wished to cite a precedent for this, it could have been R. Sa'adyah Gaon (882–942), in particular his explanation of the Jewish calendar. The standard approach is that originally the new moon was proclaimed every month on the basis of witnesses' testimony of its sighting. When this became too difficult, a permanent calendar based on calculation was established. However, R. Sa'adyah claims that the original system was indeed based on a calculated calendar, and that when witnesses testified that they had seen the new moon this was only done to blunt Sadducean criticism about the proper date.[40]

[38] We almost certainly see this approach elsewhere in Maimonides' writings as well. For example, Maimonides' claim in the introduction to his *Commentary on the Mishnah*, i. 11, that there are no disputes with regard to *halakhot lemosheh misinai*, is virtually impossible to justify. (For a discussion of *halakhot lemosheh misinai*, see *EJ*, vol. vii, col. 1167.) Levinger, *Maimonides' Techniques of Codification* (Heb.), 63 ff., cites this as an example of Maimonides responding to the needs of the masses by presenting them with an understanding of Judaism that would best be able to withstand the onslaught of Islamic polemics (or possibly Karaite assaults; see Maimonides, *Igerot harambam*, ii. 442; Baron, *Social and Religious History*, v. 22). See also my *Limits of Orthodox Theology*, 118 ff., and my *Studies in Maimonides and His Interpreters*, 85, 109–10.

[39] The assumption that certain rabbinic sages were not frank in everything they said also appears elsewhere. For example, R. Hayim Joseph David Azulai, *Shem hagedolim*, 'Ma'arekhet sefarim', s.v. 'Zohar', states that R. Jacob Emden did not really believe what he wrote in his *Mitpaḥat sefarim*, namely, that the Zohar is in large part a medieval work. According to Azulai, the reason Emden attempted to disprove the authenticity of the Zohar was to undermine the Shabateans, who were relying on certain zoharic passages. This understanding of Emden became quite popular in traditional circles, and is also shared by D. Luria, *Kadmut sefer hazohar*, 10; Nathanson, *Sho'el umeshiv*, 7th series, 'Ḥoshen mishpat', no. 54; A. I. Kook, *Otserot hare'iyah*, 264; Y. Leiner, *Ma'amar zohar harakia*, no. 16. Leiner claims that we should view Emden's denial of Maimonides' authorship of the *Guide* in the same way as his denial of the Zohar's authenticity, namely, as something he did not really believe but thought necessary to affirm in his battle against certain heretics. See also Arbel, *Aḥoti kalah*, 150, who claims that the Hazon Ish wrote something he did not really believe (namely, that Torah scholars are never improperly influenced) because he felt the times required that people should have this conviction. The same argument has been made with regard to R. Joel Teitelbaum's anti-Zionist 'proofs' from earlier rabbinic literature. See Aviner, *Aloh na'aleh*, 172–3 (citing a haredi source).

[40] All the relevant sources are found in Kasher, *Torah shelemah*, xiii, ch. 3. See also Jolles, *Hatorah vehaḥokhmah*, 207 ff.; Poznanski, 'Anti-Karaite Writings', 270 ff. An Arabic text by R. Sa'adyah Gaon on the matter appears in Zucker, 'Fragments' (Heb.), 376 n. 17. See also S. B. Lieberman, *Bishevilei haḥodesh*, ch. 3; A. Stern, 'Rabbi Sa'adyah Gaon's Teaching' (Heb.); Valter, 'Rabbi Sa'adyah Gaon's View' (Heb.); Halperin, 'Why Did Rabbi Sa'adyah Gaon Depart from the Truth?' (Heb.).

In other words, according to R. Sa'adyah the authority for the date of the new moon was always a calendar established by calculation.

This is such an astounding position that Maimonides denies that R. Sa'adyah actually believed it. Maimonides apparently did not know that R. Meshullam ben Kalonymos (tenth–eleventh centuries) and R. Hananel ben Hushiel (d. *c*.1055) also held this position,[41] but no doubt he would have explained their claims in the same way that he explained R. Sa'adyah's words: 'His purpose was to attack his opponent [i.e. the Karaites] in any possible way, *whether it was correct or not*, since he saw no other escape from the pressure of the dispute.'[42] During the geonic period there were great disputes between the Rabbanites and the Karaites about the proper dates of the holidays, and the Karaites claimed that the Rabbanite calendar was fraudulent.[43] Thus, by asserting that the calendar was not something developed by the Sages, but went all the way back to Moses at Sinai, R. Sa'adyah was able to neutralize the Karaite assault.[44]

Maimonides presumably knew of R. Sa'adyah's justification of his position, yet he cannot have taken what R. Sa'adyah wrote seriously.[45] It is significant that Maimonides thought that R. Sa'adyah would say something he did not believe in order to defend a Rabbanite position more effectively against Karaite assaults.[46] R. Hai Gaon (939–1038) also thought that R. Sa'adyah's explanation was a flimsy excuse made for the moment, which did not reflect his true opinion.[47]

[41] See Hananel ben Hushiel, *Migdal ḥananel*, 32 ff.; Bahya ben Asher, *Commentary* on Exod. 12: 2; and Y. H. Lifshitz, 'Secret of Intercalation' (Heb.). For R. Meshullam ben Kalonymos, see Moses of Coucy, *Sefer mitsvot gadol*, positive commandment no. 47.

[42] Maimonides, *Commentary on the Mishnah*, i, *RH* 2: 7 (p. 209).

[43] See e.g. Olszowy-Schlanger, *Karaite Marriage Documents*, 249–50.

[44] See Messer Leon, *Kevod ḥakhamim*, 57 ff.; Naor, *Limit of Intellectual Freedom*, 152. In the 19th cent. R. Solomon Judah Rapoport felt obliged to deny that he accepted R. Sa'adyah's position. See Greenwald, *Otsar neḥmad*, 84.

[45] Interestingly, R. Sa'adyah's position is advocated in the commentary on BT *RH* attributed to Maimonides. See Fixler, 'Polemical Language' (Heb.), 188–90. Fixler sees this as an example of an opinion that Maimonides would later strongly reject. However, most scholars do not share Fixler's assumption that this commentary was written by Maimonides. See Davidson, 'Authenticity', 114 ff.

[46] When Solomon Zeitlin made the same point, Saul Lieberman reacted strongly. See his letters to Zeitlin published in my *Saul Lieberman and the Orthodox*, 19 ff. (Hebrew section), and also S. Lieberman, 'Mishnat rishonim'. See also A. Stern, 'Rabbi Sa'adyah Gaon's Position' (Heb.), 37–8, who argues that R. Sa'adyah did indeed believe in his position.

[47] קנה הוא שדחה את אפיקורוס. See *Teshuvot hage'onim*, no. 1 (= Lewin (ed.), *Otsar hage'onim*, 'Beitsah' 4*b* (p. 4)). R. Hai's comment is based on BT *Ḥul.* 27*b*. Here it describes how one of the Sages admitted to his students that 'I brushed aside my opponent with a straw.' See also Nachshoni, *Hagut befarshiyot hatorah*, 137 ('Vayishlaḥ'), who suggests that R. Jonathan Eybeschuetz wrote something that he knew to be false, in order to more easily refute someone who was challenging an accepted halakhah. Although Nachshoni's point is incorrect with regard to the case

Certainly, this is not the only case we have of twisting the truth—if that is what R. Sa'adyah did[48]—in order to blunt the Karaites. Gerald Blidstein has pointed to a similar example in which he claims that R. Samuel ben Hofni (d. 1034) was not being truthful. R. Samuel ben Hofni claims that when dealing with a talmudic dispute, the accepted halakhic position is the one that was given at Sinai.[49] As Blidstein notes, while this type of argument makes sense in an Islamic context, where determining the reliability of a tradition is crucial, it is out of place in a Jewish context where halakhah is decided in a completely different fashion.[50] Indeed, contrary to what R. Samuel ben Hofni writes, Jewish sources never assumed that the settled halakhah reflects God's 'original intent'.[51] It therefore appears that R. Samuel ben Hofni was not frank in his presentation, and he likely intended to provide his coreligionists with an approach that could best withstand Islamic polemical assaults, even if it was not entirely accurate.

None of what I have just described will be surprising to those who are aware of the history of Jewish apologetics in Christendom. These writings also contain numerous examples of shadings of truth and sometimes even outright lies. However, for Jews living in the Christian world, such a strategy was often essential to the security of the Jewish community, whereas in R. Sa'adyah's and R. Samuel ben Hofni's cases we are dealing with a purely spiritual conflict.

When Can One Lie?

A good deal has been written on the subject of when one can depart from truthfulness, and I do not wish to repeat what has already been discussed by others.[52] Instead, I will focus on some issues that are particularly relevant to the theme of this book, as well as citing texts that are not well known.

he discusses, the fact that Nachshoni himself thought that this was an acceptable approach is more important for our purposes.

48 While Maimonides and R. Hai find R. Sa'adyah's position incomprehensible, R. Bahya ben Asher, in his comment on Exod. 12: 2, quotes it without objection.

49 See the *Introduction to the Talmud*, attributed to R. Samuel Hanagid (993–*c*.1056), at the end of tractate *Berakhot* in the Vilna Romm edition of the Talmud, p. 43*b*. We now know that it is an abridgement of a work by R. Samuel ben Hofni. See Abramson, 'From the Teachings' (Heb.), 22–3.

50 Blidstein, *Studies* (Heb.), 139 n. 17, 143.

51 That is the message of the story of the 'oven of Akhnai' (BT *BM* 59*b*). Even when God himself reveals his intention we do not listen to him, for the Torah was given to be explained through human intellect. See N. Gerondi, *Derashot haran*, 44–5, 84, 112, 198–9; Bacharach, *Ḥut hashani*, no. 53; A. L. Hakohen, *Ketsot haḥoshen*, introd. See also Englard, 'Majority Decision vs. Individual Truth'.

52 For previous discussions, see Hayim, *Torah lishmah*, no. 364; Stein, 'Behandlung'; N. Frimer, 'A Midrash on Morality'; Dratch, 'Nothing but the Truth?'; Zivotofsky, 'Perspectives on

The *locus classicus* for discussions of truthfulness is *Ketubot* 16*b*–17*a*:

Our Rabbis taught: How does one dance[53] before the bride? Beit Shammai says: 'The bride as she is.' Beit Hillel says: 'Beautiful and graceful bride.' Beit Shammai said to Beit Hillel: 'If she was lame or blind, does one say of her: "Beautiful and graceful bride?" Whereas the Torah said, "Keep thee far from a false matter" [Exod. 23: 7].' Said Beit Hillel to Beit Shammai: 'According to your words, if someone has made a bad purchase in the market, should one praise it in his [the purchaser's] eyes or deprecate it? Surely, one should praise it in his eyes.' Therefore, the Sages said: 'A man's disposition should always be pleasant with people.'

The most obvious understanding of this passage is that while Beit Shammai demands absolute truth, Beit Hillel does not.[54] In other words, while Beit Hillel would permit one to say that a bride is beautiful, even if she is not, Beit Shammai sees this as a violation of the Torah's command to keep far from a false matter. It is not that Beit Shammai requires one to say an unpleasant truth, just not to speak an untruth. Beit Shammai would also permit one to describe the bride as a 'beautiful person', in the way this expression is used when people are not speaking about someone's physical appearance.[55]

Beit Shammai thought that the verse 'Keep thee far from a false matter' was an actual command to avoid falsehood in all circumstances, while Beit Hillel disagreed. How do post-talmudic authorities regard the verse? Some important figures regard telling the truth as an obligation, and cite this verse as the proof text.[56] R. Simeon ben Tsemah Duran sees this as obvious, for, as he puts it, 'How is it possible that there would not be a positive commandment to speak the truth?'[57]

Truthfulness'; Hanokh Goldberg, 'Is It Halakhically Permissible to Lie?' (Heb.); Y. Cherlow, 'Keep Away from Falsehood' (Heb.); D. Z. Feldman, *The Right and the Good*, chs. 5 and 6; Bar Shalom, *Vayitsbor yosef*, vol. ii, no. 86; Y. Yosef, *Yalkut yosef: hilkhot kibud av va'em*, 477 ff.; Rosenfeld, 'When is Lying Permitted?' (Heb.); Y. H. Fish, *Titen emet leya'akov*; H. H. Friedman and A. C. Weisel, 'Should Moral Individuals Ever Lie?'; Frimer and Frimer, 'Women's Prayer Services', appendix, part 6.

[53] 'What does one say before her?' (Rashi).

[54] See e.g. Isaiah of Trani (the Younger), *Piskei hariaz*, 124; Yom Tov Ishbili (Ritva), *Ḥidushei haritva: ketubot*, ad loc.; Hayim, *Ben yehoyada*, ad loc.; Yellin, *Derekh tsadikim*, 13*a*–*b*; M. N. Friedman, *On Truth and Falsehood* (Heb.), 11; Anushiski, *Matsav hayashar*, i. 16*b*, 21*a*: 'In short, in order to praise a bride before her groom (after the actual marriage ceremony), it is permissible to lie in order to make him happy and to strengthen their relationship.'

[55] See Dratch, 'Nothing but the Truth?', 221.

[56] See e.g. Moses of Coucy, *Sefer mitsvot gadol*, positive commandment 107; Isaac of Corbeil, *Sefer mitsvot katan*, no. 227; Azikri, *Sefer ḥaredim*, 4: 26 (pp. 72–3): מצות עשה לדבר אמת אפילו במילי דעלמא דליכא בהו דררא דממונא שנאמר מדבר שקר תרחק משמע אפילו ליכא רק דבור בעלמא.

[57] Duran, *Zohar harakia*, 28*a*, no. 59.

Yet there are others who disagree and do not recognize a specific biblical command to tell the truth. As for 'Keep thee far from a false matter', they see this verse as only applicable to legal proceedings.[58] As Mark Dratch has pointed out, neither R. Simeon Kayara (author of *Halakhot gedolot*; ninth century), R. Sa'adyah Gaon, Maimonides, Nahmanides, nor *Sefer haḥinukh* records a commandment to tell the truth in non-judicial matters.[59]

There is a separate issue known as *geneivat da'at*, which means leaving someone with a false impression. An example given in the Talmud is when you urge someone to dine with you knowing that he will not accept, and in this way get 'credit' for the invitation.[60] This does not refer to a white lie, by which I mean a lie of no consequence. It is true that Maimonides says that 'One shall not be one thing with his mouth and another with his heart.' Yet this formulation appears to be more in the way of good advice than a prohibition,[61] and even if it is a prohibition, it does not have biblical authority.[62] For those halakhists who do not identify speaking falsely as a biblical prohibition, it is obviously easier to set the truth aside when confronted by other values.

As for Beit Shammai's objection to Beit Hillel that telling an untruth violates a biblical commandment, R. Tsevi Hirsch Chajes elaborates on Beit Hillel's reply. He asserts that the prohibition against lying was dependent for its details on the Sages. They were therefore able to decide that in this case (as well as others), where another person's feelings would be hurt, the general biblical prohibition against speaking falsely does not apply.[63]

Without such an approach, it would be very difficult to function in the real world. If one assumed that absolute truth was always required, what could you do if your friend gave you a present that you did not like? You would not be able to say, as we all do, 'I love it.' Similarly, if your friend asked you how her new haircut looked, you would be obligated to say that it makes her look

[58] See above, p. 245, where it was noted that R. Eliezer of Metz applies the verse to any damage caused to one's neighbour.

[59] Dratch, 'Nothing but the Truth?', 225.

[60] BT *Ḥul.* 94*a*.

[61] Maimonides, *Mishneh torah*, 'Hilkhot de'ot' 2: 6: אסור לאדם להנהיג עצמו בדברי חלקות ופתוי ולא תהיה אחת בפה ואחת בלב. It is not clear if the word אסור, 'forbidden', which appears in the first part of the sentence, applies to the underlined passage as well. Even if it does, the prohibition is specific to one who accustoms himself to such behaviour (להנהיג עצמו). See Rabinovitch, *Yad peshutah*, ad loc. Thus, an occasional white lie would not be technically forbidden, according to Maimonides. R. Jonah Gerondi, however, assumes that even white lies are forbidden. He includes making up stories or even changing the details of authentic stories in this judgement. See id., *Sha'arei teshuvah*, 3: 181, 183.

[62] See above, n. 34. R. Yeruham Fischel Perla assumes that there is no rabbinic prohibition against white lies. See his edition of Sa'adyah Gaon, *Sefer hamitsvot*, i. 158*a*–*b* (positive commandment 22): ואפי' איסורא דרבנן אינו ברור אצלי בזה כל דלא הוי אלא פטומי מילי בעלמא ואין בהן הפסד כלל לשום אדם, אלא דבר מגונה הוא, אבל איסורא ליכא אפי' מדבריהם . . . אין בו איסור כלל אפי' מדרבנן, אלא דמ"מ מדה מגונה ומגרעת היא לשקר בדבריו בכל ענין.

[63] Chajes, *Kol sifrei maharats ḥayes*, i. 166.

terrible. Beit Hillel's approach, on the other hand, establishes that not hurting people's feelings is a greater value than absolute truth. As Ritva comments, 'anything [said] due to the "ways of peace" is not in violation of "Keep thee far from a false matter".'[64]

Another talmudic text supporting this approach appears in *Eruvin* 53*b*, where R. Joshua ben Hananiah is described as lying to his hostess about why he would not eat her food. While the real reason was that it had been over-seasoned with salt, in order not to hurt her feelings he claimed that he was not hungry, having eaten earlier in the day. This excuse continues to be used by even the most pious when trying to avoid eating something they do not like. Fortunately for them, they are often able to point to the sumptuous synagogue kiddush to explain why they are not eating more of the Sabbath lunch meal.[65]

Despite what we have just seen, it is fascinating that some commentators were reluctant to interpret Beit Hillel's words, that one praises the beauty of all brides, in accordance with their plain sense. Thus, R. Samuel Edels claims that Beit Hillel is not really countenancing lying, since while it might be clear to those in attendance that the bride is no beauty, 'she is beautiful and graceful in his [i.e. the groom's] eyes, for if not he certainly would not have married her.'[66] R. Netanel Weil also denies that Beit Hillel sanctions lying. According to him, all Beit Hillel had in mind was to speak with equivocation, so that when one says 'beautiful and graceful', one has her actions in mind.[67] According to this understanding, while Beit Hillel would approve of equivocation, that is, using words that can be understood in more than one way, Beit Shammai would require that one's language reflect the common meaning of

[64] Yom Tov Ishbili (Ritva), *Ḥidushei haritva: ketubot*, 17*a*. See similarly Moses of Coucy, *Sefer mitsvot gadol*, positive commandment 107; Isaac of Corbeil, *Sefer mitsvot katan*, no. 226. Based on the principle just enunciated, R. Ovadyah Yosef ruled that a child whose father is mistreating his mother is permitted to tell the father (falsely) that he heard from a great rabbi that the father's behaviour is forbidden; see id., *Ma'yan omer*, iv. 123.

[65] For another example of lying related to food, see BT *Shab*. 129*a*, where R. Nahman ben Isaac tells his disciples: 'I beg of you, tell your wives on the day of blood-letting, Nahman is visiting us.' As Rashi explains, the purpose of this falsehood was so that their wives would prepare substantial meals. In other words, this was a good enough reason to permit the disciples to lie to their wives.

[66] Edels (Maharsha), ad loc. R. Judah Loew ben Bezalel (Maharal) adopts the same approach. See id., *Netivot olam*, 'Netiv ha'emet', ch. 1, p. 200: 'This is not called falsehood . . . even if the bride is not really beautiful, nevertheless she is beautiful in the eyes of the groom.'

[67] Weil, *Korban netanel*, 'Ketubot', ch. 2, 1: 4. See also B. Ashkenazi, *Shitah mekubetset*, ad loc.; Wosner, *Shevet halevi*, vol. v, no. 2; Falk, *Perishah*, 'Even ha'ezer' 65: 'Even though it is written, "Keep thee far from a false matter", we can say that what he means is that she is beautiful in her deeds.' See also R. Joseph Saul Nathanson, *Divrei sha'ul*, 'Ketubot' 17*a*, who advances an alternative explanation that the praise for the bride is a general praise about *all* brides, but not actually directed at this particular one. For more on equivocal language, see below, n. 184.

words and phrases. According to Beit Shammai, since 'beauty generally relates to physical traits rather than to character, this quality should not be applied to one who lacks physical beauty'.[68]

Elsewhere in the Talmud, *Yevamot* 65*b*, an opinion is quoted that one is permitted to deviate from the truth (i.e. lie) in the interests of peace, and R. Nathan states that one is obligated to do so.[69] In other words, the value of peaceful relations is more important than truth.[70] One of the proof texts cited in this discussion is Genesis 50: 16–17. After Jacob died, Joseph's brothers sent a message to him: 'Thy father did command before he died, saying, So shall ye say unto Joseph: Forgive, I pray thee now, the transgression of thy brethren, and their sin, for that they did unto thee evil.' Yet the Bible does not record Jacob making such a request. The Talmud understands this to mean that the brothers invented Jacob's statement in the interests of peace. Since this is recorded in Scripture without further comment, we are supposed to assume that their action was pleasing to God.[71]

In commenting on this biblical story, *Bereshit rabah* quotes R. Simeon ben Gamaliel as follows:

> Great is peace, for even the tribal ancestors resorted to a fabrication in order to make peace between Joseph and themselves. Thus it says, 'And they sent a message unto Joseph saying: Thy father did command', etc. Yet when did he command thus? We do not find that he did so.[72]

A parallel midrashic passage is more direct, going so far as to include Scripture itself as party to the falsehood: 'Reish Lakish said: Great is peace, for Scripture gave fictitious reasons in order to make peace between Joseph and his brethren.'[73] This permission to lie for the state of peace is the basis for the following common-sense ruling by R. Yitshak Yosef, the current Sephardi chief rabbi of Israel: if someone does something at his mother's request, and

[68] J. S. Cohen, 'Halakhic Parameters of Truth', 86. See also D. Z. Feldman, *The Right and the Good*, 78 ff.

[69] According to R. Israel Meir Hakohen, the halakhah is in accordance with R. Nathan's opinion. See I. M. Hakohen, *Ḥafets ḥayim*, 'Isurei rekhilut' 1: 8 (*Be'er mayim ḥayim*, n. 14). See also Palache, *Lev ḥayim*, vol. i, no. 5. Basing his opinion on Nahmanides' commentary on Gen. 18: 13, R. Moses Sofer claims that Nahmanides was not 'comfortable' with the common understanding of the talmudic passage that lying is permitted for the sake of peace. See M. Sofer, *She'elot uteshuvot ḥatam sofer*, vol. vi, no. 59. See Anushiski, *Matsav hayashar*, i. 22*b*, who responds sharply to Sofer's understanding.

[70] See also BT *Beits.* 20*a*, where Hillel lies in order to preserve peace.

[71] See also JT *Pe'ah* 1: 1. R. Hanokh Zundel ben Joseph, *Ets yosef*, on *Devarim rabah* 5: 14 writes: שהכתוב לא היה כותב השקר שלהם אם לא היה מותר לשנות מפני בקשת השלום.

[72] *Bereshit rabah* 100: 8.

[73] *Devarim rabah* 5: 14. The midrash is obviously speaking figuratively when it states that 'Scripture gave fictitious reasons', as the information given to Joseph came from his brothers, not from Scripture.

his father asks him who told him to do this, if he knows that his father will be angry at his mother if he tells the truth, he is permitted to lie.[74]

Another famous talmudic text is *Bava metsia* 23*b*–24*a*, which states that pious scholars are permitted, indeed expected, to lie in three matters: 'tractate, bed, and hospitality'. When asked if they are familiar with a tractate of the Talmud, they will conceal their knowledge.[75] When asked about their sexual life, they will also not be truthful, in order to preserve their modesty.[76] They will also not tell others what a fine host someone is, in order to prevent people from descending upon his house and demanding hospitality.

I do not know of any biblical examples where God himself speaks falsely, but we do find that he did not always tell the whole truth. Immediately following the example of Joseph and his brothers mentioned above, the Talmud, *Yevamot* 65*b*, states:

> At the school of R. Ishmael it was taught: Great is the cause of peace, seeing that for its sake even the Holy One, blessed be He, modified a statement. It is first written, '[After I am waxed old shall I have pleasure,] my lord being old also' [Gen. 18: 12] while afterwards it is written, 'And I am old' [Gen. 18: 13].

In other words, when God repeated Sarah's statement to Abraham, he left out her comment on her husband's age. To give a modern example of how this might be used, if your friend asks you what someone said about her, rather than telling her that he said she was 'pretty stupid', it would suffice to tell her 'He said you were pretty.'

Steven H. Resnicoff sums matters up as follows:

> The Talmud and later Jewish law authorities apply an expansive concept of 'promoting peace' to permit dishonest means for a variety of objectives, such as to make someone feel better, to avoid embarrassment, to prevent disclosure of a confidence with which one is entrusted, to foil an evildoer's plot, to avoid the exploitation of someone's virtues, to persuade someone as to the proper interpretation of the law, to cause someone to fulfill a commandment, or to enable someone to display personal humility.[77]

When it comes to the expansive concept of 'promoting peace' that was thought to be significant enough to permit lying, there are those who have adopted a somewhat conservative perspective. For example, *Sefer ḥasidim*,[78]

[74] Y. Yosef, *Yalkut yosef: hilkhot kibud av va'em*, 9: 49 (p. 477). Yosef's source is *Sefer ḥasidim*, no. 336.

[75] See also BT *Ket.* 77*b*, which tells how R. Joshua ben Levi lied because of his modesty. See also Gombiner, *Magen avraham* and D. Halevi, *Turei zahav* on Karo, *Shulḥan arukh*, 'Oraḥ ḥayim' 565: 6; H. S. Abraham, *Birkat shelomoh*, no. 43.

[76] This explanation is in accordance with Rashi, as was the previous example.

[77] Resnicoff, 'Lying and Lawyering', 964.

[78] No. 426.

followed by R. Abraham Gombiner,[79] states that the rule that one may lie to promote peace only applies with regard to events that have already occurred. However, with regard to what is taking place at present, or will happen in the future, one must tell the truth and deal with the consequences.[80] Because my purpose in this chapter is to chart the outer limits of what has been viewed as acceptable when it comes to falsehood and deception, I will be focusing on the more 'liberal' positions. My aim is to show just how far some rabbinic decisors were willing to go in sanctioning deviations from the truth. One must bear in mind, however, that there are often views in opposition to the ones I shall be examining. Perhaps this knowledge can serve as a counterweight to the shock that many readers will experience upon learning of some of the positions I will mention.

One 'liberal' position was expressed by R. Moses Isserles, who went so far as to say that one can even slander someone for the sake of preserving the community.[81] The particular case he was discussing concerned a terrible communal dispute that had created the possibility that the Jewish population would be expelled from the city. In what many will find a problematic decision, Isserles offered the opinion, which was then put into action, that it was acceptable to provide false information about an individual whom the government suspected of wrongdoing, if this would alleviate the situation. Although the Talmud states, with regard to giving a man up for execution in response to a demand made by non-Jews, that this is not the way of the pious,[82] Isserles defended his approach: 'Even if we did not act in accord with the way of the pious, nevertheless, we acted in accord with the law. I have proven that it is permitted to speak *leshon hara* [slander] in order to preserve peace.'

False Attribution

False attribution is another genre where a number of talmudic sages and later rabbinic figures saw mendacity as justified in the name of a larger concern. (The decision as to when this 'larger concern' should be acted upon was a prerogative of the community of scholars, as the masses were never given this leeway.) This type of falsehood is not acceptable in contemporary society. Undoubtedly, many modern readers are thus bound to feel quite troubled when seeing how a value—honesty—that they take to be sacrosanct was not regarded as such by at least some great rabbinic figures.

79 Gombiner, *Magen avraham*, on Karo, *Shulḥan arukh*, 'Oraḥ ḥayim' 156.

80 For opinions that disagree with this restrictive approach, see Palache, *Lev ḥayim*, vol. i, no. 5.

81 Isserles, *She'elot uteshuvot harama*, no. 11.

82 JT *Ter.* 8: 4.

R. Yair Hayim Bacharach acknowledges the difficulty of the passages we will examine, but advises readers, 'do not let your heart fall' upon seeing these sources. He concludes that the actions described are permissible when there is a 'higher purpose' (*tsorekh gavo'ah*), namely, to teach practical halakhah. In such cases, the sages did not feel bound by the normal requirements of honesty in attribution.[83]

The situation in rabbinic literature is complicated by the fact that in general the Sages regarded proper attribution as very important.[84] Indeed, the entire system of the Oral Law depends on authenticity in transmission, and virtually every page of the Talmud has examples of teachings recorded in the name of a particular sage.[85] R. Hanina goes so far as to say that one who quotes something in the name of another brings redemption to the world.[86] Furthermore, a dead person's lips are said to move in the grave when a Torah teaching is repeated in his name.[87]

By the same token, one is not supposed to cite something in another person's name if he never said it. Quite apart from the statement in Mishnah *Avot* 5: 7 that a wise man openly acknowledges when he has not heard something from someone else, according to the end of the post-talmudic tractate *Kalah*, one who falsely attributes a statement to a sage causes the divine presence to depart from Israel. According to the halakhic Midrash *Sifrei*, one who falsely attributes an opinion violates the biblical prohibition 'Thou shalt not remove thy neighbour's landmark' (Deuteronomy 19: 14).[88] Yet as we shall see, despite the vital importance of authentic attribution, many sages also recognized that there was indeed a time and place for false attribution.[89]

One other point must be noted. We know that the editors of the Talmud exercised a good deal of freedom in editing the various *sugyot*. As part of this

[83] Bacharach, *Ya'ir nativ*, 13.

[84] See R. Shmuel Aharon Fish's comprehensive work, *Davar beshem omro*. See also M. Rabinowitz, *Amirat davar beshem omro* and R. Margaliyot, *Shem olam*, 9 ff. Regarding an apocryphal rabbinic saying that one who does not properly attribute a teaching violates a negative commandment, see S. Ashkenazi, *Alfa beita tinyeta dishemuel ze'ira*, i. 454 ff.

[85] See e.g. M. Hakohen, *Yad malakhi*, no. 663.

[86] BT *Meg.* 15*a*.

[87] BT *Yev.* 97*a*. R. Levi Ibn Habib notes: 'From the great reward for one who says something in the name of another, that he brings redemption to the world, we learn the punishment of one who falsely attributes something to another.' Ibn Habib, *She'elot uteshuvot haralbaḥ*, no. 31 (p. 18*a*).

[88] *Sifrei devarim*, ad loc. See also JT *Naz.* 7: 1 where R. Aha states that a student who had (intentionally?) falsely attributed a teaching to him should be flogged.

[89] False attribution in Jewish literature certainly existed before the rabbinic period. I refer in particular to the pseudepigraphical works from before the Common Era that place words of prophecy and wisdom in the mouths of ancient figures. I am assuming that these are examples of false attribution, although it is also possible that the authors of these texts were convinced that the ancients spoke through their pens.

editing, material thought to be illuminating was put in the mouths of various figures. While from a modern perspective these would be examples of false attribution, from the talmudic perspective all that has been done is to expand on an authentic position, with the assumption being that the expansion follows from the original statement,[90] or that the figure being quoted could have said this, based upon what else is known of him.[91] This type of 'false attribution' is of a very different character from the other examples we will examine, where the intent is to deceive rather than to enlighten.

There are a number of talmudic examples that support false attribution.[92] *Eruvin* 51*a* describes how Rabbah and R. Joseph were discussing a halakhic matter. In order to persuade R. Joseph to accept Rabbah's opinion, the latter reported that R. Jose also shared his viewpoint. The Talmud comments upon this: 'This, however, was not exactly correct. He attributed the teaching to R. Jose with the sole object that he [R. Joseph] should accept it from him, since R. Jose was known to have sound reasons for his rulings.' Rashi explains that Rabbah did not attribute his own view to R. Jose. Rather, he knew such a halakhic teaching, which he felt was correct. Wishing others to accept it, he falsely attributed it to the great sage R. Jose. R. Paltoi Gaon (ninth century) also understands the text in this fashion, and stresses that before engaging in such false attribution one must be certain as to the halakhah.[93]

[90] See Albeck, *Mavo latalmudim*, 504 ff. Albeck cites the comment of R. Abraham ben David of Posquières (Rabad), quoted in R. Solomon ben Adret, *Ḥidushei harashba* on BT *Eruv.* 19*b*: לאו רב פפא גופיה הוא דמפרש לה אלא אנן הוא דמפרשא לן מדברי רב פפא וכיון דמדידיה מפרשא לן תלי ליה בדרב פפא. See also Tosafot, BT *BK* 73*b*, s.v. *amar*: ולא אמר אביי זה מעולם אלא בני הישיבה היו מתרצים כן אליבא דאביי לפי מה שהיו סוברים; Ehrenberg, *Devar yehoshua*, i, no. 41: 3: דאע״פ שריב״ל לא אמרה בפירוש משום דלא אצטריך לי׳ כנ״ל שפיר יכולין להכניס גם ד״ז בדברי ריב״ל כיון שהי׳ ראוי לאומרו וכה״ג לא מיחזי כשיקרא.

[91] See Frankel, *Mevo hayerushalmi*, 35*a*; Zweifel, *Saneigor*, 73; J. Kaplan, *Redaction of the Babylonian Talmud*, 154 ff.

[92] For an exhaustive discussion of the texts I deal with from BT *Eruv.* 51*a* and *Pes.* 112*a*, see Maged, *Beit aharon*, 402 ff. Regarding the larger issue of false attribution, the following articles are also helpful and do not always agree with my own perspective: L. Jacobs, 'How Much of the Babylonian Talmud Is Pseudepigraphic?'; S. Stern, 'Attribution and Authorship'; and Bregman, 'Pseudepigraphy in Rabbinic Literature'.

[93] Lewin (ed.), *Otsar hage'onim*, 'Berakhot' 27*b* (p. 61): האומר דבר שלא שמע מפי רבו אם אומרה על שמו אי לא. אם מכיר באותה שמועה שהוא כהלכה ואין מקבלין אותה ממנו אומרה משום רבו כדי שיקבלו ממנו ואם אין ברור לו שהלכה היא אל יתלה ברבו. Concerning the text from BT *Eruv.* 51*a*, it is important to note the following: while the Talmud states that R. Jose never said that which was attributed to him (and this halakhah indeed appears without a name attached to it in *Eruv.* 50*b*), in Tosefta, *Eruv.* 3: 16, R. Jose's name *is* attached to it. In other words, the editor who added 'This, however, was not exactly correct . . .' was unaware of the Tosefta that Rabbah was quoting. He therefore assumed, incorrectly, that Rabbah had provided a false attribution. (In a letter to me, R. Meir Mazuz cited this passage as one of a number that show that the Tosefta was not known by the editors of the Babylonian Talmud.)

This text, and its suggested explanations, could not be any more clear that honesty is to be sacrificed in the name of a larger goal, namely, conformity to proper halakhic behaviour. In justifying this approach from an ethical standpoint, R. Yair Hayim Bacharach writes that the originator of a statement that is later falsely attributed to someone greater than he can be assumed to be amenable to this, in order to best achieve the important task of properly establishing the halakhah.[94] Based upon what we have just seen, it is not surprising that a popular nineteenth-century work, which can be best described as an 'ethical code', writes as follows: 'If someone heard a law and it seems to him that the halakhah is in accord with this, it is permitted to repeat this law in the name of a great man so that people will accept it.'[95]

While Rashi understands the Talmud to be referring to a case in which Rabbah was acquainted with a real halakhic teaching, and it is only the attribution that is false,[96] it is possible that this understanding is intended to soften the radicalism of the passage. Unlike Rashi, one can read the talmudic text as meaning that Rabbah himself was the originator of the halakhic teaching that he falsely attributed to R. Jose. If this is so, then the meaning is that whenever one is certain of a halakhah, even if he did not hear it from someone else he can falsely attribute it, in order that the halakhah achieve wide acceptance. This understanding was shared by, among others, R. Samuel Kolin (*c*.1720–1806)[97] and R. Solomon Kluger.[98] R. Aryeh Kaplan (1934–83) explains this position as follows: 'When a rabbi is positive of his conclusions . . . [h]e may even, if the situation warrants, ascribe the decision to a great sage so that it will be generally accepted.'[99]

[94] Bacharach, *Ya'ir nativ*, 13. A different perspective is offered by R. Jacob Shalom Sofer, *Torat ḥayim*, 'Oraḥ ḥayim' 156, who states that one is only permitted to falsely attribute something to a great scholar when it is a non-halakhic matter, such as an ethical teaching.

[95] Trives, *Oraḥ meisharim*, 9: 5.

[96] See also R. David Fraenkel (*c*.1704–62), *Sheyarei korban*, 'Nazir' 7: 1 (34*a*), that it is forbidden to attribute a ruling of one's own to one's teacher, but there is no prohibition against attributing an anonymous ruling to him.

[97] Kolin, *Maḥatsit hashekel*, 'Oraḥ ḥayim' 156, s.v. *im shama*: אם יודע שהדבר ההוא דבר ברור ואין בו לפקפק ודאי או שיודע ברבו שאינו מקפיד בכזה אם כוונתו לשם שמים כי היכי דלקבלו מיניה מותר.

[98] S. Kluger, *Sefer haḥayim*, no. 156 (who even recommends false attribution): וראוי לומר דבר זה בשם חכם כדי לקבלו מני' בדבר הלכה. See also Tursh, *Moznei tsedek*, 230; A. D. Horowitz, *Kinyan torah bahalakhah*, vol. vii, no. 74 (p. 92); O. Yosef, *Yabia omer*, vol. ii, 'Ḥoshen mishpat', no. 3 (p. 270); Silver, *Emet keneh*, 35.

[99] A. Kaplan, *Handbook of Jewish Thought*, 251. Can the passage in BT *Eruv*. 51*a* be brought into line with the passage at the end of *Kalah* that states that one who falsely attributes a statement to a sage causes the divine presence to depart from Israel? Many scholars have discussed the apparent contradiction. According to R. Hayim Joseph David Azulai, the permission given in *Eruvin* to attribute something falsely only applies to a learned person who is able to arrive at halakhic decisions independently. Once he arrives at such a decision, the false attribution is designed to

R. Israel Lipschutz agrees with this approach, adding that one must be certain of the halakhah in order to attribute it to one's teacher falsely. Yet he adds that one does not have the same responsibility to another Torah scholar. Regarding the latter, it is permitted to attribute a halakhic teaching to him even if you are not certain that it is correct![100] Surprisingly, while Lipschutz attempts to show why this will not reflect poorly on the scholar who is being (falsely) quoted, he never even raises the problem of other people who will hear the false attribution of this uncertain halakhah and be led to act incorrectly as a result.

Another talmudic text that is cited to prove that false attribution is acceptable—although in this case there are a few different ways of understanding the passage—is *Pesaḥim* 112*a*. Here R. Akiva instructs R. Simeon ben Yohai: 'If you wish to be strangled, be hanged on a large tree.' As the Soncino Talmud explains, this means: 'If you must depend on an authority, see that he is a great one.'

It is unlikely that this passage refers to false attribution. In fact, R. Akiva's statement originates in a Greek proverb that has no connection to falsehood of any sort.[101] The statement probably means nothing more than if you study with a great scholar you will be able to pass on his teachings.[102] Alternatively, it could be advising someone who wishes his opinion to be accepted to find a great authority who says the same thing. The text could also be understood as a warning, that if you attribute something falsely you will be 'hanged' (punished). That is, this is a bad thing to do.[103] Even Rashi, who seems to be advis-

enable this ruling to be accepted. Tractate *Kalah*, which forbids false attribution, is referring to all other cases. See Azulai, *Maḥazik berakhah*, 'Oraḥ ḥayim' 156: 7; id., *Kise raḥamim*, 'Kalah' (end). The same approach is followed by Najar, *Simḥat yehudah*, 'Kalah' (end). For other attempted solutions, all of which affirm the validity of false attributions in certain cases, see E. Shapira, *Eliyah rabah*, 156: 2; S. Kluger, *Sefer haḥayim*, no. 156; H. Kanievsky, *She'elat rav*, ii. 16–17; S. A. Fish, *Davar beshem omro*, 151; Attiah, *Rov dagan*, 'Eruvin' 51*a*. Attiah concludes: 'Everything depends on his intention, that his intention be for the sake of heaven and not for self-interest.' See also R. Malkiel Tsevi Tenenbaum, *Divrei malki'el*, vol. ii, no. 74, who claims that false attribution is only forbidden with regard to one's primary teacher (*rav muvhak*).

[100] Lipschutz, *Tiferet yisra'el*, 'Avot' 5: 7 (*Bo'az* no. 2). R. Shmuel Wosner notes that he is aware of a number of cases in which great rabbis were upset that false teachings had been attributed to them by people who thought that this was halakhically permissible. See id., *Shevet halevi*, xiv, no. 46 (called to my attention by R. Yonason Rosman).

[101] See S. Lieberman, *Greek in Jewish Palestine*, 138–9.

[102] See R. Samuel ben Meir (Rashbam), commentary on BT *Pes.*, ad loc.; Trives, *Oraḥ meisharim*, 9: 5 n. 9. R. Hananel ben Hushiel's commentary, ad loc., has a different interpretation. See also the *Arukh*, quoted in *Masoret hashas* (in standard edns. of the Talmud), ad loc.

[103] See Menasheh of Ilya, *Alfei menasheh*, ii. 48–9 (called to my attention by R. Moshe Tsuriel); Joseph Joske of Lublin, *Yesod yosef hamevo'ar*, ch. 46, p. 216; *Sefer ḥasidim*, 'Mekor ḥesed' 977: 2; Reifman, 'Explanations' (Heb.), 41; Rogovin, 'Amar mar', 14.

ing false attribution,[104] is not entirely clear, and we cannot be sure that this is his meaning.

Yet there are a number of outstanding authorities, beginning with R. Natronai Gaon (ninth century),[105] who do indeed interpret this passage in the same way as the passage from *Eruvin* already mentioned. That is, they understand it to be advising false attribution. Among those who adopt this approach are R. Abraham Gombiner,[106] R. Yair Hayim Bacharach,[107] R. Hayim Joseph David Azulai,[108] R. Barukh Teomim-Frankel (1760–1828),[109] R. Solomon Kluger,[110] R. Moses Sofer,[111] R. Zechariah Isaiah Jolles (1816–52),[112] R. Hayim Palache,[113] R. Israel Lipschutz,[114] R. Elijah Benamozegh,[115] R. Naphtali Hertz Halevi (1852–1902),[116] and R. Hayim Hezekiah Medini.[117] Using this passage, and maintaining a distinction between scholars and the masses, R. Moses Kunitz concludes as follows: 'A scholar is permitted to lie in order to establish the truth[!] [to the extent that it is] in his power.[118] . . . But a negative commandment of the Torah forbids an *am ha'arets* [uneducated person] from ever telling a lie.'[119] What Kunitz is saying—and the other

[104] Rashi, commentary on the Talmud, ad loc.: אם בקשת ליחנק: לומר דבר שיהיה נשמע לבריות ויקבלו ממך. היתלה באילן גדול: אמור בשם אדם גדול.

[105] Natronai Gaon, *Teshuvot rav natronai gaon*, vol. ii, nos. 223–4. He assumes that a halakhah quoted by R. Ya'akov Gaon in the name of R. Yehudai Gaon is not authentic: ודאמר נמי משום רב יהודאי איכא למימר דלא אמרה מר רב יהודאי אלא מלתא אסתברא ליה ולא קבלוה בני דאריה מיניה ותליא במר רב יהודאי כדאמר [!] רבנן אם בקשתה ליחנק תתלה באילן גדול.

[106] Gombiner, *Magen avraham*, 'Oraḥ ḥayim' 156.

[107] Bacharach, *Ya'ir nativ*, 13.

[108] Azulai, *Birkei yosef*, 'Yoreh de'ah' 242: 29, 'Ḥoshen mishpat' 12: 13.

[109] Teomim-Frankel, *Ateret ḥakhamim*, 'Even ha'ezer', no. 29.

[110] S. Kluger, *Sefer haḥayim*, no. 156.

[111] M. Sofer, *She'elot uteshuvot ḥatam sofer*, vol. vi, no. 59. In this responsum, Sofer wonders if a certain rabbi has falsely quoted something in the name of Sofer's teacher, R. Nathan Adler. Rather than be outraged at this possibility, Sofer shows himself to be quite understanding, since he assumes that the false attribution was done for a good reason: ומ"ש שהרב אמר משם אמ"ו זצ"ל לא שמעתי מפיו ואולי התיר הרב לעצמו ע"ד שאמרו חז"ל רצית להחנק תתלה באילן גדול ואל תאשימהו עבור זה. It is in this context of false attribution that Sofer quotes, and agrees with, R. Jacob Emden's view of the Zohar (see below, n. 137). On the other hand, Sofer is also quoted as having said, 'I forgive you if you say my novellae [*ḥidushim*] in *your* name, but I do not forgive you if you say your novellae in *my* name.' See *Otserot hasofer*, 14 (5764), 91.

[112] *Dover meisharim*. In this book, Jolles shows that a work of talmudic notes attributed to R. Mordechai Jaffe is actually a forgery. Apparently, this forger had no nefarious motives. He simply wanted people to read what he wrote, and therefore falsely attributed it to a great sage. Jolles states (p. 7*a*): 'We should not find the author culpable for attributing his notes to the *Levush*, because he relied on the saying of R. Akiva: "If you wish to be strangled", etc.' For a similar defence of Saul Berlin and Solomon Friedlaender, who respectively forged the *Besamim rosh* and Jerusalem Talmud on 'Kodashim', see M. Abraham, *Enosh keḥatsir*, 468.

[113] Palache, *Heḥafets ḥayim*, 19: 18.

[114] Lipschutz, *Tiferet yisra'el*, 'Avot' 5: 7 (*Bo'az*, no. 2).

[115] Benamozegh, *Ta'am leshad*, 30.

[116] See Medini, *Sedei ḥemed*, ii, 'Ma'arekhet kaf', no. 8.

[117] Ibid., 'Ma'arekhet lamed', no. 108.

[118] תלמיד חכם רשאי לשקר, למען הקים האמת בכחו.

[119] Kunitz, *Hametsaref*, ii. 30.

authorities cited in this paragraph agree with him—is that scholars have the responsibility of making sure that the masses behave in accordance with halakhah. This is the highest 'truth', and in order to reach it, they are permitted to tell the masses a falsehood.

In addition to the passages from *Eruvin* and *Pesaḥim* already cited, there are a number of other rabbinic texts that show a tolerance for false attribution. A passage in the midrashic work *Tana devei eliyahu* focuses on Exodus 32: 26–7, in which, during the Golden Calf episode, we have the following description:

Then Moses stood in the gate of the camp, and said: 'Whoso is on the Lord's side, let him come to me,' and all the sons of Levi gathered themselves unto him. And he said to them: 'Thus saith the Lord, the God of Israel: Put ye every man his sword upon his thigh, and go to and fro from gate to gate throughout the camp, and slay every man his brother, and every man his companion, and every man his neighbour.'

Tana devei eliyahu comments:

I call heaven and earth to witness, however, that the Holy One said to Moses no such thing as that he was to stand at the gate of the camp and ask, 'Whoso is on the Lord's side. . . .'. Moses, righteous man that he was, justified [his attribution to God of his command to the sons of Levi] in this way: If, on my own, I were to say to Israel, 'Slay every man his brother and every man his companion, and every man his neighbour,' Israel would say, 'Did you not teach us, "A Sanhedrin that puts even one man to death in a week [of years] is called a tyrannical tribunal"?[120] Why, then, are you about to slay three thousand men in a single day?' Therefore, [in order to avert Israel's reproach of him, he attributed this command to the sons of Levi to slay the worshipers of the Golden Calf] to the Glory that is above, by 'Thus saith the Lord the God of Israel.'[121]

R. Yeruham Leiner (1888–1964) cites this passage and suggests that the Sages' permission to make false attributions is derived from this very episode.[122]

120 See Mishnah, *Mak.* 1: 10.

121 *Tana devei eliyahu* 4: 1; trans. Braude and Kapstein, 38–9. For discussion of this passage, see A. J. Heschel, *Heavenly Torah* (Heb.), ii. 143–5; Hoberman, *Ze'ev yitrof*, 368; Fisher, *Birkat eliyahu*, 25–6; Tursh, *Moznei tsedek*, 150. Among those who connect this passage to BT *Eruv.* 51*a* are Teomin-Frankel, *Ateret ḥakhamim*, 'Even ha'ezer', no. 29, and the commentary on *Tana devei eliyahu* entitled *Ramatayim tsofim* (Warsaw, 1881). (The title page says that this book was written by R. Samuel of Sieniawa (*c*.1796–1874). However, in his article 'Biography' (Heb.), 47, R. Joseph Levenstein admits that he wrote the book but due to a 'hidden reason' did not publicize his authorship. I thank R. Shmuel Ashkenazi for calling this to my attention. For sources on Levenstein, see Assaf, *Caught in the Thicket* (Heb.), 140 n. 8.)

122 See his notes printed as an appendix to Hayim ben Solomon, *Torat ḥayim*, 7. Abarbanel points to another example where he claims that Moses did not tell the truth when speaking to the nation. See his commentary on Num. 13: 1 (p. 62 in the standard edition).

The Talmud records a case where Rabbah behaves in the same fashion. *Shabat* 114*b*–115*a* explains what actions can be performed on Yom Kippur that falls on the Sabbath, in order to have food ready as soon as the fast is over. These actions are only permitted in the afternoon but not before then. The Talmud then states: 'Rabbah's household scraped pumpkins. Seeing that they were doing this [too] early, he said to them: "A letter has come from the west in Rabbi Yohanan's name that this is forbidden."'

Rashi explains that Rabbah's purpose in saying that he received a letter was to persuade his family to accept what he was telling them. In other words, Rabbah lied to his family in order to keep them from stumbling into sin.[123] R. Hayim David Halevi (1924–98) notes, 'From here one can learn that even absolute falsehood is permitted if the intention is to keep people from sinning.'[124] Commenting on this passage, R. Moses Leiter writes: 'Regarding the fact that he testified falsely about something, apparently this was common among them [the Sages], and they did not regard this as having anything to do with falsehood [*sheker*].'[125]

The same approach appears in *Pesaḥim* 27*a*. Here the Talmud explains that Samuel falsely attributed a stringent ruling of R. Judah to the Sages, in order that the people would follow this ruling. In *Bava metsia* 8*b* it states that Samuel ascribed R. Meir's viewpoint to the Sages, so that it would be accepted.[126] The *amora* (talmudic sage) Levi is described as doing the same thing in *Gitin* 20*a*. According to Rashi, this approach is found in *Kidushin* 44*b*, where an opinion of the *amora* Karna is attributed to Samuel so that Rav should take it more seriously.[127] These cases should be distinguished from many other examples in the Talmud where an individual tannaitic opinion is

[123] See the discussion of this passage in Y. H. Sofer, *Kerem ya'akov*, 13: 10.

[124] H. D. Halevi, *Aseh lekha rav*, iv. 303. However, in an unpublished responsum Halevi argued that a halakhic authority may *not* misrepresent halakhah, both because of the prohibition of avoiding falsehood as well as the concern that rabbinic authority will be undermined if the truth becomes known. See Frimer and Frimer, 'Women's Prayer Services', appendix, part 6.

[125] Leiter, *Beshulei gilyoni*, 'Shabat' 115*a*.

[126] See Rashi, ad loc., s.v. *umide'apikh*: ומשום דיחיד ורבים הלכה כרבים אפכה למתני' לאוקמה פטורא כרבנן.

[127] Rashi, ad loc., s.v. *afkhuhah*. R. Samuel Strashun (1794–1872) is very surprised by Rashi's explanation: תימה וכי משוא פנים יש בכזה והרי הש"ס מלא בפלוגתות דרב ושמואל. R. Isaiah Berlin's (1725–99) language is much sharper, even suggesting that Rashi's explanation is a later interpolation. See his *Ḥidushei hashas*, ad loc., also included in the Oz Vehadar edition of the Talmud: עמדתי מרעיד וכי ח"ו נחשד רב שהי' חסיד גדול דבשביל לחנופי לאוהבו יאמר לדינא דבר שאינו על צד האמת והלא אף אדם בינוני אינו עושה כן וכ"ש רב שהי' גדול למאוד . . . ואלולי דמסתפינ' ה"א דאיזה תלמיד כתב זה ונדפס אח"כ ברש"י. Clearly troubled by this story, R. Elijah ben Samuel of Lublin (18th cent.), *Yad eliyahu*, no. 61, questions whether those who misattributed Karna's opinion acted properly. For another example of (unintentional?) false attribution, but without any halakhic implications, see BT *Shev.* 19*a*. For other instances showing how the Talmud is often not careful with attributions, see Y. Heilprin, *Seder hadorot*, introd., pp. 72 ff.

attributed to the Sages.[128] In the latter examples the 'name change' was not designed to deceive. It merely signifies that the viewpoint of the individual *tana* (mishnaic sage) was regarded as the accepted halakhah, as it was agreed to by the majority of the Sages.[129]

Bava batra 111*a* describes how R. Huna b. Hiya was going to decide the halakhah in accordance with a particular view. When challenged, he declared that he was relying upon what R. Huna had said in the name of Rav. R. Nahman did not believe him and declared that he was going to ask R. Huna if he really held this position. Upon hearing this, R. Huna b. Hiya 'grew embarrassed'. R. Samuel ben Meir (Rashbam) explains that he was embarrassed because perhaps R. Huna no longer held this opinion or did not rely on it in practice. Yet R. Gershom (tenth–eleventh centuries) explains that he was embarrassed because he had falsely attributed the teaching to R. Huna.

According to Tosafot,[130] R. Joshua lied about his halakhic opinion, apparently in order to avoid getting into a dispute with R. Gamaliel. R. Hayim Hezekiah Medini notes that according to Tosafot,[131] R. Papa also presented false information in an argument in order to make it easier for Abaye to abandon his opinion.[132] Medini points to another talmudic passage that can be understood along the same lines. *Ḥulin* 111*b* states:

[128] These examples can be found by searching in the Talmud for the words *man ḥakhamim*. See also Judah ben Kalonymos, *Yiḥusei tana'im ve'amora'im*, 324, 364. In BT *Git*. 77*a* we see that R. Hiya altered the attribution of a teaching from R. Judah to the majority of the Sages, but the Sages were not happy with this. Maimonides himself follows this approach on at least one occasion. Whereas BT *Ber*. 34*b* attributes to Samuel the view that 'the sole difference between the present and the messianic days is delivery from servitude to foreign powers', Maimonides attributes this view to the Sages, even though Samuel's position is disputed by R. Johanan. See id., *Mishneh torah*, 'Hilkhot teshuvah' 9: 2, 'Hilkhot melakhim' 12: 2; Benedikt, *Collected Essays* (Heb.), 141, 156–7. See also *Mishneh torah*, 'Hilkhot melakhim' 11: 3, where Maimonides states that '*all the sages* of his [R. Akiva's] generation' believed that Bar Kokhba was the messiah, though there are talmudic passages that contradict this. See Aviner, *Aloh na'aleh*, 273. According to R. Isaac Berechiah, R. Menahem Azariah da Fano's (1548–1620) son, Maimonides would on occasion even switch the names of disputing sages so that his own opinion would be in line with that of the authoritative sage. See da Fano, *She'elot uteshuvot harama mifano*, no. 90. Azulai, *Ahavat david*, 84*b* (10th sermon), defends R. Isaac Berechiah's suggestion. (He is more sceptical in *Yosef omets*, no. 63.) Needless to say, this is a very radical proposal and, as far as I know, is not supported by modern scholarship. In fact, if a modern scholar made such a suggestion, it would be regarded by traditionalists as a disgraceful assault on Maimonides' integrity. Yet here are Azulai's words: ומזה למד הרמב״ם דהסברא שנראה בעיניו אמיתית הגם דלפי נסחתו אמרה תנא או אמורא שאין הלכה כמותו רב גובריה להפך השמות וסברא שהיא אמת לדעתו הוא מיחסה לתנא או אמורא שהלכה כמותו.

[129] For other examples where the Talmud, for stylistic reasons and with no intent to deceive, inserts words in the mouths of individuals, see Maged, *Beit aharon*, x. 14 ff.

[130] BT *Bekh*. 36*a*, s.v. *hei'akh*.

[131] BT *Naz*. 39*a*, s.v. *amar rav papa*.

[132] *Sedei ḥemed*, iii, 'Ma'arekhet shin', no. 27: הרי כדי להטות דעת אביי למה שהוא האמת (לסברת רב פפא) התיר לעצמו לדבר שקר.

Rabbi Eleazar was once standing before Mar Samuel, who was being served with fish upon a [meat] plate and was eating it with milk sauce. He [Samuel] offered him some but he would not eat it. He [Samuel] said to him, 'I once offered some to your Master [Rav] and he ate it, and you won't eat it.' He [R. Eleazar] then came to Rav and asked him, 'Has my master withdrawn his view?' He replied, 'Heaven forfend that the son of Abba b. Abba [Samuel] should give me to eat that which I do not hold [to be permitted].'[133]

Apparently, Samuel lied to R. Eleazar about Rav having eaten this food.[134] As Medini explains, if one assumes that it is permitted to deceive another in order to bring him to the halakhic truth, Samuel's statement to R. Eleazar is understandable.

R. Jacob Emden refers to this 'liberal' perspective on false attribution in discussing the authorship of the Zohar.[135] As is well known, this book is attributed to the second-century sage R. Simeon ben Yohai. However, Emden pointed to all sorts of problems with this attribution, at least with regard to most sections of the Zohar. How then should one understand the ascription to R. Simeon ben Yohai? Emden suggests that since the kernel of the Zohar goes back to him, despite the fact that it was actually composed much later, R. Simeon ben Yohai can still be regarded as the 'father' of the work. Another approach offered by Emden is that the Zohar (or at least the majority of it) is simply a pseudepigraphical work, written by someone in medieval times but with the appearance of a much earlier book.[136] In other words, it is a literary forgery.[137]

133 Rashi, ad loc., s.v. *delispei*, explains: לא היו דברים מעולם: 'It never happened.'

134 This is such a shocking text that all sorts of reinterpretations have been offered, though some of the reinterpretations are just as troubling. One such example is R. Issachar Ber Eylenburg's (1550–1623) suggestion that Samuel did not lie to R. Eleazar. Rather, he actually gave the food to Rav and Rav unknowingly ate it. Why would Samuel do such a thing, giving food to Rav that the latter thought was non-kosher? Eylenburg explains that Samuel knew that God does not permit a righteous person to consume non-kosher food (see BT *Yev.* 99*b*). Therefore, he conducted an experiment with Rav as the unwitting subject. If he ate the food—which he did—it could only mean that Samuel's halakhic viewpoint was correct! See Eylenburg, *Be'er sheva*, 'Ḥulin' 111*b*. (p. 81*b*). See also de Medina, *She'elot uteshuvot maharashdam*, 'Yoreh de'ah', no. 227.

135 Emden, *Mitpaḥat sefarim*, 4–5, 13–14, 174.

136 Emden was unaware of evidence that R. Moses de Leon engaged in other pseudepigraphic activity. See Wolfson, 'Hai Gaon's Letter'.

137 Although it is not well known, R. Moses Sofer, *She'elot uteshuvot ḥatam sofer*, vol. vi, no. 59, accepted Emden's judgement that most of the Zohar was composed in medieval times. Referring to Emden's *Mitpaḥat sefarim*, Sofer writes: דבר גדול דיבר הנביא ז"ל בענין זה הלא ישתוממו רואיו. Sofer is also reported to have said that if one separates what R. Simeon ben Yohai wrote from the later additions, the Zohar would only contain a few pages. See Neusatz, *Mei menuḥot*, 43*b*. R. Moses Kunitz published his *Ben yoḥai* in order to refute Emden and uphold R. Simeon ben Yohai's authorship of the Zohar. Regarding this book, Sofer is reported to have declared: ערבים עלי דברי דודים

Rather than condemn the work for this reason, Emden finds support for this pseudepigraphical attribution in the talmudic passage I have already mentioned (*Pesaḥim* 112*a*), where R. Akiva states: 'If you wish to be strangled, be hanged on a large tree.' Although we have seen that there is no need to understand this passage as meaning that one can make false attributions, this is indeed a popular interpretation and is shared by Emden.

Emden cites another talmudic text to support the legitimacy of false attribution. In *Ḥulin* 85*a* R. Hiya b. Abba cites R. Yohanan as stating that since R. Judah the Prince approved of certain views stated by individual sages, he attributed them to the Sages as a whole when he recorded these views in the Mishnah. When a view is stated in the name of the Sages it has more authority than if stated by an individual, and that was exactly R. Judah's point. He was attempting to ensure the acceptance of a view he thought to be the correct halakhah by the way in which he formulated the Mishnah.[138]

Since, as we have seen, many sages assumed that false attribution was permissible, this created a problem of credibility. Some people were understandably sceptical when certain rabbis attributed a teaching to another. As R. Yitshak Eisik Silver has noted,[139] this can be seen from *Eruvin* 17*a*. Here R. Gidal quotes Rav, and the response of his listeners to him is: 'Did Rav really say so?' R. Gidal replies: '[By] the Law, the Prophets, and the Writings, Rav said so.' As Rashi points out, the language of R. Gidal is that of an oath. But why did R. Gidal have to take an oath? Why was he not believed before this? It must be, Silver argues, that R. Gidal's interlocutors feared that he was falsely attributing the opinion to Rav, and only by means of an oath would they be convinced that he was being honest with them. This is quite startling, because

ממענות הבר יוחאי זצ״ל מהגאון היעב״ץ [!] שבס׳ מטפחות סופרי׳. See J. H. Schwartz (ed.), *Zikaron lemosheh*, 151.

[138] Despite Emden's comment, see above, pp. 262–3, where I assume that actions such as R. Judah's should not be regarded as false attribution, since the 'name change' signifies that the individual *tana*'s viewpoint is the accepted halakhah. In *Mor uketsiah*, 'Oraḥ ḥayim' 156, Emden offers an alternative approach, according to which R. Judah did not engage in false attribution. He reasons that since there were certainly other sages who agreed with the individual sage, R. Judah was justified in recording a singular opinion as that of 'the Sages'. The problem with this approach is that, based on this logic, *any* mishnaic opinion could also be recorded as the opinion of 'the Sages', and the Mishnah would be full of disputes between various groups of sages. It is obvious that only in certain circumstances, that is, when R. Judah approved of a view and assumed that it was the halakhah, did he transform the opinion of an individual sage into that of the collective Sages. See Rashi, BT *BM* 33*b*, s.v. *bimei*, and BT *Beits.* 2*b*, s. v. *man*: הוא סדר המשנה וכשראה דברי חכם וישרו בעיניו שנאן סתם ולא הזכיר שם אומרו עליהן כדי שלא יהו שנויה מפי יחיד ונראין כאילו נשנו מפי המרובים ויעשו כמותן. See also Rashi, BT *Ket.* 19*a*, s.v *genuvah*, and Azulai, *Yosef omets*, no. 63.

[139] Silver, *Emet keneh*, 36.

it means that some of the sages were sceptical of what they heard from their colleagues, a state of affairs that is difficult to imagine today.[140]

R. Zev Dov Alter Meir (Majer) also calls attention to the Talmud's readiness to alter attributions in order to ensure that a halakhah is accepted, a phenomenon that he claims 'arouses great wonder'.[141] He argues that it was this 'liberal' approach to attributions that explains a passage in the Jerusalem Talmud, *Shabat* 1: 2: 'Gidul said, "Whoever says a tradition in the name of the one who said it should imagine that the authority for the tradition is standing before him."' According to Meir, Gidul's point is that one should not rely on what someone reports in the name of a certain sage unless it is in line with what else one knows about this sage.[142] In other words, one has to be careful before accepting what one hears, since the Sages view themselves as able to diverge from the truth when necessary. While others explain the practice of false attribution as necessary in order to achieve a religious or social goal, Meir sees Gidul as warning people to be sceptical of the authenticity of rabbinic teachings.[143]

Another text worth noting in this regard appears in the Jerusalem Talmud, *Shabat* 6: 1. R. Abbahu quotes R. Yohanan as stating that it is permitted for a man to teach his daughter Greek, 'because such learning is an adornment for her'. Upon hearing this Simeon bar Ba replied: 'It is because R. Abbahu wants to teach his daughter such things that he has assigned the teaching to R. Yohanan.' Simeon bar Ba's words, although apparently not accurate in this instance,[144] show that he felt that at least one of the sages was not to be trusted when he attributed a statement to others.[145]

There are other talmudic texts that speak of sages lying. In *Bava metsia* 109*a* the Talmud describes how R. Joseph gave his tenants false information so that it would be easier for him to get them to leave.[146] In *Bava metsia* 30*b* R. Ishmael tells someone an incorrect halakhah because he does not want him to acquire some materials that R. Ishmael had declared ownerless.[147]

[140] See also BT *Yev.* 55*b*, where R. Dimi accuses Rabba bar Bar Hana of falsely reporting a teaching of R. Yohanan. R. Dimi said to his colleagues: 'Either he [Rabbah bar Bar Hana] is a liar, or I lied.' The implication is obvious.

[141] Z. D. A. Meir, *Lo ta'aneh al rav*, 13.

[142] While this is certainly an important point, especially in our day when all sorts of strange opinions are attributed to leading rabbis (*gedolim*), it is hard to see this as having anything to do with Gidul's statement.

[143] Z. D. A. Meir, *Lo ta'aneh al rav*, 17.

[144] In response to Simeon bar Ba's accusation, R. Abbahu reaffirmed the truth of his statement: 'May a curse come upon me, if I did not hear it from R. Yohanan.'

[145] See I. H. Weiss, *Dor dor vedoreshav*, i. 4, who assumes that the strong statements in talmudic literature pointing to the importance of faithful attribution, mentioned above, p. 256, were made precisely in order to counter widespread disregard of this principle.

[146] See Tosafot, BT *BM* 109*b*, s.v. *mesalkinan*.

[147] BT *BB* 55*a* mentions that the scribes of Rava, for their own economic benefit, falsely reported the halakhah. However, these scribes are not to be regarded as sages.

There is even a talmudic story that appears to be saying that a sage lied in order to prevent himself from being put to shame for having erred. According to *Berakhot* 43*b*, R. Papa once mistakenly recited certain blessings in the incorrect order (which was, however, in accord with Beit Hillel's rejected opinion). When he was challenged on this, rather than acknowledge his error he replied: 'Thus said Rava: The halakhah follows Beit Hillel.'

On this statement the Talmud comments: 'This was not correct, however; he said so only to excuse himself.'[148] If this is interpreted according to Rashi, that R. Papa made up the statement he attributed to Rava in order to spare himself embarrassment,[149] the text is quite shocking. R. Yair Hayim Bacharach responds to Rashi as follows: 'God forbid that the *tsadik* R. Papa would say something false in the name of Rava in a halakhic matter in order to excuse himself.'[150]

Yet R. Israel Lipschutz has a different perspective, and justifies R. Papa's action by calling attention to *Berakhot* 19*b*, which states: 'Great is human dignity, since it overrides a negative precept of the Torah.'[151] In other words, to prevent oneself from being embarrassed, one is permitted to lie.[152] Rashi, in fact, explains another talmudic passage similarly, stating that Rava took

[148] According to Tosafot, s.v. *hakhi*, R. Isaac Alfasi's version of the text apparently did not include this last sentence (see also R. Joel Sirkes' note, ad loc.), and the Vilna Gaon thinks it should be removed. R. Joseph Karo, *Kesef mishneh*, 'Hilkhot berakhot' 9: 3, disagrees.

[149] Rashi, ad loc., s.v. *velo hi*: לא אמר רבא הלכתא כב"ה אלא רב פפא אכסיף לפי שטעה והשמיט עצמו בכך.

[150] Bacharach, *Ya'ir nativ*, 13. See also A. I. Kook, *Igerot hare'iyah*, ii, no. 694, who offers an alternative to Rashi's understanding.

[151] Lipschutz, *Tiferet yisra'el*, 'Avot' 5: 7 (*Bo'az*, no. 2).

[152] See also Mutzeri, *Be'er mayim ḥayim*, 41*a* (second numbering), no. 27: הרי דרב פפא הוציא דבר שקר מפיו לאשתמוטי נפשיה על מאי דעבד משום כיסופא ואם כן דברי רש"י צדקו. See similarly M. Mizrahi, *Admat kodesh*, vol. ii, 'Even ha'ezer', no. 2, 'Ḥoshen mishpat', no. 25. I cannot explain why R. Papa keeps coming up in this regard, a point already noted by R. Akiva Sofer, *Sha'arei sofer*, no. 15. We have already seen that according to Tosafot, R. Papa lied so that Abaye would accept his position. See above, p. 263. Both Rashi, BT *Kid.* 72*a*, s.v. *iteta* and Tosafot, ibid., s.v. *iteta*, quote an opinion (which they reject) that after R. Papa was refused a wife from a certain district, he spread a falsehood about the personal status of these people, claiming that they had intermarried with the Cutheans. In BT *Ket.* 85*a* we see that Rava did not believe what R. Papa said. R. Yitshak Ratsaby explains: דשאני רב פפא שהוא עוסק בתורה והיא מכנסת בלבו של אדם ערמומיות . . . ומה גם, שיודע בחכמתו תירוצים וחילוקים אימתי מותר לשקר ולשנות וכיוצ"ב. See his letter in Y. Cohen, *Ukeneh lekha ḥaver*, 638–9. Just as surprisingly, Edels (Maharsha) on BT *Shab.* 140*b* claims that R. Papa issued a halakhic ruling in order to make a monetary profit thereby: ורב פפא לטובת עצמו אמרה שהוא הי' עושה שכר. See R. Samuel Strashun, ad loc., and his comment on BT *Shab.* 118*b*, and Medini, *Sedei ḥemed*, 'Ma'arekhet lamed', no. 108, who are astounded by Edels's interpretation. See also Ratsaby, 'Of What Was Rav Papa Suspected?' (Heb.), 108, who suggests that Edels is not saying that R. Papa consciously decided the halakhah so as to benefit thereby, only that since he was a beer-maker, he was unconsciously led to this position. See also my Seforim Blog post, 22 Apr. 2010. On the other hand, R. Jacob Saphir (1822–85) understands Edels literally and likes his interpretation. See id., *Even sapir*, introd., p. 2 (unpaginated).

liberties with the truth in order not to be embarrassed.[153] R. Asher ben Yehiel states: 'There are a few places in the Talmud where *amora'im* deviated [from the truth] because of embarrassment.'[154] In a different context, R. Moses Sofer writes that the implication of a comment of Rashi is that 'one is permitted to deviate [from the truth] so that young people may not laugh at him, and this is not included in "Keep thee far from a false matter".'[155] Along these lines, R. Jacob Ettlinger (1798–1871) writes that a student is permitted to lie about what his teacher said in order that his teacher should not look bad. In support of this he cites *Yevamot* 65*b*, mentioned above, which states that one can deviate from the truth for the sake of peace. By the same token, he notes, one can deviate from the truth for one's teacher's honour.[156]

In the case of R. Papa, however, in addition to lying to spare himself embarrassment (according to Rashi), there is the other problem that his action ended up affirming an incorrect halakhah. Is that also permissible in order to spare oneself embarrassment? It is because of this problem that some commentators understand R. Papa's lie to include only the false attribution of the statement to Rava, but not that R. Papa knowingly stated an incorrect halakhah.[157] According to this understanding, R. Papa really held that Beit

153 BT *AZ* 58*a*, s.v. *demei*.

154 Asher ben Yehiel, *She'elot uteshuvot harosh*, 82: 1.

155 M. Sofer, *Ḥatam sofer al hatorah*, i. 92 (Gen. 24: 35), s. v. *bamidrash*.

156 Ettlinger, *Arukh laner*, 'Makot' 15*a*. For a related issue, see R. Shmuel Wosner, *Shevet halevi*, iii, no. 96. Wosner was asked about a rabbi who normally makes the blessing over the counting of the *omer* for his congregation. However, one night when he was not at the synagogue he forgot to count. In such a case, the halakhah is that one is no longer permitted to recite the blessing on subsequent nights. Yet it would be very embarrassing for the rabbi were his congregation to learn of his error, which would be the case if he would no longer make the public blessing. Wosner rules that since this is a matter of *kevod hatorah* and *kevod hatsibur*, the rabbi can rely on the view that one can count with a blessing even if he missed a day. Along these lines, it is reported that one Sabbath R. Moses Kliers (1874–1934) learnt that the *eruv* set up by one of his colleagues was not kosher. Nothing could be done to fix the matter on the Sabbath, yet Kliers falsely told people that the *eruv* was fine, and they could thus carry. He reasoned that it is better that people carry on the Sabbath, and violate a rabbinic commandment, then that the rabbi be embarrassed by his error, as respect for the rabbi (*kevod hatorah*) is a scriptural commandment. See Perlman, *Mipi dodi*, 9–10.

157 See Y. T. L. Heller, *Ma'adanei yom tov*, 'Berakhot' 43*b* (p. 29*a* in the Vilna Talmud edn.); Azulai, *Birkei yosef*, 'Oraḥ ḥayim' 216: 12, 'Ḥoshen mishpat' 12: 13; id., *Ein zokher*, 'Ma'arekhet kuf', no. 23. See also da Fano, *She'elot uteshuvot harama mifano*, no. 5, who has a different interpretation: ורב פפא מסברא דנפשיה פליג על רבי יוחנן, ולא מחמת כסופא הוא דבעא לאשתמוטי אלא ממדת חסידות, ותלה הגדולה ברבו. R. Tsevi Elimelekh Shapira of Dynów (1783–1841) uses the 'mental reservation' approach that we will soon discuss to defend R. Papa from the charge that he spoke falsely. He claims that although Rava never stated that in the case under discussion Beit Hillel's opinion was the correct one, since with regard to *some other matter* he must have said 'the halakhah follows Beit Hillel', when R. Papa repeated this sentence to defend himself—without clarifying which case he was referring to—he was technically not stating a falsehood! See T. E. Shapira, *Magid ta'alumah*, 93*b*. The same justification is offered by Hayim, *Rav pe'alim*, vol. iii, 'Ḥoshen mishpat', no. 1.

Hillel's view was the correct one, but presumably was too shy to identify with this position publicly.[158]

R. Levi Ibn Habib (*c.*1483–1545) discusses the incident with R. Papa, and questions why the latter was so concerned about being embarrassed and did not simply admit his error. After all, Ibn Habib quotes a few talmudic passages in which sages acknowledged their mistakes, and this was always regarded as a praiseworthy act. Ibn Habib explains that in the cases where sages admitted their errors there had not yet been any practical ramifications. In such cases, there was no embarrassment in acknowledgement of error. However, in the case of R. Papa, he had already *acted* in an incorrect manner, and an acknowledgement of error in such a case would have brought him significant shame.[159]

Ibn Habib uses this point in his dispute with R. Jacob Berab of Safed (1474–1546) about the reinstitution of *semikhah* (full rabbinic ordination). Berab supported this step and even ordained a number of scholars, including R. Joseph Karo. This created a great dispute between the Safed scholars and Ibn Habib, who lived in Jerusalem. Although Ibn Habib states that he does not believe that Berab and the Safed scholars would intentionally say something false in order to support their position, he also cites the case of R. Papa, who was prepared to lie in order to spare himself the embarrassment of admitting his error. The implication of this, as clearly understood by Berab, is that one should not take the Safed scholars' defence of their position seriously, since having been shown the weakness of their viewpoint, like R. Papa they would be willing to put forth arguments they knew to be false in order to spare themselves the shame of retraction.[160]

Another relevant passage is *Kidushin* 44*a*, where R. Assi asks whether R. Abin is reliable. As R. Elijah Klatzkin explains, the context here is the fear that R. Abin would distort the truth in order to support the halakhic position he favoured.[161] The answer given R. Assi, as Tosafot understands it,[162] is that one need not suspect R. Abin of lying because in this case he would easily be exposed. Once again, it is shocking that the honesty of a talmudic sage is called into question.

158 Despite the fact that the Talmud seemingly indicates that Beit Hillel's opinion is rejected, the standard codifiers, including Maimonides, *Mishneh torah*, 'Hilkhot berakhot' 9: 3, rule in accordance with Beit Hillel. See Maged, *Beit aharon*, iii. 421–2.

159 Ibn Habib, *She'elot uteshuvot haralbaḥ*, 'Kuntres hasemikhah', 2. See also Emden, *Mor uketsiah*, 'Oraḥ ḥayim', no. 156.

160 Ibn Habib, *She'elot uteshuvot haralbaḥ*, 'Kuntres hasemikhah', 2, 29–30. Berab's comment appears here, on p. 21. Cf. Trachtman, *Shevet binyamin*, 92–3, who accuses Berab of behaving unethically in his dispute with Ibn Habib.

161 Klatzkin, *Even haroshah*, introd., p. 2*b*.

162 s.v. *kemin*.

According to Rashi, concern with scholars not telling the truth is seen in another talmudic passage as well. *Yevamot* 77*a* records that Ithna the Israelite quoted a tradition from Samuel's *beit din* permitting females from Ammon and Moab to enter the congregation of Israel.[163] The Talmud continues:

Could he [Ithna], however, be trusted [in such circumstances]? Surely R. Abba stated in the name of Rav: Whenever a learned man gives directions on a point of law [based on what he claimed to have received from his teachers], and such a point comes up [for a practical decision], he is obeyed if his statement was made before the event, but if not, he is not obeyed. Here the case was different, since Samuel and his *beit din* were still living.

Rashi explains the Talmud's answer to mean that when the matter can be readily confirmed, in such a case the scholar transmitting a teaching is believed.[164] Yet barring this, one must be concerned that the scholar will lie about what he had heard.[165]

Basing his opinion on this text, an anonymous scholar quoted by R. Solomon Luria came to a shocking conclusion, disturbing because of its lack of faith in the basic integrity of rabbis. There are two separate Hebrew names, Gershom and Gershon, and if they are interchanged on a *get* (divorce document), the *get* is invalid. This scholar—and Luria quotes his viewpoint without objection—stated that if a rabbi instructs that the name be written a certain way and later, upon being challenged, claims that this is how people who knew the divorcé told him it should be written, he is not to be believed.[166] R. Samuel Feivish (d. *c*.1703), who quotes this ruling, points out that this would not apply if the matter can be easily confirmed. Yet barring such an eventuality, even Feivish agrees that we fear that the man might be willing to lie in order to spare himself embarrassment, even though this would mean an invalid *get* with all the dire consequences this would entail.[167]

[163] Deut. 23: 4 states, 'An Ammonite or a Moabite shall not enter into the assembly of the Lord.' The tradition from Samuel's *beit din* understood this verse to refer exclusively to males.

[164] ומילתא דעביד לגלויי הוא ולא משקר בה Rashi, ad loc., s.v. *im* and *deha*. See R. Yom Tov Ishbili (Ritva), *Ḥidushei haritva: yevamot*, ad loc., who strongly rejects Rashi's explanation. Azulai, *Birkei yosef*, 'Yoreh de'ah' 242: 40, connects Rashi's explanation here with his explanation of R. Papa's behaviour in BT *Ber.* 43*b* (above, p. 267), showing that Rashi assumed that talmudic sages would sometimes lie.

[165] See also BT *Yev.* 98*a* and Rashi, ad loc., s.v. *im*, BT *Ber.* 70*b* and Rashi, ad loc., s.v. *im*, BT *Bekh.* 38*b* and Rashi, ad loc., s.v. *ein*. Rabbenu Tam, quoted in Tosafot, BT *Yev.* 77*a*, s.v. *im*, claims that we only suspect falsehood when the scholar has some connection to the case (*noge'a badavar*). Regarding this issue, see also T. H. Ashkenazi, *She'elot uteshuvot ḥakham tsevi*, no. 114.

[166] S. Luria, *Yam shel shelomoh*, 'Gitin', ch. 4, no. 29: 3.

[167] Feivish, *Beit shemuel*, 'Even ha'ezer', 'Shemot anashim venashim', s.v. *gershom* (after 'Even ha'ezer' 129). For opposition to this view, see Eisenstadt, *Pitḥei teshuvah*, ad loc. R. Ephraim

R. Abraham di Boton (sixteenth century) offers another example, which he regards as a defence of scholars who do not tell the truth in order to spare themselves embarrassment. As we have seen, the Talmud states that a scholar is permitted to lie 'in matters of a tractate'.[168] Rashi explains that if someone is asked if he knows a certain tractate of the Talmud, even if he does it is permitted to say 'no' for reasons of modesty. Yet di Boton has a different interpretation. He understands the phrase as giving permission for a scholar to lie so that he will not be embarrassed if, upon stating that he knows the tractate, he is then asked a question to which he does not have the answer.[169]

One final example: in *Bava kama* 11*b*–12*a* we find that Ulla gave one answer to a question of R. Nahman, and when the latter was no longer present, let the audience know that his answer to R. Nahman was not truthful. Upon hearing of this, R. Nahman exclaimed, 'Ulla escaped my criticism.' What motivated Ulla's falsehood? Rashi explains that Ulla was afraid that R. Nahman would challenge his viewpoint and he would not be able to defend himself.[170] So once again, according to Rashi, we see that fear of embarrassment becomes a justification for speaking falsely.

The Problem of Where to Draw the Line

Now that we have seen that there is no absolute requirement to tell the truth, we must examine the problem of where to draw the line. This is crucial, for once the door to prevarication is unlatched, as long as there are 'good reasons' for this, who can say how far it is to be opened? Different people will obviously come to different conclusions as to what these 'good reasons' should be, and I am sure readers will be surprised to learn the extent to which certain rabbinic figures have permitted falsehoods.

In some cases it is easy to determine if it is permissible to lie. We have already seen that when it comes to 'preserving peace' falsehood is permissible. This is obviously also the case when one is able to prevent injury to another.[171]

Zalman Margulies, *Tiv gitin*, 10*b* (no. 26), strongly rejects this approach, as it assumes that rabbis will lie as a matter of course in order to spare themselves embarrassment.

168 BT *BM* 23*b*.

169 A. di Boton, *Leḥem mishneh*, 'Gezelah ve'avedah' 14: 13. R. Elijah Hazan (*c*.1848–1908) states that 'if a Torah scholar altered the truth of a matter and spoke falsely because of a hidden reason, one should not reproach him because he has strong sources upon which to rely'. See id., *Ta'alumot lev*, iv. 90*b*.

170 Rashi, BT *BK* 12*a*, s.v. *ishtamtin*: ומתיירא הוא שמא אקפחנו בהלכות ובקושיות.

171 This is obvious from a Jewish standpoint, but such great thinkers as Augustine and Kant had a different perspective. They argued that falsehood is never permissible, even if an innocent life is at stake. See Bok, *Lying*, ch. 3.

When I refer to 'injury' I do not just mean physical injury. For example, if someone refuses to perform *ḥalitsah* with his sister-in-law,[172] it is entirely appropriate to tell him that if he does so he will be given money, even if one never intends to follow through on this.[173] R. Shlomo Zalman Auerbach gives another example where lying is permissible: if you know that someone is lazy and may miss his train, you can tell him that the train will be leaving earlier than the actual time. This is acceptable, and is even a mitzvah, because it is to the benefit of the other person.[174]

I do not think anyone will disagree about the *ḥalitsah* case, though the last case is a closer call. I say this because it opens up a Pandora's box, as it is often hard to determine what is to another person's benefit. The advocates of censorship believe that sparing someone the knowledge of certain historical facts and halakhic opinions is also to his benefit.

R. Hayim Palache also discusses the issue and offers instances when lying is permitted. I do not think that his examples are surprising, as they include cases when someone is trying to help another or make him feel better, as when encouraging a student, or as part of a eulogy for a great man where it is permitted 'to lie [*leshaker*] and exaggerate a bit'.[175] Yet one example Palache offers is quite interesting. He claims that in order to prevent people from being led astray by an inappropriate teacher, one can falsely state that something this teacher said is incorrect.[176] His source for this is *Berakhot* 59*a*, where R. Kattina said about a certain explanation offered by a necromancer

[172] A religious ceremony that allows a childless widow to marry someone other than her husband's brother; see Deut. 25: 5–10.

[173] See BT *Yev.* 106*a*; Mazuz, *Arim nisi*, 13 (first pagination). R. Yosef Bar Shalom points out that *dayanim* routinely tell falsehoods to people who appear before them, in order to reach a compromise. For example, they will say to one party that if he continues with his claim he will lose everything. See id., *Vayitsbor yosef*, ii. 317. The same point was earlier made by R. Abraham ben Nahman Hakohen, *Taharat hamayim*, 'Shiyurei taharah, Ma'arekhet 4', no. 35, who writes: מותר להפחידו [הבעל דין] בדברים שקרים.

[174] S. Auerbach, *Ma'adanei shelomoh*, 151–2. See ibid. 152, where Auerbach suggested other cases when it is permitted to lie. For example, if you want to drive someone home and he is reluctant to trouble you, you can tell him that you are going past his house anyway. Also, if you do not want to be disturbed, you can instruct someone in your house to tell a visitor that you are not home at present, since it could be insulting to him to be told that you are home but have requested not to be disturbed.

[175] See Palache, *Heḥafets ḥayim*, 19: 33. Regarding eulogies, Palache's point would seem to be contradicted by BT *Ber.* 62*a*. He cites as his source R. David Halevi (Taz; *c.*1586–1667), in his *Turei zahav*, 'Yoreh de'ah' 344: 1, but the Taz is more nuanced than this and even denies that the term *sheker* (falsehood) is appropriate. According to the Taz, exaggerating a person's good qualities is not a lie. He explains that since one can assume that if the deceased had had the opportunity to extend his good deeds a bit, he would have done so, therefore 'it is as if he had done so'.

[176] Palache, *Heḥafets ḥayim*, 19: 22.

that 'he is a liar and his words are false'. The Talmud comments on this: 'He did not really mean this, however . . . and the reason why he did not admit it was so that people should not go astray after him.' In other words, R. Kattina felt that it was appropriate to lie about the necromancer so that people would not assume that he was a wise man and be attracted to him. Apparently, people engaged in religious polemics and apologetics are here given carte blanche to destroy the scholarly reputation of their opponent, even to the extent of lying about the veracity of what he has asserted.

We have already seen that it is permitted to lie about the bride at the wedding, but how about before the wedding? The Hazon Ish, R. Aaron Kotler, and R. Yosef Shalom Elyashiv are quoted as permitting minor lies about the potential spouse's age if it will improve the woman's (or man's) chance of marriage. Elyashiv gave this example: if a woman is 20 years old she is permitted to say that she is 19.[177] In none of these 'liberal' opinions is there any mention that the lying party ever needs to 'come clean' with the future husband or wife.[178]

Among other noteworthy examples where falsehood is permitted by rabbinic authorities, R. Yisra'el Ya'akov Fischer (1928–2003) stated that a poor man is permitted to make believe that he is blind or crippled if this will help him collect more money.[179] R. Shlomo Zalman Auerbach asserted that some great rabbis, whom he did not name, permitted lying to donors about how many students attend a yeshiva in order to receive larger donations.[180] (Auerbach himself stated that he did not know how this could be permitted.[181]) There is even a view, incredible as it may seem, that someone collecting money to pay for publication of a book can falsely tell people that he is collecting for a poor bride! According to another view, one can use the 'poor bride' story and direct the money collected to support those studying Torah.[182]

[177] See Y. H. Fish, *Titen emet leya'akov*, ch. 5, no. 38, who also cites the opposing positions of R. Shlomo Zalman Auerbach and R. Binyamin Silber. (Fish also quotes an unnamed relative of Auerbach to the effect that on one occasion Auerbach did permit lying about a man's age, but it is hard to know if this report is accurate.) In contrast to the Hazon Ish's 'liberal' position mentioned in the text, he is quoted elsewhere as forbidding lies when it comes to potential marriages; see Karelitz, 'Halakhic Rulings' (Heb.), 736. Perhaps this stringent position refers to substantial lies.

[178] R. Herzl Hillel Yitshak concludes that while one may lie at the beginning stages of dating, the truth must be told once the couple know each other better. See id., 'Is One Permitted To Be Imprecise Regarding Age for the Purposes of Matchmaking?' (Heb.).

[179] See Y. H. Fish, *Titen emet leya'akov*, 162. Fish quotes R. Hayim Kanievsky as disagreeing with this ruling.

[180] See Anon., *Hashakdan*, ii. 102, which reports that R. Yosef Shalom Elyashiv held that charities are permitted to lie, for instance, by creating stories of how donors were recipients of various miracles, if this will encourage donations.

[181] See Y. H. Fish, *Titen emet leya'akov*, 160–1; Stepansky, *Ve'alehu lo yibol*, ii. 359.

[182] See Y. H. Fish, *Titen emet leya'akov*, 71 ff. See also R. Yehudah Shapira, *Da'at yehudah*, 162–3,

Fortunately, the opinions noted in the last paragraph are not widely held (at least as far as I know), and they are great examples of how far the slippery slope can carry you once untruths are permitted for a 'good cause'. To pick the last example mentioned, it need hardly be said that if rabbis permit themselves to use the time-honoured practice of supporting poor brides in order to raise money for another purpose, then their word will lose all credibility in the eyes of the people. As it is, based on what we have seen in this chapter, laypeople would appear to have plenty of justification for doubting the veracity of at least some of what their rabbis tell them.

R. Yitshak Eizik Silver, author of a recent book on the subject of truth, is very aware of this. He is concerned that the masses, if they see all the examples of rabbis lying that have been mentioned in this chapter, will conclude that the rabbis have created an alternative morality for themselves. In his preface, Silver acknowledges that he thought of omitting the entire chapter that deals with the times that lying is permissible. He also tells us that he did not include a section that deals with all the examples of biblical figures not telling the truth. This was omitted so that immature students would not be exposed to it, and also so that enemies of traditional Judaism would not be given ammunition. He notes that the material that he did choose to include in the book 'is only intended for *benei torah* [Torah scholars] for whom Torah is their livelihood'. In other words, it is only the Torah scholars who can handle this information and be trusted to make the judgement about when lying is permissible.[183]

Mental Reservation

We have seen many examples of falsehood, and the times when falsehood is permitted. Yet even with the permissions given, there are plenty of occasions when there is apparently a need to speak falsely, but no ready halakhic justification exists. That is where rabbinic ingenuity came in, finding a way to permit falsehood when this was thought to be important, while not technically violating the letter of the law.

This was done through the mechanism of mental reservation.[184] Mental

who rules that it is permissible to collect money for a *kolel* without telling people that the *kolel* has closed and the money will be used to pay the *kolel*'s debts. Shapira makes his ruling conditional on also using a little of the money collected to support two yeshiva students.

[183] Silver, *Emet keneh*, 3–4.

[184] Catholic theologians distinguished between two types of mental reservation: that which they called 'wide mental reservation', in which one's words themselves are equivocal, and that termed 'strict mental reservation', in which one's words, lacking any mental qualification, are indeed in opposition to the facts. See Slater, 'Mental Reservation'. I make use of both of these categories. An example of equivocal language appears in the Bible when Abraham speaks of Sarah as his sister;

reservation means that when you say something, in your mind you have added a qualification that no one other than yourself knows. It also includes equivocal language, the sense of which only you are privy to. In the case of an oath, it means that you swear according to your own intention, not the intention of the person opposite you, be he judge or claimant. It is not actually a lie, since a lie means that you say something that you do not believe. In a case of mental reservation, other people are just misunderstanding you.

President Bill Clinton's statements about Monica Lewinsky included some famous instances of this mechanism. For example, he stated, 'I did not have sexual relations with that woman.' Later he claimed that he thought that oral sex did not count, all the while knowing that this was not what everyone else assumed. In his testimony in the Paula Jones Case Deposition, Clinton claimed that he had no recollection of being alone with Lewinsky. As he later explained in his Grand Jury testimony, in a way that only a lawyer could, in his understanding he was never really alone because in his position as president, people could always be coming in.[185] In other words, Clinton was operating with a different understanding of the word 'alone' from that of everyone else.

see Gen. 20: 12 and also earlier in ch. 12. Various *midrashim* attribute equivocal language to Jacob when he takes Esau's blessing from their blind father, Isaac. While Gen. 27: 19 has Jacob saying 'I am Esau your first born', these *midrashim* read Jacob as saying, 'I am [Jacob], Esau is your first born'. See Kasher, *Torah shelemah*, ad loc. There are also a number of talmudic texts that deal with equivocal language. For example, BT *Git.* 62*a* states that R. Kahana would greet heathens with 'Peace, sir' (*shelama lemar*). As Rashi explains, his intention was to bless his teacher, but the heathen would assume that the blessing was intended for him. BT *Ned.* 62*b* states: 'A rabbinical scholar may assert, "I am a servant of fire" so as not to pay the poll tax.' While the Persians would take this statement literally and exempt him from the tax together with all other fire-worshippers, the scholar would have in mind that he worships God, who is referred to as a 'devouring fire' in Deut. 4: 24. See also *Kohelet rabati* 1: 24, which describes how R. Eliezer was accused of heresy and brought before the governor to be tried. In his defence, R. Eliezer stated: 'Faithful is the Judge concerning me.' The governor assumed that R. Eliezer had him in mind, while he was actually referring to God. This passage was cited by Maimonides in his *Igeret hashemad* as a proof that one can feign disbelief. See id., *Igerot harambam*, i. 39 ff. It must be noted, however, that in the case of R. Eliezer his life was in danger. See J. Schwartz and P. J. Tomson, 'When Rabbi Eliezer Was Arrested for Heresy'. For a more recent example, based on R. Moses Isserles' ruling in *Shulḥan arukh*, 'Yoreh de'ah' 157: 2, see R. Ephraim Oshry (1914–2003), *Divrei efrayim*, 51*a*. Oshry states that although one is not permitted to say that he is a worshipper of *avodah zarah* ('foreign worship') even upon pain of death, it was permitted during the Holocaust for people to add the letters RK illegally to their passports. These letters would be understood by others to mean Roman Catholic (Römisch Katholisch). However, the Jew, when writing the letters, could understand the 'K' to mean the Yiddish word *kein*, thus meaning 'not a Roman'. See also Oshry, *She'elot uteshuvot mima'amakim*, vol. v, no. 3; Klein, *Mishneh halakhot*, vol. ix, no. 170; Yitshak Hershkowitz, 'Theurgical Interpretation' (Heb.), 326–7; Weitman, 'Using a Non-Jew's Identity Card' (Heb.). For other examples of equivocal language, see Ibn Kaspi, *Shulḥan kesef*, 161; R. Bahya ben Asher, *Commentary* on Gen. 27: 19.

185 'It depends on how you define alone. . . . [T]here were also a lot of times when, even though

A more prosaic example would be if someone asked you, 'Have you visited Los Angeles?' You reply, 'No, I haven't visited Los Angeles,' while in your mind you add 'this year'. Thus, the questioner assumes falsely that you have never been to Los Angeles, when in reality it is only in the past year that you have not travelled there.

The doctrine of mental reservation, which arose among medieval Catholic thinkers, was greatly developed in the sixteenth century. In the popular mind it became identified with Jesuit thinkers (hence, the pejorative term 'jesuitical', meaning 'sly' or 'crafty').[186] Faced with the rigid Catholic opposition to all lying, even in matters of life and death, the notion of mental reservation became a counterweight. As can be imagined, an idea such as mental reservation is bound to be the subject of much controversy, as indeed it was, both internally within Catholicism and in Protestant–Catholic disputes.[187] One recent author has even referred to the concept as the 'most casuistical of the casuists' doctrines'.[188] Although the theologians who permitted mental reservation did so only in emergency situations, the idea was still very controversial in Catholic circles. In 1679 the doctrine of mental reservation was finally laid to rest in Catholicism when Pope Innocent XI officially condemned it.[189]

While it is true that the theoretical discussions of mental reservation are first found in Catholic writers, we do find examples of mental reservation in rabbinic literature, long pre-dating the development of the doctrine in Christianity. The Talmud, *Nedarim* 27*b*–28*a*, discusses making a vow under duress, and states that in such a circumstance one can add a mental stipulation. The example given is that if you are confronted with someone who wants to take your produce, you can claim that it really belongs to the royal house, even vowing 'May all the fruits of the world be forbidden to me, if this does not belong to the royal family.' Together with this vow, you are to stipulate mentally 'forbidden *today* for me'.[190] Tosafot comments on this as follows, offering another example of mental reservation from medieval times:

no one could see us, the doors were open to the halls, on both ends of the halls, people could hear. The Navy stewards could come in and out at will, if they were around. Other things could be happening. So, there were a lot of times when we were alone, but I never really thought we were.' See the transcript of Clinton's testimony, <http://www.washingtonpost.com/wpsrv/politics/special/clinton/stories/bctest092198_9.htm>.

186 This identification was not actually correct, as there were Jesuit thinkers, most notably Juan Azor (1535–1603) and Paul Laymann (1574–1635), who rejected the doctrine. See Sommerville, 'The "New Art of Lying"', 178–9.

187 See Zagorin, *Ways of Lying*; id., 'Historical Significance'.

188 Sommerville, 'The "New Art of Lying"', 160.

189 See Slater, 'Mental Reservation'.

190 See Maimonides, *Mishneh torah*, 'Hilkhot nedarim' 4: 1–2; Karo, *Shulḥan arukh*, 'Yoreh de'ah' 232: 14. Another example from the rabbinic period records R. Akiva using mental

When the oppressors cause the Jews living in their territories to swear that they will not go to a different city, they can swear that they will not go but have in mind 'today'. Even if they state that they will not leave all their lifetime, they can add some qualifying factor in their mind, and if they void the oath silently with their lips it certainly is a valid nullification.[191]

A midrashic text points to an example of mental reservation by the patriarch Jacob in conversation with Esau. Genesis 33 describes how the two brothers met and, according to the rabbinic understanding, Jacob was afraid of what Esau might do to him and his family. In his effort to smooth out their relations he promises to visit his brother: 'Let my lord, I pray thee, pass over before his servant; and I will journey on gently, according to the pace of the cattle that are before me and according to the pace of the children, until I come unto my lord unto Seir' (Gen. 33: 14).

On this verse a midrash states:

R. Abbahu said: We have searched the whole Scriptures and do not find that Jacob ever went to Esau to the mountain of Seir. Is it then possible that Jacob, the truthful, should deceive him? But when would he come to him? In the messianic era: 'And saviours shall come up to Mount Zion to judge the mount of Esau', etc. [Obad. 1: 21].[192]

From medieval times, there is a case in the responsa of R. Asher ben Yehiel that appears to be an example of mental reservation.[193] A Jew had loaned money to a non-Jew who left collateral with the Jew. They agreed that if the non-Jew did not pay back the money by a certain date, the collateral would belong to the Jew. The deadline passed and the Jew decided to keep the pledge.

reservation in an oath in order to find out the halakhic personal status of a child; see *Kalah*, ch. 2. See also R. Mordechai ben Hillel, *Sefer hamordekhai* on BT *Shev.* 3: 755 and R. Nissim ben Reuben (Ran), supercommentary on Alfasi, *Kid.*, 20*b* in the Alfasi pages, s.v. *amar rava*. In BT *Ber.* 58*a* it describes how a man had intercourse with a non-Jewish woman and R. Shila had him lashed. When the man complained about the lashing to the non-Jewish authorities, R. Shila stated that he had had intercourse with an ass, which would bring about the death penalty. When R. Shila was challenged by the man about his false testimony, he replied by quoting Ezek. 23: 20, which compares non-Jews to asses. In other words, when R. Shila testified to the authorities about the man having intercourse with an 'ass', he knew that they would take his statement literally while he, and he alone, understood it figuratively.

191 BT *BK* 113*a*, s.v. *noderin*. Not surprisingly, there is a note in the Vilna Talmud that states: 'This is only to save oneself from the oppressors, but otherwise it is forbidden to deceive a person in any way, God forbid, even when not taking an oath.' A section of another Tosafot that permits mental reservation in an oath was omitted from various printings, including the Vilna Romm edition. See BT *Ned.* 28*a*, s.v. *bemokhes*, in Anon., *Kevutsat hahashmatot*, ad loc., and also in the new Wagshal and Oz Vehadar Talmuds.

192 *Bereshit rabah* 78: 14.

193 Asher ben Yehiel, *She'elot uteshuvot harosh*, 8: 15.

The non-Jew then took him to court, hoping that his loss would not be enforced.[194]

R. Asher was asked if the Jew could take an oath that he did not have the non-Jew's property. This would, with certainty, ensure his victory in the case. R. Asher states that the Jew cannot swear that he was not given the collateral, as this would be a false oath. However, he is permitted to swear that he does not have anything belonging to the non-Jew in his possession. This is not regarded as a false oath, since according to both Jewish and non-Jewish law the collateral now really belongs to the Jew.

Is this an example of mental reservation? On the one hand, this is not a case where the facts are in opposition to the statement made, and are 'reconciled' via the unspoken mental stipulation known only to the speaker. Yet it is hard to argue that the language of the oath was not equivocal. R. Asher was clearly comfortable with a very legalistic approach, one that violated the spirit of the oath but not its letter.

R. Jacob di Boton (*c.*1635–87) was prepared to go further than R. Asher, as he saw mental reservation as a valid option in the case just discussed. According to di Boton, the man could swear that he did not receive the collateral and this would not be a false oath, since he could mentally stipulate, 'today I did not receive it, only last year'.[195] Similarly, R. Ephraim Navon (1677–1735) discusses a case where a non-Jewish heir demands repayment owed to his late father, but the Jewish borrower does not have the money. If non-payment would lead to the Jew being imprisoned, Navon rules that he is permitted to swear that he does not owe anything, using mental reservation.[196]

There is a well-known case in which R. Joseph Rozin, the famed Rogochover, approved of using mental reservation in an oath. When asked by his

[194] R. Asher does not explain why the loss would not be enforced. I originally assumed the meaning to be that the court would give the non-Jew more time to pay back the debt. Yet Steven H. Resnicoff is probably correct that it means that the non-Jew was now able to redeem the collateral by paying what was due. See his 'Ends and Means', 168.

[195] J. di Boton, *Edut beya'akov*, no. 80. For other relevant cases, see Elijah ben Hayim, *She'elot uteshuvot rabi eliyahu ben ḥayim*, nos. 3, 113. See ibid., no. 3 (end), where R. Samuel Jaffe states that while mental reservation is valid with oaths, this is not something that should be taught to the masses, for they will no longer treat oaths with the necessary severity.

[196] Navon, *Maḥaneh efrayim*, 'Hilkhot shevuot', no. 13. This section appears in the Constantinople, 1738 edition but has been removed from the Warsaw, 1878 edition. It is not clear if this was due to non-Jewish censorship or Jewish self-censorship. Navon's position goes much further than R. Moses Isserles' gloss on Karo, *Shulḥan arukh*, 'Ḥoshen mishpat' 283: 1, which states that if a non-Jew dies and his heirs are unaware of money owed to them by a Jew, the latter is not obligated to inform them.

son-in-law, R. Israel Citron (1881–1927), if it was permitted to swear falsely to the British authorities in Palestine that he was born in the land of Israel in order to speed up receipt of a passport, Rozin permitted him to take the oath. He based this permission on a passage in *Ketubot* 75*a* where the Talmud explains a verse in Psalms to mean that even one who only looks forward to seeing the land of Israel is regarded as if he had been born there.[197] I regard Rozin's ruling to be an example of 'mental reservation', because obviously the British official in front of whom the oath took place understood the meaning of Citron's words in a very different fashion from Citron. Only Citron knew that when he said he was 'born in Palestine' he was using an aggadic understanding of 'birth'.

Other Examples of Lying for a Good Purpose

R. Jacob Reischer (1661–1733) takes permission to lie in a completely different, and perhaps more problematic, direction.[198] He discusses a court case in which there were three judges. Two judges held one opinion, while the third judge believed that they were incorrect. Seeing that the other two judges disagreed with him, the third judge realized that his opinion would be outvoted. According to the halakhah, if one of the judges in a court case states that he does not know how to vote, two more judges are added and the proceedings begin again.[199]

The question Reischer was confronted with is whether the third judge may lie and say that he cannot come to a conclusion. This will then lead to two more judges being added, who may decide in accordance with his opinion, which he is certain is the correct verdict. Reischer's view is that this is permitted, since the judge's intention is for the sake of heaven, to establish a proper ruling. 'Even though he lies [when he says "I do not know"] . . . the halakhah is that one is permitted to deviate [from the truth] for the sake of peace, and correct law is regarded as peace, as it says, "Execute the judgement of truth and peace in your gates" [Zech. 8: 16].'[200]

R. Joseph Hayim records an extremely troubling decision in his pseudonymous work, *Torah lishmah*.[201] A woman whose father died without a will

[197] See Weingarten, 'And of Zion It Shall Be Said' (Heb.); Citron, *Ḥidushei harav tsitron-katroni*, introd., 9. It is reported that R. Joseph Hayim Sonnenfeld made exactly the same point; see S. Z. Sonnenfeld, *Ha'ish al haḥomah*, ii. 154.

[198] Reischer, *Shevut ya'akov*, vol. i, no. 138.

[199] Karo, *Shulḥan arukh*, 'Ḥoshen mishpat' 18: 1.

[200] For discussion of Reischer's view, and the authorities who disagree with him, see O. Yosef, *Yabia omer*, ii, 'Ḥoshen mishpat', no. 3.

[201] J. Hayim, *Torah lishmah*, no. 371. It is not clear if R. Joseph Hayim is discussing an actual case that came before him. For detailed analysis of the issue, see M. Schwartz, *Mishpat hatsava'ah*, no. 5.

decided to go to the secular court to be awarded part of the inheritance. She did so since she knew that according to Jewish law only her brothers were entitled to the inheritance. The question was whether it was permitted to forge a will in the father's name awarding his sons the inheritance. R. Joseph Hayim writes: 'This is certainly permitted and there is no fear of [violating the commandment] "Keep thee far from a false matter", for the Sages say that one can deviate [from the truth] on account of peace, and even more important than this is establishing the banner of Torah, and there is no greater peace than this.'

In support of the notion that lying is permitted in this sort of matter, R. Joseph Hayim cites a source not mentioned elsewhere. *Rosh hashanah* 20*a* states that 'Witnesses may be intimidated into reporting [on the thirtieth day] the new moon which has not appeared in its due time, in order that the new moon may be sanctified. Even though they have not seen it they may say, "We have seen it."' We do not need to go into the reason why the witnesses are encouraged to testify falsely in this case. More important for our purposes is the lesson R. Joseph Hayim derives from this: 'Regarding all that they [the Sages] do for society's betterment . . . one need not be concerned about [the prohibition of] falsehood, for this is included in what they said, that one can deviate [from the truth] in the interests of peace.'

R. Joseph Hayim concludes that if lying is permitted in the case of witnesses testifying about the new moon, it is certainly permitted in the case he is discussing. However, he notes that before forging the document, one must be sure that the action cannot be exposed, as this would then lead to a *ḥilul hashem* ('desecration of [God's] name'). While in the popular mind *ḥilul hashem* is usually understood to mean that non-Jews see Jews behaving improperly and get a false impression about Judaism, here R. Joseph Hayim understands *ḥilul hashem* as meaning that the non-Jews will get a *true* impression, and this will bring Judaism into disrepute in their eyes.[202]

Although I stated that R. Joseph Hayim's ruling is troubling, as it permits lying in court, the principle is easy to understand: one is permitted to lie in order to retrieve that which rightfully belongs to him. This is something that I think most people would agree with. It even finds expression in the Talmud, *Yoma* 83*b*, which describes how two sages lied to the wife of an innkeeper in

[202] We also find other examples where the *ḥilul hashem* is precisely that non-Jews will find out something about Jewish law that understandably offends them. One should therefore refrain from certain actions in order to prevent a *ḥilul hashem*, even though the actions would be permissible if such a concern was not present. See e.g. Maimonides, *Mishneh torah*, 'Hilkhot gezelah ve'avedah' 11: 43; Karo, *Shulḥan arukh*, 'Ḥoshen mishpat' 348: 2 (Isserles' comment): טעות עובד כוכבים כגון להטעותו בחשבון או להפקיע הלואתו מותר ובלבד שלא יודע לו דליכא חילול השם. This formulation comes directly from Jacob ben Asher, *Arba'ah turim*, 'Ḥoshen mishpat' 348: 3.

order to persuade her to give back their money, which had been stolen by her husband. However, in the case discussed by R. Joseph Hayim, the lying was no longer between one person and another, but also entailed false testimony in court. This is clearly an escalation of the fraud. Yet R. Joseph Hayim is not unique in his ruling. R. Yitshak Eizik Silver states: 'In a secular court . . . there are those who say that it is even permitted to lie if it is impossible [to get a Torah-mandated result] without doing so. This is only when there is no chance that they will catch you (*ḥilul hashem*).'[203]

Lying as an Educational Tool

Let us now turn to the altering of facts for educational reasons, or what can be termed 'Torah purposes'. R. Shlomo Zalman Auerbach was asked if it is permitted to tell a story that never happened if it offers the best opportunity to focus on a halakhic matter that is important for the listeners to be aware of. He answers that one can indeed do so.[204] Auerbach's questioner actually provided a good source for the ruling. *Yoma* 23*a–b* describes how R. Zadok was speaking to the people after a murder took place within the Temple. During his message, which dealt with the atoning ceremony of the *eglah arufah* (the ritual carried out when someone is killed by an unknown murderer), he made certain statements that were not in accord with halakhah. The Talmud explains that he did so 'in order to increase the weeping'.[205]

Some years earlier than Auerbach, the hasidic master R. Solomon Rabinowich of Radomsk (1803–66) also recommended to preachers that if they want to get their point across through the use of a story, they should not call the story a *mashal* (parable). They should rather call it a *ma'aseh*, that is, an

[203] Silver, *Emet keneh*, 39. The implications of this viewpoint are enormous, as anyone who accepts it can no longer be regarded as a trustworthy witness in a secular court. See also Resnicoff, 'Ends and Means', 165: 'A number of authorities also explicitly allow false testimony when a Jewish plaintiff wrongfully sues a Jewish defendant in secular court.' Resnicoff supports this statement by citing examples where halakhic authorities from earlier centuries permit lying in court in order to achieve a Jewishly just result; see 'Ends and Means', 165 ff. (I cite a number of the same sources referred to by Resnicoff.) See also H. S. Abraham, *Devar torah*, i. 249. For a contemporary halakhist who permits lying in court, see R. Eliezer Melamed, *Revivim: kovets ma'amarim*, 198 ff., who states that those arrested during protests against Israel's expulsion of settlers are permitted to falsely deny accusations made against them in order to avoid punishment.

[204] See Yadler, *Berurei halakhah me'or hashabat*, 'Peninei hamaor' II: 4 (p. 502). For the opposing position, see A. Y. Grossman, *Vedarashta veḥakarta* (2011), vol. v, 'Oraḥ ḥayim', no. 76: 4.

[205] See also Kook, *Olat hare'iyah*, i. 238, that absolute truth is not necessary when trying to inspire listeners, but that when one is conveying something as fact, then his words should be exact (called to my attention by R. Davidi Jonas).

actual event, 'because through this, the matter will make an impression'.[206] As to how this is permissible, since one is supposed to avoid falsehood, Rabinowich notes that according to one opinion in the Talmud the story of the book of Job never actually occurred but is only a parable.[207] According to Rabinowich, this shows that one can make up a story if it helps to get a point across.

I must say, however, that this is hardly a good proof. According to the opinion that Job never existed and the entire story is a parable, this information was not designed to be hidden from anyone, and there is thus no falsehood involved. In fact, the reading of the book of Job as a parable is, I would argue, the *peshat*, or simple meaning, of the text. There is obviously a great difference between a parable that everyone recognizes as such, and a story designed to instil some value when the people reading or hearing it do not know that it is made up.

Rabinowich offers another strange justification for his position. The Jerusalem Talmud states, 'All lies are bad, but lies about the Torah are good.'[208] The commentary *Penei mosheh*, by R. Moses Margolies (d. 1781), explains that this refers to the fact that, for reasons of modesty, a person is permitted to lie about how much Torah he has studied, a point I have already mentioned. Rabinowich understands the passage to mean that in Torah matters one is permitted to make up stories in order to have an impact on the listener.[209] He elaborates in a fascinating way, asking why many stories are recorded several times in rabbinic literature, with details that do not match. His explanation, which is very much in line with how modern scholars look at these stories, is that what is important is not the details but the larger message.

Finally, R. Hayim Oberlander published a responsum in the widely read rabbinic journal *Or yisra'el* which dealt with the following question:

> I am a teacher in a school that is not so haredi (but they [the students] are Sabbath observant) for children ages 8–9, and I saw that when I tell them stories of great sages, that this inspires them to fear of heaven and alacrity in observing Torah and mitzvot. My question is, since in general I change the story completely, so that it will be more exciting in order to best inspire them, and also so that they will be able to understand it better, can I continue in this fashion?[210]

There is no question that for generations people have been making up stories about great rabbis in order to provide religious inspiration for the masses,

206 Rabinowich, *Niflaot hatiferet shelomoh*, 23 (first pagination: nos. 69–70). 207 BT *BB* 15*a*.

208 JT *Ber.* 9: 5. This is the standard version. Regarding this text, and the alternative readings, see Naor, *Limit of Intellectual Freedom*, 82, 267–70.

209 מותר לומר על דבר שלא נברא שהיתה ושנבראת והוא מעשה שהיתה כדי לפעול רושם על לב שומע.

210 H. Oberlander, 'Is It Permitted to Tell Fictitious Stories?' (Heb.), 121.

and Oberlander finds a way to justify this. As long as the teacher's purpose is 'for the sake of heaven', Oberlander concludes that he is permitted to continue with his practice.[211] Yet he notes that one should not do this too often, as falsehood is not something to which pious people should be attached. Oberlander also adds that it is unnecessary to make up stories as there are plenty of true stories that are available for the teacher to use.

Since Oberlander's viewpoint is undoubtedly shared by numerous others—although it also has many important opponents[212]—one can assume that a significant number of the false '*gedolim* stories' that are bandied about are not run-of-the-mill rumours, but were intentionally created in order to inspire people. R. Elyakim Schlesinger reports that a group of Torah scholars actually admitted to him that they invented stories about the Hazon Ish, since they thought the stories would be inspiring.[213]

A Rabbinic Doctrine of the Noble Lie?

When examining the texts presented in this chapter, which show great rabbis lying in the name of a larger good, it is impossible not to think of Plato's doctrine of the Noble Lie.[214] As explained in the *Republic*,[215] a Noble Lie is a lie for a higher purpose. Plato is speaking of lying in order to preserve the temporal order. Sometimes rulers find it necessary to lie to their subjects in order to lead them in the best way. It is a paternalistic approach in which people cannot be given access to all the truths, for their own benefit and that of society at large.

It appears that some of the talmudic sages and post-talmudic authorities independently developed a conception of the Noble Lie. However, unlike

[211] See Papo, *Pele yo'ets*, 68 (letter *dalet*, s.v. *hasheker*): 'It is permitted to lie for the sake of Heaven.'

[212] See the letter in *Or yisra'el*, 30 (Tevet 5763), 244, where R. Avraham Weinberg, the Slonimer Rebbe of Benei Berak, strongly objects to Oberlander's conclusion. Anon., *Beit rabi*, 135; Wolbe, *Alei shur*, ii. 296; and R. Jacob Israel Kanievsky, quoted in A. Horovitz, *Orḥot rabenu*, i. 252, also state that it is improper to invent stories about great Torah personalities. R. Yosef Shalom Elyashiv, *Kovets teshuvot*, vol. iii, no. 28, does not think it is proper to invent stories out of thin air, but he does permit embellishing a sage's biography, which is not very different from what he claims to oppose: אכן אפשר להוסיף באופן שיש להניח שאם היה בא לידו דבר כזה היה עושה אותו, כאלו וכיוצא בזה מותר להוסיף. R. Ya'akov Ades refers to this formulation and states that it is only applicable to children's books, but that books for adults have to be accurate. Ades also raises the possibility that it is theft to sell a book to adults that is intentionally not accurate, since at least some people would not have bought the volume had they known its true nature. See Ades, *Divrei ya'akov*, 634.

[213] E. Schlesinger, *Hador vehatekufah*, 41 (second pagination).

[214] With reference to the Noble Lie, Nietzsche writes: 'Neither Manu nor Plato nor Confucius nor the Jewish and Christian teachers have ever doubted their *right* to lie.' See W. Kaufmann (ed. and trans.), *The Portable Nietzsche*, 505 (from *Twilight of the Idols*).

[215] *Laws* 2.663d–e.

Plato, the rabbinic Noble Lie was not intended to provide stability. Its point was much more exalted, for it was designed to promote spiritual values and help ensure that people's lives be conducted in accord with Jewish law. In fact, I think it is quite significant that we do not only have a conception of the Noble Lie directed towards the masses, as we have also seen that the Noble Lie is sometimes even used by one sage in speaking to another.

Redefining Truth

One way of dealing with the disconnect between the obligation to speak truthfully and the reality that departing from truth is permitted in so many cases is to redefine the meaning of 'truth'. We have seen many examples in this book where the truth has been altered. Yet is truth only to be identified with historical truth? Cannot a myth also provide all sorts of 'truths', even if it is not historically accurate?

One should bear these points in mind when examining those who offer an alternative perspective on the meaning and significance of truth. I have already mentioned R. Elijah Dessler in this regard, in Chapter 1, but it bears repeating here. In an essay entitled 'What is Truth and What is Falsehood?', Dessler, a famed *musar* teacher, adopts a utilitarian approach to the entire concept of truth. As he sees it, truth as a value must carry some positive result, since truth is by definition a positive quality. Therefore, 'truth', as understood by the Sages, means that which leads to a good result. When the Sages say that the seal of God is truth and speak of the importance of truth, they are not necessarily speaking of factual or historical truth. According to Dessler, 'truth' is not dependent upon empirical observation and evidence, but derives from religious considerations. Thus, a historically accurate description that leads to a bad result is, from a religious perspective, 'false'. By the same token, that which helps lead people to do God's will, even if it is factually false, is nevertheless to be regarded as 'truth'.[216]

There is no doubt that Dessler's expansive definition of 'truth' and 'falsehood' provides justification for all sorts of distortions, all in the name of a good purpose. Yet before one concludes that Dessler's point is merely haredi doublespeak, I must note that his view is shared by the noted philosopher Hastings Rashdall. In his classic work *Theory of Good and Evil*, Rashdall writes: 'There are even cases in which a lie has to be told in the interests of Truth itself. . . . [A] statement literally untrue must be made that a higher truth

[216] Dessler, *Mikhtav me'eliyahu*, i. 94–6. For a formulation similar to that of Dessler, see R. Yeruham Levovitz (1873–1936), *Da'at ḥokhmah umusar*, i. 113: 'The difference between truth and falsehood is measured by what results from each. If the result is true then the means to create this

may be taught or real liberty of thought and speech advanced.'[217] In other words, sometimes truth must give way to Truth. In support of this contention, Rashdall cites the Danish philosopher Harald Hoffding: 'The duty of speaking the truth amounts to this, the duty of promoting the supremacy of the truth.'[218]

I think that rationales of the sort advanced by Dessler, Rashdall, and Hoffding, even if not consciously formulated, are how the religious censors, and those who create falsehoods in the name of a larger Truth, justify their actions to themselves. As this chapter has attempted to show, such an approach can be supported by quite a few sources in the rabbinic tradition.

truth is also true.' Reflecting on how Dessler's position relates to the study of history, J. J. Schacter comments, '[C]an one not make a case that, for R. Dessler, disregarding historical accuracy in such circumstances is precisely what the truth requires, assuming, of course, that one knows the truth about what the truth requires . . .' (Schacter, 'Facing the Truths of History', 234 (ellipsis in original)).

[217] Vol. i. 194. This source was noted by Bok, *Lying*, 301 n. 9.

[218] Rashdall, *Theory of Good and Evil*, i. 194–5 n. 1. In my earlier discussion of Dessler, p. 24 above, I also referred to William James's pragmatic theory of truth.

BIBLIOGRAPHY

Websites and Blogs

Bein Din Ledin — www.bdld.info
Dei'ah veDibur — www.chareidi.org
Failed Messiah — www.failedmessiah.com
Ishim ve-Shitos — www.ishimshitos.blogspot.com
On the Main Line — www.onthemainline.blogspot.com
Oneg Shabbat (David Assaf) — www.onegshabbat.blogspot.com
Seforim Blog — www.seforim.blogspot.com
Text and Texture — text.rcarabbis.org

Printed Sources

ABARBANEL, ISAAC, *Commentary on the Torah* [Perush al hatorah] (Jerusalem, 1994).

ABBA SHAUL, BEN TSIYON, *Or letsiyon* (Jerusalem, 2005), vol. iii.

ABOAB, ISAAC [supposed author], *Magen elokim*, ed. Y. Spiegel (Petah Tikvah, 2007).

ABOAB, SAMUEL, *Sefer hazikhronot* (Venice, 1650).

ABRAHAM BEN DAVID OF POSQUIÈRES, *Hasagot*, glosses on Maimonides, *Mishneh torah*, printed in standard edns.

—— *Katuv sham*, ed. M. Z. Hasidah (Jerusalem, 1969).

—— *Katuv sham* (Jerusalem, 1990).

ABRAHAM, HAYIM SHLOMO, *Birkat shelomoh* (Brooklyn, NY, 2000).

—— *Devar torah*, 2 vols. (Monsey, NY, 2006, 2010).

ABRAHAM, MICHAEL, *Enosh keḥatsir* (Kefar Hasidim, 2008).

ABRAHAMS, ISRAEL, *Hebrew Ethical Wills* (Philadelphia, Pa., 1926), vol. i.

ABRAMOWITZ, UDI, 'The Ideology of Rabbi Tsevi Yehudah Kook in the Editing of the Works of Rabbi Abraham Isaac Kook' [Ha'ide'ologyah shel harav tsevi yehudah hakohen kuk be'arikhat kitvei hare'iyah] (MA diss., Bar-Ilan University, 2007).

—— 'The Mission, the Monopoly, and the Censorship: Rabbi Tsevi Yehudah Hakohen Kook and the Editing of Rav Kook's Writings' (Heb.), *Da'at*, 60 (2007), 121–52.

ABRAMOWITZ, Z. Y., '*Besamim rosh* in a Hasidic Mirror' (Heb.), *Tagim*, 3–4 (Elul 5732), 56–8.

ABRAMSON, SHRAGA, 'From the Teachings of Rabbi Samuel Hanagid of Spain' (Heb.), *Sinai*, 100 (1987), 7–73.

ABULAFIA, MEIR, *Yad ramah* (Jerusalem, 1994).

ADELMAN, HOWARD ERNEST, '"Law and Love": The Jewish Family in Early Modern Italy', *Continuity and Change*, 16 (2001), 283–303.

—— 'Success and Failure in the Seventeenth Century Ghetto of Venice: The Life and Thought of Leon Modena, 1571–1648' (Ph.D. diss., Brandeis University, 1985).

ADES, YA'AKOV, *Divrei ya'akov: ḥulin, toharot* (n.p., n.d.).

ADLER, MENAHEM, *A Hasmonean and His Sons* [Ḥashmona'i uvanav] (Jerusalem, 2003).

ADLER, RACHEL, 'The Virgin in the Brothel and Other Anomalies: Character and Context in the Legend of Beruriah', *Tikkun*, 3 (Nov.–Dec. 1988), 28–32, 102–5.

AGNON, SHMUEL YOSEF, *Sefer, sofer vesipur* (Jerusalem, 1978).

—— *A Simple Story*, trans. Hillel Halkin (New York, 1985).

AJDLER, J. JEAN, 'Talmudic Metrology VII: Sabbath Limits and Jewish Time Reckoning', *Badad*, 26 (2012), 21–64.

ALBECK, HANOKH, *Mavo latalmudim* (Tel Aviv, 1969).

ALDERMAN, GEOFFREY, 'The Charedi Custom of Excise', *Jewish Chronicle*, 23 Nov. 2011.

ALEXANDER SUSSKIND BEN MOSES, *Tsava'ah* (Grodno, 1794; Zhitomir, 1848; Warsaw, 1913; Vilna, 1929).

ALHARAR, MOSHE MAIMON, *Likhvodah shel torah* (Jerusalem, 1988).

ALLEN, PRUDENCE, *The Concept of Woman* (Montreal, 1985).

ALTER, ABRAHAM MORDECHAI, *Osef mikhtavim* (Augsburg, 1947).

ALTMANN, ALEXANDER, *Moses Mendelssohn* (London, 1998).

AMRAM GAON, *Seder rav amram hashalem*, ed. A. L. Frumkin (Jerusalem, 1912; Jerusalem, 1993).

ANATOLI, JACOB, *Malmad hatalmidim* (Lyck, 1866).

ANGEL, HAYYIM, 'Abarbanel: Commentator and Teacher Celebrating 500 Years of His Influence on Tanakh Study', *Tradition*, 42 (Fall 2009), 9–26.

ANON., *Afikei torah* (New York, 2009).

ANON., *Avat nefesh*, undated typescript on Otzar HaHochma (<www.otzar.org>).

ANON., *Beit rabi* (Benei Berak, 1988).

ANON., *Beit zlotshov*, 2 vols. (Jerusalem, 1999).

ANON., 'Concerning *Be'er mayim ḥayim*, the Levin–Epstein Edition' (Heb.), *Shevet miyisra'el*, 3 (2002), 28–9.

ANON., *Erets tsevi: kovets ma'amarim be'inyanei erets yisra'el* (Jerusalem, 1989).

ANON., *Hashakdan*, 3 vols. (Jerusalem, 2010–13).

ANON., *Ḥemdat yamim* (Izmir, 1731–2).

ANON., *Ḥesronot hashas* (Kraków, 1894).

ANON., *The* Igeret hamusar *Attributed to Maimonides* [Igeret hamusar hameyuḥeset leharambam], ed. H. Copperman (Jerusalem, 2007).

ANON., *Kevutsat hahashmatot* (n.p., n.d.).

ANON., *Kol bo*, ed. D. Avraham (Jerusalem, 1990), vol. ii.

ANON., *Kol hashofar* (Jerusalem, [1920]).

ANON., *Lezikhro* [in memory of R. Tsevi Yehudah Kook] (Jerusalem, 1993).

ANON., 'Maskilic Changes in the Works of R. Hayim Joseph David Azulai' (Heb.), *Hamevaser* (22 Adar 5772), 20–1.

ANON., 'Mystery: Who Published *Hilkhot hamedinah?*' (Heb.) (30 Jan. 2007), <www.inn.co.il/News/News.aspx/159012>.

ANON., *Omer hashikheḥah* (n.p., 1861).

ANON., *Orḥot tsadikim* (New York, 1982).

ANON., *Die Samson-Raphael-Hirsch-Schule in Frankfurt am Main* (Frankfurt am Main, 2001).

ANON., *Sar hatorah* (Jerusalem, 2004).

ANON., *Shemitah kemitsvatah* (n.p., 2006).

ANON., *Shivḥei habesht* (Kopys, 1815); ed. S. Horodetzky (Berlin, 1922).

ANON., *Yisa shalom* (n.p., 2012).

ANON. (ed.), *Zekhor ledavid* [David Frankel memorial volume] (Jerusalem, 2000), vol. ii.

ANUSHISKI, SHNEUR ZALMAN, *Matsav hayashar* (Vilna, 1881), vol. i.

APTOWITZER, V., *Das Schriftwort in der rabbinischen Literatur* (New York, 1970).

ARANOFF, DEENA, 'Elijah Levita: A Jewish Hebraist', *Jewish History*, 23 (2009), 17–40.

ARATAN, ISRAEL, *Torat hamidot* (Jerusalem, 1947).

ARBEL, AVRAHAM, *Aḥoti kalah* (n.p., 2007).

ARIEL, YA'AKOV, 'Conquering Curiosity' (Heb.), *Nekudah*, 114 (Tishrei 5748), 44.

ARIELI, YITSHAK, *Einayim lamishpat al masekhet berakhot* (Jerusalem, 1947; repr. 2006).

ASHER BEN YEHIEL, *She'elot uteshuvot harosh*, ed. Y. Yudelov (Jerusalem, 1994).

ASHKENAZI, BETSALEL, *Shitah mekubetset* (Jerusalem, 1999).

ASHKENAZI, NISSIM ABRAHAM, *Neḥmad lemar'eh* (Salonika, 1832).

ASHKENAZI, SHMUEL, *Alfa beita tinyeta dishemuel ze'ira*, ed. Y. Stahl (Jerusalem, 2011), vol. i.

ASHKENAZI, TSEVI HIRSCH, *She'elot uteshuvot ḥakham tsevi* (Lemberg, 1900).

ASHLAG, YEHUDAH, Commentary on R. Hayim Vital's *Ets ḥayim* (Jerusalem, 1930; London, 1967).

ASSAF, DAVID, *Beguiled by Knowledge: An Anatomy of a Hasidic Controversy* [Hetsits venifga: anatomyah shel maḥaloket ḥasidit] (Haifa, 2012).

—— *Caught in the Thicket* [Ne'eḥaz basevakh] (Jerusalem, 2006).

—— 'It is the Glory of God to Conceal a Thing' (Heb.), *Katedra*, 68 (June 1993), 57–66.

—— *The Regal Way: The Life and Times of R. Israel of Ruzhin* [Derekh hamalkhut: r. yisra'el miruzhin umekomo betoledot haḥasidut] (Jerusalem, 1997).

ATTIAH, ISAAC, *Rov dagan* (Livorno, 1823).

AUERBACH, MOSHE (ed.), *Memorial Book for Rabbi Isaac Halevy* [Sefer zikaron lerabi yitsḥak isak halevi] (Tel Aviv, 1964).

AUERBACH, SHLOMO ZALMAN, *Ma'adanei shelomoh* (Jerusalem, 2003).

AUGUSTINE, *City of God*, trans. Marcus Dods (Edinburgh, 1881).

AVINER, SHLOMO, *Aloh na'aleh*, ed. Mordechai Tsiyon (Beit El, 2012).

—— *Tsevi kodesh* (Beit El, 2005).

AVIVI, YOSEF, 'R. Hayim Vital's *Ets ḥayim, Peri ets ḥayim,* and *Nof ets ḥayim*' (Heb.), *Tsefunot,* 17 (1993), 84–91.

AVNERI, YOSSI, 'Rabbi Abraham Isaac Hakohen Kook, Rabbi of Jaffa (1904–14)' (Heb.), *Katedra,* 37 (1985), 49–82.

AVNI, M. (ed.), *Ḥazon ha'ish* (Jerusalem, 1997).

AYASH, MORDECHAI, *Beitkha shalom* (n.p. [Israel], 2009).

AZIKRI, ELEAZAR BEN MOSES, *Sefer ḥaredim* (Jerusalem, 1958).

AZULAI, HAYIM JOSEPH DAVID, *Ahavat david* (Jerusalem, 1967).

—— *Birkei yosef* (Jerusalem, 1990).

—— *Ein zokher* (Jerusalem, 1962).

—— *Kise raḥamim* (Livorno, 1803).

—— *Ma'gal tov hashalem,* ed. A. Freimann (Jerusalem, 1934).

—— *Maḥazik berakhah* (Livorno, 1785).

—— *Petaḥ einayim* (Jerusalem, 1959).

—— *Shem hagedolim* (Vilna, 1853).

—— *Shem hagedolim hashalem* (New York, n.d), vol. ii.

—— *Yosef omets* (Jerusalem, 1961).

BACHARACH, YAIR HAYIM, *Ḥut hashani* (Jerusalem, 1980).

—— *Mekor ḥayim,* ed. E. Pines (Jerusalem, 1984).

—— *Ya'ir nativ,* published in *Bikurim,* 1 (1865), 4–26.

BAHUR, ELIJAH, *see* Levita.

BAHYA BEN ASHER, *Commentary on the Torah* [Be'ur al hatorah], 3 vols., ed. C. Chavel (Jerusalem, 2006).

BAHYA IBN PAKUDA, *Ḥovot halevavot,* trans. Moses Hyamson (Jerusalem, 1962); trans. Menahem Mansoor (London, 1973); *The Duties of the Heart,* trans. Yaakov Feldman (Northvale, NJ, 1996).

BAR-ILAN, MEIR, *From Volozhin to Jerusalem* [Mivolozhin ad yerushalayim] (Tel Aviv, 1971), vol. i.

BAR SHALOM, YOSEF, *Vayitsbor yosef* (Bat Yam, 2001), vol. ii.

BARDA, DAVID, *Revid hazahav* (Tiberias, 2008), vol. ii.

BARIS, MICHAEL, 'Place and Identity: A Commentary on the First Chapter of *Pirkei avot*' (Heb.), in *Mikarmei shomron* (n.p., 2000), 283–316.

BARON, SALO WITTMAYER, *The Russian Jews under Tsars and Soviets* (New York, 1964).

—— *A Social and Religious History of the Jews,* 17 vols. (New York, 1952–83).

BARTAL, ISRAEL, 'R. Ya'akov Lifshitz's *Zikhron ya'akov*: Orthodox Historiography?' (Heb.), *Milet,* 2 (1985), 409–14.

—— 'Shimon the Heretic: A Chapter in Orthodox Historiography' (Heb.), in I. Bartal et al. (eds.), *Studies in Jewish Culture in Honour of Chone Shmeruk* [Keminhag ashkenaz upolin: sefer yovel lekhoneh shmeruk] (Jerusalem, 1993), 243–68.

—— 'True Knowledge and Wisdom: Approaches to Understanding Orthodox Historiography' (Heb.), *Zemanim,* 64 (1998), 4–14.

BASSER, HERBERT W., *Studies in Exegesis: Christian Critiques of Jewish Law and Rabbinic Responses 70–300 C.E.* (Boston, Mass., 2002).

BE'ER, SHABETAI, *Be'er esek* (Venice, 1674).

BEKHOR SHOR, JOSEPH, *Commentary on the Torah* [Perush al hatorah] (Jerusalem, 1956).

BEN-AMOS, DAN, and JEROME R. MINTZ (trans.), *In Praise of the Baal Shem Tov* (Northvale, NJ, 1993).

BEN-ARTZI, HAGGAI, 'The First Teaching Is Also Zionist' (Heb.), *Akdamot*, 6 (1999), 73–5.

—— '"The Old Will Be Renewed and the New Will Be Sanctified": Criticism of Religion and the Means of its Renewal in the Early Thought of Rav Kook' (Heb.), *Akdamot*, 3 (1997), 9–28.

BEN-DAVID, YEHUDAH LAVI, '*Ḥemdat yamim*' (Heb.), *Tsohar*, 4 (1999), 278–92.

—— *Shevet miyehudah* (Jerusalem, 2002).

BEN ISAIAH, ABRAHAM, and BENJAMIN SHARFMAN (trans.), *The Pentateuch and Rashi's Commentary* (Brooklyn, NY, 1949).

BEN-MENAHEM, ELYAKIM, introd. and commentary on Jonah, in *Da'at mikra: trei-asar* (Jerusalem, 1990), vol. i.

BEN-MENAHEM, NAFTALI, 'Maḥaloket-Beregsas', *Sinai*, 14 (1944), 152–62.

BEN-YEHUDA, NACHMAN, *The Masada Myth: Collective Memory and Mythmaking in Israel* (Madison, Wis., 1995).

BENAMOZEGH, ELIJAH, *Jewish and Christian Ethics* (San Francisco, 1873; Jerusalem, 2000).

—— *Ta'am leshad* (Livorno, 1865).

BENAYAHU, MEIR, 'R. Hayim Hezekiah Medini (Biography)' (Heb.), in Abraham Elmaleh (ed.), *Ḥemdat yisra'el* (Jerusalem, 1946), 183–212.

—— *Relations between Greek and Italian Jewry* [Hayaḥasim shebein yehudei yavan liyehudei italyah] (Tel Aviv, 1980).

—— *Yosef beḥiri* (Jerusalem, 1991).

BENEDIKT, BINYAMIN ZE'EV, *Collected Essays* [Asupat ma'amarim] (Jerusalem, 1994).

BENISCH, HAYIM P., 'An Explanation of the Calculation of the Times of Day and Night by the Hatam Sofer in the Name of His Teacher R. Nathan Adler' (Heb.), *Otserot hasofer*, 12 (2001), 59–64.

—— *Hazemanim bahalakhah*, 2 vols. (Benei Berak, 1996).

BENISCH, PEARL, *To Vanquish the Dragon* (Jerusalem, 1991).

Bereshit rabah, ed. J. Theodor and H. Albeck (Jerusalem, 1965).

BERGER, DAVID, *Cultures in Collision and Conversation* (Boston, Mass., 2011).

—— 'Jews, Gentiles and the Modern Egalitarian Ethos: Some Tentative Thoughts', in Marc D. Stern (ed.), *Formulating Responses in an Egalitarian Age* (Lanham, Md., 2005), 83–108.

—— *Persecution, Polemic, and Dialogue* (Boston, Mass., 2010).

BERGER, ISRAEL, *Eser orot* (Piotrków, 1907).

BERGER, MICHAEL S., 'Maimonides on Sex and Marriage', in Michael J. Broyde and Michael Ausubel (eds.), *Marriage, Sex, and Family in Judaism* (Oxford, 2005), 149–91.

BERGMAN, ASHER, *Toledot maran harav shakh* (Benei Berak, 2006).

BERLIN, NAPHTALI TSEVI JUDAH, *Meshiv davar* (Warsaw, 1894), vol. ii.

BERLIN, SAUL, *Besamim rosh* (Jerusalem, 1984).

BERLINER, ABRAHAM, *Aus dem Leben der deutschen Juden im Mittelalter* (Berlin, 1900).

—— *Selected Writings* [Ketavim nivḥarim], 2 vols. (Jerusalem, 1945–9).

BIN-NUN, YOEL, 'Inspiration of the Holy Spirit According to Rabbi A. I. Kook' (Heb.), in Binyamin Ish Shalom (ed.), *On the Paths of Peace: Studies in Jewish Thought Presented to Shalom Rosenberg* [Bedarkhei shalom: iyunim behagut yehudit mugashim leshalom rosenberg] (Jerusalem, 2007), 353–76.

BIRNBAUM, PHILIP, *Ha-Siddur ha-Shalem* (New York, 1949).

BLEICH, J. DAVID, 'Divine Unity in Maimonides, The Tosafists and Me'iri', in Lenn E. Goodman (ed.), *Neoplatonism and Jewish Thought* (Albany, NY, 1992), 237–54.

BLIDSTEIN, GERALD (YA'AKOV), *Studies in Halakhic and Aggadic Thought* [Iyunim bemaḥshevet hahalakhah veha'agadah] (Be'er Sheva, 2004).

BLOCH, ELIJAH MOSES, *Ruaḥ eliyahu* (Lakewood, NJ, 1954).

BLOCH, HAYIM, *Anthology of the Words and Sayings of the Sages* [Heikhal ledivrei ḥazal ufitgemeihem] (New York, 1948).

BOK, SISELA, *Lying: Moral Choice in Public and Private Life* (New York, 1999).

BOKSER, BEN ZION (ed.), *The Prayer Book* (New York, 1957).

BONFIL, ROBERT, *Rabbis and Jewish Communities in Renaissance Italy*, trans. Jonathan Chipman (London, 1993).

BONFILS, JOSEPH, *Tsafnat pane'aḥ*, ed. D. Herzog, 2 vols. (Kraków, 1912; Heidelberg, 1930).

BORSCHEL-DAN, AMANDA, 'Visiting Gershom Scholem', *Times of Israel*, 20 Feb. 2012.

BOYARIN, DANIEL, *Border Lines: The Partition of Judaeo-Christianity* (Philadelphia, Pa., 2004).

—— *Carnal Israel* (Berkeley, Calif., 1995).

—— *Socrates and the Fat Rabbis* (Chicago, 2009).

BRAND, EZRA, 'Principles of Omission of Laws in Maimonides' *Mishneh torah*' (Heb.), *Hama'yan*, 53 (Tevet 5773), 21–54.

BRAUN, SHLOMO ZALMAN, *She'arim metsuyanim bahalakhah* (New York, 1949).

BRAZIL, SHMUEL, *Besha'arei hamo'adim* (n.p., 1997).

BREGMAN, MARC, 'Pseudepigraphy in Rabbinic Literature', in Esther G. Chazon and Michael Stone (eds.), *Pseudepigraphic Perspectives: The Apocrypha and Pseudepigrapha in Light of the Dead Sea Scrolls* (Leiden, 1999), 27–41.

BREISCH, MORDECHAI JACOB, *Ḥelkat ya'akov* (Jerusalem, 1951).

BREUER, ISAAC, *Darki* (Jerusalem, 1988); German trans., *Mein Weg* (Zurich, 1988).

—— *Weltwende* (Jerusalem, 1979).

BREUER, MORDECHAI, 'Agudat Yisra'el and Western Orthodoxy' (Heb.), *Hama'yan*, 5 (Tishrei 5725 [1964]), 15–18.

—— *Asif* (Jerusalem, 1999).

—— *Modernity within Tradition*, trans. Elizabeth Petuchowski (New York, 1992).

—— *Ohalei torah* (Jerusalem, 2004).

—— 'Review of Recent Books' (Heb.), *Hama'yan*, 7 (Tishrei 5727), 64–72.

BRILL, ALAN, 'The Writings of the Vilna Gaon and Philosophical Terminology', in Moshe Hallamish et al. (eds.), *The Vilna Gaon and His Disciples* (Ramat Gan, 2003), 8–37.

BRIN, GERSHON, 'Themes in R. Judah Hehasid's Torah Commentary' (Heb.), *Te'udah*, 3 (1983), 215–26.

BRODT, ELIEZER YEHUDAH, 'The Laws of *Birkat hare'iyah* in *Ma'gal tov* by R. Hayim Joseph David Azulai (Hida) (2)' (Heb.), *Yeshurun*, 27 (2012), 907–39.

BROWN, BENJAMIN, 'From Principles to Rules and from *Musar* to *Halakhah*: The Hafetz Hayim's Rulings on Libel and Gossip', *Dine Israel*, 25 (2008), 171–256.

—— *The Hazon Ish: Halakhist, Believer, and Leader of the Haredi Revolution* [Haḥazon ish: haposek, hama'amin umanhig hamahapekhah haḥaredit] (Jerusalem, 2011).

BROYDE, MICHAEL, 'Hair Covering and Jewish Law: Biblical and Objective (*Dat Moshe*) or Rabbinic and Subjective (*Dat Yehudit*)?', *Tradition*, 42 (Fall 2009), 97–179.

BRÜLL, JACOB, *Mevo hamishnah* (Frankfurt am Main, 1876).

BUNIM, AMOS, *A Fire in His Soul* (Jerusalem, 1989).

BUNIM, IRVING, *Ethics from Sinai*, 3 vols. (New York, 1964–6).

BUXTORF, JOHANNES, *Synagoga Judaica* (Basel, 1680); online translation by Alan D. Corré, <https://pantherfile.uwm.edu/corre/www/buxdorf>.

CAPSALI, ELIJAH, *Me'ah she'arim* (Jerusalem, 2001).

CARLEBACH, ELISHEVA, *Divided Souls: Converts from Judaism in Germany, 1500–1750* (New Haven, Conn., 2001).

—— *The Pursuit of Heresy: Rabbi Moses Hagiz and the Sabbatian Controversies* (New York, 1990).

CARMILLY-WEINBERGER, MOSES, *Censorship and Freedom of Expression in Jewish History* (New York, 1977).

—— *Fear of Art: Censorship and Freedom of Expression in Art* (New York, 1986).

CARMY, SHALOM, 'Dialectic, Doubters, and a Self-Erasing Letter', in Lawrence J. Kaplan and David Shatz (eds.), *Rabbi Abraham Isaac Kook and Jewish Spirituality* (New York, 1995), 205–36.

CASPI *see* IBN KASPI

CHAJES, TSEVI HIRSCH, *Kol sifrei maharats ḥayes* (Jerusalem, 1958), vol. i.

CHAPNIK, ELAINE, '"Women Known for These Acts" through the Rabbinic Lens: A Study of *Hilchot Lesbiut*', in Miryam Kabakov (ed.), *Keep Your Wives Away from Them: Orthodox Women, Unorthodox Desires* (Berkeley, Calif., 2010), 78–98.

CHERLOW, SEMADAR, *The Tsadik is the Foundation of the World: Rav Kook's Esoteric Mission and Mystical Experience* [Tsadik yesod olam: hasheliḥut hasodit vehaḥavayah hamistit shel harav kook] (Ramat Gan, 2012).

CHERLOW, YUVAL, 'Keep Away from Falsehood' (Heb.), *Tsohar*, 1 (2000), 13–24.

CHWAT, ARI YITSHAK, 'The Question of Antinomianism and Clarification of the Concept of *bediavad* in Rav Kook's Teachings' (Heb.), unpublished.

—— 'Those Who Are Innocent According to the Bible and Guilty According to the Sages' (Heb.), *Talelei orot*, 12 (2006), 13–99.

CHWAT, EZRA, 'A Responsum on *Birkat haminim* by R. Meir the Author of *Mishpat tsedek*' (Heb.), *Yeshurun*, 14 (2004), 803–10.

CITRON, ISRAEL, *Ḥidushei harav tsitron-katroni* (Petah Tikvah, 2010).

CLEMENT OF ALEXANDRIA, *The Writings of Clement of Alexandria*, trans. William Wilson, in Alexander Roberts and James Donaldson (eds.), *Ante-Nicene Christian Library* (Edinburgh, 1867), vol. ii.

COHEN, ARYEH LEIB, 'The Ways and Opinions of the Hafets Hayim' (Heb.), in *Mikhtevei harav ḥafets ḥayim* (New York, n.d.), 3–92 (third pagination).

COHEN, DAVID, *Mishnat hanazir* (Jerusalem, 2005).

COHEN, DOVID, *He'akov lemishor* (Brooklyn, NY, 1993).

COHEN, GERSHON, 'On the History of the Controversy over Non-Jewish Wine in Italy and its Sources' (Heb.), *Sinai*, 77 (1975), 62–90.

COHEN, JACK SIMCHA, 'Halakhic Parameters of Truth', *Tradition*, 16 (Spring 1977), 83–97.

COHEN, SHALOM PINHAS, 'Maimonides' Relation to Women According to Rabbi Joseph Kafih' (Heb.), in Yosef Farhi (ed.), *Masorah leyosef*, 8 (2014), 53–71.

COHEN, YIGAL, *Ukeneh lekha ḥaver* (Holon, 2006).

CONNOR, JAMES, *The Last Judgment: Michelangelo and the Death of the Renaissance* (New York, 2009).

COOPERMAN, BERNARD, '"Trade and Settlement": The Establishment and Early Development of the Jewish Communities in Leghorn and Pisa (1591–1626)' (Ph.D. diss., Harvard University, 1976).

CORONEL, NAHMAN NATHAN, *Zekher natan* (Vienna, 1872).

DA FANO, MENAHEM AZARIAH, *She'elot uteshuvot harama mifano* (Jerusalem, n.d.).

DA SILVA, HEZEKIAH, *Peri ḥadash* (Amsterdam, 1706).

Da'at zekenim miba'alei tosafot, in standard edns. of *Mikraot gedolot* (Rabbinic Bibles).

DANZIG, ABRAHAM, *Ḥayei adam* (Vilna, 1810; Vilna and Grodno, 1819).

—— *Ḥayei adam venishmat adam hamefo'ar* (Jerusalem, 2008), vol. ii.

—— *Ḥokhmat adam* (n.p., 1970).

DANZIGER, SHLOMO, 'Rediscovering the Hirschian Legacy', *Jewish Action*, 56 (Summer 1996), 20–4.

DAVID MOSES OF CHORTKOV, *Divrei david* (Husiatyn, 1904).

DAVIDSON, HERBERT A., 'The Authenticity of Works Attributed to Maimonides', in Ezra Fleischer et al. (eds.), *Me'ah She'arim: Studies in Medieval Jewish Spiritual Life in Memory of Isadore Twersky* (Jerusalem, 2001), 111–33.

—— 'Maimonides' "Shemonah Peraqim" and Alfarabi's "Fusul al Madani"', *PAAJR*, 31 (1963), 33–50.

—— *Moses Maimonides: The Man and His Works* (Oxford, 2005).

DAVIS, AVROHOM, *The Complete Metsudah Siddur* (Brooklyn, NY, 1990).

DAVIS, JOSEPH, *Yom-Tov Lipmann Heller: Portrait of a Seventeenth-Century Rabbi* (Oxford, 2004).

DE ROSSI, AZARIAH, *Me'or einayim* (Vilna, 1863).

DE SOLA, D. A., and M. J. RAPHALL (trans.), *Eighteen Treatises from the Mishna* (London, 1843).

DE SOLA POOL, DAVID, *The Kaddish* (Leipzig, 1909).

—— (ed. and trans.), *Traditional Prayerbook for Sabbath and Festivals* (New Hyde Park, NY, 1960).

DEANESLY, MARGARET, *The Lollard Bible and Other Medieval Biblical Versions* (Cambridge, 1920).

DEBLITZKY, BETZALEL, 'Responsa of R. Joseph Hayim' (Heb.), *Mikavtse'el*, 35 (Tishrei 5769), 583–628.

DEHAN, YA'AKOV, *Dibrot ya'akov: ketubot* (n.p., 1997).

DELMEDIGO, JOSEPH SOLOMON, *Matsref leḥokhmah* (Basel, 1629).

DERSHOWITZ, YITZCHOK, *The Legacy of Maran Rav Aharon Kotler* (Nanuet, NY, 2005).

DESHEN, SHLOMO, *R. Shimon Kohen of Frankfurt* [R. shimon kohen mifrankfurt] (Jerusalem, 2003).

DESSLER, ELIJAH, *Mikhtav me'eliyahu* (Jerusalem, 2007), vol. i.

DEUTSCH, NATHANIEL, *The Maiden of Ludmir* (Berkeley, Calif., 2003).

DEUTSCH, SHAUL SHIMON, *Larger than Life: The Life and Times of the Lubavitcher Rebbe Rabbi Menachem Mendel Schneerson* (New York, 1997), vol. ii.

DI BOTON, ABRAHAM, *Leḥem mishneh*, commentary on Maimonides, *Mishneh torah*, printed in standard edns.

DI BOTON, JACOB, *Edut beya'akov* (Salonika, 1720).

DIENSTAG, ISRAEL JACOB, 'Did the Vilna Gaon Oppose Maimonides' Philosophy?' (Heb.), *Talpiyot*, 4 (1949), 253–68.

——'Maimonides' *Mishneh torah*: A Bibliography of Editions' (Heb.), in Charles Berlin (ed.), *Studies in Jewish Bibliography, History, and Literature in Honor of I. Edward Kiev* (New York, 1971), 21–108.

DISON, YONINAH, '*Orot hakodesh* Re-edited and Organized According to Four Motifs' (Heb.), *Da'at*, 24 (1990), 41–86.

DON-YIHYE, SHABETAI, *Anshei torah umalkhut* (Tel Aviv, 1967).

DRATCH, MARK, 'Nothing but the Truth?', *Judaism*, 37 (Spring 1988), 218–28.

DURAN, SIMEON BEN TSEMAH, *Magen avot*, ed. E. Zini (Jerusalem, 2000).

—— *Ohev mishpat* (Venice, 1590).

—— *Zohar harakia* (Vilna, 1879).

EDELMAN, H., *Hegyon lev* (Königsberg, 1845).

EDELS, SAMUEL (MAHARSHA), commentary on the Talmud, printed in standard edns.

EFRATI, BINYAMIN, 'Two Visits to the Hazon Ish' (Heb.), *Morashah*, 6 (1974), 62–3.

EHRENBERG, JOSHUA, *Devar yehoshua* (Jerusalem, 1970), vol. i.

EHRENREICH, HAYIM YEHUDAH, 'One Who Drinks Gentile Wine, How Does He Atone?' (Heb.), *Otsar haḥayim*, 12 (1936), 99.

EISEN, CHAIM, 'Maharal's *Be'er ha-Golah* and His Revolution in Aggadic Scholarship—in Their Context and on His Terms', *Hakirah*, 4 (Winter, 2007), 137–94.

EISENSTADT, ABRAHAM TSEVI, *Pitḥei teshuvah*, commentary on Joseph Karo, *Shulḥan arukh*, printed in standard edns.

EISENSTEIN, JUDAH DAVID (ed.), *Otsar yisra'el* (Jerusalem, 1971), vol. viii.

ELBAUM, AVISHAI, 'Alterations in *Haskamot*' (Heb.), *Hama'yan*, 38 (Tishrei 5758), 34–8.

—— and ARYEH ELBAUM, *Dabar ledor* (n.p., 1996).

ELBAUM, YA'AKOV, 'Concerning Two Textual Emendations in the *Aleinu* Prayer' (Heb.), *Tarbiz*, 42 (1973), 204–8.

ELBOGEN, ISMAR, *Jewish Liturgy: A Comprehensive Survey*, trans. Raymond P. Scheindlin (Philadelpha, Pa., 1993).

ELEAZAR ASHKENAZI BEN NATHAN HABAVLI, *Tsafnat pane'aḥ*, ed. S. Rappaport (Johannesburg, 1965).

ELEFF, ZEV, *Shirat miryam* (Baltimore, Md., 2009).

ELHANAN, YOEL [pseud.], 'How to Build Herzl's Temple: A Letter from Rabbi Abraham Isaac Hakohen Kook to Rabbi Hayim Hirschensohn' (Heb.), <www.yoel-ab.com/katava.asp?id=131>.

ELIACH, DOV, *Avi hayeshivot* (Jerusalem, 1991).

—— *Sefer hagaon*, 3 vols. (Jerusalem, 2002).

ELIASBURG, JONATHAN, *Shevil hazahav* (Vilna, 1897).

ELIEZER OF METZ, *Sefer yere'im* (Pinsk, 1935).

ELIEZRI, SAMUEL, *Melekhet shemuel* (Tel Aviv, 1962).

ELIJAH BEN HAYIM, *She'elot uteshuvot rabi eliyahu ben ḥayim* (Jerusalem, 1960).

ELIJAH BEN SAMUEL, *Yad eliyahu* (Amsterdam, 1712).

ELIJAH BEN SOLOMON ABRAHAM HAKOHEN, *Midrash talpiyot* (Izmir, 1736).

ELIYAHU, YOSEF, '*Leshon hara* between Husband and Wife' (Heb.), <www.inn.co.il/Articles/Article.aspx/7443>.

—— and RUTH ELIYAHU, *Hatorah hamesamaḥat* (Beit El, 1998).

ELON, MENACHEM, *Jewish Law*, trans. Bernard Auerbach and Melvin J. Sykes (Philadelphia, Pa., 1994), vol. iv.

ELYASHIV, SOLOMON, *Leshem shevo ve'aḥlamah*, 'Sefer hade'ah', vol. ii (Piotrków, 1912).

ELYASHIV, YOSEF SHALOM, *Kovets teshuvot* (Jerusalem, 2003), vol. iii.

EMDEN, JACOB, *Amudei shamayim* (Altona, 1745), vol. i.

—— *Derush tefilat yesharim* (Altona, 1775; Kraków, 1911).

—— *Luaḥ eresh*, ed. D. Yitzhaki (Toronto, 2001).

—— *Megilat sefer*, ed. A. Bombach (Jerusalem, 2012).

—— *Migdal oz* (Altona, 1748; Zhitomir, 1874).

—— *Mitpaḥat sefarim* (Jerusalem, 1995).

—— *Mor uketsiyah* (Jerusalem, 1996).

Encyclopaedia Judaica, 16 vols., ed. C. Roth (Jerusalem, 1972).

ENGLARD, IZHAK, 'Majority Decision vs. Individual Truth', *Tradition*, 15 (Spring–Summer, 1975), 137–52.

Entsiklopedyah talmudit, 32 vols. (Jerusalem, 1947–).

EPSTEIN, ISIDORE, *Judaism* (Baltimore, Md., 1966).

EPSTEIN, J. N., '*Mekhilta* and *Sifrei* in Maimonides' Works' (Heb.), *Tarbiz*, 6 (1935), 99–138.

EPSTEIN, YEHIEL MIKHEL, *Kitsur shelah* (Fuerth, 1653).

EPSTEIN, YEHIEL MIKHEL, *Arukh hashulḥan* (Jerusalem, n.d.).

—— *Kitvei ha'arukh hashulḥan* (Jerusalem, 2007).

ETKES, IMMANUEL, *Gaon of Vilna: The Man and His Image* [Yaḥid bedoro: hagaon mivilna—demut vedimui] (Jerusalem, 1998).

ETTLINGER, JACOB, *Arukh laner* (New York, 1950).

EUCLID, *Elements*, Hebrew trans. by Barukh of Shklov (The Hague, 1780).

EVEN, YITSHAK, *The Dispute between Sanz and Sadegora* [Maḥaloket sanz vesadigurah] (New York, 1916).

EYBESCHUETZ, JONATHAN, *Sar ha'elef* (Warsaw, 1816).

EYLENBURG, ISSACHAR BER, *Be'er sheva* (Jerusalem, 2004).

FAIERSTEIN, MORRIS M., *All Is in the Hands of Heaven: The Teachings of Rabbi Mordecai Joseph Leiner of Izbica* (Hoboken, NJ, 1989).

—— *Jewish Mystical Autobiographies: Book of Visions and Book of Secrets* (New York, 1999).

FALK, JOSHUA, *Perishah*, glosses on Jacob ben Asher, *Arba'ah turim*, printed in standard edns.

FALK, PESACH ELIYAHU, *Oz vehadar levushah* (Gateshead, 1998).

FARBER, SETH, *An American Orthodox Dreamer: Rabbi Joseph B. Soloveitchik and Boston's Maimonides School* (Hanover, NH, 2004).

FARBSTEIN, ESTHER, *Beseter ra'am: halakhah, hagut umanhigut bimei hasho'ah* (Jerusalem, 2002).

FAUR, JOSÉ, *The Horizontal Society* (Boston, Mass., 2008), vol. i.

FEINSTEIN, MOSES, *Dibrot mosheh: ketubot* (New York, 2000).

—— *Igerot mosheh*, 9 vols. (New York, 1959–2011).

FEIVISH, SAMUEL, *Beit shemuel*, commentary on Joseph Karo, *Shulḥan arukh*, printed in standard edns.

FELDMAN, DANIEL Z., *The Right and the Good: Halakhah and Human Relations* (Northvale, NJ, 1999).

FELDMAN, LOUIS, 'Masada, A Critique of Recent Scholarship', in Jacob Neusner (ed.), *Christianity, Judaism and Other Greco-Roman Cults: Studies for Morton Smith at Sixty* (Leiden, 1975), 218–48.

FELDMAN, ZVI (trans.), *Rav A. Y. Kook: Selected Letters* (Ma'aleh Adumim, 1986).

FERZIGER, ADAM, 'The Road Not Taken: Rav Shlomoh Zvi Schück and the Legacy of Hungarian Orthodoxy', *HUCA*, 79 (2003), 107–40.

FILBER, YA'AKOV, *Kokhvei or* (Jerusalem, 2003).

FINKELMAN, YOEL, *Strictly Kosher Reading: Popular Literature and the Condition of Contemporary Orthodoxy* (Boston, Mass., 2011).

FINKELSCHERER, ISRAEL, *Mose Maimunis Stellung zum Aberglauben und zur Mystik* (Breslau, 1894).

FISH, SHMUEL AHARON, *Davar beshem omro* (Jerusalem, 2006).

FISH, YA'AKOV HIZKIYAHU, *Titen emet leya'akov* (Jerusalem, 2004).

FISHER, ELIYAHU, *Birkat eliyahu* (Brooklyn, NY, n.d.).

FISHMAN, TALYA, 'Forging Jewish Memory: *Besamim Rosh* and the Invention of Pre-Emancipation Jewish Culture', in Elisheva Carlebach et al. (eds.), *Jewish History and Jewish Memory: Essays in Honor of Yosef Hayim Yerushalmi* (Hanover, NH, 1998), 70–88.

FIXLER, DROR, 'Polemical Language in Maimonides' *Commentary on the Mishnah*' (Heb.), in Yosef Eliyahu Movshovitz (ed.), *Maimonides Anthology* [Kovets harambam] (Jerusalem, 2005), 151–98.

FLATTO, SHARON, *The Kabbalistic Culture of Eighteenth-Century Prague: Ezekiel Landau (the 'Noda Biyehudah') and His Contemporaries* (Oxford, 2010).

FLECKELES, ELEAZAR, *Ahavat david* (Prague, 1800).

FLEISCHER, JUDAH LEIB, 'R. Abraham Ibn Ezra and His Literary Work in England' (Heb.), *Otsar haḥayim*, 7 (1931), 69–76, 107–11, 129–33, 160–8, 189–203.

FOGEL, MOSHE, 'The Sabbatian Character of *Ḥemdat yamim*: A New Look' (Heb.), in Rachel Elior (ed.), *The Dream and its Shattering* [Haḥalom veshivro] (Jerusalem, 2001), 365–422.

FOGELMAN, MORDECHAI, 'Practical Halakhah: *Halakhah ve'ein morin ken*' (Heb.), *Hatsofeh leḥokhmat yisra'el*, 15 (1931), 144–56.

FRAENKEL, DAVID, *Sheyarei korban*, commentary on the Jerusalem Talmud, printed in standard edns.

FRANKEL, ZECHARIAH, *Mevo hayerushalmi* (Breslau, 1870).

FRANKLIN, RUTH, *A Thousand Darknesses: Lies and Truth in Holocaust Fiction* (Oxford, 2011).

FREUNDEL, BARRY, *Why We Pray What We Pray* (Jerusalem, 2000).

FRIEDFERTIG, MORDECHAI, *Kum hithalekh ba'arets* (n.p., 2008).

FRIEDMAN, HERSHEY H., and ABRAHAM C. WEISEL, 'Should Moral Individuals Ever Lie? Insights from Jewish Law', <http://www.jlaw.com/Articles/hf_Lying Permissible.html>.

FRIEDMAN, MENAHEM, *Society and Religion* [Ḥevrah vedat] (Jerusalem, 1998).

FRIEDMAN, MENAHEM NAHUM, *On Truth and Falsehood* [Al ha'emet vehasheker] (Botoșani, 1927).

FRIEDMAN, TALI, 'Does the Public Have a Right to Know? The Censorship, Editing, and Non-Publication of Rabbi Abraham Isaac Hakohen Kook's Manuscripts' [Ha'im zekhut hatsibur leda'at: tsenzurah, arikhah, ugenizat kitvei hayad shel harav avraham yitsḥak hakohen kuk] (MA diss., Bar-Ilan University, 2011).

FRIEDMAN, TSEVI HIRSH, *Tsevi ḥemed* (Brooklyn, NY, 1960), vols. 38–40.

FRIMER, ARYEH, and DOV FRIMER, 'Women's Prayer Services: Theory and Practice', *Tradition*, 32 (Winter 1998), 5–118.

FRIMER, NORMAN, 'A Midrash on Morality or When is a Lie Permissible', *Tradition*, 13 (Spring–Summer 1973), 23–34.

FRISCH, AMOZ, 'R. Samson Raphael Hirsch's Interpretation of the Sins of the Patriarchs According to His Commentary on Genesis' (Heb.), in Moshe Ahrend and Shmuel Feuerstein (eds.), *Paths in the Bible and its Teaching* [Derakhim bamikra uvehora'ato] (Ramat Gan, 1997), 181–97.

—— 'The Sins of the Patriarchs as Viewed by Traditional Jewish Exegesis', *JSQ*, 10 (2003), 258–73.

GALINSKY, JUDAH D., and JAMES T. ROBINSON, 'Rabbi Jeruham b. Meshullam, Michael Scot, and the Development of Jewish Law in Fourteenth-Century Spain', *Harvard Theological Review*, 100 (2007), 489–504.

GANTZ, HAYIM MEIR, *Reshumim beshimkha* (Ashdod, 2007).

GANZFRIED, SOLOMON, *Kitsur shulḥan arukh* (numerous edns.); Eng. trans. Hyman E. Goldin, *Code of Jewish Law* (New York, 1961).

GARB, JONATHAN, 'Prophecy, Halakhah, and Antinomianism in Rav Kook's *Shemonah kevatsim*' (Heb.), in Zeev Gries et al. (eds.), *Shefa tal* (Be'er Sheva, 2004), 267–77.

GARBER, ZEV, 'The 93 Beit Yaakov Martyrs', in Franklin H. Littel et al. (eds.), *What Have We Learned? Telling the Story and Teaching the Lessons of the Holocaust* (Lewiston, NY, 1993), 323–49.

Gates of Prayer (New York, 1975).

GELLMAN, JEROME I., *The Fear, the Trembling, and the Fire: Kierkegaard and Hasidic Masters on the Binding of Isaac* (Lanham, Md., 1994).

GERBER, REUVEN, *The Enlightenment Revolution: The Spiritual Path of Rabbi Abraham Isaac Kook* [Mahapekhat hahe'arah: darko haruḥanit shel harav avraham yitsḥak hakohen kuk] (Jerusalem, 2005).

GERONDI, JONAH, *Igeret hateshuvah* (Jerusalem, 1962).

—— *Sha'arei teshuvah* (Jerusalem, 1967).

GERONDI, NISSIM, *Derashot haran*, ed. L. Feldman (Jerusalem, 1977).

GEWIRTZ, WILLIAM L., '*Zemannim*: On the Introduction of New Constructs in Halakhah', *TUMJ*, 16 (2012–13), 153–71.

GLICK, SHMUEL, *Kuntres hateshuvot heḥadash*, 4 vols. (Jerusalem, 2006–10).

—— 'On Alterations, Omissions, and Internal Censorship in the Responsa Literature' (Heb.), *Kuntres*, 1 (Winter 2009), 40–76.

—— *Window to the Responsa Literature* [Eshnav lesifrut hateshuvot] (New York, 2012).

GOLD, AVIE (ed.), *The Complete ArtScroll Machzor: Pesach* (Brooklyn, NY, 1994).

GOLDBERG, HANOKH, 'Is It Halakhically Permissible to Lie?' (Heb.), *Shanah beshanah* (1988), 187–95.

GOLDBERG, HILLEL, *Between Berlin and Slobodka: Jewish Transition Figures from Eastern Europe* (Hoboken, NJ, 1989).

GOLDHABER, YEHIEL, '"Come, Let Us Go and Welcome the Sabbath" (4)' (Heb.), *Kovets beit aharon veyisra'el*, 13 (Tishrei–Heshvan 5758), 119–34.

—— 'Ta'alumah ve'ayin kora lah', *Pa'amon*, 5 (2013), 51–9.

GOLDSCHMIDT, PINHAS, *Zikaron basefer* (n.p., 1995).

GOLDSTEIN, DAVID, *Dostoevsky and the Jews* (Austin, Tex., 1981).

GOLDSTEIN, MENAHEM MENDEL SEGAL, 'Studies and Clarifications of the Thought of R. Jacob Emden' (Heb.), *Or yisra'el*, 43 (Nisan 5766), 203–15.

GOLDSTEIN, MOSES, *Mas'ot yerushalayim* (Munkács, 1931).

—— (ed.), *Tikun olam* (Munkács, 1936).

—— *Yabia omer* (Jerusalem, 1924).

GOLDWASSER, DOVID, *Comrade* (Southfield, Mich., 2004).

GOMBINER, ABRAHAM, *Magen avraham*, commentary on Joseph Karo, *Shulḥan arukh*, printed in standard edns.

GOODBLATT, DAVID, 'The Beruriah Traditions', *JJS*, 26 (1975), 68–85.

GOODMAN, MORDECHAI S. (ed. and trans.), *The Sabbath Epistle of Rabbi Abraham Ibn Ezra* (Jersey City, NJ, 2009).

GOPIN, MARC, 'An Orthodox Embrace of Gentiles? Interfaith Tolerance in the Thought of S. D. Luzzatto and E. Benamozegh', *Modern Judaism*, 18 (May 1998), 173–95.

GORDON, H. L., *The Maggid of Caro* (New York, 1949).

GORDON, MARTIN L., 'The Rationalism of Jacob Anatoli' (Ph.D. diss., Yeshiva University, 1974).

GORELIK, MORDECHAI, 'On Printing the Talmud with New Translations and Commentaries' (Heb.), *Or yisra'el*, 50 (Tevet 5768), 39–40.

GOSHEN-GOTTSTEIN, MOSHE, 'The Authenticity of the Aleppo Codex', *Textus*, 1 (1960), 17–58.

GOTTLIEB, MICHAH, 'Counter-Enlightenment in a Jewish Key: Anti-Maimonideanism in Nineteenth-Century Orthodoxy', in James T. Robinson (ed.), *The Cultures of Maimonideanism: New Approaches to the History of Jewish Thought* (Leiden, 2009), 259–87.

GRAETZ, NAOMI, *Silence is Deadly: Judaism Confronts Wifebeating* (Northvale, NJ, 1998).

GREENWALD, LEOPOLD, *Aḥ letsarah* (St. Louis, 1939).

—— *Jewish Groups in Hungary* [Liflagot yisra'el behungaryah] (Deva, 1929).

—— *Maharil uzemano* (New York, 1944).

—— *Matsevat kodesh* (New York, 1952).

—— *Otsar neḥmad* (New York, 1942).

GROSS, MORDECHAI, *Om ani ḥomah* (Benei Berak, 2000), vol. ii.

GROSSMAN, AHARON YEHUDAH, *Vedarashta veḥakarta* [rabbinic novellae] (Jerusalem, 2008), vol. v.

—— *Vedarashta veḥakarta* [responsa] (Jerusalem, 2011), vol. v.

GROSSMAN, AVRAHAM, *And He Shall Rule Over You? Women in Medieval Rabbinic Thought* [Vehu yimshol bakh? Ha'ishah bemishnatam shel ḥakhmei yisra'el bimei habeinayim] (Jerusalem, 2011).

—— 'Medieval Rabbinic Views on Wife-Beating, 800–1300', *Jewish History*, 5 (1991), 53–62.

—— *Pious and Rebellious: Jewish Women in Europe in the Middle Ages* [Ḥasidot umoredot: nashim yehudiyot be'eiropah bimei habeinayim] (Jerusalem, 2001).

GRUENWALD, ELIEZER, *Keren ledavid* (Brooklyn, NY, 1969).

GRUENWALD, JUDAH, *Zikhron yehudah* (Budapest, 1923).

GRUNFELD, I., *Three Generations: The Influence of Samson Raphael Hirsch on Jewish Life and Thought* (London, 1958).

GULEVSKY, HAYIM DOV BER, *Lahat ḥerev hamithapekhet* (Brooklyn, NY, 1979).

GURFINKEL, ELI, 'Maimonides and the Kabbalah: Annotated Bibliography' (Heb.), in Avraham Elqayam and Dov Schwartz (eds.), *Maimonides and Mysticism* [Harambam benivkhei hasod] (Ramat Gan, 2009), 417–85.

GUTTEL, NERIAH, 'Craftsmanship and Art in Rabbi T. Y. Kook's Editing of Rabbi A. I. Hakohen Kook's Writings: The Introduction to *Shabat ha'arets*—a Case in Point' (Heb.), *Tarbiz*, 70 (2001), 601–24.

—— 'Heaven Forbid This Should Be Done' (Heb.), *Makor rishon* (17 Adar 5769), <http://hayamin.org/forum/index.php?topic=18845.0>.

HACKER, JOSEPH, 'The Controversy over Philosophy in Istanbul' (Heb.), in J. Hacker and Joseph Dan (eds.), *Studies in Jewish Mysticism, Philosophy, and Ethical Literature* [Meḥkarim bekabalah, befilosofyah yehudit uvesifrut hamusar vehahagut] (Jerusalem, 1986), 507–36.

—— 'Sixteenth-Century Jewish Internal Censorship of Hebrew Books', in J. Hacker and Adam Shear (eds.), *The Hebrew Book in Early Modern Italy* (Philadelphia, Pa., 2011), 109–20.

HACOHEN, RAN, 'The Hay Wagon Moves to the West: On Martin Buber's Adaptation of Hassidic Legends', *Modern Judaism*, 28 (Feb. 2008), 1–13.

Hagadah shel pesaḥ mibeit levi (brisk) (Jerusalem, 1989).

HAGIZ, MOSES, *Mishnat ḥakhamim* (Wandsbeck, 1733).

HAKAK, YOHAI, 'Holy Amnesia: Remembering Religious Sages as Super Humans or as Simply Human', *Contemporary Jewry*, 29 (2009), 215–40.

HAKOHEN, ABRAHAM BEN NAHMAN, *Taharat hamayim* ([Livorno], 1879).

HAKOHEN, ABRAHAM DOV BER, *Teshuvat ad"k* (Jerusalem, 1883).

HAKOHEN, ARYEH LEIB, *Ketsot haḥoshen* (Jerusalem, 1990).

HAKOHEN, AVIAD, 'R. Moses Hefets' *Melekhet maḥshevet*' (Heb.), *Maḥanayim*, 4 (1993), 266–75.

HAKOHEN (KAGAN), ISRAEL MEIR, *Ḥafets ḥayim* (Jerusalem, 2000).

—— *Likutei halakhot* (Warsaw, 1899).

—— *Maḥaneh yisra'el* (Warsaw, 1881), vol. ii.

—— *Mikhtevei harav ḥafets ḥayim* (New York, n.d.).

—— *Mishnah berurah*, many edns.

—— *Sefat emet* (Jerusalem, 1965).

—— *Shem olam* (Jerusalem, 1978).

—— *Shemirat halashon* (Vilna, 1879).

HAKOHEN, JOSHUA JOSEPH, *Ezrat kohanim* (Warsaw, 1873).

HAKOHEN, MALACHI, *Yad malakhi* (Benei Berak, n.d.).

HAKOHEN, TSADOK, *Tsidkat hatsadik* (Lublin, 1902; Jerusalem, 1968).

—— *Yisra'el kedoshim* (Har Berakhah, 2010).

HAKOHEN, YOSEF, *Shalom ohalekha* (Ashdod, 1998).

HALBERSTADT, YITSHAK, 'The Time of the End of the Sabbath According to the Opinion of the Hatam Sofer' (Heb.), in *Festschrift in Honour and Memory of . . . Rabbi Moses Sofer* [Sefer hayovel likhvodo ulezikhro shel . . . rabeinu mosheh sofer] (Jerusalem, 1989), 240–3.

HALEVI, DAVID BEN SAMUEL, *Turei zahav*, commentary on Joseph Karo, *Shulḥan arukh*, printed in standard edns.

HALEVI, HAYIM DAVID, *Aseh lekha rav* (Tel Aviv, 1981), vol. iv.

HALPER, SHAUN JACOB, 'Coming Out of the Hasidic Closet: Jiri Mordechai Langer (1894–1943) and the Fashioning of Homosexual–Jewish Identity', *JQR*, 101 (2011), 189–231.

HALPERIN, MORDECHAI, 'Consultation of a Witch Doctor by a Severely Ill Patient' (Heb.), *Assia*, 19 (Shevat 2005), 7–32.

—— 'Why Did Rabbi Sa'adyah Gaon Depart from the Truth?' (Heb.), *Yod'ei binah*, 5 (5771), 40–74.

HAMAMI, AVRAHAM, *Minḥat avraham* (Jerusalem, 2011).

HAMBURGER, BINYAMIN SHLOMO, *Harav yonah merzbakh* (Benei Berak, 2004).

—— *Hayeshivah haramah befiorda* (Benei Berak, 2010), vol. i.

HANANEL BEN HUSHIEL, *Commentary on the Babylonian Talmud*, printed in standard edns. of the Talmud.

—— *Migdal ḥananel* (Berlin, 1876).

HANOKH ZUNDEL BEN JOSEPH, *Ets yosef*, commentary on *Midrash rabah*, printed in standard edns.

HARAN, RAYA, 'Atarah leyoshnah: ha'omnam?', *Katedra*, 64 (1992), 98–102.

—— 'The Praises of the *Rebbe*: The Authenticity of Letters Written by Hasidim in Erets Yisra'el' (Heb.), *Katedra*, 55 (1990), 22–58.

HARFENES, YISRA'EL DAVID, *Yisra'el vehazemanim* (Brooklyn, NY, 2002), vols. ii and iii.

HARLAP, JACOB MOSES, *Tovim me'orot* (Jerusalem, 1920).

HARLAP, YAIR, *Shirat hayam* (Jerusalem, 2012).

HARVEY, WARREN ZEV, 'The Obligation of Talmud on Women According to Maimonides', *Tradition*, 19 (Summer 1981), 122–30.

HAVER, ISAAC, *Magen vetsinah* (Jerusalem, 1985).

HAVLIN, SHLOMO ZALMAN, 'New Light on the Letters of the Ba'al Shem Tov and His Disciples' (Heb.), *Yeshurun*, 23 (2010), 503–29.

HAYIM BEN BETZALEL, *Vikuaḥ mayim ḥayim* (Amsterdam, 1711).

HAYIM BEN SOLOMON, *Torat ḥayim* (Jerusalem, 1959).

HAYIM OF VOLOZHIN, *Ḥut hameshulash* (Vilna, 1882).

HAYIM, JOSEPH, *Ben yehoyada* (Jerusalem, 1902).

—— *Hod yosef* (Jerusalem, 1983).

—— *Kanun al-nisa* (Baghdad, 1906); *Ḥukei hanashim*, Hebrew trans. Ben Zion

Mutzafi (Jerusalem, 1979); *Laws for Women*, trans. Moshe Schapiro (Jerusalem, 2011).

—— *Od yosef ḥai* (Jerusalem, 1958).

—— *Rav pe'alim* (Jerusalem, 1980).

—— *Torah lishmah* (Jerusalem, 1973).

HAZAN, ELIJAH, *Ta'alumot lev* (Jerusalem, 1986), vol. iv.

HEILPRIN, ISRAEL (ed.), *Takanot medinat mehrin* (Jerusalem, 1952).

HEILPRIN, RAPHAEL, *Rashi: His Life and Commentaries* [Rashi: ḥayav uferushav], 4 vols. (n.p., 1997).

HEILPRIN, YEHIEL, *Seder hadorot* (Benei Berak, 2003).

HELLER, MARVIN J., *Printing the Talmud* (Leiden, 1999).

—— *Studies in the Making of the Early Hebrew Book* (Leiden, 2008).

HELLER, YOM-TOV LIPMANN, *Ma'adanei yom tov*, commentary on R. Asher ben Yehiel, *Piskei harosh*, printed in standard edns. of the Babylonian Talmud.

HEN, OVADYAH, *Haketav vehamikhtav* (n.p., 2006).

HENKIN, EITAM, 'The Excommunication of R. Yehiel Mikhel Pines in Jerusalem and His Ties with His Brother-in-Law R. David Friedman' (Heb.), *Hama'yan*, 49 (Tevet 5769), 19–38.

—— 'The Mystery of the "Story of Beruriah"' (Heb.), *Akdamot*, 21 (2008), 140–59.

—— 'Rabbi Abraham Isaac Hakohen Kook's *Linevokhei hador*' (Heb.), *Akdamot*, 25 (2010), 171–88.

—— 'Rav Kook's Relationship with the Keren Hayesod' (Heb.), *Hama'yan*, 51 (Tamuz 5771), 75–90.

—— 'Was a Comment about Herzl Censored in *Igerot hare'iyah*?' (Heb.), <http://www.yeshiva.org.il/midrash/shiur.asp?cat=1104&id=15824&q=>.

HENKIN, YEHUDAH HERZL, *Benei vanim* (Jerusalem, 2005), vol. iv.

—— 'Contemporary Tseni'ut', *Tradition*, 37 (Fall 2003), 1–48.

HERCZEG, YISRAEL ISSER ZVI et al. (eds.), *The Torah with Rashi's Commentary: Sapirstein Edition*, 5 vols. (Brooklyn, NY, 2003).

HERR, MOSHE DAVID, 'The Sages' Concept of History' (Heb.), *Sixth World Congress of Jewish Studies* (Jerusalem, 1977), vol. iii, pp. 129–42.

HERSHKOWITZ, YEHUDAH, 'A Note on Rabbi Jacob ben Asher's Torah Commentaries' (Heb.), *Datche*, 95 (21 May, 2010), 7.

HERSHKOWITZ, YITSHAK, 'A Theurgical Commentary on Maimonides: Rabbi Y. S. Teichtal on Acquiring Conversion Certificates' (Heb.), in Avraham Elqayam and Dov Schwartz (eds.), *Maimonides and Mysticism* [Harambam benivkhei hasod] (Ramat Gan, 2009), 323–42.

HERTZ, JOSEPH H., *The Authorised Daily Prayer Book* (New York, 1948).

—— *A Book of Jewish Thoughts* (London, 1922).

HERZOG, ISAAC, *Pesakim ukhetavim*, 9 vols. (Jerusalem, 1989).

HESCHEL, ABRAHAM JOSHUA, *Heavenly Torah as Refracted through the Generations* [Torah min hashamayim be'aspaklaryah shel hadorot] (London, 1965), vol. ii.

HESCHEL, YISRA'EL NATAN, 'On the Holy Work *Panim yafot* by R. Pinhas Horowitz' (Heb.), *Beit aharon veyisra'el*, 9 (Sivan–Tamuz 5754), 135–50.

HILDESHEIMER, MEIR, 'The Attitude of the Hatam Sofer Toward Moses Mendelssohn', *PAAJR*, 60 (1994), 141–87.

—— 'Moses Mendelssohn in Nineteenth Century Rabbinical Literature', *PAAJR*, 55 (1988), 79–133.

HILLEL, YA'AKOV MOSHE, *Ben ish ḥai* (Jerusalem, n.d.).

—— *Vayashav hayam*, 2 vols. (Jerusalem, 1994, 2000).

HILLMAN, DAVID TSEVI (ed.), *Letters of Rabbi Shneur Zalman of Lyady and His Contemporaries* [Igerot ba'al hatanya uvenei doro] (Jerusalem, 1953).

—— 'On the Kherson Letters' (Heb.), *Yeshurun*, 23 (2010), 530–47, with additional notes by S. Z. Havlin, 548–53.

—— 'Statements of Meiri written in Response to the Heretics' (Heb.), *Tsefunot*, 1 (Tishrei 5749), 65–72.

—— 'The Wording of *Birkat haminim*' (Heb.), *Tsefunot*, 2 (Tevet 5749), 58–65.

HIRSCH, SAMSON RAPHAEL, *Bema'gelei shanah*, trans. Aviezer Wolf, 4 vols. (Benei Berak, 1966).

—— *Horeb*, trans. I. Grunfeld (London, 1962).

—— *Judaism Eternal*, trans. I. Grunfeld (London, 1976), vol. ii.

—— *The Nineteen Letters*, trans. Jacob Breuer (Jerusalem, 1969); *The Nineteen Letters of Ben Uziel*, trans. Bernard Drachman (New York and London, 1899).

—— *The Pentateuch* with commentary by Samson Raphael Hirsch, trans. by I. Levy (New York, 1971).

—— *Shemesh marpe* (New York, 1992).

—— *Yesodot haḥinukh*, trans. Aviezer Wolf and Shalom Pushinsky (Benei Berak, 1968).

HIRSCHENSOHN, HAYIM, *Ḥidushei harav ḥayim hirshenson* (Jerusalem, 1926), vol. iii.

—— *Malki bakodesh*, 6 vols. (St. Louis and Seini, 1919–26).

—— *Nimukei rashi* (Seini, 1930), vol. ii.

HIRSCHOWITZ, ABRAHAM ELIEZER, *Minhagei yeshurun* (Vilna, 1899).

HOBERMAN, ZEV, *Ze'ev yitrof: devarim* (Brooklyn, NY, 2006).

HOCH, RICHARD LAWRENCE, 'The Politics of Redemption: Rabbi Tzvi Yehudah ha-Kohen Kook and the Origins of Gush Emunim' (Ph.D. diss., University of California, Santa Barbara, 1994).

HODES, JOEL ZUSMAN, *Al harishonim ve'aḥaronim* (Birmingham, 1928).

HOFFMANN, DAVID TSEVI, *Melamed leho'il* (New York, 1954), vol. ii.

—— *Der Schulchan-Aruch und die Rabbinen über das Verhältniss der Juden zu Andersgläubigen* (Berlin, 1894).

HOROVITZ, A., *Orḥot rabenu ba'al hakehilot ya'akov*, 5 vols. (Benei Berak, 1991–2005).

HOROWITZ, ABRAHAM, *Emek haberakhah* (Amsterdam, 1729).

HOROWITZ, AVRAHAM DAVID, *Kinyan torah bahalakhah* (Jerusalem, 2005), vol. vii.

HOROWITZ, ELLIOT S., 'Between Cleanliness and Godliness: Aspects of Jewish Bathing in Medieval and Early Modern Times', in Elisheva Baumgarten et al. (eds.),

Tov Elem: Memory, Community and Gender in Medieval and Early Modern Jewish Societies (Jerusalem, 2011), 29–54.

—— 'The Early Eighteenth Century Confronts the Beard: Kabbalah and Jewish Self-Fashioning', *Jewish History*, 8 (1984), 95–115.

—— *Reckless Rites: Purim and the Legacy of Jewish Violence* (Princeton, NJ, 2006).

HOROWITZ, MARYANNE CLINE, 'Aristotle and Woman', *Journal of the History of Biology*, 9 (Autumn 1976), 183–213.

HOROWITZ, MOSHE, *Shehamafte'aḥ beyado* (Jerusalem, 1989).

HOROWITZ, PINHAS ELIJAH, *Sefer haberit* (Bruenn, 1797).

HORWITZ, RIVKA (ed.), *Isaac Breuer: Studies of His Thought* [Yitsḥak breuer: iyunim bemishnato] (Ramat Gan, 1988).

HOSHEN, DALIA, *Beruria the Tannait* (Lanham, Md., 2007).

HUTNER, ISAAC, *Paḥad yitsḥak: igerot ukhetavim* (Brooklyn, NY, 2006).

IBN EZRA, ABRAHAM, *Yesod mora* (Jerusalem, 1931).

—— *Yesod mora vesod torah*, ed. Yosef Cohen and Uriel Simon (Ramat Gan, 2007).

IBN HABIB, LEVI, *She'elot uteshuvot haralbaḥ* (n.p. [Israel], 1978).

IBN KASPI, JOSEPH, *Adnei kesef* [commentary on the Prophets], ed. I. Last, 2 vols. (London, 1911, 1912).

—— *Shulḥan kesef*, ed. H. Kasher (Jerusalem, 1996).

IBN LATIF, ISAAC, 'R. Isaac Ibn Latif's *Epistle of Repentance*' (Heb.), *Hateḥiyah*, 2 (1857), 50–64 (also printed in *Kovets al yad*, 1 (1885), 45–70).

IBN ZIMRA, DAVID, *She'elot uteshuvot haradbaz* (New York, n.d.).

IDEL, MOSHE, *Kabbalah: New Perspectives* (New Haven, Conn., 1988).

—— *Language, Torah, and Hermeneutics in Abraham Abulafia*, trans. Menahem Kallus (Albany, NY, 1989).

—— 'The Writings and Teachings of R. Abraham Abulafia' [Kitvei r. avraham abulafyah umishnato] (Ph.D. diss., Hebrew University of Jerusalem, 1976).

ILAN, TAL, *Integrating Women into Second Temple History* (Peabody, Mass., 1999).

—— *Mine and Yours Are Hers: Retrieving Women's History from Rabbinic Literature* (Leiden, 1997).

IMMANUEL OF ROME, *Maḥberot imanu'el haromi*, ed. D. Yarden (Jerusalem, 1957).

Interpreter's Dictionary of the Bible, ed. George A. Buttrick, 4 vols. (New York, 1962).

ISAAC OF CORBEIL, *Sefer mitsvot katan*, ed. J. Ralbag (New York, 1959).

ISAAC BAR SHESHET, *She'elot uteshuvot harivash*, ed. D. Metzger (Jerusalem, 1993).

ISAIAH OF TRANI, *Piskei hariaz*, ed. A. Liss (Jerusalem, 1973).

ISH-SHALOM, BENJAMIN, *Rav Avraham Itzhak HaCohen Kook: Between Rationalism and Mysticism*, trans. Ora Wiskind-Elper (Albany, NY, 1993).

ISRAELI, ISRAEL, *Mitsvot zemaniyot*, ed. M. Blau (New York, 1984).

ISSERLEIN, ISRAEL, *Terumat hadeshen* (Jerusalem, 1991).

ISSERLES, MOSES, *She'elot uteshuvot harama*, ed. A. Siev (Jerusalem, 1971).

JACOB BEN ASHER, *Arba'ah turim* (*Tur*), many edns.

—— *Ba'al haturim al hatorah*, ed. Y. Reinitz (Jerusalem, 1996).

JACOB BEN ASHER, *Perush hatur ha'arokh al hatorah*, ed. Y. Reinitz (Jerusalem, 2006).

JACOB OF MARVÈGE, *She'elot uteshuvot min hashamayim*, ed. Reuven Margaliyot (Jerusalem, n.d.).

JACOB OF VIENNA, *Peshatim uferushim* (Mainz, 1888).

JACOBS, LOUIS, *Beyond Reasonable Doubt* (London, 1999).

—— *Hasidic Prayer* (New York, 1978).

—— 'How Much of the Babylonian Talmud Is Pseudepigraphic?', *JJS*, 28 (1977), 47–59.

—— *A Jewish Theology* (New York, 1973).

—— *A Tree of Life* (London, 2000).

JACOBS, MOSHE TSEVI, *Bimeḥitsat rabenu* (Jerusalem, 2004).

JAFFE, MORDECHAI, *Levush ir shushan* (Jerusalem, 2004).

—— *Levush pinat yikrat* (Jerusalem, 2000).

JAFFE, SAMUEL, *Yefeh mar'eh* (Venice, 1590).

JAKOBOVICS, BENTSIYON, *Zekhor yemot olam* (Benei Berak, 1989), vol. ii.

JAKOBOVITZ, ELHANAN, *Even shimon* (Jerusalem, 1937; Brooklyn, NY, 1993).

JAMES, WILLIAM, *Pragmatism* (New York, 1907).

JASTROW, MARCUS, *Dictionary of the Targumim, Talmud Babli, Yerushalmi and Midrashic Literature* (New York, 1971).

JOLLES, ZECHARIAH ISAIAH, *Dover meisharim* (Lemberg, 1831).

—— *Hatorah vehaḥokhmah* (Vilna, 1913).

JOSEPH JOSKE OF LUBLIN, *Yesod yosef hamevo'ar* (Ashdod, 2002).

JUDAH BEN KALONYMOS, *Yiḥusei tana'im ve'amora'im*, ed. J. L. Maimon (Jerusalem, 1963).

JUDAH HEHASID, *The Torah Commentaries of R. Judah Hehasid* [Perushei hatorah lerabi yehudah heḥasid], ed. Y. Lange (Jerusalem, 1975).

JUDAH LOEW BEN BEZALEL (MAHARAL), *Netivot olam* (London, 1961).

KAFIH, JOSEPH, Commentary on Maimonides, *Mishneh torah* (Heb.), 25 vols. (Jerusalem, 1984–96).

KAGAN, AARON, *Avodat hakorbanot* (Piotrków, 1913), vol. i.

KAGAN, ISRAEL MEIR HAKOHEN, *see* HAKOHEN (KAGAN), ISRAEL MEIR.

KAHANA, BARUCH, ELIYAHU SHLOMO RA'ANAN, and YA'AKOV BLUM (eds.), *An Index of the Commentaries on Maimonides' Mishneh Torah* [Mafte'aḥ leferushim al mishneh torah leharambam] (Jerusalem, 2005), vol. i.

KAHANA, DAVID (ed.), *Rabbi Abraham Ibn Ezra* (Heb.) (Warsaw, 1894), vol. ii.

KAHANA, MAOZ, and MICHAEL K. SILBER, 'Deists, Sabbatians, and Kabbalists in Prague: A Censored Sermon of R. Ezekiel Landau' (Heb.), *Kabalah*, 21 (2010), 349–84.

KAHANA, MENAHEM, 'Midrashic Manuscripts in the Libraries of Leningrad and Moscow' (Heb.), *Asupot*, 6 (1992), 41–70.

KALIMI, ISAAC, *The Retelling of Chronicles in Jewish Tradition and Literature* (Winona Lake, Ind., 2009).

KALIR, JOSEPH, 'The Jewish Service in the Eyes of Christian and Baptized Jews in the 17th and 18th Centuries', *JQR*, 56 (1965), 51–80.

KALMIN, RICHARD, *The Sage in Jewish Society of Late Antiquity* (New York, 1999).

KAMELHAR, YEKUTIEL ARYEH, *Dor de'ah* (Piotrków, 1935), vol. i.

KAMENETSKY, DAVID, 'Approbations by Leading Rabbis for R. Solomon Dubno's Pentateuch' (Heb.), *Yeshurun*, 8 (2001), 738–59.

—— 'The Gaon R. Menasheh of Ilya' (Heb.), *Yeshurun*, 20 (2008), 729–81.

KAMENETSKY, NATHAN, *Making of a Godol*, 2 vols. (Jerusalem, 2002).

KAMENETSKY, YA'AKOV, *Emet leya'akov* (Cleveland Heights, Ohio, 2007).

KAMIN, DAVID TSEVI, *Beit david* (Jerusalem, 1919).

KAMPINSKI, MENAHEM, *Bein shenei kohanim gedolim* (Elad, 2008).

KANIEVSKY, AVRAHAM YESHAYAHU, *Toledot ya'akov* (Benei Berak, 1995).

KANIEVSKY, HAYIM, *She'elat rav* (Kiryat Sefer, 2012), vol. ii.

KANIEVSKY, JACOB ISRAEL, *Ḥayei olam* (Benei Berak, 1957).

—— *Karyana de'igarta* (Benei Berak, 1986), vol. i.

KAPLAN, ABRAHAM ELIJAH, *Be'ikvot hayirah* (Jerusalem, 1988).

KAPLAN, ARYEH, *Handbook of Jewish Thought* (New York, 1979).

KAPLAN, DEBRA, *Beyond Expulsion: Jews, Christians, and Reformation Strasbourg* (Stanford, Calif., 2011).

KAPLAN, JULIUS, *The Redaction of the Babylonian Talmud* (New York, 1933).

KAPLAN, LAWRENCE, 'Daas Torah: A Modern Conception of Rabbinic Authority', in Moshe Sokol (ed.), *Rabbinic Authority and Personal Autonomy* (Northvale, NJ, 1992), 1–60.

—— 'The Hazon Ish: Haredi Critic of Traditional Orthodoxy', in Jack Wertheimer (ed.), *The Uses of Tradition* (New York, 1992), 145–73.

—— 'Rabbi Mordekhai Jaffe and the Evolution of Jewish Culture in Poland in the Sixteenth Century', in Bernard Dov Cooperman (ed.), *Jewish Thought in the Sixteenth Century* (Cambridge, 1983), 266–82.

—— 'Revisionism and the Rav: The Struggle for the Soul of Modern Orthodoxy', *Judaism*, 48 (1999), 290–311.

—— '*Torah u-Madda* in the Thought of Rabbi Samson Raphael Hirsch', *Bekhol Derakhekha Daehu*, 5 (Summer 1997), 5–31.

KARELITZ, ABRAHAM ISAIAH, *Emunah uvitaḥon* (n.p., 2006); *Faith and Trust*, trans. Yaakov Goldstein (n.p., 2008).

—— *Genazim ushe'elot uteshuvot ḥazon ish*, 4 vols. (n.p., [2011–14]).

—— 'Halakhic Rulings from the Hazon Ish' (Heb.), *Yeshurun*, 26 (2012), 731–6.

—— *Kovets igerot ḥazon ish*, 3 vols. (Benei Berak, 1990).

KARLINSKY, NAHUM, *Alternative History: 'Hasidic Letters from the Land of Israel'—Text and Context* [Historyah shekeneged: 'igerot haḥasidim me'erets yisra'el': hatekst vehakontekst] (Jerusalem, 1998).

—— 'The Dawn of Hasidic–Haredi Historiography', *Modern Judaism*, 27 (2007), 20–46.

KARO, JOSEPH, *Beit yosef*, many edns.
—— *Kesef mishneh*, commentary on Maimonides, *Mishneh torah*, printed in standard edns.
—— *Shulhan arukh*, Makhon Yerushalayim edn., 22 vols. (Jerusalem, 1994–2014).
KASHER, MENAHEM, M., *The Jewish Dateline* [Kav hata'arikh hayisra'eli] (Jerusalem, 1977).
—— *Maimonides and the Mekhilta derabi shimon bar yohai* [Harambam vehamekhilta derashbi] (Jerusalem, 1980).
—— *Torah shelemah*, 45 vols. (Jerusalem, 1992).
KASIRER, YITSHAK SHMUEL, *Shemitah kemitsvatah* (Beit Shemesh, 2007).
KATTINA, JACOB, *Rahamei ha'av* (Warsaw, 1874; Jerusalem, 1950).
KATZ, BEN ZION, *A Journey through Torah* (Jerusalem, 2012).
KATZ, JACOB, *Exclusiveness and Tolerance* (Oxford, 1961).
—— *Halakhah in Crisis* [Hahalakhah bametsar] (Jerusalem, 1992).
—— *Tradition and Crisis: Jewish Society at the End of the Middle Ages*, trans. Bernard Dov Cooperman (New York, 1993).
—— *With My Own Eyes*, trans. Ann Brenner and Zipora Brody (Hanover, NH, 1995).
KATZ, MEIR, 'An Alteration in the Book *Sefat tamim*' (Heb.), *Hamaor*, 21 (Apr.–May 1970), 17.
KATZMAN, ELIEZER, 'The Gaon R. Judah Leib Gordon: The Gaon of Lomza' (Heb.), *Yeshurun*, 3 (1997), 649–78.
—— 'R. Haim Liberman and the Kherson Archive' (Heb.), *Yeshurun*, 23 (2010), 567–72.
KAUFMANN, DAVID, *Geschichte der Attributenlehre in der Jüdischen Religionsphilosophie des Mittelalters* (Gotha, 1877).
KAUFMANN, WALTER (ed. and trans.), *The Portable Nietzsche* (New York, 1982).
KELLEY, DONALD R., *Faces of History: Historical Inquiry from Herodotus to Herder* (New Haven, Conn., 1999).
KELLNER, MENACHEM, *Maimonides' Confrontation with Mysticism* (Oxford, 2006).
—— 'A New and Unexpected Textual Witness to the Reading "He who kills a single person—it is as if he destroyed an entire world"' (Heb.), *Tarbiz*, 75 (2006), 565–6.
—— *Torah in the Observatory: Gersonides, Maimonides, Song of Songs* (Brighton, Mass., 2010).
KELNER, YOSEF, *Milon hare'iyah* (Jerusalem, 1999).
KIMHI, DAVID, *Commentary on the Torah* [Perush radak al hatorah] (Pressburg, 1842).
KINARTI, AMIHAI, *Ateret tsevi* (n.p., 2006).
—— *Az nidberu yir'ei hashem* (n.p., 2004).
—— *Hare'iyah veha'ahi'ezer* (n.p., 2006).
—— *Or shelomoh* (n.p., 2005).
KING, DAVID, *The Commissar Vanishes: The Falsification of Photographs and Art in Stalin's Russia* (New York, 1997).
KITSIS, GERSHON, 'A. Marcus's *Hasidism*' (Heb.), *Hama'yan*, 21 (Tishrei 5741), 64–88.

KLATZKIN, ELIJAH, *Even haroshah* (Warsaw, 1887).
KLEIN, MENASHEH, *Mishneh halakhot* (Brooklyn, NY, 2008), vol. ix.
KLUGER, BINYAMIN, *Min hamakor*, 5 vols. (Jerusalem, 1980).
KLUGER, SOLOMON, *Ha'elef lekha shelomoh*, 'Yoreh de'ah' (Jerusalem, 1968).
—— *Sefer haḥayim* (New York, 1968).
KLUGMAN, ELIYAHU MEIR, *Rabbi Samson Raphael Hirsch* (New York, 1996).
KOBLER, FRANZ, *Letters of Jews through the Ages*, 2 vols. (Philadelphia, Pa., 1953).
KOHEN, SHLOMO, *Pe'er hador* (Jerusalem, 1969), vol. ii.
KOHLER, G. Y., *Reading Maimonides' Philosophy in 19th Century Germany: The Guide to Religious Reform* (Dordrecht, 2012).
Kol haneshamah (Elkins Park, Pa., 2006).
KOLIN, SAMUEL, *Maḥatsit hashekel*, commentary on Joseph Karo, *Shulḥan arukh*, printed in standard edns.
KOOK, ABRAHAM ISAAC, *Arpilei tohar* (Jerusalem, 1983).
—— *Eder hayekar* (Jerusalem, n.d.).
—— *Ein ayah*, 5 vols. (Jerusalem, 1987–95).
—— *Ginzei re'iyah* (n.p., n.d.).
—— *Haskamot hare'iyah* (Jerusalem, 1988).
—— *Igerot hare'iyah*, 4 vols. (Jerusalem, 1962–84).
—— *Ikvei hatson* (Jerusalem, n.d.).
—— *Kevatsim miketav yad kodsho*, 2 vols. (Jerusalem, 2006, 2008).
—— *Ma'amrei hare'iyah* (Jerusalem, 1984).
—— *Me'orot hare'iyah leyeraḥ ha'eitanim* (Jerusalem, 1995).
—— *Olat hare'iyah*, 2 vols. (Jerusalem, 1939).
—— *Oraḥ mishpat* (Jerusalem, 1985).
—— *Orot* (Jerusalem, 1920); trans. Bezalel Naor (Northvale, NJ, 1993).
—— *Orot ha'emunah*, ed. M. Gurwitz (Jerusalem, 2002).
—— *Orot hakodesh*, 3 vols. (Jerusalem, 1985).
—— *Orot hateshuvah* (Jerusalem, 1924).
—— *Otserot hare'iyah*, ed. M. Tsuriel, 5 vols. (Rishon Letsiyon, 2002).
—— *Pinkas 13* (Jerusalem, 2004).
—— *Pinkesei hare'iyah*, 2 vols. (Jerusalem, 2008, 2010).
—— *Shemonah kevatsim*, 2 vols. (Jerusalem, 2004).
—— 'Teviat ein ayah', *Hamizraḥ* (1903), 352–4.
KOOK, TSEVI YEHUDAH, *Bama'arakhah hatsiburit* (Jerusalem, 1986).
—— 'Explaining Fundamental Matters in their Simplicity' (Heb.), *Amudim*, 360 (Elul 5736), 40.
—— 'Herzl' (Heb.), *Iturei kohanim* (Tamuz 5755), 35–9.
—— *Judaism and Christianity* [Yahadut venatsrut], ed. S. Aviner (Jerusalem, 2001).
—— *Linetivot yisra'el*, 2 vols. (Jerusalem, 1989 and Beit El, 2003).
—— *Nefesh hare'iyah* (Jerusalem, 2003).
—— *Or linetivati* (Jerusalem, 1989).

KOOK, TSEVI YEHUDAH, *Siḥot harav tsevi yehudah al sefer orot*, ed. S. Aviner (Jerusalem, 2006).

—— *Siḥot harav tsevi yehudah: bamidbar*, ed. S. Aviner (Jerusalem, 1993).

—— *Siḥotav shel harav tsevi yehudah hakohen kuk al perek kinyan torah*, ed. N. Rakover (Alon Shevut, 1982).

—— *Tsemaḥ tsevi* (Jerusalem, 1990).

—— and DAVID COHEN, *Dodi litsevi* (Jerusalem, 2005).

KOPPEL, ELIJAH HALEVI, 'Concerning Ben Ya'akov's Deletions from *Shem hagedolim*' (Heb.), *Ets ḥayim*, 7 (Shevat 5769), 27–33.

KOPPEL, MOSHE, DROR MUGHAZ, and NAVOT AKIVA, 'New Methods for Attribution of Rabbinic Literature', *Hebrew Linguistics*, 57 (2006), 5–18.

KORAH, SHLOMO, *Teshuvah kahalakhah* (Benei Berak, 1994).

KOSMAN, ADMIEL, 'The Central Role of the Category of *uvdin deḥol* Prohibitions in the Hatam Sofer's Halakhic Claims against Reform Leniencies in the Use of New Technological Devices on Sabbath and Festivals' (Heb.), in Daniel Gutvain and Menahem Mautner (eds.), *Justice and History* [Mishpat vehistoryah] (Jerusalem, 1999), 75–101.

KOSMAN, AVRAHAM, 'Is There a Tractate "Hanukah?"' (Heb.), *Kolmos*, 107 (Tevet 5772), 10–15, 35.

KOSSOWSKY, ISAAC, *She'elat yitsḥak* (Benei Berak, 1994).

KREISEL, HAYIM, 'Philosophical-Allegorical Interpretation of the Torah in the Middle Ages' (Heb.), in Ezra Fleischer et al. (eds.), *Meah Shearim: Studies in Medieval Jewish Spiritual Life in Memory of Isadore Twersky* (Jerusalem, 2001), 297–316.

KRINSKY, JUDAH LEIB, *Meḥokekei yehudah* (Vilna, 1928).

KUGEL, JAMES, *How to Read the Bible* (New York, 2007).

KUNITZ, MOSES, *Ben yoḥai* (Vienna, 1815).

—— *Hametsaref*, 2 vols. (Vienna and Prague 1820, 1857).

LADERMAN, SHULAMIT, 'What Do Jewish Artistic Findings Teach Us about Head Covering for Men?' (Heb.), in Gershon Bacon et al. (eds.), *Studies on the History of the Jews of Ashkenaz: Presented to Eric Zimmer* [Meḥkarim betoledot yehudei ashkenaz: sefer yovel likhvod yitsḥak (erik) zimer] (Ramat Gan, 2008), 135–56.

LANDAU, BETZALEL, *Hagaon heḥasid mivilna* (Jerusalem, 1966).

—— and NATHAN ORTNER, *The Holy Rebbe of Belz* [Harav hakadosh mibelza] (Jerusalem, 1967).

LANDAU, EZEKIEL, *Tsiyun lenefesh ḥayah: berakhot* (Prague, 1791; Żółkiew, 1824).

LANDAU, LUIS, 'Stories of Rashi Printed in the Babylonian Talmud' (Heb.), *Eshel be'er sheva*, 3 (1986), 101–17.

LANGER, RUTH, 'The Censorship of Aleinu in Ashkenaz and its Aftermath', in Debra Reed Blank (ed.), *The Experience of Jewish Liturgy: Studies Dedicated to Menahem Schmelzer* (Leiden, 2011), 147–66.

—— *Cursing the Christians* (Oxford, 2012).

LAWEE, ERIC, 'Embarrassment and Re-embracement of a Midrash on Genesis 2: 23', in Tzemah Yoreh et al. (eds.), *Vixens Disturbing Vineyards* (Boston, Mass., 2010), 192–207.

—— 'From Sepharad to Ashkenaz: A Case Study in the Rashi Supercommentary Tradition', *AJS Review*, 30 (2006), 393–425.

—— *Isaac Abarbanel's Stance toward Tradition* (Albany, NY, 2001).

—— 'The Reception of Rashi's *Commentary on the Torah* in Spain: The Case of Adam's Mating with the Animals', *JQR*, 97 (2007), 37–66.

LAZI, YEKUTIEL (ed.), *Margaliyot tovah* [*sic*] (Amsterdam, 1722).

LEIBOWITZ, BARUKH BER, *Birkat shemuel* (New York, 1972), vol. i.

LEIBOWITZ, YESHAYAHU, *Discussions on the Reasons for the Commandments* [Siḥot al pirkei ta'amei hamitsvot] (Jerusalem, 2003).

LEIFER, MORDECHAI, *Ma'amar mordekhai heḥadash* (Brooklyn, NY, 1964).

LEIMAN, SID (SHNAYER) Z., 'Censored Approbations' (Heb.), *Alei sefer*, 12 (1986), 134–5.

—— 'Rabbi Abraham Isaac ha-Kohen Kook: Invocation at the Inauguration of the Hebrew University', *Tradition*, 29 (Fall 1994), 87–92.

—— 'R. Israel Lipschutz and the Portrait of Moses Controversy', in Isadore Twersky (ed.), *Danzig, Between East and West: Aspects of Modern Jewish History* (Cambridge, Mass., 1985), 51–63.

LEINER, MORDECHAI, *Mei hashilo'aḥ* (Vienna, 1860), vol. i.

LEINER, YERUHAM, *Ma'amar zohar harakia*, printed together with David Luria, *Kadmut sefer hazohar* (New York, 1951).

LEITER, MOSES, *Beshulei gilyoni* (Jerusalem, 1967).

LEONI, ELIEZER (ed.), *Volozhin: The Book of the City and the Ets Hayim Yeshiva* [Volozhin: sifrah shel ha'ir veshel yeshivat 'ets ḥayim'] (Tel Aviv, 1970).

LERNER, M. B., 'The Formulation of a Talmudic Halakhah in the Geonic Literature' (Heb.), *Asupot*, 14 (2002), 98–112.

LEVANON, NATI, 'The *Sabbath Epistle* and Rashbam's Commentary on Genesis' (Heb.), *Datche*, 1 (29 Tishrei 5768), 5.

LEVENSTEIN, JOSEPH, 'Biography of the "Penei Yehoshua"' (Heb.), *Hapeles*, 3 (1903), 44–50.

LEVI, YEHUDAH, 'Rabbi Samson Raphael Hirsch: Myth and Fact', *Tradition*, 31 (Spring 1997), 5–22.

LEVIN, ABRAHAM DOV, *Otsar igerot kodesh* (Jerusalem, 1952).

LEVIN, JOSHUA HESCHEL, *Aliyot eliyahu* (Jerusalem, 1989).

LEVINGER, YA'AKOV, 'Concerning the Time of Halakhic Twilight and the Circumcision on the Sabbath of a Child Born Near the End of the Sabbath: The Hatam Sofer's Understanding of the Position of Rabbenu Tam' (Heb.), *Hama'yan*, 52 (Tevet 5772), 23–50.

—— *Maimonides' Techniques of Codification* [Darkhei hamaḥashavah hahilkhatit shel harambam] (Jerusalem, 1965).

LEVISOHN, JOSHUA MOSHE, 'The Early Vilna *Haskalah* and the Search for a Modern Jewish Identity' (Ph.D. diss., Harvard University, 1999).

LEVITA, ELIJAH, *Hatishbi* (Isny, 1541; Maramarossziget [1910?]; Benei Berak, 1976, 2005).

LEVOVITZ, YERUHAM, *Da'at ḥokhmah umusar* (New York, 1967), vol. i.

LEVY, AMNON, *Haḥaredim* (Jerusalem, 1988).

LEWIN, B. M. (ed.), *Alumah* (Jerusalem, 1936).

—— (ed.), *Otsar hage'onim* (Jerusalem, 2002).

LIBERMAN, HAYIM, *Ohel raḥel* (New York, 1980), vol. i.

LIEBERMAN, AVROHOM, 'Tikkunei Soferim, an Analysis of a Masoretic Phenomenon', *Hakirah*, 5 (2007), 227–36.

LIEBERMAN, SAUL, *Greek in Jewish Palestine* (New York, 1994).

—— 'Mishnat rishonim', *Talpiyot*, 2 (1945–6), 375–9.

—— 'Notes on Chapter 1 of *Kohelet rabah*' (Heb.), in *Studies in Mysticism and Religion Presented to Gershom G. Scholem* (Jerusalem, 1968), 163–79.

LIEBERMAN, SIMHAH BUNEM, *Bishevilei haḥodesh* (Safed, 2006).

LIFSHITZ, HAYIM, *Derekh ḥayim* (Sulzbach, 1703).

—— *Shivḥei hare'iyah* (Jerusalem, 1979).

LIFSHITZ, YA'AKOV HALEVI, 'The Secret of Intercalation According to Rabbenu Hananel' (Heb.), *Yeshurun*, 11 (2002), 15–42.

LIPSCHUTZ, ISRAEL, *Tiferet yisra'el*, commentary in standard edns. of the Mishnah.

LITTWACK, HILLEL, *Midevar sheker tirḥak* (New York, 2005).

LOCKSHIN, MARTIN I., 'Tradition or Context: Two Exegetes Struggle with Peshat', in Jacob Neusner et al. (eds.), *From Ancient Judaism to Modern Israel* (Atlanta, Ga., 1989), vol. iii, pp. 173–86.

LOEWENTHAL, NAFTALI, 'Women and the Dialectic of Spirituality in Hasidism', in Immanuel Etkes et al. (eds.), *Bema'gelei ḥasidim* (Jerusalem, 1999), 7–65.

LOEWINGER, SAMUEL, 'Prolegomenon', in V. Aptowitzer, *Das Schriftwort in der Rabbinischen Literatur* (New York, 1970), pp. vii–xlv.

LONZANO, MENAHEM DE, *Derekh ḥayim* (Constantinople [*c*.1575]; 2nd edn. Venice, 1618).

LORBERBAUM, JACOB, *Derekh haḥayim hashalem* (n.p., n.d.).

LOW, ZEV, 'Answer to Criticism' (Heb.), *Hama'yan*, 32 (Tamuz 5752), 44–9.

LOWENTHAL, DAVID, *The Heritage Crusade and the Spoils of History* (Cambridge, 1998).

—— 'Fabricating Heritage', *History and Memory*, 10 (1998), 5–24.

LURIA, DAVID, *Kadmut sefer hazohar* (New York, 1951).

LURIA, HANOKH ZUNDEL, *Kenaf renanim* (Pressburg, 1859).

LURIA, SOLOMON, *She'elot uteshuvot maharshal* (Jerusalem, 1969).

—— *Yam shel shelomoh* (Jerusalem, 1995).

LUZ, EHUD, *Parallels Meet: Religion and Nationalism in the Early Zionist Movement*, trans. Lenn J. Schramm (Philadelphia, Pa., 1988).

MAGED, AARON, *Beit aharon*, 11 vols. (New York, 1962–78).

MAGID, SHAUL, 'Constructing Women from Men: The Metaphysics of Male Homosexuality Among Lurianic Kabbalists in Sixteenth-Century Safed', *JSQ*, 17 (2010), 4–28.

—— *Hasidism on the Margin: Reconciliation, Antinomianism, and Messianism in Izbica/Radzin Hasidism* (Madison, Wis., 2003).

MAGIL, JOSEPH (trans.), *Linear School Bible* (New York, 1905).

MAHLER, RAPHAEL, *Hasidism and the Jewish Enlightenment*, trans. Eugene Orenstein (Philadelphia, Pa., 1985).

MAIMON, JUDAH LEIB, *Midei ḥodesh beḥodsho* (Jerusalem, 1962), vol. v.

MAIMONIDES, MOSES, *Commentary on the Mishnah*, 3 vols., ed. J. Kafih (Jerusalem, 1989).

—— *Igerot harambam*, ed. Y. Sheilat, 2 vols. (Jerusalem, 1987).

—— *Kovets teshuvot harambam*, ed. Abraham Lichtenberg (Leipzig, 1859), vol. iii.

—— *Mishneh Torah*, vol. i, trans. Simon Glazer (New York, 1927).

—— *Mishneh Torah*, ed. and trans. Moses Hyamson, 2 vols. (Jerusalem, 1937, 1962).

—— *Mishneh Torah*, trans. Eliyahu Touger (New York, 2010), vol. i.

—— *Mishneh torah*, Frankel edn., 15 vols. (Jerusalem and Benei Berak, 1975–2007).

—— *Pe'er hador*, ed. Mordechai Tama (Amsterdam, 1765).

—— *Sefer hamitsvot* (Jerusalem, 1995).

MALKA, MOSHE, *Mikveh hamayim* (Jerusalem, 1989), vol. vi.

MALONEY, LINDA M., 'The Argument for Women's Difference in Classical Philosophy and Early Christianity', in Anne Carr and Elisabeth Schüssler Fiorenza (eds.), *The Special Nature of Women?* (London, 1991), 41–9.

MANEKIN, RACHEL, 'Naphtali Herz Homberg: The Man and His Image' (Heb.), *Zion*, 71 (2006), 153–202.

MANN, VIVIAN B. (ed.), *Gardens and Ghettos: The Art of Jewish Life in Italy* (Berkeley, Calif., 1989).

MAORI, YESHAYAHU, '*Tikun soferim* and *kinah hakatuv* in Rashi's Commentary on the Bible' (Heb.), in Yaakov Elman et al. (eds.), *Netiot ledavid* (Jerusalem, 2004), 99–108.

MARCUS, AHRON, *Hasidism* [Haḥasidut], trans. M. Sheinfeld (Tel Aviv, 1954).

MARGALIYOT, ELIEZER, *Haḥayavim bamikra vezaka'im batalmud uvamidrashim* (London, 1949).

MARGALIYOT, JUDAH LEIB, *Tal orot* (Pressburg, 1843).

MARGALIYOT, REUVEN, *The Basis of the Mishnah and its Redaction* [Yesod hamishnah ve'arikhatah] (Tel Aviv, 1956).

—— *Nefesh ḥayah* (Lwów, 1932).

—— *Shem olam* (Jerusalem, 2009).

MARGOLIES, MOSES, *Penei mosheh*, commentary on the Jerusalem Talmud, printed in standard edns.

MARGOLIN, ISAIAH JOSEPH, *Hama'aseh vehamidrash* (Jerusalem, 1937).

MARGOLIYOT, HAYIM MORDECHAI, *Sha'arei teshuvah*, commentary on Joseph Karo, *Shulḥan arukh*, printed in standard edns.

MARGULIES, EPHRAIM ZALMAN, *Tiv gitin* (Vilna, 1849).

MARGULIES, ISAIAH ASHER ZELIG, *Amudei arazim* (Jerusalem, 1932).

MARTIKA, DAVID MAROKA, *Zekhut adam*, in Yehiel Brill (ed.), *Yein levanon* (Paris, 1866), 1–24 (second pagination).

MASHIAH, AMIR, *Rabbi Shlomo Zalman Auerbach's Halakhic Philosophy in a Dynamic Era of Socio-Technological Transformation* [Halakhah bitemurot hazeman bemishnato shel harav shelomoh zalman auerbakh] (Ramat Gan, 2013).

MATTATHIAS BEN MEIR, *Matat yado* (Vilna, 1882), vol. i.

MAZUZ, MEIR, *Arim nisi: yevamot* (Benei Berak, 2008).

—— 'Article on Shemitah' (Heb.), in Amnon Halevi (ed.), *Et hazamir* (Benei Berak, 2009), 291–311.

—— *Kise hamelekh* (Benei Berak, 2005).

—— *Kovets ma'amarim* (Benei Berak, 2003).

—— *Sansan leya'ir* (Benei Berak, 2012).

MEDAN, YA'AKOV, *David and Bathsheba: The Sin, the Punishment, and the Repair* [David uvat sheva: haḥet, ha'onesh, vehatikun] (Alon Shevut, 2002).

MEDINA, SAMUEL DE, *She'elot uteshuvot maharashdam* (Lemberg, 1862).

MEDINI, HAYIM HEZEKIAH, *Igerot sedei ḥemed* (Benei Berak, 2006).

—— *Sedei ḥemed*, 10 vols. (Brooklyn, NY, 1949).

MEIR OF APTA, *Or lashamayim* (Lemberg, 1860).

MEIR OF LUBLIN, *Manhir einei ḥakhamim* (Venice, 1618).

—— *She'elot uteshuvot maharam lublin* (New York, 1976).

MEIR, MORDECHAI, 'On the "Tefilah zakah"' (Heb.), in Yosef Tabory (ed.), *Kenishta*, 2 (2003), 119–38.

MEIR, YONATAN, 'Lights and Vessels: A New Inquiry into the "Circle" of Rav Kook and the Editors of His Works' (Heb.), *Kabalah*, 13 (2005), 163–247.

—— '*The Book of Visions*: Hillel Zeitlin's Mystical Diary in Light of Unpublished Correspondence' (Heb.), *Alei sefer*, 21 (2010), 149–71.

MEIR, ZEV DOV ALTER, *Lo ta'aneh al rav* (Pressburg, 1916).

MEIRI, MENAHEM, *Beit habeḥirah* (Israel, n.d.).

MEKLENBURG, JACOB TSEVI, *Haketav vehakabalah* (Leipzig, 1839).

MELAMED, ABRAHAM, 'Maimonides on Women: Formless Matter or Potential Prophet?', in Alfred Ivry (ed.), *Perspectives on Jewish Thought and Mysticism* (Amsterdam, 1998), 99–134.

MELAMED, ELIEZER, *Revivim: gedolei yisra'el udemuyot mofet* (Har Berakhah, 2010).

—— *Revivim: kovets ma'amarim be'inyenei am erets vetsava* (Har Berakhah, 2008).

—— *Revivim: nisuin, ḥinukh, mishpaḥah, vekaryerah* (Har Berakhah, 2007).

MELAMED, EZRA ZION, '*Lishna me'alya* and *kinuyei soferim* in Talmudic Literature' (Heb.), in id. (ed.), *Memorial Book for Binyamin De Vries* [Sefer zikaron lebinyamin de vries] (Tel Aviv, 1979), 119–48.

MENAHEM MENDEL OF KOTZK, *Amud ha'emet* (Tel Aviv, n.d.).

MENAHEM MENDEL OF RYMANÓW, *Ateret menaḥem* (Biłgoraj, 1910).

MENAHEM MENDEL OF VITEBSK, *Peri ha'arets* (Jerusalem, 1987).

MENASHEH OF ILYA, *Alfei menasheh* (Vilna, 1905), vol. ii.

MESSAS, JOSEPH, *Mayim ḥayim* (Jerusalem, 1985), vol. ii.

—— *Otsar hamikhtavim* (Jerusalem, 1998), vol. i.

MESSER LEON, DAVID, *Kevod ḥakhamim*, ed. S. Bernfeld (Berlin, 1899).

The Metsudah Chumash/Rashi, trans. Avrohom Davis (n.p., 1994), vol. i.

METZGER, BRUCE M., 'Literary Forgeries and Canonical Pseudepigrapha', *Journal of Biblical Literature*, 91 (1972), 3–24.

Midrash Rabbah, ArtScroll Kleinman Edition, vol. ii: *Bereishis, Parshiyos Lech Lecha Through Toldos* (Brooklyn, NY, 2012).

Mikraot gedolot haketer, 'Samuel', ed. Menahem Cohen (Ramat Gan, 1993); 'Psalms', ed. Menahem Cohen, 2 vols. (Ramat Gan, 2003).

Mikraot gedolot hamaor, 5 vols. (Jerusalem, 1990).

MILLER, JUDAH, *She'elot uteshuvot rabi yehudah miler* (Jerusalem, 1993).

MILLER, MICHAEL, *Rabbis and Revolution: The Jews of Moravia in the Age of Emancipation* (Stanford, Calif., 2011).

MINTZ, JUDAH, *Responsa* [She'elot uteshuvot mahari mints] (Munkács, 1898).

MINTZ-MANOR, OPHIR, 'Towards a Solution of the Censorship Question Regarding the Shavuot *Piyutim*' (Heb.), *Tarbiz*, 70 (2001), 637–44.

MIRSKY, YEHUDA, 'An Intellectual and Spiritual Biography of Rabbi Avraham Yitzhaq Ha-Cohen Kook from 1865–1904' (Ph.D. diss., Harvard University, 2007).

MIZRAHI, ELIJAH, *Ḥumash hare'em* (Petah Tikvah, 1994).

MIZRAHI, MOSES, *Admat kodesh* (Salonika, 1758), vol. ii.

MIZRAHI, YOSEF HAYIM, *Ḥemdat yosef* (Jerusalem, 2004).

MODENA, LEON, *Historia de' riti hebraici* (Venice, 1638); Heb. trans. *Shulḥan arukh*, trans. Solomon Rubin (Vienna, 1867).

—— *Letters of R. Judah Aryeh of Modena* [Igerot rabi yehudah aryeh mimodena], ed. Y. Boksenboim (Tel Aviv, 1984).

—— *The Works of R. Judah Aryeh of Modena* [Kitvei harav yehudah aryeh mimodena], ed. L. Blau (Budapest, 1906).

—— *Ziknei yehudah*, ed. S. Simonsohn (Jerusalem, 1956).

MOELIN, JACOB, *Maharil: minhagim*, ed. S. Spitzer (Jerusalem, 1989).

—— *Responsa* [She'elot uteshuvot maharil ḥadashot], ed. Y. Satz (Jerusalem, 1977).

MONDSHINE, AHARON, 'On the Relationship between Ibn Ezra's and Rashbam's Commentaries on the Torah: A New Examination' (Heb.), *Te'udah*, 16–17 (2010), 15–45.

—— 'Rashi, Rashbam, and Ibn Ezra on the Phenomenon of *tikun soferim*' (Heb.), in Shmuel Vargon et al. (eds.), *Iyunei mikra ufarshanut*, 8 (Ramat Gan, 2008), 409–50.

MONDSHINE, YEHOSHUA, 'The Authenticity of Hasidic Letters (2)' (Heb.), *Katedra*, 64 (2002), 79–97.

—— 'The Fluidity of Categories in Hasidim: *Averah lishmah* in the Teachings of R. Zevi Elimelekh of Dynow', in Ada Rapoport-Albert (ed.), *Hasidism Reappraised* (London, 1997), 301–20.

—— *Hatsofeh ledoro* (Jerusalem, 1987).

MONDSHINE, YEHOSHUA, '*Ḥemdat yamim* and the Hasidic Masters' (Heb.), *Heikhal habesht*, 7 (5764), 154–67; *Heikhal habesht*, 11 (5765), 174.

—— *Kerem ḥabad* (Kefar Habad, 1992), vol. iv.

—— *Likutei amarim or the Tanya: Its Editions, Translations, and Commentaries (1796–1981)* [Likutei amarim hu sefer hatanya mahadurotav, targumav uve'urav (1796–1981)] (Brooklyn, NY, 1982).

—— *Shivḥei habesht* (Jerusalem, 1982).

—— '"Silent Approbations" from Volozhin and Vilna' (Heb.), *Or yisra'el*, 16 (Tamuz 5759), 151–9.

—— 'Sipurim vegilguleihem' [series], <www.shturem.net>.

MOPSIK, CHARLES, *Lettre sur la sainteté* (Lagrasse, 1986).

MORDECHAI BEN HILLEL, *Sefer hamordekhai* on the Babylonian Talmud, printed in standard edns.

MORGENSTERN, ARYEH, *Mysticism and Messianism: From Luzzatto to the Vilna Gaon* [Mistikah umeshiḥiyut; me'aliyat haramḥal ad hagaon mivilna] (Jerusalem, 1999).

MORGENSTERN, MATTHIAS, *From Frankfurt to Jerusalem: Isaac Breuer and the History of the Secession Dispute in Modern Jewish Orthodoxy* (Leiden, 2002).

MORPURGO, SAMSON, *Shemesh tsedakah* (Venice, 1743).

MORRIS, BENNY, *The Birth of the Palestinian Refugee Problem Revisited* (Cambridge, 2004).

MORSE, RUTH, *Truth and Convention in the Middle Ages* (Cambridge, 1991).

MOSES OF COUCY, *Sefer mitsvot hagadol* (Jerusalem, 1989).

Moshav zekenim al hatorah, ed. Solomon David Sassoon (London, 1959).

MOSKOWITZ, HAYIM, 'How is Hasidism "Researched" in Modern Times?' (Heb.), *Heikhal habesht*, 29 (Nisan 5770), 175–215.

MOTOT, SAMUEL, *Supercommentary on R. Abraham Ibn Ezra* [Perush al perush heḥakham rabi avraham ibn ezra] (Venice, 1554).

MUNITZ, MEIR, 'The Editing of Rabbi Abraham Isaac Kook's *Orot*' (Heb.), *Alei sefer*, 20 (2009), 125–70.

—— 'Rav Kook's Circle and the Editing of His Works' [Ḥug hare'iyah ve'arikhat ketavav shel harav kuk] (Ph.D. diss., Bar-Ilan University, 2008).

MUNK, ELIE, 'Rabbiner Hirsch als Rationalist der Kabbala', *Nachalath Zewi*, 3 (1932), 84–92.

—— *The World of Prayer*, trans. Henry Biberfeld and Leonard Oschry (New York, 1961), vol. i.

MUTZERI, HAYIM NISIM RAFA'EL, *Be'er mayim ḥayim* (Salonika, 1794).

NACHSHONI, YEHUDAH, *Hagut befarshiyot hatorah* (Benei Berak, 1981).

NADEL, GEDALIAH, *Betorato shel r. gedalyah*, ed. Y. Sheilat (Ma'aleh Adumim, 2004).

NADLER, ALLAN, L., 'The "Rambam Revival" in Early Modern Jewish Thought: Maskilim, Mitnagdim, and Hasidim on Maimonides' *Guide of the Perplexed*', in Jay M. Harris (ed.), *Maimonides after 800 Years: Essays on Maimonides and His Influence* (Cambridge, Mass., 2007), 36–61.

—— 'The War on Modernity of R. Hayyim Elazar Shapira of Munkacz', *Modern Judaism*, 14 (1994), 233–64.

NAHMAN OF BRATSLAV, *Sefer hamidot* (Jerusalem, 1998).

NAHMANIDES, MOSES, *The Works of Nahmanides* [Kitvei ramban], ed. C. Chavel, 2 vols. (Jerusalem, 1963).

NAJAR, JUDAH, *Simḥat yehudah* (Pisa, 1816).

NAJMAN, HINDY, 'Rewriting as Whitewashing: The Case of Rewritten Bible', in Tzemah Yoreh et al. (eds.), *Vixens Disturbing Vineyards: Embarrassment and Embracement of Scriptures* (Boston, Mass., 2010), 140–53.

NAOR, BEZALEL, *From a Kabbalist's Notebook* (Spring Valley, NY, 2005).

—— *The Limit of Intellectual Freedom: The Letters of Rav Kook* (Spring Valley, NY, 2011).

—— 'Plumbing Rav Kook's Panentheism', in Moshe Z. Sokol (ed.), *Engaging Modernity: Rabbinic Leaders and the Challenge of the Twentieth Century* (Northvale, NJ, 1997), 79–89.

—— *Post-Sabbatian Sabbatianism* (Spring Valley, NY, 1999).

—— *When God Becomes History: Historical Essays of Rabbi Abraham Isaac Hakohen Kook* (Spring Valley, NY, 2003).

NATHANSON, JOSEPH SAUL, *Divrei sha'ul* (Lemberg, 1877).

—— *Sho'el umeshiv* (Jerusalem, 1995).

NATRONAI GAON, *Teshuvot rav natronai gaon*, ed. Y. Brody (Jerusalem, 1994), vol. ii.

NAVON, EPHRAIM, *Maḥaneh efrayim* (Constantinople, 1738; Warsaw, 1878; Jerusalem, 2002).

NERIYAH, MOSHE TSEVI, *Bisedeh hare'iyah* (Kefar Haro'eh, 1987).

—— *Likutei hare'iyah* (Kefar Haro'eh, 1995), vol. iii.

—— *Siḥot hare'iyah* (Tel Aviv, 1979).

NETANYAHU, BENZION, *Don Isaac Abravanel: Statesman and Philosopher* (Philadelphia, Pa., 1968).

NEUSATZ, ELIEZER LIPMANN, *Mei menuḥot* (Pressburg, 1884).

NEUWIRTH, YEHOSHUA YESHAYAH, *Shemirat shabat kehilkhatah* (Jerusalem, 1965).

NEWMAN, ARYEH, 'Women, Saints, and Heretics in Maimonides: The Challenge of Translating Judaica', *Conservative Judaism*, 59 (1997), 75–84.

NIGAL, GEDALYAH, *Magic, Mysticism, and Hasidism*, trans. Edward Levin (Northvale, NJ, 1994).

NISSIM BEN MOSES OF MARSEILLES, *Ma'aseh nisim*, ed. H. Kreisel (Jerusalem, 2000).

NISSIM BEN REUBEN (RAN), supercommentary on Alfasi's commentary on the Babylonian Talmud, printed in standard edns. of the Talmud.

NOVAK, DAVID, *Law and Theology in Judaism*, 2nd series (New York, 1976).

NOYES, GEORGE RAPALL, *Tolstoy* (New York, 1918).

NURIEL, ABRAHAM, *Concealed and Revealed in Medieval Jewish Philosophy* [Galui vesamui befilosofyah hayehudit bimei habeinayim] (Jerusalem, 2000).

OBERLANDER, GEDALIAH, 'On the Division of the Torah into Chapters' (Heb.), *Or yisra'el*, 12 (Tamuz 5758), 144–52.

OBERLANDER, GEDALIAH, *Minhag avoteinu beyadeinu* (Monsey, NY, 2006), vol. i.

OBERLANDER, HAYIM, 'Is It Permitted to Tell Fictitious Stories in Order to Arouse Listeners to Torah and the Fear of Heaven?' (Heb.), *Or yisra'el*, 29 (Tishrei 5763), 121–3.

OFER, YOSEF, 'Ketiv and Kere: The Phenomenon, its Notation, and its Reflection in Early Rabbinic Literature' (Heb.), *Leshonenu*, 70 (2008), 55–73; *Leshonenu*, 71 (2009), 1–25.

—— 'M. D. Cassuto's Notes on the Aleppo Codex' (Heb.), *Sefunot*, NS 4 (1989), 277–344.

OGEN, YITSHAK (ed.), *Asher hayah* (Tel Aviv, 1959).

OLSZOWY-SCHLANGER, JUDITH, *Karaite Marriage Documents from the Cairo Geniza* (Leiden, 1998).

ORTNER, NATHAN, *Devar ḥen* (Lod, 2006).

ORWELL, GEORGE, *Nineteen Eighty-Four* (New York, 1981).

OSHRY, EPHRAIM, *Divrei efrayim* (New York, 1949).

—— *She'elot uteshuvot mima'amakim* (New York, 1979), vol. v.

PALACHE, HAYIM, *Heḥafets ḥayim* (Izmir, 1880).

—— *Kaf haḥayim* (Salonika, 1859).

—— *Lev ḥayim* (Jerusalem, 1997), vol. i.

—— *Tokhaḥat ḥayim* (Izmir, 1874).

PAPO, ELIEZER, *Pele yo'ets* (Constantinople, 1824).

PARUSH, IRIS, *Reading Jewish Women: Marginality and Modernization in Nineteenth-Century Eastern European Jewish Society*, trans. Saadya Sternberg (Waltham, Mass., 2004).

PATSANOVSKY, JOSEPH, *Pardes yosef*, 10 vols. (Piotrków and Łódź, 1930–37); *Pardes yosef hashalem* (Benei Berak, 1993–8); *Pardes yosef hashalem vehamefo'ar* (Benei Berak, 1995).

PATSINER, ISAAC MEIR, *Parashat hamelekh* (Jerusalem, 1956), vol. ii.

PAUL, SHALOM, 'An Akkadian-Rabbinic Sexual Euphemism', in David Golinkin et al. (eds.), *Torah Lishma: Essays in Jewish Studies in Honor of Professor Shamma Friedman* (Jerusalem, 2007), pp. xi–xiii.

—— *Divrei shalom* (Leiden, 2005).

PENIRI, SASON, *Kol sason* (Ramat Gan, 2004).

PERL, GIL S., *The Pillar of Volozhin: Rabbi Naftali Zvi Yehuda Berlin and the World of Nineteenth-Century Lithuanian Torah Scholarship* (Boston, Mass., 2012).

PERLMAN, MOSES DAVID, *Mipi dodi* (Jerusalem, 1935).

PETROKOVSKY, ABRAHAM, *Piskei teshuvah* (Piotrków, 1937).

PETUCHOWSKI, JAKOB J., *Studies in Modern Theology and Prayer* (Philadelphia, Pa., 1998).

PIEKARZ, MENDEL, *Polish Hasidism* [Ḥasidut polin] (Jerusalem, 1990).

PIK, ISAIAH, *Ḥidushei hashas* (Jerusalem, 1987).

PINFER, PESAH, *Masoret hatorah vehanevi'im* (Vilna, 1906).

PISK, LEIB, *Dimyon aryeh* (Prague, 1616).

PLATO, *The Laws*, trans. R. G. Bury (Cambridge, Mass., 1967).

—— *The Republic*, trans. Allan Bloom (New York, 1968).

PLATO, MENAHEM MENDEL, *Bishevilei radin* (Petah Tikvah, 2001).

PLAUT, HEZEKIAH, *Likutei ḥaver ben ḥayim* (Pressburg, 1881), vol. iv.

POLLAK, JACOB, *Vayakem edut beya'akov* (Prague, 1595).

POPPER, WILLIAM, *The Censorship of Hebrew Books* (New York, 1899).

POSEN, RAPHAEL BINYAMIN, '"When Torah Scholars are Engaged in a Halakhic Dispute, Who Are You to Interfere?"' (Heb.), *Hama'yan*, 49 (Tishrei 5769), 53–64.

POZNANSKI, SAMUEL, 'The Anti-Karaite Writings of Sa'adiah Gaon', *JQR*, 10 (1898), 238–76.

POZNA, MEIR, 'An Explanation of the Hatam Sofer's Time Calculation' (Heb.), *Otserot hasofer*, 13 (2002), 65–79.

PROVENCAL, MOSES, *She'elot uteshuvot rabenu mosheh provintsalu* (Jerusalem, 1989), vol. i.

RABBINOVICZ, RAPHAEL NATHAN, *Dikdukei soferim* (Jerusalem, 2002).

—— *Dikdukei soferim: zera'im* (Munich, 1868).

—— *Ma'amar al hadpasat hatalmud*, ed. A. M. Haberman (Jerusalem, 1952).

RABINOVITCH, N. L., *Commentary on Mishneh torah, 'Sefer hamada'* (Heb.) (Jerusalem, 1990).

RABINOWICH, SOLOMON, *Niflaot hatiferet shelomoh* (Piotrków, 1923).

RABINOWITZ, ABRAHAM ISAAC, *Malakhei elyon* (Warsaw, [1937]; 2nd edn., Jerusalem, 1966).

RABINOWITZ, ARYEH MORDECHAI, *Sha'arei aryeh* (Jerusalem, 1958).

RABINOWITZ, DAN, 'The Two Versions of the Bach's Responsa, Frankfurt Edition of 1697' (Heb.), *Alei sefer*, 21 (2010), 99–111.

—— 'Yarmulke: A Historic Cover-Up?', *Hakirah*, 4 (2007), 221–38.

RABINOWITZ, MENAHEM MENDEL, *Ma'aseh neḥemyah* (Warsaw, 1913; Jerusalem, 1956; Jerusalem, 1987).

RABINOWITZ, MORDECHAI, *Amirat davar beshem omro* (Tel Aviv, 1960).

RABINOWITZ-TEOMIM, ELIJAH DAVID, *Ḥidushei hagaon ha'aderet* (Brooklyn, NY, 2003).

—— *Over oraḥ* (Jerusalem, 2006).

—— *Seder eliyahu* (Jerusalem, 1983).

RAFLER, MEIR, *Netivei me'ir* (Merkaz Shapira, 2013).

RAISIN, JACOB S., *The Haskalah Movement in Russia* (Philadelphia, Pa., 1913).

RAKOVER, NAHUM, *Ends that Justify the Means* [Matarah hamekadeshet et ha'emtsa'im] (Jerusalem, 2000).

RAPOPORT, CHAIM, *Judaism and Homosexuality: An Authentic Orthodox View* (London, 2004).

RAPOPORT, SOLOMON JUDAH, *Igerot shir* (Przemyśl, 1885), vol. ii.

RAPOPORT-ALBERT, ADA, 'Hagiography with Footnotes: Edifying Tales and the Writing of History in Hasidism', *History and Theory*, 27 (1988), 119–59.

RASHDALL, HASTINGS, *Theory of Good and Evil* (Oxford, 1907), vol. i.

RASHI (SOLOMON BEN ISAAC), *Commentary on the Torah*, Ariel edn., 7 vols. (Jerusalem, 1986–2005).

RATSABY, YITSHAK, *Olat yitsḥak* (Benei Berak, 1992), vol. ii.

—— 'Of What Was Rav Papa Suspected?' (Heb.), *Pa'amei ya'akov* (Adar II 5768), 103–10.

RAVITZKY, AVIEZER, *Messianism, Zionism, and Jewish Religious Radicalism* [Hakets hameguleh umedinat hayehudim] (Tel Aviv, 1993).

—— 'The Thought of R. Zerahiah b. Isaac b. Shealtiel Hen' [Mishnato shel r. zeraḥyah ben yitsḥak she'alti'el ḥen vehahagut hamaimonit–tibonit bame'ah hayud-gimel' (Ph.D. diss., Hebrew University of Jerusalem, 1978).

RAZ-KRAKOTZKIN, AMNON, *The Censor, the Editor, and the Text: The Catholic Church and the Shaping of the Jewish Canon in the Sixteenth Century*, trans. Jackie Feldman (Philadelphia, Pa., 2007).

—— 'From Safed to Venice: The *Shulhan Arukh* and the Censor', in Chanita Goodblatt and Howard Kreisel (eds.), *Tradition, Heterodoxy and Religious Culture: Judaism and Christianity in the Early Modern Period* (Be'er Sheva, 2006), 91–115.

Readings from the Holy Scriptures (Washington, DC, 1942).

RECANATI, MENAHEM BEN MOSES, *Ta'amei hamitsvot* (Lemberg, 1858).

REIF, STEFAN C., *Judaism and Hebrew Prayer* (Cambridge, 1993).

REIFMAN, JACOB, 'Explanations of Rabbinic Sayings' (Heb.), in Judah Warnheim (ed.), *Kevutsat ḥakhamim* (Vienna, 1861), 40–3.

—— 'Some More Flowers' (Heb.), *Hamagid* (11 Elul 5633), 323–4.

REISCHER, JACOB, *Shevut ya'akov* (Lemberg, 1897), vol. i.

REMER, AVRAHAM, *Gadol shimushah* ([Jerusalem], 1984; 2nd edn., Jerusalem, 1994).

RESNICOFF, STEVEN H., 'Ends and Means in Jewish Law: Lying to Achieve Economic Justice', *Jewish Law Annual*, 15 (2004), 147–88.

—— 'Lying and Lawyering: Contrasting American and Jewish Law', *Notre Dame Law Review*, 77 (2002), 937–76.

RIMON, YOSEF TZVI, '"Tosefet Shabbat": Adding Time onto Shabbat', trans. David Silverberg, <vbm-torah.org/archive/halak64/24tosefet%20shabbat.doc>.

RIPPMAN, DAVID, *Keter kehunah* (Jerusalem, 1932).

RIVKIND, ISAAC, 'Dikdukei sefarim', in *Sefer hayovel likhvod aleksander marks* (New York, 1950), 401–32.

RIVLIN, AVRAHAM, *Jonah: Prophecy and Rebuke* [Yonah: nevuah vetokhaḥah] (Kerem Beyavneh, 2006).

RIVLIN, ELIEZER, *Rabbi Joseph Zundel of Salant* [Rabi yosef zundel misalant] (Jerusalem, 1993).

RIVLIN, YOSEF, 'The Vilna Gaon's Commentary on Jonah' (Heb.), *Kiryat sefer*, 62 (1989), 920–4.

ROGOVIN, MEIR, 'Amar mar', *Halevanon*, section 'Kevod halevanon', 10 Jan. 1870, cols. 14–15.

ROSENACK, AVINOAM, 'Hidden Diaries and New Discoveries: The Life and Thought of Rabbi A. I. Kook', *Shofar*, 25/3 (2007), 111–47.

—— *The Prophetic Halakhah* [Hahalakhah hanevuit] (Jerusalem, 2007).

—— 'Who's Afraid of Rav Kook's Hidden Writings?' (Heb.), *Tarbiz*, 69 (2000), 257–91.

ROSENBAUM, M., and A. M. SILBERMANN, *Pentateuch With Targum Onkelos, Haphtaroth and Prayers for Sabbath and Rashi's Commentary*, 5 vols. (London, 1946).

ROSENBAUM, RAPHAEL (ed.), *Memorial Book for R. Moshe Lifshitz* [Sefer hazikaron lerabi mosheh lifshits] (New York, 1996).

ROSENBERG, A. J. (trans.), *Mikraot gedolot: bereshit* (New York, 1993).

ROSENBERG, AHARON, *Mishkenot haro'im* (New York, 1987), vol. iii.

ROSENBERG, AVRAHAM BARUKH, *Tsava'at aba* (Beclean, Romania, 1931).

ROSENBERG, SHALOM, and BENJAMIN ISH-SHALOM (eds.), *The World of Rav Kook's Thought* (Jerusalem, 1991).

ROSENBLOOM, NOAH H., *Hamalbim* (Jerusalem, 1988).

ROSENBLUM, YONASAN, *Reb Shraga Feivel: The Life and Times of Rabbi Shraga Feivel Mendlowitz, The Architect of Torah in America* (Brooklyn, NY, 2001).

ROSENFELD, SHLOMO, 'When is Lying Permitted?' (Heb.), *Teḥumin*, 31 (2011), 431–9.

ROSENHEIM, JACOB, *Das Bildungsideal S. R. Hirschs und die Gegenwart* (Frankfurt am Main, 1935); *Samson Raphael Hirsch's Cultural Ideal and Our Times*, trans. I. E. Lichtigfeld (London, 1951); *Rabi shimshon rafa'el hirsh: mevaser umagshim ḥazon hayahadut hanitsḥit*, trans. Hayim Weissman (Benei Berak, 1965).

ROSENSWEIG, BERNARD, 'The Unique Phenomenon that Was the Rav', in Zev Eleff (ed.), *Mentor of Generations: Reflections on Rabbi Joseph B. Soloveitchik* (Jersey City, NJ, 2008), 44–50.

ROSENTHAL, SHABETAI DOV, *To'afot re'em* (Jerusalem, 2006).

ROSEN-TSEVI, YISHAI, 'Emergent Metaphysics: The Controversy at the Merkaz Harav Yeshiva—A Critical Study' (Heb.), in Dov Schwarz and Avi Sagi (eds.), *One Hundred Years of Religious Zionism* [Me'ah shenot tsiyonut datit] (Ramat Gan, 2003), vol. iii, pp. 421–45.

ROSS, TAMAR, 'Can the Demand for Change in the Status of Women be Halakhically Legitimated?', *Judaism*, 42 (Fall 1993), 478–92.

—— *Expanding the Palace of Torah: Orthodoxy and Feminism* (Waltham, Mass., 2004).

ROTTZOLL, DIRK U., 'Kannte Avraham ibn Ezra Sh'mu'el ben Me'ir', *Frankfurter Judaistische Beiträge*, 25 (1998), 75–104.

RUBENSTEIN, JEFFREY M., *Rabbinic Stories* (New York, 2002).

RUDAVSKY, T. M., 'To Know What Is: Feminism, Metaphysics, and Epistemology', in Hava Tirosh-Samuelson (ed.), *Women and Gender in Jewish Philosophy* (Bloomington, Ind., 2004), 179–203.

RUDNIK, ISAAC, *Sedeh yitsḥak* (London, 1961).

RUSOFF, ELIJAH, *Ugat eliyahu* (Brooklyn, NY, 1960).

SA'ADYAH GAON, *Sefer hamitsvot*, ed. Y. Perla (Jerusalem, 1973), vol. i.

Sabbath and Festival Prayer Book (New York, 1946).

SACKS, JONATHAN, *Koren Siddur* (Jerusalem, 2009).

SAFRAN, BEZALEL, 'Leone da Modena's Historical Thinking', in Isadore Twersky and Bernard Septimus (eds.), *Jewish Thought in the Seventeenth Century* (Cambridge, Mass., 1987), 381–98.

SAMET, MOSHE, *Heḥadash asur min hatorah* (Jerusalem, 2005).

SAMUEL BEN MEIR (RASHBAM), commentary on BT *Pesaḥim*, printed in standard edns.

SAMUEL HANAGID, *Ben mishlei*, ed. S. Abramson (Tel Aviv, 1948).

SAPHIR, JACOB, *Even sapir* (Lyck, 1866).

SASSON, JACOB, 'The Ben Ish Hai and Women's Hair Covering: An Interesting Case of Censorship?', Text and Texture website, 16 May 2011, <http://text.rcarabbis.org/?s=Jacob+Sasson>.

SAWYER, DEBORAH F., 'Heterodoxy and Censorship: Some Critical Remarks on Wertheimer's Edition of Midrash Aleph Beth', *JJS*, 42 (1991), 115–21.

SCHACHTER, TSEVI, *Mipeninei harav* (Jerusalem, 2001).

—— 'Pearls from Our Rabbi' (Heb.), *Beit yitsḥak*, 36 (2004), 320–32.

SCHACTER, JACOB J., 'Facing the Truths of History', *TUMJ*, 8 (1998–9), 200–76.

—— 'Rabbi Jacob Emden: Life and Major Works' (Ph.D. diss., Harvard University, 1988).

—— and NORMA BAUMEL JOSEPH, 'The 93 Beth Jacob Girls of Cracow: History or Typology', in J. J. Schacter (ed.), *Reverence, Righteousness and Rahamanut: Essays in Memory of Rabbi Dr. Leo Jung* (New York, 1992), 93–130.

SCHÄFER, PETER, *Jesus in the Talmud* (Princeton, NJ, 2007).

SCHATZ, RIVKA, 'The Beginning of the Campaign against Rav Kook' (Heb.), *Molad*, 6 (1974), 251–62.

SCHEFSKI, HAROLD K., 'Tolstoi and the Jews', *Russian Review*, 41 (1982), 1–10.

SCHEINFELD, SOLOMON ISAAC, *Olam hasheker* (Milwaukee, Wis., 1936).

SCHEINHAUS, LEON, 'Alenu Leschabeach', *Ost und West* (July 1908), cols. 451–60.

SCHERMAN, NOSSON (ed.), *Chumash: Stone Edition* (New York, 1993).

—— (ed.), *Tanach: Stone Edition* (Brooklyn, NY, 1996).

—— and MEIR ZLOTOWITZ (eds.), *The Complete ArtScroll Siddur* (Brooklyn, NY, 2003).

—— (eds.), *Shir ha-Shirim* (Brooklyn, NY, 1977).

SCHICK, MOSES, *She'elot uteshuvot maharam shik* (New York, 1961).

SCHISCHA, ABRAHAM, 'Bibliographical Notes on the Works and Responsa of the Hatam Sofer' (Heb.), *Hama'yan*, 9 (Tevet 5729), 77–88.

—— 'The Order of Publication of the Vilna Gaon's Commentary on *Shulḥan arukh*, "Oraḥ ḥayim", "Yoreh de'ah", and "Even ha'ezer", and its Problems' (Heb.), *Yeshurun*, 5 (1999), 678–95.

—— 'Responsa *Zikhron yehudah*, Part 3' (Heb.), *Tsefunot*, 11 (Nisan 5751), 48–57.

SCHLESINGER, AKIVA JOSEPH, *Lev ha'ivri* (Jerusalem, 1990).

—— *Tsava'at mosheh: na'ar ivri* (Jerusalem, 1924).

SCHLESINGER, ELYAKIM, *Hador vehatekufah* (Jerusalem, 2002).

SCHLESINGER, KALMAN, 'The Controversy over Non-Jewish Wine in Italy' (Heb.), in *A Jubilee Gift: Articles in Honour of Shmuel Yosef Agnon* [Yovel shai: ma'amarim likhvod shemuel yosef agnon behagio leseivah] (Ramat Gan, 1958), 211–20.

SCHLESINGER, MOSHE YEHUDAH, 'Young Men Wearing a Tallit and Male Head Covering' (Heb.), *Yerushatenu*, 1 (2007), 111–12.

SCHMELKES, ISAAC, *Beit yitsḥak* (New York, 1960).

SCHNEEBALG, SHRAGA FEIVISH, *Shraga hame'ir* (London, 1993), vol. vii.

SCHNEERSOHN, JOSEPH ISAAC, 'A Critique of the Educational System of the German Orthodox' (Heb.), *Hahed* (Av 5688), 1–3.

—— *Igerot kodesh* (Brooklyn, NY, 1993), vol. xiii.

SCHNEERSON, MENACHEM MENDEL, *Igerot kodesh* (Brooklyn, NY, 1992), vol. xx.

SCHNITZKER, TSEVI, 'The Revealer of Secrets' (Heb.), *Hatsofeh me'erets hagar*, 1 (1911), 98–101.

SCHOLEM, GERSHOM, *The Messianic Idea in Judaism* (New York, 1971).

—— *Researches in Sabbateanism* [Meḥkerei shabta'ut], ed. Y. Liebes (Tel Aviv, 1991).

SCHÜCK, SOLOMON TSEVI, *She'elot uteshuvot rashban* (Munkács, 1900), vol. i.

SCHUSSMAN, AVIVA, 'Allegory, Theology, and Polemic in Tanhum Yerushalmi's Commentary on the Book of Jonah' (Heb.), *Pe'amim*, 59 (1994), 85–98.

SCHWAB, SHIMON, *Selected Writings* (Lakewood, NJ, 1988).

SCHWARTZ, DOV, *Amulets, Charms, and Rationalism in Medieval Jewish Thought* [Kemiot, segulot, vesikhletanut behagut hayehudit bimei habeinayim] (Ramat Gan, 2004).

—— *Challenge and Crisis in Rav Kook's Circle* [Etgar umashber beḥug harav kuk] (Tel Aviv, 2001).

—— *Emunah al parashat derakhim* (Tel Aviv, 1996); English edn.: *Faith at the Crossroads*, trans. Batya Stein (Leiden, 2002).

—— *Religious Zionism: Between Logic and Messianism* [Hatsiyonut hadatit bein higayon limeshiḥiyut] (Tel Aviv, 1999).

SCHWARTZ, HAYIM AVIHU, *Mitokh hatorah hago'elet* (Jerusalem, 1984), vol. ii.

SCHWARTZ, JOSEPH, and PETER J. TOMSON, 'When Rabbi Eliezer Was Arrested for Heresy', *JSIJ*, 10 (2012), 145–81.

SCHWARTZ, JOSEPH HAKOHEN (ed.), *Zikaron lemosheh* (Brooklyn, NY, 1990).

SCHWARTZ, MATITYAHU, *Mishpat hatsava'ah* (n.p., 2008).

SCHWARTZ, YOEL, *The Life of Rabbi Samson Raphael Hirsch* [Toledot hagaon hatsadik rabi shimshon rafa'el hirsh] (Jerusalem, 2000).

Sefer ḥasidim, ed. R. Margaliyot (Jerusalem, 1989).

SEGAL, HAGAI, 'Orot be'ofel', *Nekudah* (3 Elul 5747), no. 113, 16–27.

SEIDMAN, NAOMI, 'Elie Wiesel and the Scandal of Jewish Rage', *Jewish Social Studies*, 3 (Fall 1996), 1–19.

—— *Faithful Renderings: Jewish Christian Difference and the Politics of Translation* (Chicago, 2006).

SELA, NETA, 'R. Avraham Yosef: Do Not Name a Son "Nimrod" or "Herzl"', YNet (21 June 2007), <www.ynet.co.il/articles/0,7340,L-3415627,00.html>.

SHAMIR, YEHUDAH, 'Allusions to Muhammad in Maimonides' Theory of Prophecy in His *Guide of the Perplexed*', *JQR*, 64 (1975), 212–24.

SHAPIRA, AVRAHAM, *Ḥag hasukot* (Jerusalem, 2012).

SHAPIRA, BEN ZION (ed.), *Igerot lare'iyah* (Jerusalem, 1990).

SHAPIRA, ELIYAHU, *Eliyah rabah* (Sulzbach, 1757).

SHAPIRA, HAYIM ELEAZAR, *Divrei torah* (Jerusalem, 1998).

SHAPIRA, MEIR YEHUDAH, *Or lame'ir* (Przemyśl, 1913; New York, 2002).

SHAPIRA, TSEVI ELIMELEKH, *Magid ta'alumah* (Przemyśl, 1876).

—— *Ma'yan ganim* (commentary on Joseph Yavets, *Or haḥayim* [Lublin, 1912]).

SHAPIRA, YEHUDAH, *Da'at yehudah* (Benei Berak, 2012).

SHAPIRO, MARC B., *Between the Yeshiva World and Modern Orthodoxy: The Life and Works of Rabbi Jehiel Jacob Weinberg, 1884–1966* (London, 1999).

—— 'Of Books and Bans', *Edah Journal*, 3/2 (2003), 1–16.

—— 'Islam and the Halakhah', *Judaism*, 42 (1993), 332–43.

—— *The Limits of Orthodox Theology* (Oxford, 2004).

—— 'Samson Raphael Hirsch and Orthodoxy: A Contested Legacy' (forthcoming).

—— *Saul Lieberman and the Orthodox* (Scranton, Pa., 2006).

—— 'Scholars and Friends: Rabbi Jehiel Jacob Weinberg and Professor Samuel Atlas', *TUMJ*, 7 (1997), 105–21.

—— *Studies in Maimonides and His Interpreters* (Scranton, Pa., 2008).

—— '*Torah im Derekh Eretz* in the Shadow of Hitler', *TUMJ*, 14 (2006–7), 84–96.

SHAPIRO, MOSHE, *Afikei mayim* (n.p., 2006).

SHAPIRO, PINHAS, *Midrash pinḥas* (Lemberg, 1872).

SHASHA, AMRI, '"A Burning Spirit Upon Strong Muscles": The Body in the Thought of Rav Kook' (Heb.), *Ma'galim*, 5 (2007), 233–62.

SHASHAR, MICHAEL, 'Should the Book of Jonah be Interpreted Allegorically?' (Heb.), *Shanah beshanah* (1986), 324–9.

SHATZ, DAVID, 'Nothing but the Truth? Modern Orthodoxy and the Polemical Uses of History', in Daniel J. Lasker (ed.), *Jewish Thought and Jewish Belief* (Be'er Sheva, 2012), 27–63.

SHAVIT, YAAKOV, and MORDECHAI ERAN, *The Hebrew Bible Reborn: From Holy Scriptures to the Book of Books*, trans. Chaya Naor (Berlin, 2007).

SHEILAT, YITSHAK, 'Orot me'ofel', *Nekudah*, 114 (Tishrei 5748), 44–5, 47.

—— 'An Unknown Translation of Maimonides' *Letter on Martyrdom*' (Heb.), *Sinai*, 95 (1984), 157–64.

SHELEG, YAIR, *The New Religious* [Hadatiyim haḥadashim] (Jerusalem, 2000).

SHEM TOV BEN JOSEPH IBN SHEM TOV, Commentary on Maimonides, *Guide of the Perplexed*, printed in the standard Hebrew edn.

SHERLO, SEMADAR, *The Tsadik is the Foundation of the World: Rav Kook's Esoteric Mission and Mystical Experience* [Tsadik yesod olam: hasheliḥut hasodit vehaḥavayah hamistit shel harav kuk] (Ramat Gan, 2012).

SHERWIN, BYRON L., *Mystical Theology and Social Dissent: The Life and Works of Judah Loew of Prague* (East Brunswick, NJ, 1982).

SHMUKLER (SHAPIRO), MOSES SAMUEL, *The Life of R. Hayim of Volozhin* [Toledot rabenu ḥayim mivolozhin] (Vilna, 1909).

SHOCHET, SAUL YEDIDYAH, *Beit yedidyah* (Piotrków, 1903; Brooklyn, NY, 1992).

SHURKIN, MICHEL ZALMAN, *Harerei kedem*, 2 vols. (Jerusalem, 2000–4).

—— *Meged giv'ot olam* (Jerusalem, 1999).

Siddur Sim Shalom, ed. and trans. Jules Harlow (New York, 1989).

SIEV, ASHER, 'R. Samuel Judah Katzenellenbogen' (Heb.), *Hadarom*, 34 (1972), 177–201.

SILBER, OMER, 'Ha'arafel betaharato', *Ma'galim*, 5 (2007), 279–315.

SILMAN, SHIMON, *Scientific Thought in Messianic Times* (Brooklyn, NY, 2010).

SILVER, YITSHAK EIZIK, *Emet keneh* (printed together with id., *Mishpetei hashalom*, Jerusalem, 2005).

SILVERMAN, MORRIS (ed.), *The Complete Purim Service* (Hartford, Conn., 1947).

SIMHAH ZISSEL ZIV OF KELM, *Ḥokhmah umusar* (New York, 1957).

SIMON, URIEL, *The Ear Discerns Words: Studies in Ibn Ezra's Exegetical Methodology* [Ozen milin tivḥan: meḥkarim bedarko haparshanit shel r. avraham ibn ezra] (Ramat Gan, 2013).

—— *JPS Bible Commentary: Jonah* (Philadelphia, Pa., 1999).

SINCLAIR, DANIEL, 'Fictitious Retractions and False Attributions: The Balance between Truth and Falsehood in Halakhic Discourse', *Jewish Law Association Studies*, 22 (2012), 283–302.

SLATER, THOMAS, 'Mental Reservation', *Catholic Encyclopaedia* (New York, 1911), vol. x, <http://www.newadvent.org/cathen/10195b.htm>.

SOFER, AKIVA, *Sha'arei sofer* (Jerusalem, 1969).

SOFER, AKIVA MENAHEM, *Minhagei raboteinu vehalikhoteihem* (Benei Berak, 2009).

SOFER, HAYIM, *Kan sofer* (London, 1963).

SOFER, JACOB SHALOM, *Torat ḥayim* (Paks, 1897).

SOFER, JOSEPH TSEVI, *Toledot soferim* (London, 1963).

SOFER, MOSES, *Ḥatam sofer al hatorah* (Jerusalem, 1989), vol. i.

—— *Ḥidushei ḥatam sofer: gitin* (Vienna, 1889).

—— *Ḥidushim: seder mo'ed* (Jerusalem, 1894).

—— *Kovets teshuvot ḥatam sofer* (Jerusalem, 1973).

—— *She'elot uteshuvot ḥatam sofer*, 6 vols. ([photo reprint of the 1st edn., Pressburg/Vienna], Jerusalem, 1991).

—— *She'elot uteshuvot ḥatam sofer haḥadashot* (Jerusalem, 1989).

SOFER, SHABETAI, *Sidur*, ed. Y. Satz and D. Yitzhaki (Baltimore, Md., 1994), vol. ii.

SOFER, SOLOMON, *Ḥut hameshulash* (Paks, 1887; Munkács, 1894).

SOFER, YA'AKOV HAYIM, *Berit ya'akov* (Jerusalem, 1985).

—— *Hadar ya'akov* (Jerusalem, 2005 and 2006), vols. v and vi.

—— *Keneset ya'akov* (Jerusalem, 1989).

—— *Kerem ya'akov* (Jerusalem, 1989).

—— *Menuḥat shalom* (Jerusalem, 2003), vol. xi.

SOKOLOFF, MICHAEL, *A Dictionary of Jewish Babylonian Aramaic of the Talmudic and Geonic Periods* (Ramat Gan, 2002).

SOLOMON BEN ADRET (RASHBA), *Ḥidushei harashba: eruvin* (Jerusalem, 2008).

—— *She'elot uteshuvot harashba* (Jerusalem, 1997), vol. i.

—— *She'elot uteshuvot harashba hameyuḥasot leramban* (Jerusalem, 2001).

—— *Torat habayit ha'arokh* (Vienna, 1811).

SOLOMON BEN ISAAC *see* RASHI.

SOLOVEITCHIK, HAYM, 'Rupture and Reconstruction: The Transformation of Contemporary Orthodoxy', *Tradition*, 28 (Summer 1994), 64–131.

—— 'Two Notes on the Commentary on the Torah of R. Yehudah he-Hasid', *Turim*, 2 (New York, 2007), 241–51.

—— *'Yeinam': Principles and Pressures: Jewish Trade in Gentile Wine in the Middle Ages* ['Yeinam': Saḥar beyeinam shel goyim—al gilgulah shel halakhah be'olam hama'aseh] (Tel Aviv, 2003).

SOMMERVILLE, JOHANN, P., 'The "New Art of Lying": Equivocation, Mental Reservation, and Casuistry', in Edmund Leites (ed.), *Conscience and Casuistry in Early Modern Europe* (Cambridge, 1988), 159–84.

SONNENFELD, SHLOMO ZALMAN, *Ha'ish al haḥomah* (Jerusalem, 2006), vol. ii.

SORASKY, AHARON, *History of Torah Education* [Toledot haḥinukh hatorati] (Benei Berak, 1967).

—— *Marbitsei torah me'olam haḥasidut* (Benei Berak, 1988), vol. vi.

—— *Pe'er yisra'el* (Jerusalem, 1998), vol. i.

—— *Yesod hama'alah* (Benei Berak, 1991).

SPERBER, DANIEL, *On Changes in Jewish Liturgy: Options and Limitations* (Jerusalem, 2010).

—— *Minhagei yisra'el*, 8 vols. (Jerusalem, 1990–2007).

—— *Netivot pesikah* (Jerusalem, 2008).

SPIEGEL, SHALOM, *The Last Trial*, trans. Judah Goldin (New York, 1993).

SPIRA, NATHAN, *Yayin hameshumar* (Venice, 1660).

SPITZER, SHLOMO, 'Was *Sefer maharil* Censored?' (Heb.), *Tsefunot*, 2 (Tevet 5749), 83–5.

STAMPFER, SHAUL, *Lithuanian Yeshivas of the Nineteenth Century*, trans. Lindsey Taylor-Guthartz (Oxford, 2012).

STANISLAWSKI, MICHAEL, 'The Yiddish *Shevet Yehudah*: A Study in the "Ashkenazation" of a Spanish Jewish Classic', in Elisheva Carlebach et al. (eds.), *Jewish History and Jewish Memory* (Hanover, NH, 1998), 134–49.

STEIN, SALOMON, 'Die Behandlung des Problems der Notlüge im Talmud', *Jahrbuch der Jüdisch-literarischen Gesellschaft*, 5 (1907), 206–24.

STEPANSKY, NACHUM, *Ve'alehu lo yibol* (Jerusalem, 2001), vol. ii.

STERN, ARYEH, 'Rabbi Sa'adyah Gaon's Position on *Kidush haḥodesh*' (Heb.), *Yodei binah*, 3 (5766), 24–39.

STERN, ELIYAHU, *The Genius: Elijah of Vilna and the Making of Modern Judaism* (New Haven, Conn., 2013).

STERN, SACHA, 'Attribution and Authorship in the Babylonian Talmud', *JJS*, 45 (1994), 28–51.

STERNBERG, SHLOMO, 'Bein haShemashot', <http://www.math.harvard.edu/~shlomo/docs/beinhashemashot.pdf>.

STITSKIN, LEON, *Letters of Maimonides* (New York, 1977).

STOLLHANS, CYNTHIA, 'Michelangelo's Nude Saint Catherine of Alexandria', *Woman's Art Journal*, 19 (1998), 26–30.

STOLOW, JEREMY, *Orthodox by Design: Judaism, Print Politics, and the ArtScroll Revolution* (Berkeley, Calif., 2010).

STRASSER, JUDAH, and AARON PERL (eds.), *Mosheh alah lamarom* (Brooklyn, NY, 1989).

STRICKMAN, H. NORMAN, 'Abraham Ibn Ezra's Non-Literal Interpretations', *Hakirah*, 9 (Winter 2010), 281–96.

STRUEVER, NANCY S., *The Language of History in the Renaissance* (Princeton, NJ, 1970).

SULAM, M., 'Supplements to "Jacob Reifman, His Life and Works: General Background of His Life"' (Heb.), *Hadarom*, 21 (Nisan 5725), 142–7.

SWIFT, MOSES, '"External Books" in the Halakhah' (Heb.), in H. J. Zimmels et al. (eds.), *Essays Presented to Chief Rabbi Israel Brodie on the Occasion of His Seventieth Birthday* (London, 1967), 205–8.

Tana devei eliyahu, with commentary *Ramatayim tsofim* (Warsaw, 1881); English edn.: *Tanna Debe Eliyyahu*, trans. William G. Braude and Israel J. Kapstein (Philadelphia, Pa., 1981).

TA-SHMA, ISRAEL MOSHE, *Creativity and Tradition: Studies in Medieval Rabbinic Scholarship, Literature and Thought* (Cambridge, Mass., 2006).

—— *Halakhah, Custom, and Reality in Franco-Germany 1100–1350* [Halakhah, minhag umetsiyut be'ashkenaz 1100–1350] (Jerusalem, 1996).

—— *Keneset meḥkarim* (Jerusalem, 2004), vol. i.

—— *Keneset meḥkarim* (Jerusalem, 2010), vol. iv.

—— Review of Avraham Grossman, *The Early Sages of Ashkenaz* (Heb.), *Kiryat sefer*, 56 (1981), 344–52.

TAUSIG, YISRA'EL, *Beit yisra'el hashalem* (Jerusalem, 1981), vol. viii.

TAVYOMI, TUVIAH, *Evel kaved* (Jerusalem, 1949).

TAYLOR, DEREK, *Solomon Schonfeld: A Purpose in Life* (London, 2009).

TCHERNOWITZ, CHAIM, *Toledot haposkim* (New York, 1947), vol. iii.

TEHERANI, AVISHAI, *Amudei mishpat* (Jerusalem, 2007), vol. i.

TEITELBAUM, JOEL, *Vayo'el mosheh* (Jerusalem, 1996).

TENENBAUM, MALKIEL TSEVI, *Divrei malki'el* (Vilna, 1891), vol. ii.

TEOMIM-FRANKEL, BARUKH, *Ateret ḥakhamim* (Josefov, 1866).

TEPPLER, YAAKOV Y., *Birkat haminim*, trans. Susan Weingarten (Tübingen, 2007).

Teshuvot hage'onim (Lyck, 1864).

Teshuvot ḥakhmei provans, ed. A. Sofer (Jerusalem, 1967).

TIROSH-SAMUELSON, HAVA, 'Gender and the Pursuit of Happiness in Maimonides' Philosophy', in Elisheva Baumgarten et al. (eds.), *Tov Elem: Memory, Community, and Gender in Medieval and Early Modern Jewish Societies* (Jerusalem, 2011), 54–78.

TISHBY, ISAIAH, *Paths of Belief and Heresy* [Netivei emunah uminut] (Jerusalem, 1982).

TOAFF, ARIEL, *Love, Work, and Death: Jewish Life in Medieval Umbria*, trans. Judith Landry (London, 1998).

TOBOLSKI, ABRAHAM, *Midevar sheker tirḥak* (n.p., 1978).

Tosafot hashalem: otsar perushei ba'alei hatosafot, ed. Y. Gellis, 13 vols. (Jerusalem, 1982–2011).

TOV, EMANUEL, *Textual Criticism of the Hebrew Bible* (Minneapolis, Minn., 1992).

TRACHTENBERG, JOSHUA, *Jewish Magic and Superstition* (Cleveland, Ohio, 1961).

TRACHTMAN, BENJAMIN, *Shevet binyamin* (n.p., 1930).

TRIVES, MENAHEM, *Oraḥ meisharim* (Mainz, 1878).

TSEVIALI, BINYAMIN, 'Rabbi Abraham Isaac Hakohen Kook and His Attitude to Literature and Art' (Heb.), in Hayim Hamiel (ed.), *Be'oro* (Jerusalem, 1986), 518–27.

TSOREF, EPHRAIM, *The Life of Rav Kook* [Ḥayei harav kuk] (Jerusalem, 1947).

TSURIEL, MOSHE (ed.), *Derishat tsiyon* (Benei Berak, 2006).

—— *Leket mehegyonei hatorah* (Benei Berak, 2011).

—— *Otserot ha'agadah* (Benei Berak, 1998).

—— (ed.), *Otserot hamusar* (Jerusalem, 2002).

—— (ed.), *Otserot hatorah* (Benei Berak, 2005).

TUANA, NANCY, *The Less Noble Sex* (Bloomington, Ind., 1993).

TURSH, DOVBERISH, *Moznei tsedek* (Warsaw, 1895).

TWERSKY, ISADORE, *Rabad of Posquières: A Twelfth-Century Talmudist* (Cambridge, Mass., 1962).

TYRNAU, ISAAC, *Sefer haminhagim*, ed. S. Spitzer (Jerusalem, 1979).

URBACH, EPHRAIM, *Me'olamam shel ḥakhamim* (Jerusalem, 1988).

UZIEL, BEN ZION, *Mikhmanei uzi'el* (Tel Aviv, 1933).

VAKNIN, AVRAHAM MEIR, 'Ben Ya'akov's Deletions from *Shem hagedolim*' (Heb.), *Moriah*, 22 (Tevet 5759), 108–21.

VALLE, MOSES, *Or olam* (Jerusalem, 2001).

VALTER, SHAI, 'Rabbi Sa'adyah Gaon's View on Determining the New Moon: The Astronomical Problem and its Solution' (Heb.), *Yodei binah*, 3 (5766), 40–56.

VAN DER HORST, PIETER W., *Hellenism–Judaism–Christianity: Essays on their Interaction* (Leuven, 1998).

VEYNE, PAUL, *Did the Greeks Believe in Their Myths?*, trans. Paula Wissing (Chicago, 1988).

VIDAL OF TOLOSA, *Magid mishneh*, commentary on Maimonides, *Mishneh torah*, printed in standard edns.

VIEZEL, ERAN, *The Commentary on Chronicles Attributed to Rashi* [Haperush hameyuḥas lerashi lesefer divrei hayamim] (Jerusalem, 2010).

VITAL, HAYIM, *Likutei torah nevi'im ukhetuvim* (Vilna, 1880).
—— *Sefer haḥezyonot*, ed. A. Aescoly (Jerusalem, 1954).
—— *Sha'ar hapesukim* (Jerusalem, 1912).
VITERBO, ABRAHAM HAYIM, *Emunat ḥakhamim*, in Eliezer Ashkenazi (ed.), *Ta'am zekenim* (Frankfurt am Main, 1854).
WALDENBERG, ELIEZER, *Hilkhot hamedinah*, 3 vols. (Jerusalem, 1952–5).
—— *Tsits eli'ezer*, 22 vols. (Jerusalem, 1985).
WALK, ELIEZER LIPMAN, *Ein eli'ezer* (Jerusalem, 1928).
WALSHAM, ALEXANDRA, 'Unclasping the Book? Post-Reformation English Catholicism and the Vernacular Bible', *Journal of British Studies*, 42 (2003), 141–66.
WALTON, MICHAEL T., and PHYLLIS J. WALTON, 'In Defense of the Church Militant: The Censorship of the Rashi Commentary in the Magna Biblia Rabbinica', *Sixteenth Century Journal*, 21 (1990), 385–400.
WARHAFTIG, ITAMAR, 'Rabbi Herzog's Approach to Modernity', in Moshe Sokol (ed.), *Engaging Modernity* (Northvale, NJ, 1997), 275–319.
WASSERMAN, AVRAHAM, and EITAM HENKIN, *Striking Root* [Lehakot shoresh] (Jerusalem, 2012).
WASSERMAN, ELHANAN, *Ikveta dimeshiḥa* (New York, 1939).
—— *Kovets ma'amarim ve'igerot*, 2 vols. (Jerusalem, 2001).
—— *Yalkut ma'amarim umikhtavim* (Brooklyn, NY, 1987).
WEIDENFELD, DOV BERISH, *Dovev meisharim* (Jerusalem, 1951), vol. i.
WEIL, NETANEL, *Korban netanel*, commentary on R. Asher ben Jehiel, printed in standard edns. of the Talmud.
—— *Torat netanel* (Fuerth, 1805).
WEINBERG, JEHIEL JACOB, *Kitvei hagaon rabi yeḥi'el ya'akov veinberg*, ed. M. Shapiro (Scranton, Pa., 2003), vol. ii.
—— *Seridei esh* (Jerusalem, 1977), vol. iv.
—— 'Torat haḥayim', in Yonah Emanuel (ed.), *Harav shimshon rafa'el hirsh: mishnato veshitato* (Jerusalem, 1962), 185–99.
—— *Das Volk der Religion* (Geneva, 1949).
WEINGARTEN, SHMUEL, 'And of Zion It Shall Be Said, "This Man and That Was Born in Her"' (Heb.), *Sinai*, 87 (1980), 189–90.
—— 'Responsa That Were Concealed' (Heb.), *Sinai*, 29 (1951), 90–9.
—— 'The Temple Mount and its Sanctity' (Heb.), *Torah shebe'al peh*, 11 (1969), 148–211.
WEINGORT, AVRAHAM ABBA, *Hagadah shel pesaḥ al pi ba'al haseridei esh* (Jerusalem, 2014).
WEINMAN, TSEVI, 'Mishnah rishonah bimekomah omedet', *Akdamot*, 6 (1999), 70–1.
WEISS, HAYIM JOSEPH DAVID, *Vaya'an david* (Jerusalem, 1996), vol. iii.
WEISS, ISAAC HIRSCH, *Dor dor vedoreshav*, 5 vols. (Vilna, 1904).
—— *Zikhronotai* (Warsaw, 1895).
WEISS, RAYMOND L., and CHARLES BUTTERWORTH, *Ethical Writings of Maimonides* (New York, 1973).

WEISS, YA'AKOV GERSHON, 'An Explanation of the Times of Day and Night Quoted by the Hatam Sofer in the Name of His Teacher R. Nathan Adler' (Heb.), *Otserot hasofer*, 18 (2008), 87–92.

WEISS, YITSHAK YESHAYAH, 'The Wording of *Birkat haminim*' (Heb.), *Tsefunot*, 3 (Nisan 5749), 107–8.

WEITMAN, MIRIAM, 'Using a Non-Jew's Identity Card during the Holocaust' (Heb.), *Teḥumin*, 31 (2011), 440–53.

WENGROV, CHARLES, *Haggadah and Woodcut* (New York, 1967).

WERBLOWSKY, R. J. Z., *Joseph Karo: Lawyer and Mystic* (Oxford, 1962).

WERSES, SHMUEL, 'Mordechai Plungian: Portrait of a *Maskil* from Vilna' (Heb.), in Stanley Nash (ed.), *Between History and Literature: Festschrift for Yitshak Barzilai* [Bein historyah lesifrut: sefer yovel leyitsḥak barzilai] (Tel Aviv, 1997), 149–61.

WERTHEIM, AHARON, *Laws and Customs in Hasidism* [Halakhot vehalikhot baḥasidut] (Jerusalem, 1989).

WERTHEIMER, SOLOMON AARON (ed.), *Batei midrashot*, 2 vols. (Jerusalem, 1952, 1956).

—— *She'elat shelomoh*, 2 vols. (Jerusalem, 1932, 1934).

WESSELY, NAPHTALI HERTZ, *Sefer hamidot* (Jerusalem, 2002).

—— *Yein levanon* (Rishon Letsiyon, 2003).

WIEDER, NAPHTALI, *The Formation of Jewish Liturgy in the East and the West* [Hitgabshut nusaḥ hatefilah bamizraḥ uvama'arav] (Jerusalem, 1998), vol. ii.

WIESEL, ELIE, *Night*, trans. Stella Rodway (New York, 1960).

WILSTEIN, HAYIM, *Ḥayei hamishnah* (Jerusalem, 1928; Jerusalem, n.d.).

WOLBE, SHLOMO, *Alei shur*, 2 vols. (Jerusalem, 1988).

—— 'The Contemporary Yeshiva' (Heb.), *Moriah*, 1 (Shevat 5729), 35–8.

WOLBERSTEIN, HILAH, *Mashmia yeshuah* (Merkaz Shapira, 2010).

WOLF, ABRAHAM, 'From His Holy Words' (Heb.), *Diglenu* (Kislev 5714), 4.

WOLF, ARNOLD JACOB, 'The New Liturgies', *Judaism*, 46 (Spring 1997), 235–42.

WOLFSON, ELLIOT R., 'Hai Gaon's Letter and Commentary on *Aleynu*: Further Evidence of Moses de Leon's Pseudepigraphic Activity', *JQR*, 81 (1991), 365–409.

WOSNER, SHMUEL, *Shevet halevi*, 14 vols. (n.p., 2002–14).

WRESCHNER, YA'AKOV YERUHAM, *Seder ya'akov* (Jerusalem, 2000).

YA'ARI, AVRAHAM, *Meḥkerei sefer* (Jerusalem, 1958).

—— *Ta'alumat sefer* (Jerusalem, 1954).

YADLER, MOSHE MEIR, *Berurei halakhah me'or hashabat* (Jerusalem, 1993).

YARON, ZVI, *The Philosophy of Rabbi Kook*, trans. Avner Tomaschoff (Jerusalem, 1992).

YAVROV, NAHUM, *Niv sefatayim* (Brooklyn, NY, 2005).

YAVROV, TSEVI, *Ma'aseh ish* (Benei Berak, 2000), vol. iii.

YELLIN, ABRAHAM, *Derekh tsadikim* (Warsaw, 1911).

YELOZ, ELIJAH, *Yesh me'ayin* (Jerusalem, 1930), vol. ii.

YERUSHALMI, YOSEF HAYIM, *Haggadah and History* (Philadelphia, Pa., 1975).
—— *Zakhor: Jewish History and Jewish Memory* (Seattle, Wash., 1996).
YITSHAK, HERZL HILLEL, 'Is One Permitted To Be Imprecise Regarding Age for the Purposes of Matchmaking?' (Heb.), *Beit hilel*, 40 (Tevet 5770), 33–6.
YOM TOV ISHBILI (RITVA), *Ḥidushei haritva: ketubot*, ed. Moshe Goldstein (Jerusalem, 2008).
—— *Ḥidushei haritva: yevamot*, ed. Raphael Aharon Joffen (Jerusalem, 2008).
YOSEF, OVADYAH, 'On the Issue of Remembering Amalek' (Heb.), *Vaya'an shemuel*, 5 (2002), 7–14.
—— *Ma'yan omer*, 12 vols. (Jerusalem, 2008–13).
—— *Yabia omer*, 10 vols. (Jerusalem, 1986–2004).
YOSEF, YITSHAK, *Ein yitsḥak* (Jerusalem, 2008), vol. iii.
—— *Yalkut yosef: hilkhot bikur ḥolim ve'avelut* (Jerusalem, 2004).
—— *Yalkut yosef: hilkhot kibud av va'em* (Jerusalem, 2005).
—— *Yalkut yosef: sova semaḥot* (Jerusalem, n.d.), vol. ii.
YUVAL, ISRAEL JACOB, *Two Nations in Your Womb*, trans. Barbara Harshav and Jonathan Chipman (Berkeley, Calif., 2006).
ZABIHI, PINHAS, *Ateret paz* (Jerusalem, 2008), vol. vi.
ZACUTO, MOSES, *She'elot uteshuvot haramaz* (Venice, 1761).
ZAGORIN, PEREZ, 'The Historical Significance of Lying and Dissimulation', *Social Research* (1996), 863–912.
—— *Ways of Lying: Dissimulation, Persecution, and Conformity in Early Modern Europe* (Cambridge, 1990).
ZAKAI, AHARON, *Shelom bayit* (Jerusalem, 1991).
ZEITLIN, HILLEL, *Rabbi Nahman of Bratslav: World Weariness and Longing for the Messiah* [Rabi naḥman mibratslav: tsa'ar ha'olam vekhisufei mashiaḥ], ed. Y. Meir (Jerusalem, 2006).
ZELCER, HESHEY, 'Shemoneh Esreh in Eretz Yisrael ca. 220–250', *Hakirah*, 14 (2012), 79–121.
ZELIKOVITCH, MOSHE, *Yalkut haro'im* (Odessa, 1869).
ZEVIN, SHLOMO YOSEF, *The Festivals in Halachah*, trans. Shlomo Fox-Ashrei (Brooklyn, NY, 1981), vol. ii.
—— *Hamo'adim bahalakhah* (Jerusalem, 1980), vol. ii.
—— *Le'or hahalakhah* (Jerusalem, 2007).
ZIGELMAN, ELIEZER TSEVI, *Naḥalei emunah* (Lublin, 1935; Jerusalem, 1968; Brooklyn, NY, 1983).
ZILBERGER, JOSEPH ISAAC, *Atsei zayit* (Warsaw, n.d.), vol. ii.
ZILBERSTEIN, ABRAHAM SAMUEL TSEVI, *Karnot hamizbe'aḥ* (Biłgoraj, 1927).
—— *Korban shemuel* (St Louis, 1944; Brooklyn, NY, 1992).
ZIMMER, ERIC, 'Men's Headcovering: The Metamorphosis of This Practice', in Jacob J. Schacter (ed.), *Reverence, Righteousness, and Rahamanut* (Northvale, NJ, 1992), 325–52.

ZINBERG, ISRAEL, *History of Jewish Literature* [Toledot sifrut yisra'el] (Tel Aviv, 1958), vol. iv.

ZIVOTOFSKY, ARI, 'Perspectives on Truthfulness in the Jewish Tradition', *Judaism*, 42 (Summer 1993), 267–88.

Zohar, ed. R. Margaliyot, 3 vols. (Jerusalem, 1984).

ZOHAR, TSEVI, 'The Halakhic Work of the Sages of Iraq' (Heb.), *Pe'amim*, 86–7 (2001), 4–50.

ZUCKER, MOSHE, 'Fragments of Rabbi Sa'adyah Gaon's *Kitab tahsil al-shara'i*' (Heb.), *Tarbiz*, 41 (1972), 373–410.

ZUCKERMAN, A. YEHOSHUA, 'On Art in the Teaching of Rav Kook' (Heb.), in Benjamin Ish-Shalom and Shalom Rosenberg (eds.), *Yovel orot* (Jerusalem, 1985), 153–8.

ZUNZ, LEOPOLD, *Die Ritus des synagogalen Gottesdienstes* (Berlin, 1859).

ZWEIFEL, ELIEZER, *Saneigor* (Warsaw, 1885).

INDEX

Page numbers in **bold** refer to pages containing illustrations.